THE OLYMPIC GAMES

THE OLYMPIC GAMES

Edited by Lord Killanin and John Rodda

MACDONALD & JANE'S
LONDON

Revised edition first published in Great Britain in 1979 by
Macdonald and Jane's Limited,
Paulton House,
8 Shepherdess Walk, London N1 7LW

ISBN 0 354 08561 1 (hardback)
ISBN 0 354 08562 X (paperback)

This book was designed and produced by
George Rainbird Limited
36 Park Street, London W1Y 4DE

Printed and bound by Jarrold & Sons Ltd, Norwich

CONTENTS

INTRODUCTION
Lord Killanin

In 1971 I approached George Rainbird, for whom I had previously co-edited and written a book, with the suggestion that there was a need for an authoritative book in English on the Olympic Games. My original suggestion was for an encyclopedia. When I made this proposal I was Vice-President of the International Olympic Committee and also Chairman of the Press and Public Relations Commission. My term of office was due to end at the Games of Munich in August 1972. I believed that after the Games I would have a good deal of spare time to devote to such a book. I had no idea that at Munich I should find myself succeeding the most distinguished Olympic figure after Baron Pierre de Coubertin – Avery Brundage – as President of the IOC.

When I found myself President of the IOC, I still felt that a book covering every aspect of the Olympic Movement would be a considerable asset. Some countries, such as Germany, where much work has been done by the Carl Diem Institute are more than adequately served but in English there is very little authoritative writing. As a result, *The Olympic Games* was published in 1976 prior to the Winter Games of Innsbruck and the Olympic Games of Montreal. I am now in my penultimate year of office. In collaboration with John Rodda I have now prepared a new version of the book, thoroughly revised and updated.

In redesigning the book, chapters on individual sports have been omitted together with certain others. However, the essential information in these contributions has been included elsewhere and new chapters have been added to cover the Montreal and Innsbruck Games. I have added a substantial new chapter looking forward to the 1980 Games in Moscow and Lake Placid.

The task of assembling this new book would not have been possible had it not been for John Rodda of the *Guardian* whom I have known well because he has for so many years taken a profound interest in the Olympic Movement and has attended the Sessions of the IOC, besides the Games, during the years I have myself been active.

For the celebrations of each Games we have sought reporters of international standing who may not all like the ways of the IOC but have shown a joy in their reporting of the Games; cramming one celebration into the length we could allow provided an exercise in discipline but all of them, I feel, have achieved a précis which would never be possible in their daily reports from the Games arenas.

We are delighted to have the amazingly sharp memory of Lord Noel-Baker, who sixty-six years ago this year, ran in the Games of Stockholm; we are sad that Harold Abrahams, Olympic Champion of 1924 who died last year, was unable to revise his contribution. We are grateful that Monique Berlioux, Director of the IOC, found time to undertake the revision of the chapter on the History of the IOC and wish to thank the staff of the IOC for their help.

It is my hope, as the originator of this book and as President of the IOC, that it will fulfil a useful purpose. However, I would like to make it absolutely clear that in no place whatever has there been any form of censorship or direction given to any contributor.

The Olympic Movement has always come in for criticism ever since de Coubertin first suggested in 1894 reviving the Games but now, as in the past, the Olympic Movement draws strength from constructive comment. The increasing number of National Olympic Committees, sports and events on the Olympic programme has all helped to keep the Movement in step with social change.

At the Olympic Congress in 1981 at Baden-Baden a complete review will be made of the Olympic Movement by the IOC in conjunction with the International Federations and the National Olympic Committees together with other organizations interested in the development of the Olympic Games. I firmly believe that the future of the Olympic Movement is assured but we have to tackle realistically the problems which face it as the end of the twentieth century approaches.

Readers of this book will find an immense amount of information on the Olympic Movement. I hope that this revised edition will find its way into the hands of sports enthusiasts throughout the world and help promote the Olympic ideal and its motto *Citius*, *Altius*, *Fortius*.

Killanin

Dublin, 1979

MOSCOW AND LAKE PLACID–THE WAY AHEAD Lord Killanin

SITING THE GAMES

The Games of the twenty-second Olympiad will be held in Moscow, the first time in history that the Games have been held in a Communist country. On the other hand, the thirteenth Winter Games will be held in Lake Placid, in the United States, the foremost capitalist country. The selection of these two countries with opposing philosophies, combined with the fact that in 1984 the Games of the twenty-third Olympiad will be held in Los Angeles and the fourteenth Winter Games in Sarajevo are indications of the breadth and scope of the Games, which should and do surpass all political and ideological barriers. Over 130 nations are expected to take part in the 1980 Games with 12,000 athletes competing, 2,000 more than in 1976. The Soviet Union entered the Olympic Movement in 1951 (Imperial Russia had been recognized from 1896 to 1919), and competed for the first time in 1952 at the Games of Helsinki. It was in the days of the virtual Iron Curtain and travellers to the Games from Sweden, when passing through the southern part of Finland, had shutters put on their cars, and the Soviet team lived in a village independent from that of the rest of the athletes.

Today, thanks to the Olympic Movement, countries with very different political, religious and social views can come together in peace to compete in sport. Provided he or she is technically eligible, it is up to the individual to put him or herself forward for selection to take part in the Games. The International Olympic Movement is not a political movement and it is not the duty of the Olympic Movement to encourage revolution or effect changes in a government's policies.

Moscow was successful in its second bid in 1974 for the Games of 1980 against the candidature of Los Angeles, which hosted the Games in 1932. The exact voting figure was not disclosed but the overwhelming majority of the members of the IOC decided in favour of Moscow. There were however immediately some voices raised to complain that there would not be the necessary freedom of speech and action in Moscow for the Games to proceed normally but, overall, the decision was very well received and it was felt that the Soviet Union was prepared to open its doors to the athletes of the world in accordance with Olympic Rules. There has been a tendency in past years for countries to exploit the Games for national purposes and critics of the Soviet system protested that this tendency would be even more evident if the Games were held in Moscow but in general it was agreed that Moscow had the potential of being a great host for the Games.

Moscow has an excellent underground Metro system and multi-lane highways through the city. Although the distances between Olympic venues are considerable, as they were in Mexico, Moscow already contains many of the sporting facilities which other cities have had to build from scratch. However, this has not prevented the city from constructing new buildings and re-equipping such famous sites as the Lenin Stadium, which will be the principal venue of the Games.

Planning, in a Socialist State, has its advantages and disadvantages. There is normally a Five Year Plan and the advantage of this is shown for example in the creation of the Olympic Village, which will be part of a conurbation, eventually housing a quarter of a million people. After the Games this will become an important permanent addition to the City of Moscow. The 12,000 athletes are to be accommodated in sixteen-storey buildings, each unit consisting of two bedrooms with a living-room and other necessary facilities with accommodation for six or seven athletes. This is in direct contrast to the planning at Montreal where one of the most costly items was the construction of the Olympic Village. Modern North American planning differs in that a three-room flat consists of two bedrooms with one very large open-plan living-room. It was inevitable that this large living-room had frequently to accommodate between seven and eleven athletes and sometimes as many as fifteen.

There can be little doubt that the Moscow Games will be excellently run from a technical and administrative point of view, although everyone must face the fact that in a Socialist State there is possibly more bureaucracy than in other countries and it is interesting to compare the situation with Lake Placid which has already staged the Games (1932). The Lake Placid Organizing Committee is small, as is the community of 3,500 permanent residents. There is no doubt of their sincere desire to improve the winter sports facilities in this beautiful site (incidentally it is nearer Montreal than New York), and this has contributed to the enthusiasm of the local people. There were environmental problems which have been dealt with in a

A covered stadium with seats for 45,000 is being built in conjunction with a swimming pool on the Avenue Mir. The arena of the covered stadium which will be Europe's biggest, will house boxing and basketball during the Moscow Games.

sensible way, to the great advantage of all concerned. One of the problems of the Winter Games is that, in the past, they have been based on fairly small villages, though the last two Games were held in large cities: Innsbruck and Sapporo. Thus while Moscow has an excellent Olympic Village, Lake Placid for its part has a problem. This small community with holiday homes and limited hotel accommodation in the immediate vicinity has no suitable university or official building which might house the competitors who take part from a wide range of countries. The Federal Government therefore decided to build an open prison which during the Games will provide the athletes with accommodation. It is perhaps a little unfortunate that this will be known as the Olympic prison. The rooms are small but in other respects the facilities are extremely good.

It is very difficult accurately to cost an Olympic Games beforehand and comparisons with other Games can be misleading. For example, the Olympic Games at Munich yielded a revenue of DM 940.9 million and those of Montreal one of 126.8 million Canadian dollars. On the other hand, the capital investment depends very much on the facilities which already exist, the desires of the Organizing Committee and local authorities and the dictates of national pride. Standards demanded by competitors also continue to rise as do the requirements of officials, spectators and the media. It is in this area of increasing capital expenditure that there is the gravest concern. If the Olympic Games cannot be justified economically they may be doomed. At the same time, it must be remembered that the facilities which are bequeathed to the city in which the Games are held are a long-standing asset and should be added to the income derived from such things as the sale of seats, fund-raising, television rights, and tourists.

In the case of the Moscow Games, in addition to the City of Moscow, which will be the main centre, preliminaries in certain sports will be held in Minsk, Kiev and Leningrad, whilst the Yachting centre will be in Tallinn, in the Soviet Socialist Republic of Estonia. This is nearly 900 kilometres by air from Moscow. The holding of the Yachting events away from the main city is no novelty. They were held at some 1,000 kilometres from Munich in 1972, at Kiel, and in Kingston, Ontario, six hours' drive from Montreal in 1976. The International Olympic Committee changed its rules at the Session in Athens in 1978 to enable the selected city to share its privileges with other cities and thus lessen the burden on one centre. This is particularly important if the Games are to continue to grow. The number of countries taking part, sports, events and athletes (especially women participants) increase at each Games.

It is to be hoped that in Moscow as many National Olympic Committees as possible will be present but that they will realize that once they have entered any event they cannot withdraw a competitor for political reasons. The object of the Olympic Games is not only to bring together people who like each other, but also those who have differences, however these differences should be forgotten on the sports arena. This is the essence of the Movement and we must strive to make it a reality.

THE GAMES

The Games as we know them today were re-instituted after the Conference in the Sorbonne in Paris in June 1894 and the first of the new series took place in Athens in 1896. Baron de Coubertin, inspirer of the revived Games, was criticized as an idealist and accused of chauvinism. Since 1896 Games have taken place every four years, with the exception of the years of the two great wars.

Baron de Coubertin's name will always be associated with the new Olympic Movement. He was born in Paris on 1 January 1863 and was at heart a pedagogue with a great interest in literature, history, education and sociology. He was from a military family, which was by tradition impecunious. When he was twenty-four, he began to campaign for a new approach to education and the revival of the Olympic Games was only part of a greater plan. He was the first President of the International Olympic Committee from 1896 to 1925 and on his retirement was given the title of Honorary President. He had moved the headquarters to Lausanne and stepped down in 1914 temporarily when he went to the war and an interim president was appointed.

However, de Coubertin, although an idealist, was also a realist. He believed that 'athleticism can occasion the most noble passions or the most vile; it can develop impartiality and the feeling of honour, as can love of winning. It can be chivalrous or corrupt, vile, bestial. One can use it to consolidate peace or prepare for war.' I have always found de Coubertin's words a great comfort.

It is believed that the original Olympic Games were first held towards the end of the fourteenth century BC and were purely Greek in culture, which led them to be banned by the Emperor Theodosius in AD 393. The early Games, unlike those of today, were restricted to freemen and were certainly discriminatory in regard to race and sex. The events in the original Games included a 150-yard race in the stadium, long jumping, wrestling, discus throwing, besides chariot racing.

The first modern Olympic Games in 1896 were held in Athens in the Pan Athenaic stadium of Herodas, which had stone of white marble and was elongated so that there was a 400-metre circuit, with sharp turns. There were ten sports included in the first program: cycling, gymnastics, tennis, swimming, athletics, fencing, weightlifting, rowing, wrestling, shooting. Today there are twenty-one sports, besides a number of disciplines within each sport, for example: Swimming which has diving, swimming and water polo; Equestrianism which includes show jumping and the three-day event.

It may have been a mistake, but in the years after the war a number of new small team games, e.g. handball, softball, volleyball, which could be played in the same stadia and halls as other sports, were added to the program as options. However, once a sport is included cities bidding for the Games in future years feel obliged to include them. Enthusiasm for these sports was also spurred on by the interest after 1952 of the Eastern European countries, where sport has become an integral part of the national and political philosophy. This is something which would have pleased Baron de Coubertin who had been inspired by seeing the emphasis placed on sport in English Public Schools, especially by Dr Arnold, Headmaster of Rugby. The greatest social change in sport has been that it has moved from being a pastime for the privileged and become an absolute right for everyone of all classes and income groups. The Olympic Movement has played an important part in bringing this about, particularly in Communist countries.

PROFESSIONAL AND AMATEUR

The question of amateurism has been a bone of contention since the earliest days. One of the reasons that Tennis is not at present on the Olympic program is that the dividing line between professional and amateur has virtually disappeared. The Olympic Eligibility rules for competition are now very relaxed and allow financial subsidies for training in an effort to give equal opportunity to all. Perhaps the scope for this kind of support for the athlete has not been fully realized yet but most people see that it is desirable to keep Olympic athletes 'amateur'. The danger of professionalism is that it allows sport to become 'show business'. Then the athlete loses his freedom and becomes the instrument of the booking agent, or impresario who determines where he or she should perform and against whom, with a special eye to the gate and television receipts. The scale of the problem varies of course from sport to sport depending on its popularity, spectator interest and potential for commercial sponsorship.

The problem of amateurism has always been there but in recent years pressures have increased. I believe the IOC faces it with realism. However, after 1980 the IOC will have to take a further look at the distinction between amateur and professional in the light of the following:

1. In the Olympic Games high performance sport needs intensive training, which takes time and interferes with the competitor's normal occupation.
2. Equipment for some sports has to be made to higher and higher standards and becomes increasingly expensive. This is particularly true of sports like skiing and yachting. Horses, too, are very expensive to keep and train.
3. In countries where national pride and sporting achievement are synonymous, amateur status can be endangered. For example, in certain Eastern European States athletes may have professions or trades but be provided with special training facilities and unlimited time in which to train. However, to my mind, there is little difference between this state-aided athlete and the athlete sponsored by a private firm or organization. What is the difference between army personnel jumping in equestrian events or a top class runner, who is released on full pay by a large private company until such a time as he has passed his peak and will resume his normal professional work?

I believe the bogy of the 'state amateur' has been grossly exaggerated. The example set by certain of the Socialist countries in the development of sports facilities should be followed in the West. During the last eight to ten years there has been an improvement but many sporting facilities are still inadequate even in so-called 'industrially developed' countries.

With the spread of the Olympic Movement and of enthusiasm for sport of all kinds, it is essential that poorer countries should not have less of an opportunity for competing and winning than richer countries. It may be very difficult for a poorer National Olympic Committee or National Federation to train its athletes to Olympic standard and, in the new oil-rich countries, the building of large and impressive stadia should not obscure the equal importance of providing primary and secondary school children with sporting facilities.

After the Games in Munich the Eligibility rules were rewritten. Rule 26 now reads:

To be eligible for participation in the Olympic Games, a competitor must:

– observe and abide by the Rules of the IOC and, in addition, the rules of his or her International Federation, as approved by the IOC, even if the Federation's rules are more strict than those of the IOC.

– not have received any financial rewards or material benefit in connection with his or her sports participation, except as permitted in the bye-laws to this rule.

The Olympic International Federations are responsible for the control of their athletes not only during the Games but all the time. The Games is to them only one, admittedly very important, competition in their program. The bye-laws to Rule 26 allow broken time, and permit National Federations to receive income from advertizing provided the individual is not exploited. The object is to give the maximum opportunity to all and at the same time to endeavour to prevent illegal payments to individuals.

Returning to de Coubertin's statement which I quoted above, I am not naïve enough to believe that there exist no dishonest athletes but the aim should be sport for sport's sake and not for private gain. There have been many controversies in the past. For example, in 1948 the Swedish Equestrian team were disqualified as only officers were considered amateur. A warrant officer who had no desire to be commissioned permanently was granted a commission for the period of the Games and then reverted to original rank. Sweden lost its medals.

I know that there are many people who believe that my own interpretation of the Eligibility rule is too liberal and amongst these critics would have been my predecessor, Avery Brundage, for whose integrity I always had the greatest respect. However, I feel that one must be pragmatic and realistic and that decisions should be made in the light of changing circumstances. Perhaps International Federations are correct when they say to the IOC 'You write your Rule 26 and we will write the bye-laws, which affect each of our sports. If you like our bye-laws you accept us on the program, if you do not, you reject us.' It would certainly save a great deal of work, but then again I am frequently implored to give a lead on what can and cannot be done.

My own view is that there is nothing whatsoever against professional sport but if the Olympic Games were handed over to professionals the Olympic Movement would fall into the hands of promoters and impresarios. Occasionally in the past, as after an Olympic Games a track and field circus is begun but it rarely lasts. It is for this reason that I do not see in the near future the Olympic Games going 'open'.

OLYMPIC CEREMONIAL

Olympic protocol has always been a point of considerable discussion and controversy. In the ancient Games, which were partially religious, the Sun played an important part, as indeed did the blessings of the gods. When de Coubertin revived the Olympic Games in 1896 he realized that certain ceremonies were essential in order to create the correct atmosphere. These evolved as the Games grew but the prime moments, other than the victory ceremonies which honour the individual athletes, are the opening and closing ceremonies.

No political demonstration is permitted although it is permissible to have a religious celebration, but the last one which I can recall was at Helsinki. It always appeared to me out of place at such a secular event as the Games. The competitors and officials parade behind their flag and the name of their country in the first language of the country in which the Games are taking place. This frequently leads to disputes of a political nature as certain countries do not recognize others and the International Olympic Committee recognizes National Olympic Committees as opposed to political units. An unfortunate tradition has arisen for using the opening ceremony to display national pride, teams vying with each other for the most outstanding uniforms especially now that women athletes are so prominent.

The opening ceremony is brief. The President of the Organizing Committee is restricted to giving a three-minute speech, in which he introduces the President of the International Olympic Committee, who in his turn simply requests the Head of State to open the Games. The Head of State has always done this with the exception of the Melbourne Games, when the Queen designated Prince Philip as a special envoy. However, in the case of the Games of Montreal, the Queen opened the Games personally, speaking in both French and English but giving French precedence as French is the first language of the Olympic Movement. This was a particularly sensitive point, Quebec being a French-speaking Province of Canada.

Another important part of the opening ceremony is the transfer of the Olympic flag, presented by the city of Antwerp in 1922. This

The opening ceremony in 1912, before the Olympic flag and flame were introduced.

A view of the closing ceremony of the 1976 Olympic Games, at the Olympic Stadium in Montreal.

is held by the Olympic City until the next Olympic Games when it is handed over by that city's Mayor to the Mayor of the current host city. Again, this has to my mind become an excuse for a certain amount of jingoism but of course is very much encouraged by the television companies for its value as a spectacle. What I believe is the most important part of the Olympic Games' opening ceremony is the oath taken by the athletes, which reads as follows:

> In the name of all the competitors I promise that we shall take part in these Olympic Games, respecting and abiding by the rules which govern them, in the true spirit of sportsmanship, for the glory of sport and the honour of our teams.

Since 1968 an oath has also been taken by the judges and officials.

The victory ceremonies have also created problems for the organizers. The medals are presented by the President of the IOC or his nominee, accompanied by the President of the International Federation of the sport concerned. National Olympic Committees have requested that their own Presidents should also attend and there have been suggestions that, in view of the narrowness of the margin which often separates winner from loser, the fourth, fifth and sixth (who receive diplomas in the individual events) should also be present on the rostrum. My own personal experience is that it is difficult enough to collect the three medal winners together let alone the first six or even more in the case of team games. It has also been suggested that the ceremony should consist simply of the elevation of the Olympic flag to a fanfare, since the raising of the national flag and the playing of the national anthem undoubtedly encourages the erroneous idea that the medal table is an indication of the relative success or otherwise of political systems. It may come as a surprise to some to learn that the Olympic medals are not made of gold but are gilt. They are the property and copyright of the International Olympic Committee although they are always designed by the host city, with the IOC's approval.

I am opposed to nationalism and I would be happier if national anthems were not used at the Games, but I realize that my view is not that of the majority. There is no doubt that some of the larger powers wish to retain the present medal ceremony and many of the newer nations, although it may be some years before their anthems are played or national flag raised, eagerly await their day. Even the anthems and the flags themselves give trouble especially in countries in the process of gaining independence or changing their political systems but it is the responsibility of each National Olympic Committee to submit the anthem it wishes played, although this in its turn has led to disputes amongst members of National Olympic Committees. As regimes change so anthems change and many embarrassing situations have been caused by the wrong anthem being played in all innocence by the host city. These anthems are now often played from a tape, which at first shocked many people, but I think it is better than listening to the efforts of an inferior orchestra and of course does reduce the actual cost.

TELEVISION

It would be foolish to pretend that television is not an important force in projecting the Olympic Movement. Olympic ceremonies, particularly the opening and closing ceremony, are influenced to some extent by the demands of the television companies. They also ask that there should not be too many or too few victory ceremonies in any one hour so that throughout the day viewers will have a victory ceremony to watch. While happy to accommodate viewers, the Organizing Committee has to ensure that events are scheduled primarily for the convenience of the competitors.

The rapid growth of interest in the Olympic Games can clearly be related to the development of television. The first television pictures of the Olympic Games were transmitted from Berlin in 1936. Audiences in halls in Berlin and in other German cities watched athletics and swimming events. From that beginning of audiences of a few thousand, in 1976, 107 electronic colour cameras (part of equipment costing 100 million dollars) sent pictures via satellite round the world to audiences each day of over 800 million. In 1980 that figure will go well over a 1,000 million since the Games will be shown on television sets throughout China.

A camera used to relay the first transmission of the Games on television in 1936.

The big jump in the size of television audiences came, of course, with the introduction of satellites which could beam pictures instantaneously to every country on earth. The first time pictures of the Games were relayed from one country to another was in 1960 at Rome, and in 1964 the Tokyo Games were relayed via satellite for the first time from one continent to another.

Inevitably it took time for the International Olympic Committee to assess the advantages and disadvantages of the advent of television and even the financial benefits were not immediately realized. The highly commercial structure of television companies in the United States competing for the largest audiences from a population of 220 million is quite different from that of almost every other country. American television companies are able to set the price of their advertizing rates according to the appeal of a particular program and it quickly became apparent that the compelling nature of the Olympic Games meant that advertizers were ready to pay enormous sums in order to advertize their wares in the middle of Olympic competitions. By 1972 American television was prepared to pay 25 million dollars for the television rights to the Montreal Games plus fees for hardware and facilities. Inflation and ever greater audiences hoisted the figure for rights and hardware to 85 million dollars when the contract between NBC and the Moscow Organizing Committee was signed in 1977. The rest of the world ironically pays less than twenty percent of this sum to receive the television pictures, largely because the companies are state funded.

Television has influenced the Games in many ways. Competitors, for example, in the track and field events, wear their numbers not only on the front and back, the traditional method so that judges and timekeepers could identify them, but on the side of their shorts, so that cameras and commentators can pick them up and identify them when they pass across the screen.

Television has brought logistical problems. Space has to be found for cameras, technicians and a vast amount of equipment; studios have to be provided for the various countries who wish to take the service. There is also the much greater worry that athletes will use the television cameras to make political gestures. Members of the United States team at the 1968 Games in Mexico raised a gloved fist, the symbol of Black Power, when receiving their medals. The incident attracted world-wide publicity and the athletes were sent home. Before that, University students, academics and others had seen fit to demonstrate against the Government in the weeks leading up to the Olympic Games. It led to a bloody demonstration in which many people were killed and while the events had no direct relationship with the Olympic Games the demonstrators knew that the television cameras would give their demonstrations world-wide publicity.

In 1972 terrorists penetrated the Olympic village and killed competitors and officials of the Israeli team. Television was on hand to show the full horror of a movement intended to promote world peace being made the vehicle of hate.

Nevertheless, one of television's greatest contributions has been to bring to the world's notice the significance of the Olympic ideal. There is no way of knowing how many thousands of people, inspired by television pictures of the Games, take up some sporting activity or help others to do so. One indication is that the number of countries within the Olympic Movement has risen from 62 in 1952 to almost 140, and the number of competitors from just over 5,000 to about 12,000. In a similar fashion Winter Sports owe some of their development to television. Here, as with the summer events, all aspects of preparation and competition are covered and relayed to the viewer. No other event in the world has a television audience to match that which watches the Olympic Games.

THE ARTIFICIAL MAN

The Olympic motto – *Citius, Altius, Fortius* – Swifter, Higher,

Professor Arnold Beckett at work on the equipment used for detecting anabolic steroids.

Stronger, was adopted in 1922 on the advice of Father Didon, a Dominican and friend of de Coubertin's. I never discovered whether he had in mind man's effort physically to reach swifter, higher, stronger, or whether it refers to the Olympic Movement. I prefer the latter interpretation but I am probably wrong.

The history of the medical work of the International Olympic Committee is closely tied up with the former interpretation. In 1961 under the chairmanship of Sir Arthur Porritt (now Lord Porritt), an eminent New Zealand surgeon, a Medical Commission was formed. It had been set up because it had become obvious that there had been an increase in the number and kind of stimulants used by sportsmen. The twilight zone between protective or remedial medicine and artificial aids such as doping, whether to stimulate or depress, is narrow. Furthermore, with many events confined to women, it became necessary, although not pleasant, to introduce femininity tests to ensure only women took part in them. This is the most delicate part of the work of the IOC Medical Commission and one of considerable importance.

Together with ordinary drugs there are various far more dangerous aids to athletic performance. The most alarming is the use of anabolic steroids, by which muscle bulk can be increased rapidly and to an unnatural degree. Detection is difficult since trace of the steroids may disappear if they are taken some fourteen days or so before an event. Professor Arnold Beckett of Chelsea College, London, has been one of the pioneers in researching this area and in recent years considerable advances have been made in detecting the use of steroids, but if scientists are going to create 'artificial' athletes to compete in the Olympic Games or any international sport then the sooner the international competitions are ended the better. Sport is about the attainment of the complete man or woman, physically and mentally, by natural, and not artificial, means. Unfortunately, as rapidly as the IOC Medical Commission (and now most International Federations and many National Olympic Committees have their own Medical Commissions) detects one particular drug, others which may not be at first detectable or may be outside the definition of banned drugs are developed. One of the benefits of the Olympic Games is that there are now very good control centres spread throughout the world. These are inevitably extremely expensive to run but Moscow is building a special centre which I am informed will be the most advanced in the world. There are good centres in many places in Europe and the laboratories at the Montreal Games, under Dr Laurin, were absolutely first class. The laboratories which will be used for the Winter Games at Lake Placid, in 1980, are modelled on these. The ideal would be to have a number of centres with the same systems and standards throughout the world. The Olympic Movement will not be swayed from its belief that fair competition is worth striving for.

THE FUTURE OF THE OLYMPIC MOVEMENT

After 1980 it will be necessary for the International Olympic Committee at its Congress in Baden-Baden in 1981 to determine its future. These Congresses are needed from time to time (the last was in Varna in Bulgaria in 1973) and provide an open forum for all those who support the Olympic Movement to express their views. Since 1973 there has been a period of marking time in which the greatest change has probably come from the easing of the amateur regulations mentioned above. One serious criticism which will have to be discussed is that the Games have become too huge and successful, to the point where they might become unmanageable.

The 1984 Games have been allocated to Los Angeles but the city refused to accept full financial responsibility for staging the Games. Montreal staged the Games with unnecessary extravagance which did the Olympic Movement harm. As has been mentioned, the Olympic Games can be spread geographically and it is possible for a city to share the honour with other cities.

Some people see no point in the Olympic Games; there are others, whom I believe to be the overwhelming majority, who believe they should continue despite all the difficulties. Once again, television can play an important part. The IOC has never requested that a main stadium should be constructed to a certain size but live audiences have, of course, increased through the very fact that television has popularized the Games and it is essential that the competitions should take place in front of a live audience who can give encouragement to the athletes.

Baron de Coubertin formed the IOC as Trustees for the Olympic Movement. The National Olympic Committees which have increased from 68 in 1950, when I was elected an NOC President, to some 140 in 1979, wish to have more say in the running of their own affairs. At the same time the International Federations which are termed more democratic have also increased in number. I believe that, unfortunately, 'the democratization' of the Olympic Movement will not work as it will increase 'the politicization'. My own view is that in the next few years the IOC will have representatives from more and more countries, especially from the great continents to which competitive sport is comparatively new and this must be of benefit, not only to the Olympic Movement, but also to mankind. The Olympic Movement is not just about siting and organizing a super sports competition every four years, but has the ideal of bringing people together in peace regardless of race, religion and colour.

THE HISTORY OF THE INTERNATIONAL OLYMPIC COMMITTEE Monique Berlioux

… — Nº 1. Janvier 1896.

BULLETIN DU COMITÉ INTERNATIONAL

DES

…EUX OLYMPIQUES

229, Rue Saint-Honoré — Citius — Fortius — Altius — Rue Saint-Honoré, 229, PARIS

PROGRAMME

DES

…EUX OLYMPIQUES DE 1896

ATHÈNES

5-15 AVRIL 1896. — (24 mars-3 avril, Style grec).

SOUS LA PRÉSIDENCE DE

S. A. R. Monseigneur le Prince Royal, duc de Sparte

A. — SPORTS ATHLÉTIQUES

…ed : 100 mètres, 400 mètres, 800 mètres et 1.500 mè… 110 mètres haies. — Les règlements seront ceux …ion des Sociétés françaises de Sports Athlétiques.

…auts en longueur et en hauteur (running long et high … Saut à la perche (Pole vault) : Lancement du poids … the weight) et du disque. — Les règlements seront … l'Amateur Athletic Association d'Angleterre.

…d, dite de Marathon, sur la distance de 48 kilomè… Marathon à Athènes, pour la coupe offerte par M. Mi…al, membre de l'Institut de France.

B. — GYMNASTIQUE

…dividuels : Corde lisse en traction de bras. — Réta…nts divers à la barre fixe. — Mouvements aux an… — Barres parallèles profondes. — Saut au cheval. …ail des poids.

… d'ensemble : (Les Sociétés ne pourront présenter … inférieures à 10 gymnastes).

C. — ESCRIME ET LUTTE

…euret, sabre et épée : Amateurs ; Professeurs (civils …ires). — Un règlement spécial a été élaboré par la … l'encouragement de l'Escrime (Paris). …ine et grecque.

D. — TIR

… d'une difficulté imprévue, le programme du Tir … publié qu'un peu plus tard.

E. — SPORTS NAUTIQUES

…ourses à la voile. — L'Union des Yachts Français a … un règlement spécial.

… rameur : 2.000 mètres, sans virage, skiffs. …ameurs de couple, sans virage, yoles et outriggers. …rameurs de pointe, sans virage, yoles. …urse spéciale sera organisée pour les équipages des … …ements seront ceux du Rowing Club Italiano.

Natation : Vitesse : 100 mètres. Fond et vitesse : 500 mètres. Fond : 1,000 mètres. Jeu de water-polo.

F. — VÉLOCIPÉDIE

Vitesse : 2.000 mètres, sur piste, sans entraîneurs. 10,000 mètres, sur piste, sans entraîneurs.

Fond : 100 kilomètres sur piste avec entraîneurs.

Course de 12 heures sur piste, avec entraîneurs.

Les règlement suivis seront ceux de l'International Cyclist's Association.

G. — EQUITATION

Concours d'équitation : reprise de manège, avec et sans étriers, saut d'obstacles, voltige, haute école.

(Il ne sera tenu compte que de l'aptitude du cavalier et non de la valeur du cheval.)

H. — JEUX ATHLÉTIQUES

Lawn tennis : Simple. Double.

Cricket : Les règlements seront ceux de la All England Lawn Tennis Association et du Marylebone Cricket Club.

Fait à Athènes, le 12/24 novembre 1894.

Colonel Mano ;
Etienne Scouloudis, député, ancien ministre ;
A.-D. Soutzo, chef d'escadron de cavalerie ;
Retsinas, maire du Pirée,
vice-présidents du Comité hellène.
Paul Skouzès, trésorier.
Alexandre Mercati, Georges M. Melas, secrétaires.

Approuvé :

D. Bikelas, président du Comité International.
Baron Pierre de Coubertin, secrétaire général.
A. Callot, trésorier.

Program for the 1896 Games.

The organization of the International Olympic Committee was envisaged as a complete structure by Pierre de Coubertin.

The International Congress of Paris for the Re-establishment of the Olympic Games was convened in June 1894 in the amphitheatre of the Sorbonne – at the very heart of the French university so opposed to sport. Its success surpassed Coubertin's hopes. The opening ceremony began with the hymn to Apollo which had just been discovered in Delphi; this epic anthem created the atmosphere he needed.

On 23 June, the Congress, with the unanimous support of the seventy-nine delegates and forty-nine sports associations from twelve countries present, agreed to re-establish the Games, choosing to hold them in true Hellenic tradition at Athens in 1896.

From the outset, Coubertin laid down the structure of the organization of the Games. Once he had determined the principles and regulations, he was only involved with the main points. He wanted a group of people who would define general policy and be the guardian of the concept. This society was to be independent, international, sovereign and assured of perpetuity. It came into being from the Paris Congress, under the title of 'International Olympic Committee'. Coubertin selected the first members of this committee, which, including himself, totalled fifteen men from twelve nations.

The IOC has unquestionable powers as guide, guardian and arbiter. It is the supreme body in the Olympic Movement, the rock, the foundation stone.

Starting line in the stadium at Olympia, where the ancient Games were held.

Pierre and Marie de Coubertin.

The Olympic Movement comprises in addition the International Sports Federations, which are responsible for the management, administration, techniques and promotion of their respective sports; the athletes, who illustrate Olympism in action; the National Olympic Committees, which represent the IOC and are delegated by it to promote the Olympic Movement within their respective territories and to see that the IOC's regulations are respected there.

The IOC has four aims:

1. to promote the development of those physical and moral qualities which are the basis of sport.
2. to educate young people through sport in a spirit of better understanding, helping to build a better and more peaceful world.
3. to spread the Olympic ideal throughout the world, thereby creating international goodwill.
4. to bring together the athletes of the world in a great four-yearly festival of sport.

The IOC is a self-recruiting body. The members are co-opted. Coubertin set out what he expected of them in *Mémoires Olympiques*:

> [The Committee] was a 'self-recruiting body', with the same type of management structure as that for the Henley [Royal] regattas. But it was already . . . composed of three concentric circles: a small core of earnest and hard-working members; a nursery of willing members ready to be taught; finally, a façade of more or less useful people whose presence satisfied national pretensions at the same time as it gave prestige to the Committee as a whole.

He wanted members to be 'trustees' of the Olympic idea. They would be selected for their knowledge of sport and their national standing, since, according to de Coubertin's principle of a 'delegation in reverse', an IOC member is an ambassador from the Committee to his own country and not an ambassador of his country to the IOC.

The candidates to the IOC, who are numerous, are considered by the Executive Board which makes a recommendation to the General Assembly, called 'Session'; the Executive Board's judgment is almost always accepted.

Until 1966, the IOC members were elected for life. Since then, they must retire at the age of seventy-two. Some of course retire before that age, and in extreme cases the Committee is entitled to dismiss them.

Members must reside in their country; because of this ruling, King Constantine of Greece, elected in 1963 when he was Crown Prince, had to resign in 1974 when he left his country.

There are some unwritten rules. When the Committee was constituted, the founder nations were entitled to several representatives. There were up to four members for France and for the United States.

Some of the IOC members present at the 1896 Games. Seated (left to right): Baron Pierre de Coubertin (France), secretary D. Vikelas (Greece), president of the IOC; A. de Boutoysky (USSR). Standing (left to right): Dr W. Gebhardt (Germany), Jiri Guth-Jarkovsky (Czechoslovakia), Francois Kemery (Hungary), General Viktor Balck (Sweden).

Memorial at Olympia containing the heart of Baron Pierre de Coubertin who revived the Olympic Games in 1896.

In 1966 this figure was reduced to three; today it is two for countries which have staged the Olympic Games, or those with a long Olympic tradition, or those whose territory spreads over a large area. The tendency has been to bring IOC representation on a national scale down to one wherever possible, as has been done in the case of Belgium and the Netherlands, both having staged the Games. Lord Killanin would like the Committee to represent as many nations as possible, in particular the doors should be wide open to African countries. Many states have recently become independent and a dozen new National Olympic Committees need to be set up before the Moscow Games.

From fifteen in 1894, the IOC's membership increased to forty-eight on the eve of World War I, sixty-seven in 1936 and seventy-two in 1951, the year when the President, Sigfrid Edström, nominated for ratification by the Session the first member from an Eastern European country, Constantin Andrianov of the USSR.

In 1979, the IOC had eighty-nine members, in seventy-one countries, spread over five continents. Africa has fourteen, Asia fifteen, America nineteen, Europe thirty-eight, Oceania three. Their social origins are extremely varied, their professions run from head of state to ambassador and from professor of physical education to doctor.

There have been over 350 members since the Committee's creation, of whom more than half have taken part in the Games or top level competition as athletes. Of these, ten or so have won gold medals, among them the Marquess of Exeter (Great Britain; 400-metres hurdles, 1928), Masaji Kiyokawa (Japan; 100-metres backstroke, 1932), Julian K. Roosevelt (United States; yachting 5.5 metres, 1952), Sven Thofelt (Sweden; modern pentathlon, 1928).

At the outset and in the early years Coubertin was completely against any participation of women in Olympic events. Moreover, the founder of the Modern Games could never have imagined women playing a part in the conduct of Olympic affairs at any level. Since Lord Killanin's accession to the presidency, the idea of seeing women in the IOC has been accepted and it is likely that some women members will be elected at Sessions in the near future. The difficulty consists in finding candidates having experience within National Olympic Committees or International Federations and who are ready to accept the post.

The IOC meets at least once a year and twice in the year of the Games, just before each one is celebrated. The program of the Session, usually heavy, is governed by an agenda including the following main points: elections, co-option of new members, amendments to the Rules and Regulations, changes in the program of the Games, reports from the Organizing Committees of the Games and the National Olympic Committees, development of the Movement and reports from the Commissions. There are twelve permanent commissions dealing with such matters as finance, medicine, eligibility, press and publicity.

The Session usually adopts recommendations from the Executive Board with a show of hands. A simple majority is sufficient except for changes in the Rules, for which a majority of two-thirds is required. For elections, an absolute majority is necessary.

Every four years the Session has to select the cities which will

Les Jeux Olympiques, **program cover for the 1896 Games.**

organize the Games of the Olympiad and the Winter Games. The voting is secret, sometimes with several ballots in between sharp and lively debates. All the Sessions are accompanied by a certain amount of pomp and ceremony. For instance in 1978, in Athens, the official opening ceremony took place in the ancient theatre of Herode Atticus. The President of the Republic, the President of the Hellenic Olympic Committee and the President of the IOC delivered speeches in which the main themes of the IOC's sporting policy were indicated. The Olympic anthem, as well as the Greek national hymn, was played. Choirs and dancers completed the ceremony which was followed by the presentation of the members to the head of state. There are always a number of receptions, at which the debates of the conference table often continue in a more relaxed, informal manner.

In 1921 Coubertin appointed the first Executive Board, consisting of five members. It has grown in size and stature; it now consists of nine members, elected in full session. They are: the President, elected for eight years, then eligible for re-election for successive periods of four years; the first, second and third Vice-Presidents, elected for four years, who are not eligible for re-election and who advance by seniority of election; five members, elected for four years, eligible for re-election after one year of absence. Lord Killanin feels that this does not provide the necessary continuity to see through programs.

Apart from its task of directing the IOC, the Executive Board prepares the work of the Sessions, maintains a constant link with current problems which the Olympic Movement faces, and meets, apart from the Sessions, at least once a year. The Board is also responsible for meeting the International Federations each year and the NOCs every other year to discuss problems and development, thus ensuring the necessary unity and coordination within the Movement.

Administrative work and research are dealt with by the general secretariat, whose headquarters are in Lausanne, Switzerland. At the head of the general secretariat is a director, assisted by an international staff including translators, interpreters and librarians. The official bulletin of the IOC, the *Olympic Review*, is published monthly in three languages: French, Spanish and English.

Legends always die hard, especially where the IOC is concerned. It has been dubbed 'a closed body', but, particularly since the accession of Lord Killanin as President, every important Olympic decision has been the subject of methodical cooperation between the committee and external sports figures. This has not always been the case and arbitrary decisions, often based upon flimsy evidence or taken hastily, have damaged the image of the IOC, giving it the reputation of being out of step with sports development in modern society. The philosophy of working with external organizations was encouraged by setting up IOC commissions. Since Lord Killanin became a vice-president, the work of these commissions has widened; they have provided a way of bringing people with a particular expertise who are not IOC members into much closer touch with the Committee. The President has the prerogative of creating the commissions and appointing the chairman and members.

The original rules of the IOC stipulated that the registered office of the society should be moved every four years to the country

Program cover for the World's Fair which included the Olympic Games, 1904.

staging the next Olympic Games. But World War I brought a change. Although he was fifty-one when hostilities broke out, Coubertin enlisted in the Army and told his fellow members that he felt it was wrong that the Committee should be presided over by a soldier. He asked Baron Godefroy de Blonay, a Swiss, to take over the Presidential duties.

For a long time the Founder had been attracted to the quiet city of Lausanne. This, together with the primary concern of protecting the Olympic institution by establishing it in a country outside the world conflict, was the key to Coubertin's decision – to install the IOC headquarters in Switzerland. He decided to override objections from the members and, on 10 April 1915, in the conference room at Lausanne Town Hall, signatures were exchanged with a view to establishing the world administration centre there.

It was not until 1922, however, that the IOC actually took up its quarters in Lausanne, occupying a floor of Mon Repos manor, a comfortable mansion in which Coubertin occupied a few rooms towards the end of his life.

In 1968 the IOC moved to the Château de Vidy, a big country house on the shores of Lake Geneva.

Strangely, until recent times the IOC had no legal status. Coubertin and his successors cherished the freedom of this position. However, our modern society has compelled the IOC to become a legal entity.

The IOC flag has five interlaced rings, of which the respective colours from the pole end are blue, yellow, black, green and red, on a white background. The yellow and green rings are lower than the other three. The yellow ring links the blue and the black ones; the green links the black and red ones. Coubertin found this emblem at Delphi in 1913. 'These five rings', he wrote, 'represent the five parts of the world won over to Olympism and ready to accept its bountiful rivalries. The six colours combined in this way represent those of every nation without exception.' The IOC flag flew for the first time in Paris, in June 1914, at the Congress marking the twentieth anniversary of its foundation.

The motto adopted by the IOC, *Citius, Altius, Fortius*, made its appearance at the Antwerp Games. Its inventor was a Dominican, Father Henri Didon. This teacher, who had a great influence on Coubertin, was prior of Arcueil College, Paris. He wanted all his pupils to practise sport and at their first meeting in the open air he announced, 'Here is your watchword – *citius, altius, fortius.*'

In a way the IOC has a second motto. A religious service in St Paul's Cathedral, London, on 19 July 1908, marked the Games of the fourth Olympiad. The Bishop of Pennsylvania preached a sermon of which one phrase dazzled Coubertin: 'the important thing in the Olympic Games is not so much to have been victorious as to have taken part'.

A few days later, paying tribute to the author of this idea, Coubertin said in a speech:

> The most important thing in the Olympic Games is not to win but to take part, just as the most important thing in life is not the triumph but the struggle. The essential thing is not to have conquered but to have fought well.

These words now appear on the electronic scoreboards at opening ceremonies of the Games.

An Olympic hymn of slow and solemn beauty and classical inspiration was composed in 1896 by the Greek Spyros Samaras to words by his colleague Costis Palamas. In the 1950s there were calls for a change but the attempts to provide something better were unsuccessful and Samaras's cadences have since been linked to every Olympic festival.

Coubertin wanted the Olympic Games to be the peak of a pyramid, with national Games at the base, then continental Games. This idea did not begin to evolve until after World War I, when the IOC granted its patronage to the Latin-American Games in 1922. Since then other continental and regional Games have flourished, such as the Pan-American, Asian, Mediterranean, African, World Student Games, and many others.

When the IOC was founded, confusion reigned in the technical rules as well as in the organization of competition sports. At that time few sports had international associations or rules. The emergence of the Olympic Movement, and the desire of sportsmen to compete in the Games, gave international formalization and impetus that would not otherwise have occurred. Today sports within the Olympic program are all properly controlled and regulated.

In the early 1960s many sports federations were dissatisfied with some of the IOC's actions and decisions, particularly in relation to amateurism. They felt they should have a more significant voice and a large number (though not the powerful International Amateur Athletic Federation) formed the General Assembly of International Federations in 1967. Lord Killanin was convinced that an exchange of views would resolve the differences which had arisen between the IOC and the International Federations and this proved to be the case. Today, all Olympic International Federations (IFs) are united under the presidency of a Swiss, Thomas Keller, who is also President of the International Rowing Federation. They meet annually to discuss their common interests: their share of television rights, the sports calendar, and rules.

Coubertin was always afraid that the IOC might become isolated. Hence the National Olympic Committees (NOCs), which he wanted to establish as branches of the IOC in all countries, so as to simplify and discipline the participation in the Games of athletes from all over the world. Here too, he was not slow in defining their function nor their dangers. In July 1903 he wrote in the *Olympic Review*:

> The NOCs must not be an emanation of the main sports federations or associations of the country. . . . There is every advantage in these Committees being permanent. . . . One cannot insist too strongly on the danger of making a National Olympic Committee the main guiding cog in the sporting activity of a country.

The use of the NOC in some countries for the development of sport for political and other purposes began to worry the IOC fifty years after those words were written and still does. In 1954 the IOC laid down, in Rule 24, the conditions governing the existence of the NOCs. They must consist of representatives of at least five sports federations recognized by the corresponding International Federations. The IOC recognizes an NOC only after approving its statutes.

Official program cover for the Olympic Games, 1908.

Official program cover for the Olympic Games, 1912.

Any recognition is revocable, as in the case of South Africa, excluded from the Olympic Movement in 1970 and of Rhodesia, from which recognition was withdrawn in 1973.

There exists a powerful but delicate instrument created with the aim of establishing strong links between the IOC and other world sporting bodies: that instrument is the Olympic Congress. There was a time when the word caused some confusion as the first IOC Session was also called a congress.

Since 1925, the Congress has met under the direction of the President of the IOC. Debates, carried on over several days, do not terminate in a vote, but rather with recommendations.

A great number of observers are invited to the Congress by the IOC: IFs recognized by the Committee but which do not participate in the Games, institutions such as the United Nations, United Nations Educational, Scientific and Cultural Organization, the World Health Organization, the World Intellectual Property Organization, associations like the Association de la Presse Sportive and the Fédération Internationale de Médecine Sportive, Olympic medallists and various dignitaries.

We have already mentioned the first Congress in Paris in 1894, attended by about 2,000 people belonging to sports associations, universities and business circles, representing thirteen nations. The second, held in 1897 with calculated modesty at the Town Hall in Le Havre (the Norman port was one of the cradles of Coubertin's family), welcomed a smaller but equally select committee. The accent was laid on the philosophical, moral and educational originality of the Olympic Movement. The next Congress was held in 1905 at the Palais des Académies in Brussels. The organizer was the young Comte Henri de Baillet-Latour, who then had been a member of the IOC for two years. There were 210 participants, from twenty-one countries. An essential innovation gave the International Federations five representatives each. In May of the following year in Paris, about sixty celebrities from the worlds of art and sport studied how the Arts and Letters could be brought into the Olympic Games. This led to the introduction of the cultural program at Stockholm in 1912. This was not officially a Congress but a 'Consultative Arts, Letters and Sports Conference'. The discussions were widely talked about; Olympism was becoming highly fashionable.

Then came, in March 1913, the Lausanne Congress devoted to sports psychology and physiology, and, in June 1914, a further Olympic Congress was held in Paris. For the first time the NOCs participated *en masse* in the Congress but World War I broke out before the minutes were finalized. One of the major topics had been women's sports, to which Coubertin and the great majority of those present were opposed, in spite of the very discreet entry of women in preceding Games. This was followed by the Olympic Congress on the Olympic Regulations, held in June 1921 in Lausanne. Besides the IOC, seventy-eight delegates from the NOCs and IFs discussed everything concerning the Games and serious misunderstandings were overcome between the IOC and the IFs. Differences of opinion existed but they were just as deep between the various IFs, and between the NOCs, as between the IOC and the individual interests of other sports institutions.

The Olympic Congress at Prague in May 1925 dealt with the

regulations and the educational role of sport. Amateurism, the reduction of the program of the Games, the NOCs' powers, women's participation in Olympism, and a number of other subjects were discussed at length.

In May 1930 the ninth Olympic Congress was held at the Herrenhaus in Berlin. There were encroachments upon the IOC's prerogatives. A new definition of amateurism was adopted, as well as various modifications to the general rules of the Games and to the protocol. The IOC feared that by allowing a succession of Olympic Congresses, there would be disorder and paralysis. With World War II looming after the Games of Berlin the next Olympic Congress was a long way off.

The tenth Congress was held in Varna, Bulgaria, in 1973 after a gap of forty-three years. Under the general title of 'The Olympic Movement and its Future' it considered three fundamental themes: redefinition of the Olympic Movement, relations between the IOC, the IFs and the NOCs, and the pattern of future Olympic Games. It was recommended that Olympic Congresses should be held every eight years, the year following the Olympic Games.

The eleventh Congress is scheduled to take place in 1981 at Baden-Baden in the Federal Republic of Germany and will consider the theme 'International Cooperation'.

Since its foundation, the IOC has had seven Presidents: Demetrius Vikelas, Coubertin, the Baron Godefroy de Blonay (who took over from Coubertin during World War I), the Comte de Baillet-Latour, Sigfrid Edström, Avery Brundage and Lord Killanin.

Demetrius Vikelas, a Greek, was the first, in 1894, while Coubertin reserved for himself the position of Secretary-General. The rules then stipulated that the President should come from the country organizing the next Games, and since these were entrusted to Paris, the leadership of the IOC naturally fell to Coubertin from 1896. His colleagues 'forced him' to remain in office until 1925 and he remained a member until his death.

Henri de Baillet-Latour, of Belgium, who became an IOC member in 1903, was a natural successor to Coubertin in that from the ashes of World War I he had taken on the organization of the Games at

G. de Blonay and H. de Baillet-Latour, third and fourth IOC Presidents.

Hitler attending the 1936 Berlin Games.

Antwerp in 1920 with only a year to prepare. He also bore the burden of the Olympic celebrations in Germany.

What is often overlooked is that the Games of the eleventh Olympiad were awarded to Berlin in May 1931 by a postal vote of forty-three to sixteen, with eight abstentions. The German Olympic Committee, according to the rule existing at the time, declared that it also wanted to stage the Winter Games and selected the site of Garmisch-Partenkirchen.

Adolf Hitler acquired power on 30 January 1933. The thirty-first Session of the IOC was held in Vienna on 7–9 June of that year. Baillet-Latour officially asked the representatives of the Reich to guarantee their country's observance of the Olympic Charter or to forgo the Games. They gave the requested guarantee. The Vienna Session noted the fact that 'in principle, the German Jews would not be excluded from the Games of the eleventh Olympiad'. Of the two German members of the IOC, one, Theodore Lewald, half Jewish by birth, was President of the Organizing Committee of the Berlin Games; the other, Dr Karl Ritter von Halt, was President of the Organizing Committee of the Garmisch Games.

Hardly had the thirty-first Session closed when Hitler decided to replace Lewald and von Halt at the head of the two Organizing Committees by the State Director of Sport he had just appointed, Hans von Tschammer und Osten. Baillet-Latour immediately requested an audience with Hitler, who felt obliged to comply. 'It was in consideration of the statures of His Excellency Dr Lewald and Ritter von Halt that the IOC granted the organization of the Games to Berlin and Garmisch,' the IOC President told the German Führer. 'If our two colleagues should cease to be Presidents of the Organizing Committees, the IOC would be obliged to withdraw the Games from the two cities conditionally elected and to award them to other candidates.' Hitler gave way before this threat.

However on 15 September 1935 Hitler proclaimed the 'Nuremberg Laws' which declared Jews to be sub-human and set off a wave of persecution. Ernest Lee Jahncke, the member for the United States,

I. Sigfrid Edström, fifth IOC President.

violently opposed American participation in the Games. In doing so he made a stand against Avery Brundage, then President of both the US Olympic Committee and the Amateur Athletic Union. Brundage accused the opponents of American participation in the Games of 'betraying the athletes of the United States'.

Jahncke refused to retract and, on 30 July, the IOC agreed to Jahncke's expulsion from the IOC. It was a unanimous decision except for the abstention by the second United States delegate, W. M. Garland. Brundage was immediately elected to replace Jahncke.

At the foot of the Zugspitz, the two villages of Garmisch and Partenkirchen were arranged with characteristic Bavarian *Gemütlichkeit*. But signs 'Dogs and Jews are not allowed' had been placed outside the toilet facilities at Olympic sites. Baillet-Latour saw them and again requested an interview with Hitler. After the customary courtesies, he said, 'Mr Chancellor, the signs shown to the visitors to the Games are not in conformity with Olympic principles.' Hitler replied, 'Mr President, when you are invited to a friend's home, you don't tell him how to run it, do you.' Baillet-Latour thought for a moment and replied, 'Excuse me, Mr Chancellor, when the five-circled flag is raised over the stadium, it is no longer Germany. It is Olympia and we are masters there.' The signs were removed.

Sigfrid Edström, a Swede, took over the leadership on Baillet-Latour's death in 1942 in his double role of vice-president and native of a neutral country. He assumed his functions officially after the Session of Lausanne in 1946. Only twenty-six members were present. Edström put the wheels in motion, filled in the gaps and chose as his successor Brundage.

Brundage, elected in 1952, set out to 'make the Olympic Games the greatest social force of our time'. Often acting with despotic firmness, this Chicago builder succeeded in equipping the IOC with universal prestige and in safeguarding its unity. Under his presi-

Avery Brundage makes his last speech as IOC President at the closing ceremony of the Olympic Games in Munich, 1972.

dency, Olympism was confronted with vast and complex problems, among them those of the two Germanies, then China, and apartheid. Brundage held the office of President for twenty years and died on 7 May 1975.

At the Vienna Session of 1951 von Halt turned to promoting the reunion of the two separated parts of Germany under one flag: a fanciful idea in the middle of the cold war but there was a deep personal esteem between him and Dr Heinz Schöbel, President of the East German NOC and future member of the IOC, to which he was elected in 1966.

Dr Schöbel made a new request for the East German Committee at the Oslo and Helsinki Sessions in February and July 1952. But he failed on both occasions. At the Paris Session in 1955 the following agreement was adopted:

> It was decided by twenty-seven votes to seven that the Olympic Committee of the People's Democratic Republic of Germany (East) be recognized provisionally on the understanding that, should it prove impossible to form a unified team from both Germanies to be sent to the Melbourne Games, this recognition would lapse automatically.

Von Halt then had four interviews with the delegations of his former compatriots. Finally they came to what is known as 'the miraculous agreement'. The East German NOC was recognized on 25 January 1956 at Bonn under this title. Bonn and Pankow sent one delegation to Cortina and to Melbourne. The flag, emblem, uniform and living quarters were the same. The *chef de mission* (team leader) was chosen by the group with the greater number of athletes.

The agreement between the two Germanies lasted until the Mexico Games. It was at the Session preceding those Games that Dr Schöbel obtained, with the consent of his colleagues from the German Federal Republic, the recognition that the long separation of the two Germanies should be written into all Olympic documents in the future.

From the 1950s onwards the entry of nations of the third world and especially black Africa to the Olympic family lent momentum to the criticism of apartheid in South Africa. Its team at the Rome Games in 1960 was solely white and that escaped nobody's notice. In the following year South Africa left the British Commonwealth and set itself up as a republic, strengthening its racial laws in a country ruled by a small white minority. Some IOC members launched their offensive against apartheid through Constantin Andrianov, of the USSR. The decisive charge came at the Baden-Baden Session in 1963. Referring to that section of the Olympic charter which states 'No discrimination in them [the Games] is allowed against any country or person on grounds of race, religion or politics', the IOC called upon the South African Olympic Committee (SANOC) to oppose publicly, and in reality, all racial discrimination in sport and competition. At Innsbruck in January 1964 the IOC noted that the SANOC had not complied and withdrew its invitation for Tokyo. The South Africans' long Olympic absence had begun.

The Supreme Council for Sport in Africa (SCSA), an organization composed of members from African states, was not satisfied with the

Certificate for prize winners and officials designed by C. J. Van der Hoef, Amsterdam 1928.

Poster for the Olympic Games, Los Angeles 1932.

position and demanded South Africa's exclusion from the Movement. In Teheran in 1967 the Assembly decided to send a commission of inquiry, presided over by Lord Killanin. The Commission's detailed report consisted of a multiplicity of facts. Following tradition, they left the conclusions to be reached by the IOC members.

At Grenoble on 2 February 1968 during the Winter Games, the IOC members present considered they were too small a group to make an immediate decision and so agreed that South Africa's fate should be settled by a postal vote. The examination of the votes thirteen days later showed a small majority in favour of maintaining the SANOC within the Olympic Movement on condition that its next delegation was incontestably multi-racial, with all its athletes enjoying complete equality of treatment. Led by Abraham Ordia and Jean-Claude Ganga, the President and Secretary-General of SCSA, the sports leaders of black Africa opposed this decision and set in motion a world-wide campaign against the IOC's decision. With the South African government maintaining apartheid, the Mexican Organizing Committee became alarmed on several counts: they believed that the South African team might only be multi-racial on the surface and that there might be demonstrations. 'For every athlete we will provide a policeman' was the offer of General José de Clark of Mexico, a member of the Executive Board and Chairman of the Organizing Committee – an ironic remark in view of the bitter internal struggles Mexico was to suffer in the weeks before the Games began. But there was another more tangible threat to the Games presented by the South African problem. At one point there was a threat that forty countries, more than a third of the members, would boycott the Mexico Games. General Clark called for the Executive Board to examine the question. Brundage, on his way to Lausanne, flew to South Africa and spent two days discussing the position. In turn at the Château de Vidy the debate lasted two days. Finally, Brundage, almost crushed by over a hundred newsmen and television personnel, stood on the steps at the back of the Château and announced:

> The Executive Board is unanimously of the opinion that it would be most unwise for a South African team to participate in the Games of the nineteenth Olympiad – therefore, the Executive Board strongly recommends that you endorse this unanimous proposal to withdraw the invitation to these Games.

This second ballot gave forty-seven votes for the withdrawal of the invitation, sixteen against and eight abstentions.

However, SCSA's allies within the IOC continued to demand expulsion. The Committee decided, before taking a final decision, to hear the two parties once more in full Session. This took place in May 1970 in Amsterdam, and, after years in which SANOC's representatives had shown a personal desire to meet the IOC's requests, there was a surprising shift of position. SANOC's representative, in what many members regarded as an abusive speech, talked about IOC interference in South Africa. Those who had tried to keep open the door felt their cause was lost; South Africa was expelled by a narrow majority.

This was not the end of the problem of apartheid. Ordia and Ganga had asked the IOC to deal with the question of Rhodesia.

Posters for the celebration of the XVth Games (below) and the first to be held in the Far East (above).

The IOC considered the position in Luxemburg in September 1971. It decided that the Rhodesians could only take part in the Munich Games on condition that they had the same flag (the Union Jack) and the same anthem ('God Save the Queen') as in Tokyo. Surprisingly, the Rhodesian NOC accepted. A fortnight before the official opening of the Munich Games, the row started again. Although Rhodesia's team had already arrived and was composed of whites and blacks, almost twenty countries threatened to withdraw their teams if the Rhodesians were allowed to compete. By thirty-six votes to three and three abstentions, the Assembly withdrew the invitation extended to the Rhodesians.

At the end of World War II, the IOC had two members for China: Dr Cheting T. Wang, a supporter of Chiang Kai-shek, elected in 1922, and Dr. H. H. Kung, elected in 1939. In 1947 the IOC gave China a third representative: Shou Yi Tung, a sports educationalist. Shortly afterwards he went over to the side of Mao Tse Tung and moved to Peking.

In 1951, the Chinese Olympic Committee recognized by Lausanne retreated to Taiwan. The following year, Peking and not Taiwan sent athletes (thirty-eight men and two women) to the Helsinki Games. In spite of their doubtful position (their country had no NOC) they were allowed to compete. In 1954, a new NOC formed in Peking was recognized by the IOC under the name of 'Olympic Committee of the Republic of China'. The Olympic Committee with its headquarters in Taiwan was also still recognized.

This annoyed Peking, and in August 1958 the Olympic Committee of the People's Democratic Republic of China withdrew from the Olympic Movement. Tung submitted his resignation to the IOC, accompanied by a long diatribe. The IOC could only take note.

In May 1959, at Lord Killanin's suggestion, the IOC notified the Chinese Olympic Committee in Taiwan that it could 'no longer be recognized under this name, in view of the fact that it does not administer sport in China'. This left the door open to the other China. Taiwan adopted the name 'Olympic Committee of the Republic of China'. The IOC officially accepted this name in 1968.

In 1970 Henry Hsu from Taiwan was elected to the Assembly. His name was presented by Brundage to the Executive Board who performed its traditional role of vetting and rejected Hsu, not on any ground of personal integrity but in the belief that his election would do damage to the attempt to bring mainland China back to the Movement. Contrary to the unwritten rule to elect only those people approved by the Executive Board, Brundage put forward Hsu's name to the Assembly and he was accepted. The following year the UN expelled Taiwan and Lord Killanin has succeeded in achieving the return of the People's Democratic Republic of China to the IOC.

When Mexico City was awarded the Games at the Session in Baden-Baden in 1963 there was an outcry from some countries that competition at an altitude of 7,415 ft (2,260m) would be unfair in some events. At that height the air is thinner and in endurance events – those that last more than a minute – competitors who normally live in the lowlands are at a disadvantage. Several countries sent teams of doctors and athletes to Mexico to undertake research and finally the IOC agreed that competitors could train at altitude

for a period of six weeks before the Games. This helped but it did not bring parity between the lowlanders and those who normally lived and worked at altitude, and the results of the Games bear this out.

Although the Russian suppression in Budapest twelve days before the Games of Melbourne had brought the withdrawal of several countries which would not allow their teams to compete against Soviet athletes, Mexico was the first city in which internal strife threatened the Games and the participants.

There had been unrest within the country for several months, largely among students, who felt that a country with so much poverty should not be spending millions on the Games.

Then on 2 October, ten days before the Games were due to open and after several days at which meetings had passed off without any violence, there was the most brutal and bloody confrontation between students, academics, trades unionists and the army. At a meeting in the Plaza de las Tres Culturas, attended by over 10,000 people, there was a call for the overthrow of the Government. Suddenly, at a given signal, a green Very light, the army opened fire; with students armed and ready for such an eventuality, a battle raged for nearly five hours. No accurate figure of the dead is known but it is certainly over 260, while another 1,200 were wounded. The effect was that opposition to the Government was utterly smashed, and the guarantee from President Diaz Ordaz that there would be no interference with the Games or those taking part was met.

Under the slogan *Todo es posible con la Paz* ('Everything is possible with peace'), the Games, opening on 12 October, was a huge success. However, sadly, three victory ceremonies were the occasion for Black American medallists to demonstrate their support of 'Black Power'.

The most terrible drama in Olympic history began at the Games of Munich, in the Olympic Village at 4.30 a.m. on 5 September 1972, the eleventh day of the Games. Eight members of the Black September organization broke into 31 Connollystrasse, the building where the Israeli delegation was housed. The terrorists intended to seize the twenty-one athletes and officials staying there. One man, in raising the alarm, was killed, but enabled eight of his colleagues to get away; one more managed to escape. The eleven remaining Israelis were held hostage until just after midnight on 6 September when, together with five of the terrorists, they died. The three surviving Palestinians were captured. They were released by the Germans on 29 October, following a threat from a Palestinian commando who had hijacked a Lufthansa plane.

Terrorist on the balcony of the Israeli quarters in 1972.

From the moment a city has been given the responsibility of staging the Olympic Games, it is to its Organizing Committee that the IOC delegates its powers but the IOC retains its supreme authority. At 7.15 a.m., representatives of all the interested parties decided to set up a 'Crisis Committee', with the Bavarian State's Minister for the Interior, Bruno Merck, at its head. Just before 4 p.m. the Committee released a communiqué written and signed by Brundage and Willi Daume, Chairman of the Organizing Committee:

> The Olympic peace has been broken by an act of assassination by criminal terrorists. The whole civilized world condemns this barbaric crime, this horror. With deep respect for the victims and

as a sign of sympathy with the hostages not yet released this afternoon's sports events are being cancelled. The IOC and the Organizing Committee will hold services in commemoration of the victims in a ceremony which will take place tomorrow, 6 September 1972, at 10 a.m. in the Olympic stadium. This ceremony will demonstrate that the Olympic idea is stronger than terror or violence.

An hour later: Brundage said:

The IOC will not allow participants in the Games who are guests in the Olympic Village to be kidnapped by terrorists and taken outside the Federal Republic.

But the German authorities were later to put into operation an ill-fated plan for terrorists and hostages to leave Germany.

The first Vice-President, Lord Killanin, who had already been elected to succeed Brundage at the head of the IOC but was not to take office until the day after the end of the Games, returned from Kiel, where he had been attending the Olympic regattas, with two other members of the Executive Board, Jonkheer Herman A. van Karnebeek and Prince Takeda. Killanin and the majority of the Executive Board approved the idea of a commemorative ceremony and felt that an extraordinary Session should be held that same day.

This began at 10.10 p.m. in the large dining room of the Hotel Vierjahreszeiten, with all members present in Munich attending. They decided that whatever the turn of events the Games would carry on to the end. At 11.45 p.m. Daume told the seventy-one members present what the official German Federal Republic's government spokesman, Conrad Ahlers, had just confirmed over the telephone: all the terrorists had been either killed or captured; the Israeli hostages were all alive. The gathering joyfully passed a vote of congratulations to Brundage and Daume, also to the Federal Republic's government, and split up towards midnight.

But in the early hours of the morning this news was found to be false and only increased the horror that was unfolded, eventually, to the world's Press. The hostages and terrorists had been taken by helicopters to a military airfield where there was a waiting plane. The terrorists thought they had been tricked; firing began, hand grenades exploded, all the competitors and a policeman were killed and all but three of the terrorists.

At 10 a.m., under the weight of the awful truth, the memorial ceremony in honour of the victims opened in the packed Olympic stadium to the strains of the Funeral March from Beethoven's *Eroica* Symphony. From all parts of the world came requests to halt the Games. It was in this atmosphere that after the addresses of Daume, the head of the Israeli delegation, Shmuel Lalkin, then the Federal President Gustav Heinemann, that Brundage said:

Every civilized person recoils in horror at the barbarous, criminal intrusion of terrorists into peaceful Olympic precincts. We mourn our Israeli friends, victims of this brutal assault. The Olympic flag and the flags of all the world fly at half mast. . . . We have only the strength of a great ideal. I am sure the public will agree that we cannot allow a handful of terrorists to destroy this nucleus of international cooperation and goodwill we have in the Olympic Movement . . .

The Games in Munich lasted one more day, and now Lord Killanin had the duty to carry the torch.

Irish, Catholic, liberal, jovial, the iron hand in the cashmere glove, Lord Killanin boxed and rowed at Cambridge and was a competent rider. He had been chairman since 1950 of the Olympic Council of Ireland and was elected to the IOC in 1952. As President, he is an energetic helmsman, accustomed to storms. The motto of his family, Morris, is *Deus nobiscum quis contra nos* (If God is with us, who is against us?).

One of Lord Killanin's major struggles was against the obvious politicization of the Games. As he stated at the opening of the 1974 Session in Vienna:

> I appeal to every single sportsman and woman not to come to the Olympic Games if they wish to make use of sport for political purposes. . . . We all have our own beliefs; we all have our friends and enemies; but the aim of the Olympic Movement is to subjugate these in the fellowship which is enshrined in the intertwining Olympic rings representing the five continents of the world, wedded together in sport, peace and friendship. If this is not accomplished . . . we shall retreat into barbarism.

Less than a month before the Opening Ceremony of the Montreal Games, the IOC learnt through an official of the Ministry of Foreign Affairs in Ottawa, that the Prime Minister, Mr Trudeau, would not authorize a team from Taiwan to enter Canada and take part in the Games. Canada had a commercial agreement with the People's Republic of China and Peking threatened to put an end to this if Ottawa allowed on its soil that team calling itself 'The Republic of China'.

The abrupt decision from Ottawa violated all the promises made in the name of the Canadian Government by Mr Mitchell Sharp, Secretary of State for Foreign Affairs. The IOC proposed that the team of the Republic of China would compete under the name 'Taiwan' and parade under the Olympic flag.

Taiwan refused. Lord Killanin, and a significant number of committee members, thought of withdrawing the Games from Montreal but it was too late. Athletes from five continents were on their way, or even on the spot. Montreal and the Organizing Committee were not responsible and had fulfilled all requirements and Lord Killanin did not to wish to penalize the City. The only course open for the Executive Board was to submit a strongly worded protest: 'It is the fundamental Olympic principles which are being seriously jeopardized by the attitude of the Canadian Government.'

Then twenty African countries, and Guiana and Iraq, announced that, in accordance with a resolution of the Organization of African Unity, dated June 1976, they would boycott the Montreal Games if New Zealand took part, as a New Zealand National Rugby team had toured South Africa in 1976.

The Olympic leaders were dumbfounded. Since 1924, rugby has not been an Olympic sport and consequently the IOC has no jurisdiction over it. Besides, many rugby players from countries other than New Zealand were regularly going to South Africa. Lord Killanin, supported by the entire Executive Board, rejected the ultimatum. 'Our refusal will lead many delegations to withdraw, but nothing

Olympic stamps issued by: (above) Greece (1896), Mexico (1968), Germany (1936), German Federal Republic (1972).

(opposite) Japan (1972), Finland (1952), Paris (1924).

could be worse than abdication', he said calmly. Twenty-two NOCs withdrew their 441 athletes entered in fourteen sports the very day before the Games.

In Montreal international politics were not the only burden. There were also financial difficulties.

The IOC considers itself a non-profit-making organization. It was born and nurtured in the era of sporting patronage. Coubertin devoted his fortune to it and without the generosity of several members the IOC would not have been able to function properly.

By the end of World War II, the IOC's expenditure exceeded its income, which came only from the members' subscriptions and increasingly rare donations. So the Organizing Committee of the 1948 Games was asked to make to the IOC a contribution fixed at £2,000 for St Moritz and £5,000 for London.

The 1952 and 1956 contributions remained modest, while the obligations and expenses of the Lausanne headquarters were rapidly increasing.

The Melbourne Games could have been paid for by the sale of television rights but the companies wanted to take and not to give.

Television rights were sold by the Organizing Committee for the first time in 1960. The two Organizing Committees made a modest contribution, divided equally between the IOC and the International Federations. The NOCs protested.

It was therefore decided that from 1972 money raised from television rights would be shared as follows: two thirds to the Organizing Committee and one third to the IOC. The IOC's share would in turn be shared equally between the IFs, the NOCs and the IOC. In 1972 the IOC received nearly two million dollars from the Munich television rights, which enabled it to pay its debts and to keep going until the Games of 1976. The world television royalties from Montreal totalled $34,500,000. The Organizing Committee retained $27,700,000. Of the remaining $6,800,000, the IOC received $2,300,000, to which was added the proceeds from the Winter Games in Innsbruck, $1,200,000.

Preparation for the Montreal Games was plagued by over-expenditure, political quarrels and a series of strikes on the building sites as John Rodda describes in his chapter on the Games. However, as Lord Killanin said in Athens in 1978:

> There is no doubt at all that exaggerated costs were reported after the Games in Montreal. In point of fact, Montreal made a cash profit of 116.6 million Canadian dollars, but they did make massive capital expenditures. We do not ask that this should be done, although if there is capital expenditure which can be of long term benefit to the city it is on the plus side for posterity.

Following its defeat by Montreal for the 1976 Games and by Moscow for the 1980 Games, Los Angeles was a strong contender for the Games of 1984. Since the Games have not been held in the United States since 1932 it was likely that a city in the United States would be selected and though New York, Boston, Chicago, Atlanta and New Orleans all tried their luck, Los Angeles was finally chosen.

It has always been easy to criticize the Olympic Games, particularly as they grow ever more successful. The first modern Games in 1896 was accompanied by demonstrations by the Armenians against

the Ottoman Empire and no doubt international sport will always have to fight against nations using the Games for their own purposes. Among those organizations wishing to gain power over the Olympic Movement was UNESCO.

Until 1976, the only direct contact the IOC had with UNESCO was the celebration of Coubertin's centenary at the Sorbonne in Paris, from 19 to 24 June 1964. Later on, UNESCO tried, time and again, to hang on to the IOC's renown, and to bind the IOC to it.

Thus UNESCO organized a scientific congress prior to the Games of 1968 and 1972, in Mexico and Munich, contrary to the rule which stipulates that the chosen city cannot host any international meeting during the eight days prior to the Games and eight days afterwards. In Montreal in 1976, the IOC succeeded in having this congress held in Quebec, just as in 1980, it will be held in Leningrad instead of Moscow.

On 5 April 1976, at a meeting of Ministers of Physical Education and Sports, in Paris, Lord Killanin called for cooperation between the Olympic Movement and UNESCO. But at this very meeting international officials and ministers laid down the basis of an intergovernmental committee for sport, under the aegis of UNESCO. Up until that time UNESCO only sponsored the International Committee for Physical Education and Sport (ICHPER), intended chiefly for physical education teachers and the Fair Play trophy.

The intergovernmental committee for sport met in Nairobi from 26 October to 30 November 1976, to define its ambitions:

1. To involve itself with sport in schools, universities and wherever youth worked.
2. To have a say in top level international sporting events.

It was already greedy; nonetheless, the active elements of this interstate assembly hoped to go much further. The IOC, all the same followed its own route. The Tripartite Commission became greatly concerned with what UNESCO obviously wished to undertake and decided to publish a Manifesto which would set out the powers and terms of reference of governmental and non-governmental organizations. The Commission assigned each one its role, and issued a strong warning to the ministers and interstate bodies who were trying to seize the international competitive sport.

The world of top level sport was already well organized and no-one could intrude upon the prerogatives of others. Leaving sports in school as outside its competence, the commission claimed full responsibility in the field of high competition.

This Manifesto, issued in March 1978, caused a considerable and world-wide stir, and the attitude of UNESCO to the IOC changed. There was a movement towards a methodical division of tasks, and there are now regular meetings between the Tripartite Commission and UNESCO.

For the Olympic Movement this action by Lord Killanin was an outstanding achievement. Another one is the solution of the long-lasting problem of China.

THE OLYMPICS

I ATHENS 1896 Otto Szymiczek

Although the Olympic Games of Greece finally were extinguished after A.D. 393, their beauty and greatness lingered through the poems of Pindar and Pausanias. The interest in classical Greece in the seventeenth and eighteenth centuries brought the history of the Games to light again. Robert Dover started the Cotswold Olympic Games in England in 1636 which were held for over 200 years. In 1850 the Much Wenlock Olympic Society was founded by Dr Penny Brooke, who was later to meet Baron Pierre de Coubertin. A German archaeologist, Ernst Curtius, who did much work at Olympia, suggested in a lecture in 1852 that the Games should be revived, and Coubertin's visits to England, where he saw and understood the value of the English public-school system and of the Olympian Societies, fired him to initiate the revival of the Olympic Games.

The modern Olympic Games began, as they were to continue in many instances, in a major political and social uproar. Although the Greek people enthusiastically welcomed Coubertin's idea of reviving the ancient Games, the Greek Government, struggling with huge financial difficulties and on the verge of bankruptcy, refused any commitment to them. The idea that Athens should put on the Games was in danger of being abandoned and the Committee which Coubertin set up in November 1894 to organize the events made little progress.

It was then that the heir to the Greek throne, Constantine (1868–1923), grandfather of the Crown Prince Constantine who won a gold medal in sailing (Rome, 1960), set up a twelve-member committee, under his chairmanship, which met for the first time on 13 January 1895, the date considered as that on which the Hellenic Olympic Committee was formed. By April 1895 the committee had issued special bulletins in English, French, German and Greek, containing the rules of the events, the definition of sportsmanship and instructions for the officials of the Games.

Collections were made both in Greece and among Greeks living abroad, to obtain the necessary funds for the organization of the Games and for building sports facilities. The response was remarkable. Georgios Averoff (1818–99), one of Greece's wealthiest businessmen, donated 920,000 drachmae in gold for the reconstruction of the Panathenean Stadium in marble and the architect Anastasios Metaxas prepared the plans.

The issue of the first stamps dedicated to the Olympic theme, brought in 400,000 drs. Much of the required money was provided by the distribution of commemorative medals and the sale of tickets. A special velodrome was built at Neon Phaliron and a shooting range at Kallithea, as well as many other sports installations.

The first modern international Olympic Games began in Athens on Easter Sunday, 24 March 1896 (5 April by the new calendar), with the unveiling of the marble statue of the principal benefactor, Averoff, which had been erected in the square in front of the Panathenean Stadium.

The following day, a Greek national holiday, 80,000 people gathered in the stadium on the seats and tiers and in the surrounding hills, or crowded on the square in front of the stadium and in adjoining streets.

After the arrival of the King and Queen, Crown Prince Constantine, President of the Organizing Committee, delivered an inspired speech. King George I (1845–1913) opened the Games with the following words: 'I declare the opening of the first international Olympic Games in Athens.' Then the Olympic Anthem, composed by Spyros Samaras (1863–1917) to a poem of the National Poet Costis Palamas (1859–1943), was played. This hymn, by decision of the IOC Congress in Tokyo, in 1958, has been recognized as the official Olympic anthem. The composer himself conducted the huge choir and the bands of the Army, Navy, the Municipality of Athens and the provinces. The anthem made such an impression on the audience that it demanded an encore.

The sound of trumpets announced the arrival of the competitors and the beginning of the events. The American James Connolly won the triple jump with 13.71 m (44 ft 11$\frac{3}{4}$ in), to become the first Olympic

Athens, venue of the first Modern Olympic Games.

victor of modern times. His record was inscribed on a special board and the American flag was hoisted on a high pole before the entrance of the stadium.

During these first Olympic Games, only the first and second in each event received prizes: the first, a diploma, a silver medal and a crown of olive branches; the second, a diploma, a bronze medal and a crown of laurel. All competitors received a commemorative medal. The victors' medal had been designed by the French sculptor Jules Chaplain and the commemorative medal by the Greek painter Nikephoros Lytras (1832–1904); the diploma by the famous Greek painter Nicolaos Gyzis (1842–1901). King George I awarded all the prizes on the last day of the Games (3 April, or 16 April by the new calendar).

The 311 athletes who attended those Games came from thirteen countries: Australia (1), Austria (4), Bulgaria (1), Chile (1), Denmark (4), Germany (19), France (19), Greece (230), Great Britain (8), Sweden (1), Switzerland (1), Hungary (8), United States (14). Most of them came to Athens on their own initiative and at their own expense. The program included nine sports and forty-three events among which two were held for the first time, the marathon race, proposed by the Frenchman Michel Bréal (1832–1915), and the discus.

When it was announced that the marathon was to be included in the program, the Greek people were touched and excited; they considered it a matter of national pride to compete in and win this very Greek event, which revived the past glory of their history.

Greek children find a rooftop perch to watch the start of the marathon.

Spyros (Spyridon) Louis (Greece).

Every village began to look for outstanding runners. Two preliminary races were held, on 10 March 1896, at the Greek Championships, when there were twelve participants (only club members could take part), and on 24 March, when the entry was open to non-club members as well. In this second race thirty-eight runners entered, among them Spyros Louis, the eventual winner of the Olympic marathon, who was placed fifth.

In the Olympic marathon itself, held on 29 March in cool and cloudy weather, sixteen runners competed, including four non-Greeks, Albin Lermusiaux (France), who had previously competed in the Olympic 800 metres and had been third in the 1,500 metres, Edwin Flack (Australia), the winner of the 800 metres and 1,500 metres, Arthur Blake (United States), who had come second in the 1,500 metres, and Gyula Kellner (Hungary). At the beginning the foreigners were in the lead, but Blake dropped out in the twenty-third kilometre, Lermusiaux after the thirty-second and Flack after the thirty-seventh. Of the non-Greeks, only Kellner finished the race, in fourth place. He was awarded a special bronze medal, as the first and only foreign runner to finish.

Louis' success caused tremendous excitement. The spectators threw their straw hats in the air. Prince George ran beside Louis on the last straight from the entrance of the stadium to the finish line, and near the finish line Prince Nicholas joined them too. A Greek barber had promised to shave the winner free for life if he were Greek and a restaurant owner promised to give free meals for life, among other offers recorded.

After the Olympics, King George I asked Louis what he would like as a gift and the marathon winner asked for a horse and cart

A competitor in the high jump.

to carry water from his village, Amaroussion, to Athens because the Athens water supply was very poor and the Athenians were buying cool well water from the village. This story indicates how Louis was able to beat the well-known athletes of the time. Besides cultivating land, he had also been selling water to the Athenians, carrying his barrels on a mule from Amaroussion to Athens twice a day. Thus, without being aware of it, he was using the most modern training methods, with two sessions a day, running beside the mule at least 14 km (the distance between the village and Athens) each time, assuming that he rode his mule on the return journey. He never took part in competition after this Olympic marathon.

Track and field, weightlifting, gymnastics and wrestling events were held in the Athens Stadium. Fencing was held in the Zappeion building, shooting at the Kallithea shooting range, swimming in the Zea Bay of Piraeus, bicycling in the velodrome of Neon Phaleron and lawn tennis on courts which had been hastily arranged by the temple of Olympian Zeus. Rowing and sailing events were cancelled because of bad weather and cricket was not held because there were no participants. All events were held before enthusiastic crowds, with the main stadium filled on every day of the Games.

Various artistic events were also organized during the period of the Games: performances of ancient drama (*Medea*, *Antigone*), a torch race, receptions and concerts. The city of Athens was lavishly illuminated at night.

The first international Olympic Games of Athens proved so successful that its near-cancellation during the preparatory phase was easily forgotten. Pierre de Coubertin now witnessed the realization of his dream and with renewed ardour planned the future of the Games. If one compares the performance of today's athletes with that of competitors during the Athens Games, one sees that the first modern Olympics was quite primitive. It is, however, doubtful whether the world will again witness the sincere enthusiasm and exultation of Greek crowds who, during these days of March–April 1896, relived their historic past, of 2,500 years before.

Athens, in 1896, had given the most brilliant start to the history of the modern international Olympic Games.

II PARIS 1900 Gaston Meyer

At the end of the 1896 Games in Athens, the King of Greece, advised by an eager and successful administrator, Timoleon Philemon, claimed for Greece the exclusive right to organize future Games. Coubertin wavered for a moment but quickly realized that agreement would mean signing the death warrant of the newborn Olympic Movement.

The Greek ideal received unexpected help from the American athletes, who signed a petition asking that Athens should be the permanent home of the Games. During the closing banquet, King George developed his idea and suggested to Coubertin that he should give his consent – or resign. The Frenchman, pretending not to understand, addressed an open letter to the King; he thanked him 'and also the city of Athens and the Greek people, for the energy and the enthusiasm with which he had replied to the appeal in 1894' but confirmed that the Games of the second Olympiad would be held in Paris in 1900. There was no royal loss of face for the Crown Prince later realized the financial impossibility of monopolizing the Games for the benefit of Athens.

It was therefore in Paris that the second Olympiad was celebrated. But Coubertin said secretly to his friends: 'It's a miracle that the Olympic movement survived that celebration!'

Disappointments and difficulties were to begin after the IOC Congress at Le Havre at the beginning of 1897. Sometimes they had nothing directly to do with the Olympic Games; Coubertin's French enemies, officials of the Union of French Athletic Associations (USFSA), of which he had become secretary-general in 1890, were stubbornly contemptuous of the Games and showed their hostility on principle to the Baron's every move. He finally gave up depending on the USFSA to organize the Games. Unfortunately he had the idea of grafting the Olympic Games onto the Universal Paris Exposition of 1900, whose organizer, Alfred Picart, was a conservative official who believed sport to be a useless and absurd activity. He resented 'having an idea thrust on him' and that of incorporating the program of the second Games within the framework of the Exposition upset him.

Before the Congress of 1894 in Paris, Coubertin had proposed a grandiose project to the directors of the 1889 Universal Exposition. He planned to reconstruct the Altis of Olympia, with its temples, statues, gymnasia and stadia. Documents and works of art would be displayed there, landmarks in the history of sport, from ancient times to the present. Outside the Altis would be reproductions of the Roman baths and the Athletic Club of Chicago. The sporting events would take place in these prestigious surroundings. Picart, who succeeded the directors of the Expo 89, thanked Coubertin, filed his plan – and buried it.

However, Picart, after an ineffectual move by Alexandre Ribot, former president of the Council, agreed to include 'exhibitions of physical exercises and sports' scattered among the sixteen sections of the Expo, from the Champs-de-Mars to the Cours-la-Reine, and even at Vincennes, which was reserved for the less popular activities. The arrangements were chaotic: skating and fencing came under cutlery, rowing under life-saving, athletics under provident societies!

Charlotte Cooper (Gt Britain), first woman to win an Olympic title.

Coubertin reacted by setting up an organizing committee to establish 'international competitions for the élite'. His mistake was in assembling a committee, the majority of which were counts and marquises, presided over by the Vicomte de la Rochefoucauld. Forty members, of whom eighteen were designated stewards and placed in charge of the various sports, published the program on 29 May 1898; they repeated the program of the Athens Games, augmented by boxing, football, polo and archery.

This was welcomed enthusiastically, in France and in other countries. Henri Desgrange, who was to found the sporting daily *L'Auto*, and was at the time director of the cycle-racing stadium of the Parc des Princes at the Auteuil Gate, wrote to Coubertin: 'I have a field of 26,000 square metres, a cycle track of 666 metres, all you need for running and for tennis. I can give you everything except the Seine. . . .' Pierre Giffard's *Petit Journal* offered to take charge of the swimming competitions, and Pierre Laffitte's *Vie au Grand Air* offered its columns.

The crash came. On 9 November 1898, the USFSA declared that it would have nothing to do with the organization of a private sports meeting in 1900 but reserved its right to lend its support to an official meeting if undertaken by the State and the City of Paris.

This was echoed by the municipal councillors of Paris, who denounced the 'society of counts and marquises'.

An additional complication arose: the American section of the Exposition sent to Coubertin a high-ranking military man. He wanted Picart's permission to build, in the area reserved for the United States, a stadium in which athletes from the other side of the Atlantic would compete to 'show the other nations what real sport is'. He was unsuccessful; Picart was backed up by the American member of the IOC, William M. Sloane, who disapproved of his fellow countrymen's move.

Eventually, Coubertin resigned from the USFSA. On 22 April 1899, after petty squabbling, the Vicomte de la Rochefoucauld also resigned and the committee voted to dissolve itself.

Twelve months were left before the opening of the Games!

On 19 February 1899, Picart had decided to nominate Daniel Mérillon, president of the Shooting Federation, which was a member of the USFSA, as director-general of the sporting contests at the Exposition. Mérillon finally obtained approval of the plans at the beginning of June 1899.

Coubertin undertook a European tour, to counter suspicions, first from the Germans, who feared hostile demonstrations, then from the British (before the settlement of the 'Fashoda incident' in the Sudan, which had strained relations between the two countries), and also to calm down those who were disconcerted by the incompetence shown by the official sources, which were putting out nothing more than endless rules, regulations and memos.

Finally, it was decided to abandon all the grandiose plans, notably that of using the park of a huge château at Courbevoie, and to go right back to the beginning, to the 1898 plan that the administration had considered at the time to be 'mean and unworthy of the nation'.

The athletic events would be held on the turf of the Racing Club de France, at Croix-Catelan, in the Bois de Boulogne, and the other competitions in already existing stadia or cycle tracks. Coubertin concluded: 'There was [for these Games] much goodwill but the interesting results had nothing Olympic about them. We have made a hash of our work.'

Born in confusion, the Games rolled on from 20 May to 28 October, comprising an unbelievable muddle of sports, some officially recognized, some not recognized, world amateur championships and professional championships, scattered over the four corners of the capital. Athletics were held in the Bois de Boulogne, swimming at Asnières, yachting at Meulan, fencing at the Tuileries (Palais des Expositions), lawn tennis at the Île de Puteaux, gymnastics at Vincennes, equestrian events at the avenue de Breteuil, cycling at the Parc des Princes, shooting almost everywhere.

There was even a rugby football match between France and Germany at Vincennes, which made the police work overtime. But the public, forgetting the French defeat in the Franco-Prussian War, applauded both victors and vanquished, all the more happily because the French won, 25–16, or 27–17, depending upon which French newspapers you read the next day. Sophistication in press facilities at the Games did not arrive until several Olympiads later.

There was constant confusion. The public couldn't make head or tail of the events, and nor could the reporters. Even today it is extremely difficult to sort out the wheat from the chaff among the prizewinners. That is why reference books give the yachting results as if they were all entirely official. Association football, polo and rugby appear only as titles of contests in the official program. Cricket, croquet and golf, if one believes the final decisions of the IOC, were the only official events; there was no boxing; wrestling had disappeared and so had weightlifting.

The number of contestants had increased to 1,319 (including eleven women) as against the 311 at Athens; the number of countries competing had risen to twenty-two from thirteen.

Athletics, which were the main attraction – on average drawing 3,000 spectators each day – were held on the 500-metre grass track of the Croix-Catelan, with very light soil. Although trees got in the way of the discus and hammer, performances achieved a respectable level.

One serious incident marred the beginning of the international competitions scheduled for 14 July, Bastille Day, a national holiday in the Republic. It was feared that spectators would stay away and, without consulting the foreign delegations, the organizers decided to put off the finals planned for 14 July to the next day, a Sunday. Some Americans protested vigorously, on the grounds that it was the Lord's Day. Two of the American competitors in the 1,500 metres withdrew and the United States did not take part in the Prix des Nations, i.e. the 5,000-metres team event.

On 14 July, in the long-jump heats, Myer Prinstein cleared 7.175 m (23 ft 6½ in). He had set the world record of 7.50 m (24 ft 7¼ in) at Philadelphia on 28 April. On that day he beat his great rival, Alvin Kraenzlein, who had held the record in 1898 of 7.24 m (23 ft 9 in), and had jumped 7.43 m (24 ft 4½ in) in 1899.

Because the next day was Sunday, Prinstein was absent, and Kraenzlein won the competition with 7.185 m (23 ft 6¾ in). On the Monday, Prinstein, learning of this 'betrayal', was so angry that he attacked his rival and hit him with his fist. He consoled himself

Refreshment for a marathon competitor.

by taking the triple jump with 14.47 m (47 ft 5¾ in), defeating the victor of the 1896 Games, his compatriot James B. Connolly, later a celebrated journalist and war correspondent of *Collier's*.

Kraenzlein remains, for history, the great star of the 1900 Games. In athletics he took the 60 metres, the 110- and 200-metres hurdles, as well as the long jump.

The other American star of those Games, Ray Ewry, also holds the all-time record for Olympic victories. No fewer than ten from 1896 to 1908 (including 1906) in the standing jump, which was then discontinued. In Paris, he easily took the standing high jump, the standing long jump and the standing triple jump (1.65 m/5 ft 5 in, 3.21 m/10 ft 6½ in, 10.58 m/34 ft 8½ in respectively), each time from the Sioux, Irving Baxter, winner of the running high jump (1.90 m/6 ft 2¾ in) and the pole vault (3.30 m/10 ft 10 in) in the absence on that Sunday of his fellow countrymen Orton and Dvorak, who defeated him easily a few days later. The latter was the first man to use a bamboo pole.

Altogether, the Americans took seventeen of the twenty-three titles. Over 100 metres, the hot favourite Arthur Duffey was beaten by Frank Jarvis (USA) (11.0 sec) from Walter Tewksbury, the winner of the 200-metres (22.2 sec) and the 400-metres hurdles (57.6 sec). Over 400 metres, the crowd were confident of a French victory. But the winner was the American Maxey Long who, that autumn, had at Travers Island lowered the world record for 440 yards to 47.8 sec and then, on the racing track at Guttenberg, New Jersey, that for 440 yards straight to 47 sec.

The middle-distance events were British successes, with Alfred Tysoe over 800 metres, and Charles Bennett over 1,500 metres, the latter threatened by the Frenchman Henri Deloge. In this 1,500 metres, two of the favourites, the Americans Alexander Grant and John Cregan, withdrew. Great Britain completed its success, which became a tradition after that, with the 4,000-metres steeplechase and the team 5,000 metres. Charles Bennett, first in this event, established an official world record for 5,000 metres of 15 min 20.0 sec.

In the throwing events, only the Hungarian Rudolf Bauer, in the discus, provided competition for the Americans. The American John Flanagan, of Irish origin (like Patrick O'Callaghan and John Connolly later), who won the hammer event with 49.73 m (163 ft 2 in), was to be crowned twice more and hold the world record of 56.19 m in 1909.

At last a Frenchman won an event, the marathon. In fact, the winner, Michel Theato, did not learn until twelve years later that he had become an official Olympic champion! He recalled then that in 1900, in suffocating heat, he finished first in a marathon, run through the back streets and mews of Paris in 2 hr 59 min 45 sec. Because of scheduling errors, the course had been obstructed several times and had not been the best organized. An American, Dick Grant, who finished sixth, brought an unsuccessful lawsuit against the IOC, claiming that a cyclist had knocked him down as he was about to overtake the Frenchman.

There were also athletics events for 'non-amateurs'. The famous American Mike Sweeney, who held the high-jump record with 1.97 m (6 ft 5½ in), won the 100 metres, high and long jumps (each endowed with 250 Fr. for the winner), and also the handicap events. And the 400-metres hurdles Olympic champion, Walter Tewksbury, benefiting from a handicap of 4 metres, could not keep up with the Indian Norman Pritchard, who, with a 15-metres handicap, won in 56 sec.

In about 1965, the French Olympic Committee, in an attempt to count its living Olympic medal holders, and going by a Hungarian book by Dr Ferenc Mező, sponsored by the IOC, discovered that a certain Vasserot, ranked second in the speed cycling event, was still alive. When questioned, the veteran vaguely remembered that he had raced in 1900 on the track at Vincennes. No one had told him at the time that he had taken part in the Olympic Games. He died in 1968 as a 'silver medallist'. More thorough research, undertaken by the Austrian Erich Kamper, confirmed that the gold medal went to the Frenchman Georges Taillandier in that speed event from another Frenchman named Sanz and an American named Lake, the latter having eliminated Vasserot in the semi-final. It is conflicting evidence of this kind which unhappily leaves so many uncertainties in Olympic history.

It is very difficult to place much faith in a roll of honour painfully reconstructed in 1912 and even to take seriously certain competitions like swimming held in the muddy waters of the Seine at Asnières, in a current which swept the champions all over the place.

As for the rowing, this is how the reporter from *Sport Universal* described it: 'This sport was only practised by coarse fellows, noisy, rowdy, who, under the name of boatmen, spread terror among the peaceful riverside inhabitants . . .'

Only gymnastics, in which the Swedes distinguished themselves, found favour with the press, which otherwise hardly mentioned the events.

Monique Berlioux concluded, in her remarkable book *Olympica*,

'The name of Pierre de Coubertin was not mentioned once, by journals or by officials.'

However, during those 1900 Games, in which only the French competed in many events, women's sports made a very timid appearance. Thus, the British Charlotte Cooper, in winning the women's singles lawn-tennis tournament, became the first woman Olympic champion. The runner-up in the final was the French Hélène Prévost, whom Charlotte Cooper defeated 6–1, 6–4. Paired with the famous Reginald Frank Doherty, Charlotte Cooper also won the mixed doubles, from Hélène Prévost and Harold Mahony.

III ST LOUIS 1904 Gaston Meyer

As early as 1894 it had been tacitly agreed that the third Olympic Games should be offered to the young America. On 13 November 1900, the *New York Sun* informed its readers that the Games would be held in Chicago. But James Sullivan, secretary-general of the Amateur Athletic Union, intervened to stop the Games going to Chicago. Sullivan was secretly annoyed that he had not been chosen as a member of the IOC.

Coubertin's French enemies, supporting Messrs de Saint-Clair and Roy in their aim of laying the foundations of an 'International Union', designed to supplant the IOC and to promote future Games, had rallied Sullivan to their cause. Their Games were to take place in 1901 at Buffalo within the framework of the Pan-American Exhibition of which Sullivan was the sports organizer. After Sullivan's pronouncements, Coubertin decided to question, in writing, the people consulted by the American, among them certain members of the IOC. They all supported Coubertin; that was the end of dissidence and of Buffalo's candidature.

The fourth Session of the IOC, held at Paris on 21 May 1901, had therefore to choose between two American candidates, St Louis and Chicago. Before it, William M. Sloane, the American member, obtained from Coubertin an agreement that he would accept the presidency for ten years to strengthen the still frail Olympic Movement.

The IOC was unanimously in favour of Chicago. The Committee decided that the Games should last only twelve days, from 12 to 25

A crowded 400-metres final, for which the starter perches on a fence for a better view of the field.

Fred Winters (United States) winner of the Dumb Bell competition at the World Fair.

September 1904, and (strangely) 'that the professional events, if there are any, shall be of less importance than the amateur events'.

Meanwhile, St Louis, which was preparing to organize a giant World Fair in 1903, was forced for financial reasons to put it off until 1904. Fearing a clash with the Games at Chicago, it asked for them to be transferred to St Louis, threatening if refused to stage important athletic competitions of its own. Chicago replied in 1902, suggesting that the Games should be put off until 1905, but this Coubertin would not accept. Finally, both parties took the matter to the arbitration of the new president of the United States, Theodore Roosevelt, who was very interested in sport. He opted for St Louis; the IOC agreed, nevertheless regretting that the Games would again be attached to a World Fair, in spite of the very trying experience of 1900.

Was that the reason that Coubertin did not attend the 1904 Games and did not call a Session at St Louis? Or was it because of the difficulties and time taken in travelling? Or was it because of certain problems of protocol? The Americans, dazzled by the aristocracy of old Europe, had virtually insisted upon the presence at St Louis of all those princes, dukes and counts in the IOC, a presence likely to flatter the newly rich. Or perhaps Coubertin felt disappointed, after his first visit, at not encountering the kind of characters and society that his reading of Fenimore Cooper had led him to associate with Missouri and Mississippi.

The third Games suffered a serious setback in the number of participants, both in nations and individual competitors: twelve nations instead of the twenty-two at Paris, 617 athletes as against 1,319. Most of these were Americans, no fewer than 525; there were only ninety-two foreigners of whom forty-one were from neighbouring Canada. And these figures even include those who took part in demonstration or exhibition matches, notably in basketball, baseball, lacrosse, roque, and motorboating.

St Louis, the cotton capital founded by French traders, was celebrating the hundredth anniversary of the acquisition of Louisiana by President Thomas Jefferson from Napoleon I for $15 million. In 1904 the city already had a population of 600,000.

That year the world was on the alert. The British navy was mobilized because navigation through the Suez Canal was threatened by the prolonging of the Russo-Japanese War. In that atmo-

St Louis inhabitants watch the finish of the 200-metres hurdles race from their window, won by Harry Hillman (United States)

sphere, the Olympic celebration did not carry much weight. It even left the rest of the world indifferent. The British sent only one athlete and he was in fact Irish.

The winners of the team sports were: basketball (exhibition), the Buffalo German YMCA (United States); association football, the Gait F.C. of Ontario (Canada); lacrosse, the Shamrock Team of Winnipeg (Canada); water polo, the New York A.C. (United States) – hardly a national selection.

This time, as was to be the case in later years, athletics monopolized attention from 29 August till 3 September. In the pleasant, harmonious surroundings of Washington University, at least 2,000 spectators watched the exploits of the American athletes, under technical conditions which were at last acceptable and on a track of sufficiently good quality, 536.45 m ($\frac{1}{3}$ mile) in length, with a straight stretch of 220 yards.

There was a full program: no fewer than twenty-five competitions, of which one was a team 4-mile (6,437.32-m) event, won by the New York A.C. from the Chicago A.C., and the tug-of-war, won by the Milwaukee A.C. There were only two winners who were not American, the French Canadian policeman from Montreal, Étienne Desmarteau, who won the 56-lb (25.4-kg) weight from New York policeman John Flanagan, and the Anglo-Irishman from the Irish-American Athletic Club of New York, Thomas Kiely, who won the 'all-rounder' championship, forerunner of the decathlon; its program, in one day, consisted of, in succession, 100 yards (91.44 m), shot, high jump, 880-yard walk, hammer, pole vault, 120-yard hurdles, 56-lb weight, long jump and mile! Kiely won the walk in 3 min 59 sec, the 120-yard hurdles in 17.8 sec, the 56-lb weight and the hammer with, respectively, 8.915 m (29 ft 3 in) and 36.75 m (120 ft $6\frac{1}{2}$ in).

John Flanagan kept the hammer title, which he had won four years earlier in Paris. Another winner of the preceding Games won again at St Louis: the famous Ray Ewry, champion of all three standing jumps with 1.50 m (4 ft 11 in) in the high jump, 3.47 m (11 ft $4\frac{1}{2}$ in) in the long jump and 10.55 m (34 ft $7\frac{1}{2}$ in) in the triple jump.

There were three other triple winners of these 'American' Games at St Louis: Archie Hahn, known as the 'Milwaukee Meteor', assured himself of the 60 metres (7 sec), the 100 metres (11 sec) and in particular the 200 metres (21.6 sec); in that event, according to the regulations in force at the time, his opponents were all penalized by one yard for committing false starts. But Hahn cleared the line three metres ahead!

James Davies Lightbody, from Chicago but of Scottish origin, only eighteen and originally a sprinter, dominated the middle-distance events. On 29 August he won the steeplechase (over 2,500 m) in 7 min 39.6 sec; on 1 September he took the 800 metres in 1 min 56 sec, and finally on 3 September the 1,500 metres in 4 min 5.4 sec, beating Charles Bennett's world record, established in Paris, a performance intrinsically inferior compared with the amateur mile record of Tom Conneff (4 min 15.6 sec in 1895) and above all the 4 min 12.75 sec of Walter George, a professional, in 1885.

Harry Hillman, third 'triple winner', assured himself of, in succession, the 400 metres in 49.2 sec, the 200-metres hurdles in 24.6 sec and above all the 400-metres hurdles in 53.0 sec (a 400-metres hurdles, with the obstacles only 76 cm (30 in) high). In that race, George

The start of the 100-yd sprint, won by Zoltán von Halmay (Hungary), extreme left.

Poage, third, became the first black Olympic medallist.

Two losers of 1900 in Paris gained their revenge in St Louis. Myer Prinstein, with 7.34 m (24 ft 1 in), took the long jump after winning the triple jump with 14.35 m (47 ft 1 in). The absence of the world-record holder, the Irishman Peter O'Connor, was regrettable. His 7.61 m (24 ft 11$\frac{3}{4}$ in) would have been astounding up to Bob Beamon's 8.90 m (29 ft 2$\frac{1}{2}$ in) in 1968. When Prinstein and O'Connor met in 1906 in Athens, on the occasion of the tenth anniversary of the revival of the Games, Prinstein outdid his rival, clearing 7.20 m (23 ft 7$\frac{1}{2}$ in) against the Irishman's 7.025 m (23 ft 0$\frac{1}{2}$ in). Charles Dvorak jumped 3.50 m (11 ft 6 in) in the pole vault. But that was in the absence of the two world-record holders, the American Norman Dole and the Frenchman Fernand Gonder, who had cleared 3.69 m (12 ft 1$\frac{1}{2}$ in) the same year. In 1905 Gonder took his record to 3.74 m (12 ft 3$\frac{1}{2}$ in).

Another absent Frenchman, Marius Eynard, world-record holder for the discus of 1.923 kg (4$\frac{1}{4}$ lb) with 43.21 (141 ft 9$\frac{1}{4}$ in) since 1903, relinquished his title to Martin Sheridan. The latter, level with Ralph Rose, a 2-m and 120-kg (264-lb 8-oz or 18-stone 12-lb 8-oz) giant, winner of the shot, defeated him in a throw-off by about five feet (1.52 m) – the only time in Olympic history that a throw-off has decided this event.

Finally, the marathon event, marked with choice incidents, filled the officials with confusion. The contestants numbered thirty-one, nearly all Americans, except the Greek Demeter Velouis (sixth) and the Cuban Felix Carvajal (fifth), who led the race until the twenty-fifth kilometre but then fell behind.

In the stadium, the wait was feverish and the runners behind schedule. In blistering heat, Fred Lorz arrived uncannily cool, hardly a speck of dust on him. He was acclaimed, carried in triumph, and photographed with Alice Roosevelt, daughter of the American President. He appeared a little bewildered by all this ceremony. A quarter of an hour later, the second man appeared, staggering and

Victory in the pole vault for Charles Dvorak (United States) at 3.50m (11ft 6in).

covered in dust, another American, Thomas Hicks. Second? When the results were announced, the judges and the timekeepers who had followed the course in cars rushed at Lorz. He was vilified, disqualified, struck off the lists, and Hicks was justly acclaimed. Lorz had dropped out of the race at the fifth kilometre; a truck had given him a lift but it had broken down and Lorz, having recovered from his cramp, decided, for a joke, to continue on foot. His story was ultimately believed, and a year later he was allowed to compete again and became US marathon champion in 1905.

As for Hicks's time: 3 hours 28 min 53 sec for 40 km, no better than that of Louis or Theato. Many people realized that Hicks was doped with sulphate of strychnine and cognac, but no one, at that time, dreamed of protesting.

The swimming pool was an asymmetrical lake used in the World Fair and the starting signals were given from a raft. The distances

A sponge for Thomas Hicks (United States), the marathon winner. But is Hicks being supported?

were chaotic and the performances hardly worthy of beach swimmers today. There were peculiar strokes as well, and the plunge for distance, which the American W. E. Dickey won with 19.05 m (62 ft 6 in).

In boxing, the weight categories were indicative of future regulations. Only the Americans took part. It was the same with wrestling.

Coubertin was told of the progress of the Games by the Hungarian Ferenc Kemény, who joined him at Bayreuth. After emphasizing the fine organization, the well-arranged grounds, the respectable performances, but sparse attendance and total misunderstanding of the Olympic spirit, he went on to say: 'I was not only present at a sporting contest but also at a fair where there were sports, where there was cheating, where monsters were exhibited for a joke.' This last was an allusion to two days, called the 'Anthropological Days', on which the competitions were parodied by opposing Patagonians, Filipinos, Ainus, Turks, Coropas from Mexico, American Sioux and Syrians. With a gigantic effort, a pygmy dispatched the regulation weight three metres.

Coubertin, less upset than his informant, made excuses for the Americans, who like children, were seeking sensation rather than the development of sport through the Olympic spirit. He is supposed to have said: 'As for that outrageous charade, it will of course lose its appeal when black men, red men and yellow men learn to run, jump and throw, and leave the white men behind them.'

There was no Olympic Session at St Louis. The sixth Session was held in the banqueting room at the Mansion House, London, put at the disposal of the IOC by the Lord Mayor of London from 20 to 22 June 1904, under the patronage of HM King Edward VII. By a unanimous and solemn vote, after the withdrawal of Berlin's candidature, Rome was announced as the venue for the Games of the fourth Olympiad. But Rome's turn to stage the Games was delayed for over half a century as the Italians had to withdraw their offer.

ATHENS 1906 John Rodda

The gathering of sportsmen in Athens two years after the St Louis Olympics became known as the Interim or Extraordinary Games or the Athenian Games. They do not take an official place in the history of the Movement but they were significant in the slow process of bedding the foundations of modern Olympism.

Coubertin had opposed the Greek plan to have every Olympic Games at Athens but as a compromise he supported the Interim Games (which were also to be held in 1910) but did not give IOC patronage to them.

Coubertin and his committee, unhappy at events in the Games of Paris in 1900 and dismayed at some of the events which came into the Olympic program in St Louis, needed a change of fortune and a reassurance in their aims; the Games at Athens in some ways provided it. But they turned out to be as disappointing as those in St Louis which so many Europeans had missed, for many events were not contested; the program included athletics, weightlifting, wrestling, gymnastics, lawn tennis, association football, fencing, swimming and diving, rowing, shooting (in which there were twelve events) and cycling.

However, it was during the Games in Athens (22 April to 2 May 1906) that the Italians made it known that they would be unable to stage the Olympics in 1908. It was here, at the IOC meeting, that Britain was invited to take over the organization of the 1908 Games and the invitation was accepted. In fact, the British had planned an international sports meeting and it was the organizational structure for this event, much embellished through the birth of the British Olympic Association in 1905, that undertook the work.

IV LONDON 1908 John Rodda

The Games of the fourth Olympiad were a significant point of development in the Movement. After the enthusiasm at Athens, the disappointment of Paris and the farce of St Louis, it needed Edwardian England, with its stability and confidence from the bedrock of a flourishing Empire, to restore dignity and credibility.

It was originally intended that the Games should be staged in Rome. Instead the Italians let it be known that they could not sustain their offer and, at Athens in 1906, Lord Desborough was asked by the International Olympic Committee if London could, with only two years remaining, stage the Games. His Lordship soon discovered, through the members of the British Olympic Association, that Britain and London were ready to discharge the task. In fact, the decision to go ahead was taken on 19 November 1906 and the Games opened at Shepherd's Bush on 13 July 1908.

To build a stadium (in which athletics, cycling, swimming, fencing, gymnastics and wrestling took place) within that period and orga-

A wrestling bout at Shepherd's Bush.

Miss Q. Newall (Gt Britain) winner of the National Round.

nize the twenty-one sports on the program approved by the IOC was a remarkable feat for that time. But no other country in the world had such a vast sporting expertise. The Amateur Athletic Association had been in existence for thirty years, Henley Royal Regatta much longer, and in these two sports alone there was an organizational experience upon which the Games were to flourish.

The Games provided the first real step towards the competition of women, who had already been playing in the lawn-tennis events but now took part in a demonstration of gymnastics. There was, too, for the first time a winter sport – ice skating.

The British Olympic Association had one piece of good fortune, in coming to an agreement with the organizers of the Franco-British Exhibition who agreed to build an arena for most of the sports. If this was a worthwhile financial arrangement, the Games, in a country which already had the Boat Race, the Derby, Cup Final, Henley, the AAA Championships and the All England (lawn tennis) Championships, were sure to find a sporting appetite. The charges for the stadium were initially too high and the publicity the Games received insufficient to bring response. But gradually the news travelled and on the final day, when the marathon was run – one of the hottest days of the English summer as it turned out – there were about 90,000 people in the stadium. Olympism was realized, a little late.

The work of preparation was massive. There were twenty-one separate competitions, each with separate books of rules which had to be translated into French and German; the working out of each program, accepting the correct definitions of amateurism for each sport and defining what was meant by the term 'country' – all these were in those days the responsibility of the Organizing Committee; even the use of the metric system in a place where the Imperial measure was king, presented difficulties.

The pace and efficiency of the British Olympic Association's work impressed the IOC at its meeting in The Hague in May 1907. Many decisions were taken then, two of lasting significance, that a gold medal should be awarded to each winner, and 'the principle of English judges, with power to appoint foreign assistants was carried unanimously'. Coubertin was a supporter of this idea and came to rue it. The belief that the British, judges and adjudicators in so many facets of life, could be impartial in sport was destroyed in many eyes at these Games. The Americans believed that they were particularly hard done by and on their return home criticism of the British was flowing. The bitterness reached a point where the British published a book, *Replies to Criticism of the Olympic Games*.

At this period there was great animosity between many British and American institutions, with one regarded as a young, brash, boasting country and the other staid, snobbish and second best at most things.

James Sullivan, the leading American official, led the foray: 'They [the officials] were unfair to the Americans, they were unfair to every athlete except the British but their real aim was to beat the Americans. Their conduct was cruel and unsportsmanlike and absolutely unfair.' And one American newspaper greeted the victorious Americans on their arrival with 'despite the foul play of the British'.

The sixty-page book published by the British Olympic Association to reply to the tirade which came across the Atlantic dealt mostly with the Halswelle affair (see below) but it was set out with quotations from the Americans on one side of the page and dignified British replies on the other. Relationships between the athletic associations of the two countries were, as a result, broken off.

The restrictions of sports and entries were by today's standards of a curious kind. In most individual sports twelve was the maximum number of entries allowed for any one country. Cricket was removed from the program 'for it is not widely played' but there were positive reflections of the Victorian and Edwardian sporting order, rather than Coubertin's educative objectives. Polo, rackets and *paume* (tennis, as distinct from lawn tennis) were included, but the antithesis of the Coubertin spirit was surely to be discovered in Southampton Water – with motorboat racing. There were apparently seven boats racing for three gold medals. In fact racing was postponed from the middle of July to the end of August because the Duke of Westminster's crack 40-footer *Wolseley-Siddeley* (a commercial name which would not be tolerated in present-day Games) was in the United States racing for the British International Cup. However, the delay did not bring the Duke his Olympic gold medal. After one race was abandoned because of bad weather, three boats went from their moorings for the last race of the competition. *Daimler II* gave up before the start with engine trouble. *Wolseley-Siddeley* got away to a sound start and, after two laps of the course, was leading *Camille* (France), which started late, by almost a lap. The Duke's gold medal seemed safe but then on the third circuit His Grace went too close to Hamble Spit and 'went high and dry on the soft mud' and so *Camille*, at a speed of 18.3 knots in poor weather, went on to win.

There was, however, a far more serious contribution to the development of sport and the Olympic Movement in the Games of 1908. Events at the stadium at Shepherd's Bush were dramatic, held in the presence of members of the Royal Family, and provided an

The women's archery teams in the National Round.

Queen Alexandra presents Dorando Pietri with a gold cup.

indelible piece of Olympic history in the disqualification of Dorando Pietri (Italy) in the marathon.

Dorando, who had always been close to the leaders and saw several of them pass him and then drop out, reached the stadium in an exhausted state. The large crowd had expected to see the figure of Charles Hefferon (South Africa) come on to the track, but he had been overtaken by Dorando just outside the stadium. The Italian's equilibrium was broken apparently by the change from running on the flat ground to the slope into the stadium; this, and the fact that he turned right into the arena rather than left, took his distress to the point of collapse. The fact that like many competitors he had probably taken some form of strychnine was a contributory factor towards the collapse. Doctors attended him on the track and he was revived, but the enormous well of feeling for a man who had undergone such an ordeal precluded his immediate disqualification by removal from the track, which should have happened. Instead Dorando tottered to the line, again receiving help, to tremendous applause.

The second man to finish was John Joseph Hayes of the United States, who had also overtaken Hefferon, and the Americans duly lodged an objection which, surprisingly, took some time to consider because of conflicting evidence. But Hayes was declared the winner, while for two and a half hours Dorando was close to death. He recovered and later received an enormous gold cup from Queen Alexandra, whose gesture expressed the feelings of most spectators. The event and its attendant publicity caused a spate of marathon contests in the years that followed.

It was from this event that the distance of the marathon, 26 miles 385 yards, was established for the race started on the lawns of Windsor Castle, near to windows from where the Royal Children might see the start; from there to the finishing line at the Stadium in Shepherd's Bush was the distance which is now traditionally regarded as a marathon.

The 400 metres produced a disqualification and a sad final, twenty-

Martin Sheridan (United States) winner of the discus Greek style.

six-year-old Wyndham Halswelle taking part alone in a re-run of the final after J. C. Carpenter, one of three Americans in a four-man final, had been disqualified for obstruction. Entering the final straight, Halswelle challenged to take the lead but Carpenter moved out, from the inside edge, preventing Halswelle from passing and making the British runner move across the track. Part of the acrimony which arose from this incident – the three Americans declined to take part in the re-run – was due to the difference in racing rules between the countries, an anomaly which was to be removed in international competition by the formation of the International Amateur Athletic Federation four years later. Halswelle was probably the best runner in the field, for having recorded 48.4 sec in winning the AAA title, he repeated the time in the second round of the Games competition to set an Olympic record.

Forrest Smithson (United States) gave an indication of reaching a peak for a specific event. Before the Games he had not recorded times as fast as his American rivals, but at Shepherd's Bush he ran 15.8 sec, 15.4 sec and then 15.0 sec, a world record, in winning the 110-metres hurdles title. The 400-metres hurdles was of similar quality, Charles Bacon bringing the United States another gold medal with a time of 55.0 sec, which was then superior to the Imperial distance record, 56.1 sec. Melvin Sheppard (United States) became the only double gold medal winner in individual athletics events at the Games by taking the 800 metres by the convincing margin of nine yards and the 1,500 metres.

One event in which British traditions were upheld was the 3-mile team race, where six of the first seven men to finish were Britons. Joe Deakin, the winner, lived in London and was still running up to the week of his death, aged 93, in 1972.

In the field events Ray Ewry added to his collection of gold medals with two from the standing broad jump and standing high jump, and the only non-American winner in the field was Timothy Ahearne of the United Kingdom in the running hop, step and jump. John Flanagan kept the hammer title he won in St Louis, beating his own Olympic record with 51.92 m (170 ft 4¼ in). There were more disgruntled Americans after the first round of the tug-of-war, an event with which they were not familiar. In their heat against the Liverpool Police, at the word 'heave' the Americans were, to quote a correspondent, 'pulled over with a rush'; they then withdrew from the competition. Some Americans thought that the heavy boots which the British team wore produced an unfair advantage. There was a protest but it was not upheld. However, if heavy boots were within the Olympic spirit, was the fact that the winning British team (City of London Police) had been training together for five months?

Swimming advanced to an international orderliness as the result of the Games. The pool, specially erected in the middle of the main stadium, was 100 metres long. The program was of six races, two diving competitions and water polo. Many of the countries taking part met during the Games to form the International Swimming Federation. One of the best races was the 400 metres, in which Frank Beaurepaire (Australia) stayed with Henry Taylor (Great Britain), who had been second at Athens in 1906, but finally was beaten by three yards. Taylor also won the 1,500 metres and took a gold medal in the 4 × 200-metres relay.

The attitudes and spirit of the day among the competitors were reflected in a diving incident. D. F. Cane, of Great Britain, one of the best divers, fell flat into the water in his semi-final stage, having attempted a double somersault. He was so badly shaken that he spent several days in bed and could not complete the competition; yet the Swedes, to indicate their belief in his talents, presented him with a silver cup.

The supremacy of British rowing was seen at Henley where all the gold medals in the four races were won by oarsmen of the host country. There were plenty of exciting moments for the large crowds. In the sculling final, Harry Blackstaffe overcame Alexander McCulloch, also of Great Britain, but it was not until the last 50 yards of the lengthened course – $1\frac{1}{2}$ miles (2,414 m) as against the traditional Henley one of 1 mile 550 yards (1,198 m) – that Blackstaffe got away. It was a remarkable peak to a career, for his first sculling success, winning the London Cup, had been achieved eleven years earlier, and he had won most of the sculling prizes including the Diamonds and the Netherlands Championship. In the year of his Olympic victory he was forty.

Perhaps one of the more poignant events of the Games was the final of the eights, which still holds its place as one of the great contests over this famous stretch of water. A Leander crew of experienced men faced Belgium, which in the two previous years had won the Grand in such fashion as to challenge the very concept of British rowing. In that Leander crew was Charles Burnell, whose son was to win a gold medal at the 1948 Olympics. In the bow of the umpire's launch was Coubertin. Leander led from the first stroke, but the attack and counter-attack of the race went on with such rapidity that many observers in the grandstands thought that one crew would crack completely; eventually the Belgians conceded when really they had nothing left, but defeat by two lengths sounds unjust to their ability and application.

The boxing was heavily dominated by the British, who won all the gold medals and all the silver except one, won by Reginald Baker (Australia) in the middleweight division. Dick Gunn, at the age of

Dorando Pietri (Italy) reels towards the tape in the marathon. After the twenty-six gruelling miles from Windsor Castle his feet are dragging and his knees giving way. John Hayes (United States) is only a hundred yards behind, and officials are helping the tiny Italian past the post. Because of this he was disqualified, but was presented with a consolation cup by Queen Alexandra.

200-metres breaststroke final in the swimming pool set in the middle of the athletics arena.

thirty-eight, won the featherweight title, having taken the ABA championships of 1894, 1895 and 1896 when he retired to serve on the ABA Council. But if the eight-year rest had cost him hitting power none of the skill was missing.

The weather of July 1908 was even worse than normal for an English summer; the cyslists suffered, lawn-tennis players slipped about the All-England courts and in fact transferred to indoor courts, and if there were those who returned home dissatisfied, London's contribution had shown the Olympic Movement the enormity of the tasks which lay ahead. The 1908 Games were the first in which entries were restricted, but there was still a need for administrative regulations relating to entries and closing dates, and, above all, international regulations which were understood and accepted generally. London, though, as it was to do in even more bleak circumstances forty years later, had provided an Olympic Games which were an important stepping-stone in the Movement's life. Stockholm and Sweden learned much from the events at Shepherd's Bush in the summer of 1908; they had four years in which to prepare for the next Games and solve many of the problems.

V STOCKHOLM 1912 Lord Noel-Baker

The Stockholm Games were an enchantment – the word was Coubertin's, in the speech with which he brought them to a close. As a competitor, I thought them an enchantment and looking back, six decades, two World Wars and twelve Olympiads later, my memories enchant me still.

Partly, no doubt, it was discovering Sweden. Landing in Gothenburg, soon after the dawn of a lovely summer day, travelling by train through woods and lakes and past smiling Scandinavian farms, the charm and the excitement of our adventure grew upon us hour by hour. But it was the Games themselves, the great concourse of the teams from all the continents, the thrill and fascination of the contests, the sheer beauty of the spectacle they offered – it was these that captured our imaginations and our hearts. We went to Stockholm as British athletes; we came home Olympians, disciples of the leader, Coubertin, with a new vision which I never lost.

In 1912 not everything was as it is today. There was no Olympic Village. The teams lived in different quarters scattered around the town. The Americans were in the transatlantic liner which had brought them from New York; we thought the ship was marvellous when we went to visit them; they thought it far too cramped and small.

The British team were in a two-star hotel which formed one side of a rocky canyon, through which electric trams began to thunder at 5 a.m. We slept several in a room. The meals were ample, nourishing, but not exciting, as Scandinavian menus almost always are.

None of this mattered to us in the least. We were young; we were comfortable enough; there were no complaints to worry the managers of the team. And the moment we walked out of the hotel, we found that Stockholm had a powerful attraction that was all its own – grass and roses at almost every turn; the lovely waterfront, bathed, as I remember, every day in glittering sun; the Royal Palaces; Skansen, to us a new kind of national park; and not least the forest, then close around the city, where we went in the evenings to dance with sedate but friendly and very pretty Swedish girls. Everyone in Stockholm was eager to give us help. The Games were Sweden's great chance in international affairs, and every Swede was resolved to do his share.

There was another reason why the Stockholm Games were an enchantment, and why they remain a landmark in Olympic history. In his opening speech, in the Swedish Parliament, and with the Crown Prince of Sweden in the chair, Coubertin spoke with sharp resentment of the 'unjustified and mischievous opposition' which the IOC had had to face for many years. He said that even in Stockholm he could find 'traces of a last ditch which a belated hostility sought to dig beneath our feet'.

In London in 1908 there had been 'incidents', errors by officials,

A demonstration of glima-wrestling.

which the vultures of the chauvinist Press had been able to exploit. In Stockholm there were no incidents, no protests, nothing to allow disloyal critics to pretend that quarrels had occurred. Before the Games had ended the opposition to the Olympic Movement largely died away. The Games were what Coubertin had planned and believed that they would be – a great international festival of sporting friendship and goodwill.

In London, four years before, teams from twenty-two countries had taken part; the competitors numbered 2,035. In Stockholm, there were teams from twenty-eight countries; and the teams were larger. According to the official Swedish records of the Games, there were 3,889 competitors, a figure which includes the gymnasts of Sweden and other Scandinavian countries whose demonstrations helped to spread gymnastics around the world. This increase since the Games in London shows the great momentum which the Olympic Movement had begun to gain. In every sport in the Stockholm program the performance of the teams reflected this notable advance.

As at each celebration of the Games, athletics, for the competitors and for the public, took pride of place. The stadium had been specially built; it was used for the first time in May 1912. We thought it beautiful, as it still is, and technically perfect in plan. The cinder track, and the jumping pits and throwing circles, were designed and laid by a veteran British groundsman, Charles Perry, who had also laid the track in Athens for the 1896 Games and many others. The performances in the Games were worthy of these preparations. There were new records, and splendid contests, in almost every track and field event.

There were many men whom I recall as splendid athletes. But one runner, by his achievements, stood above the rest: Hannes Kolehmainen of Finland. Kolehmainen, in the space of a few days, won his heat and the final of the 5,000 metres; the 10,000 metres, for which no heats were run; the 8-kilometre cross-country race; and his heat of the 3,000-metre team race (the first three runners home to count). Finland did not qualify for the final of the team race, or no doubt Kolehmainen would have won that, too.

One of the most dramatic finishes of the Games. Hannes Kolehmainen (Finland) about to overtake Jean Bouin (France) in the last 30 metres of the 5,000 metres.

Sometimes a single race can ensure the triumph of an athletic meeting. This happened with the 5,000-metres final in the Stockholm Stadium. Kolehmainen was happy and smiling, a generous competitor and a modest winner. Jean Bouin was a handsome, jolly young Frenchman, already, as was evident, on cordial terms with Kolehmainen. The Swedish public took them both to their hearts. In the 5,000-metres final, these two raced away together from the gun; there was soon a large gap between them and the remainder of the field. All the way, for twelve and a half laps, they ran together, passing and repassing one another, as each tried in vain to break away. When the bell rang for the last lap, the great crowd, cheering both of them, were delirious with excitement; when they reached the final straight, Scandinavian solidarity prevailed, the spectators roared a thunderous encouragement for the Finn. Down the straight they ran side by side, first one and then the other pulling a few centimetres ahead. Perhaps my personal affection for Kolehmainen makes me remember that 5,000 metres as the most exciting race I ever saw.

I remember something else about it. In London the Finnish team had not been allowed to carry a flag in the opening parade. Finland

Hannes Kolehmainen (Finland) in the marathon.

was still part of the Russian Empire, and the Tsarist Government had insisted that they must carry the Russian flag – or none. They carried none.

In Stockholm, the Russian flag still went up for Kolehmainen's victory; and, as I shook his hand and thumped him on the back after the 5,000 metres, he turned and pointed at the flagpole and said: 'I would almost rather not have won, than see that flag up there.' He was wrong. What flag it was they hoisted was instantly forgotten; his glorious race with Bouin had struck a resounding blow for the nationalism, and in due course for the independence, of the Finns.

There were other outstanding people on the track in Stockholm: Ralph Craig, who won both the sprints, and who turned up again in London in 1948 as the Captain of the US yachting team; Hanns Braun, of Munich, who was beaten by inches in the 400 metres, and who, with luck, might have won the 800 metres; he was a marvellously graceful runner, a very gifted sculptor; he survived three years in the trenches in France and Flanders, only to be shot down and killed in a fighter aircraft in the last month of World War I; Ted Meredith, a Philadelphia schoolboy, who won the 800 metres in a new world-record time; Ralph Rose, who weighed 250 lb (113.40 kg), won the two-handed shot for the United States, and was popularly reported to eat two pounds of steak for breakfast, together with six eggs in their shells. Arnold Strode-Jackson, an Oxford undergraduate in his second year, who had run hardly any first-class races before he came to Stockholm, won the 1,500-metres final; he defeated a team of world-record-beating American milers, in a new Olympic time. Jackson was a man of immense courage and iron willpower; in World War I he was wounded four times; four times he was awarded the Distinguished Service Order for exceptional gallantry in action. On both sides of the Atlantic, he became a legendary figure

British Ladies' swimming team.

for his feats on the track and on the battlefield.

There was, too, another man who was to become a legend in his own lifetime, Jim Thorpe, an Indian whose mother was from the Potawatome tribe and named her son Bright Path and whose father was from the Sac and Fox tribe. Thorpe made a great impression on my mind and fully deserved the accolade of the greatest all-round athlete. He won the pentathlon by a massive margin, finishing first in four of the events, and then the decathlon with a score of 8,412.96 points, nearly 700 more than the second man. 'Sir,' said the King of Sweden, when presenting him with his prize, 'you are the most wonderful athlete in the world.' Thorpe's running, jumping and throwing seemed to me those of a superman.

But I remember, too, the indignation I felt when, on what I thought was a purely technical offence, he was disqualified in January of the following year and declared a professional, his name being removed from the Olympic records. It was discovered that he had been paid for playing baseball – $60 for a month. But when confronted with this sin against Olympism, Thorpe, a quiet, unassuming man, did not deny it. In fact, he did not believe he had done anything wrong. 'I did not play for the money, I played because I liked baseball,' he said.

Nothing like the track and field events in Stockholm had ever happened in athletic history before. They gave a golden glamour to the Games in the eyes of all men and women in every land. Next in prestige to athletics was the association football tournament. It was after Stockholm, and thanks to its exciting matches and the teams' demonstrations of football skill, that the game spread rapidly around the world – first in Scandinavia, but soon elsewhere – only twelve years later the Olympic champions came from Uruguay.

In Stockholm there were eleven teams, all from Europe. Britain and Denmark were notably stronger than the rest, and they fought out the final before 25,000 spectators, Britain winning by 4 goals to 2.

Each side had a player of worldwide renown. Vivian Woodward, England's Captain, had already, as an amateur among professionals, earned a reputation, first with Tottenham Hotspurs, and then with Chelsea, as the finest centre-forward in the world. His artistry, and his deadly shooting, were a feature of every game. Nils Middelboe of Denmark showed a skill and versatility that were rare; he moved up from half-back to centre-forward in the final, and beat the British goalkeeper with a brilliant goal. When these tournaments were finished, association football and FIFA were on their way to their present universality and fame.

The same was true of gymnastics, which after Stockholm were firmly established as a major Olympic sport. Thirteen nations entered teams totalling 1,275 men and women gymnasts. Five days were allotted to the contests and the displays, which all took place in brilliant sunshine in the athletics stadium.

All the Scandinavian countries, Italy, Germany and others sent large and well-trained teams of men. Among the contests were obligatory exercises on the parallel bars, on the horizontal bar, on the pommelled vaulting horse, and on the rings. The men performed prodigies of skill and strength on all this apparatus; Italy won the gold medals, in the individual (Alberto Braglia) and the team events.

I was deeply impressed by the magnificent physique of the men gymnasts, and by their strength, their skill, their discipline. But, as so often in gymnastics, it was the women who stole the show. I remember the teams of Scandinavian girls, dressed in colourful and lovely costumes, who gave displays of disciplined collective movement which had the beauty of the ballet, and which seemed somehow imbued with the glorious national spirit of the free and democratic nations of the North. It was not surprising that in the following years the gymnastic system of the Swedish master, Per Henrik Ling, 'based upon the sports and pastimes of the Swedish Vikings', spread

Matthew McGrath (United States) winner of the hammer.

rapidly to many other countries, far and near.

In Stockholm swimming also came into its own. The sensation of the swimming pool was a competitor from Honolulu, Duke Kahanamoku. He only won a single gold medal, for the 100-metres freestyle sprint. He also swam as anchor man for the United States in the 4 × 200-metres relay. But his truly magnificent physique, the perfection of his sophisticated crawl, his victory by a wide margin and his exuberant and friendly character, made him a most popular figure in the pool, in the stadium and in the streets of Stockholm.

Swimming was more truly international than it had been before. There were eighteen national teams and 223 swimmers; the swimming pool was popular with the public, and the Olympic contests had gained in 'atmosphere' and in prestige.

In the men's races, it became apparent that Australia and Japan would be bringing strong teams to future Games. In Stockholm, too, women, for the first time, were allowed to swim; their participation was a huge success, with the competitors and the public alike. In the platform diving, Swedish women took seven of the first eight places; an English girl (Isabelle White) broke the sequence.

In wrestling there were teams from seventeen nations; the official Swedish Report of the Games said that the entries were 'simply enormous' and that 'the modern technique of wrestling has been going up enormously during the last few years. Everybody following the wrestling of the 1912 Games can testify to the truth of this assertion.'

The Finns were very much 'top nation' in the wrestling contests. They took three gold medals out of five. In the fifth event, the light heavyweight, a Swede, Anders Ahlgren, wrestled with a Finn, Ivar Böhling, for nine hours, without either of them being able to get a

More women in the Olympic arena. A display by Finnish women gymnasts.

Jenö Fuchs (Hungary) and Nedo Nadi (Italy) in the sabre event.

fall. At that point the Judges declared the match a draw, and awarded no gold medal, but two silvers instead.

The modern pentathlon was a new event in the Olympic program, introduced at the instance of Coubertin. The five contests were shooting; swimming (300 metres); fencing; cross-country riding; and cross-country running (4,000 metres).

As the contests were spread over five days, they were, for well-trained men, more a test of widely differing skills than of great physical endurance. In the first event, shooting, the Swedes swept the board, taking the three first places. In the swimming race in the Olympic pool, Britain was first and sixth, but there were three Swedes in between. The fencing was spread over two days, but even so, it was a strenuous affair: a Swede was first, with twenty-four wins (that is twenty-four separate fights!); a Frenchman second with twenty-three. In the cross-country riding, the Swedes took the first five places, and they did almost as well in the cross-country running.

The first photo-finish equipment to be used at the Olympic Games.

As the final placings in the modern pentathlon depended on the results of the running, and as the start and finish were in the stadium, it might have been an exciting and exhilarating spectacle. Some of the drama was taken out of it, however, by the decision that the competitors should start at one-minute intervals. The first man home was Gösta Åsbrink of Sweden, who covered the 4-kilometre course in 19 min 01 sec. Swedes were second and fourth, with George Smith Patton of the United States (who later became a famous General in World War II) third, exactly 60 sec slower than Åsbrink.

In the light of what is said above, it is not surprising that Sweden took all the medals. But the order of these medallists was surprising; first was G. M. Lilliehöök, whose best individual placings were fourth in the riding, and fifth in the cross-country run. The silver medallist was Åsbrink, and the bronze was Georg de Laval.

There were no track cycle races but a road time trial which the Swedish Official Report called 'a veritable epoch in the history of cycle racing'. The course chosen was that of an annual Swedish event – 320 kilometres (199 miles) long. There were 121 starters, of whom ninety-three finished the course. They were dispatched at 2-minute intervals, the first at 2 a.m., the last precisely 5 hours later, at 7 a.m. The individual winner was Rudolf Lewis of South Africa in 10 hr 42 min 39.0 sec.

CANADA

C18

Right: Albert Gutterson (United States) winner of the running broad jump.

Left: Competitors in the 10,000-metres walk being watched closely to ensure they do not break contact with the ground.

Left: Wrestling. Middleweight Martin Klein (USSR) v Alfred Asikainen (Finland). A typical illustration of the unconquerable energy of these two opponents.

Towards the end of the Games, the visiting teams were amazed to see the stadium converted, in a single night, into an arena for the equestrian events – hedges, ditches, gates and all the rest. It was a demonstration of the thoroughness and the efficiency with which the Swedish Olympic Committee had prepared the Games. Much of the satisfaction which the teams derived from their events, and much of the general harmony that prevailed, was due to the care and the imagination of the Swedish hosts.

The equestrian cross-country course was thirty-three miles long; the weather was hot, and the ground was hard. But by good fortune all went well. In the three-day event, in the dressage, in the show jumping, the Swedes almost cleared the board. They captured four gold medals out of five; a Frenchman, Jean Cariou, got the fifth.

The Stockholm Games were everything that Coubertin had desired that they should be. There were no 'incidents'. The endemic chauvinist hostility, which for twenty years had been a festering sore, was temporarily silenced. In the stadium, in the pool, in every sports hall, the Olympic spirit had begun to live. The athletes had begun to know each other, and to fraternize. The officials of the national teams and of the international sporting federations had begun to form a close and powerful community of friends. Sweden had done the Olympic Movement proud; the Olympic Movement had brought Sweden an added prestige and an added glamour in the world society of states.

All this made Stockholm 1912 a decisive milestone in the history of the Olympic Games. On the last night of the Games, the Swedish organizers gave the teams and their leaders and officials a magnificent banquet in the stadium where the athletics, the gymnastics and the equestrian events had taken place. It was a fitting climax to the

Platt Adams (United States) winner of the Standing High Jump.

greatest Olympiad there had been. It furthered, as it symbolized, the unity and the fraternity of the sportsmen of the world.

It was at this banquet that Coubertin made his closing speech. As was his custom, he ended by saluting the nation who would be the hosts of the next Games:

> A great people [Germany had been chosen for 1916] has received the torch of the Olympiads from your [Swedish] hands, and has thereby undertaken to preserve, and, if possible, to quicken its precious flame. . . . May it [the sixth Olympiad] contribute, like its illustrious predecessors, to the general welfare and to the betterment of humanity! May it be prepared in the fruitful labours of peaceful times! May it be celebrated, when the day comes, by all the peoples of the world in gladness and concord.

There was a transcendent purpose in that great man's mind, which, to those who understood the facts of the international situation of 1912, and who saw the gathering storm clouds, shone out like a beacon through our golden Stockholm days.

VI BERLIN (Cancelled) 1916 John Rodda

At that point where modern Olympism had begun to walk with a firm step – at Stockholm for the celebration of the fifth Olympiad in 1912 – Europe moved towards turmoil.

The candidates for the sixth Games were Berlin, Budapest and Alexandria; Coubertin, and other members of the IOC, aware of the clouds of war and of Germany's navalism and militarism, believed that if Berlin were to be awarded the Games war might be averted. Coubertin was aware that there were strong forces in Germany which wanted peace and that, while the Kaiser liked the idea of military power, he had a personal aversion to the thought of war.

The Games at Stockholm had brought the Swedes vast, prestigious publicity. The Games for Berlin, Coubertin felt, might help the Kaiser to find support for his more peaceful inclinations.

Thus at the IOC session in Stockholm during the Games, when the candidates for the next Games came up for discussion, Coubertin's influence was seen. Jules de Muzsa, the member in Hungary, waived claim in favour of Germany; he was supported and Berlin was adopted unanimously.

The Germans, like their opponents, believed that the war would be short and in 1914 they did not withdraw from staging the Games. But as time passed the hopes of a Games in Berlin diminished. First Coubertin came under pressure to have the Games in either Scandinavia or the United States, but he declined to take this sort of initiative so long as Germany had not given up the mandate because he believed that it would further damage the Olympic Movement. He established that if an Olympiad was not celebrated it would, like the Ancient Games in Greece, still maintain its number.

War, of course, cut deep into Olympic loyalties. Theodore Cook, an IOC member in Britain, asked that the German members be expelled from certain international academic and scientific groups. Coubertin felt that this would be unwise and after consulting other members rejected the motion and Cook resigned. It was an uneasy time for the IOC for its role and future seemed uncertain. Coubertin wanted to give up the presidency but when war came he decided to stay on; in fact he took a most useful, positive step in 1915, setting up the headquarters of the Movement in Lausanne, where he had a home.

As early as its meeting in June 1914, the IOC had considered Antwerp as a candidate for 1920, which, as the carnage of man's nobility dragged on, was seen as the most appropriate place for the youth of the world to gather in more peaceful ways.

VII ANTWERP 1920 Lord Noel-Baker

Coubertin was deeply afflicted by the tragedy of the war, and by the blank Olympiad of 1916. 'Berlin' was written on his heart. But defeat never made Coubertin defeatist. He resolved that, although the date would be barely twenty months after the end of World War I, the seventh Olympiad should be celebrated at the due and proper time. A few weeks after the guns were silenced, he assembled the International Olympic Committee in Lausanne, and they decided that the Games should be in Antwerp in August 1920.

The decision was, of course, intended as a tribute of honour to the gallant Belgians, who had been the victims of unprovoked aggression five years before; it was universally popular throughout the world. But it imposed a heavy burden on the Belgian organizers. Belgium had by no means recovered from the war. After four years of struggle and of enemy occupation, they had not even in 1920 repaired the damage in the battle zone, where lovely, medieval towns like Ypres and Furnes had been totally destroyed. To prepare the stadia and the sports halls needed for the various Olympic sports, to provide for the accommodation of the teams, to arrange the social and ceremonial occasions, including royal visits, and to do all this within eighteen

Great Britain beating the United States in tug-of-war.

months of the armistice and national reconstruction, was a truly Herculean task.

By Herculean efforts, it was admirably carried out. With great difficulties to overcome, the Belgian organizers built a splendid stadium for the athletics and association football; excellent pools for the swimming and the diving; excellent grounds or sports halls for the contests; and they provided accommodation – living quarters – for the teams which I remember with lively pleasure still.

The accommodation was in the Antwerp City Schools. The catering and the food – to athletes most important – were very good; the Belgian personnel who served us were kind and willing; we were given – again important – admirable beds, eight to a classroom. It has always been a happy memory that I slept next to Bevill Rudd – he was South African, but he chose to live with the British team. The cheerful temper of the team, in our bedrooms, and at meals in the school assembly hall, made our communal life very pleasant and very welcome to us all.

The Commandant of our British team, Brigadier Kentish, D.S.O., managed to provide us with some Scottish pipers. Clad in their kilts, they performed on their bagpipes on all probable and improbable occasions. They were a source of pride to us, and of delight to all our foreign visitors.

Even more important, the Brigadier found a first-class dance band. We invited teams from other countries to evening parties, at which the school playground was our dance floor. I remember in particular a splendid evening with the Swedes, which helped me to forget the worry of the 1,500-metres heats on the following day.

There was the same feeling of relief, of release, that there was to be at Wembley after World War II. The four endless, wasted years of battle were behind us. The world had turned, and we turned with it, to better, happier things. So we all greatly enjoyed ourselves in Antwerp. But we treated our Olympic contests with the serious concentration which they required and deserved.

As always, the Opening of the Games drew an enormous crowd to the stadium. The ceremony was performed by the King of the Belgians, King Albert, an ardent mountaineer, who lost his life in a climbing accident in 1934. His wife, Queen Elizabeth, was by his side and Cardinal Mercier was there, too, to bless the Games. They were all three held in such esteem throughout the world that their presence gave a special distinction to the day. Cardinal Mercier also held a Requiem Mass of Remembrance in Antwerp Cathedral for those who had lost their lives on active service in the war.

The parade of the teams was as colourful as that in 1912, and a great deal smarter. Many competitors had learned of marching during the preceding years.

Anyone who now judges the performance in the running events should make allowance for the track. The Belgians had worked miracles in the preparation of the Games but they had not succeeded in laying the world's fastest track. The track was slow and heavy. When it rained, there were ruts and depressions in its surface; it was a constant worry to the runners from first to last.

To those who had been in Stockholm, there were tragic gaps in the ranks of the athletes – many, like the great Jean Bouin of France, and the great Hanns Braun of Germany, had lost their lives on active service.

But there were some survivors. Among them, Hannes Kolehmainen was most eminent. Eight years after Stockholm, he rounded off his magnificent career by a victory in the marathon. Nobody had expected that he could win. There was a strong field; among the most fancied were Christian Gitsham (South Africa), who had been second in Stockholm, Juris Lossman (Estonia), and Valerio Arri (Italy).

Kolehmainen showed his serious intentions from the start. He was running second at 5 kilometres, and again at 15 kilometres; between those distances he was never further back than fourth; at 30 kilometres, he took the lead, and held it to the tape. His was, I think, the most popular victory in Antwerp; I remember still the cheers that he received when he came first into the stadium. Apart from him, the experts had not been so wrong: the Estonian, Lossman, came next, outsprinting Arri for second place; Arri, to show how fresh he was, turned three somersaults on the track as he crossed the finishing line.

There were other Finns in Antwerp, worthy to belong to Kolehmainen's team. There was Paavo Nurmi, paradoxically, on his first appearance, defeated. A Frenchman, Joseph Guillemot, followed

Hannes Kolehmainen (Finland) entering the Stadium at Antwerp on his way to victory during the marathon. (At Stockholm, in 1912, Kolehmainen won the 10,000 metres run and also the cross country race).

Victor Boin (Belgium) taking the first oath on behalf of all competitors.

Yuri Lossman (Estonia) competing in the marathon.

close behind him in the 5,000 metres until they were half-way down the final straight; then he gained a lead with a sudden spurt which Nurmi could not overtake. Guillemot, who had been the victim of poison gas in the war, thus avenged France for the defeat of Bouin in Stockholm eight years before.

But that was neither the end of Nurmi nor of the Finns. Three days later, Nurmi won the 10,000 metres, doing to his conqueror, Guillemot, precisely what Guillemot had done to him. Then he won the individual title in the 8-kilometre cross-country race, and with his compatriots won the team cross-country championship for Finland as well.

Another Finn, Eero Lehtonen, took first place in the pentathlon – long jump, javelin, discus, 200 metres, 1,500 metres (no longer on the program). Lehtonen was to win the same event again, with better performances, in Paris in 1924. Finland took all three medals at Antwerp in the javelin – such a thing had never happened in any field event before.

In the discus, and in the shot again, Finns were first and second. The names of Elmer Niklander, Armas Taipale and Ville Pörhölä were to be famous later on. Antwerp was the start of Finnish pre-eminence in track and field, which reached its zenith eight years later at the Games in Amsterdam.

The United States also had its share of track and field successes. Almost as a matter of course, Americans were first and second in both the sprints: Charles William Paddock, Allen Woodring and Morris Marshall Kirksey. Likewise they won the 4 × 100-metres relay. They could claim six medals out of six for the two hurdle races: the 110 metres and 400 metres. All the six hurdlers were trained and educated in the United States, although one of them, Earl Thomson, who won the 110-metres hurdles and had learned everything he knew at Dartmouth College, N.H., had chosen to run instead for Canada, where he had been born.

The United States also won the 3,000-metres team race: it came second in the 800 metres (Earl Eby from Philadelphia) and in the steeplechase (Patrick Flynn); third in the 1,500 metres (Lawrence Shields, the US University Champion). Americans were first and second in the high jump; first and third in the pole vault; first and third in the hammer; second in the decathlon; second in the long jump.

Any other nation would have been immensely proud of such results. The Americans thought it a rather moderate success. But the standard of their achievement was shown by the fact that every athlete of any other nationality thought that, if he had beaten an American in his event, he had not come to Antwerp in vain.

As in Stockholm, other Scandinavians besides the Finns did well. The Swedes were prominent in almost everything; their most distinguished track success was achieved by Nils Engdahl, who won the bronze medal in the 400 metres, beating all the Americans. They were first and third in the long jump (William Pettersson and Erik Abrahamsson); third (the famous Bo Ekelund) in the high jump; and gained medals in other field events.

The Italians had two splendid walkers, Ugo Frigerio and Donato Pavesi. Frigerio won the gold medals for both the 3,000- and the 10,000-metres walks. He was to win the 10,000 metres again in Paris

Two medal-winning children: fourteen-year-old Aileen Riggin (United States) took the spring-board diving and Nils Skoglund (Sweden), thirteen, the silver in the plain high diving.

in 1924 – there was no 3,000 metres then. I saw Frigerio in other competitions besides the Olympic Games. His times in Antwerp were not world records, but I have always thought him the most perfect stylist among all the walkers I have ever seen. His grace and rhythm as he moved were beautiful to watch.

One of the outstanding competitors was H. F. V. (Harry) Edward, a West Indian sprinter – a man whom many other great West Indians were to emulate in years to come. Edward won bronze medals in both the 100 and 200 metres. In the 100 metres, he was the victim of grievous ill-luck. Owing to a misunderstanding of the officials' orders at the start, Edward, and two other finalists from the United States and France, had relaxed, with their back knees on the track, when the starter's gun was fired. Yards behind, Edward made a splendid effort to come third. I admired no less his cheerful, sporting spirit when a committee decided that the race must stand.

Another was Albert Hill of Britain, a railway guard, and thirty-six years old. Before the war, he had won a British 4-mile championship. He had served in the Army for the full four years of the war. In Antwerp he won both the 800 and 1,500 metres. He had a marvellous temperament, which other runners of all nationalities envied. Before a race, while others were counting aches and pains, and biting nails, Hill would have an early lunch, and then sleep soundly for three hours. This power of sleep must have helped him to win five races in five days – three rounds of 800 metres and the heat and the final of the 1,500 metres.

Both finals were exciting races, and in both he showed that he was past master in the tactics of the track. In the 1,500 metres he stayed at the rear of the leading group, but at the bell, with 400 metres still to go, he flashed into the lead and held it to the end. His was the finest double of the Games.

A third was Bevill Rudd of South Africa. He had had a very strenuous and very exacting war. He was an officer in the first tanks ever to be sent to attack enemy lines. On one of their raids, his tank broke down; he was stuck for hours between the lines, and escaped miraculously with his life. His character was strong, but so generous, and so understanding of others that it was said that 'no one ever lost a race against Bevill without feeling that he had won a friend'. He could do 10 seconds for the 100 yards, and could beat almost any miler of his day. In the 800-metres final in Antwerp, he led into the last straight; then by ill-fate he put a foot in a 'depression' in the track; he wrenched his ankle so badly that he did well to finish third, and it seemed doubtful whether he could start in the 400 later in the week. But start he did, and won the gold medal.

There was much in the Antwerp Games besides athletics to excite and to entertain the teams, the Press reporters, and the general public.

Association football was very popular. Teams from fifteen nations – fourteen from Europe, one from Egypt – took part. Britain swiftly lost the title won in Stockholm, defeated in the first round by Norway 1–3. In the final there was a scene I have never witnessed before or since. When the home team, Belgium, came on the field, it was loudly hooted by the crowd. Embarrassed Belgians told us that the Antwerp Press had bitterly attacked the selectors, because distinguished local players had been left out of the national team.

Part of rugby union football's brief contribution to the Games. United States beat France, 8-0.

The game which followed was an unhappy episode in Olympic history. Soccer was in its infancy in Europe and Latin America; the high standards of sportsmanship and fair play in the Olympic championship had not yet been built up. The referee's decisions were constantly disputed; the Czech team walked off the field in protest and a crowd of 40,000 dissatisfied spectators saw the Belgians become the victors by the disqualification of their opponents.

In 1920 lawn tennis was still an Olympic sport. The tournament was played on courts next door to the stadium, so it was very easy to watch. What most people remember is their first view of Suzanne Lenglen, who won the women's singles and, with Max Decugis, the mixed doubles. It was the beginning of nearly twelve years of French pre-eminence in the game. Suzanne Lenglen seemed to us the greatest player, man or woman, we had ever seen; some would have added: 'or whom we shall ever see'. In every stroke she had the power of 'Little Mo' – Maureen Connolly of California; but Suzanne had something else as well: her every movement was like a lovely ballerina's, and the ballet, quite as firmly as her tennis, stayed in the beholders' minds. There were other famous players in the Antwerp tournament; it was notable that the runners-up in the men's doubles were Ichiya Kamagai and Seiichiro Kashio, a brilliant couple from Japan. But 'Antwerp tennis' meant 'Suzanne Lenglen' in the impartial spectator's mind.

The modern pentathlon – Coubertin's event, to which he attached a great importance – was stoutly contested in the Antwerp Games. Again, as in Stockholm, the Swedes were very much on top, and one of them, Gustav Dyrssen, eventually won – a worthy successor to his compatriot Gustaf Lilliehöök who had triumphed eight years before.

In the swimming pools, there was an even stronger reminder of what Stockholm had produced. The picturesque swimmer from Honolulu, Duke Kahanamoku, was there again. His ebullient and attractive personality drew delighted attention wherever he chanced to go. Again he won the 100-metres freestyle for the United States, followed by his comrade from Honolulu, Pua Kela Kealoha. Again he helped the United States to win the 4 × 200-metres relay, while Warren Kealoha (Pua Kela Kealoha's brother) won the 100-metres backstroke.

There was a pointer to the future in the diving – two children: Aileen Riggin of the United States, who won the springboard diving, and Nils Skoglund of Sweden, who was second in the men's plain high diving.

The wrestling and the boxing drew their usual crowd of fans. In the freestyle competition, honours were fairly evenly divided. Finland took two gold medals, but Sweden, the United States and Switzerland each got one. The Greco-Roman contests were again a purely Scandinavian affair – Finland took three of the gold medals, Sweden the other two. The wrestling was of a higher standard than it had been eight years before.

Boxing was a more international affair. There were eight classes, from flyweight to heavyweight. The United States won three titles (Frank De Genaro, Samuel Mosberg and Edward Eagan); Britain two (Harry Mallin and Ronald Rawson, who were both to be heard of again); France, South Africa and Canada took one title each. I remember no trouble in the ring, but people began to say that the International Federation should clean up the rules.

The rowing people, like the boxers, were a happy band of brothers. Britain, which had led the world till then, was severely routed. Jack Beresford began his wonderful career by reaching the final of the single sculls; but he was beaten by Jack Kelly of the United States. American crews took two of the other races; Switzerland and Italy took one each.

Patrick Ryan (United States).

The equestrian events were, once again, almost a clean sweep for Sweden. An Italian officer, Lieutenant Tommaso Lequio, won the individual show jumping; for the rest, the Swedes were in a class by themselves.

So were the Italians in the fencing. They took two individual titles (Nedo Nadi won the foil and sabre), and all three team events, foil, épée and sabre. A Frenchman, Armand Massard, won the individual épée. The rest of the world seemed to be nowhere. In fact, that was an illusion; there were other strong teams in Antwerp besides the Italians and the French; and it became clear in Antwerp that fencing was then firmly established as an Olympic sport.

The gymnastics, not yet developed as they are today, belonged, like the fencing, to Italy; Italians won both the individual (Giorgio Zampori) and the team event.

All the cycling races were exciting – there were six of them, and six nations won one race each. A Swede, Harry Stenqvist, won the individual title in the 175-kilometres road race; but France won the team race, beating the Swedes by over six minutes on the aggregate of the riders' times, while the Swedes had an advantage over the Belgians of more than five minutes. I remember it as a close race and as a truly magnificent event.

The Antwerp Games were very much what I have called them, a postwar affair. They were an important factor in the world's psychological recovery from the war. They showed that not even a world war, lasting more than the period of a whole Olympiad, could break or weaken the Olympic Movement. Beyond question, it emerged from Antwerp stronger than it had been before. In a speech delivered in

Antwerp Town Hall to the IOC, and in the presence of King Albert, Coubertin said:

> This is what the seventh Olympiad has brought us: general comprehension; the certainty of being henceforward understood by all . . . These festivals . . . are above all the festivals of human unity. In an incomparable synthesis the effort of muscles and of mind, mutual help and competition, lofty patriotism and intelligent cosmopolitanism, the personal interest in the champion and the abnegation of the team-member, are bound in a sheaf for a common task.

VIII PARIS 1924 Vernon Morgan

Paris, having held the second Games in 1900, became the first city to celebrate them a second time. The Games of 1924 were held there at the express wish of Coubertin, who wanted to eradicate the fiasco of the 1900 Paris Olympics and to end his term as IOC President with the staging of his Games in his own country. He got them but not without reservations. Lack of cash and facilities were such that an appeal had to be made to Los Angeles to find out if it could take over the Games should Paris have to withdraw; it said it would. The financial problems in Paris eased but then the Games looked like floundering on another disaster when the Seine overflowed its banks during the winter of 1923 and much of the city was flooded.

However, the effect on Paris did not permeate to the Games and the city staged not only a celebration in which the Baron could take pride but a Games which marked the beginning of a new era in the Movement.

The previous Olympics in Antwerp had been of necessity somewhat austere, coming shortly after the end of World War I. In Paris, records of every kind were established. There were forty-four nations competing as against the previous record of twenty-nine in Antwerp

Polo match between Gt Britain and the United States.

Finnish competitors in the marathon; Hannes Kolehmainen, Albin Stenroos (the winner) and Lauri Halonen.

and although there were five fewer events (seventeen as against twenty-two) there were some 500 more participants with a tally of over 3,000, more in fact than took part in the 1928 Olympics in Amsterdam. In track and field events held in the famous Colombes Stadium, six new world records were set and fifteen Olympic records equalled or bettered. In the Tourelles pool the swimmers set two world records and equalled or beat ten previous Olympic marks.

Paris provided the first collective accommodation for athletes – huts gathered round the Colombes Stadium – but the first Olympic Village, with all the facilities which that term implies, was not built until the Games of 1932 in Los Angeles. In Paris, too, women competed in fencing for the first time; lawn tennis and rugby football were seen at the Olympics for the last time; polo made its penultimate appearance.

Huge profits were made by speculators buying and selling tickets

Harold Abrahams (Gt Britain) winning the 100 metres.

for the opening ceremony. For not only did all Paris want to see President Gaston Doumergue open the Games, but most of France, as well as people from other European countries. It was an impressive ceremony but, like others of its time, austere compared with the huge colourful opening ceremonies of the 1970s. Never before had there been a Games staged in such terrific heat; never has there been since. Colombes was variously described as a 'cauldron' and a 'furnace', and one of the refreshment stalls was dubbed *La Bonne Frite* ('the good fry'). Although there was at least one storm to relieve the intense heat, it was 45°C (113°F) on some days, notably when the 10,000-metres cross-country was run. It is not surprising that only fifteen of the thirty-eight starters finished the gruelling course, most of them in a poor physical condition. But the winner, Paavo Nurmi, was unaffected by the conditions.

Nurmi, then twenty-seven, was the hero of the Games. Not only did he win the cross-country, but three other golds: in the 3,000-metres team race (no longer held), the 1,500 metres and the 5,000 metres, the last two races on the same day within one hour of each other.

In those days runners did not have the aid of either official or unofficial times being called out at the completion of each lap. But Nurmi was as ahead of his time in his thinking about running as he was in the quality and quantity of his training and he realized that an even race was an essential economy in long-distance running. So he carried a watch in his left hand during training and competition. I'll never forget his annoyance when in the 3,000-metres steeplechase in Amsterdam in 1928 (I also took part) he fell in the water jump and damaged his watch. He would never say whether this cost him the race, in which he finished second to his team mate Toivo Loukola.

Nurmi was not the only Finn to defy the heat and show the world they had more like Hannes Kolehmainen. Ville Ritola won the 10,000 metres and the steeplechase, Albin Stenroos took the marathon, Eero Lehtonen the pentathlon (its last appearance on the Olympic program) and Jonni Myyrä the javelin.

The world long-jump record was broken but not in the long-jump competition. The new figures were set in the pentathlon! Robert LeGendre was annoyed that he had not been picked to jump for the

United States. So he was not amused when William De Hart Hubbard won the gold medal for the United States with a leap of 7.445 m (24 ft 5 in). On taking the track for the pentathlon LeGendre was reported as remarking, 'I'll show them who their best long jumper is, and what's more I'll set a new world record.' Though taking only the bronze in the pentathlon, LeGendre was as good as his word. His best leap of 7.765 m (25 ft 5 in) was over a foot further than Hubbard's winning Olympic jump, and it duly broke the world record.

Who will ever forget the great win of Harold Abrahams, the only Briton ever to have won the Olympic 100 metres, and with a new Olympic record? Eric Liddell, from Scotland, set not only an Olympic but a world record by taking the 400 metres in 47.6 sec. He took the bronze in the 200 metres but withdrew from the 100 metres, in which he had a strong chance of winning, because the heats were run on a Sunday.

Then there was Douglas Lowe (Gt Britain) in the 800 metres. Timing his effort as superbly as always, he just got home ahead of Paul Martin (Switzerland). Lowe was to repeat this performance four years later in the Amsterdam Olympics. Britain won a gold in the swimming pool too. This was through Lucy Morton in the 200-metre breaststroke.

Two gold medals came Britain's way in the boxing through the two Harrys, Mallin and Mitchell, the former winning the middleweight title and the latter the light heavyweight. Mallin was involved in the most infamous incident of the Games, being bitten in the shoulder by his French opponent, who was subsequently disqualified. The Olympic tournament was held with the referee officiating outside the ring for the first time and critics of this novel Olympic procedure said some boxers took advantage of this arrangement.

Britain won another two golds in the rowing events on the Seine, in the single sculls, and coxless fours. The victory of Jack Beresford in the single sculls was one of sweet revenge. In 1920 in Antwerp he had been pipped at the post by Jack Kelly (United States). Beresford was eager for revenge in Paris but his final opponent was not Kelly but the sculler who had beaten him for the US title, William Gilmore. The Briton showed consummate skill in a cat-and-mouse affair to win comfortably.

Women's singles tennis – Miss Kathleen McKane (Gt Britain) who came third, Miss Julie Vlasto (France) second, and the champion Miss Helen Wills (United States).

The rugby football tournament went to the United States with France and Romania the only other contestants.

The United States won both lawn-tennis singles titles in this other sport for which these Games in Paris were the last. Vincent Richards beat Henri Cochet, the local hero, in five tough sets in the men's event and Helen Wills beat Jeanne Vlasto of France in the women's without much trouble. Suzanne Lenglen, her formidable French rival, had withdrawn from the tournament at the last minute through 'indisposition'.

Even in those days they had 'unofficial' medals tables. The United States was an easy leader with forty-five medals, then came Finland with fourteen and France with thirteen.

The American successes came in nine of the seventeen sports. They won thirteen golds in the swimming, seven by their men and six by their women; twelve in track and field; five in shooting and lawn tennis in which they swept the board, winning every title; four in wrestling, two each in rowing and boxing and one in gymnastics. They also won the rugby football title. Only in gymnastics did any other country win more golds.

In track and field they won the 200 metres, both hurdles, both relays, the high jump, long jump, shot, hammer, discus, pole vault and decathlon. They were responsible for three of the six world records established.

In the men's swimming events they won the 100- and 400-metres freestyle, the 100-metres backstroke and 200-metres breaststroke, the 4 × 200-metres relay and both dives, setting a new world figure in the relay and new Olympic times in three other swimming titles. The women won the 100- and 400-metres freestyle, the 100-metres backstroke, the 4 × 100-metres relay and both dives. World records were established in the 200-metres freestyle and relay.

Their shooting victories came in the free rifle (600 metres), free

Albin Oskar Stenroos on his way to victory in the marathon.

Albert White (United States) diving.

pistol (25 metres), running deer and, in the team events, in free rifle and clay pigeon. In wrestling the golds came in the featherweight, lightweight, light heavyweight and heavyweight divisions; in boxing, the flyweight and featherweight; in rowing the double sculls and eights, and in gymnastics, the long-horse vault.

Two gold medallists of the United States boxing team later went on to win professional world titles. They were Fidel LaBarba who became the world flyweight champion, and Jackie Fields, the Olympic featherweight champion, who took the world welterweight title in 1929.

There were greats in the swimming events too, like Johnny Weissmuller (of later Tarzan fame) and Duke Kahanamoku. With Andrew Charlton, Australia began its bid to overcome the supremacy of the United States. Weissmuller's success in Paris was the more remarkable in that he was regarded during infancy as a weakling and was thought to have a heart trouble. Yet he became the first man to win the 100 metres in under a minute. Earlier that year in Miami he had broken the world record with 57.4 sec. These

Ville Ritola (France) winner of the 10,000 metres and the steeplechase.

were great Games for the Americans in swimming and diving. They won all but three of the titles in both men's and women's events, and in six took all three medals. The three events they lost were the 1,500 metres, won by Australia's Andrew Charlton, the men's plain high diving, won by Australia's Richmond Eve, and the 200-metre breaststroke for women, won by Britain's Lucy Morton, the first and the third in new Olympic times. Charlton also set a new world record.

More than half of the French medals came from cycling and fencing, sports at which the French have always excelled. Sprint gold medallist Lucien Michard went on to win the world professional title, and there has never been an easier winner of the road race than Armand Blanchonnet, who crossed the finishing line nearly ten minutes ahead of his nearest rival. The French fencing ace was Roger Ducret, who took three golds and two silvers. The French were particularly delighted that in these, their Games, they were able to avenge themselves on their chief rivals and neighbours, the Italians. In the previous Olympics in Antwerp, the Italians had swept the board, winning five titles to one by France. In Paris the score was France three, Italy one.

History was made in shooting. Finishing third in the Swedish team in the running-deer (double-shot) team event, won by Norway, was Alfred Swahn. This was his ninth Olympic medal, gained at the age of forty-five. His tally in the Olympics of 1908, 1912, 1920 and 1924 was three golds, three silvers and three bronzes. And it would certainly have been more had it been possible to hold the Games of the sixth Olympiad in 1916.

What is even more remarkable is that his father Oscar not only competed with his son in 1912 and 1920, as well as in 1908, but took six Olympic medals. Between them the Swahns won six golds, four silvers and five bronzes, a total of fifteen, a record likely to stand for all time.

IX AMSTERDAM 1928 Lord Noel-Baker

Coubertin was prevented by illness from being present at the ninth Olympic Games. So he sent a message 'to the athletes and all those taking part at Amsterdam in the Games of the ninth Olympiad'; foreseeing that he might be unable to be at Los Angeles for the tenth Olympiad in 1932, he said in his message: 'I should be wise to take the present opportunity of bidding you farewell.'

It was a harsh moment for him when he wrote those words and a grievous moment for the Olympic Movement. But in his message he called on the athletes and others at Amsterdam 'strongly and faithfully [to] keep ever alive the flame of the revived Olympic spirit and maintain its necessary principles . . . The great point is that, everywhere everyone from adolescent to adult, should cultivate and spread the true sporting spirit of spontaneous loyalty and chivalrous impartiality.' And he ended: 'Once again, I beg to thank those who have followed me and helped me to fight a forty-year war, not often easy and not always cleanly fought.'

That he should end his farewell message to the athletes and to his Olympic friends with these bitter words, shows how sharply and how deeply he had been wounded by the venomous hostility of the chauvinists who had constantly attacked him from the first moment when he proposed the revival of the ancient Games. Many of these enemies were pure chauvinists and nothing more – they found such phrases 'international good understanding' and 'festival of human unity' repellent – and, of course, 'utopian' as well. But there were others; I knew them and hated them with a youthful zest which has in no way abated today – a zest of which, I feel sure, the generous Coubertin would himself have been ashamed.

There were newspaper proprietors who hoped they could increase their circulation by exploiting or inventing quarrels and 'incidents' in international sport. There were journalists – 'sports writers' – who had never in their lives perspired for an hour from any kind of sport, but who were always ready to make trouble for those who did. There were even would-be 'intellectuals', who boasted that they found the very thought of physical effort abhorrent. These persons – I do not call them 'men' – had indeed made 'war' on Coubertin for forty years. They had done so with venom and with disloyalty which he was fully entitled to resent.

There are still such persons in the world today. In 1972, during the Munich Games, there was a brief, grotesquely foolish, and quickly stifled recrudescence of the chauvinistic attacks. Even the editors of some leading British papers thought it might pay them to join in.

Such persons no longer matter; they only show themselves to be absurd. And, indeed, they did not matter any more at Amsterdam in 1928. Coubertin's 'forty-year war, not often easy and not always cleanly fought' had in fact been won. The chauvinists had been routed, and were in disorderly and disreputable retreat.

No one said any longer that the Amsterdam Games would be 'the last'. In London, in 1908, twenty-two countries had sent national teams. The competitors numbered 2,034. Twenty years – and a world war – later, the countries were to number forty-six, and the competitors were to be a thousand more. Coubertin had won. The Games were impregnably established; the Olympic Movement had taken

sport around the world, and the world replied by giving the Olympic Movement its solid and unwavering support.

Only those who had lived, as I had, through the doubtful, crucial years, and had heard the lying slogans, as I had, naïvely mumbled by Prime Ministers and Foreign Secretaries and such, could fully understand the sense of victory we felt in Amsterdam. Something virile, noble and infinitely important had been brought to triumph. For a full month we enjoyed that triumph in famous and beautiful Amsterdam.

I saw the Games in Amsterdam from a new and different angle. I had twice been Captain of the British track team; in Amsterdam I was Deputy Commissioner for the whole British contingent. This was a most honourable appointment which I greatly valued; it carried responsibilities of various kinds.

One morning I received an urgent message from the Commissioner. Would I please be at the swimming pool at 11 a.m.? Britain was to play the Netherlands at water polo; Queen Wilhelmina of the Netherlands would be there, and it was essential that the British team should not be guilty of any fouls. I would be responsible, if there were trouble; it was my job to see there was none.

Knowing something of how water polo was too often played, I approached the pool with trepidation, not to say alarm. I assembled the British team, and gave them the lecture which the Commissioner had ordained. During the first session in the water, the referee penalized and warned several members of the British team; and the crowd – the arena was packed – began to groan. At the next interval I told the team that, if there were even one more infringement of the rules, I should carry out the Commissioner's instructions, and tell

Above: **French Ladies' team rope climbing.**

Below: **The water polo final. Germany beat Hungary 5-2.**

Mikio Oda winner of the triple jump, Japan's first gold medallist.

the referee that Britain had 'withdrawn'. In spite of the inhibitions I imposed upon them the British team were victorious by 5–3. But in the next round they met Germany, the ultimate victors in the competition. My admonitions were no less vigorous; Britain lost. Decades later, at an Olympic party in No. 10 Downing Street, I met a burly someone whose face I thought I recognized; most certainly *he* had recognized *me*! 'Ah,' he said, 'you're the chap that lost us the gold medals for water polo in Amsterdam!' That was rose-tinted speculation.

The Olympic Movement (with help from the British Empire) had taken sport around the world. In Amsterdam; Uruguay was Olympic association football champion; Argentina won two gold medals and two silver in the boxing, a gold in the swimming, and elsewhere did well; a runner from Chile was second in the marathon; India won the hockey, 3–0, against the host country, the Netherlands; 50,000 people came to see the match, and predicted that India would remain for long on top; Japan won a gold medal for the triple jump (Mikio Oda), another for the 200-metres breaststroke in the swimming, and did well elsewhere; Egypt won a gold medal in the Greco-Roman wrestling (Ibrahim Mustafa); Haiti's Silvio Cator was second in the long jump; South Africa sent Sid Atkinson to win the 110-metres hurdles, and George Weightman-Smith to break the world record in a semi-final of the same event; New Zealand's Edward Morgan won the welterweight title in the boxing.

The net of organized athletics and of other sports had indeed spread far and wide around the world. There were still no Russians and no Chinese in Amsterdam but the 'Central Powers' had returned – the ex-enemies of World War I, Germany, Austria, Hungary and Bulgaria. It was sixteen years since they had last taken part in the Olympic Games. Considering that fact, they did extremely well.

Germany, in particular, was prominent almost everywhere, winning gold medals in the equestrian events, wrestling, water polo and swimming, and several silver and bronze medals in track events.

Lina Radke won the 800-metres women's race in 2 min 16.8 sec. However, the race was not a pleasant sight; several runners collapsed either before or after the finish, and immediately officials from other countries rounded on me, from Britain, for this frightful episode. Four years before Britain had vigorously defended the inclusion of women's athletic events. The trouble with this 800 metres was that the competitors had not been properly trained; thirty-six years later Ann Packer showed the grace and beauty women could bring to this event when she won a memorable race in Tokyo.

Hungary's contribution to the Games was impressive. In the boxing, Antal Kocsis won a gold medal in the flyweight class; Lajos Keresztes won a gold in the lightweight class of the Greco-Roman wrestling; Ödön Tersztyánszky won the individual sabre in the fencing; and with other Hungarians he won the sabre team event. ('The sabre is a magnificent weapon,' Coubertin had said.)

Participation in the Games was still not universal. But the contribution of the distant continents, of the 'developing' nations, and of the 'ex-enemies' of ten years before, added greatly to the richness of the program and to the worldwide interest it evoked.

The sensation of the Amsterdam athletics lay in the fantastic

Boughéra El Ouafi (France) during the marathon.

successes of the Finns – and perhaps also the comparative non-success of the United States. The United States won no gold medal on the track for the first five days. Then Raymond Barbuti took the 400 metres. It was to be the only American individual gold medal on the track and he only won it because James Ball of Canada made all the mistakes it is possible for a runner to make in such a race. Ball apparently forgot that, as was the practice in the 400 metres in those days, he could break from the lanes in the back straight. Instead, he carried on in his lane and must have run several yards further than anyone else. Ball was beaten only by inches, and photos show him at the tape looking so wildly and so abstractedly over his left shoulder that that alone must have cost him his first place. Ball never came to the Olympic Games again; but I remember him as one of the most gifted quarter-milers there ever was.

The United States won the two relays, 4 × 100 metres and 4 × 400 metres, a very satisfying compensation. They got two places in each of the hurdles races; but Sid Atkinson of South Africa won the 110-metres high hurdles, and Lord Burghley won the 400-metres hurdles. To crown it all, Finland took the first two places in the decathlon, leaving a lone American (John Kenneth Doherty) with the bronze.

In the field events, jumping and throwing, the United States took thirteen medals out of twenty-four, including five gold. The Finns did less well in these events than they had done in Antwerp; second in the discus, third in the triple jump, was all they had to show. But their successes on the track wiped out whatever disappointment their field-events enthusiasts might have felt. They were first and third (Harri Larva and Eino Purje) in the 1,500 metres. They were first and second (Ville Ritola and Paavo Nurmi) in the 5,000 metres. They were first and second (Nurmi and Ritola – Nurmi's revenge) in the 10,000 metres. They took all three places in the 3,000-metres steeplechase (Toivo Loukola, Nurmi and Ove Andersen, first, second and third respectively). They got third place (Martti Marttelin) in the marathon.

All of these, beginning with the 1,500 metres, are events in which endurance and will-power count. The Finns have a word which combines the meaning of both endurance and will-power – *sisu*. I heard much of *sisu* when I went to visit Finland, and the Finnish Army in the line, during their 'Winter War' against the USSR in 1940. Field Marshal Mannerheim told me that *sisu* was the most important factor in the resistance they put up. I saw much of Finnish *sisu* in Amsterdam in 1928, and again in Munich eleven Olympiads after that.

But what had hit the Americans in the short events? Some whirlwinds, from quarters they did not expect.

There was a nineteen-year-old schoolboy, Percy Williams from Vancouver. He had hitch-hiked his way across Canada from west to east to take part in his country's trials for the Olympic Games; he was rewarded by a double victory in the sprints. He repeated his

Jumping competition. José Alvarez Marqués de los Trujillos (Spain) on Zalamero. Spain won the gold medal in the show jumping team event.

Protecting members of the jury from the weather at the fancy diving competition.

double victory in the 100 and 200 metres in Amsterdam. Dutch doctors and researchers had asked the 3,000 athletes in the Games to fill in forms giving measurements of their limbs, their chest, their waist, their biceps, etc., and to undergo tests of breathing, chest expansion, lifting weights and so on. I never understood the nature, perhaps the magic, of this exercise. But I was not much surprised when they revealed that, according to their tests, Percy Williams, out of the 3,000 in all the various sports, was the perfect athlete in Amsterdam.

Britain, too, produced a whirlwind – Jack London, a black medical student at London University. His homeland was British Guiana but he was universally acclaimed as 'Mr London of London'. He was a red-hot second in the 100 metres, and many people thought he might have beaten Percy Williams, if he had been entered in the 200 metres as well.

For the third places in the sprints, there were the Germans, Georg Lammers and Helmut Körnig. Joachim Büchner of Germany took third place, after Barbuti and Ball, in the 400 metres; Hermann Engelhard of Germany was third in the 800 metres, in which Erik Byléhn of Sweden was second, and Douglas Lowe of Britain first.

Lowe had won the 800 metres in Paris, and not many people thought that, after four years of pretty strenuous competition, he could win again. In fact, in Amsterdam he was at the very zenith of his glorious career; he coasted through the first two rounds and in the final was in command of the proceedings from first to last. He went into his finishing sprint around the bottom bend, led into the straight and won with an ample margin of metres to spare, in 1 min 51.8 sec, an Olympic record.

A German runner, Otto Peltzer, had beaten Lowe at Stamford Bridge in London in 1926 in a new world record time. In Amsterdam, Peltzer had been injured, was below his proper form and was eliminated in the second round. So Lowe, the most chivalrous of men, accepted an invitation to go a month later to Berlin and give Peltzer a second chance to win. The race was naturally a sensation; Peltzer had recovered and ran extremely well. But Lowe won by a narrow margin, and in a time faster than Peltzer had recorded in London the year before. This was the end of Lowe's career. He was the perfect Olympic champion, and the perfect artist on the track. He remains the most lovely mover I have ever seen.

In the equestrian events there was what amounted to a revolution. In Stockholm and in Antwerp the Swedes had virtually swept the board; in Paris, they had done extremely well, winning the individual dressage, and the team jumping – two golds out of five, the Netherlands (Adolph D. C. van der Voort van Zijp) had taken two and Switzerland (Alphonse Gemuseus) had taken one.

In Amsterdam, Sweden almost disappeared from view. A brilliant new star, Lieutenant Ferdinand Pahud de Mortanges of the Netherlands, won the individual three-day event; with his Dutch comrades, he won the three-day team event as well. The Germans (Carl Friedrich Freiherr von Langen) did the same for the individual and the team dressage. Captain František Ventura of Czechoslovakia was first in the individual jumping; Spain took the team jumping. In six equestrian events, Sweden got just two *bronze* medals, while Germany, Czechoslovakia, Norway, Poland and other new equestrian competitors were doing well. Neither the United States nor Britain won any medal at all. Later Olympiads were to continue the process which Amsterdam began, and to show that skill with horses is widely distributed around the world.

The modern pentathlon was some comfort to the Swedes. The ultimate winner was Sven Thofelt of Sweden, whose best event was the 300-metres freestyle swimming, in which he was second to Eugenio Pagnini of Italy. The 5-kilometre cross-country riding was won by another Swede, Ingvar Berg. The cross-country running was won by a Pole, Stefan Szelestowski; the fencing by a Dane, Helge

The first women's 800 metres in the Olympic Games. Lina Radke (Germany), number 762, was the winner.

Jensen; the revolver shooting by a German, Heinz Hax. So a Swede won this important gold medal; if the contest had been treated as a team event, the three Swedish competitors would have been first again, with Germany second, and the Netherlands third.

The rowing, spread over nine days on the Sloten canal, brought a revival by the British oarsmen. In the coxless fours, the British crew (First Trinity, Cambridge) won gold medals. In the coxless pairs, Britain (Terence O'Brien and Robert Archibald Nisbet) was second; in the single sculls, the best Briton, Theodore David Collet, came third. The race which gave them most satisfaction was the eights: the British crew (the Thames Rowing Club) was only beaten by the United States by a short half-length in extremely fast time. Two famous men were in the crew: Jack Beresford, who won the single sculls in Paris, at 'two', and 'Gully' Nickalls at 'seven'. The US crew were from the University of California, where there is sunshine all the year; they had in fact been rowing together for three years.

In this Amsterdam regatta, Australia (Bob Pearce) won the single sculls; the United States (Paul Costello and Charles McIlvaine) the double sculls; Switzerland the coxed pairs; Italy the coxed fours – a wide allocation of top honours around the world.

The swimming pools in Amsterdam no longer had the charming personality of Duke Kahanamoku of Honolulu. He had been beaten in Paris into second place in the 100-metres freestyle race by a new star, who shone brightly again in Amsterdam. This was none other than Johnny Weissmuller, who won the 100-metres freestyle again, and was a member of the US team in the 4 × 200-metres relay.

As always, the United States took plenty of medals in the swimming; but besides the German, the Japanese, and Alberto Zorilla (Argentina), a Swede, Arne Borg, took a gold medal in the 1,500-metres freestyle, Japan took second place in the 4 × 200-metres relay, and third place behind Weissmuller in the 100 metres; an Egyptian, Farid Simaika, took a silver medal in the high diving and a bronze in the springboard diving. The United States took the remainder of the men's events and the women's 4 × 100-metres freestyle relay, springboard and the highboard diving. In the 400-metres freestyle, Alberto Zorilla became the only Argentinian ever to win an Olympic title for his country in this sport. Arne Borg had been second four years previously having broken thirty-two world records in the space of eight years.

The gymnastics began to take on the glamour and the beauty that they have today. But the top places were changing hands. The Swiss took nearly everything; a Czech (Ladislav Vácha) won the parallel bars, a Yugoslav the rings; among the women's teams, who were competing for the first time in the Olympic Games, the Netherlands came first.

Italy did well in boxing and in fencing. In boxing Italians took three Olympic titles, Argentina took two, Hungary, the Netherlands and New Zealand one each. In fencing Italy took the team events, foil and épée. Hungary took both individual and team sabres.

India, having formed a hockey federation only three years previously, won the hockey title, the first of six successive Olympic victories stretching across almost thirty years and bringing them the tribute of being dubbed 'The Masters'.

Miguel Plaza (Chile) finishing second in the marathon.

Association football had more than its usual success: more than a quarter of a million spectators paid for entrance to the matches. Uruguay narrowly defeated Argentina in the final, 2–1. Italy defeated Egypt for the bronze medals 11–3.

In a month we had time to see something of Amsterdam – the picture galleries, the marvellous housing projects, the reclamation of the Zuider Zee, ten times as large and glorious as Mussolini's draining of the Romagna swamps, about which there was so much sycophantic talk.

But nothing diverted us for long from the greater glory of the Games. Not long before they started, Coubertin wrote the following words about the 'celebration' of Amsterdam:

> If among the great majority of the competitors each one on the last day can give himself credit for having striven in all honour, without failing for a single instant . . . then the moral gain will be won, and the IXth Olympiad will be a noble and happy milestone on the path of chivalrous progress. May it be so. It is my wish and my conviction.

It *was* so. When I left Amsterdam, I had only one regret: that Coubertin had not been there himself to see the noble, happy milestone, and to know that his great Movement was destined to grow yet greater, and most surely to endure.

X LOS ANGELES 1932 Paul Zimmerman

The year was 1932. The world was in the throes of a deep depression. The stock-market crash had driven many a financier to his grave and others to selling apples in the streets. The national bank holiday was just around the corner. It was under such inauspicious circumstances that the summer games of the tenth Olympiad took place.

The wonder is that the Los Angeles Organizing Committee was able to keep the Olympic flame ablaze. The accomplishment must go down in the history of the Movement as one of its finest hours. Under the astute and bold leadership of William May Garland the summer Games of 1932 was one of the most artistic and financially successful ever staged. When it was over and a final accounting was made it showed sixteen world records shattered, two equalled and thirty-three new Olympic marks.

The Games attracted more than $1\frac{1}{4}$ million spectators and when the final audit was made it disclosed that the Los Angeles Organizing Committee had accumulated almost $1 million surplus.

When Los Angeles first sought the Games the world was still riding post-World-War-I prosperity. There was still no hint of a financial calamity when the International Olympic Committee, in its 1923 meeting in Rome, brought Garland's long-time dream to fruition with the awarding of the games to Los Angeles for 1932.

Armed with an official letter of invitation from the mayor, Garland first appeared before the IOC at Antwerp in 1920. His quest was for the 1924 Games or the 1928 Games at the latest. Garland was told that Paris was the choice for 1924, with Amsterdam standing in the wings for 1928. The IOC members were so impressed with this persuasive man from the shores of the Pacific, however, that they elected him to membership and suggested Los Angeles bid for 1932.

Once the bid succeeded in 1923 Garland returned home and went to

Italian cyclist Attilio Pavesi pedals down the home stretch to win the Olympic 100-kilometre road race.

George Calnan, a member of the United States team pronounces the Olympic oath at the opening ceremony.

work. He headed a group of civic leaders known as the Community Development Association which erected a huge stadium. Its seating capacity was enlarged to over 100,000 by the time the Games were held.

This association became the nucleus of the Organizing Committee. In the face of growing evidence of a world financial crisis it went stubbornly about the business of preparing to stage the Games. In spite of mounting pessimism, early in 1930 it sent out embossed invitations to National Olympic Committees the world over. Aware of the growing fear around the world that the expense of sending athletes such a distance would prove prohibitive, Garland and his committee developed a bold plan.

Appearing before the Olympic Congress at Berlin in the summer of 1930, the Los Angeles representative announced that it was prepared to feed, house, entertain and locally transport every competitor for $2 a day.

With the arranged reduced steamship and railroad fares this meant, for example, that athletes from Europe could make the thirty-day round trip for only $500 each – a third of the anticipated cost. On the basis of such a promise, reservations began to roll in. However, it was not until months later, when the first of the larger contingents began to disembark at United States ports, that Garland and his staff would heave a sigh of relief.

The result of that bold stroke was that 1,500 athletes from thirty-four nations found their way to Los Angeles.

To accomplish the low cost the committee developed a novel plan. The athletes would be housed in an Olympic village, living in common bond; a plan discussed before but never implemented until the Games of 1932.

Juan Carlos Zabala, twenty-year old newsboy from Argentina wins the marathon.

Located on a hilltop, cooled by ocean breezes and only ten minutes from the Olympic stadium, the village consisted of two-room Mexican ranch-style cottages built in a circle on 250 landscaped acres. Separate dining rooms with cuisines to accommodate every world taste, a hospitality house, recreation area, hospital, fire department, and an independent policing system were included in the fenced-in privacy of the village. Women athletes were given the exclusive run of the spacious Chapman Park hotel on Wilshire Boulevard. Viewed with scepticism by some of the larger nations at the outset, the village plan was so successful and popular it has been a part of the protocol of every Olympics since.

There were other innovations. For the first time an electric photo-timing device for races was introduced; a forerunner of today's methods. Hand timing remained official but the system was used as a backstop. Very early in the Games it helped the judges determine the victor in the 100-metres dash, in which Eddie Tolan (United States) and Ralph Metcalfe (United States) finished inches apart.

The victory stand had its beginning in Los Angeles – the ceremonies of awarding medals were accompanied by the playing of national anthems while flags of the winners' countries were unfurled. Another first was the use of teletype communications between venues for the press. Each newspaper and press association had at its location in the Olympic stadium press section a private automatic printer that spewed out results from all the other events in progress; a forerunner of the refinement introduced at Tokyo where closed-circuit television receivers were installed. A free bus service supplied transport everywhere.

Under a cloudless sky on 30 July 1932, 101,000 spectators filled the Olympic stadium to capacity, cheering the world's greatest athletes as they paraded on to the field and revelling in the pomp and splendour of the opening ceremonies. For once the woes of the world were forgotten. Vice-President Charles Curtis intoned the speech of welcome and the Games many had thought never could be staged were on. After they had run their spectacular course, another capacity throng filled the Olympic stadium for the closing ceremony. At the end, with the sun setting over the Pacific, the thousands stood and joined in the haunting Hawaiian song of farewell – *Aloha*.

Detractors had said the dry, subtropical climate would prove enervating to the athletes. This fear was quickly dispelled when the program of fourteen sports began with competition in athletics. Before the largest crowds ever attracted for track and field, record-breaking performances became the rule – not the exception.

Perhaps the most startling of the many surprises in athletics was the break in Finland's dominance in the distance races. Where the Finns had taken everything from the 1,500-metres run to the marathon at Paris in 1924 and followed this with four victories in five races at Amsterdam, they were fortunate to glean two gold medals at Los Angeles.

In this, the competitors were aided and abetted by the International Amateur Athletic Federation, which, a few days before the Games opened, had decided that Paavo Nurmi was guilty of charges of professionalism. So the great runner, winner of three gold medals and two silver at Paris and Amsterdam, was relegated to the stands as a spectator.

Yasuji Miyazaki (Japan) won the gold medal in the 100-metres freestyle.

Beginning with the 1,500-metres run, the erosion of Finland's dominance was heralded. Harri Larva, victor at Amsterdam four years before, ran well back in the pack as Luigi Beccali (Italy) added a burning sprint finish to a withering early pace and crossed the finish line strides ahead of John Cornes (Great Britain) and Philip Edwards (Canada) in 3 min 51.2 sec for an Olympic record.

Only through the good graces of the judges was Lauri Lehtinen awarded the gold medal in the 5,000 metres. In a surprising performance Ralph Hill (United States) was close on the Finn's heels off the final turn down the finish stretch. As the American put on a sprint to pass, Lehtinen swerved into the second lane to cut him off. Hill then tried to go by on the inside. Lehtinen swung back, thwarting him.

The crowd gave vent to its indignation before the calming voice of the announcer, Bill Henry, saved the day for the Finn.

'Remember, please,' he implored, 'these people are our guests!'

The uproar subsided to a murmur. Hill had to be content with second place, a stride back. Since there was no official protest nor charge of foul, the judges let the victory stand. Lehtinen's time of 14 min 30.0 sec was an Olympic record.

Another setback for the Finns came in the 10,000 metres. Here Janusz Kusociński (Poland) clearly demonstrated his superiority as he ran away from Volmari Iso-Hollo and Lauri Virtanen in the Olympic record time of 30 min 11.4 sec. This was only 5.2 sec under Nurmi's world mark.

The marathon produced a similar story. Little Juan Zabala (Argentina) stayed up with the leaders through the early going. A few miles out of the Olympic stadium he forged to the front.

Although he never held a commanding lead, the diminutive South American clung to his advantage as the leaders took their final lap around the track and even had enough for a finishing spurt. His time of 2 hr 31 min 36 sec was only 19 sec faster than that of Great Britain's Sam Ferris, who came second. Armas Toivonen (Finland), who won

Eleanor Holm (United States) won the 100-metres backstroke.

the bronze, was only 36 sec behind the winner.

This was the race everyone had expected Nurmi would run to close a spectacular career.

Iso-Hollo salvaged the second gold medal for Finland in the steeplechase. This was an unusual race because the clerk of the course in charge of the lap cards became confused and every competitor ran an extra lap over the hurdles and water jumps.

There was no question of Iso-Hollo's superiority. He was far out in front at what should have been the regulation 3,000 metres and had enough left to extend this advantage over his faltering competition. Thomas Evenson (Great Britain) held off Joseph McCluskey (United States) for second. Iso-Hollo's time for the 3,460 metres was 10 min 33.4 sec compared with the Olympic record of 9 min 14.6 sec he established in the preliminaries over the correct distance.

The United States dominated the sprints as expected. Eddie Tolan became the only double victor in athletics by winning the 100 metres and 200 metres from team mates Ralph Metcalfe and George Simpson. Tolan's time of 10.3 sec for the short dash equalled the world record.

A fast starter, Tolan barely held off the closing surge of Metcalfe. The finish was so tight the judges waited until the new photo-finish pictures could be developed and viewed. Little Eddie had no trouble taking the 200-metres dash from Simpson, with Metcalfe third. His time around the turn was 21.2 sec for another Olympic mark. This trio gave way to four other sprinters in the short relay – Robert Kiesel, Emmett Toppino, Hector Dyer and Frank Wykoff. Their time of 40.0 sec, a world record, was nine-tenths of a second faster than that of Germany's quartet and emphasized the superiority of American sprinting at its best in California.

Many thought the most spectacular performance came in the 400-metres dash. Here William Carr (United States), with a sensational straightaway burst of speed, beat his team mate Ben Eastman by four yards as he cut eight-tenths of a second off the world record with a time of 46.2 sec.

Leading from starter's gun to tape, Tom Hampson (Great Britain) captured the 800-metres run in the world's fastest time of 1 min

A Los Angeles street decorated for the Olympic Games.

The Japanese and British teams are shown passing the baton in the 400-metre relay heats. Left to right: Lord Burghley (Gt Britain), Oki (Japan), Masuda (Japan), Thomas Hampson (Gt Britain). Japan won the relay heat.

49.7 sec (since middle-distance races were officially timed to one-fifth of a second in 1932, his record was rounded off to 1 min 49.8 sec). Hampson superbly judged his strength and pace as he held off the sprint finish of Alexander Wilson (Canada).

Lord Burghley (the Marquess of Exeter and for long an IOC member) travelled to Los Angeles to defend his 400-metres hurdles title and other races as well. In an ambitious program that would require him to run eight races in the span of a few days, Lord Burghley also entered the 110-metres hurdles and 4 × 400-metres relay. He decided to miss the parade at the opening ceremony, but when he learned that his leading rival in the 400-metres hurdles, Morgan Taylor, had been chosen to carry the United States flag, he also marched in the parade, in a gesture of fine sportsmanship.

All this was too much: Burghley was fifth in the high hurdles which was won by George Saling (United States) in 14.6 sec; in the 400-metres hurdles there was a surprise winner: Burghley and Taylor had been expected to battle for the gold medal but instead an Irishman, Robert Tisdall, won in 51.7 sec (officially rounded up to 51.8 sec) which would have been a world and Olympic record had he not knocked down a hurdle.

Two strides back, less than a foot apart, came Glenn Hardin (United States), Taylor and Burghley, in that order. His Lordship helped Britain take the silver medal in the 4 × 400-metres relay. In this, led by the amazing William Carr, the United States ran away from all opposition, shattering the world record with 3 min 08.2 sec.

The ways things went, only three events – the long jump, high jump and hammer – escaped the record-breaking onslaught. Only one athletics champion at Amsterdam four years before was able to win again in Los Angeles. He was the sturdy Irishman, Dr Patrick O'Callaghan, in the hammer.

A traditional American gold medal was endangered in the pole vault, in which Shuhei Nishida (Japan) kept pace with the three United States stars all the way to the top. William Miller had to set a

Left to right: Matti Järvinen, Matti Sippala, Eino Penttilä (Finland), first, second and third in the Javelin event.

world record of 4.315 metres (14 ft $1\frac{7}{8}$ in) to beat the doughty Japanese vaulter and then only by a fraction of an inch; Nishida's 4.30 m (14 ft $1\frac{1}{4}$ in) put him well ahead of the other two Americans George Jefferson and William Graber.

The greatest story in the women's athletics concerned Mildred (Babe) Didrikson. This slender eighteen-year-old high-school girl from the wide-open spaces of Texas set two world records and was deprived of equalling a third through an unusual disqualification.

She began by winning the 80-metres hurdles, the first year this women's event was held, in 11.7 sec, beating her American colleague Evelyne Hall by inches. In the javelin she achieved a distance of 43.68 m (143 ft 4 in) to beat the two German favourites, Ellen Braumüller and Tilly Fleischer.

In the high jump she and Jean Shiley, who had represented the United States at Amsterdam, tied at the record height of 1.67 m (5 ft $5\frac{1}{4}$ in). To break the tie the bar was lowered to 1.65 m (5 ft 5 in)

Painting called *Struggle* by Ruth Miller (United States) which won second prize in the Olympic art contest.

Duncan McNaughton (Canada) winning the high jump with a height of 1.97 metres (6ft 5½in).

for a jump off. First Shiley and then Didrikson cleared the bar. At the juncture the judges went into a huddle and ruled that Miss Didrikson was disqualified for diving across the bar. So the victory went to Shiley with Babe placed second.

Just as the United States dominated track and field, the Japanese men took charge in swimming. Had it not been for Clarence Crabbe they might have won the five races. Crabbe salvaged a gold medal for the United States, taking the 400-metres freestyle in the Olympic record time of 4 min 48.4 sec.

With their buoyant style of swimming, high in the water, the Japanese started off when Yasuji Miyazaki and Tatsugo Kawaishi took the gold and silver medals in the 100-metres freestyle. Miyazaki's 58.0 sec in the semi-final was an Olympic mark.

Next came Masaji Kiyokawa (he became an IOC member in 1968) who led a Japanese sweep of the 100-metres backstroke. Japan finished first and second in the 200-metres breaststroke in which Yoshiyuki Tsuruta touched first, and again in the 1,500-metres freestyle, Kusuo Kitamura winning in a new Olympic time of 19 min 12.4 sec.

The Japanese 4 × 200-metres relay team made a shambles of the world record which they improved by 37.8 sec with a mark of 8 min 58.4 sec.

The United States girls salvaged the country's pride with Helene Madison, their outstanding swimmer. She achieved a world record of 5 min 28.5 sec in the 400-metres freestyle after setting an Olympic mark of 1 min 06.8 sec in the 100 metres. Her third gold medal came on the anchor leg of the 4 × 100-metres relay in which the Americans covered the 400 metres in 4 min 38.0 sec, a world record.

The first specially designed Olympic Village, at Los Angeles.

Eleanor Holm followed Miss Madison to the victors' podium by winning the 100-metres backstroke in 1 min 19.4 sec after setting a new Olympic best of 1 min 18.3 sec in the first heat. Only Claire Dennis of Australia prevented an American sweep, with an Olympic record swim of 3 min 06.3 sec in the 200-metres breaststroke.

There was a wide distribution of laurels among the nations in other sports. French weightlifters; Swedish wrestlers; Italian gymnasts and cyclists; French, Hungarian and Italian fencers; and South African, Argentinian and United States boxers all won titles.

In rowing the United States' eight withstood a valiant closing spurt by Italy, inching to a two-tenths-of-a-second victory. It had been a three-boat race for first place, with Canada less than a length behind the United States and Italy. Great Britain was only another length behind in fourth place. The other outstanding feature of the rowing was the Australian Henry Robert Pearce's successful defence of the single sculls title he won at Amsterdam.

When all the events were over and the records complete, the Games of the tenth Olympiad, which many had despaired of ever taking place because of the ominous clouds of a world financial crisis, had earned for themselves a rightful place as one of the finest in the history of the Olympic Movement.

XI BERLIN 1936 Peter Wilson

They say first impressions are the most lasting – and the Berlin Olympic Games of 1936 were not only the first I had reported but the first I had seen. And the first impression I had of those first Games was of sitting in a hotel lounge, that of the Excelsior I think, fidgeting under the bleak gaze of three half-lifesize colour pictures of the unholy trinity of Hitler, Goering and Goebbels; it was obvious that these were to be the most political Games to date.

In 1936 there were few dictatorships. The Spanish Civil War had been in progress only two weeks by the time the Games started in Berlin on 1 August. Italy had long been under the domination of Benito Mussolini, destined to turn out a sawdust Caesar. But you needed visas, as far as I know, for no European countries apart from Russia – and you never met anyone who had been to the USSR.

But we had read accounts of German anti-Semitism and of its corollary, a colour bar which was second only in viciousness to that in force, at the time, in the Deep South of the United States. There were indeed many requests to remove the Games from Berlin, mainly from Jewish and American organizations.

Therefore it was deliciously ironic that *the* figure of the 1936 Olympic Games should be an American Negro. He was James Cleveland Owens; a condensation of his initials 'J.C.' produced the 'Jesse' by which Owens was universally known.

Owens won the 100 metres, the 200 metres, the long jump and gave the United States a winning medal in the 4 × 100-metres relay. I do not think I have ever seen such a graceful sprinter as Owens. By a trick of the eyes those legs never seemed to be coming down on the track but always rising from the cinders. The nearest approach to him I can recollect was Bobby Morrow, who, in the Melbourne Games of 1956, also won both the individual sprints and anchored the sprint relay.

But whereas Morrow flowed along the track, Owens seemed to be literally spring-toed. In none of his races was there any great drama, for his superiority was so effortless and inevitable that it reduced the

Adolf Hitler at the opening of the 1936 Games at Berlin. Left: Reich Minister Fuch, Rudolf Hess and Field Marshal von Blomberg. Right: the Crown Prince of Italy.

Jesse Owens (United States) shows power and technical excellence at the start of the 200 metres.

excitement; but if that was a loss in his races the excitement was there in the long-jump competition.

A year earlier Owens had set the world record with a leap of 8.13 m (26 ft $8\frac{1}{4}$ in) which was destined to stand for almost a quarter of a century until Ralph Boston added just 8 cm (3 in) to it in 1960. But in Berlin, Owens, who only qualified for the final jump-off with his last leap because of a mix-up, could not throw off the German, Luz Long. After four of the six jumps the Negro and his supposed hated Aryan 'superior' were tied at 7.87 m (25 ft $9\frac{3}{4}$ in). But it was Owens, not the blond Aryan, who was to prove the Superman. For, with his final jump, Owens covered a magnificent 8.06 m (26 ft $5\frac{1}{4}$ in).

Long proved himself as good a loser as Owens was a magnificent winner by walking around the infield with his conqueror after the competition was finished, showing, as was often to happen later, that whatever the politicians felt, some of the athletes, despite barriers of language, customs and background, could achieve a rapport through the *lingua franca* of sport.

Unfortunately, Hitler was no sportsman. Early in the Games the German leader had summoned to his box the first two Germans to win medals in the Games so that he could personally congratulate them. But, markedly, there were no congratulations for Owens or any of the other black athletes who were so patently and embarrassingly proving the fallacy of the theory of Aryan supremacy.

Richard D. Mandell, in *The Nazi Olympics* (1972), explains that after Hitler's original personal congratulations:

Count Baillet-Latour, president of the International Olympic

Committee, sent word to Hitler that he was merely a guest of honour at the Games. He should congratulate all or none. Hitler chose to congratulate none – in public at least. (Thereafter, he did warmly felicitate German victors, in private however.)

But in Goebbels' newspaper *Der Angriff* (The Attack) the American black athletes were referred to as 'black auxiliaries' of the American team, and their medal-scoring feats were excluded from *Der Angriff's* scoring chart.

Obnoxious as this was, with the air of general suspicion – the rooms of journalists supposed to be antagonistic were searched and the Press box at the main stadium was infiltrated by temporary occupants who were there, quite obviously, not to report on what was happening in the arena but on what was being said among foreign newspapermen – there was a reverse side to this base coin.

The Olympic Games *are*, after all, the greatest sporting event on earth and not even Hitler could completely destroy the charisma of the Games and the superb performances which were put up.

There was, for instance, the 1,500-metres final which, with Chris Chataway's world 5,000-metres record against Vladimir Kuts in London in 1954 and Herb Elliott's Olympic 1,500-metres triumph in Rome in 1960, remains one of the three greatest foot races I have ever seen.

The five men who had filled the first five places in the 1932 Los Angeles Olympic Games had qualified for the final in Berlin. They were Luigi Beccali (Italy), who four years earlier had set up a new Olympic record of 3 min 51.2 sec, Jerry Cornes (Great Britain), Phil Edwards, a black Canadian, barrel-chested Glen Cunningham who, on the voyage over, had been voted the most popular member of the

The opening ceremony at the stadium in Berlin.

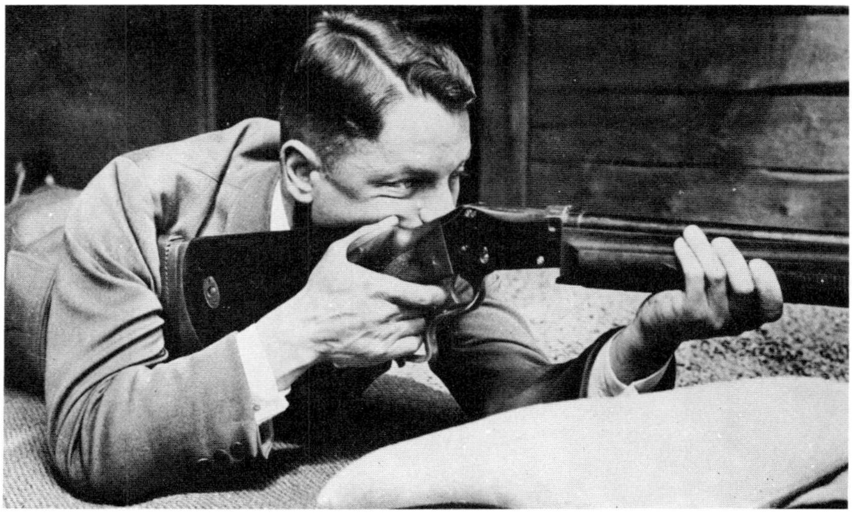

Will Røgeberg (Norway) who scored a maximum 300 pts in the smallbore rifle.

American team, and Eric Ny (Sweden).

Yet none of these was to win this race. That honour was reserved for a slim New Zealander, Jack Lovelock, an above-average lightweight amateur boxer whose running career was nearly cut short years before, when he broke a leg playing rugby football for the University of Otago in his native New Zealand. By a strange coincidence, Lovelock qualified as a doctor at St Mary's Hospital, London, to which some twenty years later, Dr Roger Bannister, the world's first sub-four-minute miler, was to be attached.

Only one thing detracted from this being the 'perfect' race and that was the absence of the wispy Sidney Wooderson (Great Britain), a perpetual and often successful rival of Lovelock's. Sadly, Wooderson had injured his left ankle and failed to qualify for the final – a disaster for the man who, in the next two years, was to hold the world records for the 800 metres, the half mile and the mile, and was, as far as looks were concerned, the most unlikely athlete ever to bring track fame to Britain.

Jerry Cornes, acting the hare, was first away, with Beccali, the title-holder, close on his heels and Fritz Schaumburg, the German champion, giving the crowd something to cheer about. At 400 metres, Cornes, running a brave race, was still in the lead, with Schaumburg and Ny coming up fast. A hundred metres later and the massive American, Cunningham, had forced his way into the lead. He was still there at 800 metres, with Ny second, Lovelock, who had moved up from sixth place, behind the Swede, and Beccali still dangerous in fourth position.

At 1,000 metres Cunningham was still ahead with Ny on the outside and Beccali pressing behind. When the bell pierced the continuous roar of the crowd, like an express train hurtling through a tunnel, the order was Ny, Cunningham, Lovelock and Beccali, but the Swede withered and faded as the field whirled into the back straight for the last time.

It was here that the race was won, for Lovelock, in the black, fern-emblazoned singlet of New Zealand, his blond hair rising like some golden helmet as he made his supreme effort, apparently extended his legs telescopically as he swept to the front. He won by a good four yards in 3 min 47.8 sec from Cunningham. Statistics are dull things but the value of this epic race was proved by the times of the first six competitors. Lovelock and Cunningham both beat the world record, held by American Bill Bonthron; Lovelock by a full second, Cunningham by 0.4 sec. Beccali, who finished third, clipped two seconds off the time which had won him the gold medal at Los Angeles four years earlier. In fact, the first five runners – young Archie San Romani (United States) was fourth and Phil Edwards fifth – broke the Olympic record, and Jerry Cornes, who finished sixth, still ran 1.2 sec faster than he had to win the silver medal at Los Angeles!

So gripping was this race that even that doyen of athletics broadcasters, Harold Abrahams, performing for a then much more sober-sided BBC so far forgot the traditional neutrality of a commentator that, as Lovelock slid into the lead, he discarded his professional sang-froid to shout:

> . . . 300 metres to go, Lovelock leads. 300 metres to go, Cunningham's gone up into second position, Lovelock!! Lovelock's out on his own about four yards ahead, Cunningham's fighting hard! Lovelock leads. Lovelock! LOVELOCK! Cunningham's second, Beccali, third. Come on, Jack. 100 yards to go. Come on, Jack. My God, he's done it!! Jack, come on. Lovelock wins. Five yards. Six yards. He wins. He's won. Hooray. Lovelock's passing the tape. Cunningham, second, Beccali, third, San Romani, fourth, Edwards, fifth, Cornes, sixth . . .

For Harold, who won the gold medal for the 100 metres in the 1924 Games, things could not have been easy in Berlin, for he is Jewish. But I think that 1,500-metres race must have made up for a lot.

For me 1936 was the start of an unsuccessful love affair with the

A hit during the final. Olympic victor Riccardi (Italy) attacks Campbell-Grey.

toughest of all track-and-field events, the marathon of 42,195 m (26 miles 385 yd). Not, I hasten to add, that I ever even contemplated running in that murderous race. But I did hope that I would see a British runner pull it off in the Olympic Games. Alas, it was not to be. In 1936, in one of the more memorable marathons, Ernie Harper (Great Britain) was second to Kitei Son, of Korea, who ran with the Rising Sun of Japan on his chest as Japan had occupied his country. Afterwards Harper told me how, through sign language, he had indicated to Son that he was going too fast too early in the race.

Now that is the sort of remark which some disappointed athletes might make after being beaten out of first place, as though to indicate that had it not been for their own sportsmanship they might have captured the first prize. But I remember at the time I completely believed Harper. And I am glad I did so for in Leni Riefenstahl's magnificent film of the 1936 Games Harper is seen gesturing to Son to slow down.

Inevitably, as I maintain they should, for they are the very spine of the Olympic Games, events on the track and field remain most vividly stamped in the memory after some four decades. There was the amusing sight of Cornelius Johnson and Dave Albritton, two lanky American blacks who only bothered to remove their track suits after a number of other competitors had been eliminated from the high jump, apparently killing time between their leaps by shooting craps against each other. In the end both did strip for action and Johnson cleared 2.03 m (6 ft $7\frac{7}{8}$ in), 3 cm ($1\frac{1}{4}$ in) higher than Albritton but 4 cm ($1\frac{7}{8}$ in) lower than the world record which they had jointly established a month earlier in New York.

Kitei Son (Korea/Japan) in the marathon and behind him Ernest Harper (Gt Britain).

The pole vault was another compelling competition. It lasted for nearly twelve hours before, round about 10.30 p.m. by floodlight (not taken for granted as it is today), Earl Meadows (United States) was finally declared the victor, having cleared 4.35 m (14 ft $3\frac{1}{4}$ in). Two Japanese, Shuhei Nishida and Suoe Oe, finished in second and third places, each having cleared 4.25 m (13 ft $11\frac{1}{4}$ in) and it was reported that they decided to share the silver and bronze medals by sawing them in half.

Without being unduly parochial, we were naturally anxious for some British successes and in fact the British did considerably better than at some subsequent Olympic Games. A gold medal went to Harold Whitlock, a motor mechanic, in the 50,000-metres walk. Outstanding on the track was Godfrey Brown, but he could not quite win the 400 metres, finishing a fifth of a second behind Archie Williams (United States) who had set a world record for the event only two months earlier. But in the 4×400-metres relay Brown anchored the British team of Fred Wolff, Godfrey Rampling – who ran the race of his life – and Bill Roberts into a magnificent gold-medal victory over the Americans, who had won this event every time except once since it had been included in the Olympics.

Nor can Don Finlay be overlooked. Four years earlier at Los Angeles he had won a bronze medal in the 110-metres hurdles and in Berlin he improved on this, a storming finish bringing him second only to the American Forrest Towns, who had already equalled his own world record of 14.1 sec in a preliminary heat. Although Finlay, a beautiful stylist, never won an Olympic or world title he stayed in the top class for year after year and no one who saw his grey

Aryan beauty and strength, a theme Leni Riefenstahl (seen on location below) propounded through part of her *Olympische Spiele*. 1936, which was not only a brilliant sporting film but remains an outstanding contribution to the art of cinema.

head – he was then forty – pass the tape first in 1949, to win his eighth AAA high-hurdles championship, will ever forget the indomitable veteran.

But while Finlay went on for years, there was one British girl who stayed at, or near, the top for literally generations. She was Dorothy Odam, later Mrs Tyler, and if ever there were a hard-luck story in athletics it was hers.

Dorothy was only sixteen in 1936, when she finished second, with the same height, 1.60 m (5 ft 3 in), to the Hungarian, Ibolya Csák. If the rules currently in operation for deciding ties had then been in force she would have won the gold instead of the silver medal. As though that were not a bitter enough disappointment, she again tied for first place in the London Olympics twelve years later – and was again placed second. I saw her again in the Helsinki Games of 1952 when she finished equal seventh, but the gold medallist's winning leap was a quarter of an inch less than Dorothy had achieved in 1948. Her final Games was in 1956 at Melbourne, when she was still good enough to finish equal twelfth.

The German efficiency did not work out in Football. Their team, which had prepared for two years, was beaten by Norway in the second round and was immediately sent home in disgrace. Peru, the only South American team – the rest were absent because of the continuing row about broken time payments – was disqualified when, after accusing Austria of making a substitution for an injured player, confusion broke out and the match was abandoned; Peru refused to take part in a replay. Austria went on to the final where they went down 2–1 to Italy who controlled the game with their short passing style.

It looked as though Germany would make a clean sweep in the rowing until two British oarsmen, Leslie (Dick) Southwood and Jack Beresford, in the double sculls, turned the tide and held the Germans in a dramatic contest. The Germans, Willy Kaidel and

Joachim Pirsch, led by a length at the halfway point, but here the British pair began the sure but steady process of outdoing their opponents, drawing level with them 200 metres from the line where the Germans, spent, stopped rowing.

The swimming events, held in the magnificent pool attached to the main Olympic stadium, were dominated by the Americans and Japanese in the men's events and the Dutch girls.

The Japanese challenge to the United States at the Games at Los Angeles, four years earlier, had been taken up, for the Americans had organized the training of their team of sixteen to a degree that had not been seen hitherto. Technically, too, they had the edge, for in freestyle their men, particularly, swam with the body in a constant horizontal position. The 100 metres, though, produced the surprise of the competition, with Ferenc Csik of Hungary winning in 57.6 sec from an outside lane and the Japanese occupying the next three places. The 400 metres produced a close contest. Shumpei Uto, like the rest of his Japanese colleagues, displayed mastery of even-paced swimming and stayed just ahead of the American champion Jack Medica. Then with about fifteen metres remaining, the American began to surge through to win by just over a second. In the 1,500 metres Noboru Terada achieved revenge for his country with a decisive win over Medica.

The most definite winner, however, was Adolf Kiefer (United States), who sliced 2.7 sec from the Olympic 100-metres backstroke record in winning a race he led from the start by more than two seconds. The closest contest came in the women's 100 metres, in which Hendrika Mastenbroek (Netherlands), in fourth place towards the end of the final length, swept through to set an Olympic record of 65.9 sec. Similar tactics brought her victory in the 400 metres, although she was a more decisive winner in this event.

Boxing produced the largest entry at an Olympics, even when the original figures of thirty-eight nations and 251 boxers dwindled to thirty-one and 191. This was caused by the International Federa-

With matchless team play and superb riding the Argentinian players (light shirts) ward off the attack of a Mexican horseman.

Above: **The Olympic Stadium and swimming pool (left).**

Below: **Captain Charles Ferdinand Pahud de Mortanges (Netherlands), winner of four Olympic equestrian gold medals.**

tion's decision to weigh in the boxers on the day of the contest for a second time, and because several countries had trials in Berlin just before the competition. The use of two rings in one hall for the elimination bouts was not satisfactory, with the crowd moving from one end of the hall to the other and the gong used for one contest distracting the competitors in the other ring. The titles were well spread, however, only Germany and France taking two gold medals, and thirteen countries represented in the first three places.

One sport which produced controversy that went on long after the Olympic flame had been extinguished was equestrianism. Many thought the course for the three-day event was far too tough. Three horses had to be destroyed, ending the chances of Denmark, Hungary and the United States in the team event. Of the fifty horses, twenty-seven completed the cross-country course and the notorious pond took heavy toll. Here the horse had to jump a fence into water and the depth was clearly uneven. Of the forty-six who attempted this, eighteen fell and ten horses unseated their riders. Some were more fortunate than others, for, as the crowd grew to watch these spectacular landings, it blocked the horses' escape from their riders.

In all this, the winning horse was appropriately named Nurmi, ridden by Ludwig Stubbendorf (Germany) who also took the team prize. The Danes were hardest hit by the failure of their third steed to finish since they placed the third and fourth rider.

The French achieved a breakthrough in cycling, providing the first two men home in the road race, Robert Charpentier and Guy Lapébie, who, with Robert Dorgebray, sixth, enabled them to win the team title as well. Charpentier and Lapébie were also first and second in the 4,000-metres team pursuit in which France was also successful.

Above: The start of the 8-metre class race on the second day of the yachting at Kiel.

Above: Jack Lovelock (New Zealand), number 467 wins the 1,500 metres.

Below: Jack Beresford (right) and Leslie Southwood (Gt Britain) after their victory in the double sculls.

Even by standards of the post-World-War-II era, the Berlin Olympics were a massive organization. Hundreds of thousands of people from every sphere of life were involved, and, for the first time, military organizations played a crucial part in the running of the Games. For example, at a festival play, on the periphery of the Games, 10,000 people were involved. The detailed organizational framework can be judged from the news bulletins which were distributed as propaganda for the Games: 3,690 newspapers and magazines received these bulletins, over 3,000 of them outside Germany; to begin with the bulletins were in five languages but ultimately fourteen languages were used. Altogether, 3,000 journalists attended the Games and there were over 150,000 foreign visitors, many of whom took back home fears that the Gathering Storm was indeed gathering.

This was also the first Olympic Games to be broadcast and televised. Television was on a closed-circuit system to halls (twenty-five in Berlin) throughout the country and over 160,000 people watched the daily transmissions from the four main Olympic sites.

Sadly, though, the overall memory of the 1936 Games was the *'Deutschland über alles'* atmosphere engendered by Hitler and the Nazis. Everywhere the eye was affronted by flags upon flags, bearing the crooked cross, like so many weeds among the flower beds of less provocative devices; everywhere the ear was assailed by loudspeakers playing martial music or relaying the hysterical *Sieg heil* responses of the thoughtless multitudes to the appearance of the Führer. There have been other Games where tragedy has intruded – but never again, I hope, will there be a world festival of sport where the prevailing air was so odiously chauvinistic and military.

XII TOKYO/HELSINKI (Cancelled) 1940
John Rodda

In 1936 the International Olympic Committee awarded the Games of the twelfth Olympiad to Japan, Tokyo to stage the summer events and Sapporo those of the winter program. It was another crucial step forward for the Olympic Movement, giving the Games to a country in Asia and one, at that time, which, to much of the Western World, still had a mystique and romanticism about it. The Japanese Olympic Committee began preparations immediately and many of the technical experts who had worked on the Games in Berlin accepted invitations to help them.

By 1938 the IOC was calling upon the Japanese to give assurances that the Games could go on unimpaired, for the Indo-China War had begun. The Japanese Olympic Committee refused to resign their intentions until their government stopped their preparations. By that point sixteen sites had been built or reserved in Tokyo for a program of eighteen sports and art competitions which were to have been held from 24 August to 8 September.

The IOC turned to Helsinki; the Finns accepted and began to prepare, only to be overtaken by war.

The IOC, having already nominated St Moritz to stage the Winter Games, met in London in June 1939 and, reflecting the optimism of the time, moved the Winter Games on to Garmisch-Partenkirchen when the Swiss would not maintain an undertaking relating to the skiing events. The Swiss supported the International Ski Federation (FIS) which refused to compete in Alpine skiing because the IOC did not regard skiing instructors as amateurs. The decision showed the IOC to be completely insulated from the political events within Germany and the strong overtones produced at the Berlin Games. In fact, the Germans continued their preparations at Garmisch until 22 November 1939, two months after war in Europe had begun. Helsinki's hopes lasted until May 1940, when it asked the IOC President, Baillet-Latour, to inform all the Federations that it was unable to stage the Games, but wished '. . . to express the sincere hope that Finland will be given the privilege to organize the next Olympic Games'.

XIII LONDON (Cancelled) 1944 John Rodda

The International Olympic Committee had received candidates for the 1944 Games from Budapest, Lausanne, Helsinki, Athens and London for the Summer Games, and St Moritz and Oslo for the Winter Games; Belgrade had also indicated willingness to stage the Games of 1948. At the IOC Session in June 1939, London was awarded the Games over Detroit, Lausanne and Rome. The Winter Games went to Cortina d'Ampezzo. But both were cancelled.

In 1942 the President of the IOC, the Belgian Comte Henri de Baillet-Latour, died; the office passed automatically to Sigfrid Edström who, as a Swede, was conveniently from a neutral country. In 1946 the IOC members, by a postal vote, awarded the Games of the fourteenth Olympiad to London and St Moritz.

XIV LONDON 1948 Harold Abrahams

Soon after the end of World War II, the International Olympic Committee decided that it would be possible to hold the fourteenth Games in 1948, and early in 1946 the Games were awarded to London. In spite of five years of war and enormous difficulties produced by shortage of materials, rationing of food, clothes and other essentials, the organization met with universal approval. The number of countries represented, fifty-nine, and the number of competitors, almost 4,500, were the highest to date. Of these countries, forty-two placed at least one competitor in the first six. Improvisation was the theme – a special temporary track was laid at Wembley Stadium for the athletics; many of the buildings from the 1924 Empire Exhibition were adapted for Press, radio and television, while the athletes were housed in school buildings and in service camps in Uxbridge and Richmond Park. The expenditure amounted to under £600,000 which included about £200,000 for the temporary work at Wembley and other venues and services provided by government departments. Receipts from 'gates' – there were often over 80,000 spectators at Wembley – meant that overall income exceeded expenditure by between £10,000 and £20,000.

Strong winds and heavy seas were responsible for many upsets during the yatching events at Torquay. The photo shows J. J. Herbulot (France) frantically baling out as his Firefly class boat begins to sink. The boat finally overturned but both were recovered.

Both radio and television transmission were naturally greater in extent than ever before. Although in 1948 the number of television sets in action in Britain was approximately 80,000, the number of viewers probably exceeded half a million.

In track and field events there is almost always at least one competitor whose performances are automatically linked with a particular Games, for example Paavo Nurmi in 1924 and Jesse Owens in 1936. Without doubt thirty-year-old Fanny Blankers-Koen (Netherlands) followed them in 1948. She competed in the 1936 Olympics and during World War II in the occupied Netherlands set world records for the 100 yards, high and long jumps and equalled that for the 80-metres hurdles; in June 1948 she had added the world's 100-metres record to her collection. At Wembley, she broke the tape eleven times (including a heat and final in the sprint relay); her victories in the two sprints being clear, her only struggles were in the 80-metres hurdles and in the relay.

In the former it was Maureen Gardner (Great Britain), who had almost failed to reach the final, who was well away and it was not until the sixth hurdle that Mrs Blankers-Koen caught her gallant rival. Both athletes were credited with a new Olympic record of 11.2 sec. In the relay Mrs Blankers-Koen ran a brilliant 'anchor' stage and brought victory to her country almost literally with her last stride. Had she competed in the long jump, she would almost certainly have won this event, included in the Games for the first time, since the winner, Olga Gyarmati (Hungary) beat a very modest field by four inches, nearly two feet short of Mrs Blankers-Koen's world record.

Emil Zátopek (Czechoslovakia) made his début at the 1948 Games. A few weeks earlier he had run within two seconds of the world 10,000-metres record held by Viljo Heino (Finland). This event was the outstanding competition of the first day and Zátopek took the lead after eight laps from Heino, who retired soon afterwards. Zátopek won by over three-quarters of a minute with a time, which,

Gt Britain (Richard Burnell and Bert Bushnell) winning the double sculls from Denmark and Uruguay at Henley-on-Thames.

though almost half a minute slower than the world record, beat the previous Olympic best by more than 10 sec. There was much speculation whether Zátopek would win the 5,000 metres, too, the double having been accomplished only once before, in 1912. In his heat he and Erik Ahldén (Sweden) were well over 100 metres ahead in the last lap and so had qualified but they raced on as if their lives depended on the issue. The struggle was unnecessary and may well have affected Zátopek's running in the final two days later. By half distance the contest was between Zátopek, Gaston Reiff (Belgium), Willem Slijkhuis (Netherlands) and Ahldén. With four laps to go, Reiff broke away from the others, and at the bell, though palpably tiring, was twenty yards ahead of the Dutchman, with Zátopek another thirty yards away. With about 300 yards to go, Zátopek sprinted, caught Slijkhuis and with every stride gained feet on Reiff. With less than ten yards to go, Reiff suddenly sensed danger from the shouting of the crowd and won by about a couple of strides in the new Olympic record time of 14 min 17.6 sec. Twenty years later, Zátopek told me that he was overwhelmed by his 10,000-metres victory, thought the 'double' impossible and, with two laps to go, had felt content to be third. Then he suddenly decided to go after Slijkhuis and with renewed strength all but beat Reiff. His last lap must have been achieved in about sixty seconds – phenomenal running for those days.

It was almost an accepted fact that the United States, with three finalists in both the 100 and 200 metres, should dominate the sprints. Four of the six finalists in the 100 metres were world-record holders and it was ironic that the final winner should be Harrison Dillard, world-record holder for the 120-yards hurdles, who had failed to qualify in the American team for that event, and gained selection for the 100 metres by finishing third behind Barney Ewell and Mel Patton, though Ewell thought he had won. The photo-finish picture (this minutely accurate apparatus was first used at Wembley) left no doubt at all about the result.

Though no male athlete succeeded in being a dual Olympic champion, Arthur Wint (Jamaica) won gold and silver medals, and the American Mal Whitfield from Texas won a gold and a bronze. As in 1932 and 1936, the final of the 400 metres was a contest between Britain, the Empire and the United States. Herbert McKenley (Jamaica) started faster than his opponents and at half-distance was at least five yards ahead of Wint. But, slowly at first and later not so slowly, Wint gained upon his rapidly tiring colleague, caught him twenty yards from the tape and won by two yards, equalling the Olympic record of 46.2 sec. Whitfield, who three days earlier had beaten Wint in the 800 metres, was third.

The men's 110-metres hurdles was a veritable triumph for the United States despite the absence of Dillard. Though William Porter hit three hurdles, his pefect rhythm was not seriously affected and he won in the new Olympic record time of 13.9 sec, ahead of his two compatriots Clyde Scott and Craig Dixon. In the 400 metres, Roy Cochran, who in 1939 had won the United States title in 51.9 sec, did this time at Wembley in his semi-final, a new Olympic record, equalled by the Swede Rune Larsson in the other semi-final. But Cochran was quite supreme in the final, winning from Duncan White (Ceylon) by seven yards in 51.1 sec.

The Americans maintained their unbeaten record in the pole vault, the concluding stages of which took place in a downpour, compelling the competitors to shelter in the tunnel between their vaults.

Hungary gained its first victory in men's athletics since 1900 when Imre Németh won the hammer by 1.8 m (5 ft 11 in) with a throw just over one foot (0.42 m) short of the Olympic record: in the discus Italy finished first and second, Adolfo Consolini beating Giuseppe Tosi by exactly one metre, both Italians beating the previous Olympic record.

Perhaps the greatest performance by an American at Wembley came in the decathlon, from Robert Mathias, seventeen and a half and competing in only his third ten-event competition. Mathias, a fine all-round athlete, was a competent football and basketball performer. At the end of the first five events he was third, 49 points behind Enrique Kistenmacher (Argentina) and 32 behind Ignace Heinrich (France). Conditions on the second day could hardly have been worse for the competitors, who started at 10.30 a.m. and finished under floodlight over twelve hours later. The almost incessant downpour caused them to spend most of the day sheltering from the rain except when actually competing. Mathias went into the lead with three events to go, throwing the discus almost 3 metres (10 ft) further than any other opponent. Before the 1,500 metres, the final event, Mathias led by 261 points over Floyd Simmons (United States) and 328 over Heinrich. Hardly able to force his tired body round the $3\frac{3}{4}$ laps of the stadium, he finished in 5 min 11 sec, the third slowest of the contestants. But his lead after nine events was sufficient to enable him to win by 165 points, to the obvious delight of his mother, father and two brothers who, after travelling 6,000 miles, stayed to the damp, dark end to share in his triumph.

There was plenty of drama on the final day. In the 4×100-metres relay, the United States finished a good eight yards ahead of Great Britain, but when it was announced that the American team had been disqualified for passing the baton outside the 20-metre zone, Great Britain's only 'victory' was received almost in silence by a

The photo-finish for the 100 metres final shows that Harrison Dillard (United States), bottom, was clearly the winner.

crowd that did not want to win that way. Two days later, after the Jury of Appeal had examined the film of the race, the referee's decision was reversed. The United States also won the 4 × 400-metres relay, but, alas for Jamaica, Arthur Wint suffered from cramp in the third stage and had to retire.

There was, as ever, drama in the marathon. Étienne Gailly, a twenty-one-year-old Belgian paratrooper, led from six to eighteen miles and was five seconds behind Delfo Cabrera of Argentina with a mile to go. By a supreme effort Gailly passed Cabrera 200 yards from the entrance of the stadium, and he entered it hardly able to drag one foot after the other. In the final lap of the track he was overhauled, first by Cabrera, then by Tom Richards (Great Britain).

Most of the vast crowd stayed to watch twenty-eight-year-old Dorothy Tyler (Great Britain) engage in what seemed an endless duel against the black American high jumper Alice Coachman. Twelve years before, as a sixteen-year-old schoolgirl in Berlin, Dorothy had cleared the same height as the winner, but had to be content with second place in the jump off held to decide the contest. Now she and Miss Coachman were the only two left in at 1.66 m (5 ft $5\frac{1}{2}$ in). Both cleared that height. Up went the bar to 1.68 m (5 ft $6\frac{1}{4}$ in) for a new Olympic record. After taking several minutes to make her attempt, Miss Coachman got over and Mrs Tyler failed.

But she got over at her second attempt. Neither could clear 1.70 m (5 ft 7 in) and Miss Coachman was the Olympic champion, having cleared the tying height at her first jump.

This was only the second occasion on which basketball featured in the Games as a competition and, as at Berlin in 1936, the United States won. Twenty-three countries took part in what were regarded as the World Championships, staged at Harringay. The level of play was extremely high and many of the matches very close. Four of the games were won by a single point and no fewer than twenty-seven by six points or less.

After a close match against Argentina in the first round, which the United States won by 59 points to 57, the American team, with several players over 1.98 m (6 ft 6 in) tall and one of 2.0 m (7 ft), met France in the final, winning 65–21. The French were a little lucky to reach the final; the draw in the quarter-finals favoured them since they were in a different half from the Mexicans, who had defeated them in the first round. In the quarter-final they beat Chile by only one point. Throughout the event the United States won all its eight matches and scored 524 goals against 256.

Twenty-seven countries with eighty-six crews provided a record entry for the seven rowing events which took place over the most famous rowing course in the world at Henley. This had been widened to take three crews instead of the usual two. In the single sculls, Jack Kelly Jr (United States), who had won the Diamonds in 1947, was keen to emulate his distinguished father who had won the Olympic title in 1920, although barred from Henley the same year. Jack Kelly Sr's club, the Vesper Boat Club of Philadelphia, had been banned from Henley in 1905 because its eight were not amateurs according to the Henley rules, and the ban had not been lifted by 1920. Jack Kelly Jr was, however, eliminated in the semi-final by Edouardo Risso (Uruguay) by a narrow margin. The winner was the holder of the Diamonds, Mervyn Wood (Australia), who easily defeated Risso by nearly fourteen seconds in 7 min 24.4 sec.

Great Britain had two victories, in the coxless pairs and double sculls. The United States was also a double victor, in the coxed fours and eights, winning the latter for the sixth Olympics in succession. Denmark gained its first Olympic title ever, beating Italy in the coxed pairs but Italy beat Denmark in the coxless fours.

In the six Olympiads since the modern pentathlon had been introduced into the Games in 1912, Swedish competitors had dominated, having lost the gold medal only once and having gained thirteen medals out of a possible eighteen; 1948 was no exception. The Swedish captain, William Grut, won with a record score of 16 points, the previous being eighteen in 1920 and 1924, when there were fewer competitors than in 1948. Grut won the riding with no faults and followed this, again in first place among forty-five competitors, in the fencing with twenty-eight wins. In the shooting, although he had all twenty shots on target, as did thirty-one competitors, his score of 190 put him in fifth place. He won the swimming (4 sec ahead of the second competitor) and finally had his lowest position of the contest in the cross-country, finishing eighth. No other competitor in this event has ever occupied first position in three of the five events.

The swimming events at Wembley have been described as the

greatest swimming tourney in Olympic history. New Olympic records were set in eight events and equalled in another. The United States made a clean sweep in the six men's events, fifteen of its eighteen representatives reaching the finals. The Americans also dominated the diving, winning all four titles for the fifth successive time. Mrs Victoria Draves won the springboard diving with the last dive of the contest, and in the high diving she was third at the end of the compulsory dives but took first place by two magnificent voluntary ones.

There was one world record, in the men's 4 × 200-metres relay, in which a United States team including Walter Ris (winner of the 100-metres freestyle from fellow-American Alan Ford) and the first two in the 400 metres, William Smith and James McLane (the latter also winner of the 1,500 metres), beat the previous record, set by the Japanese in 1936, by over five seconds. Ris beat the Olympic record in the 100-metres freestyle by one-fifth of a second. In the 400-metres freestyle, McLane beat the previous Olympic record in his heat, but in the final lost to fellow American William Smith, who beat him by 2.4 sec and also took 1.2 sec off McLane's recent record. McLane, however, easily proved best in the 1,500 metres, defeating the Australian John Marshall by over twelve seconds.

In the women's swimming, Greta Andersen (Denmark) won the 100-metres freestyle. Ann Curtis (United States) won the 400 metres before producing a remarkable last leg in the 4 × 100-metres relay to give the United States victory; she was timed over her stint at 64.4 sec, one-fifth of a second inside the world record, though this was not recognized as it was made in a relay.

The weightlifting was the most representative ever, with 120 competitors from thirty countries taking part in the six divisions. The United States, which previously had taken only one victory, won four titles, Egypt capturing the other two. The bantamweight, held for the first time, was won by Joseph De Pietro (United States); 1.42 m (4 ft 8 in) tall, he had such short arms that he was only just able to raise the bar above his head in the snatch. The lightweight produced some of the most thrilling lifting of the whole competition. With one attempt in hand, Ibrahim Shams (Egypt) had to lift 147.6 kg ($325\frac{1}{2}$ lb) to win. Actually he achieved 147.4 kg (325 lb), which, with an overall total of 360.0 kg ($793\frac{1}{2}$ lb), meant that he tied with Attia Hamouda, but was awarded the gold because he was 1.36 kg (3 lb) lighter than his fellow Egyptian.

The middleweight winner was Frank Spellman (United States), who beat his fellow American nineteen-year-old Peter George. George, the youngest competitor in the sport, set Olympic records in the snatch and jerk, but just failed with his final attempt in the jerk to exceed his previous best by some 5.5 kg (12 lb). Had he succeeded he would have been Olympic champion.

The United States won both the light heavyweight and the heavyweight classes. The former went to Stan Stanczyk, who easily beat the Olympic records in the press, snatch and jerk and, of course, in the overall total. In the heavyweight John Davis got $997\frac{1}{2}$ lb (452.5 kg), within 4 lb (1.81 kg) of the 1,000 lb (453.6 kg) total, a mark he was to exceed four years later.

The victories of Turkey in the Greco-Roman wrestling were unexpected, for it is freestyle wrestling which has always been popular in that country and though the skill of Turkish wrestlers in

Fanny Blankers-Koen (Netherlands) clearing the last obstacle to win the 80-metres hurdles.

the past had been limited, their strength had always made up for such deficiencies in technique. In the freestyle welterweight, Yaşar Dogu (Turkey) won four of his five contests by falls, while the featherweight Gazenfer Bilge, also of Turkey, the European champion, won five out of his six fights by falls.

In the beautiful setting of Torbay, the opening ceremony for the yachting, which concluded with the arrival of the last of 107 runners who had brought the Olympic torch from Wembley, was a most impressive occasion. The five events, each with six days' racing, produced a great series of contests of rare excitement. The United States was the only country to win more than one title and nine of the twenty-five countries competing gained medals. Norway, Sweden and Denmark were prominent in the Dragon class, the United States and Cuba in the Star. On the final day's racing, the Norwegian crew had to gain third place to win the Dragon class; this it achieved by only three seconds. In the Swallow, the first time this event had been included, Stewart Morris (Great Britain) had to

THE IMPORTANT THING IN
THE OLYMPIC GAMES IS NOT
WINNING BUT TAKING PART.
THE ESSENTIAL THING IN
LIFE IS NOT CONQUERING
BUT FIGHTING WELL.
BARON de COUBERTIN

The Torch-bearer, the last of the runners bringing the Olympic Flame from Greece, arriving at the Wembley Stadium during the opening ceremony. Above him on a board the 'second' motto of the Olympic Games first formulated in 1908 by Baron Pierre de Coubertin.

finish at least fourth to win; this he did with ten seconds to spare. The American crew in the Dragon class included the 1912 dual athletics sprint champion, Ralph Craig.

With 206 competitors from thirty-nine nations, the boxing entry was the biggest since 1924. Argentina, Hungary and South Africa each won two weights, Czechoslovakia and Italy one each. The contests, held at the Empress Hall and at Wembley, were carried out with no serious incident and with exemplary behaviour by the competitors. By contrast, the judging and refereeing was, to say the least, in many cases indifferent, chiefly because of the lack of experienced officials due to World War II.

George Hunter (South Africa), winner of the light heavyweight, was awarded the Val Barker Trophy for the most stylish display in the whole of the Olympic boxing. Never was an honour more richly deserved. He boxed impeccably and correctly, with the knuckle part of the closed glove, and showed a wide variety of punches in his winning bouts.

In at least four of the five cycling events, the forecasts of most of the experts went awry. In the 1,000-metres sprint, twenty-eight-year-old Reg Harris (Great Britain), who had been wounded in the Western Desert but had proved himself to be the outstanding rider in Europe by winning the world title in 1947, succumbed in the final to Mario Ghella (Italy), losing both heats by 3 and 1½ lengths. Harris also had to be content with second place in the 2,000-metres tandem; he and Alan Bannister defeated Ferdinando Terruzi and Renato Perona of Italy in the first race, but lost the next two, the final one by only 15 cm (6 in) in almost complete darkness. The program had fallen badly behind and without floodlights at the Herne Hill track it was only possible to see the white of the British riders' singlets on the back straight in the final race. Journalists had to use matches and torches to send their final reports by telephone for the booths were not equipped with lights. In the 4,000-metre team pursuit, Italy, the favourite, lost to France; in the final, in which both teams appeared jaded after strenuous semi-finals, the four French riders maintained good team formation, while the Italians split up before the end. France won by nearly forty seconds, in 4 min 57.8 sec, some three seconds slower than its time in the semi-final.

Fast times in the 1,000-metres time trial were impossible owing to the heavy and damp weather. The favourite, Jacques Dupont (France) won from Pierre Nihant (Belgium) with one second to spare, but in a time nearly five seconds slower than his previous best.

In the equestrian events, though Sweden was announced as the winner of the team dressage with nearly 100 points more than France, a year later the International Equestrian Federation (FEI) disqualified the Swedish team because one of its members, Gehnäll Persson, was non-commissioned although he had been entered as an officer (at that time the rules of the International Equestrian Federation limited the competition to officers, a restriction later dropped). The individual dressage was won by Hans Moser (Switzerland), with one of the most remarkable horsemen ever, fifty-four-year-old Captain André Jousseaume (France), second. Captain Jousseaume had already won a gold and silver medal in 1932 and 1936 respectively in the team competition and was to win a bronze in the individual event in 1952. In five Olympics spanning twenty-four years, he finished fifth three times in the individual contest in addition to his silver and bronze medals.

Fencing attracted the largest entry of any Games and the very heavy program necessitated fencing for long hours on most of the thirteen days of the competition. The Games will long be remembered for the severity and intensity of the competition and especially for the atmosphere of good fellowship and good sportsmanship which prevailed throughout.

In the men's individual foil the Frenchman Jehan Buhan, whose brilliant fencing played the leading part in his country's victory in the team event, did not lose a fight in the final. His runner-up was another Frenchman, Christian d'Oriola, who had won the world title the year before at the age of eighteen and who was to win the gold medal in 1952 and 1956.

In the women's foil Ilona Elek (Hungary), in her forty-second year, was to retain the title she had gained in Berlin. Her runner-up, Karen Lachmann (Denmark), who had also competed in Berlin and, like Elek, had won all five qualifying bouts, was defeated 4–2 in the final. Elek's sister Margit finished sixth. Another veteran, thirty-two-year-old Ellen Müller-Preis of Austria, winner in 1932 and third in 1936, again won the bronze medal.

Of the seventeen teams which helped to make the association football competition the most variegated ever held in Britain, the two strongest, Sweden and Yugoslavia, reached the final, in which the Swedes, who throughout the competition scored a total of twenty-two goals to three despite missing many 'sitters' in the early stages, won 3–1. Perhaps the best game in the series was in the semi-final between Sweden and Denmark, when the Danes dominated the match for much of the first half and scored the first goal. In the seventeenth minute Sweden equalized with one of the most extraordinary goals ever seen: except for the Swedish centre forward, Gunnar Nordahl, who had taken refuge there to avoid being off-side, the Danish goal was empty and Henry Carlsson, the Swedish inside left, headed the ball into the net, where it was caught by Nordahl after it had crossed the line.

It was originally planned that the gymnastics should be held in Wembley Stadium, but the rainstorms compelled a last-minute transfer to the Empress Hall. The entry of sixteen men's and eleven women's teams made it essential to have many events (both men's and women's) decided simultaneously, so the arena resembled several three-ringed circuses, making the spectators almost cross-eyed as they tried to see as much as they could of everything happening at once. Finland beat Switzerland in the men's team combined exercises and won the individual pommelled horse, Switzerland the rings, parallel and horizontal bars and Hungary the individual floor exercises. In the solitary women's event (combined exercises) Czechoslovakia gained a fine victory despite the fact that one of the team died in London soon after the team's arrival.

XV HELSINKI 1952 Peter Wilson

The 1940 Olympics had been offered to Helsinki after Tokyo had been banned from holding the Games because of the Sino-Japanese War, but World War II delayed Finland's opportunity to be host until 1952. The Games in Helsinki were regarded as the happiest and conducted in the spirit closest to the original Olympic ideals. To competitors from outside Scandinavia, Finland was still very much a land of mystery. All that most visitors to Helsinki knew about the host nation was that it had fought very bravely against the Russians in 1939–40, that in summertime it had a very long day and a very short night, and that in Paavo Nurmi it had produced perhaps the greatest athlete of all time.

There was one blot but this was clearly not the fault of the Finns. The Russians, unexpectedly entering the Games for the first time since 1912, were allowed to set up a separate Olympic Village for their competitors, along with those from Hungary, Poland, Bulgaria, Romania and Czechoslovakia.

This broached the Olympic spirit and it is hard to understand how the International Olympic Committee, which had strained at so many gnats, allowed itself to swallow this particular camel. Probably they were anxious to accommodate the lost sheep which had returned.

Incidentally, one amusing incident was connected with the 'Eastern camp'. At one stage it looked as though the USSR was going to skate home in the unofficial point-scoring system. In fact, so sure of victory were the Russians that they had a large board constructed showing the relative positions of the various competing countries.

But right at the end, the United States came with a rush, winning no fewer than five gold medals in the boxing, and as soon as the Russian officials saw that they were going to be overhauled they began to dismantle the scoreboard. Unfortunately for the Russians,

1,500 metres final. Josef Barthel (Luxembourg), number 406, won with Robert McMillen (United States), number 992 and Werner Lueg (Germany), number 739 coming second and third. Fourth was Roger Bannister.

while their 'demolition' job was in progress, a representative of one of the US news agencies came into the camp and sent out the story under the heading, 'Russians caught with points down!'.

There was another 'incident', this time at the opening ceremony. This has become so diverse that spectators are never quite sure what is coming next. And this explains why a rather plump lady, partly veiled and wearing what appeared to be a flowing white nightdress, was able to get onto the track, complete a half circuit of it, and actually ascend the official rostrum and begin a speech with what sounded something like 'Peace'.

But lack of breath, because of her girth and her exertion, and the timely action of the one senior Finnish official who did know that she was not part of the official ceremony stopped her at that point. She was removed by the police, who later announced that she was a mentally deranged German girl who had come to address 'Humanity', as was also an enthusiastic Sunday newspaper journalist who asked so many questions, in English, of the uncomprehending Finnish police that they decided he must, at least, be her accomplice! Fortunately he was released sooner than 'The Angel of Peace'.

But there was one part of the opening ceremony which was truly memorable, when the Olympic flame was borne into the arena on the last lap of its long journey from Greece.

For a moment there was stillness as the crowd looked in silence at the trim but middle-aged figure carrying the torch. Then one mighty roar went up from thousands of throats, from everyone, in fact, except those who were so overcome that they could only weep.

The torch-bearer was Paavo Nurmi, the man who had done as much as any other single athlete to popularize track and field events and, with Sibelius and Field-Marshal Mannerheim, was the most famous of his countrymen.

Although he had been reported as racked with rheumatism, the fifty-five-year-old runner moved as featly as ever until he had completed his lap. Then, after igniting a huge candelabra at the side of the track, Nurmi handed over the torch to his countryman, Hannes Kolehmainen, who had won gold medals for the 5,000 metres, 10,000 metres and the cross-country – in the Stockholm Games of 1912. The sixty-two-year-old warrior lit a second flame on top of the stadium tower.

It was rumoured at the time that the International Olympic Committee had not altogether approved of the selection of Nurmi as torch-bearer. That was hardly surprising for the International Amateur Athletic Federation, the senior sports federation, had declared the Finn ineligible to compete in the 1932 Los Angeles Games – for alleged breaches of amateurism – where he might well have added to his total of medals. But anyone who knew the stern independence of the Finns would have known that it would take more than an unspoken veto by the IOC to make them abandon their hero.

The Games indicated that the world was recovering strength after the war and finding a new sophistication, for Olympic records were broken on nearly 100 occasions.

There was, of course, only one 'Man of the Games' at Helsinki: the magnificent Czech Emil Zátopek, who triumphed, like some revitalized Nurmi, in the 5,000 metres and 10,000 metres and also in the marathon, a race in which he had never before competed.

Jean Boiteux (France) won the 400 metres freestyle. His father, eager to congratulate him, fell into the pool and is being helped out.

The 100-metres final was one of the most exciting – and controversial – that I have ever watched. The first four men, Lindy Remigino (United States), Herb McKenley (Jamaica), McDonald Bailey (Great Britain) and Dean Smith (United States) were all credited with the same time, 10.4 sec, one-fifth of a second outside the world record.

To this day I am not convinced that the gold medal for this race went to the right man. At the time I wrote: 'From my seat, three yards beyond the finishing tape and about twenty-five feet above, it looked as though McKenley had won by a whisker.' One of my abiding memories is of McKenley remaining behind in a deserted stadium, still studying the photo-finish picture of the race and commenting: 'I feel certain I won. Yes, even after studying the picture of the photo-finish until my eyeballs nearly fell out!' But, to a suggestion that he might protest, he replied: 'No. I don't want to win on a protest – or on a photograph. I want to win on my legs.'

Roger Bannister (Great Britain) had been one of the most confident tips for the 1,500 metres, although he was still nearly two years away from his unforgettable achievement of being the first sub-four-minute miler.

Unfortunately in Helsinki there was such a large entry for the 1,500 metres that an additional round had to be run so that there were races on three successive days – a schedule which Bannister, never the most robust of runners, would certainly not have chosen. He was not particularly impressive in the semi-final, which was won by a virtually unknown runner from Luxembourg, Josef Barthel.

In the final Bannister made his customary 'killing-off burst' some 300 yards from the finish but he could not sustain it and both Robert McMillen (USA) and Werner Lueg (Germany) finished ahead of him.

903

Emil Zátopek (Czechoslovakia), holder of four Olympic gold medals, winning the 5,000 metres in 1952.

But ahead of them all, although he was given the same time as the American (since 1,500-metres races were timed only to a fifth of a second at that time), was the unconsidered little Barthel, 3.3 seconds faster than his previous best, the only athletics winner from the Grand Duchy in the history of the Olympic Games. Barthel on the winner's pedestal, tears streaming down his face, as his National Anthem was played – after the band had found the music – was one of the memorable sights of the Games.

And so to Zátopek. No one was particularly surprised when he won the first gold medal of the Games by taking the 10,000 metres. He had after all, won the gold in this event four years earlier in London. In the meantime he had set up a new world record for the distance and although he did not approach this in Helsinki he still won as he liked, by over 90 yards from Alain Mimoun, a French Algerian.

The 5,000 metres was different. In fact Zátopek was beaten in his heat. That needs some explanation – indeed, in those days, whenever Zátopek was beaten it needed more than a bit of explanation!

Zátopek was determined that a Russian competitor, Aleksandr Anufriev, should win this heat. So much so that he kept waving the Soviet athlete on, with a lap to go, and even risked disqualification by actually pushing him home on the last lap.

It was, of course, very different in the final. Then there was no time for playing. The shorter distance was always more of a challenge to Zátopek, and it was not for nearly another two years that he finally beat the world record put up by Gunder Hägg back in 1942.

The final lap of the Helsinki 5,000 metres provided another great athletics memory. With little more than half a furlong to go, Chris Chataway (Great Britain), then a twenty-year-old Oxford undergraduate, was leading. But as they straightened into the last run-in you could see Chataway's face salt-white against his red hair, and working with the effort of keeping going.

All at once Herbert Schade, the German, was past Chataway with Zátopek and Mimoun haring after him – and Chataway, exhausted and possibly brushed by one of them, was lying sprawled half on the track, half on the infield.

Zátopek had to give it everything he had to win in 14 min 06.6 sec, just 0.8 sec ahead of Alain Mimoun; who else? For Mimoun always seemed to be the 'bridesmaid' to Zátopek in those days.

Having already run nearly $12\frac{1}{2}$ competitive miles, in two 5,000- and one 10,000-metres races, Zátopek was now faced with bringing his total up to 62.2 km, slightly over $38\frac{5}{8}$ miles in eight days, with his final race, the marathon.

But that was not all. Although he had never run the distance before he was so confident that he was able to joke about it beforehand.

On the same day that Emil had won the 5,000 metres, his wife, Dana, had won the women's javelin event; Sándor Barcs in his excellent book *The Modern Olympics Story* (1964) relates: 'When he was asked whether he was tired, and if he would enter the marathon race, he said: "At present, the score of the contest in the Zátopek family is 2–1. This result is too close! To restore some prestige I will try to improve on it – in the marathon race." '

It was obvious from the start that this was going to be a personal duel between Britain's Jim Peters, who a few months earlier had set

Dana Zátopkova, Emil's wife, (Czechoslovakia) won the women's javelin event.

a world's best time of 2 hr 20 min 42 sec (there is no world record in the marathon because of the varying difficulty of the courses) and the apparently irresistible Czech.

At first the cheers came from the Englishman's supporters when, a mile from the stadium, Peters was seen to be leading by about 100 yards; but they were soon hushed as the red singlet of Zátopek was seen licking along after him like some all-consuming flame.

Did Peters set too fast a pace? Probably. The same fault was to crucify him in the agonizing Commonwealth Games marathon at Vancouver two years later. But had he not set such a killing rate Zátopek might have won even more easily. I think the answer was that no runner then competing could have beaten Zátopek on that day.

As it was, Peters led at five, ten and fifteen kilometres but, by the half-way mark, Gustaf Jansson (Sweden) was leading from Zátopek with Peters third. Shortly after that, Zátopek took the lead which he was never to surrender. By the 15-mile mark he was 30 yards clear of the Swede with Peters 300 yards adrift. Round about the 20-mile mark Peters was attacked by cramp, sat by the roadside for a time, tried to continue but collapsed again and had to be brought back by car.

In the meantime Zátopek, clearly enjoying the whole 'outing', continued on his way, chatting to cyclists, policemen and enthusiasts lining the route – whether they understood him or not did not matter, his body spoke for him.

It would be idle to say that he showed no signs of strain. If Zátopek had had to run for a bus his face would have been twisted in agony; nevertheless, he ran into the stadium just over $2\frac{1}{2}$ minutes ahead of the second man, Reinaldo Gorno, of Argentina. He had taken 6 min 16 sec off the previous Olympic best for the race and had won by some 750 yards.

I have always believed this to be the greatest Olympic achievement I ever saw in the eight Summer Games which I covered professionally – just marginally eclipsing Jessie Owens' four athletic golds in 1936.

The exploits of Zátopek tended to blur some startling individual performances which were significant breakthroughs in their event. Charles Moore of the United States was expected to win the 400-metres hurdles long before he arrived in Helsinki, so distinctive had been his form in the United States, and he was not to let down the tipsters. He began with a victory in 51.8 sec, then broke the 1948 Olympic record by R. B. Cochran of 51.1 sec by three-tenths of a second, and, in the final, where he ran in the difficult outside lane, again recorded 50.8 sec to win by half a second.

Of those who retained their titles in the athletic stadium, Bob Mathias, the decathlon champion, was the most conclusive. He set a world record of 7,887, the largest single increase in points since the 1920s.

In the women's competition there were world records in the 80-metres hurdles, 4 × 100-metres relay and shot, while that for the 100 metres was equalled. There was no single outstanding woman, like Fanny Blankers-Koen of the 1948 Olympics, but the Australian women overcame the difficulty of travelling from their winter to the northern hemisphere summer and finding their best form. Marjorie Jackson took both sprint titles for Australia and Shirley Strickland was the winner of the 80-metres hurdles.

But athletics for once did not eclipse all the other sports in Helsinki, where some truly remarkable things happened in the boxing ring.

Paavo Nurmi (Finland) carrying the Olympic torch into the arena.

Floyd Patterson (United States) left, who was to become the youngest-ever professional world heavyweight champion in 1956, competed in Helsinki as a middleweight.

For instance, two of the competitors subsequently won the richest prize in sport, the professional world heavyweight championship. Yet the one who was to win it first, Floyd Patterson (United States), competed in Helsinki as a middleweight; and Ingemar Johansson (Sweden), who was to take the professional title from him, nearly seven years later, was disqualified in the final of the heavyweight competition in Helsinki, and failed so completely to put up any sort of fight that his silver medal was withheld. Patterson made pugilistic history by being the only man up until that time to regain the professional title – achievement made all the more sweet because it was from the Swede that the American black recaptured it.

Yet had it not been for the introduction of two new weights for the Helsinki Games I think it is more than possible that Patterson might never have won an Olympic gold medal – and if he hadn't triumphed in Helsinki his professional future would have probably been much more dubious.

The two new weights which were introduced for the first time were the light middle and the light welter, and the introduction of the light middle meant that László Papp, the Hungarian who had won the middleweight gold medal in London four years previously, was now able to shed several pounds, without the worry of giving weight away.

In one of the preliminary rounds Papp knocked out Ellsworth 'Spider' Webb, an American black who later, after turning professional, stopped future world middleweight champions Joey Giardello and Terry Downes, as well as outpointing future double world champion, Dick Tiger.

Papp was at his peak then, more experienced than he had been in London, not so old as he was in the Melborne Games of 1956 – although even then he was good enough to beat, in the final, José Torres, who was later to win the world professional light-heavyweight title.

In the swimming pool, which had been built for the Games of 1940, the spread of medals was greater than in any previous Games. The Hungarian women and the American men left the greatest impact with the former's relay team shattering the world record by nearly three seconds. Within that world record Éva Novák (Hungary) swam her 100-metres leg in 65.1 sec, which was 1.7 sec faster than her countrywoman Katalin Szőke's winning time in the individual 100 metres; Miss Novák was not entered for that event.

Joan Harrison became the first South African Olympic swimming champion when she held off the world-record holder, Geertje Wielema of the Netherlands, a hot favourite to win, in the 100-metres backstroke.

The Yachting events provided sporting history. The organizing committee, realizing that the Firefly Class, a single-hander, was unpopular, held a competition to find a new boat suitable for Olympic sailing. The winner was Ricard Sarby, a Swede, with his Finn boat, and this competition has remained an Olympic class ever since.

XVI MELBOURNE 1956 Neil Allen

The year of 1956 was not a happy time for much of the world. 'The year of disgrace' is how it has been described in one Olympic book. Whatever one's political views, the 'revolution' or 'rebellion' in Hungary and the 'invasion' or 'action' in the Suez Canal zone left mankind trembling on the brink of a major war with the possibility of atomic weapons being used. Looking back, it seems remarkable that the Melbourne Games were held at all. In 1949 the IOC only had the margin of one vote in favour of Melbourne being the host and it was a nasty shock, much later, when the Australian Government's strict laws on quarantine meant that its country could not organize the Olympic equestrian events.

In violation of the Olympic charter, it was reluctantly decided that the equestrian sports would be held in another country. Between 10 and 17 June, teams from twenty-nine countries rode and jumped in the Stockholm stadium which, forty-four years earlier, had been the scene of the fifth Summer Olympics. Even so there was a worrying moment for the Swedes when a fire broke out near the Olympic stables. Fortunately all the horses were led to safety and Sweden was eventually rewarded for its work as substitute Olympic host by individual and team gold medals in the dressage and individual in the *concours complet.*

The build-up to the Melbourne Olympics proper included a spate of disputes over television and filming of the competitions and so many reports that the main facilities would not be built in time that Avery Brundage, President of the IOC, flew out to investigate. As the opening Olympic day drew nearer, and fighting continued in Hungary, it was astonishing to learn that the Hungarians would be represented at Melbourne, even though many of their competitors had had to shelter in the cellars of their team hotel in Budapest. Then the Dutch Olympic Committee decided unanimously that the Netherlands would not participate because 'events in Hungary had spoiled the festive Olympic atmosphere'. Three days later, on 9 November, the People's Republic of China withdrew from the Games because the

Republic of China (Taiwan) had been allowed to compete, saying, 'The Chinese Olympic Committee, the All China Athletic Federation, solemnly declares that the Chinese people and the Chinese athletes cannot tolerate this scheme of artificially splitting China.'

The Dutch Olympic officials agreed to donate 100,000 guilders (£10,000 then) to Hungarian sufferers from the fighting in their country and the Spanish Sports Federation decided it was not fitting for Spanish athletes to compete at Melbourne 'while the liberty of peoples is being trampled on'. Egypt withdrew, after demanding that nations 'guilty of cowardly aggression against Egypt' should be expelled from the Games and Lebanon also pulled out in protest against the 'Australian attitude' towards the Middle East crisis. Brundage meanwhile insisted, 'We are dead against any country using the Games for political purposes, whether right or wrong. The Olympics are competitions between individuals and not nations.'

Few Games have been organized under such a cloud of depressing world news as that of 1956 but Australian charm, courtesy and efficiency swept aside the usual minor disagreements and teething problems. No modern Olympic Games has been entirely free from trouble outside the realm of sport and it was a triumph for the people of Melbourne that such an admirable spirit pervaded both the Olympic village at Heidelberg and the city itself.

In spite of the stormy political weather, there was sunshine and blue skies at the Melbourne Cricket Ground when the sixteenth Games of the modern era were opened by HRH the Duke of Edinburgh. For all the talk of withdrawals, sixty-seven countries were represented in the great bowl as spectators shielded themselves with newspapers. One of the biggest cheers, as the parading teams marched in, was for the Hungarians, half dressed in sea-blue suits and half in blazers and flannels because they were short of supplies after their unexpected arrival. On the results board was the statement: 'The Olympic Movement tends to bring together in a radiant union all the qualities which guide mankind to perfection.'

One incident on that opening day which was to be remembered twelve years later, when the Mexico Olympics were almost upon us, was the lighting of the Olympic flame. It was done by a young Australian named Ron Clarke, already holder of the world junior mile record. Clarke suffered burns on his uplifted arm that day as bravely as he was to accept his fate, in the 1960s, of being a multiple world-record breaker who never won an Olympic gold medal.

It was Clarke's speciality, the 10,000 metres, which opened the first act of the 1956 Olympics and it proved to be one of the classic long-distance races. The two giants were Vladimir Kuts, a stocky Soviet ex-marine, and Gordon Pirie, a tall, skinny London bank clerk. In June 1956 Pirie had beaten Kuts over 5,000 metres in Norway and set a world record of 13 min 36.8 sec. But two months later, Kuts had shown his great strength by taking more than 12 sec off the 10,000-metres record with 28 min 30.4 sec.

The battle, then, between a bludgeon and a rapier was clearly set down as the two men swiftly detached themselves from the rest of the field and Kuts threw down the gauntlet with 61.4 sec for the first of the twenty-five laps. Head hunched forward, Kuts tried remorselessly to draw the sting from Pirie's finish with a long burst on the fifth lap and, before the end, another six brutal accelerations. Each time

Pirie, as if drawn by elastic, went with the Russian, but the British runner's strength ebbed.

It was at the end of the twenty-first lap that Pirie suddenly wilted and gradually slipped back to eighth, as Kuts, now relieved of his persistent shadow, galloped away for a magnificent victory. Years later, the Russian told how the turning point for him in the 10,000 metres was the moment when, on the twentieth lap, he stole a look back at Pirie and saw the British runner's face was glazed with exhaustion.

Kuts gained a magnificent double on the Melbourne Cricket Ground – one which was not destined to be achieved again over 5,000 metres and 10,000 metres until the 1972 Olympics. But for many, the outstanding athletic figure of the 1956 Games was the American sprinter Bobby Joe Morrow. At twenty-one, this 6 ft 1½ in (1.87 m) Texan impressed us most of all by the margin with which he won his titles. Though the timing in the 100 metres gave both Morrow and his runner-up the same time of 10.5 sec, against the wind, the photo-finish timings (not used officially) had Morrow more than 0.1 sec in front. In the 200 metres Morrow was pressed by the 1952 champion, Andy Stanfield (United States), but came through magnificently in the straight to win by more than a yard in 20.6 sec, an Olympic record. Finally Morrow achieved his life ambition of emulating the 1936 hero Jesse Owens with a third gold sprint medal in the 4 × 100-metres relay on the anchor leg. Ironically, the fastest running of the Melbourne Games may well have been that of Leamon King on the second relay leg for the United States. King had twice equalled the then world 100-metres record of 10.1 sec the previous month but in the American 'sudden death' Olympic trials, back in June, he had finished fourth and therefore was selected only for the team event.

Morrow was the spearhead of an American men's athletics team which took fifteen gold medals in twenty-four events – one more gold than at Helsinki in 1952. They had a clean sweep of gold, silver and bronze in the 200 metres, the 110-metres and 400-metres hurdles and the discus, and finished first and second in five other events. In spite of the lack of encouragement for women's track and field events in the United States, the Americans also gained a gold medal in the high jump by Mildred McDaniel with a world record leap of 1.76 m (5 ft 9¼ in), a silver medal in the long jump by seventeen-year-old Willye White who was to finish eleventh in the 1972 Games, and bronze awards for a sprint relay team which included a sixteen-year-old named Wilma Rudolph who was to win three golds four years later in Rome.

The only individual men's world athletics record during the Games came in the javelin. A head wind was proving troublesome to the throwers. In the fourth round a Norwegian named Egil Danielsen at first stopped at the end of his approach run without throwing. The next time, however, he came striding through, and his red steel Seefab spear went sailing on and on, with a long, late, low trajectory until I thought it might even strike the pole vaulters at the other end of the ground. The measurement was 85.71 m (281 ft 2½ in) but one did not need the measuring tape to know that this was a major break-through in a spectacular event.

The 400 metres was won in only 46.7 sec, thanks as much to the running of semi-finals on the same day as the final as to the cold, windy weather. But the 800 metres and 1,500 metres and steeplechase were all memorable for various reasons. The 800 metres was as much as a classic as the 10,000 metres, with a dramatic sight in the home straight as Britain's slightly built Derek Johnson headed the deep-chested American Tom Courtney for about thirty of the last thirty-five metres. Courtney was so exhausted by his eventual narrow victory that he had to receive medical attention.

The 1,500 metres provided an unexpected winner in Ron Delany of Ireland as well as one of the most competitive races at this distance. John Landy (Australia), bitter about being branded as front runner without a finish, lay back during a race marked, in all but its final stages, by a closely packed field. Also 'sitting' was Delany, who was fourth with 200 metres to go as Britain's Brian Hewson made a break. But once Delany did take off, with his high-stepping knee action and shrugging shoulders, he rocketed away unanswerably, covering the last 400 metres in 53.8 sec,the final 100 metres in 12.9 sec and bursting through the tape to fall on his knees in prayer. Running up to him with congratulations, and then checking respectfully for a moment, was the bronze-medal winner Landy who the twenty-one-year-old Delany said later had given him invaluable advice when they met in the United States.

For the British reporters the steeplechase was bound to be a big story when their own little-regarded Chris Brasher, who had only scraped into the team, was a clear winner. Then the rest of the world's press became rather more interested when it was announced that the winner was not Brasher but Hungary's Sándor Rozsnyói who had finished 2.4 sec behind. Later came the news that Brasher had been disqualified for impeding Ernst Larsen (Norway) while crossing a hurdle. It was not until 7.5 p.m., three hours after the start of the race, that Brasher's agonized appeal was upheld though he did not have his victory ceremony until the following day. It was Britain's first Olympic athletics gold medal since 1932. But what I remember most warmly is that the three men who stood to gain from Brasher's disqualification, Rozsnyói, Larsen and the fourth finisher Heinz Laufer (Germany), all instantly offered Brasher their support in his protest.

The outstanding woman athlete at Melbourne was an eighteen-year-old Sydney girl named Betty Cuthbert who made up for the lack of any gold by Australian males in winning the 100 metres and 200 metres and producing, characteristically open-mouthed, a tremendous sprint on the last leg of the 4 × 100-metres relay to overhaul a determined British team. Australia also took the 80-metres hurdles through Shirley Strickland (de la Hunty) who, running on the same winning relay team as Betty Cuthbert, ended a unique Olympic career spanning three Games in which she had won three gold, one silver and three bronze medals.

Melbourne's athletics also saw the beginning of a famous sporting romance when the hammer-throwing champion, Harold Connolly of the United States, fell in love with, and later married, Czechoslovakia's discus winner, Olga Fikotová. My most pleasant memory of the athletics is at the end of the marathon, won by Alain Mimoun of France at thirty-six years of age after three silver medals on the track in the Games of 1948 and 1952. The man who had beaten him each time was the great Emil Zátopek (Czechoslovakia) but on that sun-

Ron Delany (Ireland) wins the Olympic 1,500 metre race in the record time of 3 min 41.2 sec. The silver medal went to Walter Richtzenhain (Germany) and the bronze medal to John Landy (Australia) (partially obscured by Delany's arm).

splashed evening of 1 December 1956 it was Mimoun who waited deliberately, waving aside photographers until Zátopek trotted home sixth and Mimoun could embrace his old rival and friend.

For many, the end of the athletics meant the Games were virtually over. But certainly not for the Australian hosts who had purposely arranged the program of sports so that the climax was the sport in which they had the highest hopes. Every one of the 5,500 seats in the swimming and diving complex (costing about £500,000) was booked months before the opening of the Games and the Melbourne public were even ready to queue to pay in order to watch teams in training.

Australian interest and support received a rich reward with eight gold, four silver and two bronze medals in the swimming events, compared with two gold, four silver and five bronze by the Americans who had dominated the previous Games in swimming. For the purists, it was even more impressive that in Melbourne the Australians won every one of the men's and women's freestyle events since they are the most developed races. Such a clean sweep had not been achieved since the Antwerp Olympics of 1920. In both men's and women's 100-metres front crawl Australia won all three medals.

Behind the success of the Australians lay a scheme of preparation so intensive that it included a twelve-week training camp from late July in Townsville where the Australian midwinter temperature was perfect for open-air training. At the same time a revolution in training methods was being advocated by the physiologist Forbes

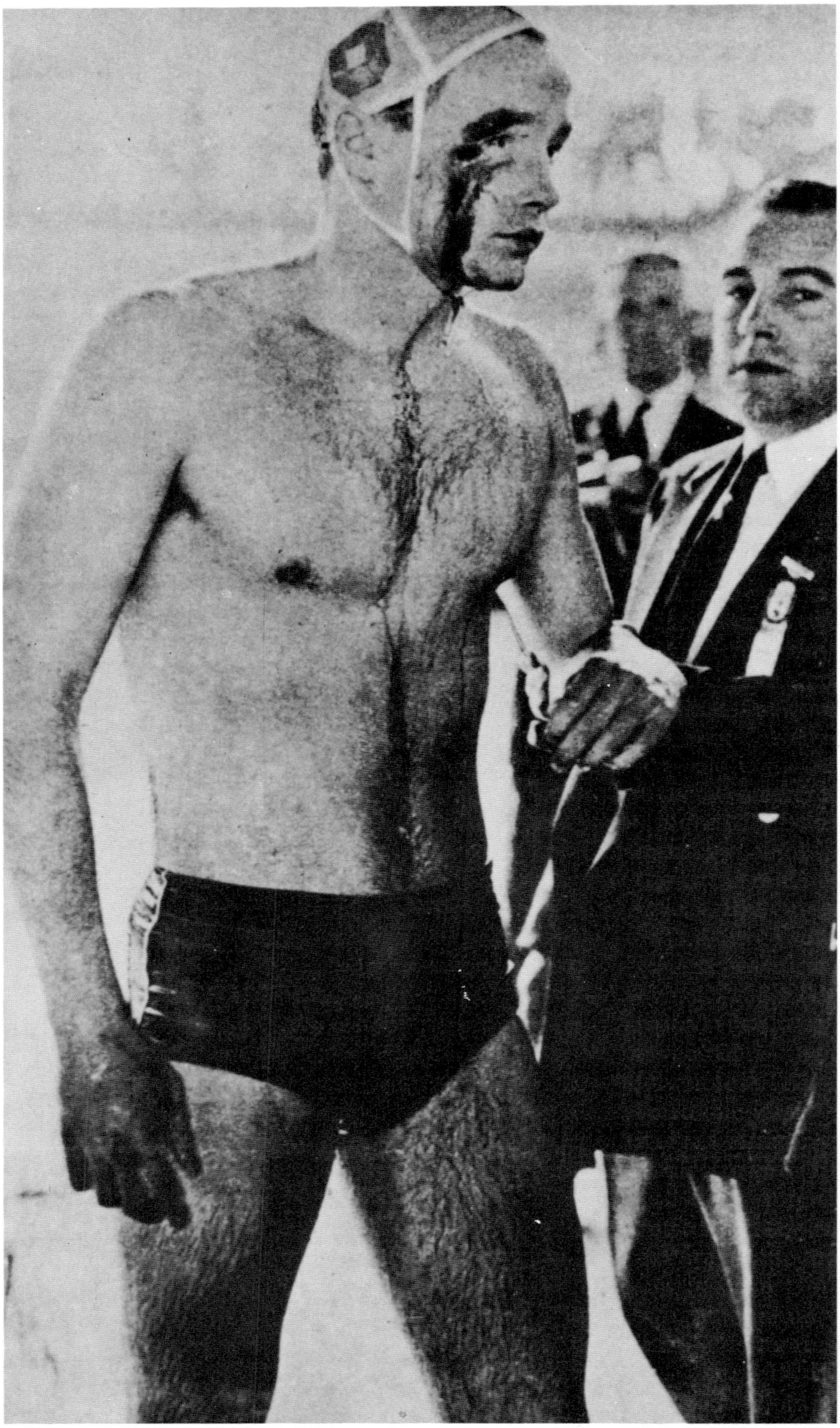

The Melbourne Games came soon after the Soviet repression of the Hungarian revolution. The Soviet and Hungarian water-polo teams brawled in their match, Hungarian Ervin Zador left the pool with a cut eye.

Carlile and refinements in technique suggested by coaches like Frank Guthrie.

With this background it was not surprising that Jon Henricks led his fellow Australians John Devitt and Gary Chapman to the first three places in the 100-metres freestyle and that there was the same national domination in the women's sprint, narrowly won by a young girl named Dawn Fraser who was to win this Olympic crown twice more. Born in England but brought up in Australia was seventeen-year-old Murray Rose, who took the 400-metres freestyle with a burst in the third 100 metres which was too much for Japan's Tsuyoshi Yamanaka. For me the highlight of the swimming was the 1,500 metres in which Rose and Yamanaka also had to face the American George Breen who had achieved a new world record of 17 min 52.9 sec in his heat. In the final Breen set the pace until 850 metres, when Rose made one of his typical mid-race bursts and gradually moved away, only for Yamanaka (Breen now languishing back in third place) to make a remarkable but unsuccessful counter-attack in the final two lengths. Rose had become the first swimmer since Johnny Weissmuller in 1924 to win two freestyle Olympic titles. Britons, meanwhile, were able to rejoice in their first swimming victory since 1924, when Judy Grinham took the 100-metres backstroke by a touch from Carin Cone (United States).

The boxing program, held at the West Melbourne stadium, had neither the glamorous setting nor quite the hyper-efficient organization of the swimming. But the finals had much appeal for the public. Terry Spinks (flyweight) and Dick McTaggart (lightweight) both won gold medals for Britain with McTaggart also taking the Val Barker trophy as the best stylist of the whole competition. Britain's team of seven also won one silver and one bronze medal which is worth noting. The USSR, technically very sound, had three champions and the United States, like Britain, two.

The American boxing team was reduced by miscalculations about weight limits and their Helsinki triumphs of 1952 were reflected only by James Boyd (light heavyweight) and Peter Rademacher (heavyweight) who took less than a round to beat Lev Mukhin of the USSR. Rademacher's punching drew gasps from the crowd.

The only final decision with which there was serious disagreement was at welterweight in favour of the Romanian southpaw Nicolae Linca over Freddie Tiedt (Ireland). But nothing in the tournament raised the pulse like the light-middleweight final. For sheer emotion, it possibly surpassed any other event in the whole of the 1956 Olympics. The reason was twofold. László Papp was attempting his third successive gold medal in Olympic boxing, having been middleweight champion in London in 1948 and light-middleweight winner in Helsinki in 1952. The second reason was that Papp was Hungarian and the sympathy of many people in Melbourne was with the competitors of the Hungarian team.

Papp's opponent was José Torres, Puerto Rican born but representing the United States and later world professional light-heavyweight champion. I thought that Torres took the first round with left leads against his southpaw opponent. But in the second round the packs of Hungarian supporters nearly lifted the roof off the stadium when Papp exploded a beautifully timed left hook to the jaw which sent Torres skittering across to the ropes. From then on the American was a beaten man though Papp, carrying his thirty years with care, refused to sail in and take unnecessary risks. When the Hungarian, having boxed even better in the third and last round, got the points decision, he was also awarded an ovation and some of his countrymen and women wept tears of joy.

There was a much less happy occasion a few days later in a water-polo match between Hungary, eventually outstanding champions once again in spite of a talented Yugoslav team, and the USSR. As Hungarian spectators booed, Russian players became rough and eventually the Hungarian Ervin Zádor climbed out of the water with a split eyebrow. At one stage it seemed that spectators might intervene but police restored order and Hungary won 4–0.

Looking back over the whole program of sports, I recall India beating Pakistan for the hockey title in a temperature of about 85°F (29.4°C); the emergence of a new school of athleticism, rather than pure technique, making some impression in the fencing (though Britain's Gillian Sheen won on classic lines in the foil); and weight-lifting having the third biggest entry of all the sports. What I missed because one could not see everything, even in those calmer times, was the heavyweight lifting final in which American Paul Anderson won only by virtue of a lighter bodyweight than Humberto Selvetti of Argentina. The next year Anderson lifted more weight than any other human when he raised 6,270 lb (2,844 kg) off trestles with his back.

When we came to the final evening, and discarded newspapers blew round the stadium, the Philistines could claim that the USSR had 'won' the Games with ninety-eight medals, thirty-seven of them gold, to seventy-four (thirty-two gold) by the United States. For my part, I do not think it is nostalgia for the past which makes me choose the following headline as epitomizing the spirit of the 1956 Olympics which had only just escaped cancellation: 'Melbourne's Family Affair. Going to Olympic Games Has Been Great Fun.' So it was.

XVII ROME 1960 Terry O'Connor

Rome, from where the order ending the Ancient Games was sent, became host of the Modern Celebration in 1960. The new and the old were never so closely together in Olympism. Wrestling took place in the Basilica of Maxentius, where two thousand years before similar competitions were held. In the Terme di Caracalla gymnastics were held, thus bridging another sporting canyon between the ancient and modern. The marathon, which started before the Capitol, finished by the Arch of Constantine. But modern Rome indelibly imprinted its image upon the events with athletics, swimming and hockey in the Foro Italico, Mussolini's creation, while within the sporting complex of EUR, the magnificent Sports Palace, for boxing, and the Velodrome, for cycling, were examples of Rome's sporting architecture created specifically for these Games.

Within less than an hour, on 2 September 1960, New Zealand athletes Murray Halberg and Peter Snell captured two of the blue-riband events, the 5,000 metres and the 800 metres, at the seventeenth Olympic Games. During a celebration in which the United States failed to dominate the track and field events as it had for the past half century, it was significant that New Zealand, with a population of less than 3,000,000, should produce two champions. It was a welcome indication of the international spread of world-class talent.

Rome's intense heat took its first grim toll in the Olympic Games when a twenty-two year old Danish cyclist, Knud Enemark Jensen collapsed while taking part in the 100-kilometres time trial team race. It was later established that drugs contributed to his death.

The older of the two runners wearing the famous all-black shorts and singlet emblazoned with a silver fern was twenty-seven-year-old Halberg. He did not look like a champion due to a withered arm which was a legacy of a school Rugby injury, but, as often happens, he compensated with an indomitable spirit. Like so many other Olympic champions, he proved that physical handicaps can be overcome.

Halberg, like his colleague Snell, was coached by Arthur Lydiard, whose ideas had a tremendous impact on athletic training during the period before and after Rome. Like many successful 5,000-metre runners, Halberg had progressed from the shorter distances. Therefore he had the basic speed and the long training runs ordered by Lydiard added to the stamina he was to need on that sweltering September day in Rome.

Viktor Kapitonov (USSR) narrowly defeats Livio Trape (Italy) in the road race.

Kazimierz Zimny, a tenacious little Polish runner, led the twelve runners into the opening stages of the race and in the heat it was obvious that the time would not be exceptionally fast. In fact it was one of only four track events at Rome in which the Olympic record was not improved.

Time was of no concern to Halberg. He was satisfied to be last at 1,000 metres, reached in 2 min 41.2 sec. He had travelled 11,000 miles from a country where losers are not recognized. Before the race he outlined his philosophy when he said:

> I am not concerned about records – only winning. So many men have lost races worrying about the time or opposition. In the Olympic Games you can never be sure who is the most dangerous rival and therefore it is better to concentrate on your own performance. Even if you break a world record it does not last, but you can never take away an Olympic title.

By 2,000 metres Halberg had moved up to fifth position but he was still biding his time while the lead switched between Zimny and the Australian Albert Thomas. With no one capable of breaking up the field as Vladimir Kuts (USSR) had done in Melbourne four years earlier, it was possible for Halberg to settle in. As so often in a 5,000 metres, the early and middle stages were a preliminary to the grand finale.

Coming into the home straight with just over three laps left, Halberg struck. He used the long stretch of track to stun his rivals with an electrifying burst of speed, and by the time he reached the mark indicating that three laps were left had opened a gap of ten yards. This was increased to twenty yards with 800 metres left.

Over the last lap when Halberg's head sagged and he appeared to be in trouble it seemed that he might have attacked too soon. Behind him Hans Grodotzki (Germany), urged on by many of his own supporters, was hacking back the lead. It was fascinating to watch the fast-moving German bearing down on the frail man in black.

The noise of the crowd awakened Halberg to the danger of the situation, and he somehow summoned up the strength to go on to win by eight yards and then collapse as he clutched the tape, which in that moment was his tangible reward as victor. His last lap of 73 sec was the slowest in the race but he would not have cared if his final time had been more than 14 min. It was in fact 13 min 43.4 sec, with Grodotzki second and Zimny third.

Before the Rome athletics began, the twenty-one-year-old barrel-chested Snell was virtually unknown, although he had beaten two well-known Australians Tony Blue and Herb Elliott over 800 metres. Halberg had warned that Snell could well prove himself the strongest man in the two-lap event and this was the case in the final.

The draw for the 800-metres final, from the inside, was Manfred Matuschewski (Germany), Roger Moens, the world-record holder (Belgium), Christian Wägli (Switzerland), George Kerr (Jamaica), Paul Schmidt (Germany); Snell was on the outside. For the first time since 1896 no American runner was in the final. As expected,

The end of India's thirty-two year domination of hockey in the Olympics, Pakistan winning 1-0.

Livio Berruti (Italy) winner of the 200 metres. Lester Carney (United States) came second and Abdoulaye Seye (France) third.

Wägli, a tall, upright runner, took the lead, going through the first lap in 52.3 sec, but, on the final straight, drooped and wilted under the pressure of being chased by such a talented field.

Impatiently Moens took up the running, followed by the smoothly moving Kerr. Coming aggressively down the final stretch, Moens looked certain to crown a fine career with an Olympic title. In a moment of panic he turned right to see how closely Kerr was placed. It was at that second that Snell, coming through on the inside with a tremendous finish, caught Moens. The Belgian tried to hang on but could not match someone at the beginning of a great athletics career. Snell won in the Olympic record time of 1 min 46.3 sec, with Moens two-tenths of a second behind.

At Rome the 1,500 metres was won by another athlete from the southern hemisphere, Herb Elliott. Every generation produces a sportsman who completely dwarfs his rivals and such a man was the bronzed Australian, who was never beaten over the 1,500 metres or mile. At the age of twenty, in 1958, he had set world records at both distances.

Although work had lured him away from athletics for a long time before Rome, few believed that he could not achieve the dream of winning an Olympic title which he had held since he was a teenaged spectator at the Melbourne Olympic Games four years before. He was coached by Percy Cerutty, who was determined that he should achieve not only victory but a world record to ensure an unforgettable Olympic memory. Concentration and an ability to escape from virtually all human inhibitions were the secrets of Elliott's superiority. Never did he display this in a more ruthless manner than at

Rome. As he nursed himself into the race, he was prepared to stay at the back of the field for two-thirds of the course, but then, goaded by the waving of a white towel by Cerutty as a signal that a world record was possible, he took off with a devastating burst and finished with a final 400 metres in 55 sec. Michel Jazy (France) and István Rózsavölgyi (Hungary), second and third respectively, admitted that they felt completely outclassed. Elliott won by an unbelievable margin of 20 yd (18.29 m) in a world time of 3 min 35.6 sec. No wonder he was called 'the human deer'.

An indication of how the United States' grip on the Olympic athletic arena had been loosened was seen in the sprints, which were won by two Europeans. Armin Hary captured the 100 metres for Germany's first Olympic track title, and the bespectacled Italian Livio Berruti won a popular local victory over 200 metres. The Latin excitement at this triumph was illustrated when a 280-lb (126.84 kg) Italian journalist near me collapsed at the end of the race and took an hour to recover.

The Italians made full use of the facilities of their ancient capital to stage the most colourful of Olympic marathons and were rewarded with a dramatic climax. The main stadium was not used and sixty-nine starters began their long haul amid chaotic crowd scenes beneath the Capitol Hill, centre of the ancient Roman Empire, and finished under the moon and torchlights along the Appian Way, almost under the Arch of Constantine.

Such a setting would have been memorable in itself but the race not only produced a world-best time of 2 hr 15 min 16.2 sec but created the first Ethiopian Olympic champion, Abebe Bikila, a barefooted runner who was a member of Emperor Haile Selassie's Personal Guard. It was also the first time that Africans filled the first two places, as behind Bikila was a Moroccan soldier, Rhadi Ben Abdesselam. Bikila's father had fought against the troops of Mussolini in 1935 and it was ironic that Bikila should choose Rome to make his conquest. Another athlete trained by Lydiard, Barry Magee of New Zealand, finished third.

In the 10,000 metres, Pyotr Bolotnikov (USSR) ran a shattering 57.8-sec last lap, breaking Vladimir Kuts' Olympic record to take the title, but he never managed to make the same impression as his countryman who had won two gold medals four years earlier.

This was also a high period for Polish athletics: the very talented Zdzislaw Krzyszkowiak won the 3,000-metres steeplechase and the artistic Józef Szmidt took the triple jump, both with Olympic records.

In the 400-metres hurdles, Glenn Davis (United States) was one of the three athletes to retain his Olympic title, but he was disappointed not to be challenged this time by Gert Potgieter (South Africa) who had been eliminated by a serious car accident in Germany two weeks before the Games opened. This was to be the last occasion on which South Africans competed in the Olympic Games because the apartheid policies of their government meant that their National Olympic Committee could not subscribe to the principles of the Olympic Movement. In the 110-metres hurdles, in which the Americans again took the first three positions, Lee Calhoun held his title.

The United States was prevented from winning its traditional gold medal in the 4 × 100-metres relay by a disqualification and the title

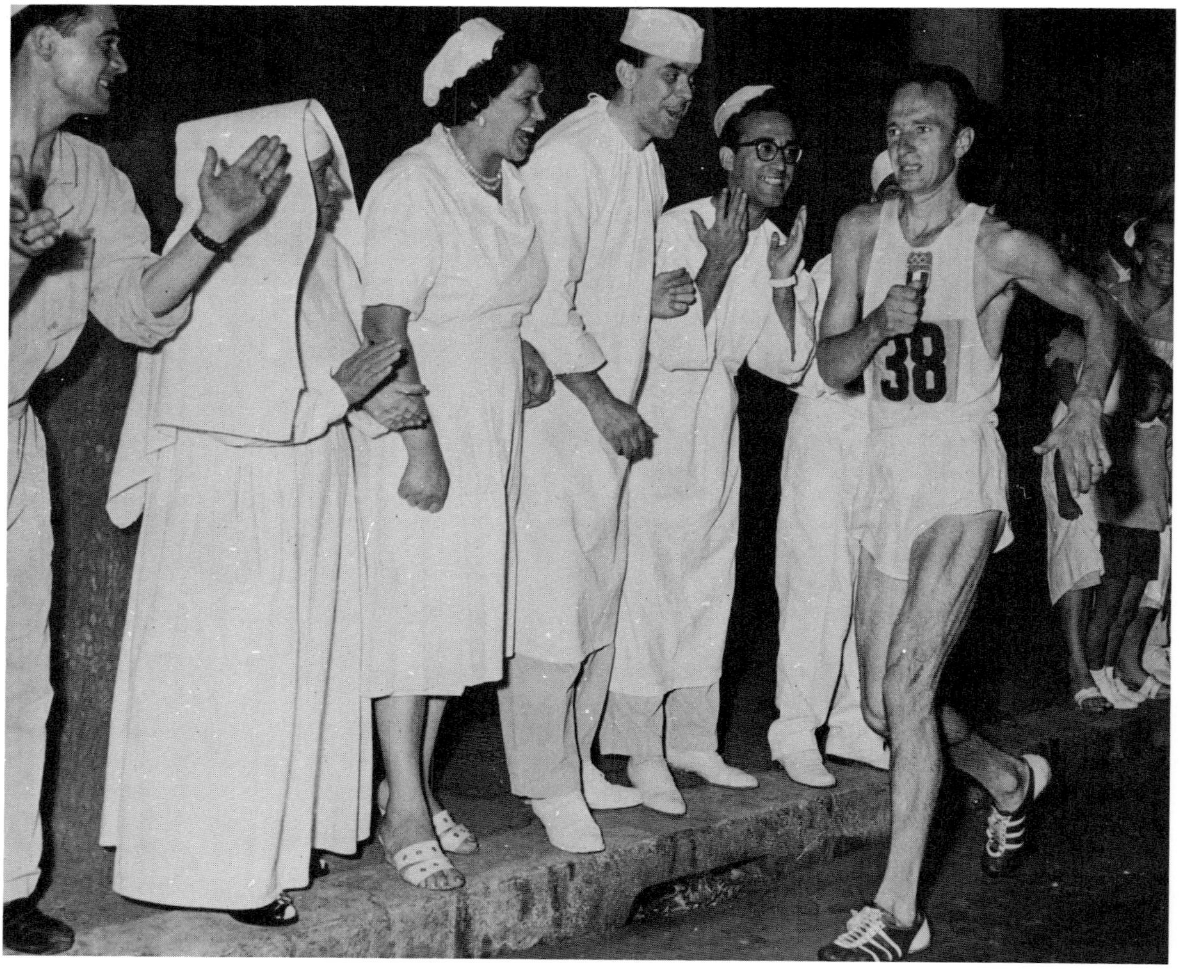

Abdon Pamich won the silver medal in the 50 kilometres walk.

went to Germany. Britain reached the semi-finals when Nigeria was disqualified in the heat, and then took the bronze medal when the United States was ruled out. Both disqualifications were for exchanging the baton outside the zone limit.

Britain's only athletic gold medal was won by the tiny Don Thompson, called 'little mouse' by the Italians. He won the 50,000-metres walk after training for the Rome temperature in his own bathroom.

In the field events there was a titanic clash in the shot with Bill Nieder (United States) taking the title from defending champion Parry O'Brien (United States). Nieder was only in Rome as a replacement for the injured Dave Davies. For the first time 7 ft (2.13 m) was cleared in the Olympic high jump and the world-record holder John Thomas (United States) was beaten into third position by two Russians, Robert Shavlakadze and Valeri Brumel. The lead repeatedly changed hands in the decathlon before Rafer Johnson (United States) beat Chuan-Kwang Yang (Republic of China/Taiwan) by a mere 58 points, to set another Olympic record.

In 1960 there were only ten women's events in track and field and the USSR claimed six, but the heroine was the pretty twenty-year-old black Wilma Rudolph (United States), who won three gold medals in the sprints and relay. As a child, Wilma, a member of a Tennessee family of nineteen, was crippled by polio. There was no trace of any disability as she poured elegantly over the 100-metres stretch in 11.0 sec and the 200 metres in 24.0 sec. Such was the acceleration of this long-legged girl that even her poor starting could not aid her rivals.

In the field events only the Romanian Iolanda Balaş prevented the Russians winning all the gold medals. There was a double triumph for the Press sisters with Irina winning the 80-metres hurdles and Tamara the shot. Nina Ponomareva, who had won the discus at Helsinki in 1952 under her maiden name of Romashkova, collected her second title.

American swimmers had vowed after winning only five gold medals (two men's and three women's) in Melbourne that it would be different in Rome. It certainly was. They won eleven and broke five world records. This time the Australians suffered disappointment. Bad weather had upset their preparations at home and then most of their young stars suffered from 'Roman tummy' on arrival. It was therefore left to the veterans Dawn Fraser, John Devitt, Murray Rose, John Konrads and David Theile to ensure that they were the second swimming nation.

The only other country among the forty-eight represented that won a swimming gold medal was Great Britain. To achieve this, nineteen-year-old Anita Lonsbrough from Yorkshire had to fight a close battle, in what many considered the race of the tournament, the 200-metres breaststroke against the blonde Wiltrud Urselmann (Germany). At the halfway stage Miss Urselmann was 2 sec ahead but by the last turn the two girls were level. At the beginning of the last 50 metres, the British girl edged ahead and held off a long challenge to break the world record in 2 min 49.5 sec. Miss Urselmann was timed at 2 min 50.0 sec, also inside the world record.

Ingrid Krämer, a seventeen-year-old German girl, won the springboard and highboard diving events. She was the first non-American to take the springboard title since it was included in the Games in 1920 and the first to win the highboard since 1920.

The floodlit pool provided a perfect setting for the events and it was regrettable that a place of such beauty and friendliness should have been the scene of a bitter controversy over the decision to award the 100-metres freestyle title to John Devitt (Australia). Over the last ten metres the Australian was in the lead but Lance Larson (United States) put in an incredible burst and appeared to touch a hand ahead. This view was confirmed by the timings of 55.0, 55.1 and 55.1 sec but these were calculated to average 55.2 sec like Devitt's. Two of the first-place judges gave Devitt the verdict but two silver-medal judges named him second. Slow-motion television came out in favour of Larson but Devitt kept the gold medal. A tie would have been a fair decision but this was not permitted by FINA laws. It was the last Olympic swimming competition in which electronic timing was not used.

In the women's events the astonishing American squad of teenagers dominated, with Chris Von Saltza, aged sixteen, winning the 400-metres freestyle, Carolyn Schuler, seventeen, the 100-metres butterfly, and Lynn Burke, seventeen, the 100-metres backstroke.

They combined with others to win the 4 × 100-metres freestyle and 4 × 100-metres medley relays, both in world-record times.

Boxing took place in the beautiful Palazzo dello Sport, and Italian spectators, burning newspapers to make torches under the magnificent dome, watched six of their countrymen compete for ten of the gold medals. This made the finals night unforgettable. It seemed the stadium would be set alight when heavyweight Franco de Piccoli (Italy), took only 1 min 30 sec to knock out the portly Russian European champion Andrei Abramov in the quarter-final.

In the light-heavyweight division, Cassius Clay, later Muhammad Ali, was first hailed as a 'world' champion. He was only eighteen but already displayed the showmanship which later became his trademark as a professional. In the final he met the veteran Zbigniew Pietrzykowski (Poland). The Pole succeeded in luring him into indiscretions in the first round but at the end of the second, Clay shook off his relaxed mood and lashed Pietrzykowski four times on the head. Then, in the final round, Clay really tightened up, putting his punches together, and it needed all Pietrzykowski's courage to stay on his feet.

Again a regrettable feature of the boxing was the standard of judging. Although judgment in boxing has to be partly a matter of opinion, there were instances where contests were marked 60–57 by one of the five judges and 57–60 by another. This meant that the first judge saw Boxer A as the winner of all three rounds while the other marked the same man as the loser of the same three rounds.

Overshadowing the cycling events was the death of the Danish competitor Knud Jensen in the road race. It was later confirmed that the use of drugs had been a contributory factor. As a result, the International Cycling Federation became the first international body to adopt a doping control. It was in the road race that the USSR prevented Italy achieving a 'grand slam' of victories, but it needed an inches victory by Viktor Kapitonov over Livio Trapè.

Vyacheslav Ivanov (USSR) was the only competitor in the rowing events to retain an Olympic title but his victory in the single sculls was disappointingly easy because the one man who would have provided stern opposition, Stuart Mackenzie of Australia, was missing. Between the Olympic years Mackenzie had gained three major victories over Ivanov but he suffered a relapse after a stomach operation. European oarsmen dominated the other events.

The rowing events introduced a new word to the dictionary of the sport. Because it was physically impossible to erect overhead steering markers on Lake Albano, the six racing lanes were individually buoyed the length of the course and what is known as the 'Albano' system has been used ever since.

In the association football tournament it looked as if Yugoslavia might fail in its fourth successive Olympic final when its captain Milan Galič was sent off for arguing with the referee after what appeared to be a legitimate goal was disallowed. At that stage Yugoslavia led by 2–0; the Danes, finally beaten 3–1, took second place and Hungary third.

In basketball the United States gained its fifth Olympic win in a row, with the USSR second for the third time, but history changed in the hockey tournament in which India was unthroned after thirty-two years' supremacy by Pakistan.

Wrestling was held in the magnificent Basilica of Maxentius.

In canoeing, Sweden was the leading country, with Gert Fredriksson appearing for the first time and winning gold medals in two events; it was for him the beginning of a long Olympic association over a period of twelve years during which he won six gold medals and a special Olympic trophy.

There were so many competitors in the weightlifting events that competitions sometimes lasted until 4 a.m. The USSR added to its tally of gold medals by winning five titles, while Turkey continued its success in wrestling with seven gold medals.

The Bay of Naples provided a perfect setting for the yachting and it seemed fitting that in such waters Crown Prince Constantine of the Hellenes should be at the helm of *Nirefs* to win the gold medal in the Dragon class.

Of all the memories left after the celebration of the seventeenth Olympiad, none was more beautiful than the closing ceremony – a tribute to the vision and poetry of the Latins. Even when the Olympic flame was extinguished, the torchlights of burning newspapers filled the sky and pointed to the future and Tokyo 1964.

XVIII TOKYO 1964 Vernon Morgan

It is not easy to find the correct epithet to describe the Games of the eighteenth Olympiad, staged in Tokyo in 1964. There is no doubt that at the time these were the greatest modern Olympics. They were also joyous and were named the 'Happy' Games by one veteran reporter. Their success should not be judged by monetary profit or loss; nor by the standard of the performances during the Games. Personally I would say that the success of a Games depends on the feelings of all – organizers, officials, competitors and public at the closing ceremony. Let the opening be joyous and the closing sad. In spite of the frolicking at the closing ceremony at Tokyo – which many interpreted as an expression of thanks – my belief is that the general majority were sad that it was all over, and that they were forced to reconcile themselves with the saying that 'all good things come to an end'.

None was more impressed by the Tokyo Olympics, nor more sad to leave Japan than Avery Brundage, President of the IOC, who has more experience of the Olympic Games than any man alive. He not only said the Games were a success but a phenomenal success. There is little doubt that in spite of their great size, these Games evoked less criticism from every quarter than perhaps any other. Everyone appeared to enjoy themselves; the smiling Japanese did indeed seem to spread a spirit of happiness everywhere. As Brundage declared, 'The entire nation from newsboy to industrial tycoon adopted the Games

Elation of the Olympic champion Valeri Brumel (USSR) after his winning jump of 2.18m (7ft 1¾in).

Ann Packer (Gt Britain) winning the 800 metres in a new world and Olympic record of 2 min. 01.1 sec.

as his own project and went out of his way to please the visitors.'

One of the highlights of the Games was the consistently large crowd in the main stadium. On one dark wet day, the rain fell steadily from leaden skies as some of the qualifying rounds of field events were taking place; had the terraces been empty one would not have been surprised. But instead they were nearly full; it was unique in Olympic history. Thousands sat huddled under their umbrellas, the rain dripping from them and their raincoats. Such was the enthusiasm and fortitude of the Japanese that they were still there, mostly soaked, for the afternoon's major events. That was the spirit of the 1964 Olympics in Tokyo.

Japan was the first country in the Far East to be given a Games. It had been awarded the 1940 Olympics but withdrew in 1938. Immediately Tokyo had been allocated the 1964 Games, easily defeating its rivals, Detroit, Vienna and Brussels for this honour, the Japanese set about their task to make them the greatest ever, and above all to show the world that though harsh things might have been said about them as a result of World War II, they were at heart human and a friendly nation. It is my belief that it was the latter task that was ever uppermost in the minds of the Japanese hosts.

And how well they succeeded in both their aims. There is no doubt that from a national point of view the Tokyo Olympics could not have been a greater success. But at an enormous financial cost. If one considers every yen spent on Tokyo after it had been given the Games,

Robert Hayes (United States); his rolling, lumbering style bemused the connoisseurs of sprinting.

Emiko Miyamoto (Japan) number 2 and Katsumi Matsumura (Japan) number 5, leap to block a shot from Danuta Kordaczuk (Poland) in women's volleyball game at the Komazawa volleyball court.

the cost probably exceeded £1,000 million. Even the £30 million spent on just staging the Games was a staggering figure.

All the efforts of the Japanese to make a success out of the 1964 Olympics looked at one time as if they might be sabotaged – by politics. This was over the GANEFO (Games of the New Emerging Forces) affair. Indonesia, which had been suspended by the IOC over the question of the admission of competitors from Israel and Taiwan to the fourth Asian Games in 1962 of which it was the host, and was therefore ineligible for the Tokyo Olympics, decided to hold its own GANEFO Games in Jakarta in 1963. And it persuaded the People's Republic of China, no longer a member of the IOC, to take part. Before these Games were held the IOC warned that no persons taking part in these Games were eligible to take part in the Tokyo Olympics. The Indonesians, having had their suspension removed, and North Koreans took no notice of this edict and travelled to Tokyo hoping to take part and banking on the Japanese being able to persuade the IOC to change its mind. The Japanese did not. However much they

Valeri Brumel (USSR) clears 7 feet 1⅞in in winning the gold medal in Olympic high jumping.

would have liked the Indonesians and North Koreans to take part, the Japanese realized the dire consequences of fighting the IOC on this matter. Even at this late stage the Games could have been ruined. But though permission to take part was given to both Indonesian and North Korean competitors who had not competed in the GANEFO both teams decided to return home. Tokyo got out of it remarkably well, for the situation was at one time ugly. Sport had triumphed over politics. And it appeared to do so during the competitions.

Just how much their eighteenth Olympiad was appreciated by the members of the IOC was shown by the award to the Tokyo Metropolitan Government of the Olympic Cup 'for their efforts in the successful preparation of the Games'; to the Japanese Olympic Committee the Count Bonacossa Trophy 'for its endeavours over the five years before the Games commenced'; and the Diploma of Merit to Dr Tenzo Kange 'for his creative designing of the National Gymnasium'. The gymnasium contained not only the superb unique swimming pool but the picturesque basketball arena.

Apart from their huge cost the Tokyo Olympics set new records for the Games. No fewer than ninety-four nations took part as against the previous highest figure of eighty-four attained in the previous Olympiad in Rome. Tokyo also beat Rome's record in the number of events, with 163 against 150.

And what of the Games themselves? It is sad to some people, but none the less a fact, that it is no longer true to say that the taking part and not the winning is what matters. Gradually the Olympics have become an arena for the gladiators, and there are those who think the last Olympics staged in the Coubertin spirit were in Helsinki in 1952. Now the aim of all, or at least the majority, is not merely to take part but to win, even if it means cheating. Thus records fall like autumn leaves in each succeeding Olympics and the

Tokyo Games were no exception in this respect.

In a galaxy of talent the outstanding man was the Ethiopian marathon runner Abebe Bikila, and the leading woman the Australian 'mermaid' Dawn Fraser. Bikila had surprised the world by winning the marathon in the previous Games in Rome in a time nearly a quarter of an hour faster than the previous Olympic best. He showed this to be no fluke by winning as he liked in Tokyo, beating his Rome time by some three minutes.

The most remarkable aspect of Bikila's victory was the fact that he took part at all. Five weeks before the marathon he had an operation for appendicitis. It was not thought possible for him to recover sufficiently even to compete, let alone win. But this lean little man was tough. In less than two weeks after the removal of his appendix he had started to train and by the day of the race he was fit again for the 26 miles 385 yards. He let the others do the pacemaking for the early miles but then forged ahead and was virtually unchallenged in winning in the new Olympic time of 2 hr 12 min 11.2 sec. He was more than four minutes ahead of his nearest rival at the finish, Basil Heatley (Great Britain), who took the silver medal by overhauling the Japanese Kokichi Tsuburaya on the final circuit of the track. When Emil Zátopek won the marathon in the 1952 Olympics in Helsinki everyone was astonished to see him so fresh. But in Tokyo he was outdone by Bikila, who jogged onto the grass at the end of the race and provided the crowd with a demonstration of callisthenics. A really great Olympian.

Dawn Fraser, though now at the ripe old age for a sprint swimmer of twenty-seven, won the 100-metres freestyle for the third successive Olympiad, and in doing so set a third successive Olympic record. Eighteen-year-old Don Schollander (United States) set three world and four Olympic records in winning his four gold medals, the 100-

Kon Ichikawa (Japan) right, directing the shooting of his film of the 1964 Games in Tokyo.

metres freestyle, 400-metres freestyle, the 4 × 100-metres relay and 4 × 200-metres relay. His toughest race was the 100 metres, when he beat Bobby McGregor (Gt Britain) by little more than a touch. He could have had a fifth gold had he been picked for the anchor leg of the medley relay but Steve Clark was given the final (freestyle) leg. Schollander, of Swedish extraction, attended to detail in preparation but there were a few eyebrows raised when he shaved not only his body but his fair head to reduce all possible friction and so become as streamlined as possible. The Games brought an end to the career of Bob Kiputh, whose coaching of American swimmers began with Bachrach and Weissmuller forty years earlier. For the first time, a Russian girl, Galina Prosumenshchikova, won a swimming title, taking the gold in the 200-metres breaststroke.

In athletics, Peter Snell of New Zealand, winner of the 800 metres at Rome, retained that title and took the 1,500 metres – the first double in these events since Albert Hill of Britain in 1920; while the New Zealander's victory in the previous Olympiad had been something of a surprise, he was among the favourites at Tokyo, but his head as well as his heart and legs got him the gold. His tactics were superb, and the way he challenged round the final curve took one

Peter Snell (New Zealand) elated after taking the 800 metres in an Olympic record of 1 min 45.1 sec. The figure lying on the track is G.E Kerr (Jamaica) who finished fourth.

back to 1936 and the Berlin Games when his similarly black-vested compatriot Jack Lovelock dashed through the field to win the 1,500-metres title. In Rome Snell only just scraped through by two-tenths of a second in the new Olympic time of 1 min 46.3 sec. In Tokyo, in beating his own Olympic record in returning 1 min 45.1 sec he had five-tenths of a second in hand. Snell had fewer problems in getting his double in the 1,500 metres. But once again it was his perfect judgment that helped him to get another gold. His final time was not all that shattering, but he ran the last lap in the remarkable time of 53.2 sec, with 25.4 sec for the final 200 metres to win by some ten metres.

Hardly less remarkable than Bikila's feat was the performance of the American Al Oerter in the discus. He too triumphed over the physical handicaps that looked like preventing him from winning in three consecutive Olympics. In Melbourne in 1956 he had won with an Olympic record of 56.36 m (184 ft 11 in); in Rome in 1960 he had bettered this in winning with a throw of 59.18 m (194 ft $1\frac{3}{4}$ in). The discus man slipped a disc in 1964 but he looked fit enough to defend his title when he got to Tokyo. But then misfortune struck again. This time, slipping in the wet, he fell heavily and severely damaged his ribs. When it came to the day of competition he was not only heavily strapped but also had to be given a pain-killing injection. In spite of this he actually beat his own Olympic record in qualifying. Yet in the final he had to wait until his penultimate throw of 61.00 m (200 ft $1\frac{1}{2}$ in) to get the gold, snatching victory from his Czechoslovak rival Ludvik Danek by little more than a foot.

The men's 100-metres title, which had only three times not been won by someone from the American continent, went back there. From the first round Bob Hayes gave cause for little doubt that he would win, but the connoisseurs of sprinting were bemused by his rolling, lumbering style. It was never more apparent than in the final, where he seemed bent upon the running and overlooked the starting. Enrique Figuerola of Cuba and Harry Jerome of Canada got away best and in most sprinting events had enough advantage at 30 metres to have been fighting for the gold. But then Hayes had got into his stride and thundered past them to equal the world record of 10.0 sec and win by a fifth of a second.

The Americans, having regained this prize, invaded a new province, by taking, for the first time, the 5,000-metres and 10,000-metres titles. Bob Schul, playing a skilful waiting game in the shorter event, outmanoeuvred his more experienced European rivals. After a slowish early pace it looked as though Michel Jazy, France's world-record breaker at a mile, would be strong enough to win, but in the final lap he was caught first by Harald Norpoth of Germany and then off the final bend by Schul.

The 10,000 metres left a feeling of some dissatisfaction for so many runners were lapped that those challenging for the medals on the final laps were impeded. It was the last occasion on which this race was run without heats. Ron Clarke of Australia, Billy Mills of the United States and Mohamed Gammoudi of Tunisia were the men in contention. Clarke was slightly impeded by a lapped runner as they swept into the final circuit and Gammoudi dashed to the front. As the Tunisian opened up his stride, Clarke went with him, with Mills on their heels. In the final straight Mills had much the better finish and he streaked past them both to record an unexpected victory.

In the boxing ring Joe Frazier began his climb to world fame with a gold medal in the heavyweight division; while in the unlimited weight of the judo competition, included in the Olympics for the first time, it was a Dutchman, Anton Geesink, who brought a cold embarrassing silence to the hall when he became the only overseas winner in the sport that the Japanese really believed was their preserve.

The sport that really developed in Tokyo, largely due to television presentation, was gymnastics. The hall was packed night after night with a pretty blonde Czech, Vera Čáslavská, who won three titles, as the main attraction.

History repeated itself in the equestrian events. In the 1952 Olympic Games in Helsinki Great Britain had begun the final event, the Grand Prix jumping, without a single gold medal. But a faultless last round by Harry Llewellyn on Foxhunter gave Britain the team gold. The individual gold on this occasion was won by a French officer, Pierre Jonquères d'Oriola. In Tokyo, France came to this last final event also without one gold medal. Again it was a horse that came to his country's rescue, for the aptly named Lutteur (Fighter) enabled the same rider, d'Oriola, at forty-four one of the oldest competitors in the Games, to win his second gold, and France's only one in Tokyo.

Few sports have arrived in the Olympic arena with such sensation as did Volleyball in 1964. The Japanese women's team had already gained wide popularity, and for their match in the final against the Soviet Union, the Japanese television networks achieved for the first and probably the last time audience ratings in excess of ninety per cent. As one writer said at the time: 'People clung to their television sets to watch the game, leaving the public bath-houses almost deserted, the Ginza nearly empty and the Toll switchboard out of action.'

XIX MEXICO CITY 1968 John Rodda

The Games of the nineteenth Olympiad in Mexico City caused anger in certain areas of the sporting world which led to some useful physiological research, very nearly precipitated a revolution and provided in the end some vivid memories.

When the IOC, at its meeting in Baden-Baden in 1963, awarded the Games to Mexico City, which is situated at a level of over 2,134 m (7,000 ft), very few people understood the significance of competition in the endurance events at this height. It quickly became clear that there would be a disparity between those who lived at altitude and those who came from sea level and whose bodies could not react in the same manner in high-class competition. The disparity was large enough to bring a degree of unfairness. Several countries undertook physiological investigation and the work of the British Olympic Association brought a proposal from the IOC that a period of four weeks in the last three months before the Games could be spent in training at high altitude to acclimatize. It was an unsatisfactory compromise for many countries allowed their athletes to train at altitude for much longer periods.

In Mexico City itself there had been discontent with the régime, particularly from students, many of whom felt that for a country with much poverty it was wasteful and misguided to be spending vast sums on the Olympic Games. The students used the event to draw attention to their cause. Their brushes with authority in the months before the Games produced an alarming-looking situation: three weeks before the Games were due to begin there were tanks on the road outside the University (the source of the trouble) opposite the main Olympic stadium. After several demonstrations and with the protest movement growing in momentum throughout the country and clearly involving far more than student life, the Army crushed the opposition on the night of 2 October – ten days before the Games were due to start. At a demonstration of 10,000 people in the Square of the Three Cultures in Mexico City, the military surrounded the square and opened fire. In the bitter battle which followed, lasting five hours, more than 260 were killed and 1,200 injured. There was no further trouble and the Games went on without interference.

The effects of competition in thin air were soon to be seen. Three of the first four men in the 10,000 metres lived at high altitude and the winning time was almost a minute slower than the Olympic record. In the 5,000 metres the same theme could be traced, with the second-, third- and fourth-placed runners, men from the mountains. It blurred the emergence of Africa's talent, Naftali Temu (Kenya) winning the 10,000 metres, Mamo Wolde (Ethiopia) taking the silver and later winning the marathon, Kipchoge Keino (Kenya) winning the 1,500 metres and taking the silver medal in the 5,000 metres and two of his compatriots, Amos Biwott and Ben Kogo, placing first and second in the steeplechase.

Misuse of the Olympic arena. The US 4 × 400-metres relay team give the black power salute when receiving their medals; from left: Lee Evans, Larry James, Ron Freeman, and Vince Matthews.

Irena Szewińska (Poland) winning the 200 metres and breaking her own world record with 22.5 sec.

There was another side effect of the altitude, seen in its most distorted form in the long jump, which Bob Beamon (United States) won with a prodigious leap of 8.90 m (29 ft $2\frac{1}{2}$ in). The world record was 8.35 m (27 ft $4\frac{3}{4}$ in). Beamon's jump came in the opening round and destroyed the competitive spirit in the rest, apart from Klaus Beer (German Democratic Republic). Beamon, who only in Mexico had listened to Ralph Boston, his colleague and previous medal-winner, about using a stride pattern in his approach run, bounded down the runway and seemed to run on into the air rather than stamp his foot on the board and lift up. When he cut the sand a world record seemed certain but the moments were long and hanging until the scoreboard flashed out its historic figures 8.90. In addition to Beamon's undoubted talent, there was another factor: twenty-seven per cent less atmospheric pressure and twenty-three per cent less air density. This assistance means that potential world-record breakers are not going to surpass Beamon's leap without the special circumstances he enjoyed. The triple jump gave another example of help provided by reduced resistance, for the world record was broken nine times during the competition with Viktor Saneev (USSR) winning the event in the final round with a jump of 17.39 m (57 ft $0\frac{3}{4}$ in).

Most people consider the hero of the Mexico Olympics to be Al Oerter (United States) who won the discus title for the fourth consecutive time. His throwing during the season had been well behind his best and that of Jay Silvester (United States), the world-record holder. The opening throws of the competition had been modest and then rain fell to halt the event; this was a break in concentration and preparedness that the less experienced competitors could not cope with, but on resumption, with the circle wet and the air heavy with

Right: **Győző Kulcsár (Hungary) and Grigori Kriss (USSR) in the final of the individual épée event. Kriss won the bout but Kulcsár took the gold medal and Kriss the silver.**

Kipchoge Keino (Kenya) wins the 1,500 metres in 3 min 34.9 sec.

dampness, Oerter reached 64.78 m (212 ft 6½ in), a personal best throw. This completely destroyed his opponents, who believed that this sort of distance in these conditions was beyond them. They all faltered but, in the fifth and sixth round, Oerter, with little speed across the circle but whip from his throwing arm again reached distances beyond the mark achieved by the silver medallist Lothar Milde (German Democratic Republic).

Many contests on the track were tinged with doubt because of altitude. Ron Clarke, Australia's multi-world-record holder, exemplified the spirit and hopelessness of the honest lowlanders. He struggled to stay in contention with the leaders in the 10,000 metres run at a pace two minutes slower than his world record but, with two laps remaining and when he was in fourth place, the oxygen debt suddenly became too great and he took 2 min 18 sec to run the last two laps, rather than something close to two minutes, collapsing onto the verge and needing oxygen for revival.

The contest for first place evolved into one between Mamo Wolde (Ethiopia), Mohamed Gammoudi (Tunisia) and Naftali Temu (Kenya). These three were in contention two laps from home when Wolde struck and opened a wide gap. Gammoudi tailed off but across the final 250 metres Temu surged back and caught the Ethiopian who had nothing left for a counter-attack. But Wolde was to take a gold medal – in the marathon. At least this event showed that Abebe Bikila (winner in 1960 and 1964) had human frailties after all. A foot injury had made him a doubtful starter and although he ran he dropped out after 17 km. Wolde made his decisive thrust when he still had 10 km to run and it showed the ebbing strength of those around him. On the long climb back to the stadium he took a lead of almost three minutes; many of those behind had found the blazing sun too much.

The most decisive winner in the track and field at Mexico was David Hemery (Great Britain) in the 400-metres hurdles. This was an event in which the thin air helped, for the first seven men in the final broke the previous Olympic record, but Hemery made them look second class as he led from the second hurdle and came into the straight three strides ahead of anyone else. At the last obstacle his leading foot had touched down after the hurdle before those behind were rising on the other side. His time was 48.1 sec, slicing seven-tenths of a second from the record set earlier in the year and beating the previous Olympic mark, set by Glenn Davis (United States) in 1960, by 1.2 sec; it was a performance to put him among the great Olympians.

The search for new techniques or improvements on old ones, particularly in field events, never ceases but there has never been a more dramatic success than the new style of high jumping introduced by Dick Fosbury (United States) and appropriately dubbed the Fosbury Flop. Most Olympic winners either straddled the bar, one foot following the other, or used a western roll in which both feet crossed the bar together. Fosbury revolutionized the event by running in on a curved approach and then at the point of take-off

David Hemery (Gt Britain) winner of the 400-metres hurdles.

Dick Fosbury (United States) introduced a new style of high jumping which became known as the Fosbury flop.

turning to go over the bar backwards, stretching the back and flipping the legs upwards. Fosbury's style was not decisive because Ed Caruthers, using the straddle, matched his fellow American as the bar was raised to each new height until at 2.24 m (7 ft $4\frac{1}{4}$ in) Fosbury got over on his third attempt; Caruthers failed narrowly.

In the women's competition, Irena Szewińska-Kirszenstein (Poland) added to her Olympic medal collection, which had begun in Tokyo. She finished third, behind the two Americans, Wyomia Tyus and Barbara Ferrell, in the 100 metres. In the 200 metres she won and broke her own world record with 22.5 sec.

The women's 400 metres brought an unexpected gold for France when the long-haired Colette Besson, in the last two strides, overhauled Lillian Board (Great Britain). In the 80-metres hurdles Maureen Caird (Australia) who was only seventeen, beat her more favoured colleague Pam Kilborn and trounced the East Europeans. Another surprise came in the high jump, in which Miroslava Rezková (Czechoslovakia), collecting several failures at the earlier heights, finally achieved the winning height at her third attempt.

The Americans dominated the swimming and diving even more than they had done in Tokyo. They won more medals than the other countries put together, twenty-three gold, fifteen silver and twenty bronze from a total of 102. Perhaps an even greater example of their superiority is shown in the number of finalists, eighty-one out of a possible ninety. Beside this avalanche the few successes of the other countries tend to stand out. Roland Matthes (German Democratic Republic) won both backstroke titles, and the 100 metres by the remarkable margin of 1.5 sec; the Australian Michael Wenden took both freestyle sprint titles, setting a world record of 52.22 sec at 100 metres and beating Don Schollander (United States) by three-fifths of a second over 200 metres – a contest where Wenden's rugged power was just sufficient to overcome Schollander's economical style. Vladimir Vasin of the Soviet Union closed a run of American victories in the springboard diving which began in 1920.

Elsewhere in the men's events there was an almost unbroken succession of American victories, often backed up by the silver and bronze medals as well. In the women's events the pattern was much

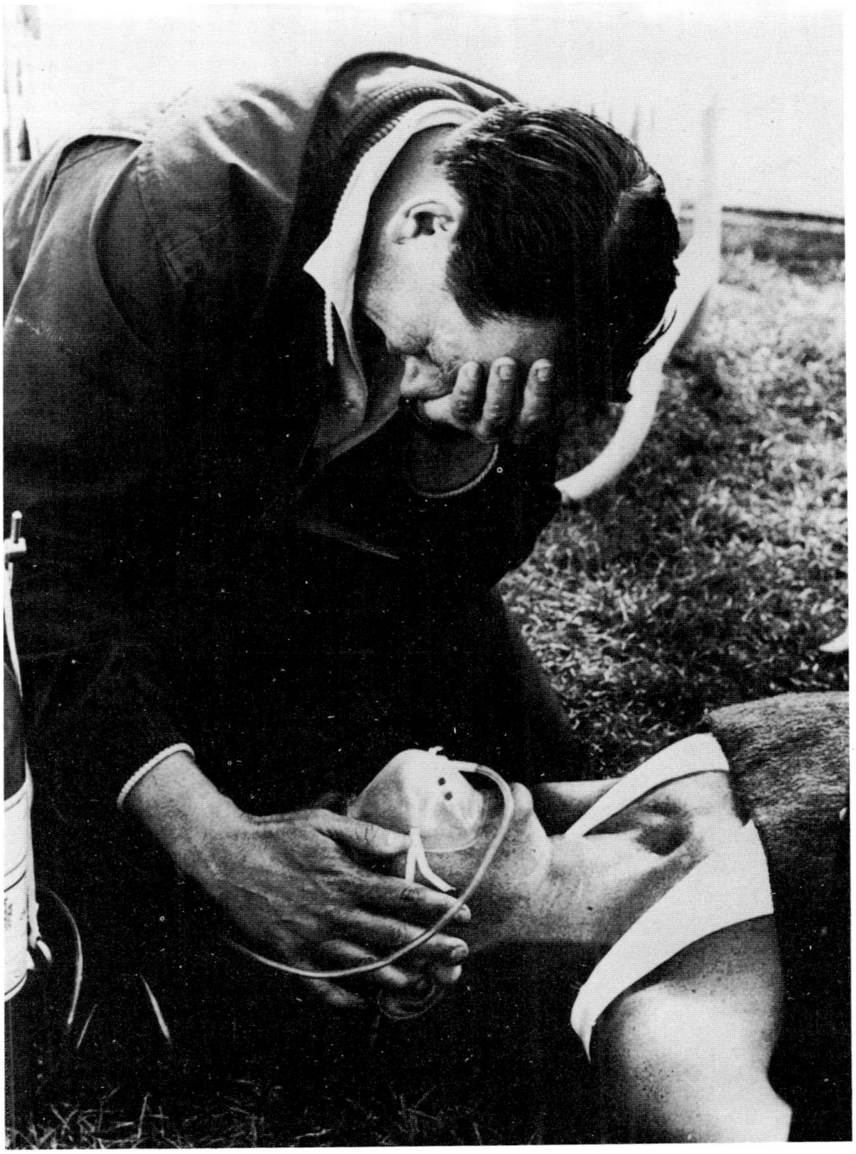

Dr Brian Corrigan weeps as he administers oxygen to Ron Clarke (Australia) after the latter had collapsed as he crossed the finish line in the men's 10,000 metres event. Clarke holder of the world record for the 10,000 metres, finished far behind the rest of the field, as, like many other competitors in endurance events, he was adversely affected by the high altitude.

Enriqueta Basilo, the first woman to light the Olympic Flame, runs up the ninety steps towards the bowl at the opening of the 1968 Games at Mexico City.

the same even though one of the firmest favourites, Catie Ball, holder of four world records, was well below her best in the 100-metres breaststroke and unable to start in the 200 metres, because of a virus infection. After all the preparation, the daily hours of slogging up and down a pool, such a handicap was a crushing event. In the 100-metres event it brought opportunity for Djurdjica Bjedov (Yugoslavia) who held off Galina Prosumenshchikova (USSR), winner of the 200-metres event in Tokyo. Miss Prosumenshchikova also lost her title; in the longer event she led at the halfway point and seemed safely on her way to victory when suddenly she faded and was overhauled by Sharon Wichman (United States) and Bjedov. Debbie Meyer (United States) won three gold medals, the 200 metres narrowly, the 400 metres comfortably and the 800 metres, a new event in the Games, by the massive margin of 11.7 sec.

The Olympics does not only call together the youth of the world as the equestrian event showed. Bill Steinkraus of the United States, in his forty-fourth year, rode Snowbound to victory in the individual jumping Grand Prix event. He had a clear first round (where there were fourteen obstacles) and had four faults in the second (six obstacles). The three-day event held at Avandro, 100 miles from Mexico City, produced another outstanding performance from a veteran rider. Derek Allhusen (Great Britain), who had previously competed in the 1948 Olympics in London, at fifty-four took the silver medal on Lochinvar, and led his team to victory. He also took the silver medal in the individual event and had a clear round in the final event, the show jumping. In the individual event Jean-Jacques Guyon won with 38.86 penalty points.

Mohammad Nassiri won Iran's first Olympic gold medal in weightlifting, with an Olympic record of 367.5 kg (810 lb) in the bantamweight division; after taking the silver medals in the three previous Olympics, Yugoslavia finally won the water-polo competition; in the boxing the Eastern Europeans were not quite so formidable as had been expected and George Foreman took a crucial step towards becoming world heavyweight boxing champion, when he won the gold medal.

In gymnastics, held in the magnificent arena with such a dull name, the Municipal Auditorium, its steeply tiered seats turning the audience into a choir which responded to every move on the floor or apparatus, Vera Čáslavská (Czechoslovakia) was the dominating figure. She added four gold medals to the three she won in Tokyo, which made Olympic history, and then, to ensure her place in the Movement's annals, she became, as far as anyone can tell, the first competitor to marry during the period of the Games. Miss Čáslavská went back to Prague as Mrs Odložil, the wife of the man who finished eighth in the athletics 1,500-metres final. Perhaps it was the excitement of approaching this new state of life which lifted Miss Čáslavská but she reached a new peak, winning the horse vault and asymmetrical bars, finishing joint first in the floor exercises and second on the beam. The Japanese men were stronger in gymnastics than in Tokyo, winning eleven individual medals.

There was not much of the Olympic spirit about the final of the Association Football Tournament. Hungary defeated Bulgaria, but three of the losing side and one Hungarian were sent off.

At Xochimilco there were also problems for the oarsmen and canoeists relating to the high altitude. It was particularly alarming for the oarsmen; if a runner feels unwell because of lack of oxygen he can slow down or drop out, but for the oarsman, in the middle of a crew, this is difficult and dangerous. He is likely to collide with the man in front or behind, incurring the risk of someone being pitched overboard. Sixteen men had to be resuscitated with oxygen during the Repêchage heats.

XX MUNICH 1972 John Rodda

An Olympiad is four years but what name should be given to the span from 6 May 1966 to 6 September 1972? At the beginning there was the elation of a city awarded the task of staging the Games; amid the potted azaleas of the Excelsior Hotel in Rome, Willi Daume, IOC member in Germany, and Karl Heinz Vogel, Mayor of Munich, spoke of their hopes, ambitions of a new vision for the Games. Six years later, on that September morning they joined thousands more in the Olympic stadium in a memorial to the eleven Israeli competitors and officials who died as a result of action by Palestinian terrorists.

The Olympic arena and its periphery has often been abused by

A remarkable contribution to Olympic history was made by New Zealand, in the eights.

cheats and charlatans, but this time the competitors' village was used for the very antithesis of the Olympic spirit by those who trespassed there to commit murder and blackmail.

To draw the blind on this horror and turn to contemplate the riches and successes of the Munich Olympics is difficult but before and after the bloodshed and mourning Munich saw rise many new Olympian peaks. The preparation of the city was one of luxury and lavishness, which had a counter-productive side since, with the news of the final bill of £300 million, others shrank from the idea of being host.

The main complex, with the village alongside the athletic stadium, swimming pool and several other arenas, was like a self-contained town. The steel masts thrusting into the air held a translucent canopy across the main stadium and pool and, as David Lacey, association football correspondent of the *Guardian*, wrote, 'gave the impression that here was a circus that would never leave town'.

Lasse Virén, a gangling Finnish policeman with a wispy beard, achieved a rare, and in the intense competition of modern athletics, an unexpected double victory on the track. He followed Hannes Kolehmainen (1912), Emil Zátopek (1952) and Vladimir Kuts (1956) in winning the 5,000 metres and 10,000 metres at one Games, and moreover, heats were required for the longer distance for the first time. In the final of the 10,000 metres Virén always stayed with the leading group but just before the halfway point Mohamed Gammoudi of Tunisia, running in front of him, fell and Virén went down. The Finn got up and, remarkably, shook off the jarring effect which such a fall brings; the rhythm and pace returned and in the final thrust across the last 600 metres he shook off Mariano Haro of Spain and then Emiel Puttemans of Belgium. Virén's enormous stride took him ahead and to the winning line in a faster time by one second than the world record of Ron Clarke (Australia).

To have won, after falling, and to have broken such a world record would have satisfied most champions, but the Finn steeled himself for the following day when he was to qualify for the 5,000-metres final. This contained a vastly experienced field and the weight of conjecture was that one of the fresh men, not someone who had gone through the mill of the 10,000 metres, would win. Virén, though, showed mental and physical depth by the nature of his running. He was, perhaps, fortunate that no one tried to burn off the opposition from the front with a fast pace, but he showed his tactical wit by ignoring some of the early half-hearted breaks but moving up when Steve Prefontaine (United States), the most competent front runner among the finalists, chose to break. This came with four laps remaining and Gammoudi, the titleholder, Ian Stewart (Great Britain) and Puttemans, were all in contention at the bell, when Virén began to make his effort; at that moment champions carry an aura about them and the inferiority becomes manifest in others. Along the final straight Virén was unchallenged; the Finnish flags dotted in the crowd acknowledged his feat and the resurgence of his country's distance running which spanned back to the first occasion when the Games were in Germany – in 1936; Finland had won both titles then.

Second-round handball match between Czechoslovakia and the USSR. Czechoslovakia eventually won the silver medal, Yugoslavia the gold.

The men's sprinting had something of a schoolboy magazine touch about it. Three Americans were lounging in one of the rooms at their quarters watching the afternoon athletics on television when suddenly the second round of the 100 metres, in which they were supposed to be taking part, began. They dashed to the stadium but only one arrived in time for his race. It was one of several American disasters at the Munich Games and it deprived the winner of the 100 and 200 metres, Valeri Borzov (USSR), of the credit those victories deserved. Borzov has been described as a man-made sprinter; it would be closer to accuracy to say that he is a natural athlete, highly intelligent, capable of understanding the technicalities of sprinting which take him closer to perfection.

The Americans were bruised again in the 1,500 metres, where Jim Ryun, the world-record holder, fell in his heat. In fact he should not have run in that particular race since his best time submitted by the American team management for seeding purposes was that of a mile, not 1,500 metres; that error took him into the same qualifying race as Kipchoge Keino, who beat him in the Mexico final.

Again the blue-and-white flag of Finland came out for the final as Pekka Vasala timed his attack superbly after Keino had tried to surprise the field with a burst, two laps from home. Although the Kenyan's legs were four years older than at Mexico he still managed to hold off all the young bloods with the exception of the Finn, who won in 3 min 36.3 sec, by half a second. In the 800 metres, the Americans were compensated for their mismanagement and ill fortune. Dave Wottle had tantalized the crowd in the heats, with his tactic of staying at the back of the field until late in the race and then swooping to victory. It was almost as much a distinguishing characteristic as the peaked golf cap he wore; that, and the fact that he and his bride chose Munich at Olympic time for their honeymoon, emphasized his casual attitude.

Wottle seemed to have overplayed his waiting game in the final when he was last and did not begin his attack until well inside the last 300 metres. There was a vast amount of running to be done to get to the front and Yevgeni Arzhanov (USSR) was moving powerfully and confidently in the lead. Wottle swept past the strung-out field, closed on the Russian but just did not have sufficient space between him and the finishing line to win, unless – and then in the last two strides Arzhanov was overtaken by disaster as he slipped and, in falling forward, lunged at the line as Wottle came up to him. The two waited in a vacuum of agony for the official verdict; Wottle won by three hundredths of a second.

Athletically Africa forged another breakthrough; running is a simple basic expression of athleticism, but the technical events of the sport offer another challenge. That was met and conquered by a man with a smile to match his enormous stride, John Akii-Bua from Uganda, whose technical perfection and power in the 400-metres hurdles not only took the gold medal, but broke David Hemery's world record, set in the 1968 Olympics in Mexico, with 47.82 sec.

The field events in the men's competition provided moments of drama and surprise. The unbroken run of American victories in the pole vault from 1896 was ended through the technical finesse of Wolfgang Nordwig, a slightly built East German, and with a controversy over the type of fibreglass pole permitted. Bob Seagren, the

Olga Korbut (USSR) winning over the crowd with her charm and expertise.

Mary Peters (Gt Britain) during the long jump event. She won a gold medal in the Pentathlon with a world record total of 4,801 pts.

American world-record holder and defending champion, was not allowed to use the type of pole he preferred and at the end of his competition thrust the one he was obliged to use into the hands of an athletic official; an incident which among other things showed how vital the sophistication of equipment is in the struggle.

For the first time since 1956 there was a new champion in the discus. Al Oerter was no longer in the American team and the runner-up to him in 1964 and bronze-medal winner in 1968, Ludvik Danek of Czechoslovakia, duly took over the mantle. But only after a harrowing competition. The Czech went into the circle for the final round lying in fifth position, but his last throw, 64.40 m (211 ft 3in) took him safely clear.

The javelin provided similar drama and joy for the hosts. Yanis Lusis, the Russian holder of the title, established his presence with two long early throws both beyond 88.40 m (290 ft); but Klaus Wolfermann got close to him in the fourth round and then, to a crescendo of roars, sent the spear 90.48 m (296 ft 10 in). Lusis responded magnificently but his next throw fell 2 cm (1 in) short of the German's.

The organization of athletics in the German Democratic Republic, a country of 17 million people, was well known before the Munich Games and their success in the women's section of the competition was evidence of it. From fourteen events the Germans took twelve medals, including six gold. The powerful limbs of Renate Stecher dominated the sprinting and the slim pale frame of Monika Zehrt provided similar output in both the 400 metres and the 4 × 400-metres relay. If the East Germans' efficient style was admired it was the response to inspiration which drew the greatest applause. Mary Peters, from the troubled city of Belfast in Northern Ireland, exuded joy through every event in the pentathlon, an expression that was quickly caught by the crowd and returned, forging the strongest rapport between competitor and spectator at the athletics. Miss Peters, with a kiss and a hug for everyone, when her two-day competition was over, won the gold medal with a world-record score of 4,801 points.

While for the home crowd there had been the anticipated victory in the long jump of Heide Rosendahl, one of the delights of the athletics came in the triumph of Ulrike Meyfarth, a sixteen-year-old schoolgirl, in the high jump. Miss Meyfarth, who is 1.93 m (6ft 4 in) tall, set a world record of 1.92 m (6 ft 3½ in) which was 11 cm (4½ in) higher than she had ever achieved before, with her flop style of jumping.

The Olympic swimming-pool water bubbled and frothed as thirty world and eighty-four Olympic records were broken or equalled. But out of the bath there was turmoil of a different kind. One winner was disqualified for taking drugs and there were accusations of competitors advertising equipment in the arena, specifically against Mark Spitz of the United States; an IOC investigation led to his exoneration. Spitz took his place in Olympic history by winning seven gold medals, a remarkable achievement but one which did prompt the suggestion (which has been made about gymnastics) that the swimming program might be reduced because of a similarity of events. Spitz won the 100-metres and 200-metres freestyle, the 100-metres and 200-metres butterfly, and helped the United States to win the 4×100-metres, 4×200-metres, and 4×100 metres medley relays; in all his finals a world record was set. The United States was the dominant swimming nation with seventeen gold medals from a possible twenty-nine while only four other nations, Australia, the German Democratic Republic, Japan and Sweden provided champions.

In the eight-day program there were many tense and rich moments, with one of them the victory in the 1,500-metres freestyle of Mike Burton (United States), who at twenty-five was, in swimming terms, a veteran. His superb judgment brought him through to first position with 300 metres remaining and he won in a world-record time of 15 min 52.58 sec, 46.3 sec faster than his winning time four years previously at the Games of Mexico City.

Roland Matthes (GDR) retained his two backstroke titles in a style that looked even more effortless than it was four years earlier. The men's 400-metres final brought a new dimension to this distance and a bitterness afterwards. At the halfway mark only seven-tenths of a second separated the eight finalists and Rick DeMont (USA), fourth at halfway, moved up to second and then began his final attack with 100 metres remaining. He swam that stretch in 58.22 sec, the fastest 100 metres of anyone in the final but Brad Cooper of Australia was with him until the final stroke. DeMont finished ahead of him by one-hundredth of a second but a dope test proved positive and the American was disqualified. He had taken ephedrine which was on the list of banned drugs, because, he said, of asthma. It was a decision which rankled and troubled those who took it because of the apparent lack of vigilance within the American team, but winning by such a narrow margin only stressed the enormity of any advantage which might be obtained.

Olympic history was made at the basketball hall. The United States, winner of every competition hitherto were beaten in the final three seconds by the USSR. There was confusion as the Americans took the lead for the first time in the match at 50–49 and an off-court horn sounded. Finally an FIBA delegate overruled the referee and ordered the final three seconds to be replayed. In that time the Russians hurled the ball from one end of the court to the other where Aleksandr Belov tipped it in for an astounding win. The Americans were so disgusted that they left Munich without accepting their silver medals.

Cuban power and artistry spanned fourteen full days of the boxing competition – with rarely a spare seat at any session. The crowds gave shrill vent to decisions with which they disagreed, but the overriding memory is of the Cubans skilfully punching their way to three gold medals out of the eleven to be won; altogether they had five men in the semi-finals and their outstanding champion was the heavyweight Teofilo Stevenson who won his title in less than six rounds of boxing.

The Indian subcontinent's long domination of the hockey was ended by the German Federal Republic. Although there were some exciting and wholesome contests in the early rounds (there were seventy matches altogether) the final provided another of Munich's stained memories. The Pakistan team did not take defeat in the final in the Olympic spirit and, after abuse of officials and assault of a doctor they turned the medal presentation into a mockery. The

Jim Ryun (United States) falls in a heat of the 1,500 metres with Billy Fordjour (Ghana). Vitus Ashaba (Uganda) is number 912.

912

Pekka Vasala (Finland) winning the 1,500 metres from Kipchoge Keino (Kenya).

International Hockey Federation (FIH) took swift action and the players involved were banned from any further Olympic competition. The German tactics throughout the final of close marking certainly taxed the patience of their opponents and spoiled the game from the spectators' point of view but brought the Germans the results they wanted for they completely suppressed the individual brilliance of the Pakistanis.

Archery returned to the Olympic program for the first time since 1920. At the Englischer Garten, with its sunshades and gay marquees, there was a gentle and easy atmosphere but there was no doubt about the quality of the sport. One of the youngest competitors, eighteen-year-old John Williams of the United States, won the men's event with a world-record score and established his supremacy by the end of the first day. The women's title was also won by an American, but Doreen Wilber was not such an overwhelming champion as her compatriot.

The British made Olympic history in the equestrian events, where they retained the team title in the three-day event, something not achieved since 1928, when the Netherlands won for the second time in Amsterdam. Britain too provided the individual winner of the three-day event, Richard Meade, riding Laurieston.

Those who are worried by the intensity of nationalistic aid and support towards winning the gold medals were delighted with the outcome of the major event in the rowing, the eights, where New Zealand's crew, who had to raise £20,000 towards their country's Olympic appeal, had a spirit and toughness that was sufficient to overcome the power of both Germanies and the USSR. The New Zealanders staggered their opponents with starting power, for by a quarter of the course they led by two seconds; attacks from behind came over the next 1,200 metres and were resisted, and finally the New Zealanders had power enough to be the fastest eight across the last 500 metres. Another New Zealand crew was involved in a titanic struggle and just lost; the coxless four looked shaped handsomely to take the gold with a solid lead as they reached the final 500 metres but then the crew from the German Democratic Republic, one which had been winning World and Olympic titles since 1966, began the long tantalizing process of overhauling which was accomplished in the last two, or at the most three strokes. That final 500 metres was a great Olympic occasion.

In the canoeing, a new, spectacular section was added, the slalom, which simulates wild water canoeing on mountain torrents. For this occasion, a special course was built at Augsburg and it proved a compelling attraction, with crowds of 30,000 watching. It was also another showpiece for the German Democratic Republic for they won every class. The IOC regarded it as an expensive extra and the racing was not included in the Montreal program.

Suddenly, amid the contests, the Games were brought to a juddering halt and suspended for twenty-four hours. In the early hours of 5 September, members of a Palestinian terrorist group climbed over the wire surrounding the village and broke into the quarters

Competitors line up with bows strung at the start of the women's archery contest. Archery returned to the Olympic scene for the first time in fifty-two years.

Kazimierz Deyna scores the winning goal for Poland against Hungary in the association football final.

of the Israeli team. One Israeli died in the initial attack and another ten were held hostage. Throughout the day there were demands and negotiations. Crowds gathered at the wire perimeter of the village to watch and glimpse the hooded figures; ice-cream and hot-dog vendors came to sustain them; television cameras were positioned so that the anguish of those immediately involved was shared by the hundred million. Finally, after fifteen hours, hostages and captors were hoisted by helicopter to a nearby airfield to be flown to the Middle East. But as the occupants of the helicopters alighted there was shooting, hand grenades were exploded and the helicopters were burned out. Altogether thirteen people died.

The following morning in the Olympic stadium a memorial service to the Israelis began with the Munich Opera House Orchestra playing Beethoven's *Egmont* Overture; in the afternoon sport was resumed. The horror and sadness remained to the end of the Games but with it also a burning in many breasts that, whatever happened, Coubertin's conception should be preserved.

XXI MONTREAL 1976 John Rodda

The Montreal Games were marred by financial extravagance that cost the taxpayers of the city and the State of Quebec dear; by the race to get the main facility, the athletic stadium, in working order in time for the opening by Her Majesty the Queen; and by the absence from that ceremony and the competitions which followed of twenty-two African countries, and Guyana for one political reason, and the Republic of China (Taiwan) for another. The African boycott, announced less than forty-eight hours before the Games were due to begin, came as a result of New Zealand's rugby tour of South Africa, while the athletes of the Republic of China were refused entry to Canada by Pierre Trudeau the Prime Minister, because his country did not recognize Taiwan. Eventually the tide of financial and political problems which threatened the Olympic Movement as dangerously as it had ever been threatened, receded. The sportsmen took their places in the various arenas and showed that the desire to win an Olympic title is unwavering among the youth of the world, and that never had there been a greater need for sophisticated electronic timing and measuring devices to determine placings in the many sports where just a part of a second or less than an inch separated winner and loser.

The main stadium was so immense it threatened to dwarf the competitors. Two men, however, stood out since they were so often there, demonstrating their excellence and winning two gold medals each. Lasse Virén of Finland achieved the unprecedented distinction of successfully defending the 5,000- and 10,000-metres titles while Alberto Juantorena of Cuba became the first man to win the 400 metres and 800 metres at one Games. Juantorena had already made an impact upon the one-lap event and was, by the beginning of the Games, the fastest man in the world over the distance in that year. His nine-foot stride was an enormous asset though it dislocated the

Jacek Wszola (Poland) clears the bar of his winning Olympic high jump, earning the gold medal.

Alberto Juantorena (Cuba), the first man to win the 400 metres and 800 metres at one Games.

smoothness of his running in the early stages of a race; he took a long time, sometimes as much as 50 metres to reach his natural gearing and by then he was out-of-step with the rest of the field. Yet the power of his running was overwhelming and in the final he won by two strides. Before that, however, Juantorena had demonstrated a new talent by winning the 800-metres title in the world-record time of 1 min 43.5 sec. Before reaching Montreal, the Cuban had raced on only four occasions over 800 metres, but a scientifically researched training programme in Cuba, generously supported by the German Democratic Republic, had shown Juantorena the full scope of his capability. Juantorena grasped the race from the outset and virtually ran the rest off their feet apart from Ivo Van

Edwin Moses (United States) winning the 400-metres hurdles.

574

Don Quarrie (Jamaica) winner of the 200 metres came second in the 100 metres to Hasely Crawford (Trinidad).

Bruce Jenner (United States) long time favourite for the decathlon.

Damme of Belgium who was to take the silver medal also in the 1,500 metres; tragically, Van Damme was killed in a car crash before the year's end.

Three athletes, Kolehmainen of Finland in 1912, Emil Zátopek of Czechoslovakia in 1952 and Vladimir Kuts of the Soviet Union in 1956, had previously won both the 5,000 and the 10,000 metres at one Olympic Games before Lasse Virén of Finland achieved it in 1972. That, coupled with the adulation which Paavo Nurmi received in Finland in the twenties and thirties, provided Virén with the incentive and motive to attempt a unique double. In the 10,000 metres his rivals seemed to make the task easier for a slow early pace – 14 min 8.9 sec for the first 5,000 metres – preserved Virén's finishing speed. By 8,000 metres only Virén and Carlos Lopez of Portugal were at the front and Virén's finishing lap, 51 sec, brought

John Walker (New Zealand) throwing his arms up in the air as he reached the finishing line of the 1,500 metres.

him a winning time of 27 min 40.4 sec, which was only two seconds slower than his world-record performance which had won him the gold medal four years previously. By the final of the 5,000 metres the tall, lean Finn was exercising a Svengali-like hold over his competitors. Virén really took charge of the race and although five men were about him as he went into the last lap none could match the strength and speed of his finish.

Having failed to hold their place in the sprints and the 400 metres, the Americans were to lose further prestige when they failed, for the first time since the Games of 1928, to take a medal in the 100 metres, an event which they have won twelve times. The victory here brought especial delight since it provided Trinidad and Tobago with their first Olympic champion Hasely Crawford, while Don Quarrie from Jamaica, at the other end of the Caribbean, who was second, then went on to win the 200 metres.

Standards in the 400-metres hurdles have risen dramatically. At Mexico in 1968, David Hemery improved the Olympic record by 1.2 sec to 48.1 sec, John Akii-Bua of Uganda clipped it back to 47.82 sec in Munich in 1972 and in Montreal a man who took up the event only twelve months before the Games, Edwin Moses of the US, won by over a second in 47.64 sec. The elation experienced by the spectators was dampened, as in the 1,500 metres final, with sadness that no African athlete was competing. In the hurdles event, Akii-Bua was missing; in the 1,500 metres, Filbert Bayi of Tanzania, the world-record holder, was missing, and thus unable to take part in the much talked about contest with John Walker of New Zealand, who won.

In the women's events only one of the gold medals was won by an athlete from outside Eastern Europe, and the GDR gathered nineteen

Miklos Nemeth (Hungary) launching the spear away to a world record. His father won the hammer title in 1948.

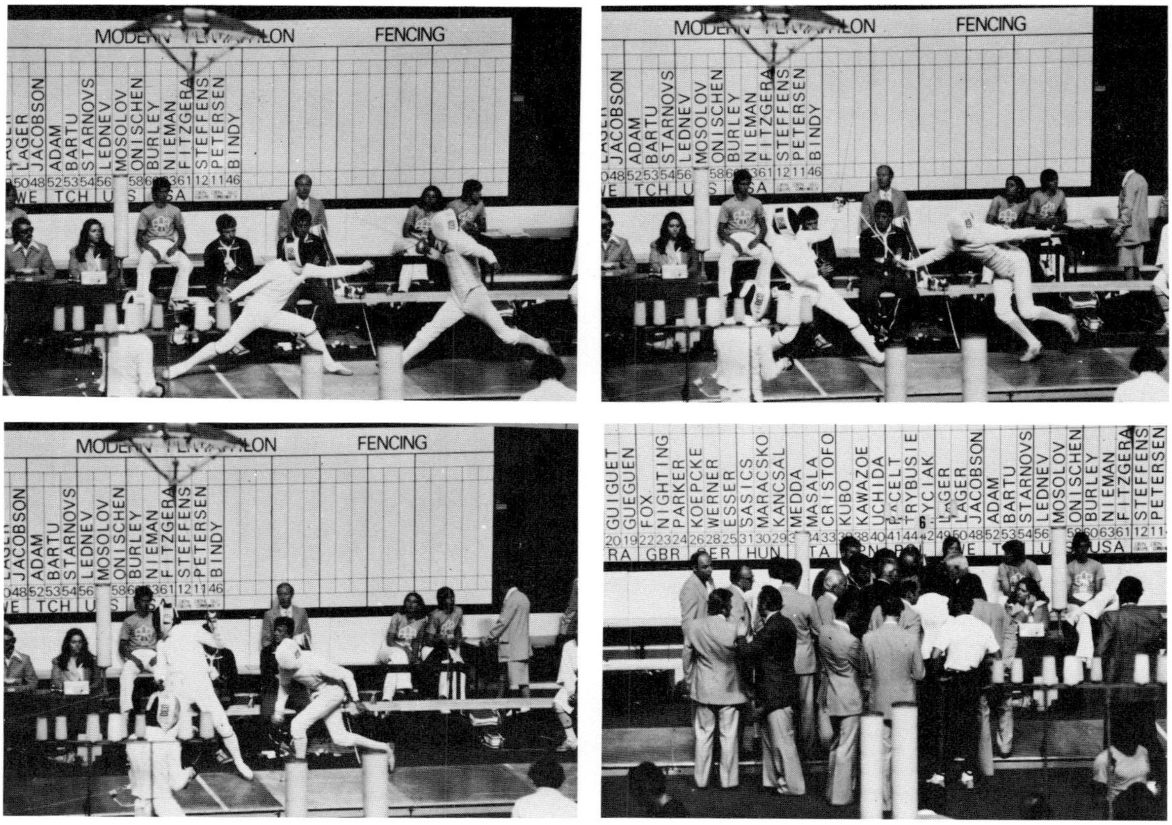

The Onischenko affair. Boris Onischenko (USSR) (on the left) taking part in the fencing event of the modern pentathlon. It was discovered that his weapon had been rigged to complete the circuit to the scoring light when no hit was in fact registered. He was disqualified.

medals in all. There were some sparkling new young faces but those who recall earlier Olympics warmed to the victory in the 400 metres of thirty-year-old Irena Szewińska of Poland. She became the first woman to win medals at four Games. In the 800 metres, four girls broke the existing world record and the winner, Tatyana Kazankina, then went on to take the 1,500 metres title as well. Annegret Richter, of West Germany, stood up for the rest of the world, winning the 100 metres, breaking the world record in her semi-final and taking the silver medal in the 200 metres and the short relay.

The most tantalizing event though was the pentathlon where three women finished within five points. Everything depended upon the final event, the 200 metres, and Sigrum Siegel and Christine Laser finished with the same number of points, 4,745; but Miss Siegel took the gold medal because she was placed ahead of Miss Laser in more of the five events.

In the field events, Viktor Saneev won the triple jump for the third time, joining John Flanagan in the hammer (1900 to 1908) and Al Oerter in the discus (1956 to 1968) to have won this number of field events; the Soviet champion hopes to maintain his form to win in Moscow and so equal Oerter's record of four wins. The winner of the javelin stirred some memories. Miklos Németh of Hungary launched the spear away to a world record, 94.58 m (310 ft $3\frac{3}{4}$ in), with his first throw, sufficient to join his father Imre, winner of the hammer title in 1948, amongst Olympic Champions.

The United States was edged aside in two events where it has a strong tradition, the high jump and pole vault. In Munich they lost the latter event for the first time in the history of the Games, and in Montreal they were pushed back into the bronze medal position. After seven hours of competition, much of it in the rain, three men had cleared 5.50 m (18 ft 0½ in), the Olympic record, but it was a competition of untypical results with men passing heights they would not normally tackle as others gathered failures which count if the ultimate height is cleared by more than one person. In the end it was Poland's Tadeuss Slusarski's record of higher earlier jumps which gave him the victory. The wet conditions almost certainly deprived Dwight Stones, the world-record holder, of a gold medal in the high jump. He was unable to use his fast approach and finished third. The crowd, however, was riveted by the jumping of Greg Joy of Canada, who, on the final day of the athletics, held the last chance of bringing his country a gold medal. It was not to be, for the man who mastered the conditions was a nineteen-year-old Pole, Jacek Wszola, who cleared 2.25 m (7 ft 4$\frac{9}{16}$ in). Three days afterwards Stones went to Philadelphia and in dry conditions broke his own world record with a leap of 2.32 m (7 ft 7⅜ in).

The decathlon, always the scene of terrible disappointments and errors that seem magnified out of all proportion in the final accounting, produced a blissful winner in Bruce Jenner of the US, a long-time favourite to win who fulfilled all expectations. In the first five of the ten events he achieved personal best marks and on the second day was always in command. Yet he never let up and ran the 1,500 metres, the final test, in 4 min 12.61 sec to finish with a world-record score of 8,618 points.

The withdrawal of the African nations was no more felt than in the boxing arena where an original entry of 370 was reduced by 90 and brought some thin sessions in the preliminary rounds. In the end, however, there was a handsome American revival with the United States taking five of the eleven titles plus a silver and bronze medal. There were some inconsistencies in the judging with the classic style of boxing nurtured in Europe not perhaps receiving the rewards it deserved. The outstanding American was Leon Spinks who was, in 1978, to go on to win the world heavyweight title from Muhammed Ali. At Montreal Spinks was in the light heavyweight division. In the final he faced a man of considerable reputation for his heavy hitting, Sixto Ssoria of Cuba, but in a grimly hard contest Spinks pounded the Cuban to defeat in the third round. Certainly it seemed that the American had been inspired by the bout immediately before his own, when his brother Michael became the middleweight title holder by defeating Rufat Riskiev of the Soviet Union. Teofilo Stevenson of Cuba, the defending heavyweight champion, thundered onwards, but in the final he faced a Romanian Mircea Simon bent upon caution and self-preservation which, admirable in the normal context of amateur boxing, was so exaggerated as to produce something of a stalemate of a contest.

The swimming events crystallized almost to a contest between the United States and the German Democratic Republic and, so far as the gold medals were concerned, only three other countries, Britain, USSR and, in a diving event, Italy, intervened. The argument which some IOC members put forward several years ago that some swimming events are a duplication seemed to be borne out. Four of the finalists in the men's 100-metres freestyle reached a similar position in the 200 metres; three from the 400-metres final were in the 1,500-metres last round; half the backstroke finalists over 100 metres also reached the 200-metres event while in the breaststroke there were five 'doubles'! No one made the sort of impact which Mark Spitz (US) winning seven medals in Munich achieved, but Kornelia Ender (GDR) took four golds and her team eleven out of thirteen. The American men, however, won all but the 200 metres breaststroke where David Wilkie of Britain was successful and even there the Americans must take some credit since Wilkie had trained and competed in the United States for several years. John Naber, with five medals including four gold, was the most successful of the Americans. Altogether twenty-two world records were broken, but in most instances the new figures merely replaced those set in various national trials just before the Games.

After their dramatic defeat in the final seconds of the Olympic basketball tournament in Munich by the USSR, the Americans went to Montreal determined to regain their place as leaders in this sport. The countries were seeded apart, but ultimately this gladiatorial encounter did not materialize for in the semi-final stage Yugoslavia, who had during the previous four years built up a considerable reputation, overcame the Soviet Union; their defeat was one of the most compelling matches of the tournament, with the Yugoslavs ahead by 15 points early on, the scores level at half time, and Yugoslavia winning 89/84 and thus qualifying for the final. Here the Yugoslavs were unable to raise their game to the pitch of the semi-final for the Americans were always in control, winning 95/74.

Montreal's cycling stadium must rank among the most beautiful Olympic buildings; whereas in the past the Olympic cycle program has not always drawn large crowds, in Montreal every seat was taken even for the preliminary rounds. In the sprint Daniel Morelon of France won his third gold medal in the event, but not before losing his first race in the final to Anton Tkac of Czechoslovakia. West Germany provided the best pursuitor, Gregor Braun, twenty, taking the individual event while in the team event he was one of the quartet which beat its rivals by considerable margins in every round and achieved the fastest time, 4 min 20.10 sec, in overcoming Czechoslovakia in the quarter-final.

There was something of a Western revival in fencing although the main spoils went to the Soviet Union.

There has been for some years disquiet about the Olympic soccer tournament and its relation with the professional World Cup. In the final at Montreal, sixteen of the players from Poland and the German Democratic Republic had taken part in the World Cup Finals at Munich two years previously. The imbalance created by some countries having a specific dividing line between amateurs and professionals while some have no professional football and, in the case of Eastern Europe, no professional sport, undoubtedly makes a nonsense of the tournament. Set against that, however, was the quality of the final game before the largest crowd of any of the events, over 71,000, which the East Germans won 3–1.

Japan only just maintained a supremacy in judo, largely because of the success of the Soviet Union and the fact that the world is fast acquiring the skills which seemed once firmly held in the Far

East home of the sport.

In shooting, some Olympic history was made. Margaret Murdock (US) became the first woman to win a medal in this sport. She took the silver in the small-bore rifle achieving the same score as the winner Larry Basham, but losing first place on a count back; Basham in fact asked the IOC to award two gold medals, to which they agreed, but this is against the International Shooting Union's rules.

In the Olympic track event Paul Cerutti of Monaco who finished near the end of the field was discovered to have taken amphetamines and was disqualified.

The gymnastics competitions were dominated by the Eastern European countries and Japan. The USSR took the women's team title for the seventh successive Games while Japan maintained their unbeaten record in men's championships at Olympic and world level which now goes back to 1960. Nadia Comaneci, of Romania, followed Olga Korbut as the star attraction of the nightly gymnastic sessions in The Forum where every one of the 1,600 seats was taken, while around the world people wondered at the grace and confidence which she displayed. She achieved a maximum score of ten points for the first time in the history of the Games and she achieved the maximum no less than six times, winning the combined title, the asymmetrical bars and the beam. Her counterpart in the men's events was Nikolai Andrianov who took four individual gold medals to add to the one he took in 1972.

The modern pentathlon championship is remembered for some phenomenal running by the British team which took them, in the final event, from fifth to the gold medal placing and for the Onischenko affair. The Soviet competitor Boris Onischenko was an international competitor of long standing but he was dismissed from the competition in ignominy when it was discovered that his faulty épée – the indicator light was flashing before the weapon touched the opponent – was not faulty but had been tampered with. Onischenko was disqualified and went home immediately and the Soviet team, with two men in the first eight, was eliminated.

Birger Ruud (Norway) outstanding Olympic Champion in ski jumping seen here in 1932.

LAKE PLACID 1980

THE CAMPAIGN TO BOYCOTT THE GAMES
John Rodda

The International Olympic Committee's session before the opening of the Winter Games, was, in the words of the President Lord Killanin, the most crucial since the first one in 1894. The United States Government led the campaign to remove, cancel, or boycott the Moscow Olympic Games and brought pressure to bear on their own Olympic Committee and tried to influence other Governments.

For six days, the Lake Placid Resort Hotel, a rambling building which was formerly a private club, provided the focal point not only of the Olympic movement but unhappily, the division which exists in the world. The Soviet intervention in Afghanistan was threatening the very life blood of the Olympic Movement.

Robert Kane, the president of the US Olympic Committee pleaded a case before the IOC for moving the Games from Moscow. But it was a case that was so obviously presented in the terms of the US State Department that most of the seventy members present listened in quiet sympathy for a man torn between his allegiance to the Olympic Movement and the demands of his Head of State.

Political interference in Olympic matters however reached its worst form when Cyrus Vance, Secretary at the US State Department stepped up to pronounce the opening of the Session. This is an occasion for Olympic words, music and hymns, with protocol being observed. Vance cast these cherished traditions brutally aside and delivered a political harangue about the boycott. Only three or four of the IOC members applauded the speech and for some it was a great strain to remain in their seats.

If the IOC members who then went in to debate the question needed a point of polarisation this was it. Their very foundation was being attacked. After two days in which over half the members present spoke on the question, they announced that the Games would go on in Moscow. It must have been difficult for some of them, particularly the two US members, Douglas Roby and Julian Roosevelt who had both bravely spoken out against political interference. The unanimity of the IOC position was gained by subtle strategy. They did not vote on or support a resolution, but in supporting a long statement by the President who set out the athletes' obligations to the Moscow Organizing Committee, the IOC showed their sensitivity to events beyond their control. If people in some parts of the world were slightly bewildered at what the IOC had done, they also came to understand its independence and the value of that independence. But the United States was unshaken in its resolve to stop the Games in Moscow.

INTRODUCTION John Samuel of *The Guardian*

Lake Placid was awarded the thirteenth Winter Games at the International Olympic Committee's Vienna congress in November 1974 when, at the same time, Moscow was awarded the Summer Games in preference to Los Angeles. Lake Placid, having badgered away without success since 1962, was the only bidder for the Winter Games.

Lake Placid had previously hosted a successful Games in 1932 on a budget of $1.1 million. This time it promised a simple 'no frills' Games, in the same spirit as 1932 but on a budget of $80 million. Many facilities had to be renovated and some new ones had to be installed since, in 1932, there had been no Alpine races and only 330 athletes from 17 nations had competed. At that time, the Winter Olympics were essentially games for a minority of strictly amateur sportsmen.

The sports on the 1932 program included speed and figure skating, ice-hockey, Nordic skiing and bobsleigh, with the introduction of the two-man as well as the four-man bob. In 1980, Lake Placid had to provide for 1,400 athletes from 37 countries. This time there were eight sports, with biathlon and luge in addition to the Alpine skiing which was introduced in 1936. Lake Placid was also required to provide for the 'Olympic family' of over 6,000 comprising athletes, coaches, officials, organizers and media. Thus a town whose population had decreased over five decades from 2,930 to 2,731 had to provide for up to three times that number within its confines, and another 35,000 people commuting to events from a variety of towns and villages in upper New York State. That was not all. A huge, invisible public, fed by a media host outnumbering the athletes, waited avidly for every scrap of news.

The Games of 1980 were to be watched by 500 million people on television all over the world, with at least as many more following the action in their newspapers and magazines. Yet the 'north country boys' who had instituted the bid still thought the village idea a valid one. The Reverend J. Bernard Fell, subsequently the executive director of the organizing committee, said, 'We want to keep it all in perspective; after all, they are just games.' However, to top European Alpine skiers, the Olympic Games are not just games, they are part of a commitment which can set them up for life.

Lake Placid's own attitudes were also not unaffected by commercial possibilities. Part of the community wanted to preserve its quiet ways, another understandably wished to see the town benefit from the business the Games would bring. The former ski jumper, Art Devlin, a strong Olympic advocate, told the *Washington Post*, 'We have to make a living. Our livelihood comes from six weeks a year (the summer tourist season). Our only hope of upgrading the community and not putting smokestacks up or cutting down the trees was the Olympics. The Olympics are something clean and pure. Sport is the only way to put us back on the map. We were dying, badly.'

The Lake Placid organizers, in the event, could not prevent a certain amount of chaos and confusion. The Games relied wholly on a bus system in a cordoned off area, yet at one point all the buses were operating on one phone and no more than 30 of the 300 buses needed were actually running.

Occasionally, competitors suffered, but not often. They were given priority from the outset. Fears about the Olympic village were groundless. It was a place of colour and good atmosphere. However, the failure to cope adequately with the spectators and the press was a great disappointment, and if the weather had ever turned truly hard, the consequences would have been disastrous, as the State appreciated in taking emergency measures during the first week. A special task force worked seventy-two hours almost without sleep to get the buses running properly. By the second week, everyone could concentrate on the competition and there were many brilliant and moving moments: Tikhonov, the Russian biathlete, member of four gold-medal-winning teams, being thrown in the air for joy by his team mates; the hug a victorious American ice-hockey player gave one of the disconsolate Russians; the delight of the British with Robin Cousins' gold medal and the widely expressed commiseration with Jan Hoffmann of the German Democratic Republic, who skated the program of his life but failed by a fraction. . . .

Competitors from the German Democratic Republic, with strong motivation, maximum utilization of training facilities and a scientific approach, showed that, although they came from a country with little snow, they could win more medals than competitors from a country with no shortage of snow such as the Soviet Union.

If the Olympic movement survives the many perils of the modern world, the thirteenth Winter Games of Lake Placid will have made a powerful contribution.

LAKE PLACID DIARY

Lord Killanin and Reverend J. Bernard Fell at the opening ceremony

Wednesday 13 February

Teams from thirty-seven countries marched into the Lake Placid High School arena, two miles from the village, dressed for weather which might vary from pouring rain to 20° below freezing. The one absent country was Taiwan; the Chinese Taipeh Olympic Committee, having lost actions in the New York courts against the Lake Placid Organizing Committee, withdrew from the Games. It wished to compete as 'the Republic of China' and use the old national flag and anthem. 'The Republic of China' is no longer recognized by the United States Government or the United Nations organization as a political entity. The IOC had requested a non-political flag and anthem. Therefore, the President of the IOC proposed that this team compete under the Olympic flag and anthem in order that all Chinese compete together but the Taipeh Olympic Committee declined to do so.

The People's Republic of China was represented for the first time and was cordially received by a crowd of about 24,000, many of whom short-circuited the transport problems by walking to the arena. In spite of the political situation, the large USSR team was received in the same spirit as the others. The crowd demonstrated the most vociferous support (the US team excepted) for the Canadian contingent.

The Reverend J. Bernard Fell introduced Lord Killanin, President of the IOC and the US Vice-President, Walter H. Mondale, who

Charles Morgan Kerr (United States) lighting the Olympic Flame

formally opened the Games. The Olympic Hymn was followed by the presentation of the Winter Games flag by the Mayor of Innsbruck, Dr Alois Lugger, to the Mayor of Lake Placid, the Honorable Robert Peacock. After a skating exhibition, the Olympic torch was borne into the arena by Charles Morgan Kerr on the last stage of its journey from Greece.

The Olympic oath on behalf of the athletes was taken by the twenty-one-year-old speed skater, Eric Heiden, an apt choice in view of his achievements. Terry McDermott, who won the 500-metre speed skating gold medal in 1964, took the oath on behalf of the officials.

It was a quietly impressive ceremony. Overcast skies prevented the most spectacular act, the skywriting of the Olympic rings and an 'I love New York' message in letters 1,000 feet tall. But helium balloons scattered millions of flowers, and thousands of homing pigeons were released; in all, there was plenty of spectacle. The only regret was the first major failure of the bus system, so that many spectators had to walk back, while others from more distant places had to wait hours before their buses could be located. The traffic snarled up into an almost immovable jam.

Thursday 14 February

On the first full day of competition, the first gold went to the USSR in the 30-kilometre cross-country at Mount Van Hoevenberg, followed quickly and less predictably by the Austrian triumph in the men's downhill at Whiteface Mountain and the Dutch triumph in the women's 1,500-metre speed skating.

It was merely one of the seemingly endless confusions that marked the start of the Games that the winner of the 30-kilometres cross-country, Nikolai Zimyatov, and his fellow Russian silver medallist, Vasili Rochev, were fast asleep in the village when they should have been attending the medals ceremony that evening in the auditorium off Main Street on the frozen Mirror Lake. Somehow, the Russians were not informed of the arrangements! The IOC member who should have been making the medal presentations failed to show up because of transport difficulties and when Lord Killanin substituted for him at the last moment, the silver medal he was presenting to the Austrian downhiller, Peter Wirnsberger, slipped from its case as an official was offering it, and had to be retrieved from the snow. There were no flags raised because the poles were too big for the holes drilled in the ice, and in any case they had arrived without halyards!

Lake Placid, which had been almost devoid of snow before the Games, perversely received six to eight inches of snow the first day of the Games proper. This added a further strain on the resources of the already hard-pressed organizers. The two-man bobsleigh event had to be stopped after every five runs for the course to be cleared of snow, and the transport of competitors, officials and media people was further impeded.

All the same, there was some outstanding and extraordinary sport. Leonhard Stock, a twenty-one-year-old reserve downhiller, produced such fast times in training that Austria's chief coach, Karl Kahr, had to reverse an earlier decision and include him in the

Leonhard Stock (Austria) who had come to Lake Placid only as a reserve, won his first gold in a major downhill event

team. This must have upset the four who thought they were already chosen – Werner Grissman, Peter Wirnsberger, Harti Weirather and Sepp Walcher. In the end, the Austrians dropped their world champion, Sepp Walcher, having earlier eliminated the 1976 Olympic champion, Franz Klammer. Stock made it all worthwhile when he won in outstanding style, taking the bumpy turns of the first quarter quicker and better than anyone thanks to his giant slalom turning skills, and maintaining his speed on the steep quarter and the so-called 'flats' that make up the last half of the course. His 1 min 45.50 sec for the course of 3,009 metres gave him a clear margin over Wirnsberger.

The first women's gold medal was won by Annie Borckink, a twenty-eight-year-old nurse from Eibergen, Holland. The previous summer Borckink had suffered an injury which had made her consider retirement but she eventually decided to compete for one more season and this was her first international win. Both she and the silver medallist, Ria Visser, an eighteen-year-old also from Holland, turned in times well above their personal bests.

The cheer of the day, and one that seemed to re-echo all over Lake Placid, so desperate were Americans for good news, was the USA's 7–3 ice-hockey victory over Czechoslovakia, the former world champions and favourites for the silver medal. Instantly, American sports buffs recalled their last Olympic triumph, at Squaw Valley in 1960, when defeat of the Czechs by 9–4 gave them their last ice-hockey gold medal.

Friday 15 February

This was the day Eric Heiden, America's supreme favourite for the gold, began his speed skating assault on all five titles – the 500, 5,000, 1,000, 1,500 and 10,000 in that order. He could have been paired with any one of the thirty-six other speed skaters in the 500 metres. He drew Evgeni Kulikov of the USSR, world record holder over the distance and gold medallist at Innsbruck four years previously. The 500 was potentially Heiden's weak race and he had been beaten only a few days before by a fellow American in the world sprint championships. It is a distance that admits no slip, but it was the thirty-year-old and not the twenty-one-year-old, who made the mistake. At 100 metres, with the gold-suited Heiden lagging slightly, Kulikov half stumbled, his right arm dropping almost to the ice as he steadied himself. Heiden eased ahead, Kulikov fought back in the second straight but Heiden came off the final bend like the breeze to win in 38.03 sec with Kulikov a mere sliver of time – thirty-four hundredths of a second – behind.

In the women's 500 metres, Karin Enke from the German Democratic Republic, a figure skater turned to speed skating, set a new Olympic mark with 41.78 sec, forty-two hundredths of a second behind Leah Mueller of Dousman, Wisconsin.

Speed skating, outside the Olympic Games, is a minority among minority sports in the United States. There is only one other outdoor rink in the country, at West Allis, Wisconsin, set among industrialized stacks but now providing America with outstanding heroes and heroines. As *The New York Times* remarked, 'Heiden is to ice what Mark Spitz was to chlorinated water.'

Heiden's exploits in the speed skating rink took place in the shadow of the futuristic arena, home of the figure skating and ice-hockey. 'Good luck Tai and Randy', streamed on a banner across the full width of a hotel balcony facing the arena. It was to seem sadly ironic by nightfall.

Rumours that Randy Gardner had a leg strain had begun to circulate among a few American pressmen before the short program. Gardner acknowledged that he had some discomfort, 'but I'll be all right'. With Tai Babilonia, he represented America's pair skating challenge in the most dramatized of all Russian-American confrontations. Would Irina Rodnina and Aleksandr Zaitseve, absent last year because Rodnina was having a baby, re-assume world domination over the Americans who took the world championship in 1979 in their absence? But for this, Irina, had been world and/or Olympic champion every year since 1969 in an unparalleled career, first with Aleksei Ulanov, now with Zaitseve.

As the Americans took to the ice in their stylish maroon outfits, the arena erupted. In the milling around of the warm-up with three other pairs, Gardner suddenly fell. Then he fell a second time. The crowd went silent. Gardner came back again, failed to complete a sitspin and, after a few words with coach, John Nicks, and US team manager, Paul George, left the ice. George walked clumsily across the ice to inform the German Federal Republic's referee, Hermann Schiechtl, of the US pair's withdrawal from the 1980 Olympics.

Team physician, Tony Daly, explained later that Gardner had pulled a groin muscle two weeks before, and the injury had slowly improved. However, two days before the competition, Gardner injured a hip flexor muscle in practice and, in spite of treatment, the injury had not improved as had been hoped. Regardless of the danger to herself, Babilonia had continued to support Gardner's attempts to go through with the competition. Babilonia was in tears as she ran down the ramp off the ice. 'She felt she had let everyone down,' said Nicks. 'Me as coach and everyone who supported her. She couldn't understand that she hadn't let anyone down. Randy's mood was one of resignation. He had to realize in the back of his mind he had serious problems.'

The short program went on. Russian pairs took the first three places with Rodnina and Zaitseve leading fairly comfortably, but the competition was now sadly depleted.

Out on the biathlon trails of Mount Van Hoevenberg, the USSR took the second cross-country event, the women's 5 kilometres. Raisa Smetanina, a twenty-seven-year-old school teacher, although five seconds behind the time of the Finnish woman, Hilkka Riihivuori, at the halfway mark, made up ten seconds to win her third Olympic gold medal.

Saturday 16 February

Eric Heiden took the 5,000 metres on the second leg of his journey into speed skating history, and American sporting legend. To do this, he had to beat the world record holder, Kai Arne Stenshjemmet. The Norwegian pushed him hard, but tired over the last two laps. 'I think I used my arms too soon, in the last but one lap instead of the final one and it tired me too soon,' he said. Heiden, pressed to say whether he would like to win five golds like Mark Spitz, told newspapermen, 'It just goes in one ear and out the other. In the 1,000 metres I have a chance to do really well. As I've said all along, the 10,000 metres is pretty much up in the air because we haven't had any competition in it.'

On the bob run, Eric Schaerer of Switzerland, world two-man champion for two years, made amends for Innsbruck in 1976 where he won a silver and bronze by taking the two-man gold on the Mount Van Hoevenberg track. Schaerer broke the course record with his 1 min 1.87 sec first run. He showed supreme judgment of line, much helped at the start by the shove of Josef Benz. They made a contrasting pair, Schaerer a wealthy estate broker, and Benz a postman, but together they certainly delivered.

The 20-kilometre biathlon went for the third successive Olympics to the USSR. Anatoli Aljabiev, from Leningrad, a lieutenant in the Russian army, was the only competitor to show perfect marksmanship in the twenty shots over the four ranges interspersing the cross-country running. In biathlon, as one American competitor put it, 'you have to run like a rabbit then turn into stone for the shoot.' Penalty minutes are added to the cross-country running time for every miss (one minute if it is an inner rather than a bull, two minutes for a complete miss). Aljabiev, who won the pre-Olympics in 1979, kept up a medium tempo to his running to ensure an accurate shoot. Frank Ullrich of the German Democratic Republic ran faster by 2 min 49 sec but his three penalty points cost him the gold. With Eberhard Rosch, also of the German Democratic Republic, coming third, it was the first time in Olympic history that there was no Scandinavian in the first three places.

Italy's chance of breaking the German Democratic Republic's grip on the Olympic luge ended sadly for the leader going into the final run, Ernst Haspinger. The Italian held a half-second lead over Bernhard Glass and needed only a moderate run to win. But, three-quarters of the way down the 1,000 metre course, he ran too high and slid off his luge. He banged his fists on the ice in anger as he slid to a stop, and walked away in tears. Twenty-two-year-old Glass from Oberhof in the German Democratic Republic made the best run of the day, 43.48 sec, to win the gold.

Vera Zozlulia took the USSR's first gold medal in the Olympic luge with an outstanding final run of 39.12 sec. Zozlulia, the 1978 world champion, set a course record of 38.97 sec in the opening heat and never relinquished her lead.

Annemarie Moser-Pröll (Austria), in the downhill event, on her way to a gold medal

Sunday 17 February

The greatest woman skier of her decade, Annemarie Moser-Pröll of Austria, finally achieved the accolade of an Olympic gold medal when she won the downhill on Whiteface Mountain. On a sunny, bitterly cold day, with the temperature minus 26° at the top, Mrs Moser vanquished her great rivals, Hanni Wenzel of Liechtenstein and Marie Thérèse Nadig of Switzerland, respectively silver and bronze medallists, with a time of 1 min 37.52 sec which shattered the course record. The wind scoured the new snow and so polished the piste that Mrs Moser's superb gliding technique, and skill with the turns at the top, came fully into play.

Marie Thérèse Nadig (Switzerland) came third after a very hard contest in the downhill event

Irina Rodnina and Aleksandr Zaitseve (USSR) going out in style. This was their last season

Injuries while training upset her plans for the season and, of the seven World Cup downhills prior to the Olympics, Miss Nadig had won six and Mrs Moser only one. The Olympics, then, became her special target; but how far, people wondered, had winning become a habit for Miss Nadig? Did she have some kind of jinx on the Austrian girl, having deprived her of the gold in both the downhill and giant slalom at Sapporo?

Miss Nadig missed Innsbruck in 1976 because of flu and Mrs Moser because she was tending her dying father. Indeed it was assumed she had retired after an absence of twenty months, but the lure of racing drew her back.

Now at twenty-six, Mrs Moser beat her twenty-five-year-old rival and an extraordinary record was achieved. It was her thirty-fourth victory in sixty-four downhill races. Eleven other times she had come second or third. In all she had won fifty-one major races.

Out on the cross-country trails there was more drama. Juha Mieto, the 1.9 m (6 ft 5 in) Finnish giant, waited, khaki army blanket over his shoulders, as Thomas Wassberg of Sweden, starting four and a half minutes after him in the 15-kilometre cross-country, poled furiously for the finish line. In 1972, Mieto had missed the bronze by six hundredth of a second. Now the twenty-three-year-old Swede was across the line and taking the gold from him by the narrowest ever Nordic ski margin – one hundredth of a second. 'If I were giving out medals, I'd take a gold one for myself and ask for another one for Juha', he remarked.

The injury that meant the withdrawal of world champions, Tai Babilonia and Randy Gardner from the pair skating eased the path of Irina Rodnina and Aleksandr Zaitseve of the USSR, who won their second consecutive Olympic gold. They finished with 147.26 points and received no mark under 5.8 in the five-minute free skating which accounted for seventy-five per cent of the marks. There was one shout of 'Go home', quickly followed by a gasp and booing, but there were no further incidents. The Russian couple were not quite at their best, and Rodnina looked tired at the finish, but they were worthy champions.

Monday 18 February

The major news of Monday was the arrival of buses in regular and reliable numbers. The State, with the help of experts, took over the running of the system so as not to leave crowds at risk in freezing conditions. A change in the weather helped. Temperatures reached 24° and 375 buses, generally kept waiting to a minimum, though there were still pockets of trouble. The US army put in nine extra warming tents to make seventeen in all at the competition sites.

It was a relatively quiet day. Ulrich Wehling of the German Democratic Republic, seeking his third gold, took a formidable lead in the 70-metre jumping section of the Nordic combined and Ingemar Stenmark of Sweden lay handily in third place in the first leg of the giant slalom. In the women's 10 kilometres, twenty-four-year-old medical student, Barbara Petzold, took the German Democratic Republic's first gold in the cross-country. The failure of the Russian women to reach the first three places set a precedent of another kind.

Ingemar Stenmark (Sweden) racing to victory in the giant slalom

Andreas Wenzel winning a second silver for Liechtenstein

Tuesday 19 February

This was the day when three of the bankers for gold medals succeeded. Ingemar Stenmark in the giant slalom, Ulrich Wehling in the combined 70-metre ski jump and 15-kilometre cross-country running, and Eric Heiden in the 1,000-metres speed skating finished on the winners' podium against all the pressures of favouritism.

For Heiden it was becoming something of a habit after his successes in the 500 and 5,000 metres. This time he started first with Gaston Boucher of Canada, and towed him into a silver medal. His own time was 1 min 15.18 sec, one and a half seconds faster than the Canadian, and was never caught by the field of forty-one.

Stenmark, starting behind Andreas Wenzel of Liechtenstein and Hans Enn of Austria in the second leg of the giant slalom, produced one of his famous late charges to win handsomely by over half a second. Wenzel, at twenty-one two years his junior, took an Olympic silver to follow his world championship silver two years before. Enn was third.

The Swede's reputation as a solitary man is based on his shy, almost deerlike presence. His home village of Tärnaby, not far below the Arctic circle, has 700 inhabitants. It is unique for a world champion of such eminence to come from such a surrounding, with none of the competitive pressures of an Alpine country like Switzerland or Austria. His Olympic victory was his fifteenth in succession in giant slalom at world level. Stenmark brings two great qualities to skiing: an advanced technique whereby he stays balanced over the top of his skis where others are rocking, and an ability to carve a turn without trace of a skid even on bumps and rolls – as well as a desire to be the equal on skis of his countryman the tennis champion, Björn Borg.

Twenty-seven-year-old Ulrich Wehling took his third gold medal in successive Olympics in the same event, an unprecedented achievement. He was ninth in the 15-kilometres running, but such was his ascendancy in the 70-metre jumping of the previous day that he shook off all opposition. Only Sixten Jernberg, the great Swedish cross-country runner, had previously achieved gold medals in three successive games at Cortina in 1956, Squaw Valley in 1960, and Innsbruck in 1964 but in different events.

The Russian world champions, Gennadi Karponosov and Natalya Linichuk, took the ice dancing gold medal without being at their best. The crowd were much more impressed by the Hungarians who train in Britain, Krisztina Regoczy and Andras Sallay who took the silver.

Wednesday 20 February

On the day the President reaffirmed the American Government's decision to boycott the Moscow Olympic Games, United States' athletes at Lake Placid enjoyed great success. The US ice-hockey victory of 4–2 over the German Federal Republic put them into the play-offs with the Soviet Union, Sweden and Finland. Although Finland and Canada each finished with three victories and two defeats, the Finns went on to beat Canada in their match. In the preliminary competition the Swedes won one section from the United

Evgeny Beliaev striving to get the USSR a gold in the 4 x 10-kilometre relay cross-country event

States on goal average. The US was 2–0 down to the Germans, but fought back to win. The youngest team in the competition – the average age was twenty-two – they were, to many Americans, the wonder of the Games. Herb Brooks, their coach, sold them as strongly as he once sold insurance, and the first play-off against the Soviet Union on Friday was looked forward to as eagerly as Eric Heiden's next speed skating event.

In that shiny oval, Beth Heiden finally achieved a medal, a bronze in the 3,000 metres. Twenty-year-old Beth had suffered much in comparison with her brother. She has never held an equivalent dominance in women's speed skating, and even the bronze was a sweet and sour moment. Asked what had saddened her, tears welled and she said, 'It got in the way of our family and that really made me mad.' Little Beth – she is only 1.57 m (5 ft 2 in) – agreed with the girl she had been paired with, the winner of the race, Eva Bjørg Jensen of Norway, that she did not have the fight of the previous year. 'I like to skate for myself and this year, I feel I have to skate for the press.' She kept quiet about achilles tendon problems which had affected her build-up.

Russia's great strength in cross-country skiing was demonstrated again at Mount Van Hoevenberg when the Russians took their third gold medal of this Games in cross-country and their second in the history of the 4×10-kilometre relay event. A fine run by Per Knut Aaland turned a 24 sec deficit into a one point advantage for Norway at the halfway mark, but Evgeny Beliaev, 15-kilometre silver medallist at Innsbruck, took a 52 sec lead over Ove Aunli; and Nikolai Zimyatov, the 30-kilometre winner here, skied the second fastest leg of the day for a total time of 1 hr 57.03 sec.

Thursday 21 February

Robin Cousins (Great Britain). Top marks for artistic impression helped to win him the gold

Robin Cousins followed another Briton, John Curry, as men's figure skating champion with an outstanding, if slightly flawed, display in the arena. Cousins, the European champion, may have been the best skater of the competition, but three of the judges thought Jan Hoffmann the best skater of the night. Five of the judges awarded Cousins first place votes, another judged the two men equal on first places, but preferred Cousins on second places, so the Briton was champion.

Where Hoffmann jumped and spun with what he described as the best performance of his long career, Cousins made three triple jumps in a beautifully shaped display but he missed his fourth. His artistic dominance was unchallenged, only one judge failing to mark him 5.9, but he made one error on landing and Hoffmann surpassed him on technical merit. It was a tense, dramatic evening, with Scott Hamilton, one of three Americans in the final group, outshining the others and drawing the reception of the night from his home crowd. Cousins, who trains in Denver, also has many American fans although he comes from Bristol and, in the end, he received tremendous acclamation on the winner's podium. His worst choreography that night was when he tripped as he stepped up to receive his gold medal from Lord Killanin.

On the speed skating oval, Eric Heiden made Olympic history when he recovered from a near-fall on a track made more slippery by rain, to win his fourth gold, this time in the 1,500 metres. He became the first male athlete to win four gold medals in Winter Games history – Lydia Skoblikova of the USSR had achieved the same at Innsbruck in 1964, also in speed skating.

At Whiteface mountain, Hanni Wenzel of Liechtenstein achieved a gold in the women's giant slalom to follow her downhill silver medal, and the strains of the familiar national anthem rang out in Lake Placid – the melody of Liechtenstein's anthem is the same as Britain's. The tiny principality was earning its first gold medal and the Wenzel family, its third honour – Andreas had won the silver in the men's giant slalom.

One of the cross-country surprises of the Games was the German Democratic Republic's 4×5 kilometres victory, its first in this event, over the USSR, winner of three of the previous four Olympic relays.

Friday 22 February

In one of the most remarkable upsets in ice-hockey history, the USA gave the USSR its first defeat in Olympic hockey since 1964, when Mark Johnson and their captain, Mike Eruzione, scored two goals inside two minutes for a 4–3 victory.

As at Squaw Valley in 1960, when they beat the USSR in the semi-finals and Czechoslovakia for the gold medal, the Americans showed spirit and played to a team pattern that overcame all their rawness. Before they went out they were told by coach Herb Brooks, 'You were meant to be here. You were born to be here. For this moment. Let's have the puck and the possession.' President Carter called them in their dressing room to wish them luck and to tell them, 'You reflect all the ideals of our society.'

An already keyed-up team was in a stadium where the crowd, almost demented with excitement, was chanting 'U-S-A . . . U-S-A'. The Russians were clearly nervous in the midst of such tension and

USSR v USA. The ice-hockey match that set the USA on its way to winning a long awaited gold medal

Phil Mahre (United States), now recovered from a severe accident on the same course in 1979, takes the silver medal

their coach, Viktor Tikhonov, substituted goalminder Vladimir Myshkin for the experienced Vladislav Tretiak. Mark Johnson scored an equalizer at 2–2 with only a fraction of a second left to the first period.

Although outshot 30–10 in the first two periods, solid goal-tending by Jim Craig restricted the Russians to a single further goal. Johnson equalized with Vladimir Krutov sent off for high sticking. Finally, Eruzione picked up a loose puck to fire a shot past Myshkin from 30 feet with ten minutes remaining.

This was the USSR's sixth defeat in forty-six games since the country started competing in Olympics in 1956. The American amateurs achieved a win where the National League All Stars had failed the previous year. The Russian coach, Tikhonov, said at a news conference that this was a particularly difficult tournament with some very good teams all trying their hardest to beat the USSR. Long after the game, crowds were still thronging Main Street yelling 'U-S-A'. On television, ABC's Jim McKay described it as the biggest celebration since the end of World War II. That evening, President Carter invited the entire American Olympic team to lunch at the White House on the Monday after the Games.

Out at Mount Van Hoevenberg, the Russians quietly went about winning the 4 $\times$7.5-kilometre biathlon relay with the German Democratic and Federal Republics coming second and third. Aleksandr Tikhonov, a thirty-three-year-old major, ended his brilliant biathlon career with his fourth gold medal in successive Olympics as a member of the team.

At Whiteface mountain, Ingemar Stenmark took his second gold in the special slalom, but America had more to cheer with Phil Mahre making a remarkable comeback from a severe injury on the same slopes a year earlier to take the silver medal. Mahre, twenty-two, had the fastest time on the first run, but Stenmark made his usual devastating second run and Mahre, having made a couple of mistakes, had to be content with second place. (In the World Cup race a year ago, Mahre fractured his left ankle in four places and shattered the roof of the weight-bearing ankle joint. Seven screws and a plate secured the injury.)

Hanni Wenzel bringing Liechtenstein into the limelight with her second gold. The Wenzel family won two gold and two silver medals during the Games

Saturday 23 February

To put his ultimate seal on these Games, Eric Heiden won the 10,000 metres in the world record time of 14 min 28.13 sec for his fifth gold medal – another record.

His time was over six seconds faster than the record set by Viktor Leskin of the USSR at Alma Ata in 1977, and more than fifteen seconds better than his previous best. Only one other skater, Ivar Ballangrud of Norway in 1936, has ever won both the 500 and 10,000 metres. Only one skater other than Heiden even attempted both events. Heiden, relaxed and casual, is retiring from speed skating to go into sports medicine. Clearly, however, he has the personality to become another Mark Spitz.

The last major day of the Games brought Hanni Wenzel of Liechtenstein her second gold medal, in the special slalom to follow the giant slalom, plus the silver in the downhill, a performance to equal that of Rosi Mittermaier at Innsbruck in 1976.

Jouko Tormanen (Finland) soaring through the sky to win the gold medal in the 90-metre ski jump

The USSR, too, gained its sixth Nordic gold medal, in the classic 50-kilometre distance, and matched its performance of 1976. Nikolai Zimyatov, who won the 30 kilometres and anchored the relay team for three golds, gaily told a news conference that he had made up for the USSR's ice-hockey defeat by the USA. He said he had hummed the folk song, 'Kalinka' time after time to keep his rhythm on his 31-mile run through the forest. Norway went away without a Nordic victory, her old pre-eminence now a matter for for the records.

Hanni Wenzel's three medals at this Games, plus her bronze in 1976, gave her a special place in the records – no Alpine skier, man or woman, has achieved four. The German-born Liechtensteiner may not have the charisma of Rosi Mittermaier, but she has plenty of character.

The 90 metres produced a genuine surprise; twenty-five-year-old Laplander, Jouko Tormanen, the No 4 in Finland's team, without a major victory in his life, caught a breeze which lifted his giant skis 114.5 and 117 metres to win on style and distance points from Hubert Neuper of Austria. Tormanen twice caught a favourable wind eddying up the valley, but so had most of the early starters. There was one horrific-looking fall, but Jan Holmlund of Sweden managed to land on his side not his head and got away with a broken collar bone.

Annet Poetzsch of the German Democratic Republic, having established a good lead in the school figures, coasted to victory in the women's figure skating. Although outshone in the free skating by Denise Biellmann of Switzerland and Linda Fratianne of the USA who took the silver, Miss Poetzsch's program included two triple jumps. Biellmann, who finished fourth, did four to pull up from twelfth place.

Sunday 24 February

One of the epic tales of the thirteenth Games finished in triumph for the US ice-hockey team when they defeated Finland 4–2 in the final before a delighted crowd. About 10,000 fans, chanting 'U-S-A' in great volleys of sound, would later be able to say they had been there. Millions more watched on television. ABC estimated that three-quarters of the population had watched all or some of the day- and night-time coverage during the two weeks.

Nothing caught the imagination of the US public more than the efforts of their ice-hockey team. Overnight, these players, mostly collegiate, became famous and so did their coach, Herb Brooks. 'Fathers and mothers love their children like I love this hockey team', said Brooks.

After the game, the president called them in their dressing room; he told them that between the ice-hockey match and Iran and the economy he had barely known which way to turn. His daughter, Amy Carter, was there for the final fling. So was Vice-President Mondale and so, in spirit, was the American nation.

The US team won not brilliantly but well, twice coming from behind. The Americans scored twice in the last seconds to equal Sweden 2–2 in a group game before the Games had formally begun. At the end of the first period against Finland they trailed 1–0. They

Eric Heiden (United States) being carried shoulder high after winning his fifth gold medal

trailed 2–1 after the second. Three goals in the final period brought the crowd time and again to its feet. First Phil Verchota whipped a low shot past the Finnish goalminder. Then Mark Johnson, one of the stars, fed Robby McClanahan and his shot flew through a mass of bodies. Still it was not over. Two penalties had to be fought through. Then another. Johnson came on, just caught the puck before the blue line shot picked up his own rebound, and tucked it away for the goal that ended the argument. The stadium crowd went wild.

Later, in the final event of the Games, the USSR beat Sweden 9–2 for the silver medal. Above the Indian Ocean, two Soviet fighters approached too close to the aircraft carrier *Coral Sea* for the Americans' comfort. A fighter went up to intercept. The Russians suddenly broke radio silence. 'Congratulations on your ice-hockey victory,' the voice said in English.

On the bob run that morning, Meinhard Nehmer of the German Democratic Republic added a third gold to his impressive record, piloting a four-man faster than anyone in history in the final race of his career. The thirty-nine-year-old army lieutenant twice went under one-minute in the four heats, the bobbing equivalent of Roger Bannister's four-minute mile. Nehmer's total of 3 min 59.92 sec may stand for a long time.

Meantime, the International Bobsleigh and Toboggan Federation took specimen runners from all bobs to investigate allegations that a compound was being baked onto runners of some teams to improve running performance by about thirty-five hundredths of a second. Quick or slow runners, nothing could detract from Nehmer's performance in driving a bob faster than anyone in the world.

The closing ceremony in the Olympic Arena followed a skating exhibition in which all the major stars of the Olympic competitions unbuttoned their most flamboyant routines to the delight of the 8,500 people packed into the auditorium.

About 200 of the 1,700 competitors mingled for the closing ceremony that followed. Lord Killanin, in a particularly striking speech, spoke memorably of the contribution sport made to understanding between nations. He referred with unusual force in his speech to 'the holocaust which could be upon us if we are not careful'.

The throng on the ice then gave itself over to a joyous and wholehearted farewell to the Games. There was the enduring drama of the flag borne from the arena flanked by fifty-two torchbearers. For a moment the only light in the arena was the Olympic flame. Slowly the flame was doused and the arena was left momentarily in darkness to reflect upon the events on which it had shone. Once again the lights flared and to banners, balloons and music the assembly slowly broke up. Outside fireworks lit the sky. Slowly, sadly, people realized all was over.

OLYMPIC MEDAL WINNERS

Gold	Silver	Bronze

Biathlon

10km ($6\frac{1}{4}$ miles) cross-country race with two shooting exercises.

Gold	Silver	Bronze
F. Ullrich *GDR* 32min 10.69sec	V. Aliken *URS* 32min 53.10sec	A. Aljabiev *URS* 33min 09.16sec

20km ($12\frac{1}{2}$ miles) cross-country race with four shooting exercises.

Gold	Silver	Bronze
A. Aljabiev *URS* 1hr 08min 16.31sec	F. Ullrich *GDR* 1hr 08min 27.79sec	E. Rosch *GDR* 1hr 11min 11.73sec

Biathlon Relay

4 x 7.5km ($4\frac{1}{2}$ miles) with two shooting exercises.

Gold	Silver	Bronze
URS 1hr 34min 3.27sec	GDR 1hr 34min 56.99sec	*GER* 1hr 37min 30.26sec

Bobsleighing

Two-Man Bob

Gold	Silver	Bronze
SUI 4min 09.36sec	GDR 4min 10.93sec	GDR 4min 11.08sec

Four-Man Bob

Gold	Silver	Bronze
GDR I 3min 59.92sec	SUI 4min 0.87sec	GDR II 4min 0.97sec

Ice Hockey

Gold	Silver	Bronze
USA	URS	SWE

Luge

Single-Seater (Men)

Gold	Silver	Bronze
B. Glass *GDR* 2min 54.80sec	P. Hildgartner *ITA* 2min 55.37sec	A. Winkler *GER* 2min 56.55sec

Two-Seater (Men)

Gold	Silver	Bronze
H. Rinn/N. Hahn *GDR* 1min 19.331sec	P. Gschnitzer/ K. Brunner *ITA* 1min 19.606sec	G. Fluckinger/ K. Schrott *AUT* 1min 19.795sec

Single-Seater (Women)

Gold	Silver	Bronze
V. Zozlulia *URS* 2min 36.5sec	M. Sollmann *GDP* 2min 37.66sec	I. Amantova *URS* 2min 37.82sec

Figure Skating (Men)

Gold	Silver	Bronze
R. Cousins *GBR* 189.48pts	J. Hoffmann *GDR* 189.72pts	C. Tickner *USA* 187.06pts

Figure Skating (Women)

Gold	Silver	Bronze
A. Poetzsch *GDR* 189.0pts	L. Fratianne *USA* 188.30pts	D. Lurz *GER* 183.04pts

Figure Skating (Pairs)

Gold	Silver	Bronze
I. Rodnina & A. Zaitseve *URS* 147.26pts	M. Charselova & S. Shakrai *URS* 143.80pts	M. Mager & U. Bewersdorf *GDR* 140.52pts

Ice Dancing*

Gold	Silver	Bronze
N. Linichuk & G. Karponosov *URS* 205.48pts	K. Regoczy & A. Sallay *HUN* 204.52pts	J. Moisayeva & A. Minenkov *URS* 201.86pts

Speed Skating (Men)

500 Metres

Gold	Silver	Bronze
E. Heiden *USA* 38.03sec	E. Kulikov *URS* 38.37sec	L. De Boer *HOL* 38.48sec

1,000 Metres

Gold	Silver	Bronze
E. Heiden *USA* 1min 15.18sec	G. Boucher *CAN* 1min 16.68sec	F. Roenning *NOR* 1min 16.91sec V. Lobanov *URS* 1min 16.91sec

Hoffman, Cousins and Tickner respectively silver, gold and bronze medallists in the figure skating

1,500 Metres

Gold	Silver	Bronze
E. Heiden *USA* 1min 55.44sec	K. A. Stenshjemmet *NOR* 1min 56.81sec	A. Andersen *NOR* 1min 56.92sec

5,000 Metres

Gold	Silver	Bronze
E. Heiden *USA* 7min 02.29sec	K. A. Stenshjemmet *NOR* 7min 03.28sec	T. Oxholm *NOR* 7min 05.59sec

10,000 Metres

Gold	Silver	Bronze
E. Heiden *USA* 14min 28.13sec (world record)	P. Kleine *HOL* 14min 35.03sec	T. Oxholm *NOR* 14min 36.60sec

Speed Skating (Women)

500 Metres

Gold	Silver	Bronze
K. Enke *GDR* 41.78sec	L. Mueller *USA* 42.26sec	N. Petruseva *URS* 42.42sec

1,000 Metres

Gold	Silver	Bronze
N. Petruseva *URS* 1min 24.10sec	L. Mueller *USA* 1min 25.41sec	S. Albrecht *GDR* 1min 26.46sec

1,500 Metres

Gold	Silver	Bronze
A. Borkink *HOL* 2min 10.95sec	R. Visser *HOL* 2min 12.35sec	S. Becker *GDR* 2min 12.38sec

3,000 Metres

Gold	Silver	Bronze
E. B. Jensen *NOR* 4min 32.13sec	S. Becker *GDR* 4min 32.79sec	B. Heiden *USA* 4min 33.77sec

Alpine Skiing (Men)

Downhill

Gold	Silver	Bronze
L. Stock *AUT* 1min 45.50sec	P. Wirnsberger *AUT* 1min 46.12sec	S. Podborski *CAN* 1min 46.62sec

Giant Slalom

Gold	Silver	Bronze
I. Stenmark *SWE* 2min 40.74 sec	A. Wenzel *LIE* 2min 41.49sec	H. Enn *AUS* 2min 42.51sec

Slalom

Gold	Silver	Bronze
I. Stenmark *SWE* 1min 44.26sec	P. Mahre *USA* 1min 44.76sec	J. Luethy *SUI* 1min 45.06sec

Alpine Skiing (Women)

Downhill

Gold	Silver	Bronze
A. Moser-Pröll *AUT* 1min 37.52sec	H. Wenzel *LIE* 1min 38.22sec	M. T. Nadig *SUI* 1min 38.36sec

Giant Slalom

Gold	Silver	Bronze
H. Wenzel *LIE* 2min 41.66sec	I. Epple *GER* 2min 42.12sec	P. Pelen *FRA* 2min 42.41sec

Slalom

Gold	Silver	Bronze
H. Wenzel *LIE* 1min 25.09sec	C. Kinshfer *GER* 1min 26.50sec	E. Hess *SUI* 1min 27.89sec

Nordic Skiing (Men)

15 Kilometres Cross-Country

Gold	Silver	Bronze
T. Wassberg *SWE* 41min 57.63 sec	J. Mieto *FIN* 41min 57.64sec	O. Aunli *NOR* 42min 28.62sec

30 Kilometres Cross-Country

Gold	Silver	Bronze
N. Zimyatov *URS* 1hr 27min 2.80sec	V. Rochev *URS* 1hr 27min 34.22sec	I. Lebanov *BUL* 1hr 28min 03.87sec

50 Kilometres Cross-Country

Gold	Silver	Bronze
N. Zimyatov *URS* 2hr 27min 24.60sec	J. Mieto *FIN* 2hr 30min 20.52sec	A. Zavylov *URS* 2hr 30min 51.52sec

4 x 10 Kilometres Relay

Gold	Silver	Bronze
URS 1hr 57min 3.46sec	NOR 1hr 58min 45.77sec	FIN 2hr 00min 00.18sec

Ski Jumping

70 Metres Jump

Gold	Silver	Bronze
A. Innauer *AUT* 266.3pts	H. Yaqi *JPN* 249.2pts	M. Deckert *GDR* 249.2pts

90 Metres Jump

Gold	Silver	Bronze
J. Tormanen *FIN* 271.0pts	H. Neuper *AUT* 262.4pts	J. Puikkonen *FIN* 248.5pts

Nordic Combined

15-km (9.3 miles) cross-country and jumping.

Gold	Silver	Bronze
U. Wehling *GDR* 432.200pts	J. Karjalainen *FIN* 429.500pts	K. Winkler *GDR* 425.320pts

Nordic Skiing (Women)

5 Kilometres Cross-Country

Gold	Silver	Bronze
R. Smetanina *URS* 15min 06.92sec	H. Riihivuori *FIN* 15min 11.96sec	K. Jeriova *TCH* 15min 23.44sec

10 Kilometres Cross-Country

Gold	Silver	Bronze
B. Petzold *GDR* 30min 31.54sec	H. Riihivuori *FIN* 30min 35.05sec	H. Takalo *FIN* 30min 45.25sec

4 x 5 Kilometres Relay

Gold	Silver	Bronze
GDR 1hr 2min 11.10sec	URS 1hr 3min 18.30sec	NOR 1hr 4min 13.50sec

*Ice Dancing 1976

Gold	Silver	Bronze
L. Pakhomova & A. Gorshkov *URS* 209.92pts	I. Moiseeva & A. Minenkov *URS* 204.88pts	C. O'Connor & J. Millns *USA* 202.64pts

Photographs in this section by Leo Mason

THE WINTER OLYMPICS

INTRODUCTION John Rodda

For many years the relationship between the IOC and the Sports on the Winter program was at the best uneasy, at worst barely tolerable because of a divergence of view and interpretation of the amateur laws. The Avery Brundage years tended to emphasize the division and the expulsion of Karl Schranz of Austria from the Olympic Village at Sapporo in 1972, laid open the wound. In 1976, the relationship changed when Innsbruck, having taken over the Games after Denver's withdrawal, saved the IOC's reputation from further change. Then Lake Placid, trying to scale down the Games to the style many IOC members wish to see, further improved the situation.

The popular version of the root of the trouble is that Coubertin was opposed to a separate Games for winter events because they would bring about disunity within the Olympic Movement. That was a contributory factor to the discord, which was more closely related, however, to the strength of winter sports.

Snow sports in the first quarter of the twentieth century were really confined to the Scandinavian countries. The Nordic Games had been organized every four years from 1901 to 1917, then in 1922 and 1926. The main events were Nordic skiing (cross-country events), ski jumping and bandy, a Nordic variety of ice hockey. With these and other smaller competitions and the annual Holmenkollen Week in Norway winter sports as the Scandinavian nations understood them were organized in a style similar to the Summer Olympics.

Holmenkollen was as much a cult as a sporting event; competing there was as much a pilgrimage as anything else. Sir Arnold Lunn, the creator of downhill ski racing and the slalom and the most influential figure in the sport, was contributing a chapter to this book when he died in 1974. He wrote of Holmenkollen from personal experience:

> I myself felt that there was something which, for want of a more accurate description, could be described as a mystique about Holmenkollen and which recalled the mystique of the classic Olympics, restricted as Herodotus wrote, 'to those who had common temples and sacrifices and like ways of life'.

It was then not surprising that if Coubertin and his colleagues were suspicious of what effect winter sports might have on the Games, the Nordic sportsmen believed that only at Holmenkollen could the 'immortal garland' be won. The Norwegian attitude had, too, the unfortunate effect of delaying the formation of the International Ski Federation, largely because the Norwegians felt that no world championship could replace their events.

The opposition to the Scandinavian countries' containment of winter events grew, however, particularly after the introduction of the Alpine 'package tour' by an Englishman, Henry Lunn, father of Sir Arnold Lunn. These quickly became popular and by 1914 at the Olympic Congress in Paris (after figure skating had been included in the 1908 London Games) there was a much stronger demand for separate Winter Games, with support coming this time from Norway. The first Games after World War I, at Antwerp in 1920, conceded ground with the inclusion of skating and ice hockey.

The year of 1924 was the most significant in winter sports; an International Winter Sports Week at Chamonix, France, first given patronage by the International Olympic Committee, was two years later accorded the title of 'First Winter Games'. In 1924 also, after the events of Chamonix, the International Ski Federation (FIS) was founded.

As Coubertin had foreseen, winter sports and specifically downhill skiing were to bring the Olympic Movement continuing trouble.

The first confrontation came in 1935 when the IOC told FIS that ski teachers would be excluded from the Games in 1936. Under FIS rules, teachers were not professionals and since the IOC rules took the Federations' rulings on amateurism this was the sort of contradiction in attitude that undermined the standing of the IOC. Many members of FIS were not so much angry at the IOC's contradiction of its own rules as by the exclusion of teachers and the inclusion of the German team which had been training together for months and was far more professional than the teachers from other countries. After the Games at Garmisch-Partenkirchen, FIS resolved to withdraw from future Games unless ski teachers were allowed to compete, a decision that was confirmed two years later. But whether that decision would have been put into effect was never tested because of World War II.

From 1952 onwards the Winter Games had a more dangerous and consistent opponent – Avery Brundage, the President of the IOC. Never was his dislike for the Games concealed; never did he miss an opportunity to point out the commercial overtones of skiing which, with the Games as a valuable advertising source, was developing throughout the world as a vast new leisure activity.

The dialogue between FIS and the IOC, about advertising and about the amount of time skiers spent in training (particularly those from the lowland countries), seemed to lurch through the 1960s from one explosion to another. In 1968 at Grenoble Brundage felt that the betrayal by FIS was ultimate, when, in the belief that skiers would not carry advertising material, he discovered at the eleventh hour that they were to do so – on their skis – and no changes to the equipment were made.

Four years later, Brundage was instrumental in disqualifying Karl Schranz of Austria, at Sapporo, when Schranz, in the Olympic Village, said that he was making thousands of dollars from skiing.

Sir Arnold Lunn succinctly summed up, in one of his last writings, the problems which the IOC had faced for forty years in skiing and to a lesser degree in other sports over a longer period:

The greater the prestige of the event and the greater the financial rewards to the victorious amateurs, the greater the risk of unpleasant incidents and unfriendly relations between rival teams. The importance of the Olympic Games is so manifest that their supporters can afford to be realistic. Those who remember the nature of man will realize that Coubertin's dream is far less likely to be fulfilled in the Olympic Games than in less important events.

While skiing caused the IOC much concern, the Olympic skating rinks were used by some individuals to raise their contractual price for ice shows, once they had won their Olympic medal; and the expensive installation of bob runs at Winter Games sites, for what is a little-practised sport, was criticized for being against the Olympic rule that a sport must be widely engaged in if it is to be maintained on the Olympic program. And then in 1971 the Winter Games image suffered another blow when Denver, which was chosen in 1970 to stage the Winter Games, withdrew from its commitment because of opposition from environmentalists and conservationists and because the State of Colorado would not guarantee full financial support.

THE CELEBRATIONS OF THE WINTER GAMES

John Samuel

The Winter Olympic Games came into being amid muddle and acrimony. The first Games, at Chamonix in 1924, were only accorded their status retrospectively, officially at the IOC meeting at Lisbon in May 1926. The previous year at its meeting in Prague, the IOC acknowledged the success of the 'Chamonix International Winter Sports Week', as it was termed at the time, and a charter worked out by the Executive Commission was formally submitted to the IOC by the Marquis de Polignac on 27 May 1925 and accepted. At the same meeting St Moritz successfully canvassed for the next Winter Games. Thus, a rather difficult infant came into the world. The charter read:

> The International Olympic Committee will carry out a special cycle of the Olympic Winter Games, which have to take place in the same years as the Summer Games. They will be called the first, second, third Winter Games etc., and are subject to all rules of the Olympic protocol. The prizes, medals and diplomas must be different from those of the Olympic Summer Games, and the term 'Olympiad' shall not be used in this connection. The IOC will select the place for the Olympic Winter Games and will reserve priority to the country arranging the Summer Games of that particular Olympiad provided that the latter can furnish sufficient guarantee of its ability to organize the Winter Games in their entirety.

The pairing of Summer and Winter Games in the same country was a pleasing notion which was not long sustained. Amsterdam, which staged the 1928 Summer Games, might provide ice rinks in abundance, but not mountains, and St Moritz in Switzerland was chosen for the first time. The United States was able to stage both Games in 1932, at Los Angeles and Lake Placid, and Germany did the same in 1936, at Berlin and Garmisch-Partenkirchen. But already the options were running out. World War II interfered with plans for twin events in Japan, the Summer Games in Tokyo and the Winter in Sapporo, and although London was able to stage the 1948 Summer Games, the winter events went to St Moritz again. No single country has since held both events in the same year, not least because of the problems of costs. Only a wealthy community has been able to stage the Winter Games since the war. Grenoble's overall budget in 1968 was $200 million, although this included major civic improvements, such as road, airport and housing works, which benefited the Olympic events but were truly long-term investments for the entire area. Sapporo's overall budget in 1972 was higher than Grenoble's, but the true figure for the thirteen Olympic sites was more like $50 million than the more frequently quoted $250 million.

Nevertheless, by the 1970s, the element of gigantism in Winter Games costing was embarrassing for the Olympic movement, and hard to reconcile with the philosophy of amateur sport. The staging of all Games had become a matter of high professionalism, with the world's press and television following every move in the game, and inventing a few of their own.

The Winter Games have tended to highlight the problems of wealthier countries. Recreations on mountainsides at 5,000 to 10,000 feet, or on artificial ice which has to be frozen layer by layer on artfully constructed concrete beds, tend to be costly of time, place and equipment. Minor industries grow up round them, merging into the major industry of tourism. Avery Brundage, president of the IOC from 1952 to 1972, believed the Winter Games had no place in the Olympic Movement because of these physical characteristics which in their turn encouraged commercialism and professionalism. When Denver, having successfully canvassed for the 1976 Games, withdrew in late 1972 because a Colorado state referendum refused further funds, many believed that the Winter Games were on their deathbed. But Innsbruck, Lake Placid, the Mont Blanc region and Tampere (Finland) were all prepared to take over the Games at short notice.

The instinct to slide on snow and ice is basic to mankind, and to develop skill and pleasure in doing so is a legitimate aspect of recreation. Winter sports are primarily for the participant rather than the spectator, television audiences notwithstanding, and all these factors tend to balance the argument whether or not the Winter Games truly comply with Olympic concepts. The limited number of countries with adequate mountains and snow cover for Nordic and Alpine skiing has bothered some critics. But easier transport, increasing leisure time and natural growth have meant that after 294 competitors (13 women) and 16 countries at Chamonix in 1924 the Games drew 1,128 (217 women) and 35 nations at Sapporo in 1972. Events themselves had diversified from 14 at Chamonix to 35 in Japan and these were figures achieved in spite of the long journeys involved for most of the competitors.

One of the stronger arguments for winter sports is that there is a long history of participation by both sexes. Ice skating, especially, has led in this respect. In the eighteenth century Marie-Antoinette skated with the Chevalier de St Georges, one of the greatest skaters of his time, and in the Netherlands in the winter of 1768–9 Casanova related how he donned skates to pursue a high society maiden. The first skating club as such was founded in Edinburgh, some say as early as 1642. Skating was included in the list of desirable Olympic contests at the 1894 Paris congress, partly because the sport had been the first to institute World and European Championships.

Although combining athletic and aesthetic qualities to a degree unmatched until gymnastics made its mark in the Summer program, ice skating has rarely been less than controversial because of the subjective nature of its judging. The great majority of sports have an objective outcome in terms of time or points or goals scored. Ice skating is marked according to personal opinion but an element of the partisan, whether of style or country, is rarely missing – it would be less than human if it was, judgments so often being based on familiarity.

Alpine skiing, which after World War II took over the centre stage in Winter Olympic Games, in fact was only introduced into Olympic competition as late as 1936.

In June 1914, immediately before the outbreak of World War I, pleas were raised on all sides for a Winter Games at the congress of National Olympic Committees in Paris. A representative of the Norwegian Skiing Federation, in a remarkable departure from previous Norwegian attitudes, proposed the inclusion of skiing in the Olympic program. Germany, Austria, Switzerland and Canada also pushed for the inclusion of ice and snow sports. Antwerp, in 1920, not only included figure skating in the Summer Games program, but also ice hockey, won by Canada, represented by a club team, the Winnipeg Falcons. A bitter fight was still to come, however. At the Lausanne meeting of the IOC in 1921 an advisory committee report showed Norway and Sweden totally opposed to the introduction of the Winter Games advocated by France, Switzerland and Canada. The Scandinavian representatives went so far as to deny all other countries the right to deal with questions of winter sport.

Mr Sigfrid Edström, the Swedish member of the IOC and later President of the Committee, somewhat embarrassed, said he had no objections to the IOC granting its patronage to the winter sports week at Chamonix. The Marquis de Polignac emphatically rejected the idea that the Scandinavian countries alone cultivated winter sports, and quoted Switzerland, Canada and France in particular. He then put a motion which read:

> The Congress suggests to the International Olympic Committee that in all countries where Olympic Games are held and where it is also possible to organize winter sports competitions, such competitions should be put under the patronage of the IOC and arranged in accordance with the rules of the international sports associations concerned.

A lively discussion followed, at the end of which Coubertin startled the proponents of winter sports by stating that the Marquis de Polignac's motion could not be put to the vote as it was contrary to an earlier decision by the IOC. He proposed a winter sports congress in 1922, arranged by the International Skating Union, to

Skating. Nicolai Panin (USSR), the holder in perpetuity of the special figure title, an event requiring elaborate patterns cut in the ice that has never been held since 1908.

investigate the Marquis's suggestion. The winter sports protagonists immediately recognized this as a delaying procedure, and Polignac's motion was eventually put to the vote and carried. The way was opened for the first Winter Games. At the French Olympic Committee meeting in Paris in June 1922, international associations and commissions were represented. An International Ski Commission, predecessor of the International Ski Federation, came into being in 1911. Chamonix was chosen from among other French resorts and on 20 February 1923 a contract was signed. The municipality of Chamonix undertook to complete the necessary installations by 1 November 1923, to keep them in shape for at least thirty years, and in that time to let them to the Olympic Committee or French sports associations for a maximum ten per cent of the gross takings from events taking place. In exchange, the French Olympic committee undertook to pay to Chamonix forty per cent of the gross takings from the International Sports Week, with a guaranteed minimum of half a million francs.

I CHAMONIX 1924

Most Winter Games have had to survive actual or threatened disruption by the weather, and Chamonix in 1924 was no exception. On 23 December there was not a flake of snow anywhere in the resort. The next morning there was a layer 1.10 m (3 ft 8 in) deep, and 36,000 sq m (43,000 sq yd) had to be cleared from the skating rink, mostly by the shovel load, for efficient snow ploughs did not then exist. A week before the start, rain turned the ice stadium into a lake. But, on the eve of the Games, a hard frost set in and the opening ceremony was held without hitch.

The 294 competitors from sixteen countries (Estonia was represented in the procession but no Estonian competed) took part in fourteen events, the sixteen pioneers being: Austria, Belgium, Canada, Czechoslovakia, Finland, France, Great Britain, Hungary, Italy, Latvia, Norway, Poland, Sweden, Switzerland, the United States and Yugoslavia.

The first Winter Games skiing hero was the twenty-nine-year-old Norwegian, Thorleif Haug, who won three gold medals in the 18-km and 50-km Nordic skiing and the Nordic combination. He also won a bronze medal in the special jumping, a success still unrivalled, though Toni Sailer (Austria), in the Alpine skiing at Cortina in 1956, and Jean-Claude Killy (France), again in Alpine skiing at Grenoble in 1968, each gained three gold medals.

The Finn, Clas Thunberg, had an even greater haul than Haug in the speed skating, with three gold medals, one silver and one bronze.

II ST MORITZ 1928

Winter sports came of age during the 1920s, and St Moritz in 1928 reflected this with 494 competitors from twenty-five countries. Once again the organizers were reminded of the uncertainties of winter weather when a warm wind from the south set in to disrupt events, or, in the case of the 10,000-metres speed skating, cause their cancellation. On the morning of the 50-km cross-country skiing race the temperature was around —17.8°C (0°F) when the skiers made their first wax tests. By the afternoon, and in spite of St Moritz's high altitude (1,850 m, or 6,066 ft, above sea level) the thermometer rose to 25°C (77°F). The skill and luck that goes into waxing now became all important, and Sweden emerged best, Per Erik Hedlund, Gustav Jonsson and Volger Andersson winning all three medals. It was an indication of the gruelling nature of the race that a quarter of the skiers had to give up, and Hedlund's winning time was almost 70 minutes slower than Haug's in winning the same race at Chamonix. The weather was unremitting, and it rained all the following day and night – a phenomenon rarely known in the Engadine at this time of year – so that every competition on 15 February had to be postponed. Suddenly the weather changed, hard frost set into the watery snow, and the Games were saved.

They were outstanding Games for figure skating. The Swede, Gillis Grafström, achieved his third and last Olympic gold medal, but it was now that the Norwegian girl, Sonja Henie, not yet sixteen, who had already won a World Championship in 1927, confirmed her domination with her first Olympic gold. The United States won both the five-man bob and the tobogganing on the Cresta Run.

It was during the Games of St Moritz that Sir Arnold Lunn, of Great Britain, persuaded the International Skiing Federation (FIS) to include downhill and slalom competitions experimentally in international competition. The way was open for Alpine skiing to take over its important role, although eight years elapsed before the first Olympic competitions in this style were held.

III LAKE PLACID 1932

Lake Placid, New York, a newly established resort close to the Canadian border, was only 568 m (1,862 ft) high and subject to changeable snow conditions. In fact snow had to be brought by the truckload from Canada to help repair the cross-country tracks, a circumstance derided by some Europeans at the time, although winter-sport resorts throughout the world came to respect the need for artificial snow-making and other devices to defeat variable weather. For the first time figure skating was held at an indoor arena, but another revolution, massed starts in speed skating, was less successful. The Americans and Canadians, encouraged by the spectators, enjoyed the free-for-all of the massed starts and took 10 of the 12 available medals. The Europeans, accustomed to starting in pairs and the best times counting, were eclipsed. They insisted on the traditional starts being restored for the World Championships which took place on the same rink immediately after the Games, and the Norwegian, Ivar Ballangrud, won the 1,500, 5,000 and 10,000 metres to prove the European point.

The bobsleigh brought the innovation of two-man sleds, but there were a number of accidents on the course. When Deutschland II became unserviceable it was replaced by an American bob and its team recruited from Germans living in the USA who were untrained as serious bob competitors. The special ski jump also provided diversions. Sudden cold followed rain to save the event, but in the outrun of the jump hill a small pool remained which many competitors could not avoid and so they took an involuntary bath. Soaked competitors complained bitterly as they waited for their second jump on the tower open to the merciless winds. Hans Beck of Norway caused a surprise by jumping 5 m (16 ft 4$\frac{7}{8}$in) farther than his fellow countryman, Birger Ruud, the FIS champion the year before, on the first jump, but Ruud, with a mighty effort, outjumped Bech by 5.50 m (18 ft 0$\frac{1}{2}$ in) on the second to take the first of his gold medals in a remarkable Olympic career.

IV GARMISCH-PARTENKIRCHEN 1936

The staging of a Winter Games close to a big population area, the support given by the Nazi regime anxious to assert itself, and the introduction of Alpine skiing all combined to make the fourth Winter Games the first with a truly mass following. There were 755 competitors from twenty-eight countries, and half a million paying spectators. The special ski jump, the concluding event, was watched by 150,000 people. Trains had left Munich at intervals of ten minutes from 11 p.m. until 10 a.m., and many thousands more came from Innsbruck. The weather was favourable to a remarkable degree. Rain fell regularly until the eve of the Games. Then there was providential snow and frost, which ensured good conditions for all the events, with the rain returning as soon as the Games were finished.

Although Sir Arnold Lunn and his supporters had by now won their fight for the inclusion of Alpine skiing, medals were awarded only for the combined positions in men's and women's events, and not for the individual races in slalom and downhill. The irony was that Norway, the principle opponents to Alpine skiing in the committee meetings, should at once succeed on the slopes, for Birger Ruud, the ski-jumping king, won the men's downhill and Laila Schou Nilsen, an outstanding speed skater and tennis player, the women's downhill. Ruud, who had raced frequently in Germany, Austria and Switzerland from 1935 to 1937 while on business there, had benefited from the fact that ski instructors had been ruled out of the Games, but it was still an extraordinary feat. He was pushed into fourth place overall, the winner being Franz Pfnür (Germany), but Miss Nilsen finished with the bronze medal.

In the speed skating, Ballangrud made amends for the disappointments at Lake Placid with three gold medals and a silver, and in figure skating Karl Schäfer, from Vienna, and Sonja Henie again demonstrated their superb talent. But Miss Henie's ten-year domination was coming to an end. The English skater, Cecilia Colledge, who had competed at Lake Placid at the age of eleven, was close behind her now, and soon afterwards Miss Henie turned professional, leaving Miss Colledge to go on and take the World Championship in 1937. Another remarkable run ended when Canada, victor in each of the previous Olympic ice-hockey competitions, was beaten by Britain 2–1. Although Britain, with a team primarily of British-born Canadians, only drew 0–0 against the United States, the Americans lost 0–1 to Canada. Britain thus gained one of the most extraordinary gold medals in Winter Games history.

The IOC meeting in Berlin in 1936 adopted Sapporo, on Japan's

most northerly island of Hokkaido, as the Winter Games centre for 1940, but because of the Sino-Japanese war and World War II, Sapporo had to wait until 1972 before it staged the Games. Both Oslo and St Moritz offered and then withdrew candidature for 1940 after Japan officially waived its claim in July 1938. The position was complicated by the first of many disputes between FIS and the IOC over amateur rules, with the FIS refusing to compete in Alpine skiing because the IOC deemed instructors inadmissible. Garmisch offered to stage the Games again, and, although the war clouds were gathering, the IOC, meeting in London in June 1939, agreed. In spite of the outbreak of war on 1 September, German preparations went on until 22 November 1939, when the assignment for Games due to take place on 2–11 February of the following year was formally relinquished.

V ST MORITZ 1948

The separation of Summer and Winter Games as distinct organizational entities proved to be the postwar pattern. London staged the Summer Games and St Moritz the Winter. Although Germany and Japan were not admitted, twenty-eight countries competed at St Moritz, the same number as at Garmisch-Partenkirchen, with 636 men and 77 women competitors. Alpine skiing had grown considerably since 1936. At Garmisch-Partenkirchen the 18 kilometres had been contested by racers from twenty-two countries, and the men's Alpine event from twenty-one nations. At St Moritz the figures were fifteen and twenty-five respectively. Furthermore gold medals were now being awarded for downhill and slalom, so there were six Alpine contests – three each for men and women – as opposed to the five traditional Nordic events.

The almost inevitable disputes and problems with the weather flawed but did not spoil an otherwise joyful winter sports reunion. Once again the *Föhn* (warm wind) set in after the Games had begun in excellent weather, and ice-hockey matches and the 10,000-metres race suffered postponements because of poor ice. But it was not as severe as in 1928 and the program was successfully completed with Henri Oreiller (France) gaining the most medals with victories in the men's downhill and combination, and a bronze in the special slalom. Oreiller was both a well-known skier and motor-rally and racing driver, and tragically met his death in a race at Montlhéry, France, on 7 October 1962. Ski racing in 1948 still had much simplicity, and one of the spectacles of the Games was the American girl, Gretchen Fraser, winning the special slalom with twin plaits flying. She was then twenty-nine, an age at which most racing skiers of the 1970s would have retired.

There was sentiment to other performances. John R. Heaton won the silver medal on the Cresta Run twenty years after gaining second place to his brother, Jennison. Birger Ruud took the silver in the ski jump sixteen years after his first Olympic victory and twelve years after his second. The Norwegians took all three medals in the ski jump chiefly due to their style, for the winner, Petter Hugsted, was outjumped by both the Finn, Matti Pietikäinen, later World Champion, and the American, Gordon Wren. The principal

1936. Speed skating, Garmisch-Partenkirchen. Ivar Ballangrud (Norway), inside, won three gold medals that year.

dispute was in ice hockey, to which the United States sent two teams. The American Hockey Association team was admitted in spite of the protests of the US Olympic Committee, the AHA team being affiliated not to the Olympic Committee but to the International Ice Hockey Association. The AHA team finished fourth, but was subsequently disqualified because of the lack of affiliation. Canada took the gold medal again, but only on a better goal average compared with Czechoslovakia. The European challenge in ice hockey had begun. Sweden dominated the cross-country skiing, and in the men's figure skating, the eighteen-year-old American Richard Button, with his fine jumping, set a new athletic standard.

VI OSLO 1952

Norway, the homeland of skiing, at last was host to a Winter Games and a sense of occasion pervaded events from beginning to end. The Olympic flame was brought not from Greece but from the hearth of the house in Morgedal, southern Norway, where Sondre Norheim (1825–97), the outstanding pioneer of modern skiing, was born. Norheim's introduction of primitive heel bindings and a shaped ski meant a giant leap forward in ski jumping and turning technique. At the end of a relay run over the 220 kilometres from Morgedal to Oslo, Eigil Nansen, a grandson of the explorer Fridtjof Nansen, whose book, *The First Crossing of Greenland* (1890), had given modern skiing its most important intellectual impetus, lit the Olympic flame in the Bislet Stadium.

For the first time, a capital city in which winter sports held an outstanding place was playing host, and 561,407 spectators watched a record number of thirty nations competing. The weather was excellent, and the climax was undoubtedly the Holmenkollen ski jump, which Arnfinn Bergmann won for Norway before 130,000 highly critical and knowledgeable spectators. Almost equalling this, however, was the giant slalom victory of another Norwegian, Stein Eriksen, who also took the silver in the special slalom. There was considerable irony in this after Norway's early opposition both to the Winter Games concept and the adoption of Alpine skiing. Hjalmar Andersen added to the Norwegian delight by winning the 1,500-metres, 5,000-metres and 10,000-metres speed-skating events. Richard Button, with the first triple rotation jump, again won the men's figure skating, and Jeanette Altwegg (Great Britain), having won the women's, unlike many of her predecessors, gave up not to become a professional but to help run the Pestalozzi Children's Village in Switzerland. Germany won both the two-man and four-man bob, but with competitors so large that the International Bobsleigh Federation had to change its rules to limit the weight of teams and try to create equal conditions.

The Olympic Ski-Jump. Horse-drawn sledges brought spectators from nearby St. Moritz. To the right of the take-off is the tower for the umpires.

VII CORTINA D'AMPEZZO 1956

Cortina set some important landmarks in the history of Olympic winter sport. It was the first televised Winter Games, and a whole new world was introduced to the colour and pageantry of the 'five-

ring circus' and to the ice and snow heroes of the mountain countries. The firework display which ended the Games seemed to set the magical peaks of the Dolomites aflame, though, alas, black-and-white television hardly did it justice. Anton (Toni) Sailer, the twenty-year-old Austrian Alpine skier, dominated the Games beyond compare. Indeed to many people these were Sailer's Games. The beauty, skill, speed and daring of Alpine skiing were personified in the young Kitzbüheler, who won all three Alpine events by extraordinary margins – the giant slalom by 6.2 sec, the special slalom by 4.00 sec and the downhill by 3.5 sec. He was only the fifth winter sportsman to win three gold medals at a single games – the others were the Scandinavian athletes Thorleif Haug, Clas Thunberg, Ivar Ballangrud and Hjalmar Andersen – and the impetus he gave to the ski holiday industry is incalculable.

The USSR was represented for the first time, and at once caused a surprise by taking the ice-hockey tournament, with Canada a disconsolate third. It was to be the start of a long period of Russian domination. Russians also excelled in the speed skating, in which Norway failed to gain a gold medal for the first time since 1932. Norway was also eclipsed in the ski jumping; the Finns, arms held back in the new, aerodynamic 'drop' style, instead of forward in front of their heads, took both gold and silver medals. The best Norwegian was ninth. Franz Kapus (Switzerland) became the oldest gold medal winner at forty-six in piloting his four-man bob to victory, and the United States had two men on the medals rostrum when Hayes Alan Jenkins, first, and his brother David, third, were honoured after the men's figure-skating championship. Another American, Ronald Robertson, took the silver, and to round off the American triumph, Tenley Albright and Carol Heiss were first and second in the women's figure-skating competition.

VIII SQUAW VALLEY 1960

Squaw Valley set another Winter Olympic precedent by being the first purpose-built centre for the Games, and a monument to the extraordinary entrepreneurial skill of Alexander Cushing, an American who persuaded the IOC to choose Squaw Valley – by thirty-two votes to thirty for Innsbruck – when all that existed there was a tourist hostel. Even many IOC members were hazy on the whereabouts of Squaw Valley, at an altitude of 1,900 m (6,230 ft) on the east side of the Sierra Nevada, about 200 miles (320 km) from San Francisco. It was attacked variously after the choice. Artificial obstacles were added to make the downhill course more of a test, which was against FIS rules, and the Scandinavians complained that an altitude of 2,000 m (6,650 ft) was too high for the cross-country skiers. The organizers refused to build a bob run because only nine countries were interested in competing. In spite of the attacks, the Games were a great success, the best example after World War II of a 'village' event, with the competitors in close touch and not overborne by transport and communication problems in a big-city complex.

There were two innovations to set against the loss of the bob: biathlon, a 20-km cross-country ski run interspersed by four series of rifle-shooting tests, and women's speed-skating events, which had not been held since demonstrations in 1932. Lidia Skoblikova won the 1,500 metres and 3,000 metres (she was to go on to Innsbruck in 1964 to win four gold medals in four successive days). The Nordic skiing events were dominated by Sixten Jernberg (Sweden) and Veikko Hakulinen (Finland); Jernberg won the 30 kilometres and came second in the 15 kilometres, and Hakulinen, now over thirty-five, took a bronze and silver and in the last leg of the 4 × 10-kilometres relay made up a lag of 22 seconds to win by a ski length from Haakon Brusveen, the Norwegian winner of the 15 kilometres.

All the figure-skating gold medals went to North America, and the United States won the ice-hockey championship for the first time – an indication, perhaps, of the psychological and physical advantages of 'playing at home', certainly in sports that draw the spectators. The Alpine skiing medals were shared around, in contrast to those at Cortina, but one of the chief surprises was in the Nordic combination (15-km cross-country running and 70-metres jumping) where Georg Thoma (Germany) became the first non-Scandinavian to take the gold medal.

IX INNSBRUCK 1964

Innsbruck, as the first of a series of big-city Winter Games, set several new fashions. A number of events, including the slaloms and giant slaloms at Axamer-Lizum, the Nordic cross-country at Seefeld, and the bob and tobogganing at Igls, were at satellite centres up to 25 km (15½ miles) from the city centre. Because of its convenience geographically, Innsbruck could welcome a record number of 1,186 competitors, and over a million spectators. Transport and communications problems were posed and answered with considerable effort and enterprise. These were the first fully computerized Games, and where for example at Cortina the figure-skating results had taken eight hours to compile, here it was done in seconds by IBM machines. The operation cost IBM £500,000, but the total budget for the Austrian authorities was nearer £12 million. At the very last moment the one missing link was the most elementary of all – snow! The Austrian army had to haul nearly 20,000 cubic metres of snow from bowls and slopes far up 2,500-m (8,200-ft) mountains so that Nordic and Alpine ski trails could be adequately packed. On the other hand, the Austrian economy, so heavily dependent on tourist income, benefited incalculably from the publicity. Opponents of the Winter Games, among them the President of the IOC, Avery Brundage, were quick to point out the commercial factors affecting individual competitors. In particular Brundage objected to those Alpine skiers who displayed their skis, all of them carrying brand names prominently, for newspaper photographers. Never before had the Winter Games received such publicity. Newspaper and radio men outnumbered competitors, and thirty-four television networks were represented.

Women took a prominent part in these Games. The Goitschel sisters of France had an extraordinary family duel in the Alpine skiing. Marielle won the giant slalom with Christine second. She then won the first leg of the slalom, also ahead of her sister, but

Christine won the second leg and the competition overall. Austrian women recovered their self-respect by taking all three medals in the downhill, won by Christl Haas. Other outstanding women competitors were Lidia Skoblikova, the Russian speed skater, with gold medals in the 500, 1,000, 1,500 and 3,000 metres, and her fellow countrywoman, Klaudia Boyarskikh, first in the 5- and 10-km Nordic skiing. Sixten Jernberg, of Sweden, at thirty-five, was the man of the Games, gaining his ninth medal in three Olympics as a member of the victorious Swedish 4×10-km team. He had earlier won the skiing marathon, the 50 km. The USSR took the largest number of medals, including the ice hockey, in which Sweden and Czechoslovakia gained the silver and bronze respectively, with the United States and Canada trailing. The Russian pairs skaters, Oleg Protopopov and Ludmila Belousova, took their country's first figure-skating medal. Brundage, for all his opposition to the principle of Winter Games, was impressed enough to remark at the closing ceremony: 'The Innsbruck Games have shown how much the human will is capable of achieving.'

If reminder were needed that modern man was well capable of honouring Olympic codes, then there was no better example than in the two-man bob. Eugenio Monti (Italy), many times world champion but never, at that point, an Olympic champion, effectively destroyed his own chances when he whipped out a bolt from his own bobsleigh at the completion of his run and got it up to the start for Tony Nash (Great Britain), whose own bolt had sheered. Nash went on to win the gold medal. Less happily two men were killed during training, an Australian skier, Ross Milne, and a Polish-born tobogganist in the British team, Kay Skrzypecki.

X GRENOBLE 1968

No amount of controversy – and Grenoble had more than its share – could hide the personal accomplishments of athletes such as Jean-Claude Killy (France), who, like Sailer in 1956, won all three Alpine gold medals; Nancy Greene (Canada), who took the giant slalom gold and special slalom silver; and Eugenio Monti (Italy), nine times world bob champion, and finally, at the age of forty, possessor of an Olympic gold.

Grenoble, with 1,293 competitors from thirty-seven nations, and hosts of journalists, cameramen, TV and radio personnel, was an operation of its time – politicized, computerized and, to the chagrin of Brundage, commercialized. Its budget was $200 million, but more than half of this went into permanent facilities such as housing and motorways. But the scale of building directly linked with the Games was still formidable, especially the Olympic indoor ice stadium, a superb modern arena, designed to seat nearly 12,000, no pillars to obstruct the view, and, unlike the bob run at Alpe d'Huez, available to a large community for countless years ahead. Grenoble suffered, as did Innsbruck, problems of transport with satellite sites up to 40 km (25 miles) away, and the bobbers were forced to live in Alpe d'Huez hotels, far from the Olympic village, awaiting pre-dawn calls. The run proved highly unsatisfactory, sited on the open mountainside without shade from the sun, and safe bobbing was only possible in the hour or so before dawn.

1964. Tormod Knutsen (Norway) winner of the Nordic combined event at Innsbruck.

1964
INNSBRUCK
25

Tony Nash (Gt Britain) who, with Robin Dixon (Gt Britain), won the two-man bob in 1964.

In the committee rooms there was further trouble. The IOC tried to curb advertising and commercial exploitation by banning the use of trade names on skis and other equipment. But many leading skiers, and their national teams, were heavily reliant on sponsorship from the equipment manufacturers, and after threats of revolt against this ruling a compromise was reached whereby skiers remove their equipment before being photographed or televised.

Finally, Killy won his third gold medal in the special slalom amid bitter controversy, for it involved the outstanding skiers of the two leading Alpine countries, Austria and France, and the reverberations were to affect the Games of Sapporo four years later. In the first instance Killy was involved in a revolt by leading skiers against the principle of an elimination slalom, introduced by FIS only for Olympic Games and World Championships. The eliminations were intended to reduce the field – special slalom, being over a shorter course, can be practised in more parts of the world than downhill or giant slalom, thus attracting a bigger entry – and starting positions in the competition proper. Top skiers argued that handicap points gained over a whole season ought to be the only criterion, but this ignored the disadvantages to skiers not able to ski regularly on the FIS circuit. The problem, which was close to the heart of the amateur–professional conflict, was side-stepped by the cancellation of the eliminating contests because of bad weather. If anything the fog was even thicker on the following day, and in all normal circumstances the race would have been postponed, but this was the last-but-one day of the Games and no one wanted a conflict on the last day between the 90-metre jumping and the special slalom. So, with the procrastinations unfortunately compounding problems, the slalom took place, with the skiers taking off as and when the mist momentarily cleared. Killy had the fastest first run, but after going first in the second run his overall time still looked vulnerable. In the German-speaking countries there was considerable popular support for Karl Schranz, Austria's veteran skier, who had gained every honour except an Olympic gold medal. Schranz began his second run, but missed gates 18 and 19 of the course of 69 gates and gave up. He claimed he had been distracted by a shadow a few gates below him, and after three witnesses had said that a course policeman had crossed the track at Gate 21 (about 50–60 ft or 15–18 m farther down) Schranz was allowed another run. His time for this would have given him the gold medal, but the French protested that Schranz could not have seen interference at such a range. The jury, which had to decide whether Schranz missed the gate because of interference or whether he did so before the interference was apparent, voted 3–1 to accept the protest, with one abstention.

There was another major incident when three East Germans, including Ortrun Enderlein, the 1964 Olympic women's champion, were disqualified from the single-seater tobogganing for heating the runners of their sleds over an open fire in an effort to obtain greater speed. More happily, Franco Nones (Italy), in winning the 30-km cross-country skiing race, became the first *Langlauf* medal holder from a country outside Scandinavia and the USSR. The Protopopovs, at thirty-five and thirty-two respectively, took their second Olympic gold medal on one of the few sentimental occasions of a Games which posed rather too many of the problems of the times.

XI SAPPORO 1972

If Grenoble was big, then Sapporo financially was bigger. If Grenoble was controversial, then Sapporo produced major confrontation. It ended with the expulsion of Karl Schranz, Austria's leading skier, whose early ticket home brought him a hero's welcome from a crowd in Vienna estimated at over 200,000. The Austrian team was withdrawn in protest, then re-entered, after Schranz had pleaded that he did not wish to be responsible for his team mates missing their chance of Olympic competition and medals after so much striving.

Schranz was expelled by the IOC by twenty-eight votes to fourteen for permitting the use of his name and pictures in commercial advertising. He was one among many – Brundage said he had a 'black list' of forty names – but he was singled out, according to the president, because he was 'the most blatant and the most verbose we could find'. On the eve of the Games, in the Olympic village, Schranz gave an interview to Will Grimsley, sports editor of the American agency, Associated Press, which appeared in the English language newspaper, the *Japan Times*. In it Schranz said that if Brundage's ideas were followed to their true conclusion then the Olympics would only be for the very rich. 'This thing of amateur purity is something that dates back to the nineteenth century when amateur sportsmen were regarded as gentlemen and everyone else was an outcast. The Olympics should be a competition of skill and strength and speed – and no more.' This appeared one day before the

Bernhard Russi (Switzerland) on his way to victory in the 1972 Olympic downhill.

Annemarie Pröll (Austria), the favourite for the downhill and giant slalom, came second in both events to Marie-Thérèse Nadig (Switzerland).

IOC executive met to consider the recommendation of Hugh Weir's eligibility committee. The timing could not have been more unfortunate, but Brundage had to face much hostile press and television questioning of the decision to make an example of one man. Schranz, he said, was not allowed to state his case because the IOC dealt with groups and not individuals. In this instance, however, it was an individual who was punished.

Sapporo, while highlighting many of the problems of a modern Olympic Games, at the same time provided a memorable setting and a gracious welcome. Situated on Hokkaido, the most northerly island of Japan, it had grown from a sparse settlement to a city of a million and more in only a hundred years, and was anxious now to establish itself in world eyes, and also with millions of Japanese, looking for new ways to enjoy their increasing money and leisure, as a ski centre. The outlay of $555,556,000 from 1967 to 1972 on the Olympic Games thus had long-term implications over and above ten days of snow and ice sport. The fact that 3,000 press, television and radio personnel outnumbered competitors by more than two to one was a matter of high significance. The data-processing centre alone cost £365,000, the broadcasting facilities £121,000 – thirteen different programs with sixty commentaries could be sent out simultaneously. The Japanese electronics industry undoubtedly benefited directly or indirectly. Sapporo, too, is famous for its Snow Sculpture Festival at Otaru Park, with creatures of legend sculpted in snow and ice, and beautiful flowers preserved in showcases of diamond-like ice – all there and gone in a few days. Thus Mount Eniwa, a virgin mountain of 4,000 ft (1,220 m) glittering with silver birches, could be manipulated by 15,000 men, 850 bulldozers and six tons of explosives for two downhill races, the men's and women's, adorned with two cable cars capable of transporting 330 people an hour, and a chair-lift, and then returned to its beautiful pristine state, as required by the conservation laws, within weeks of the Games being over. The cost of this operation alone was about £2 million. The bob run on Mount Teine, which also staged the slalom and giant slalom races but was never to be used again, cost another £2 million.

Mount Teine set another record. Overlooking the Sea of Japan, which divides Hokkaido from the Siberian mainland, it was the first Winter Games site with an ocean view. In theory the climate should have been temperate. In fact, with the juxtaposition of the Siberian high- and the Pacific low-pressure weather systems, Sapporo was subject to violent changes of weather. Waxing of skis, always a tricky art, became a matter of almost neurotic concern. Undoubtedly Swiss research and organization in this area contributed to their domination of Alpine skiing – six medals, including three golds, of the eighteen available. Austria suffered bitter disappointment with Annemarie Pröll, the outstanding favourite for the downhill and giant slalom, bearing a considerable psychological burden after

1972. USSR defeating the United States at Sapporo.

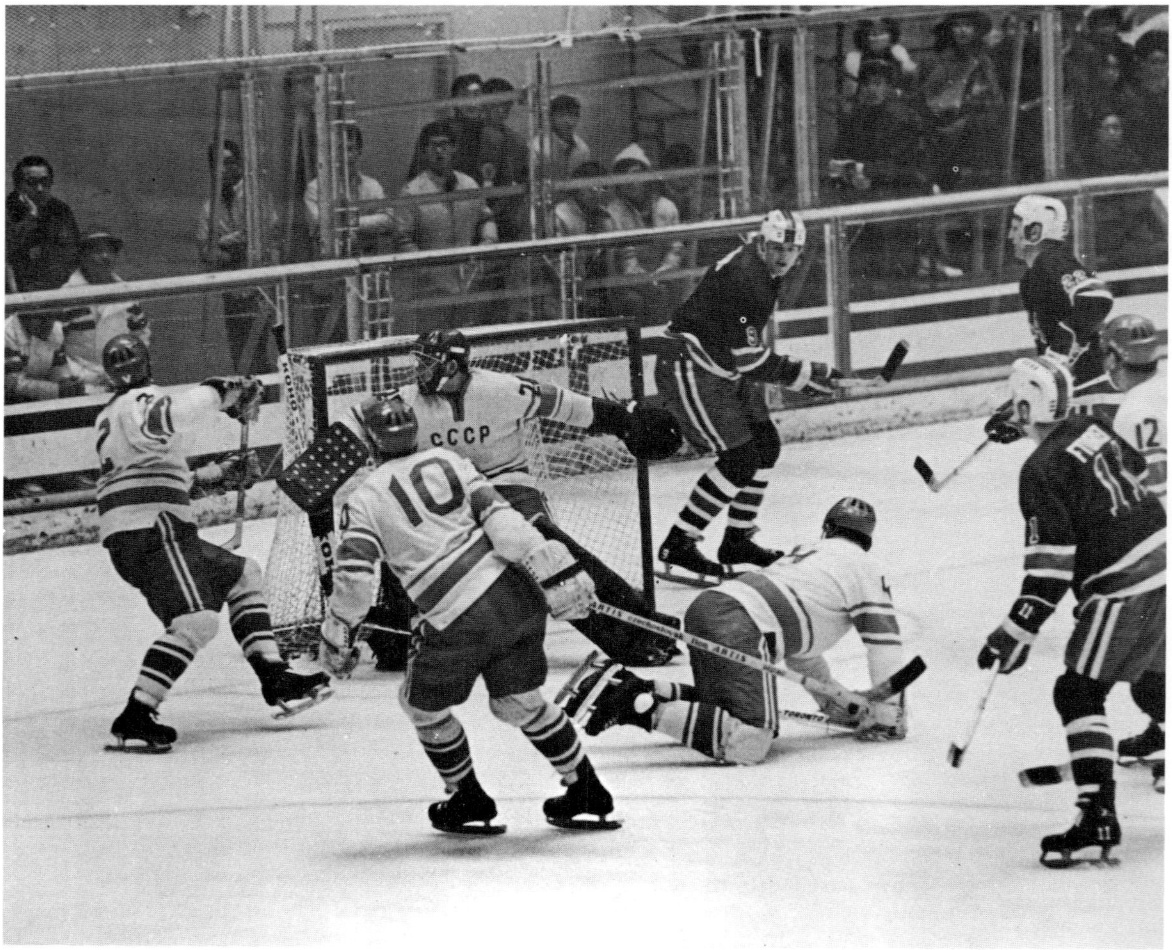

1972. Irina Rodnina and Aleksei Ulanov (USSR) winning the pairs skating gold medal.

Schranz's expulsion, and coming second in both events to Marie-Thérèse Nadig (Switzerland), who had never before won a major race. Bernhard Russi, the Swiss World Champion, won the men's downhill, and Gustav Thoeni (Italy), another great world figure, the

1972. Japan's first skiing medal, Yukio Kasaya taking the 70-metre jump at Sapporo.

giant slalom, but the special slalom again proved an outsider's race, Francisco Fernández Ochoa providing Spain with its first Winter Olympic gold medal. It represented, too, the increasing geographical spread of winter sports, although Alpine skiing's popularity was scarcely represented in its six events as against Nordic skiing's ten.

The USSR took eight medals in cross-country events, including four in the women's, and Norway seven, but the outstanding surprise was the success of the Japanese in ski jumping. In the 70 metres they took all three medals, and another Japanese skier won the jumping section of the combined jumping and cross-country competition. Wojciech Fortuna gave Poland an unexpected gold medal in the 90-metre jump, his longest jump being 111 metres (365 feet).

In spite of his first fall in a major competition for four years, Ondrej Nepela (Czechoslovakia) won the men's figure skating. Trixi Schuba (Austria), an immaculate tracer of figure eights, won the women's competition on possibly the last occasion a skater of her style could do so. After 1972 the rules were changed which accorded the free-skating section of the individual competition a higher proportion of the marks. Irina Rodnina and Aleksei Ulanov, from Moscow, won the pairs competition, but this also was in the nature of a farewell. The Western press was much intrigued by a romantic involvement between Ulanov and Ludmila Smirnova, who partnered Andrei Suraikin to the silver medal. Russian skating officials denied that it was of any consequence, but Ulanov later married Miss Smirnova and became her partner in international competition.

The USSR took the ice-hockey gold medal for the third successive Games, but the competition was the worse for Canada's refusal to participate because of amateur–professional arguments. Ard Schenk (Netherlands) became only the third speed skater in Olympic history to take three titles when he won the 10,000 kilometres to add to the 5,000 and 1,500. The Chicago suburb of Northbrook provided two gold medallists in the women's speed skating, Anne Henning in the 500 metres and Dianne Holum in the 1,500 metres, which meant all three gold medals gained by the United States were won by girls – Barbara Ann Cochran's gold in the Alpine skiing special slalom was won by the smallest margin in Olympic history, two-hundredths of a second.

Japan's *sayonora*, or goodbye, was expressed touchingly and warmly at the closing ceremony, but the last word was with its weather, which closed in so violently with gale, snow, rain and thaw on the day afterwards that many competitors were marooned in the Olympic village or waited many hours at Sapporo airport with planes unable to take off. A few days earlier and the Games, which had survived a few minor ups and downs with the weather, would have been ruined.

XII INNSBRUCK 1976

High on a plinth at the Bergisel 90-metre jumping stadium, two Austrian winter sports stars, Joseph Feistmantl, the 1964 Olympic luge champion, and Christl Haas, the 1964 women's downhill gold medallist, touched off Olympic flames to right and left, and 55,000 people cheered. Olympic history was being made. No city had previously hosted a Winter Olympic Games twice.

Innsbruck, with only three years to prepare, organized perhaps the most successful Games in modern times. Watched by more than 1½ million spectators on the spot, and 600 million on television, 'The Simple Games', as they were shrewdly christened by the organizers, produced great performances and champions, and a minimum of unhappy incidents.

The International Olympic Committee Executive Board, faced with the withdrawal of Denver after a Colorado state referendum had refused further funds for the staging of the Games, in February 1973 chose Innsbruck above Lake Placid (USA), Tampere (Finland) and the Mont Blanc region (France) because of its known expertise. Innsbruck wanted and needed the Games, had all the facilities, knew how to handle logistical problems, and had the financial backing of government, province and city. Lord Killanin, in announcing the Board's decision, said there were many people critical of the eligibility of winter sports for the Olympic Movement because of the small number of countries involved and the commercialism. 'The commercialism will be watched very carefully, and much will depend on the attitude of Innsbruck,' he said.

The choice of Innsbruck was in fact a truce. It repaired the damage to Austrian pride following the expulsion of the skier, Karl Schranz, from Sapporo by Avery Brundage. It represented, too, more liberal attitudes by the IOC towards the problems of financing major sports and sportsmen while demanding reasonable restraints. The amendment of Rule 26, permitting a full-time commitment and broken-time payments, brought the World Cup skiers and Russian ice-hockey players legally into the Olympic fold.

Innsbruck in the end spent 230 million schillings (approximately

Rosi Mittermaier winning her first ever Downhill competition at Innsbruck 1976.

$17 million) in adding to, or modernizing, its Olympic sites, plus personnel costs and technical facilities. The overall costs, including 250 million schillings (nearly $20 million), of Austrian television, was 599 million schillings ($44 million) with a planned deficit of 60 million schillings. The Austrian army was extensively employed – 144,712 men putting in 1,354,218 hours' work in preparing and running events according to the organizers' meticulously kept statistics. They also contributed heavily to the extensive security measures made necessary by the attack at Munich. It was a major accomplishment that the omnipresent soldiers and policemen did not corrode the spirit and style of the Games.

So the organizers kept their side of the bargain. A country of seven million proved it could host a Winter Games at reasonable cost. Austria, with its huge dependence on tourism, and winter sports travel in particular, had a desperate need of success on the snow or ice. On the first day of serious competition, Franz Klammer gave them that with an epic victory in the downhill ski race. The eve of the Games, which were being watched closely for commercialism, brought one of the smartest public relations stunts by a ski manufacturer. The company, which had spent 400,000 marks developing a new ski, kept it under wraps until the third and fourth training runs of the downhill. Then, with a fanfare, it was announced that Klammer would use it. The Wonder Ski had a spatule, or large hole, in the toe, designed to reduce the amount of air balling under the normal, solid, upturned tip. It was both a sales stunt and a gambit in the psychological war. Bernhard Russi, Klammer's great Swiss rival, gold medallist at Sapporo, said simply: 'There are no wonder skis. Only facts'. And his was the time Klammer had to beat as the 22-year-old from Mooswald, winner of 12 of the previous 16 World Cup downhills, hurled himself down the 3.1 kilometres of Patscherkofel's zig-zagging snow chute. At the interval Klammer was two-tenths of a second behind Russi, and nearly 70,000 Austrians on the course, and six million glued to their television screens, suffered heart flutter as his interval time was intoned . . . 1 min 13.24 sec, nearly two tenths slower than Russi. Instinctively Klammer knew he had to let everything go in the bottom half. He cornered the infamous Bear's Neck with a line sharper and more controlled than anyone's. Down through the finishing schuss the crowd roared him on to victory.

Austria ended the twelfth Games as she began it, with Karl Schnabl's birdlike descent in the 90-metre stadium providing a marvellous finale. Alpine success, which Austria takes as a birthright, otherwise eluded her. Rosi Mittermaier, born a few metres over the Austrian border in Reit im Winkl, West Germany, was one of the reasons, but no one grudged Mittermaier her unprecedented two golds and a silver. If any one person's ability and character summed up the Games it was Mittermaier's. Her victory on the first Sunday of the Games was her first ever in downhill. When, more predictably, she won the special slalom on the following Wednesday, the world's eye was on her. Could she win the giant slalom and repeat the feat of Jean-Claude Killy in 1968 and Toni Sailer in 1956 and win three Alpine golds? She failed, but only by twelve hundredths of a second, to Kathy Kreiner of Canada, the tiniest margin in any race of the Games. Whatever the influence of commercialism, Alpine skiing came out of the Games well because of the personality and style of Mittermaier. Athletic but feminine, direct but charming, she won everything except the three golds. 'Who could be unhappy with two gold medals and a silver!' she said.

The Soviet Union and East Germany collected forty-six of the 111 medals, with the rest split among fourteen of the thirty-five countries taking part. East Germany achieved their seven gold, five silver and seven bronze medals with no competitor in Alpine ski. Their outstanding achievements were at Igls, where they won every title in

15
ALPIN

Franz Klammer (Austria) beat his rival Bernhard Russi in the Downhill ski race, 1976.

luge and bob, and at Seefeld, the Nordic centre, where Ulrich Wehling took the combined 70-metre jump and 5-kilometre run for the second successive Olympics, and Hans-Georg Aschenbach confirmed their 70-metre jumping supremacy by taking the individual event. Of Russia's twenty-seven medals, thirteen (six gold, two silver, five bronze) were gained at Seefeld. In only four Nordic events – 50-kilometres cross-country, the seven combined, and both jumps – did they fail to gain a medal. An element of the unpredictable still flavoured competition. Bill Koch, in the 30 kilometres, gained the United States' first Nordic medal without a single US media man to thrust a mike or tape recorder in his face.

Ice skating produced its usual mixture of drama, beauty and controversy. Dancing, introduced for the first time against the better instincts of many purists, was won decisively by Ludmila Pakhomova and Aleksandr Gorshkov, of Russia. The pairs title went to Irina Rodnina and Aleksandr Zaitseve, Miss Rodnina having also won it in 1972, paired with Alexei Ulanov, who afterwards eloped with the silver medallist, Ludmilla Smirnova. John Curry, of Britain, won the men's title after a widely quoted criticism by him and Toller Cranston, Canada's bronze medallist, of the prejudices of judges who downmarked balletic styles. Dorothy Hamill succeeded fellow Americans Peggy Fleming and Carol Heiss as women's champion.

Speed skating, so often the sport producing multi-medal champions, spread its favours around. Tatiana Averina became the first double gold medallist of the Games by winning the 1,000 and 3,000 metres events. Then Sheila Young, from Detroit, took home gold, silver and bronze to add to her world championship at cycling. The men's events produced no Ard Schenk. Sten Stenson (Norway) and Piet Kleine (Holland) each took a gold and silver however.

Lacking Sweden and Canada, the ice-hockey tournament was a two-horse race between the Soviet Union, seeking their fourth successive Olympic title, and Czechoslovakia. The Czechs were badly hit by the influenza which swept the Olympic village, and then had the 3–1 victory against Poland removed from them because a player took 'flu medication containing a banned drug. In the final, emotion-charged game, the Czechs needed to beat the unbeaten Russians for the gold. Quickly going 2–0 up they were still 3–2 ahead in the final period when Novak was penalized for cross checking. Yakushev equalized and Karlamov scored the winner four minutes from time with Novak still in the sin bin.

The one other drug incident involved Russia's most famous woman cross-country skier, Galina Kolakova, winner of five medals in previous Olympic Games. Tested after what would have been her sixth medal, the 5 kilometres bronze, she was found to have minute traces of a banned substance from the use of a nasal spray for a streaming cold. Her medal was taken away, but the offence was considered trifling enough to permit starts in the 10 kilometres and 4 × 5 kilometres relay, for which she earned bronze and gold respectively.

WHO'S WHO IN THE OLYMPIC GAMES

The editors would have liked to include in this section a biography of every Olympian who has mounted the middle position of the prizewinners' podium; regrettably we did not have space for so many entries. Instead we have had to be selective, choosing those champions who have reached some higher distinction. Some qualifiers do not appear only because all our research proved fruitless.

The abbreviations for names of countries are the official ones used by the International Olympic Committee and listed on page 268. A name appearing in SMALL CAPITALS within an entry indicates that a separate biography of that person will be found in this section of the book. Olympic medals are listed at the end of each entry.

Alexeev, Vasily (URS)

B. Pokravo-shishkino, Ryazan, 7 Jan. 1942. Alexeev, 1.86 m (6 ft $1\frac{1}{4}$ in) tall and often weighing 162.5 kg (359 lb or 25 stone 9 lb), was the most successful weightlifter of the 1970s, taking every Olympic and world super-heavyweight title between 1970 and 1977. This feat of eight consecutive gold medals has only been equalled in the sport by the United States' John Davis (1946–53) and Tommy Kono (1952–59). Between these dates, Alexeev never lost a competition, broke over one hundred world records and at Olympic Games was almost unchallenged. In Munich, his most formidable opponents, Belgium's Serge Reding missed all his presses and the United States' Ken Patera dropped his snatches, allowing Alexeev to use weights well within his grasp to take the title by 30 kg (66 lb) with an Olympic record total of 640 kg (1,410$\frac{3}{4}$ lb). Alexeev's total belief in his own ability – he has invariably trained at whim sometimes in the middle of the night – always gave him confidence at the major events. In Montreal, both Khristo Plachkov (BUL) and Gerd Bonk (GDR) had raised superior totals before the Games, but Plachkov withdrew because of sickness and Bonk failed to produce anything like his best form. Alexeev went steadily on to take the gold medal with 440 kg (969$\frac{3}{4}$ lb) including a world record clean and jerk, the movement in which he had always excelled, with 255 kg (562 lb). He lost his world title in 1978 at Gettysburg when he was unable to finish a jerk of 240 kg (529 lb) because of a damaged hip tendon.

Gold weightlifting super-heavyweight 1972, 1976

Anderson, Gary L. (USA)

B. Holdrege, Neb., 8 Oct. 1939. He won eleven individual and ten team gold medals in international competition during the 1960s. A rare left-handed shooter, Anderson taught himself to shoot. He was the first American in over forty years to win the free rifle event in two consecutive Olympic Games.

Gold free rifle 1964, 1968

Andrianov, Nikolai (URS)

B. Vladimir, 14 Oct. 1952. The most consistent and successful male gymnast of recent years, Andrianov has dominated his section of the sport since 1975,

Nikolai Andrianov (URS), 1976

when he took five gold medals and a silver at the European championships. He had made his Olympic début three years earlier at Munich, at the age of 19, and won the floor exercise.

By the time of Montreal he was a far more confident performer, and although the men's competition there was somewhat overshadowed in the public eye by the perfection of Nadia COMANECI, Andrianov took four gold medals, including the combined exercises. Overall victories in the 1977 World Cup and 1978 World championships reinforced his stature, and his remaining ambition is to

successfully defend his Olympic title in Moscow.
Gold combined exercises (individual) 1976; floor exercises 1972, 1976; rings 1976; vault 1976
Silver combined exercises (team) 1972, 1976; parallel bars 1976
Bronze vault 1972; pommelled horse 1976

Astakhova, Polina (URS)

B. Donetsk, Ukraine, 30 Oct. 1936. This seemingly fragile Russian gymnast would have won even more honours if she had not been a contemporary of Larisa LATYNINA. At Tokyo (1964) she finished only 0.033 pt behind Latynina in an event won by Vera ČÁSLAVSKÁ (TCH). On the asymmetrical bars Čáslavská seemed likely to finish first but missed a pirouette off the top bar and fell, thus allowing Astakhova to take the title.
Gold asymmetrical bars 1960, 1964; combined exercises (team) 1956, 1960, 1964
Silver floor exercises 1960, 1964
Bronze combined exercises (individual) 1960, 1964

Babashoff, Shirley (USA)

B. Whittier, California, 31 Jan. 1957. Her two Olympic gold medals came in the relays – 4 × 100-metres freestyle in 1972 and 1976. But Miss Babashoff also won five silver medals in freestyle events during her career.

In 1972 she was runner-up in the 100-metres and 200-metres freestyle, but was on the winning team that broke the world record in the freestyle relay; though she helped the USA to qualify for the final of the medley relay she was replaced for the final, missing another team gold.

In the 1976 Games she was runner-up to Kornelia ENDER in the 200-metres freestyle and to Petra Thumer in the 400-metres and 800-metres freestyle. Her greatest moment was when she brought the United States' team home ahead of GDR in the 4 × 100-metres freestyle relay, the only victory by the American women at those Games and one in world record time.
Gold 4 × 100-metres 1972, 1976
Silver 100-metres freestyle 1972; 200-metres freestyle 1972, 1976; 400-metres freestyle 1976; 800-metres freestyle 1976; 4 × 100-metres medley 1976

Shirley Babashoff (USA), 1976

Baillet-Latour, Comte Henri de (BEL)

B. 1 Mar. 1876; d. Brussels, 6 Jan. 1942. Became an IOC Member in 1903; responsible for organizing the Games in Antwerp (1920) for which there was only one year to make preparations. It was largely his energy in the management of this task that led his colleagues to elect him to the Presidency of the IOC, succeeding COUBERTIN in 1925. He tried to keep commercialism and politics out of the Olympic Movement, the latter notably in Berlin, in 1936. He was President of the IOC until his death.

Balaş, Iolanda (ROM)

B. Timisoara, 12 Dec. 1936. World's outstanding woman high jumper from 1958 to 1966, she set the first of her fourteen world records in this event in July 1956. At the 1956 Olympics she finished fifth but was European Champion in 1958 and 1962 and won the Olympic title with 1.85 m (6 ft $0\frac{3}{4}$ in) in 1960 and with 1.90 m (6 ft $2\frac{3}{4}$ in) in 1964. She was 1.85 m (6 ft $0\frac{3}{4}$ in) tall but found it impossible to use any style but a version

Iolanda Balaş (ROM), 1964

of the old-fashioned 'scissors'. Otherwise she might well have raised the record higher than her 1.91 m (6 ft $3\frac{1}{4}$ in) in 1961.
Gold high jump 1960, 1964

Balczó, András (HUN)

B. Kondoros, 16 Aug. 1939. Probably the greatest all-rounder in the history of modern pentathlon. He first competed in the 1960 Olympics, where he was placed fourth, only 15 pts behind the silver medallist, and won a gold in the team event. In spite of being the reigning World Champion, he was not in the Hungarian team in Tokyo. As well as his Olympic achievements, he won the world title in 1963, 1965, 1966, 1967 and 1969.
Gold modern pentathlon (individual) 1972, (team) 1960, 1968
Silver modern pentathlon (individual) 1968, (team) 1972

Ballangrud, Ivar (NOR)

B. Lunner, Hadeland, 7 Mar. 1904; d. Trondheim, 6 June 1969. In his first years in competitive speed

skating his best distances were 5,000 metres and 10,000 metres. Later he was also an excellent sprinter. As well as his Olympic successes, he won the World Championship four times, the European Championship four times, was Norwegian Champion five times, and set five world records in the 1,500 metres, 5,000 metres (three times) and 10,000 metres.
Gold 500 metres 1936; 5,000 metres 1928, 1936; 10,000 metres 1936
Silver 1,500 metres 1936; 10,000 metres 1932
Bronze 1,500 metres 1928

Beamon, Robert (USA)
B. Jamaica, N.Y., 29 Aug. 1936. Achieved possibly the outstanding single Olympic athletics performance with his long jump of 8.90 m (29 ft $2\frac{1}{2}$ in), which added 55 cm ($21\frac{1}{2}$ in) to the world record at Mexico City on 18 October 1968. Beamon was a sometimes unpredictable but undoubtedly talented jumper who could run 100 yd in 9.5 sec and, before the 1968 Games, had cleared 8.33 m (27 ft 4 in). On his greatest day he had speed, spring and height; the following wind was right on the limit, for record ratification, of 2 metres per second (4.47 mph) and at the altitude of 2,260 m (7,415 ft), resistance is some 20 per cent less than at sea level. Even so, he was staggered at his accomplishment and never again did better than 8.20 m (26 ft 11 in). He turned professional in 1973.
Gold long jump 1968

Robert Beamon (USA), 1968

Belote, Melissa (USA)
B. Washington, D.C., 16 Oct. 1956. Miss Belote was only fifteen when she won three swimming gold medals at Munich. She had broken the world record for 200-metres backstroke at Chicago a month before the Games and had won both backstroke finals in the US Olympic trials. In Munich she twice broke the world record for 200-metres backstroke, with 2 min 20.58 sec in her heat and 2 min 19.19 sec in the final – the first woman to beat 2 min 20 sec for the event. She also won the 100-metres backstroke in the Olympic record time of 1 min 5.78 sec and shared in another world record as a member of the medley relay winning team; her time on the backstroke stage was 1 min 6.24 sec.
Gold 100-metres backstroke 1972; 200-metres backstroke 1972; 4 × 100-metres medley relay 1972

Belousova, Ludmila (URS)
see PROTOPOPOV

Beresford, Jack (GBR)
B. Chiswick, 1 Jan. 1899; d. 3 Dec. 1977. Although weighing only some $72\frac{1}{2}$ kg (160 lb) Beresford was the most successful Olympic oarsman and sculler of all time, competing in five consecutive Games; in 1939 he was preparing for a sixth appearance in the 1940 Games, when war intervened. In 1949 he was awarded the Olympic Diploma of Merit by the IOC.
Gold single sculls 1924; coxless fours 1932; double sculls 1936
Silver single sculls 1920; eights 1928

Bianchetto, Sergio (ITA)
B. Torre (Padova), 16 Feb. 1939. From his first cycling race in 1955 his talent was recognized and at seventeen he was selected as first reserve for the 1956 Italian Olympic team. Although twice world sprint champion, in 1961 and 1962, his Olympic gold medals were won on a tandem. In both instances it was his rare aggression and exceptional skill in handling a cycle that gave him the medal. In 1960 he was partnered by an old school friend Giuseppe Beghetto; in 1964 he rode with Andrea Damiano.
Gold 2,000-metres tandem 1960, 1964
Silver individual, 1,000-metres sprint 1964

Bikila, Abebe (ETH)
B. Mout, Ethiopia, 7 Aug. 1932; d. 25 Oct. 1973. Celebrated as the first man to win the Olympic marathon twice, Bikila should also be remembered as the first athletics gold medal winner from black Africa. In 1960 he was completely unknown outside his own country though he had just run a marathon in 2 hr 21 min 23 sec in the high altitude of Ethiopia which may, through its process of

Abebe Bikila (ETH), 1960

lung ventilation, have played a considerable part in his successes. Running barefoot through the floodlit streets of Rome, Bikila pulled away from his only real challenger, Rhadi Ben Abdesselam (MAR), in a world's best time of 2 hr 15 min 16.2 sec. The bemused press then discovered that this was only the third marathon run by this member of the Imperial Guard of Emperor Haile Selassie.

Four years later, this time wearing shoes, Bikila ran in the 1964 marathon on 21 October, although on 16 September he had had his appendix removed and had not been able to resume training until 27 September.

Sadly, in 1968 Bikila had to drop out after ten miles with an injured leg. Tragically, he received such severe injuries in a car accident in 1969 that he was unable to walk again. He bravely took up competitive paraplegic sport, including archery, but what had become a bitter struggle ended with his death at only forty-one years of age.
Gold marathon 1960, 1964

Blankers-Koen, Francina (HOL)

B. Amsterdam, 26 Apr. 1918. Between 1938 and 1951 she set world records in seven different events: 100 yards and 100 metres, 220 yards, 80-metres hurdles, high jump, long jump and pentathlon. She was sixth equal in the 1936 Olympic high jump. Because of World War II she was thirty by her next Games in 1948. She made the most of her chance with four gold medals, in spite of increasing emotional fatigue – just thirteen years after starting athletics as an 800-metres runner. In the European Championships of 1938, 1946 and 1950 she won eight medals and five titles.
Gold 100 metres 1948; 200 metres 1948; 80-metres hurdles 1948; 4 × 100-metres relay 1948

Bleibtrey, Ethelda (USA)

B. Waterford, N.Y., 27 Feb. 1902. It was possible to win only three gold medals in the women's swimming events at the 1920 Olympics, which Miss Bleibtrey achieved. She was the first woman to win three Olympic titles in any sport and she would probably have won four if there had been a backstroke event in the Games at that time, for she was the holder of a world record in that event in 1920. She set world records in the 100-metres freestyle (1 min 13.6 sec) and the now defunct 300-metres freestyle (4 min 34.0 sec). She set seven world records in her career.
Gold 100-metres freestyle 1920; 300-metres freestyle 1920; 4 × 100-metres freestyle relay 1920

Bogdanov, Anatoli (URS)

B. Leningrad, 1 Jan. 1931. One of the best shooters in free and smallbore rifle events in the 1950s, he was the first Soviet Olympic Champion, won twenty-five gold medals at the Olympic Games, World and European Championships and held the world record 1954–9. He took up shooting in 1950 and two years later won the free rifle event at the Olympic Games at Helsinki.
Gold free rifle 1952; smallbore rifle three positions 1956

Borzov, Valeri (URS)

B. near Lvov, 20 Oct. 1949. The only European to have won both the Olympic 100- and 200-metres titles, which he did almost effortlessly in 1972. A remarkably polished runner, Borzov was said to be a sprinter made rather than born, by a group of Kiev physiologists and coaches. This does less than justice to his coolness under pressure which gave him a perfect competitive record in major championships from 1968 to 1974, when he won both European junior titles. Only a year later he equalled the European senior record for the 100-metres event of 10 sec.

At Munich Borzov was deprived of the chance of racing against the two fastest Americans, Eddie Hart and Reynaud Robinson, because they failed to

Valeri Borzov (URS), 1972

turn up on time for their quarter-final races. But even so Borzov looked unbeatable in the final.

After the Olympic Games of 1972 Borzov suffered both a psychological reaction and a muscle injury but in 1974 in Rome he retained his European 100-metres title. In 1977 he married the Soviet gymnast Ludmila TURISCHEVA.
Gold 100 metres 1972; 200 metres 1972
Silver 4 × 100-metres relay 1972, 1976
Bronze 100 metres 1976

Boyarskikh, Klaudia (URS)

B. Verkhnyaya Pyshma, Sverdlovsk, 11 Nov. 1939. Teacher of physical education and the best woman skier of the mid-1960s. While a student she took part in athletics and then skiing. She won a prize at the international skiing competitions in Kavgolovo in 1963, three gold medals at the Winter Olympic Games in 1964 and two at the World Championships in 1966. She also won the

women's Holmenkollen events in 1965 and 1967.
Gold 5 kilometres 1964; 10 kilometres 1964; 3 × 5-kilometres relay 1964

Braglia, Alberto (ITA)
B. Campogalliano, Modena, 23 Mar. 1883; d. 5 Feb. 1954. Regarded as Italy's first Olympic gold medal winner but this was at the Interim Games in Athens in 1906 where, in gymnastics, he was joint champion in pentathlon and hexathlon. His reputation as one of the greatest gymnastics technicians grew and was confirmed in 1908 in London and maintained to 1912 in Stockholm, where he took the individual prize and helped Italy to win the team event. He achieved equal success in coaching; as the chief coach to the 1932 Italian Olympic team, he played a part in Italy's greatest triumph in the sport, winning four gold medals at one Games.
Gold combined exercises (individual) 1908, 1912, (team) 1912

Brenden, Hallgeir (NOR)
B. Trysil, 10 Feb. 1929. In the Oslo Olympics he won the gold medal for the 18-km cross-country skiing and repeated the victory in 1956. He was Norwegian champion in the 30-km cross-country three times, and in the 15-km six times. He was also a good track-and-field athlete, holding the Norwegian record for the 3,000-metres steeplechase.
Gold 18-kilometres cross-country 1952; 15-kilometres cross-country 1956
Silver 4 × 10-kilometres relay 1952, 1960

Brundage, Avery (USA)
B. Detroit, Mich., 28 Sept. 1887; d. Garmisch-Partenkirchen, 7 May 1975. Orphaned by the age of eleven, he was brought up by an uncle and aunt. He graduated from the University of Illinois in engineering with a first-class degree. He was also an outstanding athlete, a member of the University basketball team and intercollegiate discus champion. He competed in the Games at Stockholm in 1912 and was three times US all-round champion. He formed the Avery Brundage Company in 1915, which constructed a number of skyscrapers and other big buildings around Chicago. He was active in sports administration from an early age, holding the position of President of the Amateur Athletic Union of the United States for seven terms and the Presidency of the US Olympic Committee for twenty-five years. He became a member of the IOC in 1936, Vice-president in 1945 and President in 1952; he resigned in 1972. He gathered one of the finest Asiatic art collections in the world, estimated to be worth $50 million, and presented it in 1954 to the city of San Francisco, which built a museum to house it.

Brunet, Pierre and Andrée (Joly) (FRA)
Pierre b. Paris, 28 June 1902; Andrée b. Paris, 16 Sept. 1901. Pierre Brunet competed in singles and pairs figure-skating events before World War II. He was eighth in the Winter Games men's championship at Chamonix (1924), seventh in the 1928 Winter Games at St Moritz, and ninth in the World Championship in 1931. It was, however, as a pair skater, in association with Andrée Joly, that he achieved most renown. In addition to their Olympic achievements they were European Champions in 1932 and won the world title four times in alternate years, 1926, 1928, 1930 and 1932. They then turned professional and went to the United States, where Pierre Brunet has coached such famous figure skaters as Carol Heiss (1960 Olympic Champion), Donald Jackson (1962 World Champion), and Janet Lynn.

Their son, Jean-Pierre, was one of the only two skaters to beat Richard BUTTON.
Gold figure skating (pairs) 1928, 1932
Bronze figure skating (pairs) 1924

Burton, Michael (USA)
B. Des Moines, Iowa, 3 July 1947. Only swimmer to have won the 1,500-metres freestyle at two successive Games, in 1968 he set Olympic records by substantial margins in the 1,500-metres and 400-metres freestyle, even though the altitude of Mexico City was said to be against fast times at 400 metres and greater distances. He made his reputation as a swimmer capable of prodigious feats of self-punishment as a member of Sherman Chavoor's squad at Arden Hills, Calif., where he was a contemporary of Mark SPITZ and Debbie MEYER. At the age of thirteen, Burton, whose sporting activity up till then had been largely cross-country running, was involved while cycling in an accident with a truck. He severed tendons under his right knee and the ball joint of his hip was forced into his rib cage. Doctors said that he would never be able to compete in sports again, but advised him to do a little swimming to strengthen his leg muscles.

The first of Burton's seven world records was his 16 min 41.6 sec for 1,500-metres freestyle in 1966. The last of his five world records in that event brought him the Olympic title in 1972 (15 min 52.58 sec).

Burton, who also set two world records for 800-metres freestyle, became a club coach and a member of the US Olympic Committee.
Gold 400-metres freestyle 1968; 1,500-metres freestyle 1968, 1972

Button, Richard Totten (USA)
B. Englewood, N.J., 18 July 1929. A graduate of Harvard Law School, Button was US Figure Skating Champion 1946–52, winner of the European title in 1948 (then an Open championship), runner-up in his first World Championship in 1947, five times World Champion, 1948–52, and twice an Olympic champion. In his entire championship career, from the 1943 US Mid-Atlantic novice event (his first title) to the 1952 Winter Games, he was beaten

Richard Totten Button (USA), 1952

only twice – by Jean-Pierre Brunet in the 1943 US Eastern States novice championship, and by Hans Gerschwiler (Switzerland) in the 1947 World Championship in Stockholm.

Button brought a new, dynamic style to free skating and pioneered the multi-rotation jumps. He performed the first triple jump (a triple loop) in a championship in the 1952 Winter Games. He turned professional in 1952 and later became a television skating commentator. His other interests include lawn tennis, sailing, music and drama. On 10 March 1973 he married Slavka Kohout, a pupil of Pierre BRUNET and trainer of Janet Lynn, a distinguished fellow American.
Gold figure skating 1948, 1952

Calhoun, Lee Q. (USA)
B. Laurel, Miss., 23 Feb. 1933. Only man to win the Olympic 110-metres hurdles twice, he tied with Jack Davis for first place in the 1956 US Olympic trials and then at Melbourne had an almost equally close battle with Davis, both men being level from the eighth hurdle, before inspection of the official photo-finish, gave victory to Calhoun in 13.5 sec. In 1958 he was suspended by the Amateur Athletic Union for appearing with his bride on a television 'give away' show and receiving nearly £1,000 worth of gifts. After missing a season he returned to the track to set a world high-hurdles record of 13.2 sec and at Rome won a second gold medal, again in a photo-finish, with a spectacular body lean.
Gold 110-metres hurdles 1956, 1960

Capilla Pérez, Joaquin (MEX)
B. Mexico, D.F., 23 Dec. 1928. The first Mexican to win an Olympic diving title, in 1956, eight years after his first Olympic medal. In 1948 and 1952 he was fourth in the springboard event. His brother Alberto was also in the Mexican diving team at the 1952 and 1956 Games. Joaquin was the Pan-American Games springboard and highboard champion in both 1951 and 1955.
Gold highboard diving 1956
Silver highboard diving 1952
Bronze highboard diving 1948; springboard diving 1956

Čáslavská, Vera (TCH)
B. Prague, 3 May 1942. Miss Čáslavská, one of the most glamorous and successful women gymnasts, won eleven Olympic medals. In all she collected twenty-two titles in Olympics, World and European Championships between 1959 and 1968. Initially an ice skater, 1.60 m (5 ft 3 in) tall, she displayed remarkable dexterity in nationwide gymnastic trials at the age of fifteen. Miss Cáslavská made her international début at the 1958 World Championships, taking a silver medal in the team competition. It took her six years of steady progress before she finally defeated Larisa LATYNINA (URS) in the combined exercises competition in 1964. The pair shared in many memorable events, in which Miss Čáslavská's sparkling personality was offset by the marginally superior technical precision of her Russian rival. But at the 1964 Games Miss Čáslavská was a clear winner overall. In 1968 she retained her title in spite of the determined opposition of Zinaida Voronina (URS) and the nineteen-year-old Natasha Kuchinskaya (URS), who had threatened Miss Čáslavská's supremacy at the 1966 World Championships. Her floor exercises routine to the tune of the 'Mexican Hat Dance' entranced the spectators and was one of the most memorable moments of those Games. She announced her retirement after the victory ceremony and married Josef Odložil, the 1964 Olympic 1,500-metres silver medallist, in a ceremony in Mexico City, during the Games, that attracted enormous crowds and publicity.
Gold combined exercises (individual) 1964, 1968; beam 1964; horse vault 1964, 1968; asymmetrical bars 1968; floor exercises 1968
Silver beam 1968; combined exercises (team) 1960, 1964, 1968

Vera Čáslavská (TCH), 1968

Miroslav Cerar (YUG), 1964

Cerar, Miroslav (YUG)
B. Ljubljana, 28 Oct. 1939. A gymnast from the age of ten. He studied law in Ljubljana. At the Moscow World Championships in 1958, he was third in the pommelled horse; and until 1970 he was unbeaten in that discipline, winning the event and the parallel bars at the 1962 World Championships. In 1966 he was again World Champion on the pommelled horse and third on the parallel bars; in 1970 he took the pommelled horse title again. He was the Yugoslav Champion for thirteen successive years.
Gold pommelled horse 1964, 1968
Bronze horizontal bar 1964

Chand, Capt. Dhyan (IND)
B. Allahabad, 28 Aug. 1905. The greatest of all hockey players, he learned the game in the Indian Army and had a dazzling international career between 1926 and 1936, days when Indian hockey was incomparably the best in the world. Chand played centre forward in the teams which won the Olympic gold medal in 1928 and 1932, and captained India to win a third successive Olympic title in 1936. In those three tournaments, India scored an aggregate of 102 goals to three. During a tour of New Zealand in 1935, Chand scored 201 goals out of an aggregate of 584. In 1947–8 he made his parting appearance at international level as captain of the team which India sent on a goodwill demonstration tour of East Africa. The magic touch of Chand was all his own, a gift of nature.
Gold hockey 1928, 1932, 1936

Chukarin, Viktor (URS)
B. Mariupol (now Zdhanov), 9 Nov. 1921. Chukarin established his country in the forefront of gymnastics by winning a total of seven Olympic gold medals. He was especially gifted on the parallel bars, winning the 1954 world title on this apparatus as well as an Olympic gold medal. He led the first USSR Olympic gymnastics team in 1952. He tied for the world title with his compatriot Valentin Muratov two years later but finished first in 1956.
Gold combined exercises (individual) 1952, 1956; pommelled horse 1952; long horse vault 1952; parallel bars 1956; combined exercises (team) 1952, 1956
Silver parallel bars 1952; rings 1952; floor exercises 1956
Bronze pommelled horse 1956

Comaneci, Nadia (ROM)
B. Gheorghe Gheorghiu-Dej, 12 Nov. 1961. The first gymnast ever to be awarded a maximum 10.0 mark in Olympic competition, this tiny and daring girl, who looked even younger than her fourteen years, brought the closest approach to perfection seen in the gymnastics arena to Montreal in 1976.

After her history-making mark, achieved on the asymmetrical bars in the team competition, she was awarded a score of 10.0 six more times during the Games, and won three individual gold medals, including the overall title. Her winning score on the bars, 20.0, is unbeatable on current rules, and could only be equalled by a gymnast achieving, as Comaneci did, 10.0 three times on separate days in the Olympic tournament.

Unknown internationally little more than a year before the Games, she first sprang to prominence by taking four of the five gold medals at the 1975 European championships at the astonishing age of thirteen.

Her performances there, and at Montreal, heralded a revival of Romanian gymnastics and a strong challenge to the Soviet supremacy. But after the Olympics her natural physical development hindered her gymnastic progress, and she even fell from the bars, her favourite apparatus, during the 1978 World championships.
Gold combined exercises (individual) 1976; asymmetrical bars 1976; beam 1976
Silver combined exercises (team) 1976
Bronze floor exercises 1976

Costello, Paul V. (USA)
B. Philadelphia, Pa., 27 Dec. 1899. The first man to win three consecutive Olympic sculling titles. In 1920 and 1924 he partnered Jack KELLY, Sr; in 1928 Costello was partnered by Charles McIlvaine.
Gold double sculls 1920, 1924, 1928

Coubertin, Baron Pierre de (FRA)
B. Paris, 1 Jan. 1863; d. Geneva, 2 Sept. 1937. Coubertin showed a profound interest in literature, history, education and sociology. He gave up a career in the Army, which broke a family tradition and, declining a career in politics, launched a campaign for broadening and restructuring education when he was twenty-four. The revival of the Olympic Games was but a small part of this work. He was President of the International Olympic Committee 1896–1925 and on his retirement was given the title of Honorary President. In 1912 at Stockholm, under the pseudonym Georg Hohrod

and Martin Eschbach, he won an Olympic gold medal for literature with his *Ode to Sport*.

In addition to teaching sport and the development of its techniques, he was the author of several historical works. He is buried in Lausanne, but his heart was interred at Olympia in a marble monument commemorating the revival of the Games.

Craig, Ralph C. (USA)
B. Detroit, Mich., 21 June 1889; d. Alexandria, Va., 24 July 1972. In 1912 Craig won gold medals in the 100 and 200 metres with times of 10.8 sec and 21.7 sec respectively. He equalled the world 220-yards record in 1910 and 1912, and also won three American intercollegiate sprint titles. At Stockholm (1912) there were eight attempts at getting the field away for the 100-metres final before Craig pulled away in the last half of the race ahead of Alvah Meyer. In the 200 metres, Meyer, the American champion, was eliminated in the semi-finals and it was left to Craig to take the title. Craig was also a member of the US Olympic yachting team in 1948.
Gold 100 metres 1912; 200 metres 1912

Cuthbert, Betty (AUS)
B. Merrylands, near Sydney, 20 Apr. 1938. Rare example of a teenage athletics champion re-establishing herself as an Olympic winner, she was undoubtedly the heroine of the 1956 Olympics. She was injured during the 1960 Olympics. But at Tokyo she successfully moved up a distance to 400 metres and won her fourth gold medal in 52.0 sec. She broke sixteen world records including performances at 100 yards, 200 metres, 220 yards and 440 yards between 1956 and 1963 and will be remembered for her slim build, sunny temperament and great determination.
Gold 100 metres 1956; 200 metres 1956; 4 × 100-metres relay 1956; 400 metres 1964

Betty Cuthbert (AUS), 1956

Daniels, Charles M. (USA)
B. 12 July 1884; d. 9 Aug. 1973. Daniels won six swimming medals in 1904 and 1908. A colourful personality inside the sport and out, he set seven world records in various events between 1907 and 1911.

In the 1904 Games, aged nineteen, he won the freestyle events over 220 yards and 440 yards, was runner-up in the 100 yards, and third in the 50 yards, which was in the Olympic program for the first and last time. His performances were regarded in his day with almost as much reverence as were Mark SPITZ's sixty-eight years later. At the Interim Games in Athens in 1906 he won the 100-metres freestyle.

Perhaps his greatest contribution to the sport was the way he influenced swimmers with his use of the crawl.
Gold 220-yards freestyle 1904; 440-yards freestyle 1904; 4 × 50-yards relay 1904; 100-metres freestyle 1908
Silver 100-yards freestyle 1904
Bronze 4 × 200-metres freestyle relay 1908; 50-yards freestyle 1904

Davis, Glenn A. (USA)
B. Wellsburg, W. Va., 12 Sept. 1934. The only man to win the Olympic 400-metres hurdles twice, in 1956 and 1960. Davis, a talented all-rounder in high school, did not turn to the 400-metres hurdles until April 1956 but in just two months he had cut the world record by 0.9 sec down to 49.5 sec. At Melbourne he won his gold medal in 50.1 sec with a strong finish and in Rome his winning time was 49.3 sec, just 0.1 sec slower than the world record he had set in 1958, when he also set new world records for 440 yards flat (45.7 sec) and 440-yards hurdles (49.9 sec). He showed astonishing versatility and stamina in two-day meetings at Oslo (200 metres in 21.1 sec, 400-metres hurdles in 49.8 sec, 100 metres in 10.3 sec, flat 400 metres in 45.6 sec) and Warsaw 400 metres in 45.5 sec, 400-metres hurdles in 49.8 sec, and 400-metres relay leg in 45.1 sec). His last race was the third stage of the American 4 × 400-metres relay team in Rome which he ran in 45.4 sec – a vital contribution as his team set a world record of 3 min 02.2 sec. He later became a professional American footballer.
Gold 400-metres hurdles 1956, 1960; 4 × 400-metres relay 1960

De La Hunty (Strickland), Shirley (AUS)
B. Guildford, Western Australia, 18 July 1925. Up until 1976 she

Shirley De La Hunty (AUS), 1956

had won more Olympic medals than any other woman in athletics; three gold, one silver and three bronze. She was the first woman to beat 11 sec for the 80-metres hurdles and also had a world record in the flat 100 metres at 11.3 sec. As late as 1960 she ran 100 yards in 10.9 sec.
Gold 80-metres hurdles 1952, 1956; 4 × 100-metres relay 1956
Silver 4 × 100-metres relay 1948
Bronze 100 metres 1948, 1952; 80-metres hurdles 1948

Desjardins, Pete (USA)

B. St. Pierre, Canada, 10 Apr. 1907. He became an American citizen after moving to Miami Beach, Fla. with his family as a child. He was an economics graduate of Stanford University, which had the finest diving instruction facilities in the early 1920s in the United States, following two other Olympic champions from that school, Clarence Pinkston and Albert WHITE. Only 1.60 m (5 ft 3 in) tall, Desjardins was runner-up to White in the 1924 Olympic springboard event. In 1928 he became the only Olympic diving competitor to get the maximum ten points.
Gold springboard diving 1928, highboard diving 1928
Silver springboard diving 1924

Dibiasi, Klaus (ITA)

B. Solbad Hall, Austria, 6 Oct. 1947. In Dibiasi's childhood his family moved from Austria to Bolzano, Italy; both his parents were Italian. At seventeen he won the Olympic silver medal for highboard, an achievement which moved the inhabitants of Bolzano to build an indoor diving tank for him. Four years later he became the first Italian to win an Olympic diving title. He was coached by his father, a former Italian springboard champion. In the 1966 and 1974 European Championships he won three titles. At the 1976 Games Dibiasi became the first diver to win a gold medal at three successive celebrations. After achieving this feat in the highboard he announced his retirement.
Gold highboard diving 1968, 1972, 1976
Silver highboard diving 1964; springboard diving 1968

Didrikson, Mildred (USA)

B. Port Arthur, Tex., 26 June 1914; d. 27 Sept. 1956. In the 1932 Olympics she won the 80-metres hurdles, with a world record. In the high jump, she and fellow American Jean Shiley both cleared 1.65 m (5 ft 5¼ in) for a new world record but a judge decided that Didrikson, who went over 1.67 m (5 ft 5¾ in), had been jumping all afternoon with an illegal diving style and she was placed second. It was not until 1939 that the rules which had led to this peremptory ruling were changed. 'Babe' Didrikson later became famous under her married name of Zaharias as a golfer and won seventeen international titles between 1934 and 1950.
Gold 80-metres hurdles 1932; javelin 1932
Silver high jump 1932

Diem, Carl (GER)

B. Würzburg, 24 June 1882; d. Cologne, 17 Dec. 1962. His enthusiasm for the Olympic idea, which he first encountered at the Interim Games in Athens in 1906, and his friendship with COUBERTIN provided Olympism with some fertile thinking and ensured that Germany played a continuing part in the Olympic Movement.

Diem was able to realise many of Coubertin's ideals in Germany. He was the outstanding administrator and organizer of sport in Germany during the first half of the century. He was leader of Germany's Olympic team for the Games of 1912, 1928 and 1932; he ordered the construction of the stadium in Berlin intended for the Games of 1916 which were cancelled. He was General Secretary of the organization for the Games from 1931 and among many aspects provided the artistic direction; among his innovations was the torch relay from Olympia which he organized with his friend Jean Ketseas. He lost influence in Germany with the rise of the Nazis but after Coubertin's death continued to produce the *Olympic Review* and was a prolific writer, producing over 2,000 works, essays, articles and books, on the Olympic Movement. Olympic youth tours and the founding of the International Olympic Academy were largely the result of his vision. He never lost vitality for new ideas, for in 1955 he began the Golden Plan in Germany which ensured that outstanding athletes there had every opportunity to fulfil Olympic ambition.

Mildred Didrikson (USA), 1932

Dillard, Harrison W. (USA)

B. Cleveland, Ohio, 8 July 1923. Inspired by the sight of the victory celebration for Jesse OWENS following the 1936 Olympics, Dillard became a specialist high hurdler and, between May 1947 and June 1948, had eighty-two sprint and hurdles races without defeat. In the 1948 US Olympic trials he fell in the hurdles and failed to finish, though he did qualify as third

string in the 100-metres flat; in an extraordinary upset he won the final in London in 10.3 sec to equal Owens' Olympic record – particularly fitting since Owens had presented him with his 1936 Olympic shoes. In 1952, Dillard returned to his first love to win the high hurdles. At only 1.78 m (5 ft 10 in) Dillard was short for a high hurdler but had great speed between the fences. He won five US outdoor titles and set world records for both the 120- and 220-yards hurdles.
Gold 100 metres 1948; 4 × 100-metres relay 1948, 1952; 110-metres hurdles 1952

Edström, J. Sigfrid (SWE)
B. Gothenburg, 21 Nov. 1870; d. Stockholm, 18 Mar. 1964. Was an outstanding administrator in Scandinavian sport, and a good sprinter, running the 100 metres in 11 sec. After studying and working in technology in Zürich, he helped to combine the various branches of sport in Sweden under one administration. He was one of the organizers of the 1912 Games in Stockholm and took the lead in founding the International Amateur Athletic Federation, of which he was President 1912–46. He was elected member of the IOC in 1920 and held a number of offices in it before becoming President 1946–52.

Elek, Ilona (HUN)
B. Budapest, 17 May 1907. Her domination of women's fencing, in the foil, straddled the period of World War II. She won a world title in 1933 in Budapest and took a winning team medal in the World Championships of Rome in 1955, finishing fifth in the individual event. Her style was sometimes described as dull but she had a compelling desire to win. In addition to her Olympic medals which, spanning twelve years, indicate her extraordinary powers of strength and resilience, she won eleven gold medals in World Championships, five silver and one bronze.

Herb Elliott (AUS), 1960

Gold foil (individual) 1936, 1948
Silver foil (individual) 1952

Elliott, Herb (AUS)
B. Perth, 25 Feb. 1938. From the age of sixteen until his retirement from athletics this Australian prodigy was never beaten over one mile or 1,500 metres. Elliott first made his mark in 1957 with world junior track records. Inspired by the coaching of Percy Cerutty, he ran his first mile in under 4 min before he was twenty, in 1958. The same year he lowered the world records in the mile to 3 min 54.5 sec and the 1,500 metres to 3 min 36.0 sec and won the British Commonwealth Games titles over 880 yards and the mile; he rejected an offer to turn professional. At the 1960 Olympics he crushed the opposition in the 1,500 metres and won in a world-record time of 3 min 35.6 sec. It was among the most sweeping of all modern Olympic victories.
Gold 1,500 metres 1960

Elvstrøm, Paul (DEN)
B. Copenhagen, 25 Feb. 1928. His approach to small-boat sailing, a belief that fitness from land training was a way to win, revolutionized competitive sailing. The first of his four gold medals was won at Torbay in 1948 and at Acapulco in 1968 he was fourth in the Star class.

He realized that hanging over the side of the boat for a longer period than his opponents gave him an advantage and the only way to achieve this was through physical fitness. He was also a student of weather lore and relished the idea of going out on stormy days to learn more about his craft and how to handle it. He won eleven World Championships in seven different classes between 1957 and 1974. He wrote several books and in 1954 started a company, Elvstrøm Sails, with branches throughout the world; he also built pleasure boats. It was these activities which brought him under scrutiny by the IOC Eligibility Commission in 1972.
Gold yachting Firefly 1948; Finn 1952, 1956, 1960

Ender, Kornelia (GDR)
B. Plauen, Vogtland, 25 Oct. 1958. Her four gold medals and a silver at the 1976 Games made Miss Ender the greatest woman swimmer ever. Twenty minutes after winning the Olympic title in the 100-metres butterfly, equalling her world record (1 min 00.13 sec), Miss Ender took her place in the final of the 200-metres freestyle and, with a world record of 1 min

Kornelia Ender (GDR), 1976

59.26 sec, she captured that title as well. She also set a world record in winning the 100-metres freestyle (55.65 sec) and contributed to another when swimming the freestyle stage in GDR's winning medley relay team (4 min 07.95 sec). A silver medal and European record came in the 4 × 100-metres freestyle in which the USA women won their only gold medals of the 1976 swimming events.

In 1973 Miss Ender won the award as the outstanding swimmer of the first World Championships. Her four victories came in the 100-metres butterfly, 100-metres freestyle, 4 × 100-metres freestyle relay and 4 × 100-metres medley relay, the last three in world record time. She was also second in the 200-metres individual medley. In the World Championships two years later she retained her titles, setting world records in the 100-metres butterfly and 4 × 100-metres freestyle, and was second in the 200-metres freestyle.

She retired from major competition after Montreal and married fellow Olympic champion, Roland MATTHES.

Gold 100-metres freestyle 1976; 200-metres freestyle 1976; 100-metres butterfly 1976; 4 × 100-metres medley 1976

Silver 200-metres individual medley 1972; 200-metres freestyle 1976; 4 × 100-metres freestyle 1972, 1976; 4 × 100-metres medley 1972

Engel-Krämer, Ingrid (GDR)

B. Dresden, 29 July 1943. She competed in the diving events at three Olympic Games; as Miss Krämer in 1960 she became the first non-American winner of the springboard diving title and completed the double on highboard; as Mrs Engel she retained the springboard title in 1964 and was runner-up on highboard; and in 1968 (divorced and remarried) as Mrs Gulbin she finished fifth in the springboard.

In her first major international competition, the 1958 European Championships in Budapest, the fifteen-year-old Miss Krämer was on the point of victory in the springboard, but failed with her last dive and finished fourth. She won both springboard and highboard in the 1962 European Championships. She carried the flag for the united German team at the opening ceremony of the 1964 Olympic Games. She became the first woman gold medallist of those Games when she retained the springboard title, in spite of complaining that the water was too cold; she took a hot shower

Ingrid Engel-Krämer (GDR), 1960

Ray Ewry (USA), 1908

between each dive.

Gold springboard diving 1960, 1964; highboard diving 1960

Silver highboard diving 1964

Ewry, Ray C. (USA)

B. Lafayette, Ind., 14 Oct. 1873 or 1874; d. 29 Sept. 1937. Ewry won ten Olympic gold medals (including two in 1906) in the now-abandoned standing high, long and triple jump events. He was paralysed as a boy but dedicated exercising developed unusual strength in his legs. His standing long jump record of 3.47 m (11 ft $4\frac{7}{8}$in) remained on the official world record list until the event was discarded in 1938. He was fifteen times an American athletics champion.

Gold standing high jump 1900, 1904, 1908; standing long jump 1900, 1904, 1908; standing triple jump 1900, 1904

Exeter, Sixth Marquess of; David George Brownlow Cecil Lord Burghley (GBR)

B. Feb. 1905. He competed in the Games of 1924, 1928 and 1932, winning a gold medal in the

400-metres hurdles at Amsterdam and silver medals in both the 110-metres hurdles and the 4× 400-metres relay in Los Angeles.

Doyen of the International Olympic Movement, he first became a member of the International Olympic Committee in 1933. He was elected Vice-President from 1952 to 1956 and stood for the Presidency in 1964. From 1946 to 1976 he was President of the International Amateur Athletic Federation.
Gold 400-metres hurdles 1928
Silver 110-metres hurdles 1932, 4×400-metres relay, 1932

Faggin, Leandro (ITA)
B. Padova, 18 July 1933; d. 5 Dec. 1970. A natural track cyclist, Faggin dominated world pursuit cycling for a dozen years. He set new records three times for riding 5,000 metres unpaced, as an amateur and as a professional. His great stamina enabled him to set an Olympic record for 1,000 metres at Melbourne and then lead his colleagues to gold medals in the 4,000-metres team pursuit. Between the World Championships in 1954 and his bronze medal as a professional in 1968, he collected twelve medals, including those for three world professional championships.
Gold 1,000-metres time trial 1956; 4,000-metres team pursuit 1956

Flack, Edwin (AUS)
B. 1874. Australia's first great middle-distance runner, he had travelled from Australia, where he was mile champion, to work as an accountant in England and decided, in the casual atmosphere of those early days, to take his month's holiday competing in the Olympics. Light-heartedly, he rented a flat in Athens with two British competitors and they cooked for themselves. The day after his 800-metres victory, Flack ran in the marathon and was in the lead but dropped out at 35 kilometres.
Gold 800 metres 1896; 1,500 metres 1896

John Flanagan (USA), 1904

Flanagan, John J. (USA)
B. Limerick, Ireland, 9 Jan. 1868; d. Ireland, 1938. The father of modern hammer throwing, Flanagan raised the world record in sixteen instalments from 44.47 m (145 ft 10½ in) in Ireland in 1895 to 56.20 m (184 ft 4 in) in 1909 after emigrating to the United States. His best Olympic record (1908) was 51.92 m (170 ft 4¼ in). He was fourth in the discus at St Louis in 1904 and second in throwing the 56-lb (25.40-kg) weight. Until the advent of Al OERTER, Flanagan was the only Olympic athlete to win three successive gold medals in a standard event.
Gold hammer 1900, 1904, 1908
Silver 56-lb weight 1904

Forberger, Frank (GDR)
B. Meissen, 5 Mar. 1943. Member of the Einheit Dresden coxless four, with Dieter GRAHN, Frank RÜHLE and Dieter SCHUBERT, the most successful rowing crew of the post-World-War-II period. They were World Champions in 1966 and 1970, and European Champions in 1967 and 1971. They were, in fact, never beaten in an Olympic, World, or European Championship regatta.
Gold coxless fours 1968, 1972

Fraser, Dawn (AUS)
B. Balmain, N.S.W., 4 Sept. 1937. The only swimmer to have won an Olympic title in the same event at three successive Games. Although she had the advantage of a lean, boylike figure, not everything in Miss Fraser's physical make-up was in her favour when, aged fourteen she first came to the attention of her coach Harry Gallagher. Throughout her swimming life she suffered from bronchial asthma.

Miss Fraser's name appears on the world record lists thirty-nine times. She beat a twenty-year-old world record when she returned 1 min 4.5 sec for 100-metres freestyle in February 1956. Her progress after that was remarkable and eight years later she brought the time down to 58.9 sec, which stood for eight years as the world record though Shane GOULD (AUS) equalled it in 1971. Her best world records for 200-metres and 220-yards freestyle were achieved in the same swim – 2 min 11.6 sec at Sydney, 1960. She was an all-rounder of considerable ability and won Australian titles in butterfly and individual medley.

In all three of her Olympics she reached the final of the 400-metres freestyle, her best placing being second in 1956 and her fastest time 4 min 47.6 sec in 1964.
Gold 100-metres freestyle 1956, 1960, 1964; 4×100-metres freestyle relay 1956
Silver 400-metres freestyle 1956; 4×100-metres freestyle relay 1960, 1964; 4×100-metres medley relay 1960

Fredriksson, Gert (SWE)
B. Nyköping, 21 Nov. 1919. Besides his Olympic achievements he also won seven gold medals in World Canoeing Championships, over 500, 1,000 and 10,000 metres. Seventeen years old when he began canoeing, his best competition years were stunted because of World War II.

No other canoeist has struck such fear into his opponents and

none has been at the top so long. He had the remarkable capacity, rare in canoeing, of being able to attack at any point in the race, and his acceleration was phenomenal. Although in nineteen years there were defeats, he always sought an opportunity to meet the conqueror and none of these return matches was lost.
Gold kayak singles 1,000 metres 1948, 1952, 1956; 10,000 metres 1948, 1956; kayak pairs 1,000 metres 1960
Silver kayak singles 10,000 metres 1952
Bronze kayak singles 1,000 metres 1960

Gaiardoni, Sante (ITA)
B. Villafranca, 29 June 1939. Short and immensely muscled, he was one of a school of Italian cycling sprinters. At twenty-one he reached his athletic peak for the Games in Rome, where he beat the world professional record in establishing a new time for the standing-start 1,000-metres time trial of 1 min 7.27 sec. He was also the outstanding sprint cyclist of these Games. As a professional, he was only able to win one world title, a sprint championship in 1963 at Liège. He married an opera singer and retired in 1971.
Gold 1,000-metres time trial 1960; individual 1,000-metres sprint 1960

Gaudin, Lucien (FRA)
B. Arras, Pas-de-Calais, 27 Sept. 1886; d. 23 Sept. 1934. Gaudin had an extraordinary fencing career from 1904 to 1929; he was French foil champion from 1906 to 1914, World Champion in foil in 1904 and European Champion in épée in 1928. He won his two individual Olympic gold medals at the age of forty-two.
Gold foil (individual) 1928, (team) 1924; épée (individual) 1928, (team) 1924
Silver foil (team) 1920, 1928

Gaudini, Giulio (ITA)
B. Rome, 28 Sept. 1904; d. Rome, 6 Jan. 1948. This great fencer competed at four Olympic Games, from 1924 to 1936. At Paris (1924) he was a member of the Italian foil team which came fourth. Besides his Olympic victories, he was also World Champion in individual foil in 1929 and 1934 and a member of the winning foil teams of 1929, 1930, 1931, 1934 and 1935 as well as of the team that won the sabre in 1938.
Gold foil (individual) 1936, (team) 1928, 1936
Silver foil (team) 1932; sabre (individual) 1932, (team) 1932, 1936
Bronze foil (individual) 1928, 1932

Geesink, Anton (HOL)
B. Utrecht, 6 Apr. 1934. The first to defeat the Japanese at the sport they invented. Geesink, 1.98 m (6 ft 6 in) and 121 kg (266 lb or 19 stone) dominated judo from 1961, when he took his first world title, until his retirement in 1967. Ability to combine skill and speed in spite of his huge size also brought him eighteen European individual titles between 1952 and 1967. He was particularly gifted at ankle techniques which require exact timing, was versatile on the ground and was also a determined trainer. Geesink finished third in the first World Championships in Tokyo in 1956 but five years later defeated the three Japanese entrants to take the title. The Japanese were determined to get their revenge when the sport appeared on the Olympic program for the first time in Tokyo. Geesink twice defeated Akio Kaminaga, whom he had beaten in the quarter-final of the World Championship in 1961, to win the Open gold medal. It was a significant moment in sporting history because it ended Japanese invincibility. After his retirement in 1967 Geesink devoted himself to teaching.
Gold judo open (unlimited weight) 1964

Anton Geesink (HOL) v Akio Kaminaga (JPN), 1964

Gillan, James Angus (GBR)
B. Aberdeen, 11 Oct. 1885. Gillan was the first man to gain two Olympic gold medals for rowing. He was a member of the Magdalen College, Oxford, coxless four, which, in 1908, won both the Visitors' and Stewards' Challenge Cups at Henley Royal Regatta, and proceeded, a month later, to win the Olympic title. In Stockholm he won his second gold medal, rowing for the Great Britain eight.
Gold coxless fours 1908; eights 1912

Goitschel, Marielle (FRA)
B. Ste Maxime, 28 Sept. 1945. Marielle, the younger of two sisters, both Olympic ski champions, matured at an early age, winning the overall World Championship at Chamonix in 1962 at sixteen. Her strongest discipline was the slalom and when she finished second to her sister, Christine, at Innsbruck she said she had sacrificed her chance of gold as it already belonged to the family, settling for a steady second run that brought a silver medal. She duly won the giant slalom, with her sister this time in second place. Four years later, with her sister no longer in competition, she won the Olympic gold medal for slalom at Grenoble, but her six-year-old reign as World Champion ended there.

Shane Gould (AUS), 1972

Gold giant slalom 1964; slalom 1968
Silver slalom 1964

Golubnichi, Vladimir (URS)

B. Sumy, 2 June 1936. He had a remarkable career in Olympic walking. A Ukraine school teacher, he set his first world track record in 1955 at only nineteen and first entered the Soviet team in 1959. He became European Champion in 1974 after being third in 1972 and second in 1966.
Gold 20-kilometres walk 1960, 1968
Silver 20-kilometres walk 1972
Bronze 20-kilometres walk 1964

Goodell, Brian Stuart (USA)

B. Stockton, California, 2 April 1959. The first man since 1912 to score a world-record double in the Olympic 400-metres and 1,500-metres freestyle, Goodell won those events at the 1976 Games. He set world records at both distances at the USA Olympic trials that year.

In the final of the Olympic 400-metres he defeated the world champion, his countryman Tim Shaw, in 3 min 51.93 sec. In the final of the 1,500-metres he held fire while Bobby Hackett (USA) set the pace and, at 1,200 metres, Steve Holland (Australia) took it up. Goodell took up the challenge over the last two lengths, winning in 15 min. 02.40 sec.
Gold 400-metres freestyle 1976; 1,500-metres freestyle 1976

Gould, Shane (AUS)

B. Brisbane, 4 Sept. 1956, One of the greatest woman swimmers, Miss Gould was the first woman to win three Olympic swimming gold medals in individual events in world-record times at one Games.

She first got her name on the world-record lists at the age of fourteen in 1971 when she equalled Dawn FRASER's long-standing mark for 100-metres freestyle with 58.9 sec. On the following day she took the world record for 200-metres freestyle for herself with 2 min 6.5 sec. By 12 December 1971, she became the first woman ever to hold every world freestyle record from 100 metres to 1,500 metres. She completed her set in Sydney with 17 min 00.6 sec for 1,500 metres, more than 18 sec faster than the previous best.

By the 1972 Olympic Games, Miss Gould was regarded with such awe by the American swimmers that they wore tee-shirts at Munich bearing the motto 'All that glitters is not Gould' in an attempt to boost their own morale. It was claimed on her behalf that she might win all five individual events in which she entered. Though she failed narrowly in this, she still dominated the women's events, winning the 200-metres freestyle (2 min 3.56 sec), 400-metres freestyle (4 min 19.04 sec), and 200-metres individual medley (2 min 23.07 sec), all in world-record time. She could not cope with the American Sandy Neilson's fast start in the 100-metres freestyle and finished third in 59.06 sec and another American, Keena Rothhammer, beat her in the 800-metres freestyle.

Miss Gould was a contemporary of another Australian Olympic champion, Gail Neall, at Turramurra High School, Sydney. She was the first Olympic champion of the outstanding Australian coach Forbes Carlile.
Gold 200-metres freestyle 1972; 400-metres freestyle 1972; 200-metres individual medley 1972
Silver 800-metres freestyle 1972
Bronze 100-metres freestyle 1972

Grafström, Gillis (SWE)

B. Stockholm, 7 June 1893; d. Potsdam, 14 Apr. 1938. An architect, professionally (and a poet, painter and etcher), Grafström was noted for the elegance and musical feeling of his free figure skating. He originated the Grafström spin (on the back outside edge of the skate) and the flying sitspin, and was the first to make the 'Axel Paulsen' a controlled jump. He won three Olympic gold medals, the first at Antwerp, where he broke a skate and, being unable to get a replacement, went into the town and bought an old-fashioned curly-toed one. At Lake Placid, aged thirty-eight, he took the silver medal after an accident in which he collided with a photographer on the ice. Grafström was a highly individualistic character who skated for his own aesthetic satisfaction and could never be bothered much with competitive skating outside the Olympic Games. He never deigned to enter the European Championships and skated only three times for the world title, in 1922, 1924 and 1929, winning every time.
Gold figure skating 1920, 1924, 1928
Silver figure skating 1932

Grahn, Dieter (GDR)

B. Zobten, 20 Mar. 1944. Member of the unbeaten Einheit Dresden coxless four. See FORBERGER, Frank
Gold coxless fours 1968, 1972

Grishin, Yevgeni (URS)

B. Tula, 23 Mar. 1931. The best sprinter in speed skating in the 1950s and early 1960s. A member of the USSR national cycling team in 1952, he was in the USSR national speed-skating team 1952–68 and held the world record at 500 metres and 1,500 metres 1955–8. European Champion in 1956, he won the bronze medals at the 1954 and 1955 World Championships, the USSR Champion

title ten times over different distances 1956–65, and was the first skater to cover 500 metres in less than 40 sec. He is the present coach to the sprinters of the USSR national team.
Gold 500 metres 1956, 1960; 1,500 metres 1956, 1960
Silver 500 metres 1964

Grønningen, Harald (NOR)
B. Lensvik, 9 Oct. 1934. In 1968, aged thirty-three, he won the 15-kilometres cross-country skiing race in Grenoble and also the 4 × 10-kilometres relay. For twenty years he was among the leading cross-country skiers. He won the 15-kilometres race at Holmenkollen twice, in 1960 and 1961.
Gold 15-kilometres cross-country 1968; 4 × 10-kilometres relay 1968
Silver 15-kilometres cross-country 1964; 30-kilometres cross-country 1964; 4 × 10-kilometres relay 1960

Grøttumsbraaten, Johan (NOR)
B. Sørkedalen, Oslo, 24 Feb. 1899. He took part in skiing events in three Winter Games, winning medals each time. For fifteen years among the best skiers in the world in the combined and 18-kilometres cross-country events, he won the Holmenkollen combined event (the King's Cup) five times. In all he won ten King's Cups in Norway. He was also World Champion twice in the combined event (1926 and 1931) and once in the 18-kilometres cross-country in 1926.
Gold combined event 1928, 1932; 18-kilometres cross-country 1928
Silver 18-kilometres cross-country 1924
Bronze 50-kilometres cross-country 1924; combined event 1924

Gulbin, Ingrid (GDR)
see ENGEL-KRÄMER, Ingrid

Hahn, Archie (USA)
B. Dodgeville, Wis., 14 Sept. 1880; d. 21 Jan. 1955. Winner of three sprint titles at the St Louis Olympics of 1904. His 200-metres time of 21.6 sec was an Olympic record until 1932, though he was fortunate in his final in that his three rivals were all penalized one yard for making a false start after he had been somewhat restive on his marks. He also won the 100 metres in 1906 at the Interim Games in Athens.
Gold 60 metres 1904; 100 metres 1904; 200 metres 1904

Hall, Lars (SWE)
B. Karlskrona, 30 Apr. 1927. Individual winner of the modern pentathlon in 1952 and 1956, the only person to win successive individual gold medals. He won the World Championship in 1950 and 1951.
Gold modern pentathlon (individual) 1952, 1956
Silver modern pentathlon (team) 1952

Haug, Thorleif (NOR)
B. Årkvisla, near Drammen, 28 Sept. 1894; d. Drammen, 12 Dec. 1934. This outstanding skier was almost thirty years old before he had the opportunity of taking part in the Olympics, since they were not held until 1924. In Chamonix Haug won three gold medals and in the jumping event took the bronze. Fifty years after this first Olympic Winter Games, in 1974, in Oslo, it was discovered that in the official results there had been a miscalculation in the special jumping: Haug had 18.00 points and his fellow Norwegian Anders Haugen, who had emigrated to the United States and represented that country, had 17.91. Haug's points should have been 17.81 and so the bronze medal was presented to the eighty-six-year-old Haugen by Haug's daughter. Haug won the famous 50-kilometres race at Holmenkollen six times and the King's Cup there (for the combined event) three times. His memory was honoured in Drammen with a lifesize stone statue erected in 1946.
Gold 18-kilometres cross-country, 50-kilometres cross-country and combined event 1924

Thorleif Haug (NOR), 1924

Hencken, John (USA)
B. Culver City, California, 29 May 1954. The most bemedalled breaststroke swimmer in Olympic history, Hencken won the 200-metres breaststroke at the 1972 Games and the 100-metres breaststroke four years later.

In the 1972 Games he broke the world record for 100 metres in the first semi-final with 1 min 05.68 sec, losing it a few minutes later to Nobutaka Taguchi (Japan) who took the second semi-final. Taguchi improved on that record in the final, Hencken winning the bronze medal. Hencken led throughout the final of the 200 metres, resisting challenges from Wilkie and Taguchi, and setting a world record (2 min 21.55 sec).

At the first World Championships the following year, he set a world record for 100 metres twice on the same day, but lost the world record for 200 metres to Wilkie in the final. In Hencken's absence, Wilkie won both breaststroke titles in the 1975 World Championships. These two rivals of USA collegiate competition had their last and greatest confrontation in a major event at Montreal in 1976. Each won his speciality in world record time, Hencken's gold medal for 100 metres coming in 1 min 3.11 sec.

Hencken was a member of the winning United States medley relay teams at the 1972 and 1976 Games, each time sharing in world records. A member of the Santa Clara Club where he was coached by Mitch Wey, Hencken won his first AAU age-group medal at the age of ten. His coach at Stanford University was Jim Gaughran.

Gold 100-metres breaststroke 1976; 200-metres breaststroke 1972; 4 × 100-metres medley relay 1972, 1976
Silver 200-metres breaststroke 1976
Bronze 100-metres breaststroke 1972

Henie, Sonja (NOR)

B. Oslo, 8 Apr. 1912; d. 12 Oct. 1969. The outstanding figure in the history of skating, for she later turned her skills to good professional account and won a host of new admirers throughout the world by way of films. She became Norwegian Champion in 1924. Competing in the Winter Olympics at Chamonix (1924), before her twelfth birthday, she was last of eight competitors, but she won the title at her second attempt, at St Moritz (1928). After twice retaining her title, she turned professional and was given a contract by the Hollywood company, 20th Century Fox. In the World Championships she was fifth in 1924 and in 1926 she was runner-up in the women's event and fifth in the pairs with Arne Lie. She was never beaten again. She won ten World titles, 1927–36 (a record equalled only by Ulrich Salchow of Sweden), six European, 1931–6, and three Olympic titles.

She made eleven films between 1938 and 1960. With her third husband, Niels Onstad, a fellow Norwegian, she founded the

Sonja Henie (NOR), 1936

Henie-Onstad collection of modern paintings which they presented to Norway. Miss Henie developed leukaemia in 1969 and died in an aircraft which was carrying her from Paris to Oslo for medical treatment.

Gold figure skating 1928, 1932, 1936

Hickcox, Charles (USA)

B. Phoenix, Ariz., 6 Feb. 1947. The most successful male swimmer of the 1968 Games, Hickcox scored a double in the individual medley events, was runner-up in the 100-metres backstroke, and won another gold medal as a member of the US medley relay team. Hickcox, 1.90 m (6 ft 3 in) tall, was a backstroke stylist who, as he became stronger physically, developed as the world's best individual medley swimmer. While at Indiana University, he set world records in the 200-metres and 400-metres individual medley during the US Olympic trials of 1968 at Long Beach. With the problems created by the altitude of Mexico City, his individual medley double there was the more meritorious. The fact that the bronze medallist in the 200-metres medley, John Ferris, collapsed at the medal ceremony and was given oxygen illustrated the physical effort required from a lowlander for events of 200 metres and longer.

Hickcox also had a good year in 1967, winning gold medals at the World Student Games in Tokyo in the 100-metres and 200-metres backstroke and as a member of the US team in the medley relay with world records in each. In his career he set five world records in individual events and shared in two in medley relays.

Gold 400-metres individual medley 1968; 200-metres individual medley 1968; 4 × 100-metres medley relay 1968
Silver 100-metres backstroke 1968

Hill, Albert George (GBR)

B. Tooting, London, 24 Mar. 1889; d. Canada, 8 Jan. 1969. He gained the extraordinary double, at thirty-one, of the 800 and 1,500 metres in the Antwerp Olympics

Albert Hill (GBR), 1920

Clarence Houser (USA), 1928

with a program of five races in four days, ten years after winning his first British title. His winning times were 1 min 53.4 sec and 4 min 01.8 sec. He was helped considerably by his British colleague, Philip Noel-Baker, who was pacemaker in the longer race.
Gold 800 metres 1920; 1,500 metres 1920
Silver 3,000 metres (team) 1920

Houser, Clarence (USA)
B. 25 Sept. 1901. The first discus thrower to demonstrate the value of rotating speed in the circle. In 1926 he set a world discus record of 48.20 m (158 ft $1\frac{3}{4}$ in). He was the last man to win both shot and discus in the Olympics.
Gold discus 1924, 1928; shot 1924

Iso-Hollo, Volmari (FIN)
B. Ylöjärvi, 1 May 1907; d. Heinola, 23 June 1969. The only man who twice won the Olympic steeplechase, at Los Angeles and Berlin. At Los Angeles he set an Olympic record of 9 min 14.6 sec in his heat so it was puzzling when his winning time in the final was announced as 10 min 33.4 sec. In fact the official scoring the laps had been taken ill, his substitute missed a lap and the field ran 460 extra metres. Four years later he set a world's best ever time of 9 min 3.8 sec. An outstanding 10,000-metres runner who gave Janusz Kusociński (POL) a tough battle in the 1932 Olympic event before losing by just 1.2 sec, he was third in the 1936 race when Finland took all three Olympic medals. His Olympic steeplechase record was not beaten until 1952.
Gold 3,000-metres steeplechase 1932, 1936
Silver 10,000 metres 1932
Bronze 10,000 metres 1936

Ivanov, Vyacheslav (URS)
B. Moscow, 30 July 1938. The outstanding single sculler post World War II. After winning both the European Championship and Olympic single sculls in 1956, he had to be content with European bronze medals in the next two seasons. But in 1959 he took the European title, in 1960 a second Olympic gold medal, in 1961 the European, and 1962 the first World Championship sculling title. In 1963 he dropped to fourth place in the European Championships, but returned, in 1964, to regain his European title, and to win his third consecutive Olympic gold medal in Tokyo.
Gold single sculls 1956, 1960, 1964

Janz, Karin (GDR)
B. Hartmannsdorf, 17 Feb. 1952. Although lacking the balletic grace of such Russian contemporaries as Ludmila TURISCHEVA or Olga KORBUT, this gifted East German gymnast possessed such technical expertise that she challenged Miss Turischeva strongly for the Olympic combined exercises title at Munich. At the Mexico Games (1968) she was a member of the East German team placed third. She improved steadily over the following four years and in Munich, together with her compatriot Erika Zuchold, pressed the USSR for the team title.
Gold horse vault 1972; asymmetrical bars 1972
Silver asymmetrical bars 1968; combined exercises (individual) 1972, (team) 1972
Bronze combined exercises (team) 1968; beam 1972

Jernberg, Sixten (SWE)
B. Limedsforsen, 6 Feb. 1929. His total of four gold medals, three silver and two bronze is the largest ever won by a skier in the Olympic Winter Games. He also won the World Championships in 1958 and 1962 in the 50-kilometres cross-country event and in the 4×10-kilometres relay.
Gold 50-kilometres cross-country 1956, 1964; 30-kilometres cross-country 1960; 4×10-kilometres relay 1964
Silver 15-kilometres cross-country 1956, 1960; 30-kilometres 1956
Bronze 15-kilometres cross-country 1964; 4×10-kilometres relay 1956

Johansson, Ivar (SWE)
B. Norrköping, 31 Jan. 1903. As well as his Olympic achievements, he was European Champion at middleweight in Greco-Roman wrestling in 1934, 1935 and 1937–9, and in freestyle in 1934–5 and 1937. In 1932 he was nominated as Sweden's best athlete.
Gold wrestling Greco-Roman welterweight 1932, middleweight 1936; freestyle middleweight 1932

Vyacheslav Ivanov (URS), 1956

Alberto Juantorena (CUB), 1976

Jousseaume, André (FRA)
B. Yvré l'Evêque, Sarthe, 27 July 1894; d. Paris, 26 May 1960. One of the greatest French riders, from the famous Cadre Noir at Saumur, he had a military career, becoming a colonel in 1952. He took part in four Olympic Games over a span of twenty years and won five medals; he was twelfth in the three-day event in 1948.
Gold dressage (team) 1932, 1948
Silver dressage (team) 1936, (individual) 1948
Bronze dressage (individual) 1952

Juantorena, Alberto (CUB)
B. Cuba, 3 Dec. 1951. The first man to win both the 400 metres and 800 metres at a single Olympic Games. In Montreal he also established a world record of 1 min 43.5 sec and one of the fastest runs for 400 metres at sea level, of 44.7 sec. He later improved his world 800-metres record by 1/10th of a second in Sofia. Juantorena who turned to track and field from basketball has a stride of 9 ft. In 1977 he won 26 of 27 races winning again the 400 and 800 metres in the World Cup in Düsseldorf.
Gold 400 metres 1976; 800 metres 1976

Kahanamoku, Duke Paoa (USA)
B. Honolulu, Hawaii, 24 Aug. 1890; d. Honolulu, 22 Jan. 1968. He and Johnny WEISSMULLER, whose swimming careers overlapped, shared the distinction of being the only men to win the 100-metres freestyle at two successive Olympic Games.

There are at least two versions of how Kahanamoku got his Christian name of Duke. One is that he acquired the name because he was born in Princess Ruth's palace in Honolulu during a visit by HRH Prince Alfred, Duke of Edinburgh, the second son of Queen Victoria. Another is that he was named after the Duke of Wellington. He became Sheriff of Honolulu.

When he retained the Olympic title in the 100-metres freestyle in 1920 it was in a re-swim after the Australians protested that their competitor William Herald had been boxed in by an American the first time (this was before lane ropes were used). Kahanamoku's winning time in the original swim, 1 min 0.4 sec, was the third and last of his world records in that event. Weissmuller prevented him from gaining a hat-trick of gold medals in the 100-metres freestyle when he beat him by 2.4 sec in the 1924 final with a time of 59 sec. Like his conqueror, Kahanamoku became a film actor. An expert at surfing, he introduced that sport to many parts of the world.
Gold 100-metres freestyle 1912, 1920; 4 × 200-metres freestyle relay 1920
Silver 100-metres freestyle 1924; 4 × 200-metres freestyle relay 1912

Duke Paoa Kahanamoku (USA), 1920

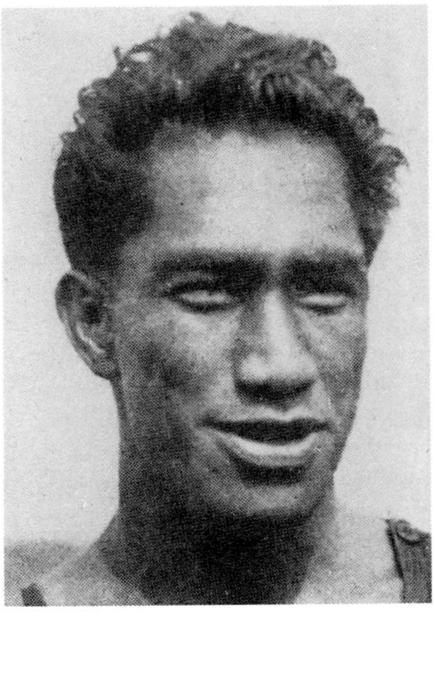

Sawao Kato (JPN), 1972

Kárpáti Rudolf (HUN)
B. Budapest, 17 July 1920. Sabre champion of Hungary in 1948 and 1955, he won two individual world titles, in 1954 and 1959, and was also a member of the World Champion sabre team of 1953, 1954, 1955, 1957 and 1958. Kárpáti is leader of the Hungarian People's Army Central Artistic Ensemble.
Gold sabre (individual) 1956, 1960, (team) 1948, 1952, 1956, 1960

Kato, Sawao (JPN)
B. Niigata Prefecture, 11 Oct. 1946. In Mexico, although trailing behind Mikhail Voronin (URS) and Akinori NAKAYAMA (JPN) after the compulsory exercises, this diminutive gymnast, 1.62 m (5 ft 4 in) tall and 53.5 kg (118 lb or 8 stone 6 lb), produced an inspiring 9.9 mark on the floor

exercises to give him the overall title. Kato was an all-rounder, not a specialist; in fact he won only two medals (a gold on the floor exercises and a bronze on the rings) in individual items. He was an easier winner in Munich, where he also collected separate awards on the parallel bars, pommelled horse and horizontal bar. His original routine and perfection of movement brought him victory by 0.075 pt from Eizo Kenmotsu in a clean sweep by the Japanese of the combined exercises medals.
Gold combined exercises (individual) 1968, 1972, (team) 1968, 1972; floor exercises 1968; parallel bars 1972
Silver pommelled horse 1972; horizontal bar 1972
Bronze rings 1968

Kealoha, Warren Paoa (USA)
B. Honolulu, Hawaii, 3 Mar. 1903; d. 8 Sept. 1972. One of several famous swimmers from Hawaii. He was the first to retain an Olympic backstroke title, doing so in 1924. When he broke the world record for 100-metres backstroke in 1920 he began a period of US domination in that event that continued until Gilbert Bozon (FRA) became the holder in 1952. Kealoha broke the record four times in six years, bringing it down from 1 min 15.6 sec to 1 min 11.4 sec, a remarkable improvement. In 1923 he set another world record, for the now-discontinued 150-yards backstroke. The man he succeeded on this record list was Johnny WEISSMULLER. The backstroke styles of these two swimmers were the subject of much technical discussion. Weismuller used a bent-arm recovery, and Kealoha, straight-arm.

Kealoha, who twice won the US freestyle sprint championship, had victories over Johnny Weissmuller and Duke KAHANAMOKU on front crawl. He returned 1 min 15.2 sec in winning the Olympic 100-metres backstroke title in 1920 when, aged sixteen, he was the youngest member of the US team.
Gold 100-metres backstroke 1920, 1924

Keino, Kipchoge (KEN)
B. Kipsano, 17 Jan. 1940. Black Africa's first Olympic track champion showed remarkable range as a runner for ten years from 1962 when he first competed internationally. At the Tokyo Olympics he ran in both the 1,500 and 5,000 metres and finished fifth in the longer event. The following season he made an exciting breakthrough with 3,000 and 5,000 metres world records and ran a 3-min 54.2-sec mile. By 1968, when the Olympics went to Mexico City, it was obvious that his ability, together with the fact that he lived at a high altitude similar to that of Mexico, would bring him medals. He amazed everyone by running in the 10,000 metres (dropping out before the finish), heat and final of the 5,000 metres, in which he finished second, and two preliminary rounds of the 1,500 metres before he crushed Jim Ryun (USA) in the final with an extraordinary time, in oxygen-thin air, of 3 min 34.9 sec. At Munich Keino had lost a little of his speed, and so finished second in the 1,500 metres. But he still had his canniness and won the steeplechase, which he had never taken seriously before, in a fast time of 8 min 23.6 sec, after deliberately slowing the early pace in order not to be dropped by better hurdlers. In 1973 he turned to professional athletics in the United States.
Gold 1,500 metres 1968; 3,000-metres steeplechase 1972
Silver 5,000 metres 1968; 1,500 metres 1972

Kipchoge Keino (KEN), 1972

Keleti, Ágnes (HUN)
B. Budapest, 9 June 1921. Only a weakness on the vault prevented Miss Keleti from winning more gymnastic honours during the 1950s. In particular, a lapse on the vault at the Melbourne Olympics probably led to her losing the gold medal to Larisa LATYNINA (URS). Mrs Latynina's steadiness brought her the title by 0.30 pt. Although lacking the skill of many of her successors, Miss Keleti, with her compatriot Margit Korondi, was the chief opponent to the USSR's domination of the sport. She was one of several Hungarians who chose not to return to Hungary after the 1956 Games and during the 1960s was coach to the Israeli national team.
Gold floor exercises 1952, 1956; beam 1956; asymmetrical bars 1956; exercise with portable apparatus (team) 1956
Silver combined exercises (individual) 1956, (team) 1952, 1956
Bronze asymmetrical bars 1952; exercise with portable apparatus (team) 1952

Keller, Erhard (GER)
B. Günzburg, 24 Dec. 1944. The most famous German speed skater, he won his first Olympic race at Grenoble. In 1971 he was World Champion in the sprint event (500 metres and 1,000 metres) and from 1967 to 1972 set five world records in the 500 metres (39.5 sec, 39.2 sec, 38.42 sec, 38.30 sec and 38.00 sec). He was also one of the best 1,000-

metres skaters. In the summer of 1972 he became a professional and is a successful television commentator.
Gold 500-metres speed skating 1968, 1972

Kelly, John B. (USA)
B. Philadelphia, Pa., 4 Oct. 1890; d. Philadelphia, 20 June 1960. Kelly is the only man to have won two Olympic sculling titles on the same day – at the Antwerp Games, where he narrowly beat Jack BERESFORD (GBR) in the single sculls, and, in partnership with Paul COSTELLO, won the double sculls. The latter success he repeated in Paris.

In 1920 Kelly was the centre of controversy, when Henley Royal Regatta refused his entry for the Diamond Sculls. This was not, as was subsequently sometimes claimed, because he was a manual labourer (bricklayer), but because Henley, at that time, had a standing resolution not to accept any entries from the Vesper Boat Club of Philadelphia, due to a previous infringement of their amateur status rules. However, the Henley Stewards did indicate that they thought it doubtful, quite apart from his membership of Vesper, whether Kelly would be eligible under their rules, which, unlike the Olympic rules, did classify all manual labourers as non-amateur.
Gold single sculls 1920; double sculls 1920, 1924

John Kelly (USA), 1920

Killanin, 3rd Baron; Michael Morris, Bt (IRL)
B. 30 July 1914. He was educated at Eton, the Sorbonne, Paris and Magdalene College, Cambridge (MA). At school he boxed and rowed. On leaving Cambridge, he joined the London *Daily Express* and subsequently transferred to the *Daily Mail.* In 1937–8 he was War Correspondent in the Sino-Japanese War; on returning to Europe, he became Assistant Political and Diplomatic Correspondent to the *Daily Mail* and wrote the political column in the *Sunday Dispatch.* In 1938 he volunteered and served throughout World War II in the King's Royal Rifle Corps, being Brigade Major 30th Armoured Brigade; he took part in the invasion of Normandy, for which he was made a Member of the Order of the British Empire (Military Division).

In 1952 he was associated with John Ford, making *The Quiet Man*, and subsequently produced a number of other films, including *The Rising of the Moon, The Playboy of the Western World* and *Gideon's Day.* He was also associated with the production of *Young Cassidy* and *Alfred the Great.* He edited and contributed to *Four Days*, a book on the Munich crisis; he is also the author of *Sir Godfrey Kneller*, a life of the eighteenth-century painter, and, with Professor Michael Duignan, edited *Shell Guide to Ireland*, besides contributing to European and United States newspapers. He joined the Board of Irish Shell & BP Limited in 1947 and is a Director of a number of other companies.

Killanin was elected President of the Olympic Council of Ireland in 1950 and a Member of the International Olympic Committee in 1952, becoming a Member of the Executive Board in 1967, Vice-President in 1968 and President in 1972.

Killanin is a member of the Irish Turf Club (Steward 1973–5) and a member of the Irish National Hunt Steeplechase Committee. He was elected a Member of the Royal Irish Academy in 1952 and made LL.D by the National University of Ireland, 1975.

His decorations include: Grand Cross of the Order of Civil Merit (Spain); 1976; Grand Officer of the Order of Merit of the Republic of Italy 1973; Grand Officer of the Order of the Republic (Tunis) 1978; Grand Officer of the Order of the Phoenix of Greece 1978; Knight of Honour and Devotion, Sovereign Order of Malta 1943; Commander of the Order of Olympic Merit (Finland) 1952; Commander of the Order of the Grimaldis 1961; Grand Cross of the German Federal Republic 1972 (Commander); Star of the Sacred Treasure (Second Class) Japan 1972; Order of the Madara Rider, Bulgaria; Commander of the Order of Sports Merit (Ivory Coast) 1977; Officer of the Legion of Honour (France) 1974; Member of the Order of the British Empire (Mil. Division); Chevalier Order of Duarte Sanchez y Mella, Dominican Republic 1977; Star of Solidarity 1st Class (Italian) 1957; Medal Miroslav Tyrs, Czechoslovakia 1970. Besides medals and decorations from Austria, Brazil, Colombia and the USSR.

In 1945 he married Sheila Mary Dunlop, MBE, and has four children.

Killy, Jean-Claude (FRA)
B. St Cloud, 30 Aug. 1943. Killy emulated at Chamrousse (near Grenoble) the Olympic skiing triple gold medal triumph of Toni SAILER at Cortina (1956), but with much less conviction than the Austrian, winning the slalom and giant slalom by less than a tenth of a second. The slalom, furthermore, followed the disqualification of another famous Austrian, Karl Schranz, and led to much acrimony. Schranz, given a second chance on his second run (he claimed to have been baulked first time), finished with a better time but many hours later a jury ruled that his claim to a second

chance was invalid.

Killy promptly turned professional to exploit his triple triumph, mostly by way of endorsements. He has since dabbled in films, motor racing and professional ski racing but without any great distinction. He competed at Innsbruck (1964) and was third in the World Championship based on the three Olympic results. He won the World Championship in 1966, but was first in only one event, the downhill. He retained the World Championship two years later with three first places. Although, like that of the Goitschel sisters, his name is closely associated with Val d'Isère, his early life was spent in Alsace. He derives his name from Irish mercenaries in the Napoleonic wars, Killy being a corruption of Kelly.
Gold downhill, slalom and giant slalom 1968

Kirszenstein, Irena (POL)
see SZEWIŃSKA, Irena

Kokkinen, Väinö (FIN)
B. Hollola, 25 Nov. 1899; d. Kuusankoski, 27 Aug. 1967. His wrestling expertise came from his push-overs while standing and merciless nelsons. He won the European Championship of 1930 and was silver medallist in 1925, 1929, 1931 and 1933 (the latter in the middle-heavyweight division).
Gold wrestling Greco-Roman middleweight 1928, 1932

Kolb, Claudia (USA)
B. Hayward, Calif., 19 Dec. 1949. Associated with the swimming centre of Santa Clara throughout her career, it was as a member of its team that she achieved the first of her eleven world records, swimming the breaststroke stage in a medley relay at Los Altos in July 1964. A few days later she set her first world record in an individual event (1 min 17.9 sec for 100-metres breaststroke). In 1966 she became the first holder of the world record for 200-metres individual medley (2 min 27.8 sec). She broke that record four times in the course of the next two years, finishing with 2 min 23.5 sec, which was still a world-class time in 1974 as was the last of her four world records for 400-metres individual medley (5 min 4.7 sec).
Gold 200-metres individual medley 1968, 400-metres individual medley 1968
Silver 200-metres breaststroke 1964

Kolehmainen, Johannes Petteri ('Hannes') (FIN)
B. Kuopio, 9 Dec. 1889; d. Helsinki, 11 Nov. 1966. The first outstanding Finnish Olympic champion runner, he set a world record of 14 min 36.6 sec in winning the 5,000 metres in Stockholm, after a memorable race with Jean Bouin (FRA), as well as the 10,000 metres in 31 min 20.8 sec. At Antwerp he won the marathon over 42,750 m ($26\frac{1}{2}$ miles) in 2 hr 32 min 35.8 sec. In 1912 he also won the now abandoned 8,000-metres cross-country event for the Finnish team and set a world record for 3,000 metres of 8 min 36.8 sec in a heat of the team 3,000-metres event. If World War I had not prevented the 1916 Games from being held, he would surely have more Olympic medals to his credit.
Gold 5,000 metres 1912; 10,000 metre 1912; marathon 1920; 8,000-metres cross-country (individual) 1912
Silver 8,000-metres cross-country (team) 1912

Hannes Kolehmainen (FIN), 1912

Olga Korbut (URS), 1972

Korbut, Olga (URS)
B. Grodno, near Minsk, 16 May 1955. Probably the most famous gymnast the world has known, the catalyst of the sport's growth, and the direct inspiration of millions of youngsters, the little Soviet girl owed her initial fame to an Olympic disaster rather than triumph. At Munich in 1972, watched by a worldwide television audience, numbering hundreds of millions, Korbut lost rhythm and concentration on the asymmetrical bars, and scored only 7.5 out of 10; her previous lowest mark had been 9.4. The seventeen-year-old's subsequent

tears of desolation, captured in close-up by the cameras, took her into hearts everywhere, and her return to win gold medals on the beam and in the floor exercises (as well as a team gold) was an outcome worthy of Hollywood.

She was tiny, 149 m (4 ft 11 in) tall, weighing 38 kg (84 lb or 6 stone), courageous and an innovator. Her backward somersault on the four-inch wide beam was regarded as being too dangerous by some officials, but it is now virtually a standard move in international competition

Dogged by injury, particularly to her ankles, Korbut's Olympic appearance in Montreal in 1976, when she took second place to COMANECI on the beam, was her final world competition, and in 1977 she retired to marry Soviet pop singer Leonid Borkevich.
Gold combined exercises (team) 1972, 1976; beam 1972; floor exercises 1972
Silver asymmetrical bars 1972; beam 1976

Kraenzlein, Alvin (USA)

B. 12 Dec. 1876; d. 6 Jan. 1928. He set world records in the high and low hurdles and the long jump, and at the 1900 Olympics in Paris gained victories in the 60-metres, 110-metres and 200-metres hurdles and then the long jump, in which he beat the qualifying mark of Myer PRINSTEIN by a bare centimetre. Kraenzlein's world records include 23.6 sec for the low hurdles, unbeaten for twenty-five years, 15.2 sec for the high hurdles and a long jump of 7.43 m (24 ft $4\frac{1}{2}$ in).
Gold 60-metres hurdles 1900; 110-metres hurdles 1900; 200-metres hurdles 1900; long jump 1900

Krämer, Ingrid (GDR)

see ENGEL-KRÄMER, Ingrid

Kulakova, Galina (URS)

B. Logachi, Udmurt, 29 April 1942. A teacher of physical education and the best woman cross-country skier of her time. In fifteen Olympic and World Championship events between 1968 and 1976 she only twice failed to gain a medal, in the 1968 Olympic 10 kilometres where she was sixth and the 1976 Olympic 5 kilometres where her bronze medal was taken away. A test revealed traces of a banned substance from the use of a nasal spray for a cold. The offence was considered minimal enough to permit her to compete in the 10 kilometres and 3 x 5 kilometres in which she took bronze and gold respectively.
Gold 5 kilometres 1972; 10 kilometres 1972; 3 x 5-kilometres relay 1972, 1976
Silver 5 kilometres 1968
Bronze 3 x 5-kilometres relay 1968; 10 kilometres 1976

Kulej, Jerzy (POL)

B. Czestochowa, 19 Oct. 1940. Began by being more interested in swimming and football but at nineteen represented Poland in the European boxing championships and later became European Champion at light welterweight in 1963 and 1965. At Mexico City this policeman's victory was a split-points decision over Enrique Regueiferos (CUB) who started strongly before Kulej's experience and determination allowed the Pole to weather the storm.
Gold boxing light welterweight 1964, 1968

Kuts, Vladimir (URS)

B. Aleksino, Ukraine, 7 Feb. 1927; d. 16 Aug. 1975. The outstanding distance runner at the 1956 Melbourne Olympics. In the 10,000 metres he had a classic battle with Gordon Pirie (GBR) controlling the pace from the front until the last five laps when Kuts went away. Strongly built for a distance runner, Kuts showed the aggression of a former amateur boxer in his tactics from the day in 1954 when he ran away from the rest of Europe over 5,000 metres. In four attempts he lowered the world record for this event from 13 min 57.2 sec to 13 min 0.35 sec and set the 10,000-metres time of 28 min 30.4 sec.

Vladimir Kuts (URS), 1956

Gold 5,000 metres 1956; 10,000 metres 1956

Lagutin, Boris (URS)

B. Moscow, 24 June 1938. He started boxing in 1955 and was European light middleweight champion in 1961 and 1963. He won his first international in 1960. At Tokyo he won his first Olympic title in a ferocious clash with Joseph Gonzales (FRA). Four years later the thirty-year-old Lagutin won a unanimous points decision over Rolando Garbey (CUB) after Garbey had been down twice in the first round.
Gold boxing light middleweight 1964, 1968
Bronze light middleweight 1960

Lane, Alfred P. (USA)

B. 26 Sept 1891. Achieved remarkable success in the 1912 Olympics when, at the age of twenty and after only two years of competitive experience, he won three gold

medals, more than any other competitor in shooting. In the 1912 team 50 metres he scored 509 pts, 34 more than the second best.
Gold rapid-fire pistol 1912; free pistol 1912; team pistol (50 metres) 1912, 1920, (30 metres) 1920
Bronze free pistol 1920

Larsson, Gunnar (SWE)

B. Malmö, 12 May 1951. A swimmer with great competitive flair, but it took coaching in the United States to enable him to fulfil his potential. This he did so well that he scored a double in the taxing individual medley events at the 1972 Olympic Games in Munich. His victory in the 400-metres individual medley caused a change in the swimming rules. A remarkable breaststroke leg in 1 min 18.1 sec put him well in the race. After a breathtaking finish to the final leg, the freestyle, Larsson and Tim McKee (USA) were shown as equal first in 4 min 31.98 sec. Further reference to the electronic timekeeper showed that Larsson had won by 0.002 sec. Or had he? Some argued that the slight variation in length of the lanes made it unreasonable to divide by such fine margins. Now times are taken only to hundredths of a second. Larsson added the title for 200-metres individual medley in the world-record time of 2 min 07.17 sec, again beating the favourite Gary Hall (USA).
Gold 200-metres individual medley 1972; 400-metres individual medley 1972

Latynina, Larisa (URS)

B. Kherson, Ukraine, 27 Dec. 1934. This spectacular gymnast took nine Olympic titles (a total equalled by Mark SPITZ and only exceeded by Ray EWRY), five silver and four bronze medals. Her complete record in all major events shows her domination of the sport between her début in 1954 and her retirement twelve years later. In Olympics, World and European Championships she took twenty-four gold medals, fifteen silver and five bronze. What makes this feat even more astonishing is that her career was interrupted by her giving birth to two children.

Mrs Latynina was renowned for her technical proficiency. Her ease in moving from one intricate position to another gave the sport a new concept. Moreover her desire for perfection meant that she kept on improving, forcing her contemporaries to raise their standard as well. Her best event, the floor exercises, in which she won three Olympic gold medals, emphasized this grace of movement. Her efforts and example firmly established the USSR's prominence in the women's branch of the sport.

Larisa Latynina (URS), 1960

Gold combined exercises (individual) 1956, 1960, (team) 1956, 1960, 1964; horse vault 1956; floor exercises 1956, 1960, 1964
Silver asymmetrical bars 1956, 1960; beam 1960; combined exercises (individual) 1964; horse vault 1964
Bronze exercise with portable apparatus (team) 1956; horse vault 1960; beam 1964; asymmetrical bars 1964

Lee, Sammy (USA)

B. Fresno, Calif., 1 Aug. 1920. His parents were Korean. The first male diver to retain an Olympic highboard diving title, Lee had the satisfaction of seeing one of his pupils, Bob Webster (USA), also complete an Olympic double on highboard (1960 and 1964). Lee won his first US titles in 1942. In 1948 he won the Olympic highboard event by more than seven points from Bruce Harlan (USA), who took the springboard event with Lee in third place. In 1952 Lee was an even more convincing winner of the highboard from Joaquin CAPILLA PÉREZ (MEX), who succeeded him as champion. In 1953 Lee received the Sullivan Award as the United States' outstanding amateur athlete. He is a doctor of medicine and has been honoured by the US Swimming Hall of Fame.
Gold highboard diving 1948, 1952
Bronze springboard diving 1948

Lemming, Erik (SWE)

B. Gothenburg, 22 Feb. 1880; d. 5 June 1930. At nineteen he set a world javelin record of 49.31 m (161 ft 9¾ in) in 1899, then broke it nine times, pushing it up to 62.32 m (204 ft 5½ in) in 1912. He was fourth equal in the pole vault and fifth in the high jump in the Paris Olympics (1900), and in London (1908) he won both the orthodox javelin event with 54.83 m (179 ft 10½ in) and the javelin freestyle (he held the spear in the middle) with 54.44 m (178 ft 7½ in). In 1912 he retained his standard title with 60.64 m (198 ft 11½ in) and in the aggregate (two-handed)

javelin event finished fourth.
Gold javelin 1908, 1912; freestyle javelin 1908

Lightbody, James D. (USA)
B. Pittsburgh, Pa., 17 Mar. 1882; d. Charleston, S.C., 2 Mar. 1953. In St Louis, on an oval-shaped $1\frac{1}{2}$-lap track he won the 800 metres in 1 min 56.0 sec and 1,500 metres in the then world-record time of 4 min 05.4 sec. In the shorter event it is said he watched the field as a hawk does a chicken before running wide round the others over the second lap and finally taking the lead in the last 30 metres. At the same Games he won the 2,500-metres steeplechase and was second in the 6,437-metres (4-miles) team race for Chicago AA. At the 1908 Games in London he was eliminated in the 1,500-metres heats.
Gold 800 metres 1904; 1,500 metres 1904; 2,500-metres steeplechase 1904
Silver 4 miles (team)

Linsenhoff, Liselott (GER)
B. Frankfurt, 27 Aug. 1927. One of Germany's great dressage riders, she won both her Olympic gold medals riding the famous Swedish stallion Piaff. She was individual European Champion in 1969 and 1971 and a member of the winning team in 1973; in World Championships she was placed second in the individual event in 1970 and 1974 and was a member of the winning team in 1974.
Gold dressage (individual) 1972, (team) 1968
Silver dressage (team) 1956, 1972
Bronze dressage (individual) 1956

James Lightbody (USA), 1904

Lowe, Douglas (GBR)
B. Manchester, 7 Aug. 1902. One of the outstanding middle-distance tacticians of the 1920s. He was a schoolboy champion over 880 yards but while at Cambridge University matured so swiftly that he was able to win his first Olympic Gold medal before he had ever won a British title. His win in Paris in 1 min 52.4 sec came after a prolonged battle in the final straight with Paul Martin (SUI). In 1926, in the British championships, Lowe lost a thrilling race over 880 yards to Otto Peltzer (GER), who set a new world record of 1 min 51.6 sec. Just before the Amsterdam Olympics the world 800-metres record was lowered to 1 min 50.6 sec by Sera Martin (FRA) and the Americans had a strong contender for Lowe's title in Lloyd Hahn. One Olympic semi-final was won by Hahn in 1 min 52.6 sec but Lowe cannily qualified nearly five seconds slower. In the final Hahn set the pace but Lowe launched an irresistible attack on the last backstraight and won in 1 min 51.8 sec, a personal and Olympic record.
Gold 800 metres 1924, 1928

McCormick (Keller), Patricia (USA)
B. Seal Beach, Calif., 12 May 1930. The only diver, man or woman, who has scored a double at two Olympic Games. In 1952 she succeeded Vicky Draves (USA) as double Olympic champion, winning both titles by substantial margins, and repeated her success at the Melbourne Games five months after the birth of her son. She was one of the first to be honoured by the US Swimming Hall of Fame.
Gold springboard diving 1952, 1956; highboard 1952, 1956

Mallin, Harry (GBR)
B. London, 1 June 1892; d. Lewisham, 8 Nov. 1969. Mallin never lost an amateur contest and was British champion for five years (1919–23).

In the Paris Games he figured in one of the most unusual boxing controversies. In a contest with Roger Brousse (FRA) the British boxer seemed to have done enough to have won on points. But as soon as the last round was ended, Mallin tried to complain to the referee that he had been bitten on the chest. Before he could make himself understood the bout was awarded on points to Brousse. A protest launched by a Swedish official brought forward medical evidence that Mallin had been bitten, and Brousse was disqualified though the jury declared the foul had not been intentional. In the final Mallin narrowly outpointed John Elliott (GBR).
Gold boxing middleweight 1920, 1924

Mangiarotti, Edoardo (ITA)
B. Renate Veduggio (Milan), 7 Apr. 1919. The passion which some Italians show towards fencing is shown through Mangiarotti; his father already having one son who showed the skills which were to make him a World Champion, changed Edoardo to a left-handed fencer in order that he would be the best ever left-handed fencer. The ploy worked; Edoardo began winning world titles in Paris in 1937 and, in spite of the interruption of World War II, was still in winning teams until the Games of 1960.
Gold épée (individual) 1952,

(team) 1936, 1952, 1956, 1960; foil (team) 1956
Silver foil (individual) 1952, (team) 1948, 1952, 1960; épée (team) 1948
Bronze épée (individual) 1948, 1956

Mankin, Valentin (URS)

B. Belokorovichi, Zhitomir area of the Ukraine, 19 Aug. 1938. A military man and one of the best sailors in the Finn and Tempest classes in the 1960s–70s, he won the USSR Championships for the first time in 1959 and held his title in 1961, 1962, 1963, 1967 (Finn), 1970, 1972, 1974 (Tempest). He was the first Soviet sailor to win a World Championship, in the Tempest class in 1973.
Gold yachting Finn 1968; Tempest 1972

Mäntyranta, Eero (FIN)

B. Pello, Finnish Lapland, 20 Nov. 1937. The outstanding cross-country skier in the 1960s, he took part in the competitions at Sapporo (1972) and was placed nineteenth in the 30 kilometres. He won the World Championship at 30 kilometres in 1962 and 1966 and World Championship silver medal at 50 kilometres in 1966. In the Holmenkollen Games in Norway he won the 15-kilometres race in 1962, 1964 and 1968. In the Salpausselkä Games in Finland he won the 15-kilometres race in 1964. Mäntyranta was a splendid technician on the ski tracks and a sound competitor who knew how to prepare himself for major races.
Gold 15-kilometres cross-country 1964; 30-kilometres cross-country 1964; 4 × 10-kilometres relay 1960
Silver 15-kilometres cross-country 1968; 4 × 10-kilometres relay 1964
Bronze 30-kilometres cross-country 1968; 4 × 10-kilometres relay 1968

Mastenbroek, Hendrika ('Rie') (HOL)

B. Rotterdam, 26 Feb. 1919. Dutch competitors won four of the five swimming gold medals open to women in the 1936 Games, Miss Mastenbroek taking two individual titles and swimming in the freestyle relay. In her first international season, she won the 400-metres freestyle (5 min 27.4 sec) and the 100-metres backstroke (1 min 20.3 sec) at the 1934 European Championships; she was also a member of the winning Dutch freestyle relay squad. Later that year she set the first of her seven world records in individual events, returning 1 min 16.8 sec for 100-metres backstroke at Düsseldorf. She also held world records for 440-yards freestyle, 200-metres backstroke, and 400-metres backstroke (5 min 48.8 sec in this event, records for which ceased to be recognized in 1948). She twice swam in Dutch quartets that broke the world record for the 4 × 100-metres freestyle relay.
Gold 100-metres freestyle 1936; 400-metres freestyle 1936; 4 × 100-metres freestyle relay 1936
Silver 100-metres backstroke 1936

Mathias, Robert B. (USA)

B. Tulare, Calif., 17 Nov. 1930. In winning the Olympic decathlon at London, Mathias, aged seventeen and a half, became the youngest ever athletics gold-medal winner. It was astonishing that someone so young should win this exhausting ten-events test over two days. At the end of the competition Mathias told his father 'never again, never again'. But he beat the world decathlon record in 1950 before doing so again in retaining his Olympic title (the first athlete ever to do this in the decathlon) at Helsinki. His performances there were 10.9 sec (100 metres), 6.98 m or 22 ft 11 in (long jump), 15.30 m or 50 ft 2½ in (shot), 1.90 m or 6 ft 3 in (high jump), 50.2 sec (400 metres), 14.7 sec (110-metres hurdles), 46.89 m or 153 ft 9¾ in (discus), 4.00 m or 13 ft 1½ in (pole vault), 59.21 m or 194 ft 2½ in (javelin), 4 min 50.8 sec (1,500 metres).

A boyhood victim of anaemia, Mathias was never beaten in the ten decathlons he contested from 1948 until 1956. In a post-Olympic meeting in 1952, he ran the high hurdles in 13.8 sec, at that time a mark beaten by only nine men. In 1953 he forfeited his amateur status by appearing in a film about his career. In 1972 he was re-elected to the United States Congress but defeated for re-election in 1974.
Gold decathlon 1948, 1952

Robert Mathias (USA), 1948

Matthes, Roland (GDR)

B. Pössneck, 17 Nov. 1950. From April 1967, when he was beaten by Joachim Rother (GDR), until 31 August 1974, when he lost to John NABER (USA) in a match between the United States and the German Democratic Republic, at Concord, Calif., Matthes was undefeated in backstroke events. Thus, for nearly seven and a half years, during which he scored backstroke doubles at two Olympic Games and at the first ever World Championships, Matthes dominated world swimming in that stroke and influenced its development.

He has a reputation for ekeing out energy evenly to win a race in individual events. His approach to swimming relays is different – his world records for 100-metres backstroke have been achieved when swimming the first stage of the medley relay for his country.

He has beaten the 100-metres backstroke record six times and equalled it once and has lowered the 200-metres backstroke record from 2 min 9.04 sec to 2 min 1.87 sec.

A highly versatile swimmer, Matthes also set the European record for 100-metres butterfly (55.7 sec). In 1970 he was European record holder for the 200-metres individual medley (2 min 12.8 sec) and has been one of the world's leading front-crawl swimmers. Matthes's coach at the Turbine Club of Erfurt is a woman, Marlies Grohe, who first noted his ability in backstroke.

Gold 100-metres backstroke 1968, 1972; 200-metres backstroke 1968, 1972
Silver 4 × 100-metres medley relay 1968, 1972
Bronze 4 × 100-metres freestyle relay 1972; 100-metres backstroke 1976

Meade, Richard (GBR)

B. Chepstow, 4 Dec. 1938. Britain's first individual equestrian gold medallist when he triumphed on Laurieston at Munich, contributing greatly to his team's victory in the process. It was his third Olympics. At Tokyo (1964), on Barberry, he was leading at the end of the second stage of the three-day event but dropped back to eighth after the show-jumping test. In Mexico (1968) he finished fourth on Cornishman V and was one of the gold-medal winning team.

With one exception he has been in the British team each year since 1964 and has participated in five victories – two Olympic gold medals, one world and two European titles. He was individual runner-up in two World Championships, on Barberry (1966) and The Poacher (1970). In 1974, riding Wayfarer, he was in the team which finished second in the World Championships at Burghley, placing individual seventh.

Gold three-day event (individual) 1972, (team) 1968, 1972

Richard Meade (GBR), 1972

Medved, Aleksandr (URS)

B. Belaya Tserkov, Ukraine, 16 Sept. 1937. His performance in becoming the first man to win wrestling gold medals at three successive Olympics makes him one of the greatest wrestlers in history. Between 1962 and his retirement after the Munich Games (1972) he lost the Olympic or World title on only one occasion – the 1965 World Championships when he drew with Ahmer Ayik (TUR) and conceded the gold medal on fewer bad marks.

What made his career even more remarkable was that he rarely weighed more than 105 kg (231 lb or 16½ stone) and sometimes fought competitors more than 63.5 kg (140 lb or 10 stone) heavier than himself.

He was initially a light heavyweight, taking the gold medal at the Tokyo Games (1964). Two years later he moved up to heavyweight. At Mexico (1968) he was helped by an injury to his leading rival, Wilfried Dietrich (GER). In Munich (1972) he had to use all his experience to keep clear of the formidable strength of Chris Taylor (USA), who weighed 190.5 kg (420 lb or 30 stone). Although the second lightest man in the class he retained his title.

Gold wrestling freestyle light heavyweight 1964; heavyweight 1968; super heavyweight 1972

Meyer, Deborah (USA)

B. Annapolis, Md., 14 Aug. 1952. Miss Meyer was the first swimmer, man or woman, to win three gold medals for individual events in one Olympic Games. The freestyle events over 200 metres and 800 metres were added to the Olympic women's program for the 1968 Games in Mexico and Miss Meyer won them both as well as the 400-metres freestyle. Her Olympic treble was the more meritorious since she went down with a stomach upset on the morning of her second final, that for 200 metres.

She set sixteen world freestyle records during her career; three of them came in the 1968 US Olympic trials at the Los Angeles Coliseum: 2 min 06.7 sec for 200 metres; 4 min 24.5 sec for 400 metres; and 9 min 10.4 sec for 800 metres. In 1970, shortly before her retirement, she improved the record for 400 metres to 4 min 24.3 sec. Her career at the top merely spanned three years from 1967.

She was coached by Sherman Chavoor at the Arden Hills Club. In addition to her achievements at Olympic distances, she made the 1,500-metres freestyle her preserve, breaking the world record four times and having a best performance of 17 min 19.9 sec in a

Aleksandr Medved (URS) v Wilfried Dietrich (GER), 1968

long-course pool.
Gold 200-metres freestyle 1968; 400-metres freestyle 1968; 800-metres freestyle 1968

Miez, Georges (SUI)
B. Töss, Zürich, 2 Oct. 1904. His life has been devoted to gymnastics, beginning at the age of thirteen and becoming an international competitor at eighteen. From then onwards he was a competitor, instructor, propagandist for his sport and even a designer of gymnastic apparatus and trousers, as well as a writer on apparatus. He won more world and Olympic medals than any other Swiss sportsman. He competed in the World Championships of 1931, winning the free exercises, and defended that title in 1934, winning also the horizontal bar title and a team prize.
Gold combined exercises (individual) 1928, (team) 1928; horizontal bar 1928; floor exercises 1936
Silver pommelled horse 1928; floor exercises 1932; combined exercises (team) 1936
Bronze combined exercises (team) 1924

Mittermaier, Rosi (GER)
B. Reit im Winkl, 5 Aug. 1950. Rosi Mittermaier became the first woman skier to win two golds and a silver medal in the three Alpine events of a Winter Olympic Games at Innsbruck in 1976. Her opening victory was the first downhill win in a skiing career begun in 1967. She had become famous as a champion runner-up, injury also intervening at critical moments. With Annemarie Moser-Pröll, the outstanding woman skier of her generation, temporarily retired, and Marie-Therese NADIG, double gold winner at Sapporo, not at her fittest, Rosi took her opportunity superbly and with a modesty which charmed everyone. 'The main thing to remember is not to take sport too seriously,' she said, after winning her second gold in the special slalom. 'I have learned that because I have been beaten too often.' She failed to win her third gold, and thus match the feats of Toni SAILER and Jean-Claude KILLY, by only twelve-hundredths of a second, or about 12 centimetres, the winner being the eighteen-year-old Canadian, Kathy Kreiner.
Gold downhill 1976, slalom 1976
Silver giant slalom 1976

Mockridge, Russell (AUS)
B. Melbourne, 18 July 1930; d. Melbourne, 13 Sept. 1958. A quiet man who had studied for the church, Mockridge had the heart of an amateur long after he had become a professional cyclist, and was an outstanding all-rounder.

Beginning as a sprinter, he was the first amateur to win the Open Grand Prix of Paris (1951). He went to the other end of competitive cycling to complete the Tour de France (2,600 miles or 4,184 km) in 1955. He raced in the London Olympics (1948), but did not win medals until 1952 in Helsinki, where he set a new record for the 1,000-metres time trial and won the tandem sprint with Lionel Cox. He was killed in a car crash.
Gold 1,000-metres time trial 1952; 2,000-metres tandem 1952

Morelon, Daniel (FRA)
B. Bourg en Bresse, 28 July 1944.

Daniel Morelon (FRA), 1972

Generally considered the most outstanding Olympic cyclist. In amateur sprint cycling he won medals at eight out of ten World Championships, including six world titles. He has always had the knack of winning by a narrow margin, thus making his opponents look better than they were. He is also the fastest unpaced cyclist, with a time of 10.72 sec (42 mph or 67.6 kph) for a 200-metres flying start, set in Zürich in 1966.
Gold 1,000-metres individual sprint 1968, 1972; 2,000-metres tandem 1968
Silver 1,000-metres individual sprint 1972
Bronze 1,000-metres individual sprint 1964

Morrow, Bobby (USA)
B. Harlingen, Tex., 15 Oct. 1935. The outstanding sprinter at the Melbourne Olympics, Morrow is considered as one of the supreme competitors over 100 and 200 metres. Between 1955 and 1958 he lost only one championship race. He held individual world records for the 100 yards (9.3 sec) and 200-metres turn (20.6 sec) and as late as 1960 narrowly missed being selected for the US team. In 1956, as a student at Abilene Christian College, he won the US Olympic sprint trials in 10.3 sec and 20.6 sec. At Melbourne he proved as great a sprinter as any yet seen in the Games. He went through four rounds of the 100 metres undefeated and won the final, against a wind of 5 metres per second, in 10.5 sec. In the 200 metres he ran with a bandaged thigh but unleashed an unanswerable burst of power to win in the Olympic record time of 20.6 sec. In the 4 × 100-metres relay he gained his third gold medal with a fine last stage which made up for two indifferent baton exchanges. The following year Morrow equalled the then world 100-yards record of 9.3 sec three times and lost only one race all season.
Gold 100 metres 1956; 200 metres 1956; 4 × 100-metres relay 1956

Mortanges, Charles Ferdinand Pahud de (HOL)
B. The Hague, 13 May 1896; d. 8 April 1971. As a winner of two consecutive individual gold medals in Olympic three-day events, General (as he became) de Mortanges held an equestrian record which still stands after forty years. As a Lieutenant in the Dutch Hussars, he rode in four Olympic events, making his début at Paris where he finished fourth on Johnny Walker as one of his country's gold-medal winning team. At Amsterdam, where the Dutch team was again successful, he won his first individual medal, riding Marcroix. At Los Angeles he triumphed again with the same horse, the Dutch team then taking the silver medal. He also rode Marcroix, then seventeen years old, at Berlin (1936), but was unplaced although completing the course. Marcroix, an Anglo-Norman palomino, is believed to be the only horse to have competed in three successive Olympic three-day events.
Gold three-day event (individual) 1928, 1932, (team) 1924, 1928
Silver three-day event (team) 1932

Jonni Myyrä (FIN), 1924

Myyrä, Jonni (FIN)
B. Savitaipale, 13 July 1892; d. 22 Jan. 1955. A pioneer in the Finnish school of javelin throwing, he achieved a world record of 62.57 m (205 ft 3½ in) in 1915 and eventually raised it to 66.10 m (216 ft 10½ in) in 1919 before winning the Olympic titles in 1920 and 1924 with 65.78 m (215 ft 9½ in) and 62.96 m (206 ft 6½ in). Myyrä, who started his Olympic career by finishing eighth in the 1912 Games, had an unofficial throw of 67.96 m (222 ft 11 in) in 1925, at the age of thirty-three.
Gold javelin 1920, 1924

Naber, John (USA)
B. California, 20 Jan. 1956. Shared with Kornelia ENDER the honour of being the most successful swimmer of the 1976 Games, winning four gold medals and a silver. Naber, 1.98 m (6 ft 6 in) tall, ended the Olympic run of Roland MATTHES (GDR) who had scored a backstroke double at the two previous Games.

On the way to his first Olympic title Naber beat Matthes in a semi-final of the 100-metres backstroke and improved the latter's world and Olympic records by 0.11 sec with 56.19 sec. Matthes, lacking training after an appendix operation, was third in the final won by Naber in 55.49 sec, another world record. Naber became the first swimmer to beat two minutes for 200-metres backstroke when he won that final in 1 min 59.19 sec, with Americans filling the other two medal places. In the 200-metres freestyle final, Naber led at 100 metres in 54.46 sec and was still alongside the eventual winner Bruce Furniss at the final turn. He took the silver medal in 1 min 50.50 sec, 0.21 sec behind Furniss. His other gold medals came in the relays.
Gold 100-metres backstroke 1976; 200-metres backstroke 1976; 4 × 200-metres freestyle 1976; 4 × 100-metres medley 1976
Silver 200-metres freestyle 1976

Nadi, Nedo (ITA)
B. Livorno, 9 June 1893; d. Rome, 29 Jan. 1940. The greatest and most versatile fencer of the century, he won more international success in this sport than anyone. He was initially taught foil in his father's gymnasium at an extremely young age, but at fifteen he was skilful in the other weapons. He started international competition in 1911 and in 1912 at Stockholm won the gold medal in foil without suffering a single defeat in the course of the final. This victory in an event which

John Naber (USA), 1976

Nedo Nadi (ITA), 1920

usually requires many years of preparation and international experience was considered one of the outstanding achievements in the history of fencing. At Antwerp (1920) Nadi accomplished the biggest feat of his career, winning five gold medals – still one of the most outstanding feats in the history of the modern Games. After becoming a professional and teaching in Buenos Aires, he returned to Europe and, against all precedent, was reinstated as an amateur so that from 1935 until his death he was President of the Italian Fencing Federation.
Gold foil (individual) 1912, 1920, (team) 1920; épée (team) 1920; sabre (individual) 1920, (team) 1920

Nadig, Marie-Thérèse (SUI)

B. Tannenboden, 8 Mar. 1954. In 1972 Miss Nadig sprang almost from nowhere to win two Olympic skiing gold medals at Sapporo. Although Swiss junior champion in 1970, she accomplished little of international significance in 1971, yet her results in the winter of 1971–2 progressively improved and she reached her peak just in time for the Sapporo Games. Annemarie Pröll (AUT) was the favourite for both downhill and giant slalom, but Miss Nadig confounded her both times. She had the stocky build that characterizes the downhill specialists, 1.63 m (5 ft $4\frac{1}{4}$ in) tall and weighing 65 kg (143 lb 7 oz).

In the six years from 1972 to 1978 she was five times placed in the first three of the downhill World Cup overall result list. She won the pre-Olympic World Cup downhill in 1975 in Innsbruck and the World Cup downhill in 1975 in Jackson Hall, USA.
Gold downhill and giant slalom 1972

Nakayama, Akinori (JPN)

B. Aichi Prefecture, 1 Mar. 1943. One of the most successful Japanese gymnasts of the late 1960s. He finished first in the parallel bars and floor exercises in his World Championships début in 1966. Although twenty-nine by the Munich Games (1972), unusually old for a leading competitor, he showed that he was still a superb all-round athlete.
Gold rings 1968, 1972; parallel bars 1968; horizontal bar 1968; combined exercises (team) 1968, 1972
Silver floor exercises 1968, 1972
Bronze combined exercises (individual) 1968, 1972

Neckermann, Josef (GER)

B. Würzburg, 5 June 1912. Owner of one of Europe's largest department stores and President of the Stiftung Deutsche Sporthilfe (a foundation to aid high-performance sportsmen) and a member of the West German National Olympic Committee and sports Federation. He became World Dressage Champion in 1966 (individual and team).
Gold dressage (team) 1964, 1968
Silver dressage (individual) 1968, (team) 1972
Bronze dressage (individual) 1960, 1972

Norelius, Martha (USA)

B. Stockholm, Sweden, 20 Jan. 1908; d. 1955. Her father represented Sweden in the Interim Games in Athens (1906), but Miss Norelius was brought up in the United States, where she was first coached by her father and then by Louis de B. Handley, who, as coach to the New York Women's Swimming Association, also trained other US Olympic gold medallists in Ethelda BLEIBTREY and Aileen Riggin. Miss Norelius was the first woman to win an Olympic gold medal for the same event at successive Games: in the 400-metres freestyle in 1924 in 6 min 02.2 sec and in 1928 in 5 min 42.8 sec (a world record). She won sixteen US titles and had nineteen world amateur records ratified. After the 1928 Games she became a professional. Her world records were all in freestyle events from 200 metres to a mile. She married Joseph Wright, a Canadian oarsman who won the 1928 Olympic silver mdeal for double sculls.
Gold 400-metres freestyle 1924, 1928; 4 × 100-metres freestyle relay 1928

Nurmi, Paavo Johannes (FIN)

B. Turku, 13 June 1897; d. Helsinki, 2 Oct. 1973. Nurmi set, altogether, twenty-two world records in athletics from distances between 1,500 metres and 20 kilometres and those feats together with his Olympic performances and his style of training brought a fundamental change in attitude towards middle- and long-distance running.

Nurmi began running when he was about nine years old and at fifteen he was fired with the exploits of Hannes KOLEHMAINEN (FIN). Running from then onwards became Nurmi's overriding passion and he set out to emulate Kolehmainen. In 1920 he began holding a stopwatch as he ran, both in training and competition, and this played a crucial part in his development.

William Parry O'Brien (USA), 1956

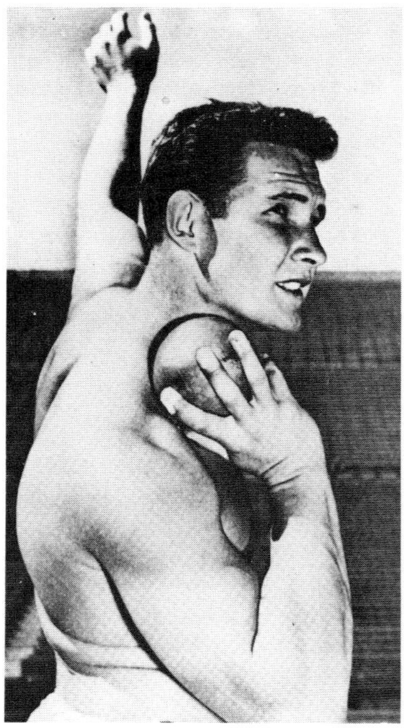

It helped judgment of pace, which eluded many other runners, it conserved energy and gave him greater confidence.

At the 1924 Olympics he won all four of his races, two of them, the 1,500 metres and 5,000 metres within an hour and a half; a few weeks previously he set world records for those distances within the space of an hour.

He was upset at being left out of the 10,000 metres in the 1924 Games, and while a fellow countryman, Ville Ritola, was winning the event in a world-record time of 30 min 23.2 sec, Nurmi was said to have been on a training run over the same distance, which he completed in 29 min 58 sec. Four years later, he won the 10,000 metres again and he would probably have taken a medal in the marathon at Los Angeles in 1932 had he not been disqualified from athletics for alleged professionalism. That decision embittered him, although it was rescinded for domestic competition, until his death. There is a bronze statue of him outside the Olympic stadium in Helsinki and he carried the torch into that arena at the Games of 1952.

Gold 1,500 metres 1924; 5,000 metres 1924; 10,000 metres 1920, 1928; 3,000 metres (team) 1924; cross-country (individual) 1920, 1924, (team) 1920, 1924
Silver 5,000 metres 1920, 1928; 3,000-metres steeplechase 1928

O'Brien, William Parry (USA)

B. Santa Monica, Calif., 28 Jan. 1932. Will be remembered by close students of athletics as the man who pioneered the step-back style of shot putting in which the competitor starts with his back towards the direction of the throw and gains more time to apply force. O'Brien was Olympic champion at only twenty, retained the title and was fourth in 1964. Between 1953 and 1955 he beat the world record fourteen times and became the first man to beat 18.29 m (60 ft). It was in 1966, still competing at thirty-four, that he achieved the greatest putt of his life 19.7 m (64 ft $7\frac{1}{2}$ in). He was eighteen times US national or collegiate champion and between 1952 and 1956 had 116 consecutive victories.

Gold shot 1952, 1956
Silver shot 1960

O'Callaghan, Patrick (IRL)

B. Kanturk, Co. Cork, 28 Jan. 1906. A year after he began specializing in the hammer throw, O'Callaghan astonished the experts by winning the gold medal in Amsterdam (1928) with a throw of 51.39 m (168 ft 7 in). He defended the title in 1932 but only won the gold medal with his last throw, 53.92 m (176 ft 11 in). He was an all-round athlete and probably one of his finest performances was never recognized officially; in 1937 from a circle six inches too small and with a hammer six ounces overweight he achieved a throw of 59.56 m (195 ft 5 in), 1.83 m (6 ft) further than the world record set twenty-four years earlier by the Irish-American Patrick Ryan.

Gold hammer 1928, 1932

Patrick O'Callaghan (IRL), 1932

Al Oerter (USA), 1968

Oerter, Alfred A. (USA)

B. Astoria, N.Y., 19 Sept. 1936. Often cited as the supreme Olympic athletics competitor on his four successive gold discus medals. He was American high-school discus record holder in 1954 and two years later surprised many, at only twenty, by winning his first Olympic title with a record throw of 56.36 m (184 ft 11 in). In spite of all the pressure he again had a personal record, this time of 59.18 m (194 ft $1\frac{3}{4}$ in) in taking his second gold medal at Rome. For his third Olympics, at Tokyo, he was seriously handicapped by torn cartilages in his lower rib cage. He came out for the final with his ribs heavily taped and his right side packed in ice to prevent internal haemorrhage. Yet he still won. Four years later, at Mexico City, the rain swamped the throwing circle but Oerter, now thirty-two, adjusted his technique by leaving out preliminary swings and had the best three throws of his whole career, including a winning 64.78 m (212 ft $6\frac{1}{2}$ in). Four times the world-record holder in the discus, Oerter strongly condemned the use of illegal anabolic steroids, saying, 'The Olympics are unique. There is no job, no amount of power, no money to approach the meaning

of the Olympic experience.'
Gold discus 1956, 1960, 1964, 1968

Okano, Isao (JPN)
B. Ibaragi Prefecture, 20 Jan. 1944. A graduate of the Chuo University, Tokyo, he started judo while attending middle school. After winning the middleweight class at the Tokyo Games (1964), while at university, he also won the World title in Rio de Janeiro the following year in the middleweight class. He belongs to the orthodox school of judo with its principle based on faith that 'softness can subdue wrath'. He established a private judo school, the *Shoki-Jiku* ('school of righteous mind') in 1969 and succeeded in gathering disciples not only in Japan but from Europe, the United States and South America.
Gold judo middleweight 1964

Ono, Takashi (JPN)
B. Akita Prefecture, 26 July 1931. The first of the outstanding Japanese gymnasts, Ono led his country's assault on the USSR's male domination of the sport. In 1956 he finished only 0.05 points behind Viktor CHUKARIN (URS) in the combined exercises competition and produced a splendid performance on the horizontal bar where he obtained 19.60 out of a possible 20 points for victory. His control and suppleness earned him widespread appreciation.

Four years later Ono again failed to take the gold medal by 0.05 points – from another Russian, Boris SHAKHLIN. However, Ono had considerable compensation in winning the gold medal in the horizontal bar and vault and bronze on the rings and parallel bars. He also led Japan to its first team triumph, a title it has not lost since in either Olympics or World Championships. By 1964, he had been surpassed but still took a gold medal in the team event.
Gold horizontal bar 1956, 1960; long-horse vault 1960; combined exercises (team) 1960, 1964
Silver combined exercises (individual) 1956, 1960; pommelled horse 1956; combined exercises (team) 1956
Bronze long-horse vault 1952; parallel bars 1956, 1960; rings 1960

Oriola, Christian d' (FRA)
B. Perpignan, Eastern Pyrénées, 3 Oct. 1928. With Lucien GAUDIN, the greatest French fencer of all time. Four times World Champion in foil, in 1947, 1949, 1953 and 1954, he took four team World titles, in 1947, 1951, 1953 and 1958. He allowed his comrade Jehan Buhan, sixteen years older, to take the gold medal in the 1948 Games. He rebelled against the introduction of the electric foil but took up competition again in 1958 and at Rome (1960) was seventh. He carried the flag for the French delegation. Ten times Champion of France, from 1952 to 1970, he was awarded the Legion of Honour in 1971. He is first cousin of Pierre Jonquères d'ORIOLA.
Gold foil (individual) 1952, 1956, (team) 1948, 1952
Silver foil (individual) 1948, (team) 1956

Oriola, Pierre Jonquères d' (FRA)
B. Corneilla del Vercol, Eastern Pyrénées, 1 Feb. 1920. The only rider to have won two individual gold medals for show jumping, the first riding Ali Baba at Helsinki (1952) and the other on Lutteur B at Tokyo (1964) when the French took the team silver. After World War II, he was one of the first French riders to move into a hitherto military preserve and make an international reputation: his early successes included the Zürich Grand Prix in 1946 and the first postwar King George V Gold Cup in London in 1947. He won the men's World Championship on Pomone at Buenos Aires in 1966 after finishing second in 1953 and third in 1954.
Gold show jumping (individual) 1952, 1964
Silver show jumping (team) 1964, 1968

Osborn, Harold (USA)
B. Butler, Ill., 13 Apr. 1899; d. Los Angeles, 5 Apr. 1975. Remarkable both for his versatility and long career. In Paris he set a world high-jump record of 2.04 m (6 ft $8\frac{1}{4}$ in) and won the Olympic title with a Games record of 1.98 m (6 ft 6 in). Then he became the first athlete to win the Olympic decathlon with a world-record score. He is still the only man to combine an individual victory with one in the decathlon. In the Amsterdam Olympics (1928) he finished only fifth in the high jump but his Olympic record in this event was not beaten until 1936. In the same year he finished his career with a world indoor best of 1.68 m (5 ft 6 in) for the standing high jump. Altogether he won eighteen US titles in six different events.
Gold high jump 1924; decathlon 1924

Ostermeyer, Micheline (FRA)
B. Rang de Fliers, 23 Dec. 1922. Third in the French discus championship of 1948, she was a most unexpected winner of the Olympic title in London that year; she was only entered as an afterthought following her initial selection for the shot, which she also won at Wembley, and the high jump, in which she was third. Winner of a Paris Conservatoire piano prize, she celebrated her Olympic victories with an impromptu recital of Beethoven at France's team headquarters.
Gold shot 1948; discus 1948
Bronze high jump 1948

Owens, James Cleveland ('Jesse') (USA)
B. Danville, Ala., 12 Sept. 1913. One of the greatest of all track and field athletes, certainly in the first half of the twentieth century. His combination of grace, speed, spring and power has been captured forever on film. He is also

James Cleveland ('Jesse') Owens (USA), 1936

remembered for his record breaking and especially his feat on 25 May 1935 at Ann Arbor, Michigan, when he beat or equalled six world records within forty-five minutes. Apart from 100 yards in 9.4 sec and 220 yards in 20 3 sec, his records that day included his single long jump of 8.13 m (26 ft 8¼ in) which was to last for twenty-five years.

Possessing great natural ability, Owens says he was motivated towards winning an Olympic title by meeting American sprinter Charley Paddock in 1928, just as eight years later the success of Owens drove Harrison DILLARD (USA) towards victory. At Ohio State University Owens had his technique polished by coach Larry Snyder as he approached the peak of a career which was to bring him nine world records in seven events and an unbeaten run over 200 metres.

At Berlin, on 2 August 1936, Owens opened his marvellous golden chapter in the Olympic book with a 100-metres heat in 10.3 sec, which, because it was wind-assisted, could not be a Games record. Before the week was over he had won the 100 metres in 10.3 sec, the 200 metres in 20.7 sec, the fastest ever at that time round a full turn, the long jump with 8.06 m (26 ft 5¼ in), an Olympic record, and anchored the American 4 × 100-metres relay team to a new world record of 39.8 sec. His only serious challenge came in the long jump where he was level with Luz Long (GER) until the fifth round. Owens turned professional soon after the Olympics.

Gold 100 metres 1936; 200 metres 1936; long jump 1936; 4 × 100-metres relay 1936

Papp, László (HUN)

B. Budapest, 25 Mar. 1926. The outstanding champion in Olympic boxing history. Papp said once that his hardest bout in the Olympics was in 1948 against Johnny Wright (GBR). But his peak may well have been his third victory in 1956 against José Torres (USA) who later became world professional light-heavyweight champion. Papp won the European professional middleweight title in 1962 and was unbeaten until he finally retired. He combined both technical skill and a powerful punch and successfully coached the Hungarian teams.

Gold boxing middleweight 1948; light middleweight 1952, 1956

Pattisson, Rodney Stuart (GBR)

B. Campbeltown, Scotland, 5 Aug. 1943. The first Briton to win two consecutive gold medals for yachting. At Acapulco (1968) he helmed his Flying Dutchman *Super . . . docious* and was crewed by Iain Macdonald Smith; they had five firsts and one second, incuring only three penalty points, the lowest number of points by the winner in any class in an Olympic regatta. This was the first yachting gold medal for Britain for twenty years. At Kiel (1972), Pattisson helmed his Flying Dutchman *Superdoso*, with Chris Davies as crew. From 1968 to 1972, Pattisson held the Flying Dutchman World and European Championships. His success has been based on the belief that racing sailors should be physically fit. He began each day with a long training run. His boat is always immaculate and he pays much attention to detail and to the meticulous tuning of his boat.

Gold yachting Flying Dutchman 1968, 1972

Silver yachting Flying Dutchman 1976

László Papp (HUN), 1948

Rodney Stuart Pattisson (GBR), and Chris Davies, 1972

Pearce, Henry Robert (AUS)

B. 30 Sept. 1905. Son of a professional waterman at Hammersmith, London, who later emigrated to Australia. He completely dominated single sculling, and so confident was he that, on occasions, he would scull with, and coach his opponents. It was probably this confidence, rather

than any real threat from any contemporary scullers, which accounted for the fact that he did not always win by large margins. Besides his Olympics successes, he won the British Empire title, against Jack BERESFORD (GBR), in 1930 at Hamilton, Ontario, and then became a Canadian citizen. The following year he won the Diamond Sculls at Henley Royal Regatta. He retained his qualification as an Australian for Olympic purposes. He turned professional in 1933, and took the world professional sculling title.
Gold single sculls 1928, 1932

Pihlajamäki, Kustaa (FIN)

B. Nurmo, 7 Apr. 1902; d. Helsinki, 10 Feb. 1944. From an outstanding family of wrestlers, he was very tough, quick and versatile. He was equally competent in freestyle and Greco-Roman. Many wrestling experts regard him as the best lightweight wrestler of all time. He competed in four Olympics and won the European Championship in Greco-Roman style in 1930, 1931, 1933, 1934, 1937, 1938, 1939, and in freestyle in 1931 and 1937. He represented Finland in forty-one international matches, of which he won thirty-eight. There is a monument to him in Helsinki. His brothers, Arvi (b. 1904; d. 1940) and Paavo (b. 1911) were Finnish freestyle champions many times.

Kustaa Pihlajamäki (FIN) v Erken (TUR), 1936

A cousin, Hermanni Pihlajamäki (b. 1903) won an Olympic gold medal in the freestyle featherweight division in 1932 and a bronze in 1936 in the lightweight class.
Gold wrestling freestyle bantamweight 1924, featherweight 1932, 1936
Silver featherweight 1928

Poynton-Hill, Dorothy (USA)

B. Salt Lake City, Utah, 17 July 1915. Miss Poynton was barely thirteen when she competed in her first Olympic Games at Amsterdam, yet won the silver medal for springboard diving. As Mrs Hill, she won the springboard bronze medal in 1936, but her real talent was seen from the highboard. An attractive blonde, she opened her own aquatic club in Los Angeles, where she had learned her diving.
Gold highboard diving 1932, 1936
Silver springboard diving 1928
Bronze springboard diving 1936

Press, Irina (URS)

B. Kharkov, 10 Mar. 1939. She started athletics in 1955 and entered the Russian team in 1958. Her Olympic pentathlon victory brought with it a world-record score (her eighth record in this event), and she finished fourth in the 80-metres hurdles and sixth in the shot, won by her sister Tamara. She retired before the 1966 European Championships.
Gold 80-metres hurdles 1960; pentathlon 1964

Press, Tamara (URS)

B. Kharkov, 10 May 1937. Six times world-record holder in both the shot and discus and also winner of three European titles. She retired before the 1966 European Championships.
Gold shot 1960, 1964; discus 1964
Silver discus 1960

Prinstein, Myer (USA)

B. 1878; d. 10 Mar. 1928. The only man to win the Olympic long jump and triple jump on the same day (1904). In 1900 he had been first in the triple jump, too, but having competed in the qualifying round of the long jump, was prevented by his college, Syracuse, from taking part in the final because it was on a Sunday. He finished second in that event with his qualifying mark of 7.175 m (23 ft $6\frac{1}{2}$ in) to 7.185 m (23 ft $6\frac{7}{8}$ in) by Alvin KRAENZLEIN (USA). In 1904 Prinstein was also fifth in the 400 metres and the 60 metres. His best long jump was 7.50 m (24 ft $7\frac{1}{4}$ in) in 1900. He also won the long jump at the 1906 Interim Games in Athens.
Gold long jump 1904; triple jump 1900, 1904
Silver long jump 1900

Tamara Press (URS), 1964

Protopopov, Oleg and Ludmila (Belousova) (URS)

Oleg, b. Leningrad, 16 July 1932; Ludmila, b. Ulyanovsk, 22 Nov. 1935. After serving in the Soviet Navy from 1951 to 1953, Oleg Protopopov took third place in the 1953 Russian pair championship with Margarita Bogoyavlenskaya. Until 1957 Ludmila Belousova's partner was Yuri Nevski. The Protopopovs began skating as a pair in 1957, and were married in the same year. They were runners-up for both World and European titles in 1962, 1963 and 1964, and were European and

World Champions four times, from 1965 to 1968. In the Olympic Games they were ninth at Squaw Valley (1960) and champions at Innsbruck (1964) and Grenoble (1968). By 1969 they were beyond their peak at thirty-six and thirty-three respectively and lost their European and World titles to Aleksei Ulanov and Irina Rodnina (URS). They turned professional and won a lucrative competition promoted by Richard BUTTON in Tokyo in 1973.
Gold figure skating (pairs) 1964, 1968

Rezantsev, Valeriy (URS)

B. Novo-Moscovsk, 8 Oct. 1948. A highly successful and skilful Greco-Roman wrestler during the 1970s, Rezantsev finished first in the light-heavyweight classes at both the 1972 and 1976 Games. His ability to disturb an opponent's balance with a sudden unexpected turn gave him a domination of the class during the decade.
Gold wrestling Greco-Roman light-heavyweight 1972, 1976

Richards, Robert E. (USA)

B. Champaign, Ill., 20 Feb. 1926. A remarkably consistent pole vaulter although only 1.76 m (5 ft $9\frac{1}{2}$ in) tall, Richards was nine times American champion. In 1956 Richards, a preacher nicknamed 'The Vaulting Vicar', only qualified for the Olympic final on his third and last attempt. He was three times American decathlon champion and represented the United States in that event at Melbourne in 1956.
Gold pole vault 1952, 1956
Bronze pole vault 1948

Oleg and Ludmila (Belousova) Protopopov (URS), 1964

Richthoff, Johan (SWE)

B. Limhamn, near Malmö, 1898. He began as a cooper and became a minister in the Swedish free church and a campaigner against alcohol. He weighed 112 kg (17 stone 9 lb or 247 lb) and was an excellent technician. He was a professional catch-wrestler in the United States 1932–3.
Gold wrestling freestyle heavyweight 1928, 1932

Rose, Iain Murray (AUS)

B. Nairn, Scotland, 6 Jan. 1939. The Rose family emigrated to Sydney, Australia, when Murray was a baby. At the time of his greatest success, 1956, when he won his first three Olympic gold medals, he was acclaimed as the best Australian swimmer ever. In individual events and relays, Rose's contribution always being on front crawl, his name appears on the world-record lists fifteen times. His first world record was 9 min 34.3 sec for 880-yards freestyle at Sydney in January 1956; more than eight and a half years later he set his last, returning 8 min 55.5 sec in the same event at Vancouver.

At Melbourne Rose won the 400-metres freestyle and the 1,500-metres freestyle as well as being a member of the winning Australian team in the 4 × 200-metres freestyle relay to become the youngest triple gold medal winner up to that time. In 1960 he retained the 400-metres title, the only man ever to have done so. Curiously in each of these victories he beat Tsuyoshi Yamanaka (JPN) by 3.1 sec.
Gold 400-metres freestyle 1956, 1960; 1,500-metres freestyle 1956; 4 × 200-metres freestyle relay 1956
Silver 1,500-metres freestyle 1960
Bronze 4 × 200-metres freestyle relay 1960

Rose, Ralph W. (USA)

B. Louisville, Ky., 17 Mar. 1884; d. 16 Oct. 1913. Literally a giant by

Ralph Rose (USA), 1912

the standards of the early Olympics, Rose was 1.96 m (6 ft 5 in) and 106.6 kg (235 lb). Only twenty when he won his first Olympic shot title in St Louis with 14.81 m (48 ft 7 in), between 1907 and 1909 he beat the world record four more times, eventually reaching 15.56 m (51 ft $0\frac{3}{4}$ in), and was unbeaten for nineteen years. He also had an unratified mark of 16.56 m (54 ft 4 in) in 1909, as well as another unofficial world record of 54.38 m (178 ft 5 in) for the hammer event.
Gold shot 1904, 1908; two-handed shot 1912
Silver discus 1904; shot 1912
Bronze hammer 1904

Rosendahl, Heide (GER)

B. Hückeswagen, 14 Feb. 1947. The victim of ill fortune in the 1968 Olympics, when illness and injury deprived her of any medals, she became the darling of the West German crowd at Munich by winning the long jump, finishing second in the pentathlon and then anchoring the German sprint relay team to victory in world-record-equalling time. The daughter of a national discus champion, she set a world long-jump record of 6.84 m (22 ft $5\frac{1}{2}$ in) in 1970.
Gold long jump 1972; 4 × 100-metres relay 1972
Silver pentathlon 1972

Heide Rosendahl (GER), 1972

Rudolph, Wilma (USA)
B. Clarksville, Tenn., 23 June 1940. Outstanding athletics champion of the 1960 Olympics, with victories in the 100 and 200 metres and the 4 × 100-metres relay. She was the seventeenth of nineteen children and once said that she learned to run fast because she wanted to get to the dining table first. At only four she became paralysed and did not learn to walk normally until she was seven. Yet at sixteen she won a bronze Olympic medal as a member of the US 4 × 100-metres relay team at Melbourne. She came to Rome as holder of the world 200-metres record but even so she amazed spectators by the wide margins with which she won both sprints. In the 100 metres her time of 11.0 sec was ineligible for world-record ratification because the following wind was just over the permissible limit. In 1961 she lowered her 100-metres record to 11.2 sec.
Gold 100 metres 1960; 200 metres 1960; 4 × 100-metres relay 1960
Bronze 4 × 100-metres relay 1956

Wilma Rudolph (USA), 1960

Rühle, Frank (GDR)
B. Dehna, 5 Mar. 1944. Member of the unbeaten Einheit Dresden coxless four. See FORBERGER, Frank
Gold coxless fours 1968, 1972

Ruska, Willem (HOL)
B. Amsterdam, 29 Aug. 1940. Twice World Champion between 1967 and 1971, he won European titles from 1965 to 1972 and is the only *judoka* to have won two Olympic titles in one Olympic Games. He started in the sport when he was twenty and after training for seven years won his first world title in Salt Lake City, Utah. He participates in a variety of other sports and although he has a body weight of 110 kg (242 lb or 17 stone 4 lb) he ran 100 metres in 11 sec. He is now coach of the Dutch judo team.
Gold judo heavyweight 1972, open 1972

Ruud, Birger (NOR)
B. Kongsberg, 23 Aug. 1911. He took part in three Olympic Winter Games, the first time in 1932 and the third time sixteen years later in 1948, when he was the coach to the Norwegian ski-jumping team. During training in the days before the competition he was added to the team and justified this late selection by winning the silver medal in special jumping; he was thirty-six. Ruud is perhaps the most famous ski jumper in the world. In addition to his Olympic medals, he took the gold medal in the World Championships in 1931, 1935 and 1937 and was US champion in 1938. Twice he held the world record in ski jumping, in 1926 in Ødnesbakken, Norway, achieving 76.5 m (251 ft), and in 1934 in Planica, Yugoslavia, with 92.0 m (301 ft 10 in).
Gold special ski jumping 1932, 1936
Silver special ski jumping 1948

Sailer, Anton ('Toni') (AUT)
B. Kitzbühel, 17 Nov. 1935. Sailer is the outstanding Alpine skier in Olympic history and still a national hero. His feat of winning all three gold medals in one Games has since been emulated by Jean-Claude KILLY (FRA) but Sailer's record is much the more impressive, since he triumphed by substantial margins – 3.5 sec in the downhill, 4.0 sec in the slalom and 6.2 sec in the giant slalom. These results placed him in a class apart from his contemporaries. He was World Champion on the strength of his Cortina performances, a title he retained two years later, though on that occasion he won only two races, being second in the slalom, not his strongest discipline.

Sailer's was a brief, meteoric career spanning only four seasons at international level. His first big success was the Lauberhorn Cup at Wengen (downhill and combined) in 1955 and his last the World Championships in 1958. Handsome as well as athletic, he later moved into the world of motion pictures, but with only moderate success, and he came back to ski racing in 1972 as director of the Austrian Alpine teams.
Gold downhill, slalom and giant slalom 1956

Viktor Saneev (URS), 1976

St Cyr, Major Henri (SWE)

B. Stockholm, 15 Mar. 1902. The only rider to win two individual gold medals for dressage, on Master Rufus at Helsinki (1952) and on Juli at Stockholm (1956). Each performance contributed to the Swedish team victory. He came close to winning a bronze at London in 1948 and at Rome in 1960. He competed at Berlin in 1936 when he was one of the Swedish three-day-event team. In this sphere he was three times Swedish National Champion, in 1935, 1937 and 1939. Following his triumph at Helsinki, he won the World Championship in dressage at Wiesbaden in 1953. In 1956 he took the Olympic oath on behalf of all riders at the Equestrian events, which because of Australian quarantine rules, were held in Stockholm.
Gold dressage (individual) 1952, 1956, (team) 1952, 1956

Saneev, Viktor (URS)

B. Sukhumi, 3 Oct. 1945. Initially a long jumper, he switched to the triple jump in 1967 and in 1968 won the Olympic gold medal with an extraordinary world record of 17.39 m (57 ft 0¾ in). He won the European title in 1969 and though he lost it to Jörg Drehmel (GDR) in 1971, he retained his Olympic title in 1972. Later that year he regained the world record he had lost to Pedro Pérez (CUB) with an effort of 17.44 m (57 ft 2¾ in). He was European Champion again in 1974. He high jumped 1.90 m (6 ft 2¾ in) when aged seventeen.
Gold triple jump 1968, 1972, 1976

Schäfer, Karl (AUT)

B. Vienna, 17 May 1909. A brilliant figure skater who ended the Olympic supremacy in 1932 of the legendary Gillis GRAFSTRÖM (SWE), Schäfer had the generosity to say afterwards: 'Yes, I beat him, but he is still the world's greatest skater.' Schäfer was a rare all-rounder who competed in both Winter and Summer Games, for he was a good enough swimmer to be chosen for Austria in 1928 and 1932, finishing fourth in the 1928 breaststroke.

Schäfer first broke through to the top of ice skating with third place in both the European and World Championships of 1927. In 1928 he moved up a place in both events and was fourth in the Winter Games of 1928. After finishing second again in the World Championship of 1929, he went on to win that title from 1929 to 1936. He was known as 'the man who never fell'.
Gold figure skating 1932, 1936

Schenk, Ard (HOL)

B. Anna Paulowna, 16 Sept. 1944. The most advanced speed skater in the world, from 1970 until he became professional in 1972 he was unbeaten.

In 1972 he won the World Championship, the European Championship and the three longest distances in the Olympic Games in Sapporo, beating his opponents decisively. In the 500 metres he fell. He won the European and World Championships three times, set nineteen world records and created a class of his own through his remarkable physique, outstanding technique and strength.
Gold 1,500 metres, 5,000 metres and 10,000 metres 1972
Silver 1,500 metres 1968

Ard Schenk (HOL), 1972

Schollander, Donald Arthur (USA)

B. Charlotte, N.C., 30 Apr. 1946. His technique on front crawl was considered the best ever developed. It helped him to win five Olympic gold medals, three titles in the 1967 Pan-American Games and eleven titles in individual events at the US championships. Always swimming front crawl, he set thirteen world records in individual events and eight in relays when representing either the Santa Clara Club or the United States. His best long-course times were: 100 metres 52.9 sec; 200 metres 1 min 54.3 sec and 400 metres 4 min 11.6 sec. He was particularly associated with the 200-metres freestyle, nine of his world records being set in that event, the first (1 min 58.8 sec) in Los Angeles in 1963 and the last (1 min 54.3 sec) at Long Beach in 1968.

The 1964 Olympic Games in Tokyo brought Schollander to the attention of a wider public. He was the first swimmer to win four gold medals at one Games.

Though he never held the world record for 100-metres freestyle and claimed not to be a sprinter, Schollander won the Olympic title in 1964 by a tenth of a second after a magnificent race with Bobby McGregor (GBR). His win

Don Schollander (USA), 1968

in the 400-metres freestyle set a world record of 4 min 12.2 sec and helped the United States to win both the freestyle relays in world-record times.
Gold 100-metres freestyle 1964; 400-metres freestyle 1964; 4 × 100-metres freestyle relay 1964; 4 × 200-metres freestyle relay 1964, 1968
Silver 200-metres freestyle 1968

Schubert, Dieter (GDR)
B. Pirna, 11 Sept. 1943. Member of the unbeaten Einheit Dresden coxless four. See FORBERGER, Frank
Gold coxless fours 1968, 1972

Schwarzmann, Alfred (GER)
B. Fürth, 23 Mar. 1912. The most successful gymnast of the 1936 Olympic Games in Berlin. Sixteen years later when forty years old he won a silver medal at the Olympics in the horizontal bar competition.
Gold combined exercises (individual) 1936, (team) 1936; long-horse vault 1936
Silver horizontal bar 1952
Bronze horizontal bar 1936, parallel bars 1936

Shakhlin, Boris (URS)
B. Ishim, Kazakhstan, 27 Jan. 1932. Although rather large for a competitive gymnast, 1.71 m (5 ft 7½ in) tall and weighing 70 kg (154 lb or 11 stone), Shakhlin's strength and precision brought him ten individual and team titles in Olympics and World Championships between 1954 and 1964.

Shakhlin's height and reach made him particularly successful on the horizontal bar. He was second in this event at the 1954 World Championships and after numerous honours in the following ten years won the gold medal on this apparatus at the Tokyo Games. His powerful forearms and long legs also helped him to win two Olympic gold medals and a world title on the pommelled horse. But his ability in these comparatively rugged movements meant that he was less adaptable for the floor exercises and in his long career he failed to finish in the first three of this event at Olympics or World Championships. His outstanding moment came in the 1960 Olympics when a determined display prevented the Japanese from capturing the combined exercises title for the individual event.
Gold pommelled horse 1956, 1960; combined exercises (individual) 1960; long-horse vault 1960; parallel bars 1960; horizontal bar 1964; combined exercises (team) 1956
Silver combined exercises (individual) 1964, (team) 1960, 1964; rings 1960
Bronze horizontal bar 1960; rings 1964

Melvin Sheppard (USA), 1908

Sheppard, Melvin W. (USA)
B. Almonesson, N.J., 5 Sept. 1883; d. 1942. Sheppard was an important catalyst in middle-distance racing because of his readiness to set a fast pace. In London (1908) Sheppard went through the first 400 metres of the 800 metres in 53 sec and held on to win in the world-record time of 1 min 52.8 sec. Four years later, at Stockholm, he took the field through the opening lap in 52.4 sec but was overhauled by nineteen-year-old James ('Ted') Meredith (USA) who set world records both at 800 metres (1 min 51.9 sec) and 880 yards (1 min 52.5 sec).
Gold 800 metres 1908; 1,500 metres 1908; 4 × 400-metres relay 1908, 1912
Silver 800 metres 1912

Silva, Adhemar Ferreira da (BRA)
B. São Paulo, 29 Sept. 1927. The outstanding Olympic athlete from the South American continent. He was world-record holder for the triple jump 1950–3 and 1955–8, with a personal best distance of 16.56 m (54 ft 4 in). He finished fourteenth at Rome (1960), at the age of thirty-two, having made his biggest Olympic impact in Helsinki where he four times beat his own world record in the final.
Gold triple jump 1952, 1956

Skoblikova, Lidia (URS)
B. Zlatoust, Chelyabinsk, 8 Mar. 1939. She was reaching her peak when ice speed-skating events for women were introduced to the Olympic program at Squaw Valley (1960). Four years later she took every gold medal at Innsbruck, a unique achievement. In 1963–4 she was also placed first in every World Championship event.
Gold 500 metres 1964; 1,000 metres 1964; 1,500 metres 1960, 1964; 3,000 metres 1960, 1964

Snell, Peter (NZL)
B. Opunake, 17 Dec. 1938. The only middle-distance runner to

Peter Snell (NZL), 1964

win three Olympic individual gold medals, Snell was an unexpected winner of the 800 metres at Rome (1960) and then achieved the incredible double of both 800 and 1,500 metres, after qualifying heats in both events, at Tokyo (1964).

A good lawn-tennis player, Snell did not take up running seriously until he was eighteen and came under the guidance of the New Zealand coach Arthur Lydiard. Long-distance training greatly increased Snell's strength though he was seriously handicapped by a stress fracture of a foot in the months before the Rome Olympics.

In the post-Olympic season of 1960, Snell ran a remarkable 880-yards relay leg in 1 min 44.8 sec. The following summer he combined, in just one hour, an 880 yards in 1 min 47.2 sec with a mile relay leg in 4 min 1.2 sec. Early in 1962 he set a world mile record of 3 min 54.4 sec and a week later also ran records for 880 yards (1 min 45.1 sec) and 800 metres (1 min 44.3 sec). He was the first man for twenty-five years to hold both half-mile and mile records.

By 1964 Snell was an experienced racer but still not sure whether he would be capable of doubling up in the Olympic 800 and 1,500 metres. But when he won his 800-metres semi-final at Tokyo in 1 min 46.1 sec his confidence returned. He took the final in 1 min 45.1 sec, and five days later the 1,500 metres in 3 min 38.1 sec after a powerful last lap in 52.7 sec. In November 1964 Snell lowered his mile record to 3 min 54.1 sec. He retired in 1965, the epitome of the strong, silent hero.

Gold 800 metres 1960, 1964; 1,500 metres 1964

Solberg, Magnar (NOR)

B. Sokndal, 4 Feb. 1937. The only man to win two gold medals in biathlon (20-kilometres cross-country and shooting).

Gold biathlon (individual) 1968, 1972

Silver 4 × 10-kilometres biathlon relay 1968

Spitz, Mark (USA)

B. Modesto, Calif., 10 Feb. 1950. At Munich, Spitz won seven gold medals in the swimming events, a record number in any sport at a single Games. The previous best was the five golds won by the Italian fencer, Nedo NADI, at the 1920 Games in Antwerp. The previous highest tally in swimming was Don SCHOLLANDER's four in 1964. Schollander and Spitz were great rivals, for their careers overlapped, and until the 1972 Games, Schollander had been considered the better competitor.

Spitz's comparative failure in the 1968 Games – two relay gold medals – brought him almost as much publicity as did his vindication as a competitor four years later. Sherman Chavoor, the coach at Arden Hills Club with whom Spitz achieved his best results, has claimed that Spitz had to contend with anti-Semitism during his career even from fellow members of US teams. This and his nervous disposition may have contributed to his early setbacks.

Spitz broke or equalled world records thirty-two times in his career. Best known for his performances at 100- and 200-metres freestyle and butterfly, he had considerable potential at longer distances, setting three world records for 400-metres freestyle and even coming within four-tenths of a second of breaking the world record for 1,500-metres freestyle in 1966. His best world records were 51.22 sec for 100-metres freestyle; 1 min 52.78 sec for 200-metres freestyle; 54.27 sec for 100-metres butterfly; and 2 min 00.70 sec for 200-metres butterfly. During the 1972 Olympic Games he set six world records.

A poster of Spitz, on which he is standing in his swimming suit and wearing his Olympic medals, brought him $10,000 and royalties of 15¢ on every one sold. He thus became a professional and later a reputed dollar millionaire through various commercial ventures.

Gold 100-metres freestyle 1972; 200-metres freestyle 1972; 100-metres butterfly 1972; 200-metres butterfly 1972; 4 × 100-metres freestyle relay 1968, 1972; 4 × 200-metres freestyle relay 1968, 1972; 4 × 100-metres medley relay 1972

Silver 100-metres butterfly 1968

Bronze 100-metres freestyle 1968

Stecher (Meissner), Renate (GDR)

B. Süptitz, 12 May 1950. She was double Olympic sprint champion at the 1972 Munich Olympics with remarkable times of 11.07 sec (100 metres) and 22.40 sec (200 metres), the latter equalling the world record. 1971 European double champion, she set world records of 10.8 sec (100 metres) and 22.1 sec (200 metres), both hand timed, during the 1973 season. Noted for strength and unusually powerful build, she was remarkably consistent as a racer as well as a record breaker.

Gold 100 metres 1972; 200 metres 1972

Silver 4 × 100-metres relay 1972

Steinkraus, William C. (USA)

B. Cleveland, Ohio, 12 Oct. 1925. He won the United States' first

show-jumping gold medal riding Snowbound at Mexico in 1968, his fourth Olympic ride. His début was at Helsinki in 1952, when his team took a bronze medal. A silver team medal followed eight years later at Rome but at Tokyo he was unfortunate when his intended partner, the highly rated Sinjon, was a last-minute withdrawal through lameness. He captained the US equestrian team from 1955 until his retirement at the end of 1972, leading the squad to two successes (1966 and 1968) in the President's Cup, the season's team championship. Grand Prix in London and New York and two King George V Gold Cups in London were among many individual triumphs.
Gold show jumping (individual) 1968
Silver show jumping (team) 1960, 1972
Bronze show jumping (team) 1952

Stevenson, Teofilo (CUB)
B. Dlicias, 23 Mar. 1952. The outstanding amateur boxer of the 1970s. A heavyweight, he won the Olympic title at Montreal in 1976 where crowds were awed by the power of his punching and the deftness of his technique more often associated with the lighter weights. He also won the World title in Havana (1974), Belgrade (1978) and since 1971 has been beaten by only two men, Duane Bobick (USA) in the 6th Pan-American Games, Cali, Colombia, and Igor Visoliski (URS), three times.
Gold heavyweight 1972, 1976

Strickland, Shirley (AUS)
see DE LA HUNTY

Štukelj, Leon (YUG)
B. Maribor, 12 Nov. 1898. Studied law and took part in gymnastic events for fourteen consecutive years, ending with his last competition in Berlin (1936) at the age of thirty-eight. He won five gold, two silver and four bronze medals in World Championships

Leon Štukelj (YUG), 1924

1922–31. In the Olympics he was also fourth in the long-horse vault and rings in 1924.
Gold combined exercises (individual) 1924; horizontal bar 1924; rings 1928
Silver rings 1936
Bronze combined exercises (individual) 1928, (team) 1928

Swahn, Alfred Gomer Albert (SWE)
B. Uddevalla, 20 Aug. 1879; d. Stockholm, 16 Mar. 1931. Son of Oscar SWAHN. Not surprisingly, after the dedication of his father, he began shooting at twelve and was brought up on running-deer shooting; for twenty years he was the best Swede in the event. He competed in the Games of 1908, 1912, 1920 and 1924, winning three gold, three silver and three bronze medals.
Gold running-deer single shot (individual) 1912, (team) 1908, 1912
Silver running-deer single shot (individual) 1920, (team) 1924, double shot (team) 1920
Bronze clay pigeon (team) 1920; running-deer double shot (individual) 1924, (team) 1924

Swahn, Oscar Gomer (SWE)
B. Tanum, Bohuslän, 20 Oct. 1847; d. Stockholm, 1 May 1927. Legendary rifleman with sixty-five years of competition, he started shooting in 1863 in Uddevalla. He competed in the Olympic Games in 1908, 1912 and 1920, winning three gold, one silver and two bronze medals, all in his speciality, running deer. He qualified for the Games of 1924 at the age of seventy-seven but had to remain at home because of ill health. He won more than 500 first prizes in competitions, all of which he donated to the Army Museum in Stockholm.
Gold running-deer single shot (individual) 1908, (team) 1908, 1912
Silver running-deer double shot (team) 1920
Bronze running-deer double shot (individual) 1908, 1912

Szewińska (Kirszenstein), Irena (POL)
B. Leningrad, 24 May 1946. She has achieved a wide range of records. When only eighteen, at the Tokyo Olympics, she finished

Left to right: Alfred Swahn, Ake Lundeberg, Oscar Swahn, Olof Arvidsson (SWE), 1912

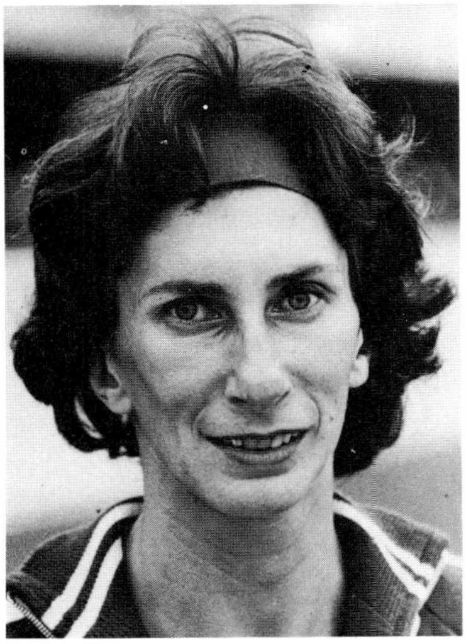

Irena Szewińska (Kirszenstein) (POL), 1976

second in both the long jump and 200 metres and was a member of Poland's victorious sprint relay team. At Mexico City she won the 200 metres in a world-record time of 22.5 sec and was third in the 100 metres. She dropped the baton in the relay. At Munich, although not quite back to full racing fitness after the birth of a son, she was third over 200 metres. An intelligent and modest champion, she had a further remarkable season in 1974 when she won the European 100 and 200 metres ahead of the formidable Renate STECHER and became the first woman to beat 50 sec for 400 metres.
Gold 4 × 100 metres relay 1964; 200 metres 1968; 400 metres 1976
Silver long jump 1964; 200 metres 1964
Bronze 100 metres 1968; 200 metres 1972

Szmidt, Józef (POL)

B. Michálkowice, 28 Mar. 1935. The first triple jumper to surpass the barriers of 55 ft and 17 metres with 17.03 m (55 ft $10\frac{1}{2}$ in) in 1960, which remained unbeaten for eight years. In spite of suffering several leg injuries, he ran 100 metres in 10.4 sec, long jumped 7.84 m (25 ft $8\frac{3}{4}$ in), was seventh in the triple jump at Mexico City (1968) with a remarkable 16.89 m (55 ft 5 in) and continued to compete internationally until 1972. He was European Champion in 1958 and 1962.
Gold triple jump 1960, 1964

Takács, Károly (HUN)

B. Budapest, 21 Jan. 1910. Between 1929 and 1938 he shot right-handed; he was a member of the Hungarian national team which won the world title in Lucerne in 1939, having a year earlier lost his right hand in a hand-grenade explosion and having learned to shoot with his left.
Gold rapid-fire pistol 1948, 1952

Tediashvili, Levan (URS)

B. Gegmoubani, Georgia, 15 Mar. 1948. One of the most formidable freestyle wrestlers of the 1970s, 'Teddy' took gold medals in different weight categories in the 1972 and 1976 Games. His fine standing techniques included a fluent outside clip, with which he bowled over many opponents, but he was also adept at moving into advantageous positions on the mat. Tediashvili first represented the Russian team in 1971 when he took the world title. The following year, he competed in the 82-kg category in Munich and won the gold medal with a series of conclusive points victories. Between Munich and Montreal, Tediashvili took all three world freestyle titles (and also a world sambo crown in 1973).
Gold wrestling freestyle middleweight 1972; light-heavyweight 1976

Józef Szmidt (POL), 1960

Károly Takács (HUN), 1956

Tewksbury, John Walter (USA)

B. Ashley, Pa., 21 Mar. 1876; d. Tunkhannock, Pa., 25 Apr. 1968. Brought the ability of a top-class sprinter to the rather underdeveloped 400-metres hurdles, previously thought of as a European speciality, beating the French favourite, Henri Tauzin, in 57.6 sec at the Paris Olympics of 1900. Seven days later Tewksbury won the 200-metres flat by 5 metres in 22.2 sec.
Gold 200 metres 1900; 400-metres hurdles 1900
Silver 60 metres 1900; 100 metres 1900
Bronze 200-metres hurdles 1900

Theile, David (AUS)

B. Maryborough, Queensland, 17 Jan. 1938. Theile won the first of his two Olympic titles for 100-metres backstroke in a world-record time of 1 min 02.2 sec; his

margin of victory, 3.0 sec over another Australian, John Monckton, was the greatest in this event in the history of the Games. Theile retained the Olympic title in 1 min 01.9 sec in 1960. After winning the Australian 110-yards backstroke title in 1955 and 1956 he studied medicine at the University of Queensland for two years, missing the British Commonwealth Games of 1958. He regained the national title from Monckton in 1959 and held it in 1960. He never had much success at distances over 100 metres.
Gold 100-metres backstroke 1956, 1960
Silver 4 × 100-metres medley relay 1960

Thorpe, Jim (USA)
B. Shawnee, Okla., 28 May 1888; d. Carlisle, Pa., 28 Mar. 1953. An Olympic legend, not only because of his prowess as an all-rounder, but also because he was disqualified from his 1912 Olympic decathlon and pentathlon victories when it was revealed that he had accepted small sums of money for playing holiday baseball three years before. An extraordinarily talented athlete, Thorpe was also fourth in the Olympic high jump and seventh in the long jump. His best individual performances included under 49 sec for 440 yards, the high hurdles in 15 sec, equalling the world record, and a high jump of 1.96 m (6 ft 5 in), only 1.6 cm (⅝in) lower than the world record. Thorpe's total points score in the 1912 Stockholm Olympic decathlon, held over three days rather than the now compulsory two days, was not beaten for fifteen years.

Jim Thorpe (USA), 1912

Thunberg, Clas Arnold Robert (FIN)
B. Helsinki, 5 Apr. 1893; d. 28 Apr. 1973. The world's outstanding speed skater of the 1920s. He would probably have won more than five Olympic medals had he decided to compete in 1932 but the Americans used the mass start style of racing, with which he and many other Europeans did not agree, so he did not go to the United States. In addition to many World and European Championships, he broke four world records, the first 42.8 sec for 500 metres in 1929 when he was thirty-five; the others were 42.6 sec for 500 metres, 1 min 28.4 sec for 1,000 metres and 5 min 19.2 sec for 3,000 metres. He adopted Paavo NURMI's attitude to his sport, training throughout the year. He was a man of tremendous will-power.
Gold 500 metres 1928, 1,500 metres 1924, 1928; 5,000 metres 1924; best all four distances 1924
Silver 10,000 metres 1924
Bronze 500 metres 1924

Timoshinin, Aleksandr (URS)
B. Moscow, 20 May 1948. Timoshinin has had an unusual rowing career, encompassing two gold medals, yet apparently with only limited success in other events. In 1968 he was partnered by Anatoli Sass. Dropped from the Soviet team in 1969, he reappeared, with Edward Zhdanovich, to finish fourth in the 1970 World Championships. He was absent again in 1971, but in 1972 won the Diamond Sculls at Henley Royal Regatta, and then teamed up with Gennadi Korshikov, to win his second Olympic gold medal. In 1973 Timoshinin and Korshikov finished second in the European Championships. In 1974 they won the double sculls at Henley.
Gold double sculls 1968, 1972

Tolan, Eddie (USA)
B. Denver, Col., 29 Sept. 1908; d. Detroit, Mich., 31 Jan. 1967. He was the first man to be officially credited with a time of 9.5 sec for 100 yards – on 25 May 1929. Known as 'The Midnight Express', Tolan was short and stocky but had remarkably fast leg speed. In the 1932 American Olympic trials he was twice beaten by Ralph Metcalfe but two weeks later, when it really mattered, Tolan was the man on form. Film of the race indicates that Tolan won by 2.5 cm (an inch). In the 200-metres final Tolan set an Olympic record of 21.2 sec.
Gold 100 metres 1932; 200 metres 1932

Trentin, Pierre (FRA)
B. Créteil, 15 May 1944. A big, burly man, Trentin is a leather craftsman and found time between setting up and running his own business to become one of the world's leading cyclists. He began competing when he was fourteen. Three years later he was the French junior champion and then entered the track championships, more or less on a whim. He was a sprint finalist that year, twelve months later he won the bronze medal in the World Championship and again in 1963. Fighting to keep his weight down he nevertheless won three World cycling Championships in the following three years, reaching his peak in the rarefied atmosphere at Mexico (1968). There he set a world amateur record for the kilometre, 1 min 3.91 sec and was also successful on a tandem with Daniel MORELON.
Gold 1,000-metres time trial 1968; 2,000-metres tandem 1968
Bronze 1,000-metres time trial 1964; 1,000-metres sprint 1968

Tsuruta, Yoshiyuki (JPN)
B. Kagoshima Prefecture, 1 Oct. 1903. The only swimmer ever to have scored a double victory in Olympic breaststroke events. His time in 1928 was 2 min 48.8 sec which beat the Olympic record by the substantial margin of 7.8 sec and compared favourably with the world record of 2 min 48 sec set by the German Erich Rademacher in a 25-yard (22.86 m) pool.

The following year Tsuruta set his only world record, 2 min 45 sec for 200-metres breaststroke in the 25-metre pool at Kyoto. His victory in the Los Angeles Games (1932) was part of the greatest Olympic performance by Japanese competitors.
Gold 200-metres breaststroke 1928, 1932

Turischeva, Ludmila (URS)
B. Grozny, 7 Oct. 1952. Although the quiet and dignified Turischeva often had to play second fiddle to the more excitable KORBUT and COMANECI in terms of world recognition, her achievements were more substantial than both of them. After making her Olympic début at Mexico City in 1968 (where she was a member of the winning Soviet team for the first of three successive Olympics), she became overall world champion in 1970, and began a five-year reign as the supreme all-round woman gymnast. At the 1973 European championships and 1975 World Cup she took all four individual golds as well as the combined title; in 1972 it was Turischeva (and not Korbut, as many people erroneously remember) who was overall Olympic champion, despite not winning any individual apparatus gold.

As women's gymnastics started to produce much younger competitors at pre-pubic stage of development, Turischeva championed the more feminine traditional image of LATYNINA and ČÁSLAVSKÁ, and her floor routine was a masterpiece of expressive ballet and technical excellence.

After Montreal, where she was overall bronze medallist, Turischeva gracefully bowed, at twenty-four, to the emergence of younger rivals, and retired to coach. In 1977 she married the former Olympic sprint champion Valeri BORZOV.
Gold combined exercises (individual) 1972; combined exercises (team) 1968, 1972, 1976
Silver floor exercises 1972, 1976; vault 1976
Bronze combined exercises (individual) 1976; vault 1972

Ludmila Turischeva (URS), 1972

Tyus, Wyomia (USA)
B. Griffin, Ga., 29 Aug. 1945. The only athlete, male or female, to win an Olympic sprint title twice. At the 1964 Olympics she cut her personal record for 100 metres down by 0.3 sec in her heat when equalling the world record of 11.2 sec by Wilma RUDOLPH. In the 4 × 100-metres relay she ran the second stage for the US team which won the silver medals. She was still only twenty-three when she defended her title in 1968 and had meanwhile set an 11.1-sec world record for 100 metres. In the final she again lowered the world record, to 11 sec. In the 4 × 100-metres relay she anchored the US team for her third gold medal plus a world-record time of 42.8 sec. During her career she beat or equalled world records twice at 100 yards and four times at 100 metres.
Gold 100 metres 1964, 1968; 4 × 100-metres relay 1968
Silver 4 × 100-metres relay 1964

Väre, Eemeli Ernesti (FIN)
B. Kärkölä, 28 Sept. 1885; d. Kärkölä, 31 Jan. 1974. He became interested in wrestling at the beginning of the century in St Petersburg (now Leningrad), Russia, as he saw the performances of the world's best wrestlers in the local circuses. Training hard and developing new wrestling holds, he soon turned out to be one of the best of his period on the mat. In the middleweight class he won the World Championship in 1911 and a European Championship in 1912.
Gold wrestling Greco-Roman lightweight 1912, 1920

Virén, Lasse (FIN)
B. Myrskyla, 22 July 1949. With the 1,500-metres winner, Pekka Vasala, Virén revived the Finnish Olympic running supremacy at the Munich Games of 1972 by taking both the 5,000 metres (13 min 26.4 sec) and 10,000 metres (27 min 38.4 sec). In the longer race he survived a fall just before halfway and yet recovered to cover the final 800 metres in 1 min 56.2 sec, and beat the world record by one sec. He became only the fourth man in the history of the modern Olympics to win both these titles in one Games. This rather shy village policeman followed up his Olympic medals with a world record of 13 min 16.4 sec for 5,000 metres in 1972 to add just

Lasse Virén (FIN), 1976

the right footnote to his racing style and zest.
Gold 5,000 metres 1972, 1976; 10,000 metres 1972, 1976

Walasiewicz, Stanislawa (POL)

B. Wierzchownia, 11 Apr. 1911. Later known as Stella Walsh in the United States, where she was taken at the age of two, she held the world 200-metres record in athletics at 23.6 sec for sixteen years after starting competition in 1926. She was sixth in the 1932 Olympic discus event. She represented Poland in the 1946 European Championships, after winning over forty US titles, and ran 400 metres in 61.3 sec as late as 1960.
Gold 100 metres 1932
Silver 100 metres 1936

Stanislawa Walasiewicz (POL), 1932

Weissmuller, Johnny (USA)

B. Windber, Pa., 2 June 1904. Until Mark SPITZ, Weissmuller was always the winner of ballots for 'the greatest swimmer ever'. The issue is still arguable. Weissmuller won three Olympic gold medals in 1924 and two more four years later. Five of Spitz's events were not on the Olympic program in those days and so Weissmuller might have a case for equal ranking with Spitz.

He was the physical prototype of the modern swimmer – 1.90 m (6 ft 3 in) with a strong, tapering frame. Weissmuller and his coach at the Illinois Athletic Club, William Bachrach, strove scientifically for the perfection of the American crawl. He rode higher in the water than any other swimmer of his day and his breathing pattern was unusual in its day, turning to either side and watching the opponents without interfering with his stroke, the main strength of which was the pull-in under the body.

Johnny Weissmuller (USA), 1924

Weissmuller swam about 500 yards (457.2 m) a day in training, which would be derisory today. He won fifty-two US titles, had twenty-eight world records ratified, holding them from 100 yards to 880 yards freestyle inclusive and also for 150 yards backstroke.

His records were notable for their longevity. He began breaking world records at the age of seventeen. Perhaps his most celebrated one was 51 sec for the 100 yards which stood for seventeen years (at the age of thirty-six, as a professional, he covered the same distance in 48.5 sec). He was the first man to swim 100 metres in under a minute (58.6 sec in 1922); the first to beat five minutes for 440-yards freestyle (4 min 57 sec in 1923).

Weissmuller became the best-known of the screen Tarzans. Because of the reshowing of his best films on television Weissmuller is probably better known today than he was at the height of his swimming career.
Gold 100-metres freestyle 1924, 1928; 400-metres freestyle 1924; 4 × 200-metres freestyle relay 1924, 1928
Bronze water polo 1924

Wenden, Michael Vincent (AUS)

B. Liverpool, N.S.W., 17 Nov. 1949. Wenden's international career lasted from the British Commonwealth Games of 1966 to those of 1974. In all that time he was among the world's best front-crawl sprinters.

He broke his right leg in 1963 when jumping a fence and, unable to play football, turned to swimming, building up his right leg by use of isometric exercises. This aspect of his preparation for swimming developed and he became an apostle of land conditioning. His coach Vic Arneil shaped his frame by isometrics, Wenden's body being tapered from powerful shoulders to unusually slim legs. Though light in weight he had remarkable strength, a necessary attribute because of the 'windmill' stroke he employed.

He had six world records in his career, the highlight of which came at the Olympic Games in 1968. Wenden was reputed to have trained up to 15,000 metres a day before the Games and such unprecedented work for a sprinter paid off in the defeat of the Americans. He won the 100-metres freestyle in a world record of 52.2 sec and the 200-metres freestyle in 1 min 55.2 sec defeating the holder of the world record, the remarkable Don SCHOLLANDER.

Gold 100-metres freestyle 1968; 200-metres freestyle 1968
Silver 4 × 200-metres freestyle relay 1968
Bronze 4 × 100-metres freestyle relay 1968

Westergren, Carl (SWE)

B. Malmö, 13 Oct. 1895; d. 5 Aug. 1958. He began wrestling in 1911 and was World Champion in middleweight A in 1922, European Champion in middleweight B in 1925 and in heavyweight in 1930–1. He took part in the Olympic Games in 1920, 1924, 1928 and 1932; his speciality was the back-hammer and he invented the 'Westergren roll'.

Gold wrestling Greco-Roman middleweight A 1920; middleweight B (light heavyweight) 1924; heavyweight 1932

White, Albert C. (USA)

B. Oakland, Calif., 14 May 1895. White was the first diver to win springboard and highboard titles at the same Olympic Games, 1924. A member of Stanford University school, whose students took all the men's diving medals at the 1924 Games, he has been honoured by the Swimming Hall of Fame at Fort Lauderdale, Fla. He never lost a lowboard diving contest in the United States.

Gold springboard diving 1924, highboard diving 1924

Whitfield, Malvin G. (USA)

B. Bay City, Tex., 11 Oct. 1924. With beautiful style – his favourite burst in the third 200 metres of two-lap races made him look as though he was running downhill – and his brilliant competitive record, Whitfield was the world's best over 800 metres for six years. Between June 1948 and June 1954 he suffered only two defeats, both in early season. Though he set world records for both 880 yards (1 min 48.6 sec) and 1,000 metres (2 min 20.8 sec), he was much more concerned about winning than times. Only one hour after his kilometre world record he set an American record of 46.2 sec for 440 yards. His range, greater than that of any other runner of his time, covered 10.7 sec for 100 metres to 4 min 12.6 sec for the mile. In 1948 he won the American Olympic trials at both 400 and 800 metres on the same day. In the Wembley 800-metres final he set an Olympic record of 1 min 49.2 sec. He retired in 1956 after failing to qualify for the US team for Melbourne.

Gold 800 metres 1948, 1952; 4 × 400-metres relay 1948
Silver 4 × 400-metres relay 1952
Bronze 400 metres 1948

Wigger, Lones W., Jr (USA)

B. Great Falls, Mont., 25 Aug. 1937. A major in the US Army, Wigger is the only American to win Olympic gold medals in the 50-metre three-position smallbore rifle and in the 300-metre free rifle. He began shooting on his family's Montana ranch.

Gold smallbore rifle, three positions 1964; free rifle 1972
Silver smallbore rifle, prone 1964

Williams, Percy (CAN)

B. Vancouver, 19 May 1908. His double sprint victory at Amsterdam, when he was only twenty, was surprising to those who did not appreciate that he had won the Canadian trials in 10.6 sec. In the Olympic 100-metres final there were three false starts before Williams was away fastest and kept the lead to win in 10.8 sec; in the 200 metres he pulled away in the last 30 metres to win in 21.8 sec. On 9 August 1930 he set an official time of 10.3 sec for the 100 metres.

Gold 100 metres 1928; 200 metres 1928

Winkler, Hans Günter (GER)

B. Wuppertal-Barmen, 24 July 1926. He won more gold medals for show jumping than any other rider. His individual triumph and first team medal was at Stockholm in 1956, riding his famous mare Halla, only four years after his international début. He wrenched a riding muscle in the first round and rode the second, without fault, in considerable pain.

He won the World Championship in 1954 and retained it the next year, each time on Halla. In European Championship contests he has won once, been second once and third three times.

Gold show jumping (individual) 1956, (team) 1956, 1960, 1964, 1972
Silver show jumping (team) 1976
Bronze show jumping (team) 1968

Yarygin, Ivan (URS)

B. Ust-Kanzas, Kemerovo, 7 Nov. 1948. This immensely forceful Russian heavyweight freestyle wrestler took titles in both the Munich 1972 and Montreal 1976 Games. He made his début in 1970, finishing second in the European Championships. 1.88 m (6 ft $1\frac{3}{4}$ in) tall, his strength and persistent attacking brought him a number of conclusive victories. In Munich, he pinned all of his opponents, never being taken further than the second round, a rare feat in the sport. His gold medal in Montreal was less easily acquired but he displayed both calmness and skill against Russ Hellickson (USA) in the crucial fifth series

bout which the Russian won 19–13, despite the crowd's tremendous support for the American.
Gold wrestling freestyle heavyweight 1972, 1976

Zátopek, Emil (TCH)

B. Koprivnice, Moravia, 19 Sept. 1922. Zátopek will always be remembered in Olympic history for his three victories in the 5,000 metres (14 min 06.6 sec), 10,000 metres (29 min 17.0 sec) and marathon (2 hr 23 min 03.2 sec) at Helsinki (1952). It was his first marathon. Zátopek was the father of the rugged school of modern interval training, the logical successor to NURMI but a man who relied on shattering mid-race surges rather than level-pace running to beat the opposition. He caught the imagination with facial grimaces and contorted upper body and was capable of a withering final burst as he showed with a last lap of 58.1 sec in the Helsinki 5,000 metres. He was unbeaten over 10,000 metres between 1948 and 1954, a total of thirty-eight consecutive victories, and broke all world records between 5,000 and 30,000 metres. He was the first man to beat 29 min for the 10,000 metres and to run more than 20,000 metres in one hour. He loved the Olympics and his fellow men and in return was one of the most popular of all Olympic champions. His wife Dana was Olympic javelin champion in 1952.
Gold 10,000 metres 1948, 1952; 5,000 metres 1952; marathon 1952
Silver 5,000 metres 1948

Emil Zátopek (TCH), 1952

Mark Spitz (USA), 1972

US

OLYMPIC MEDAL WINNERS

The following statistics relate to events currently in the Olympic program. For these records we have drawn on many sources including the Official Reports, the records of the International Sports Federations and of many National Olympic Committees. In the early Games, the times and distances were not always recorded. There was no Official Report of the Paris Games in 1900 and there is controversy over the records of many of the events. No Official Report of the Antwerp Games in 1920 was produced immediately after the Games. The Belgian Olympic Committee compiled one in 1959 from its archives.

The following official Olympic abbreviations have been used for the names of countries in this section:

AFG	Afghanistan
AHO	Netherlands Antilles
ALB	Albania
ALG	Algeria
ARG	Argentina
ARS	Saudi Arabia
AUS	Australia (or Australia, representing a combined team from Australia and New Zealand in the years up to and including 1912)
AUT	Austria
BAH	Bahamas
BAR	Barbados
BEL	Belgium
BER	Bermuda
BIR	Burma
BOL	Bolivia
BRA	Brazil
BUL	Bulgaria
CAF	Central Africa
CAN	Canada
CEY	Ceylon (up to 1972)
CGO	Congo Republic
CHA	Chad
CHI	Chile
CIV	Ivory Coast
CMR	Cameroon Republic
COK	Congo Kinshasa
COL	Colombia
CRC	Costa Rica
CUB	Cuba
DAH	Dahomey
DEN	Denmark
DOM	Dominican Republic
ECU	Ecuador
EGY	Egypt (or United Arab Republic)
ESP	Spain
ETH	Ethiopia
FIJ	Fiji
FIN	Finland
FRA	France
GAB	Gabon
GBR	Great Britain
GDR	German Democratic Republic 1968 on
GER	German Federal Republic (Germany until 1968)
GHA	Ghana
GRE	Greece
GUA	Guatemala
GUI	Guinea
GUY	Guyana
HAI	Haiti
HBR	British Honduras
HKG	Hong Kong
HOL	Netherlands
HON	Honduras
HUN	Hungary
INA	Indonesia
IND	India
IRL	Ireland
IRN	Iran
IRQ	Iraq
ISL	Iceland
ISR	Israel
ITA	Italy
ISV	Virgin Islands
JAM	Jamaica
JOR	Jordan
JPN	Japan
KEN	Kenya
KHM	Cambodia
KOR	South Korea
KUW	Kuwait
LBA	Libya
LBR	Liberia
LES	Lesotho
LIB	Lebanon
LIE	Liechtenstein
LUX	Luxembourg
MAD	Madagascar
MAL	Malaysia
MAR	Morocco
MAW	Malawi
MEX	Mexico
MGL	Mongolia
MLI	Mali
MLT	Malta
MON	Monaco
MRI	Mauritius
NCA	Nicaragua
NEP	Nepal
NGR	Nigeria
NIG	Niger
NOR	Norway
NZL	New Zealand
PAK	Pakistan
PAN	Panama
PAR	Paraguay
PER	Peru
PHI	Philippines
POL	Poland
POR	Portugal
PRK	North Korea
PUR	Puerto Rico
RHO	Rhodesia
ROC	Republic of China
ROM	Romania
RUS	Russia until 1917
SAL	El Salvador
SEN	Senegal
SIN	Singapore
SLE	Sierra Leone
SMR	San Marino
SOM	Somali Republic
SRI	Sri Lanka (formerly Ceylon)
SUD	Sudan
SUI	Switzerland
SUR	Surinam
SWE	Sweden
SWZ	Swaziland
SYR	Syria
TAN	Tanzania
TCH	Czechoslovákia
THA	Thailand
TOG	Togoland
TRI	Trinidad and Tobago
TUN	Tunisia
TUR	Turkey
UAR	United Arab Republic
UGA	Uganda
URS	USSR
URU	Uruguay
USA	United States of America
VEN	Venezuela
VNM	Viet Nam
VOL	Upper Volta
YUG	Yugoslavia
ZAI	Zaire
ZAM	Zambia

Other abbreviations for countries used in this section are:

ANT	Antilles (West Indies)
BOH	Bohemia
ENG	England
EST	Estonia
LAT	Latvia
LIT	Lithuania
RUS	(Tsarist) Russia
SAF	South Africa
SCO	Scotland
WAL	Wales

A few other usages need elucidation. We spell all personal names as the owner would himself, complete with accents. Transliteration from Cyrillic follows recommended current Anglo-American practice. We have not been consistent in the presentation of married women's names, generally preferring to follow the system used in the competitor's country of origin since her name is generally known in that form. (This may be married name only, maiden name followed by married name, with or without a hyphen, or married name followed by maiden name, with or without a hyphen. Another convention adopted here is to show the maiden name in parentheses.) The official results of the Olympic Games are today recorded using the metric system, although in the early years some events were first recorded in feet and inches and pounds. As far as possible, we have gone back to the results as originally recorded. For the conversion of metric measurements into feet and inches and pounds (and *vice versa*) we have used the *Metric Conversion Table* compiled by Bob Sparks and Charles Elliott (Arena Publications Ltd), officially approved by the International Amateur Athletic Federation, and *Cassell's Concise Conversion Tables* by Stephen Naft and Ralph de Sola, revised by P. H. Bigg. Conversion factors: 1 inch=0.0254 metre; 1 pound avoirdupois=0.45359 kilogram (British Standard 350).

The abbreviations used in measurements follow British Standard 350. Other abbreviations used are: flts faults; pts points; nda no data available.

Approximate Metric Guide

1 metre (m)	3ft 3½in
100m	109yd 1ft 1in
200m	218yd 2ft 2in
400m	437yd 1ft 4in
800m	874yd 2ft 8in
1,000m	1,093yd 1ft 10in
1,500m	1,640yd 1ft 3in
1609.3m	1 mile
3,000m	1 mile 1,520yd 2ft 6in
5,000m	3 miles 188yd 0ft 2in
10,000m (10km)	6 miles 376yd 0ft 4in
15km	9 miles 564yd 0ft 9in
20km	12 miles 752yd 0ft 8in
30km	18 miles 1,130yd 1ft 0in
50km	31 miles 119yd 2ft 10in

	Gold	Silver	Bronze

Archery (Men)

Double Men's International Round (36 arrows each at 90, 70, 50 and 30 metres). Not held before 1972.

	Gold	Silver	Bronze
1972	J. Williams *USA* 2,528 pts	G. Jervill *SWE* 2,481 pts	K. Laasonen *FIN* 2,467 pts
1976	D. Pace *USA* 2,571 pts	H. Michinaga *JPN* 2,502 pts	G. C. Ferrari *ITA* 2,495 pts

Archery (Women)

Double Women's International Round (36 arrows each at 70, 60, 50 and 30 metres). Not held before 1972.

	Gold	Silver	Bronze
1972	D. Wilber *USA* 2,424 pts	I. Szydlowska *POL* 2,407 pts	E. Gapchenko *URS* 2,403 pts
1976	L. Ryon *USA* 2,499 pts	V. Kovpan *URS* 2,460 pts	Z. Rustamova *URS* 2,407 pts

Association Football

Not held before 1900.

	Gold	Silver	Bronze
1900	GBR	FRA	BEL
1904	CAN	USA	USA
1908	GBR	DEN	HOL
1912	GBR	DEN	HOL
1920	BEL	ESP	HOL
1924	URU	SUI	SWE
1928	URU	ARG	ITA
1932	*Not held*		
1936	ITA	AUT	NOR
1948	SWE	YUG	DEN
1952	HUN	YUG	SWE
1956	URS	YUG	BUL
1960	YUG	DEN	HUN
1964	HUN	TCH	GER
1968	HUN	BUL	JPN
1972	POL	HUN	GDR & URS
1976	GDR	POL	URS

Athletics (Men)

100 Metres

	Gold	Silver	Bronze
1896	T. Burke *USA* 12.0sec	F. Hofmann *GER* 12.2sec	A. Szokolyi *HUN* 12.6sec
1900	F. Jarvis *USA* 11.0sec	J. W. Tewksbury *USA* 11.1sec	S. Rowley *AUS* 11.2sec
1904	A. Hahn *USA* 11.0sec	N. Cartmell *USA* 11.2sec	W. Hogenson *USA* 11.2sec
1908	R. Walker *SAF* 10.8sec	J. Rector *USA* 10.9sec	R. Kerr *CAN* 11.0sec
1912	R. Craig *USA* 10.8sec	A. Meyer *USA* 10.9sec	D. Lippincott *USA* 10.9sec
1920	C. Paddock *USA* 10.8sec	M. Kirksey *USA* 10.8sec	H. Edward *GBR* 11.9sec
1924	H. Abrahams *GBR* 10.6sec	J. Scholz *USA* 10.7sec	A. Porritt *NZL* 10.8sec
1928	P. Williams *CAN* 10.8sec	J. London *GBR* 10.9sec	G. Lammers *GER* 10.9sec
1932	E. Tolan *USA* 10.3sec	R. Metcalfe *USA* 10.3sec	A. Jonath *GER* 10.4sec
1936	J. Owens *USA* 10.3sec	R. Metcalfe *USA* 10.4sec	M. Osendarp *HOL* 10.5sec
1948	H. Dillard *USA* 10.3sec	H. N. Ewell *USA* 10.4sec	L. La Beach *PAN* 10.4sec
1952	L. Remigino *USA* 10.4sec	H. McKenley *JAM* 10.4sec	E. M. Bailey *GBR* 10.4sec

	Gold	Silver	Bronze
1956	B. Morrow *USA* 10.5sec	W. T. Baker *USA* 10.5sec	H. Hogan *AUS* 10.6sec
1960	A. Hary *GER* 10.2sec	D. Sime *USA* 10.2sec	P. Radford *GBR* 10.3sec
1964	R. Hayes *USA* 10.0sec	E. Figuerola *CUB* 10.2sec	H. Jerome *CAN* 10.2sec
1968	J. Hines *USA* 9.9sec	L. Miller *JAM* 10.0sec	C. Greene *USA* 10.0sec
1972	V. Borzov *URS* 10.14sec	R. Taylor *USA* 10.24sec	L. Miller *JAM* 10.33sec
1976	H. Crawford *TRI* 10.06sec	D. Quarrie *JAM* 10.08sec	V. Borzov *URS* 10.14sec

200 Metres

Not held before 1900.

	Gold	Silver	Bronze
1900	J. W. Tewksbury *USA* 22.2sec	N. Pritchard *IND* 22.8sec	S. Rowley *AUS* 22.9sec
1904	A. Hahn *USA* 21.6sec	N. Cartmell *USA* 21.9sec	W. Hogenson *USA* nda
1908	R. Kerr *CAN* 22.6sec	R. Cloughen *USA* 22.6sec	N. Cartmell *USA* 22.7sec
1912	R. Craig *USA* 21.7sec	D. Lippincott *USA* 21.8sec	W. Applegarth *GBR* 22.0sec
1920	A. Woodring *USA* 22.0sec	C. Paddock *USA* 22.1sec	H. Edward *GBR* 22.2sec
1924	J. Scholz *USA* 21.6sec	C. Paddock *USA* 21.7sec	E. Liddell *GBR* 21.9sec
1928	P. Williams *CAN* 21.8sec	W. Rangeley *GBR* 21.9sec	H. Körnig *GER* 21.9sec
1932	E. Tolan *USA* 21.2sec	G. Simpson *USA* 21.4sec	R. Metcalfe *USA* 21.5sec
1936	J. Owens *USA* 20.7sec	M. Robinson *USA* 21.1sec	M. Osendarp *HOL* 21.3sec
1948	M. Patton *USA* 21.2sec	H. N. Ewell *USA* 21.1sec	L. La Beach *PAN* 21.2sec
1952	A. Stanfield *USA* 20.7sec	W. T. Baker *USA* 20.8sec	J. Gathers *USA* 20.8sec
1956	B. Morrow *USA* 20.6sec	A. Stanfield *USA* 20.7sec	W. T. Baker *USA* 20.9sec
1960	L. Berutti *ITA* 20.5sec	L. Carney *USA* 20.6sec	A. Seye *FRA* 20.7sec
1964	H. Carr *USA* 20.3sec	P. Drayton *USA* 20.5sec	E. Roberts *TRI* 20.6sec
1968	T. Smith *USA* 19.8sec	P. Norman *AUS* 20.0sec	J. Carlos *USA* 20.0sec
1972	V. Borzov *URS* 20.0sec	L. Black *USA* 20.19sec	P. Mennea *ITA* 20.30sec
1976	D. Quarrie *JAM* 20.23sec	M. Hampton *USA* 20.29sec	D. Evans *USA* 20.43sec

400 Metres

In 1908 a re-run was ordered after J. C. Carpenter USA *was disqualified in the final. Halswelle was the only competitor.*

	Gold	Silver	Bronze
1896	T. Burke *USA* 54.2sec	H. Jamison *USA* 55.2sec	F. Hofmann *GER* nda
1900	M. Long *USA* 49.4sec	W. Holland *USA* 49.6sec	E. Schultz *DEN* 15yd behind
1904	H. Hillman *USA* 49.2sec	F. Waller *USA* 49.9sec	H. Groman *USA* 50.0sec
1908	W. Halswelle *GBR* 50.0sec		
1912	C. Reidpath *USA* 48.2sec	H. Braun *GER* 48.3sec	E. Lindberg *USA* 48.4sec
1920	B. Rudd *SAF* 49.6sec	G. Butler *GBR* 49.9sec	N. Engdahl *SWE* 50.0sec
1924	E. Liddell *GBR* 47.6sec	H. Fitch *USA* 48.4sec	G. Butler *GBR* 48.6sec
1928	R. Barbuti *USA* 47.8sec	J. Ball *CAN* 48.0sec	J. Büchner *GER* 48.2sec
1932	W. Carr *USA* 46.2sec	B. Eastman *USA* 46.4sec	A. Wilson *CAN* 47.4sec
1936	A. Williams *USA* 46.5sec	A. G. Brown *GBR* 46.7sec	J. LuValle *USA* 46.8sec
1948	A. Wint *JAM* 46.2sec	H. McKenley *JAM* 46.4sec	M. Whitfield *USA* 46.9sec
1952	G. Rhoden *JAM* 45.9sec	H. McKenley *JAM* 45.9sec	O. Matson *USA* 46.8sec
1956	C. Jenkins *USA* 46.7sec	K. F. Haas *GER* 46.8sec	V. Hellsten *FIN* & A. Ignatiev *URS* 47.0sec
1960	O. Davis *USA* 44.9sec	C. Kaufmann *GER* 44.9sec	M. Spence *SAF* 45.5sec
1964	M. Larrabee *USA* 45.1sec	W. Mottley *TRI* 45.2sec	A. Badeński *POL* 45.6sec
1968	L. Evans *USA* 43.8sec	L. James *USA* 43.9sec	R. Freeman *USA* 44.4sec
1972	V. Matthews *USA* 44.66sec	W. Collett *USA* 44.80sec	J. Sang *KEN* 44.92sec
1976	A. Juantorena *CUB* 44.26sec	F. Newhouse *USA* 44.40sec	H. Frazier *USA* 44.95sec

800 Metres

	Gold	Silver	Bronze
1896	E. Flack *AUS* 2min 11.0sec	N. Dáni *HUN* 2min 11.8sec	D. Golemis *GRE* nda
1900	A. Tysoe *GBR* 2min 01.2sec	J. Cregan *USA* 2min 03.0sec	D. Hall *USA* nda
1904	J. Lightbody *USA* 1min 56.0sec	H. Valentine *USA* 1min 56.3sec	E. Breitkreutz *USA* 1min 56.4sec
1908	M. Sheppard *USA* 1min 52.8sec	E. Lunghi *ITA* 1min 54.2sec	H. Braun *GER* 1min 55.2sec
1912	J. Meredith *USA* 1min 51.9sec	M. Sheppard *USA* 1min 52.0sec	I. Davenport *USA* 1min 52.0sec
1920	A. Hill *GBR* 1min 53.4sec	E. Eby *USA* 1min 53.6sec	B. Rudd *SAF* 1min 54.0sec
1924	D. Lowe *GBR* 1min 52.4sec	P. Martin *SUI* 1min 52.6sec	S. Enck *USA* 1min 53.0sec
1928	D. Lowe *GBR* 1min 51.8sec	E. Byléhn *SWE* 1min 52.8sec	H. Engelhard *GER* 1min 53.2sec
1932	T. Hampson *GBR* 1min 49.7sec	A. Wilson *CAN* 1min 49.9sec	P. Edwards *CAN* 1min 51.5sec
1936	J. Woodruff *USA* 1min 52.9sec	M. Lanzi *ITA* 1min 53.3sec	P. Edwards *CAN* 1min 53.6sec
1948	M. Whitfield *USA* 1min 49.2sec	A. Wint *JAM* 1min 49.5sec	M. Hansenne *FRA* 1min 49.8sec
1952	M. Whitfield *USA* 1min 49.2sec	A. Wint *JAM* 1min 49.4sec	H. Ulzheimer *GER* 1min 49.7sec
1956	T. Courtney *USA* 1min 47.7sec	D. Johnson *GBR* 1min 47.8sec	A. Boysen *NOR* 1min 48.1sec
1960	P. Snell *NZL* 1min 46.3sec	R. Moens *BEL* 1min 46.5sec	G. Kerr *JAM* 1min 47.1sec
1964	P. Snell *NZL* 1min 45.1sec	W. Crothers *CAN* 1min 45.6sec	W. Kiprugut *KEN* 1min 45.9sec
1968	R. Doubell *AUS* 1min 44.3sec	W. Kiprugut *KEN* 1min 44.5sec	T. Farrell *USA* 1min 45.4sec
1972	D. Wottle *USA* 1min 45.9sec	Y. Arzhanov *URS* 1min 45.9sec	M. Boit *KEN* 1min 46.0sec
1976	A. Juantorena *CUB* 1min 43.50sec	I. Van Damme *BEL* 1min 43.86sec	R. Wohlhuter *USA* 1min 44.12sec

1,500 Metres

	Gold	Silver	Bronze
1896	E. Flack *AUS* 4min 33.2sec	A. Blake *USA* 4min 35.4sec	A. Lermusiaux *FRA* 4min 36.0sec
1900	C. Bennett *GBR* 4min 06.2sec	H. Deloge *FRA* 4min 06.6sec	J. Bray *USA* 4min 07.2sec
1904	J. Lightbody *USA* 4min 05.4sec	F. Verner *USA* 4min 06.8sec	L. Hearn *USA* nda
1908	M. Sheppard *USA* 4min 03.4sec	H. Wilson *GBR* 4min 03.6sec	N. Hallows *GBR* 4min 04.0sec
1912	A. Jackson *GBR* 3min 56.8sec	A. Kiviat *USA* 3min 56.9sec	N. Taber *USA* 3min 56.9sec

	Gold	Silver	Bronze
1920	A. Hill *GBR* 4min 01.8sec	P. Baker *GBR* 4min 02.4sec	L. Shields *USA* 4min 03.1sec
1924	P. Nurmi *FIN* 3min 53.6sec	W. Schärer *SUI* 3min 55.0sec	H. Stallard *GBR* 3min 55.6sec
1928	H. Larva *FIN* 3min 53.2sec	J. Ladoumègue *FRA* 3min 53.8sec	E. Purje *FIN* 3min 56.4sec
1932	L. Beccali *ITA* 3min 51.2sec	J. Cornes *GBR* 3min 52.6sec	P. Edwards *CAN* 3min 52.8sec
1936	J. Lovelock *NZL* 3min 47.8sec	G. Cunningham *USA* 3min 48.4sec	L. Beccali *ITA* 3min 49.2sec
1948	H. Eriksson *SWE* 3min 49.8sec	L. Strand *SWE* 3min 50.4sec	W. Slijkhuis *HOL* 3min 50.4sec
1952	J. Barthel *LUX* 3min 45.1sec	R. McMillen *USA* 3min 45.2sec	W. Lueg *GER* 3min 45.4sec
1956	R. Delany *IRL* 3min 41.2sec	K. Richtzenhain *GER* 3min 42.0sec	J. Landy *AUS* 3min 42.0sec
1960	H. Elliott *AUS* 3min 35.6sec	M. Jazy *FRA* 3min 38.4sec	I. Rózsavölgyi *HUN* 3min 39.2sec
1964	P. Snell *NZL* 3min 38.1sec	J. Odložil *TCH* 3min 39.6sec	J. Davies *NZL* 3min 39.6sec
1968	K. Keino *KEN* 3min 34.9sec	J. Ryun *USA* 3min 37.8sec	B. Tümmler *GER* 3min 39.0sec
1972	P. Vasala *FIN* 3min 36.3sec	K. Keino *KEN* 3min 36.8sec	R. Dixon *NZL* 3min 37.5sec
1976	J. Walker *NZL* 3min 39.17sec	I. Van Damme *BEL* 3min 39.27sec	P. H. Wellmann *GER* 3min 39.33sec

5,000 Metres

Not held before 1912.

	Gold	Silver	Bronze
1912	H. Kolehmainen *FIN* 14min 36.6sec	J. Bouin *FRA* 14min 36.7sec	G. Hutson *GBR* 15min 07.6sec
1920	J. Guillemot *FRA* 14min 55.6sec	P. Nurmi *FIN* 15min 00.0sec	E. Backman *SWE* 15min 13.0sec
1924	P. Nurmi *FIN* 14min 31.2sec	V. Ritola *FIN* 14min 31.4sec	E. Wide *SWE* 15min 01.8sec
1928	V. Ritola *FIN* 14min 38.0sec	P. Nurmi *FIN* 14min 40.0sec	E. Wide *SWE* 14min 41.2sec
1932	L. Lehtinen *FIN* 14min 30.0sec	R. Hill *USA* 14min 30.0sec	L. Virtanen *FIN* 14min 44.0sec
1936	G. Höckert *FIN* 14min 22.2sec	L. Lehtinen *FIN* 14min 25.8sec	H. Jonsson *SWE* 14min 29.0sec
1948	G. Rieff *BEL* 14min 17.6sec	E. Zátopek *TCH* 14min 17.8sec	W. Slijkhuis *HOL* 14min 26.8sec
1952	E. Zátopek *TCH* 14min 06.6sec	A. Mimoun *FRA* 14min 07.4sec	H. Schade *GER* 14min 08.6sec
1956	V. Kuts *URS* 13min 39.6sec	G. Pirie *GBR* 13min 50.6sec	D. Ibbotson *GBR* 13min 54.4sec
1960	M. Halberg *NZL* 13min 43.4sec	H. Grodotzki *GER* 13min 44.6sec	K. Zimny *POL* 13min 44.8sec
1964	R. Schul *USA* 13min 48.8sec	H. Norpoth *GER* 13min 49.6sec	W. Dellinger *USA* 13min 49.8sec
1968	M. Gammoudi *TUN* 13min 05.0sec	K. Keino *KEN* 14min 05.2sec	N. Temu *KEN* 14min 06.4sec
1972	L. Virén *FIN* 13min 26.4sec	M. Gammoudi *TUN* 13min 27.4sec	I. Stewart *GBR* 13min 27.6sec
1976	L. Virén *FIN* 13min 24.76sec	D. Quax *NZL* 13min 25.16sec	K. P. Hildenbrand *GER* 13min 25.38sec

10,000 Metres

Not held before 1912.

	Gold	Silver	Bronze
1912	H. Kolehmainen *FIN* 31min 20.8sec	L. Tewanima *USA* 32min 06.6sec	A. Stenroos *FIN* 32min 21.8sec
1920	P. Nurmi *FIN* 31min 45.8sec	J. Guillemot *FRA* 31min 47.2sec	J. Wilson *GBR* 31min 50.8sec
1924	V. Ritola *FIN* 30min 23.2sec	E. Wide *SWE* 30min 55.2sec	E. Berg *FIN* 31min 43.0sec
1928	P. Nurmi *FIN* 30min 18.8sec	V. Ritola *FIN* 30min 19.4sec	E. Wide *SWE* 31min 00.8sec
1932	J. Kusociński *POL* 30min 11.4sec	V. Iso-Hollo *FIN* 30min 12.6sec	L. Virtanen *FIN* 30min 35.0sec
1936	I. Salminen *FIN* 30min 15.4sec	A. Askola *FIN* 30min 15.6sec	V. Iso-Hollo *FIN* 30min 20.2sec
1948	E. Zátopek *TCH* 29min 59.6sec	A. Mimoun *FRA* 30min 47.4sec	B. Albertsson *SWE* 30min 53.6sec
1952	E. Zátopek *TCH* 29min 17.0sec	A. Mimoun *FRA* 29min 32.8sec	A. Anufriev *URS* 29min 48.2sec
1956	V. Kuts *URS* 28min 45.6sec	J. Kovács *HUN* 28min 52.4sec	A. Lawrence *AUS* 28min 53.6sec
1960	P. Bolotnikov *URS* 28 min 32.2sec	H. Grodotzki *GER* 28min 37.0sec	D. Power *AUS* 28min 38.2sec
1964	B. Mills *USA* 28min 24.4sec	M. Gammoudi *TUN* 28min 24.8sec	R. Clarke *AUS* 28min 25.8sec
1968	N. Temu *KEN* 29min 27.4sec	M. Wolde *ETH* 29min 28.0sec	M. Gammoudi *TUN* 29min 34.2sec
1972	L. Virén *FIN* 27min 38.4sec	E. Puttemans *BEL* 27min 39.6sec	M. Yifter *ETH* 27min 41.0sec
1976	L. Virén *FIN* 27min 40.38sec	C. Sousa Lopes *POR* 27min 45.17sec	B. Foster *GBR* 27min 54.92sec

Marathon

The standard distance of 42,195m (26 miles 385yd) was established in 1908 and has been retained since 1924. In other years the distance has varied.

	Gold	Silver	Bronze
1896	S. Louis *GRE* 2hr 58min 50.0sec	C. Vasilakos *GRE* 3hr 06min 03.0sec	G. Kellner *HUN* 3hr 06min 35.0sec
1900	M. Theato *FRA* 2hr 59min 45.0sec	E. Champion *FRA* 3hr 04min 17.0sec	E. Fast *SWE* 3hr 37min 14.0sec
1904	T. Hicks *USA* 3hr 28min 53.0sec	A. Corey *USA* 3hr 34min 52.0sec	A. Newton *USA* 3hr 47min 33.0sec
1908	J. Hayes *USA* 2hr 55min 18.4sec	C. Hefferon *SAF* 2hr 56min 06.0sec	J. Forshaw *USA* 2hr 57min 10.4sec
1912	K. McArthur *SAF* 2hr 36min 54.8sec	C. Gitsham *SAF* 2hr 37min 52.0sec	G. Strobino *USA* 2hr 38min 42.4sec
1920	H. Kolehmainen *FIN* 2hr 32min 35.8sec	Y. Lossman *EST* 2hr 32min 48.6sec	V. Arri *ITA* 2hr 36min 32.8sec
1924	A. Stenroos *FIN* 2hr 41min 22.6sec	R. Bertini *ITA* 2hr 47min 19.6sec	C. DeMar *USA* 2hr 48min 14.0sec
1928	M. El Ouafi *FRA* 2hr 32min 57.0sec	M. Plaza *CHI* 2hr 33min 23.0sec	M. Marttelin *FIN* 2hr 35min 02.0sec
1932	J. Zabala *ARG* 2hr 31min 36.0sec	S. Ferris *GBR* 2hr 31min 55.0sec	A. Toivonen *FIN* 2hr 32min 12.0sec
1936	K. Son *JPN* 2hr 29min 19.2sec	E. Harper *GBR* 2hr 31min 23.2sec	S. Nan *JPN* 2hr 31min 42.0sec
1948	D. Cabrera *ARG* 2hr 34min 51.6sec	T. Richards *GBR* 2hr 35min 07.6sec	E. Gailly *BEL* 2hr 35min 33.6sec
1952	E. Zátopek *TCH* 2hr 23min 03.2sec	R. Gorno *ARG* 2hr 25min 35.0sec	G. Jansson *SWE* 2hr 26min 07.0sec
1956	A. Mimoun *FRA* 2hr 25min 00.0sec	F. Mihalič *YUG* 2hr 26min 32.0sec	V. Karvonen *FIN* 2hr 27min 47.0sec
1960	A. Bikila *ETH* 2hr 15min 16.2sec	R. Ben Abdesselam *MAR* 2hr 15min 41.6sec	B. Magee *NZL* 2hr 17min 18.2sec
1964	A. Bikila *ETH* 2hr 12min 11.2sec	B. Heatley *GBR* 2hr 16min 19.2sec	K. Tsuburaya *JPN* 2hr 16min 22.8sec
1968	M. Wolde *ETH* 2hr 20min 26.4sec	K. Kimihara *JPN* 2hr 23min 31.0sec	M. Ryan *NZL* 2hr 23min 45.0sec
1972	F. Shorter *USA* 2hr 12min 19.8sec	K. Lismont *BEL* 2hr 14min 31.8sec	M. Wolde *ETH* 2hr 15min 08.4sec
1976	W. Cierpinski *GDR* 2hr 09min 55.0sec	F. Shorter *USA* 2hr 10min 45.8sec	K. Lismont *BEL* 2hr 11min 12.6sec

110 Metres Hurdles

In 1896 the distance was 100m (100yd 28ft).

	Gold	Silver	Bronze
1896	T. Curtis *USA* 17.6sec	G. Goulding *GBR* 17.7sec	
1900	A. Kraenzlein *USA* 15.4sec	J. McLean *USA* 15.5sec	F. Moloney *USA* nda
1904	F. Schule *USA* 16.0sec	T. Shideler *USA* 16.3sec	L. Ashburner *USA* 16.4sec

	Gold	Silver	Bronze
1908	F. Smithson *USA* 15.0sec	J. Garrels *USA* 5yd	A. Shaw *USA* nda
1912	F. Kelly *USA* 15.1sec	J. Wendell *USA* 15.2sec	M. Hawkins *USA* 15.3sec
1920	E. Thomson *CAN* 14.8sec	H. Barron *USA* 15.1sec	F. Murray *USA* 15.2sec
1924	D. Kinsey *USA* 15.0sec	S. Atkinson *SAF* 15.0sec	S. Pettersson *SWE* 15.4sec
1928	S. Atkinson *SAF* 14.8sec	S. Anderson *USA* 14.8sec	J. Collier *USA* 14.9sec
1932	G. Saling *USA* 14.6sec	P. Beard *USA* 14.7sec	D. Finlay *GBR* 14.8sec
1936	F. Towns *USA* 14.2sec	D. Finlay *GBR* 14.4sec	F. Pollard *USA* 14.4sec
1948	W. Porter *USA* 13.9sec	C. Scott *USA* 14.1sec	C. Dixon *USA* 14.1sec
1952	W. H. Dillard *USA* 13.7sec	J. Davis *USA* 13.7sec	A. Barnard *USA* 14.1sec
1956	L. Calhoun *USA* 13.5sec	J. Davis *USA* 13.5sec	J. Shankle *USA* 14.1sec
1960	L. Calhoun *USA* 13.8sec	W. May *USA* 13.8sec	H. Jones *USA* 14.0sec
1964	H. Jones *USA* 13.6sec	H. B. Lindgren *USA* 13.7sec	A. Mikhailov *URS* 13.7sec
1968	W. Davenport *USA* 13.3sec	E. Hall *USA* 13.4sec	E. Ottoz *ITA* 13.4sec
1972	R. Milburn *USA* 13.24sec	G. Drut *FRA* 13.34sec	T. Hill *USA* 13.48sec
1976	G. Drut *FRA* 13.30sec	A. Casanas *CUB* 13.33sec	W. Davenport *USA* 13.38sec

400 Metres Hurdles

Not held before 1900.

	Gold	Silver	Bronze
1900	J. W. Tewksbury *USA* 57.6sec	H. Tausin *FRA* 58.3sec	G. Orton *CAN* nda
1904	H. Hillman *USA* 53.0sec	F. Waller *USA* 53.2sec	G. Poage *USA* nda
1908	C. Bacon *USA* 55.0sec	H. Hillman *USA* 55.3sec	L. Tremeer *GBR* 57.0sec
1912	*Not held*		
1920	F. Loomis *USA* 54.0sec	J. Norton *USA* 54.3sec	A. Desch *USA* 54.5sec
1924	F. M. Taylor *USA* 52.6sec	E. Vilén *FIN* 53.8sec	I. Riley *USA* 54.2sec
1928	Lord Burghley *GBR* 53.4sec	F. Cuhel *USA* 53.6sec	F. M. Taylor *USA* 53.6sec
1932	R. Tisdall *IRL* 51.7sec	G. Hardin *USA* 51.9sec	F. M. Taylor *USA* 52.0sec
1936	G. Hardin *USA* 52.4sec	J. Loaring *CAN* 52.7sec	M. White *PHI* 52.8sec
1948	R. Cochran *USA* 51.1sec	D. White *CEY* 51.8sec	R. Larsson *SWE* 52.2sec
1952	C. Moore *USA* 50.8sec	Y. Lituyev *URS* 51.3sec	J. Holland *NZL* 52.2sec
1956	G. Davis *USA* 50.1sec	E. Southern *USA* 50.8sec	J. Culbreath *USA* 51.6sec
1960	G. Davis *USA* 49.3sec	C. Cushman *USA* 49.6sec	R. Howard *USA* 49.7sec
1964	R. W. Cawley *USA* 49.6sec	J. Cooper *GBR* 50.1sec	S. Morale *ITA* 50.1sec
1968	D. Hemery *GBR* 48.1sec	G. Hennige *GER* 49.0sec	J. Sherwood *GBR* 49.0sec
1972	J. Akii-Bua *UGA* 47.82sec	R. Mann *USA* 48.51sec	D. Hemery *GBR* 48.52sec
1976	E. Moses *USA* 47.64sec	M. Shine *USA* 48.69sec	E. Gavrilenko *URS* 49.45sec

3,000 Metres Steeplechase

Not held before 1900. In 1900 and 1904 the distance was 2,500m; in 1908 it was 3,200m. In 1932 the distance in the final was 3,460m due to an error on the part of an official.

	Gold	Silver	Bronze
1900	G. Orton *CAN* 7min 34.4sec	S. Robinson *GBR* 7min 38.0sec	J. Chastanié *FRA* nda
1904	J. Lightbody *USA* 7min 39.6sec	J. Daly *GBR/IRL* 7min 40.6sec	A Newton *USA* 30yd
1908	A. Russell *GBR* 10min 47.8sec	A. Robertson *GBR* 10min 48.4sec	J. L. Eisele *USA* 11min 00.8sec
1912	*Not held*		
1920	P. Hodge *GBR* 10min 00.4sec	P. Flynn *USA* 100yd	E. Ambrosini *ITA* 130yd
1924	V. Ritola *FIN* 9min 33.6sec	E. Katz *FIN* 9min 44.0sec	P. Bontemps *FRA* 9min 45.2sec
1928	T. Loukola *FIN* 9min 21.8sec	P. Nurmi *FIN* 9min 31.2sec	O. Andersen *FIN* 9min 35.6sec
1932	V. Iso-Hollo *FIN* 10min 33.4sec	T. Evenson *GBR* 10min 46.0sec	J. McCluskey *USA* 10min 46.2sec
1936	V. Iso-Hollo *FIN* 9min 03.8sec	K. Tuominen *FIN* 9min 06.8sec	A. Dompert *GER* 9min 07.2sec
1948	T. Sjöstrand *SWE* 9min 04.6sec	E. Elmsäter *SWE* 9min 08.2sec	G. Hagström *SWE* 9min 11.8sec
1952	H. Ashenfelter *USA* 8min 45.4sec	V. Kazantsev *URS* 8min 51.6sec	J. Disley *GBR* 8min 51.8sec
1956	C. Brasher *GBR* 8min 41.2sec	S. Rozsnyói *HUN* 8min 43.6sec	E. Larsen *NOR* 8min 44.0sec
1960	Z. Krzyszkowiak *POL* 8min 34.2sec	N. Sokolov *URS* 8min 36.4sec	S. Rzhishchin *URS* 8min 42.2sec
1964	G. Roelants *BEL* 8min 30.8sec	M. Herriott *GBR* 8min 32.4sec	I. Belyaiev *URS* 8min 33.8sec
1968	A. Biwott *KEN* 8min 51.0sec	B. Kogo *KEN* 8min 51.6sec	G. Young *USA* 8min 51.8sec
1972	K. Keino *KEN* 8min 23.6sec	B. Jipcho *KEN* 8min 24.6sec	T. Kantanen *FIN* 8min 24.8sec
1976	A. Garderud *SWE* 8min 08.02sec	B. Malinowski *POL* 8min 09.11sec	F. Baumgartl *GDR* 8min 10.36sec

4 x 100 Metres Relay

Not held before 1912.

	Gold	Silver	Bronze
1912	GBR 42.4sec	SWE 42.6sec	
1920	USA 42.2sec	FRA 42.6sec	SWE 42.9sec
1924	USA 41.0sec	GBR 41.2sec	HOL 41.8sec
1928	USA 41.0sec	GER 41.2sec	GBR 41.8sec
1932	USA 40.0sec	GER 40.9sec	ITA 41.2sec
1936	USA 39.8sec	ITA 41.1sec	GER 41.2sec
1948	USA 40.6sec	GBR 41.3sec	ITA 41.5sec
1952	USA 40.1sec	URS 40.3sec	HUN 40.5sec
1956	USA 39.5sec	URS 39.8sec	GER 40.3sec
1960	GER 39.5sec	URS 40.1sec	GBR 40.2sec
1964	USA 39.0sec	POL 39.3sec	FRA 39.3sec
1968	USA 38.2sec	CUB 38.3sec	FRA 38.4sec
1972	USA 38.19sec	URS 38.50sec	GER 38.79sec
1976	USA 38.33sec	GDR 38.66sec	URS 38.78sec

4 x 400 Metres Relay

Not held before 1912.

	Gold	Silver	Bronze
1912	USA 3min 16.6sec	FRA 3min 20.7sec	GBR 3min 23.2sec
1920	GBR 3min 22.2sec	SAF 3min 24.2sec	FRA 3min 24.8sec
1924	USA 3min 16.0sec	SWE 3min 17.0sec	GBR 3min 17.4sec
1928	USA 3min 14.2sec	GER 3min 14.8sec	CAN 3min 15.4sec
1932	USA 3min 08.2sec	GBR 3min 11.2sec	CAN 3min 12.8sec
1936	GBR 3min 09.0sec	USA 3min 11.2sec	GER 3min 11.8sec
1948	USA 3min 10.4sec	FRA 3min 14.8sec	SWE 3min 16.0sec
1952	JAM 3min 03.9sec	USA 3min 04.0sec	GER 3min 06.6sec
1956	USA 3min 04.8sec	AUS 3min 06.2sec	GBR 3min 07.2sec

	Gold	Silver	Bronze
1960	USA 3min 02.2sec	GER 3min 02.7sec	ANT 3min 04.0sec
1964	USA 3min 00.7sec	GBR 3min 01.6sec	TRI 3min 01.7sec
1968	USA 2min 56.1sec	KEN 2min 59.6sec	GER 3min 00.5sec
1972	KEN 2min 59.8sec	GBR 3min 00.5sec	FRA 3min 00.7sec
1976	USA 2min 58.65sec	POL 3min 01.43sec	GER 3min 01.98sec

20 Kilometres Walk

Not held before 1956.

	Gold	Silver	Bronze
1956	L. Spirin *URS* 1hr 31min 27.4sec	A. Mikenas *URS* 1hr 32min 03.0sec	B. Yunk *URS* 1hr 32min 12.0sec
1960	V. Golubnichi *URS* 1hr 34min 07.2sec	N. Freeman *AUS* 1hr 34min 16.4sec	S. Vickers *GBR* 1hr 34min 56.4sec
1964	K. Matthews *GBR* 1hr 29min 34.0sec	D. Linder *GER* 1hr 31min 13.2sec	V. Golubnichi *URS* 1hr 31min 59.4sec
1968	V. Golubnichi *URS* 1hr 33min 58.4sec	J. Pedraza *MEX* 1hr 34min 00.0sec	N. Smaga *URS* 1hr 34min 03.4sec
1972	P. Frenkel *GDR* 1hr 26min 42.4sec	V. Golubnichi *URS* 1hr 26min 55.2sec	H. Reimann *GDR* 1hr 27min 16.6sec
1976	D. Bautista *MEX* 1hr 24min 40.6sec	H. Reimann *GDR* 1hr 25min 13.8sec	P. Frenkel *GDR* 1hr 25min 29.4sec

50 Kilometres Walk

Not held before 1932.

	Gold	Silver	Bronze
1932	T. Green *GBR* 4hr 50min 10.0sec	J. Dalinsh *LAT* 4hr 57min 20.0sec	U. Frigerio *ITA* 4hr 59min 06.0sec
1936	H. Whitlock *GBR* 4hr 30min 41.1sec	A. Schwab *SUI* 4hr 32min 09.2sec	A. Bubenko *LAT* 4hr 32min 42.2sec
1948	J. Ljunggren *SWE* 4hr 41min 52.0sec	G. Godel *SUI* 4hr 48min 17.0sec	T. Johnson *GBR* 4hr 48min 31.0sec
1952	G. Dordoni *ITA* 4hr 28min 07.8sec	J. Doležal *TCH* 4hr 30min 17.8sec	A. Róka *HUN* 4hr 31min 27.2sec
1956	N. Read *NZL* 4hr 30min 42.8sec	Y. Maskinskov *URS* 4hr 32min 57.0sec	J. Ljunggren *SWE* 4hr 35min 02.0sec
1960	D. Thompson *GBR* 4hr 25min 30.0sec	J. Ljunggren *SWE* 4hr 25min 47.0sec	A. Pamich *ITA* 4hr 27min 55.4sec
1964	A. Pamich *ITA* 4hr 11min 12.4sec	P. Nihill *GBR* 4hr 11min 31.2sec	I. Pettersson *SWE* 4hr 14min 17.4sec
1968	C. Höhne *GDR* 4hr 20min 13.6sec	A. Kiss *HUN* 4hr 30min 17.0sec	L. Young *USA* 4hr 31min 55.4sec
1972	B. Kannenberg *GER* 3hr 56min 11.6sec	V. Soldatenko *URS* 3hr 58min 24.0sec	L. Young *USA* 4hr 00min 46.0sec
1976	*Not held*		

High Jump

	Gold	Silver	Bronze
1896	E. Clark *USA* 1.81m (5ft 11¼in)	J. Connolly *USA* 1.65m (5ft 5in)	R. Garrett *USA* 1.65m (5ft 5in)
1900	I. Baxter *USA* 1.90m (6ft 2¾in)	P. Leahy *GBR/IRL* 1.78m (5ft 10⅛in)	L. Gönczy *HUN* 1.75m (5ft 8⅞in)
1904	S. Jones *USA* 1.80m (5ft 11in)	G. P. Serviss *USA* 1.78m (5ft 10in)	P. Weinstein *GER* 1.78m (5ft 10in)
1908	H. Porter *USA* 1.90m (6ft 3in)	C. Leahy *GBR/IRL*, I. Somodi *HUN* & G. André *FRA* 1.88m (6ft 2in)	
1912	A. Richards *USA* 1.93m (6ft 4in)	H. Leische *GER* 1.91m (6ft 3¼in)	G. Horine *USA* 1.89m (6ft 2⅜in)
1920	R. Landon *USA* 1.94m (6ft 4⅜in)	H. Muller *USA* 1.90m (6ft 2¾in)	B. Ekelund *SWE* 1.90m (6ft 2¾in)
1924	H. Osborn *USA* 1.98m (6ft 6in)	L. Brown *USA* 1.95m (6ft 4¾in)	P. Lewden *FRA* 1.92m (6ft 3⅝in)
1928	R. King *USA* 1.94m (6ft 4⅜in)	B. Hedges *USA* 1.91m (6ft 3¼in)	C. Ménard *FRA* 1.91m (6ft 3¼in)
1932	D. McNaughton *CAN* 1.97m (6ft 5½in)	R. Van Osdel *USA* 1.97m (6ft 5½in)	S. Toribio *PHI* 1.97m (6ft 5½in)
1936	C. Johnson *USA* 2.03m (6ft 7⅞in)	D. Albritton *USA* 2.00m (6ft 6¾in)	D. Thurber *USA* 2.00m (6ft 6¾in)
1948	J. Winter *AUS* 1.98m (6ft 6in)	B. Paulsen *NOR* 1.95m (6ft 4¾in)	G. Stanich *USA* 1.95m (6ft 4¾in)
1952	W. Davis *USA* 2.04m (6ft 8⅜in)	K. Wiesner *USA* 2.01m (6ft 7⅛in)	J. Telles da Conceição *BRA* 1.98m (6ft 6in)
1956	C. Dumas *USA* 2.12m (6ft 11½in)	C. Porter *AUS* 2.10m (6ft 10⅝in)	I. Kashkarov *USA* 2.08m (6ft 9⅞in)
1960	R. Shavlakadze *URS* 2.16m (7ft 1⅛in)	V. Brumel *URS* 2.16m (7ft 1⅛in)	J. Thomas *USA* 2.14m (7ft 0¼in)
1964	V. Brumel *URS* 2.18m (7ft 1¾in)	J. Thomas *USA* 2.18m (7ft 1¾in)	J. Rambo *USA* 2.16m (7ft 1in)
1968	R. Fosbury *USA* 2.24m (7ft 4¼in)	E. Caruthers *USA* 2.22m (7ft 3½in)	V. Gavrilov *URS* 2.20m (7ft 2⅝in)
1972	Y. Tarmak *URS* 2.23m (7ft 3¾in)	S. Junge *GDR* 2.21m (7ft 3in)	D. Stones *USA* 2.21m (7ft 3in)
1976	J. Wszola *POL* 2.25m (7ft 4½in)	G. Joy *CAN* 2.23m (7ft 3¾in)	D. Stones *USA* 2.21m (7ft 3in)

Long Jump

	Gold	Silver	Bronze
1896	E. Clark *USA* 6.35m (20ft 10in)	R. Garrett *USA* 6.18m (20ft 3¼in)	J. Connolly *USA* 6.11m (20ft 0½in)
1900	A. Kraenzlein *USA* 7.185m (23ft 6¾in)	M. Prinstein *USA* 7.17m (23ft 6½in)	P. Leahy *GBR* 6.95m (22ft 9½in)
1904	M. Prinstein *USA* 7.34m (24ft 1in)	D. Frank *USA* 6.89m (22ft 7¼in)	R. Stangland *USA* 6.88m (22ft 7in)
1908	F. Irons *USA* 7.48m (24ft 6½in)	D. Kelly *USA* 7.09m (23ft 3¼in)	C. Bricker *CAN* 7.08m (23ft 3in)
1912	A. Gutterson *USA* 7.60m (24ft 11¼in)	C. Bricker *CAN* 7.21m (23ft 7¾in)	G. Åberg *SWE* 7.18m (23ft 6¾in)
1920	W. Pettersson *SWE* 7.15m (23ft 5½in)	C. Johnson *USA* 7.09m (23ft 3¼in)	E. Abrahamsson *SWE* 7.08m (23ft 2¾in)
1924	W. D. H. Hubbard *USA* 7.44m (24ft 5in)	E. Gourdin *USA* 7.28m (23ft 10½in)	S. Hansen *NOR* 7.26m (23ft 9¾in)
1928	E. Hamm *USA* 7.73m (25ft 4½in)	S. Cator *HAI* 7.58m (24ft 10½in)	A. Bates *USA* 7.40m (24ft 3¼in)
1932	E. Gordon *USA* 7.64m (25ft 0¾in)	C. L. Redd *USA* 7.60m (24ft 11¼in)	C. Nambu *JPN* 7.45m (24ft 5¼in)
1936	J. Owens *USA* 8.06m (26ft 5¼in)	L. Long *GER* 7.87m (25ft 9¾in)	N. Tajima *JPN* 7.74m (25ft 4¾in)
1948	W. Steele *USA* 7.82m (25ft 8in)	T. Bruce *AUS* 7.55m (24ft 9¼in)	H. Douglas *USA* 7.54m (24ft 9in)
1952	J. Biffle *USA* 7.57m (24ft 10in)	M. Gourdine *USA* 7.53m (24ft 8½in)	O. Földessy *HUN* 7.30m (23ft 11½in)
1956	G. Bell *USA* 7.83m (25ft 8¼in)	J. Bennett *USA* 7.68m (25ft 2¼in)	J. Valkama *FIN* 7.48m (24ft 6½in)
1960	R. Boston *USA* 8.12m (26ft 7¾in)	I. Roberson *USA* 8.11m (26ft 7¼in)	I. Ter-Ovanesyan *URS* 8.04m (26ft 4½in)
1964	L. Davies *GBR* 8.07m (26ft 5¾in)	R. Boston *USA* 8.03m (26ft 4¼in)	I. Ter-Ovanesyan *URS* 7.99m (26ft 2¾in)
1968	R. Beamon *USA* 8.90m (29ft 2½in)	K. Beer *GDR* 8.19m (26ft 10½in)	R. Boston *USA* 8.16m (26ft 9¼in)
1972	R. Williams *USA* 8.24m (27ft 0½in)	H. Baumgärtner *GER* 8.18m (26ft 10in)	A. Robinson *USA* 8.03m (26ft 4¼in)
1976	A. Robinson *USA* 8.35m (27ft 4¾in)	R. Williams *USA* 8.11m (26ft 7¼in)	F. Wartenberg *GDR* 8.02m (26ft 3¾in)

Triple Jump

	Gold	Silver	Bronze
1896	J. Connolly *USA* 13.71m (44ft 11¾in)	A. Tuffère *FRA* 12.70m (41ft 8in)	I. Persakis *GRE* 12.52m (41ft 1in)
1900	M. Prinstein *USA* 14.47m (47ft 5¾in)	J. Connolly *USA* 13.97m (45ft 10in)	L. P. Sheldon *USA* 13.64m (44ft 9in)
1904	M. Prinstein *USA* 14.35m (47ft 1in)	F. Englehardt *USA* 13.90m (45ft 7¼in)	R. Stangland *USA* 13.36m (43ft 10½in)
1908	T. Ahearne *GBR/IRL* 14.91m (48ft 11¼in)	J. G. MacDonald *CAN* 14.76m (48ft 5in)	E. Larsen *NOR* 14.39m (47ft 2¾in)

	Gold	Silver	Bronze
1912	G. Lindblom *SWE* 14.76m (48ft 5in)	G. Åberg *SWE* 14.51m (47ft 7¼in)	E. Almlöf *SWE* 14.17m (46ft 5¾in)
1920	V. Tuulos *FIN* 14.50m (47ft 7in)	F. Jansson *SWE* 14.48m (47ft 6in)	E. Almlöf *SWE* 14.27m (46ft 10in)
1924	A. Winter *AUS* 15.52m (50ft 11¼in)	L. Bruneto *ARG* 15.42m (50ft 7¼in)	V. Tuulos *FIN* 15.37m (50ft 5in)
1928	M. Oda *JPN* 15.21m (49ft 10¾in)	L. Casey *USA* 15.17m (49ft 9¼in)	V. Tuulos *FIN* 15.11m (49ft 7in)
1932	C. Nambu *JPN* 15.72m (51ft 7in)	E. Svensson *SWE* 15.32m (50ft 3¼in)	K. Oshima *JPN* 15.12m (49ft 7¼in)
1936	N. Tajima *JPN* 16.00m (52ft 6in)	M. Harada *JPN* 15.66m (51ft 4½in)	J. P. Metcalfe *AUS* 15.50m (50ft 10¼in)
1948	A. Åhman *SWE* 15.40m (50ft 6¼in)	G. Avery *AUS* 15.37m (50ft 5in)	R. Sarialp *TUR* 15.02m (49ft 3½in)
1952	A. F. da Silva *BRA* 16.22m (53ft 2½in)	L. Shcherbakov *URS* 15.98m (52ft 5¼in)	A. Devonish *VEN* 15.52m (50ft 11in)
1956	A. F. da Silva *BRA* 16.35m (53ft 7¾in)	V. Einarsson *ISL* 16.26m (53ft 4¼in)	V. Kreyer *URS* 16.02m (52ft 6¾in)
1960	J. Szmidt *POL* 16.81m (55ft 1¾in)	V. Goryayev *URS* 16.63m (54ft 6¾in)	V. Kreyer *URS* 16.43m (53ft 10¾in)
1964	J. Szmidt *POL* 16.85m (55ft 3½in)	O. Fedoseyev *URS* 16.58m (54ft 4¾in)	V. Kravchenko *URS* 16.57m (54ft 4¼in)
1968	V. Saneev *URS* 17.39m (57ft 0¾in)	N. Prudencio *BRA* 17.27m (56ft 8in)	G. Gentile *ITA* 17.22m (56ft 6in)
1972	V. Saneev *URS* 17.35m (56ft 11¼in)	J. Drehmel *GDR* 17.31m (56ft 9½in)	N. Prudencio *BRA* 17.05m (55ft 11¼in)
1976	V. Saneev *URS* 17.29m (56ft 8¾in)	J. Butts *USA* 17.18m (56ft 4⅜in)	J. C. de Oliviera *BRA* 16.90m (55ft 5⅜in)

Pole Vault

	Gold	Silver	Bronze
1896	W. Hoyt *USA* 3.30m (10ft 10in)	A. Tyler *USA* 3.25m (10ft 8in)	E. Damaskos *GRE* 2.85m (9ft 4¼in)
1900	I. Baxter *USA* 3.30m (10ft 10in)	M. B. Colkett *USA* 3.25m (10ft 8in)	C. A. Andersen *NOR* 3.20m (10ft 6in)
1904	C. Dvorak *USA* 3.50 (11ft 6in)	L. Samse *USA* 3.43m (11ft 3in)	L. Wilkins *USA* 3.43m (11ft 3in)
1908	A. Gilbert *USA* & E. Cooke *USA* 3.71m (12ft 2in)		E. Archibald *CAN* 3.58m (11ft 9in)
1912	H. Babcock *USA* 3.95m (12ft 11½in)	F. Nelson *USA* & M. Wright *USA* 3.85m (12ft 7½in)	
1920	F. Foss *USA* 4.09m (13ft 5in)	H. Petersen *DEN* 3.70m (12ft 1¾in)	E. Myers *USA* 3.60m (11ft 9¾in)
1924	L. Barnes *USA* 3.95m (12ft 11½in)	G. Graham *USA* 3.95m (12ft 11½in)	J. Brooker *USA* 3.90m (12ft 9½in)
1928	S. Carr *USA* 4.20m (13ft 9½in)	W. Droegemuller *USA* 4.10m (13ft 5½in)	C. McGinnis *USA* 3.95m (12ft 11½in)
1932	W. Miller *USA* 4.32m (14ft 1⅞in)	S. Nishida *JPN* 4.30m (14ft 1¼in)	G. Jefferson *USA* 4.20m (13ft 9½in)
1936	E. Meadows *USA* 4.35m (14ft 3¼in)	S. Nishida *JPN* 4.25m (13ft 11¼in)	S. Oe *JPN* 4.25m (13ft 11¼in)
1948	O. G. Smith *USA* 4.30m (14ft 1¼in)	E. Kataja *FIN* 4.20m (13ft 9½in)	R. Richards *USA* 4.20m (13ft 9½in)
1952	R. Richards *USA* 4.55m (14ft 11¼in)	D. Laz *USA* 4.50m (14ft 9¼in)	R. Lundberg *SWE* 4.40m (14ft 5¼in)
1956	R. Richards *USA* 4.56m (14ft 11½in)	R. Gutowski *USA* 4.53m (14ft 10¼in)	G. Roubanis *GRE* 4.50m (14ft 9¼in)
1960	D. Bragg *USA* 4.70m (15ft 5in)	R. Morris *USA* 4.60m (15ft 1¼in)	E. Landström *FIN* 4.55m (14ft 11¼in)
1964	F. Hansen *USA* 5.10m (16ft 8¾in)	W. Reinhardt *GER* 5.05m (16ft 6¾in)	K. Lehnertz *GER* 5.00m (16ft 5in)
1968	R. Seagren *USA* 5.40m (17ft 8½in)	C. Schiprowski *GER* 5.40m (17ft 8½in)	W. Nordwig *GDR* 5.40m (17ft 8½in)
1972	W. Nordwig *GDR* 5.50m (18ft 0½in)	R. Seagren *USA* 5.40m (17ft 8½in)	J. Johnson *USA* 5.35m (17ft 6½in)
1976	T. Slusarski *POL* 5.50m (18ft 0½in)	A. Kalliomaki *FIN* 5.50m (18ft 0½in)	D. Roberts *USA* 5.50m (18ft 0½in)

Shot

Weight 7.257kg (16lb) from a circle of 2.135m (7ft); in 1896 and 1900 a square of 2.135m (7ft).

	Gold	Silver	Bronze
1896	R. Garrett *USA* 11.22m (36ft 9¾in)	M. Gouscos *GRE* 11.20m (36ft 9in)	G. Papasideris *GRE* 10.36m (34ft 0in)
1900	R. Sheldon *USA* 14.10m (46ft 3in)	J. McCracken *USA* 12.85m (42ft 2in)	R. Garrett *USA* 12.37m (40ft 7in)
1904	R. Rose *USA* 14.81m (48ft 7in)	W. Coe *USA* 14.40m (47ft 3in)	L. Feuerbach *USA* 13.37m (43ft 10½in)
1908	R. Rose *USA* 14.21m (46ft 7½in)	D. Horgan *GBR* 13.62m (44ft 8¼in)	J. Garrels *USA* 13.18m (43ft 3in)
1912	P. McDonald *USA* 15.34m (50ft 4in)	R. Rose *USA* 15.25m (50ft 0½in)	L. Whitney *USA* 13.93m (45ft 8½in)
1920	V. Pörhölä *FIN* 14.81m (48ft 7in)	E. Niklander *FIN* 14.15m (46ft 5¼in)	H. Liversedge *USA* 14.15m (46ft 5in)
1924	C. Houser *USA* 14.99m (49ft 2½in)	G. Hartranft *USA* 14.90m (48ft 10½in)	R. Hills *USA* 14.64m (48ft 0½in)
1928	J. Kuck *USA* 15.87m (52ft 0¾in)	H. Brix *USA* 15.75m (51ft 8in)	E. Hirschfeld *GER* 15.72m (51ft 7in)
1932	L. Sexton *USA* 16.01m (52ft 6¼in)	H. Rothert *USA* 15.67m (51ft 5in)	F. Douda *TCH* 15.61m (51ft 2½in)
1936	H. Wöllke *GER* 16.20m (53ft 1¾in)	S. Bärlund *FIN* 16.12m (52ft 10¾in)	G. Stöck *GER* 15.66m (51ft 4½in)
1948	W. Thompson *USA* 17.12m (56ft 2in)	J. Delaney *USA* 16.68m (54ft 8¾in)	J. Fuchs *USA* 16.42m (53ft 10½in)
1952	P. O'Brien *USA* 17.41m (57ft 1½in)	D. Hooper *USA* 17.39m (57ft 0¾in)	J. Fuchs *USA* 17.06m (55ft 11¾in)
1956	P. O'Brien *USA* 18.57m (60ft 11¼in)	W. Nieder *USA* 18.18m (59ft 7¾in)	J. Skobla *TCH* 17.65m (57ft 11in)
1960	W. Nieder *USA* 19.68m (64ft 6¾in)	P. O'Brien *USA* 19.11m (62ft 8¼in)	D. Long *USA* 19.01m (62ft 4¼in)
1964	D. Long *USA* 20.33m (66ft 8½in)	R. Matson *USA* 20.20m (66ft 3¼in)	V. Varju *HUN* 19.39m (63ft 7½in)
1968	R. Matson *USA* 20.54m (67ft 4¾in)	G. Woods *USA* 20.12m (66ft 0¼in)	E. Gushchin *URS* 20.09m (65ft 11in)
1972	W. Komar *POL* 21.18m (69ft 6in)	G. Woods *USA* 21.17m (69ft 5½in)	H. Briesenick *GDR* 21.14m (69ft 4¼in)
1976	U. Beyer *GDR* 21.05m (69ft 0¾in)	E. Mironov *URS* 21.03m (69ft 0in)	A. Barisnikov *URS* 21.00m (68ft 10¾in)

Discus

Weight 2kg (4lb 6.547oz) from a circle of 2.50m (8ft 2½in).

	Gold	Silver	Bronze
1896	R. Garrett *USA* 29.15m (95ft 7¾in)	P. Paraskevopoulos *GRE* 28.96m (95ft 0in)	S. Versis *GRE* 28.78m (94ft 5in)
1900	R. Bauer *HUN* 36.04m (118ft 3in)	F. Janda-Suk *BOH* 35.25m (115ft 7¾in)	R. Sheldon *USA* 34.60m (113ft 6in)
1904	M. Sheridan *USA* 39.28m (128ft 10½in)	R. Rose *USA* 39.28m (128ft 10½in)	N. Georgantos *GRE* 37.68m (123ft 7½in)
1908	M. Sheridan *USA* 40.89m (134ft 2in)	M. H. Griffin *USA* 40.70m (133ft 6½in)	M. Horr *USA* 39.45m (129ft 5¼in)
1912	A. Taipale *FIN* 45.21m (148ft 4in)	R. Byrd *USA* 42.32m (138ft 10in)	J. Duncan *USA* 42.28m (138ft 8½in)
1920	E. Niklander *FIN* 44.69m (146ft 7½in)	A. Taipale *FIN* 44.19m (144ft 11½in)	A. Pope *USA* 42.13m (138ft 2½in)

	Gold	Silver	Bronze
1924	C. Houser *USA* 46.16m (151ft 5in)	V. Niittymaa *FIN* 44.95m (147ft 5½in)	T. Lieb *USA* 44.83m (147ft 1in)
1928	C. Houser *USA* 47.32m (155ft 3in)	A. Kivi *FIN* 47.23m (154ft 11½in)	J. Corson *USA* 47.10m (154ft 6½in)
1932	J. Anderson *USA* 49.49m (162ft 4½in)	H. J. Laborde *FRA* 48.47m (159ft 0½in)	P. Winter *FRA* 47.85m (157ft 0in)
1936	K. Carpenter *USA* 50.48m (165ft 7½in)	G. Dunn *USA* 49.36m (161ft 11in)	G. Oberweger *ITA* 49.23m (161ft 6in)
1948	A. Consolini *ITA* 52.78m (172ft 2in)	G. Tosi *ITA* 51.78m (169ft 10½in)	F. Gordien *USA* 50.77m (166ft 7in)
1952	S. Iness *USA* 55.03m (180ft 6½in)	A. Consolini *ITA* 53.78m (176ft 5in)	J. Dillion *USA* 53.28m (174ft 9½in)
1956	A. Oerter *USA* 56.36m (184ft 11in)	F. Gordien *USA* 54.81m (179ft 9in)	D. Koch *USA* 54.40m (178ft 5½in)
1960	A. Oerter *USA* 59.18m (194ft 1¾in)	R. Babka *USA* 58.01m (190ft 4¼in)	R. Cochran *USA* 57.16m (187ft 6½in)
1964	A. Oerter *USA* 61.00m (200ft 1½in)	L. Danek *TCH* 60.52m (198ft 6½in)	D. Weill *USA* 59.49m (195ft 2in)
1968	A. Oerter *USA* 64.78m (212ft 6½in)	L. Milde *GDR* 63.08m (206ft 11½in)	L. Danek *TCH* 62.92m (206ft 5in)
1972	L. Danek *TCH* 64.40m (211ft 3in)	L. J. Silvester *USA* 63.50m (208ft 4in)	R. Bruch *SWE* 63.40m (208ft 0in)
1976	M. Wilkins *USA* 67.50m (221ft 5½in)	W. Schmidt *GDR* 66.22m (217ft 3in)	J. Powell *USA* 65.70m (215ft 6⅝in)

Hammer

Weight 7.257kg (16lb) from a circle of 2.135m (7ft): in 1900 from a 9ft circle. Not held before 1900.

	Gold	Silver	Bronze
1900	J. Flanagan *USA* 49.73m (163ft 2in)	T. Hare *USA* 49.13m (161ft 2in)	J. McCracken *USA* 42.46m (139ft 3½in)
1904	J. Flanagan *USA* 51.23m (168ft 1in)	J. DeWitt *USA* 50.26m (164ft 11in)	R. Rose *USA* 45.73m (150ft 0½in)
1908	J. Flanagan *USA* 51.92m (170ft 4¼in)	M. McGrath *USA* 51.18m (167ft 11in)	C. Walsh *USA* 48.50m (159ft 1½in)
1912	M. McGrath *USA* 54.74m (179ft 7in)	D. Gillis *CAN* 48.39m (158ft 9in)	C. Childs *USA* 48.17m (158ft 0½in)
1920	P. Ryan *USA* 52.88m (173ft 5½in)	C. H. Lind *SWE* 48.43m (158ft 10½in)	B. Bennett *USA* 48.25m (158ft 3½in)
1924	F. Tootell *USA* 53.30m (174ft 0in)	M. McGrath *USA* 50.84m (166ft 9½in)	M. Nokes *GBR* 48.88m (160ft 4in)
1928	P. O'Callaghan *IRL* 51.39m (168ft 7in)	O. Skiöld *SWE* 51.29m (168ft 3in)	E. Black *USA* 49.03m (160ft 10in)
1932	P. O'Callaghan *IRL* 53.92m (176ft 11in)	V. Pörhölä *FIN* 52.27m (171ft 6in)	P. Zaremba *USA* 50.33m (165ft 1½in)
1936	K. Hein *GER* 56.49m (185ft 4in)	E. Blask *GER* 55.04m (180ft 7in)	F. Warngård *SWE* 54.83m (179ft 10½in)
1948	I. Németh *HUN* 56.07m (183ft 11½in)	I. Gubijan *YUG* 54.27m (178ft 0½in)	R. Bennett *USA* 53.73m (176ft 3½in)
1952	J. Csermák *HUN* 60.34m (197ft 11½in)	K. Storch *GER* 58.86m (193ft 1in)	I. Németh *HUN* 57.74m (189ft 5in)
1956	H. Connolly *USA* 63.19m (207ft 3½in)	M. Krivonosov *URS* 63.03m (206ft 9½in)	A. Samotsvetov *URS* 62.56m (205ft 3in)
1960	V. Rudenkov *URS* 67.10m (220ft 1¾in)	G. Zsivótzky *HUN* 65.79m (215ft 10in)	T. Rut *POL* 65.64m (215ft 4½in)
1964	R. Klim *URS* 69.74m (228ft 10in)	G. Zsivótzky *HUN* 69.09m (226ft 8in)	U. Beyer *GER* 68.09m (223ft 4½in)
1968	G. Zsivótzky *HUN* 73.36m (240ft 8in)	R. Klim *URS* 73.28m (240ft 5in)	L. Lovász *HUN* 69.78m (228ft 11in)
1972	A. Bondarchuk *URS* 75.50m (247ft 8in)	J. Sachse *GDR* 74.96m (245ft 11in)	V. Khmelevski *URS* 74.04m (242ft 11in)
1976	Y. Sedyh *URS* 77.52m (254ft 4in)	A. Spiridonov *URS* 76.08m (249ft 7½in)	A. Bondarchuk *URS* 75.48m (247ft 7¾in)

Javelin

Not held before 1908.

	Gold	Silver	Bronze
1908	E. Lemming *SWE* 54.83m (179ft 10½in)	A. Halse *NOR* 50.57m (165ft 11in)	O. Nilsson *SWE* 47.10m (154ft 6¼in)
1912	E. Lemming *SWE* 60.64m (198ft 11½in)	J. Saaristo *FIN* 58.66m (192ft 5½in)	M. Koczán *HUN* 55.50m (182ft 1in)
1920	J. Myyrä *FIN* 65.78m (215ft 9½in)	U. Peltonen *FIN* 63.50m (208ft 4in)	P. Johansson *FIN* 63.10m (207ft 0in)
1924	J. Myyrä *FIN* 62.96m (206ft 6½in)	G. Lindström *SWE* 60.92m (199ft 10½in)	E. Oberst *USA* 58.35m (191ft 5in)
1928	E. Lundkvist *SWE* 66.60m (218ft 6in)	B. Szepes *HUN* 65.26m (214ft 1in)	O. Sunde *NOR* 63.97m (209ft 10½in)
1932	M. Järvinen *FIN* 72.71m (238ft 6½in)	M. Sippala *FIN* 69.80m (229ft 0in)	E. Penttilä *FIN* 68.70m (225ft 4½in)
1936	G. Stöck *GER* 71.84m (235ft 8½in)	Y. Nikkanen *FIN* 70.77m (232ft 2in)	K. Toivonen *FIN* 70.72m (232ft 0in)
1948	T. Rautavaara *FIN* 69.77m (228ft 11in)	S. Seymour *USA* 67.56m (221ft 8in)	J. Várszegi *HUN* 67.03m (219ft 11in)
1952	C. Young *USA* 73.78m (242ft 0½in)	W. Miller *USA* 72.46m (237ft 8½in)	T. Hyytiäinen *FIN* 71.89m (235ft 10½in)
1956	E. Danielsen *NOR* 85.71m (281ft 2½in)	J. Sidlo *POL* 79.98m (262ft 4½in)	V. Tsibulenko *URS* 79.50m (260ft 10in)
1960	V. Tsibulenko *URS* 84.64m (277ft 8in)	W. Krüger *GER* 79.36m (260ft 4½in)	G. Kulcsár *HUN* 78.57m (257ft 9¼in)
1964	P. Nevala *FIN* 82.66m (271ft 2in)	G. Kulcsár *HUN* 82.32m (270ft 0½in)	Y. Lusis *URS* 80.57m (264ft 4½in)
1968	Y. Lusis *URS* 90.10m (295ft 7in)	J. Kinnunen *FIN* 88.58m (290ft 7½in)	G. Kulcsár *HUN* 87.06m (285ft 7½in)
1972	K. Wolfermann *GER* 90.48m (296ft 10in)	Y. Lusis *URS* 90.46m (296ft 9in)	W. Schmidt *USA* 84.42m (276ft 11in)
1976	M. Németh *HUN* 94.58m (310ft 3¾in)	H. Siitonen *FIN* 87.92m (288ft 5½in)	G. Megelea *ROM* 87.16m (285ft 11⅝in)

Decathlon

Consists of ten events on two consecutive days; 100 metres, long jump, shot, high jump, 400 metres, on the first day; 110-metres hurdles, discus, pole vault, javelin, 1,500 metres, on the second day. Not held in its present form before 1912,

	Gold	Silver	Bronze
1912	H. Wieslander *SWE* 7,724.495 pts	C. Lomberg *SWE* 7,413.510 pts	G. Holmér *SWE* 7,347.855 pts

	Gold	Silver	Bronze
1920	H. Lövland *NOR* 6,803.355 pts	B. Hamilton *USA* 6,771.085 pts	B. Ohlson *SWE* 6,580.030 pts
1924	H. Osborn *USA* 7,710.775 pts	E. Norton *USA* 7,350.895 pts	A. Klumberg *EST* 7,329.360 pts
1928	P. Yrjölä *FIN* 8,053.290 pts	A. Järvinen *FIN* 7,931.500 pts	J. K. Doherty *USA* 7,706.650 pts
1932	J. Bausch *USA* 8,462.230 pts	A. Järvinen *FIN* 8,292.480 pts	W. Eberle *GER* 8,030.800 pts
1936	G. Morris *USA* 7,900 pts	R. Clark *USA* 7,601 pts	J. Parker *USA* 7,275 pts
1948	R. Mathias *USA* 7,139 pts	I. Heinrich *FRA* 6,974 pts	F. Simmons *USA* 6,950 pts
1952	R. Mathias *USA* 7,887 pts	M. Campbell *USA* 6,975 pts	F. Simmons *USA* 6,788 pts
1956	M. Campbell *USA* 7,937 pts	R. Johnson *USA* 7,587 pts	V. Kuznetsov *URS* 7,465 pts
1960	R. Johnson *USA* 8,392 pts	C. K. Yang *ROC* 8,334 pts	V. Kuznetsov *URS* 7,809 pts
1964	W. Holdorf *GER* 7,887 pts	R. Aun *URS* 7,842 pts	H. J. Walde *GER* 7,809 pts
1968	B. Toomey *USA* 8,193 pts	H. J. Walde *GER* 8,111 pts	K. Bendin *GER* 8,064 pts
1972	N. Avilov *URS* 8,454 pts.	L. Litvinenko *URS* 8,035 pts	R. Katus *POL* 7,984 pts
1976	B. Jenner *USA* 8,618 pts	G. Kratschmer *GER* 8,411 pts	N. Avilov *URS* 8,369 pts

Athletics (Women)

100 Metres

Not held before 1928.

	Gold	Silver	Bronze
1928	E. Robinson *USA* 12.2sec	F. Rosenfeld *CAN* 12.3sec	E. Smith *CAN* 12.3sec
1932	S. Walasiewicz *POL* 11.9sec	H. Strike *CAN* 11.9sec	W. von Bremen *USA* 12.0sec
1936	H. Stephens *USA* 11.5sec	S. Walasiewicz *POL* 11.7sec	K. Krauss *GER* 11.9sec
1948	F. Blankers-Koen *HOL* 11.9sec	D. Manley *GBR* 12.2sec	S. Strickland *AUS* 12.2sec
1952	M. Jackson *AUS* 11.5sec	D. Hasenjager *SAF* 11.8sec	S. Strickland *AUS* 11.9sec
1956	B. Cuthbert *AUS* 11.5sec	C. Stubnick *GER* 11.7sec	M. Matthews *AUS* 11.7sec
1960	W. Rudolph *USA* 11.0sec	D. Hyman *GBR* 11.3sec	G. Leone *ITA* 11.3sec
1964	W. Tyus *USA* 11.4sec	E. Maguire *USA* 11.6sec	E. Klobukowska *POL* 11.6sec
1968	W. Tyus *USA* 11.0sec	B. Ferrell *USA* 11.1sec	I. Szewińska-Kirszenstein *POL* 11.1sec
1972	R. Stecher *GDR* 11.07sec	R. Boyle *AUS* 11.23sec	S. Chivas *CUB* 11.24sec
1976	A. Richter *GDR* 11.08sec	R. Stecher *GDR* 11.13sec	I. Helten *GER* 11.17sec

200 Metres

Not held before 1948.

	Gold	Silver	Bronze
1948	F. Blankers-Koen *HOL* 24.4sec	A. Williamson *GBR* 25.1sec	A. Patterson *USA* 25.2sec
1952	M. Jackson *AUS* 23.7sec	B. Brouwer *HOL* 24.2sec	N. Khnykina *URS* 24.2sec
1956	B. Cuthbert *AUS* 23.4sec	C. Stubnick *GER* 23.7sec	M. Matthews *AUS* 23.8sec
1960	W. Rudolph *USA* 24.0sec	J. Heine *GER* 24.4sec	D. Hyman *GBR* 24.7sec
1964	E. Maguire *USA* 23.0sec	I. Kirszenstein *POL* 23.1sec	M. Black *AUS* 23.1sec
1968	I. Szewińska-Kirszenstein *POL* 22.5sec	R. Boyle *AUS* 22.7sec	J. Lamy *AUS* 22.8sec
1972	R. Stecher *GDR* 22.40sec	R. Boyle *AUS* 22.45sec	I. Szewińska-Kirszenstein *POL* 22.74sec
1976	B. Eckert *GDR* 22.37sec	A. Richter *GER* 22.39sec	R. Stecher *GDR* 22.47sec

400 Metres

Not held before 1964.

	Gold	Silver	Bronze
1964	B. Cuthbert *AUS* 52.0sec	A. Packer *GBR* 52.2sec	J. Amoore *AUS* 53.4sec
1968	C. Besson *FRA* 52.0sec	L. Board *GBR* 52.1sec	N. Pechenkina *URS* 52.2sec
1972	M. Zehrt *GDR* 51.08sec	R. Wilden *GER* 51.21sec	K. Hammond *USA* 51.64sec
1976	I. Szewińska-Kirszenstein *POL* 49.29sec	C. Brehmer *GDR* 50.51sec	E. Streidt *GDR* 50.55sec

800 Metres

Not held before 1928.

	Gold	Silver	Bronze
1928	L. Radke *GER* 2min 16.8sec	K. Hitomi *JPN* 2min 17.6sec	I. Gentzel *SWE* 2min 17.8sec
1932-1956	*Not held.*		
1960	L. Shevtsova *URS* 2min 04.3sec	B. Jones *AUS* 2min 04.4sec	U. Donath *GER* 2min 05.6sec
1964	A. Packer *GBR* 2min 01.1sec	M. Dupureur *FRA* 2min 01.9sec	A. Chamberlain *NZL* 2min 02.8sec
1968	M. Manning *USA* 2min 00.9sec	I. Silai *ROM* 2min 02.5sec	M. Gommers *HOL* 2min 02.6sec
1972	H. Falck *GER* 1min 58.6sec	N. Sabaite *URS* 1min 58.7sec	G. Hoffmeister *GDR* 1min 59.2sec
1976	T. Kazankina *URS* 1min 54.94sec	H. Chtereva *BUL* 1min 55.42sec	E. Zinn *GDR* 1min 55.60sec

80 Metres Hurdles

Not held before 1932.

	Gold	Silver	Bronze
1932	M. Didrikson *USA* 11.7sec	E. Hall *USA* 11.7sec	M. Clark *SAF* 11.8sec
1936	T. Valla *ITA* 11.7sec	A. Steuer *GER* 11.7sec	E. Taylor *CAN* 11.7sec
1948	F. Blankers-Koen *HOL* 11.2sec	M. Gardner *GBR* 11.2sec	S. (Strickland) de la Hunty *AUS* 11.4sec
1952	S. (Strickland) de la Hunty *AUS* 10.9sec	M. Golubnichaya *URS* 11.1sec	M. Sander *GER* 11.1sec
1956	S. (Strickland) de la Hunty *AUS* 10.7sec	G. (Köhler) Birkemeyer *GER* 10.9sec	N. Thrower *AUS* 11.0sec
1960	I. Press *URS* 10.8sec	C. Quinton *GBR* 10.9sec	G. (Köhler) Birkemeyer *GER* 11.0sec
1964	K. Balzer *GER* 10.5sec	T. Ciepla *POL* 10.5sec	P. Kilborn *AUS* 10.5sec
1968	M. Caird *AUS* 10.3sec	P. Kilborn *AUS* 10.4sec	C. Cheng *ROC* 10.4sec

In 1972 this event was changed to 100 Metres Hurdles.

100 Metres Hurdles

Not held before 1972.

	Gold	Silver	Bronze
1972	A. Ehrhardt *GDR* 12.59sec	V. Bufanu *ROM* 12.84sec	K. Balzer *GDR* 12.90sec
1976	J. Schaller *GDR* 12.77sec	T. Anisimova *URS* 12.78sec	N. Lebedeva *URS* 12.80sec

4 x 100 Metres Relay

Not held before 1928.

	Gold	Silver	Bronze
1928	CAN 48.4sec	USA 48.8sec	GER 49.0sec
1932	USA 47.0sec	CAN 47.0sec	GBR 47.6sec
1936	USA 46.9sec	GBR 47.6sec	CAN 47.8sec
1948	HOL 47.5sec	AUS 47.6sec	CAN 47.8sec

	Gold	Silver	Bronze
1952	USA 45.9sec	GER 45.9sec	GBR 46.2sec
1956	AUS 44.5sec	GBR 44.7sec	USA 44.9sec
1960	USA 44.5sec	GER 44.8sec	POL 45.0sec
1964	POL 43.6sec	USA 43.9sec	GBR 44.0sec
1968	USA 42.8sec	CUB 43.3sec	URS 43.4sec
1972	GER 42.81sec	GDR 42.95sec	CUB 43.36sec
1976	GDR 42.55sec	GER 42.59sec	URS 43.09sec

4 x 400 Metres Relay

Not held before 1972.

	Gold	Silver	Bronze
1972	GDR 3min 23.0sec	USA 3min 25.2sec	GER 3min 26.5sec
1976	GDR 3min 19.23sec	USA 3min 22.81sec	URS 3min 24.24sec

1,500 Metres

Not held before 1972.

	Gold	Silver	Bronze
1972	L. Bragina *URS* 4min 01.4sec	G. Hoffmeister *GDR* 4min 02.8sec	P. Cacchi *ITA* 4min 02.9sec
1976	T. Kazankina *URS* 4min 05.48sec	G. Hoffmeister *GDR* 4min 06.22sec	H. Klapezynski *GDR* 4min 06.09sec

Pentathlon

Consists of five events on two consecutive days; 80-metres hurdles (100-metres hurdles after 1968), shot, high jump, on the first day; long jump and 200 metres on the second. Not held before 1964.

	Gold	Silver	Bronze
1964	I. Press *URS* 5,246 pts	M. Rand *GBR* 5,035 pts	G. Bystrova *URS* 4,956 pts
1968	I. Becker *GER* 5,098 pts	L. Prokop *AUT* 4,966 pts	A. T. Kovács *HUN* 4,959 pts
1972	M. Peters *GBR* 4,801 pts	H. Rosendahl *GER* 4,791 pts	B. Pollak *GDR* 4,768 pts
1976	S. Siegl *GDR* 4, 745 pts	C. Laser *GDR* 4,745 pts	B. Pollak *GDR* 4,740 pts

High Jump

Not held before 1928.

	Gold	Silver	Bronze
1928	E. Catherwood *CAN* 1.59m (5ft $2\frac{3}{4}$in)	C. Gisolf *HOL* 1.56m (5ft $1\frac{1}{2}$in)	M. Wiley *USA* 1.56m (5ft $1\frac{1}{2}$in)
1932	J. Shiley *USA* 1.65m (5ft $5\frac{1}{4}$in)	M. Didrikson *USA* 1.65m (5ft $5\frac{1}{4}$in)	E. Dawes *CAN* 1.60m (5ft 3in)
1936	I. Csák *HUN* 1.60m (5ft 3in)	D. Odam *GBR* 1.60m (5ft 3in)	E. Kaun *GER* 1.60m (5ft 3in)
1948	A. Coachman *USA* 1.68m (5ft $6\frac{1}{4}$in)	D. (Odam) Tyler *GBR* 1.68m (5ft $6\frac{1}{4}$in)	M. Ostermeyer *FRA* 1.61m (5ft $3\frac{1}{4}$in)
1952	E. Brand *SAF* 1.67m (5ft $5\frac{3}{4}$in)	S. Lerwill *GBR* 1.65m (5ft $5\frac{1}{4}$in)	A. Chudina *URS* 1.63m (5ft 4in)
1956	M. McDaniel *USA* 1.76m (5ft $9\frac{1}{4}$in)	T. Hopkins *GBR* & M. Pisaryeva *URS* 1.67m (5ft $5\frac{3}{4}$in)	
1960	I. Balaş *ROM* 1.85m (6ft $0\frac{3}{4}$in)	J. Jóźwiakowska *POL* & D. Shirley *GBR* 1.71m (5ft $7\frac{1}{4}$in)	
1964	I. Balaş *ROM* 1.90m (6ft $2\frac{3}{4}$in)	M. Brown *AUS* 1.80m (5ft 11in)	T. Chenchik *URS* 1.78m (5ft 10in)
1968	M. Rezková *TCH* 1.82m (5ft $11\frac{3}{4}$in)	A. Okorokova *URS* 1.80m (5ft $10\frac{3}{4}$in)	V. Kozyr *URS* 1.80m (5ft $10\frac{3}{4}$in)
1972	U. Meyfarth *GER* 1.92m (6ft $3\frac{1}{2}$in)	Y. Blagoyeva *BUL* 1.88m (6ft 2in)	I. Gusenbauer *AUT* 1.88m (6ft 2in)
1976	R. Ackerman *GDR* 1.93m (6ft 4in)	S. Simeoni *ITA* 1.91m (6ft $3\frac{1}{4}$in)	Y. Blagoyeva *BUL* 1.91m (6ft $3\frac{1}{4}$in)

Long Jump

Not held before 1948.

	Gold	Silver	Bronze
1948	O. Gyarmati *HUN* 5.70m (18ft $8\frac{1}{4}$in)	N. S. de Portela *ARG* 5.60m (18ft $4\frac{1}{2}$in)	A. B. Leyman *SWE* 5.58m (18ft $3\frac{3}{4}$in)
1952	Y. Williams *NZL* 6.24m (20ft $5\frac{1}{2}$in)	A. Chudina *URS* 6.14m (20ft $1\frac{3}{4}$in)	S. Cawley *GBR* 5.92m (19ft 5in)
1956	E. Krzesinska *POL* 6.35m (20ft 10in)	W. White *USA* 6.09m (19ft $11\frac{3}{4}$in)	N. (Khnykina) Dvalishvili *URS* 6.07m (19ft 11in)
1960	V. Krepkina *URS* 6.37m (20ft $10\frac{3}{4}$in)	E. Krzesinska *POL* 6.27m (20ft $6\frac{3}{4}$in)	H. Claus *GER* 6.21m (20ft $4\frac{1}{2}$in)
1964	M. Rand *GBR* 6.76m (22ft $2\frac{1}{4}$in)	I. Szewińska Kirszenstein *POL* 6.60m (21ft $7\frac{3}{4}$in)	T. Shchelkanova *URS* 6.42m (21ft $0\frac{3}{4}$in)
1968	V. Viscopoleanu *ROM* 6.82m (22ft $4\frac{1}{2}$in)	S. Sherwood *GBR* 6.68m (21ft 11in)	T. Talysheva *URS* 6.66m (21ft $10\frac{1}{4}$in)
1972	H. Rosendahl *GER* 6.78m (22ft 3in)	D. Yorgova *BUL* 6.77m (22ft $2\frac{1}{2}$in)	E. Suranová *TCH* 6.67m (21ft $10\frac{3}{4}$in)
1976	A. Voigt *GDR* 6.72m (22ft $0\frac{3}{4}$in)	K. McMillan USA 6.66m (21ft $10\frac{1}{8}$in)	L. Alfeeva URS 6.60m (21ft $7\frac{3}{4}$in)

Shot

Weight 4kg (8lb 13oz) from a circle of 2.135m (7ft). Not held before 1948.

	Gold	Silver	Bronze
1948	M. Ostermeyer *FRA* 13.75m (45ft $1\frac{1}{2}$in)	A. Piccinini *ITA* 13.10m (42ft $11\frac{1}{4}$in)	I. Schäffer *AUT* 13.08m (42ft $10\frac{3}{4}$in)
1952	G. Zybina *URS* 15.28m (50ft $1\frac{1}{2}$in)	M. Werner *GER* 14.57m (47ft $9\frac{1}{2}$in)	K. Tochenova *URS* 14.50m (47ft $6\frac{3}{4}$in)
1956	T. Tyshkevich *URS* 16.59m (54ft 5in)	G. Zybina *URS* 16.53m (54ft $2\frac{3}{4}$in)	M. Werner *GER* 15.61m (51ft $2\frac{1}{2}$in)
1960	T. Press *URS* 17.32m (56ft 10in)	J. Lüttge *GER* 16.61m (54ft 6in)	E. Brown *USA* 16.42m (53ft $10\frac{1}{2}$in)
1964	T. Press *URS* 18.14m (59ft 6in)	R. Garisch *GER* 17.61m (57ft $9\frac{1}{4}$in)	G. Zybina *URS* 17.45m (57ft 3in)
1968	M. Gummel *GDR* 19.61m (64ft 4in)	M. Lange *GDR* 18.78m (61ft $7\frac{1}{2}$in)	N. Chizhova *URS* 18.19m (59ft $8\frac{1}{4}$in)
1972	N. Chizhova *URS* 21.03m (69ft 0in)	M. Gummel *GDR* 20.22m (66ft $4\frac{1}{4}$in)	I. Khristova *BUL* 19.35m (63ft 6in)
1976	I. Christova *BUL* 21.16m (69ft $5\frac{1}{8}$in)	N. Chizhova *URS* 20.96m (68ft $9\frac{1}{4}$in)	H. Fibingerova *TCH* 20.67m (67ft $9\frac{3}{4}$in)

Discus

Weight 1kg (2lb 3.274oz) from a circle of 2.50m (8ft $2\frac{1}{2}$in). Not held before 1928.

	Gold	Silver	Bronze
1928	H. Konopacka *POL* 39.62m (129ft $11\frac{3}{4}$)	L. Copeland *USA* 37.08m (121ft $7\frac{7}{8}$in)	R. Svedberg *SWE* 35.92m (117ft $10\frac{1}{4}$in)
1932	L. Copeland *USA* 40.58m (133ft $1\frac{3}{4}$in)	R. Osburn *USA* 40.12m (131ft $7\frac{1}{2}$in)	J. Wajsówna *POL* 38.74m (127ft $1\frac{1}{4}$in)
1936	G. Mauermayer *GER* 47.63m (156ft $3\frac{1}{4}$in)	J. Wajsówna *POL* 46.22m (151ft $7\frac{3}{4}$in)	P. Mollenhauer *GER* 39.80m (130ft $6\frac{7}{8}$in)
1948	M. Ostermeyer *FRA* 41.92m (137ft $6\frac{1}{8}$in)	E. Gentile Cordiale *ITA* 41.17m (135ft $0\frac{7}{8}$in)	J. Mazeas *FRA* 40.47m (132ft $9\frac{1}{2}$in)
1952	N. Romashkova *URS* 51.42m (168ft $8\frac{1}{2}$in)	Y. Bagryantseva *URS* 47.08m (154ft $5\frac{5}{8}$in)	N. Dumbadze *URS* 46.29m (151ft $10\frac{1}{2}$in)
1956	O. Fikotová *TCH* 53.69m (176ft $1\frac{1}{2}$in)	I. Beglyakova *URS* 52.54m (172ft $4\frac{1}{2}$in)	N. (Romashkova) Ponomareva *URS* 52.02m (170ft 8in)
1960	N. (Romashkova) Ponomareva *URS* 55.10m (180ft $9\frac{1}{4}$in)	T. Press *URS* 52.59m (172ft $6\frac{1}{2}$in)	L. Manoliu *ROM* 52.36m (171ft $9\frac{1}{2}$in)
1964	T. Press *URS* 57.27m (187ft $10\frac{1}{2}$in)	I. Lotz *GER* 57.21m (187ft $8\frac{1}{2}$in)	L. Manoliu *ROM* 56.97m (186ft 11in)
1968	L. Manoliu *ROM* 58.28m (191ft $2\frac{1}{2}$in)	L. Westermann *GER* 57.76m (189ft 6in)	J. Kleiber *HUN* 54.90m (180ft $1\frac{1}{2}$in)

	Gold	Silver	Bronze
1972	F. Melnik *URS* 66.62m (218ft 7in)	A. Menis *ROM* 65.06m (213ft 5in)	V. Stoeva *BUL* 64.34m (211ft 1in)
1976	E. Schlaak *GDR* 69.00m (226ft $4\frac{3}{8}$in)	M. Vergova *BUL* 67.30m (220ft $9\frac{5}{8}$in)	G. Hinzmann *GDR* 66.84m (219ft $3\frac{5}{8}$in)

Javelin

Not held before 1932.

	Gold	Silver	Bronze
1932	M. Didrikson *USA* 43.68m (143ft 4in)	E. Braumüller *GER* 43.49m (142ft $8\frac{5}{8}$in)	T. Fleischer *GER* 43.00m (141ft $1\frac{1}{2}$in)
1936	T. Fleischer *GER* 45.18m (148ft $2\frac{3}{4}$in)	L. Krüger *GER* 43.29m (142ft $0\frac{3}{8}$in)	M. Kwasniewska *POL* 41.80m (137ft $1\frac{1}{4}$in)
1948	H. Bauma *AUT* 45.57m (149ft 6in)	K. Parviänen *FIN* 43.79m (143ft $8\frac{1}{8}$in)	L. Carlstedt *DEN* 42.80m (140ft $5\frac{1}{8}$in)
1952	D. Zátopková *TCH* 50.47m (165ft 7in)	A. Chudina *URS* 50.01m (164ft $0\frac{7}{8}$in)	T. Gorchakova *URS* 49.76m (163ft $3\frac{1}{8}$in)
1956	I. Yaunzeme *URS* 53.86m (176ft $8\frac{1}{2}$in)	M. Ahrens *CHI* 50.38m (165ft $3\frac{1}{2}$in)	N. Konyaeva *URS* 50.28m (164ft $11\frac{1}{2}$in)
1960	E. Ozolina *URS* 55.98m (183ft 8in)	D. Zátopková *TCH* 53.78m (176ft $5\frac{1}{4}$in)	B. Kalediene *URS* 53.45m (175ft $4\frac{1}{2}$in)
1964	M. Peneş *ROM* 60.54m (198ft $7\frac{1}{2}$in)	M. Rudas *HUN* 58.27m (191ft 2in)	Y. Gorchakova *URS* 57.06m (187ft $2\frac{1}{2}$in)
1968	A. Németh *HUN* 60.36m (198ft $0\frac{1}{2}$in)	M. Peneş *ROM* 59.92m (196ft 7in)	E. Janko *AUT* 58.04m (190ft 5in)
1972	R. Fuchs *GDR* 63.88m (209ft 7in)	J. Todten *GDR* 62.54m (205ft 2in)	K. Schmidt *USA* 59.94m (196ft 8in)
1976	R. Fuchs *GDR* 65.94m (216ft $4\frac{1}{8}$in)	M. Becker *GER* 64.70m (212ft $3\frac{1}{4}$in)	K. Schmidt *USA* 63.96m (209ft $10\frac{1}{8}$in)

Basketball (Men)

Not held as a competition before 1936.

	Gold	Silver	Bronze
1936	USA	CAN	MEX
1948	USA	FRA	BRA
1952	USA	URS	URU
1956	USA	URS	URU
1960	USA	URS	BRA
1964	USA	URS	BRA
1968	USA	YUG	URS
1972	URS	USA	CUB
1976	USA	YUG	URS

Basketball (Women)

Not held as a competition before 1976.

	Gold	Silver	Bronze
1976	URS	USA	BUL

Boxing

From 1952 both losing semi-finalists have been awarded bronze medals.

Light Flyweight

Not held before 1968. Weight limit 48kg (105lb 13oz).

	Gold	Silver	Bronze
1968	F. Rodríguez *VEN*	Y. J. Jee *KOR*	H. Marbley *USA* & H. Skrzypczak *POL*
1972	G. Gedo *HUN*	U. G. Kim *PRK*	R. Evans *GBR* & E. Rodríguez *ESP*
1976	J. Hernandez *CUB*	B. U. Li *PRK*	P. Pooltarat *THA* & O. Maldonado *PUR*

Flyweight

Not held before 1904. In 1904 weight limit 47.6kg (105lb); 1920–36 50.8kg (112lb); from 1948 51kg (112lb 6oz).

	Gold	Silver	Bronze
1904	G. Finnegan *USA*	M. Burke *USA*	
1908–1912	*Not held*		
1920	F. De Genaro *USA*	A. Petersen *DEN*	W. Cuthbertson *GBR*
1924	F. LaBarba *USA*	J. Mackenzie *GBR*	R. Fee *USA*
1928	A. Kocsis *HUN*	A. Appel *FRA*	C. Cavagnoli *ITA*
1932	I. Énekes *HUN*	F. Cabañas *MEX*	L. Salica *USA*
1936	W. Kaiser *GER*	G. Matta *ITA*	L. Laurie *USA*
1948	P. Perez *ARG*	S. Bandinelli *ITA*	S. A. Han *KOR*
1952	N. Brooks *USA*	E. Basel *GER*	A. Bulakov *URS* & W. Toweel *SAF*
1956	T. Spinks *GBR*	M. Dobrescu *ROM*	J. Caldwell *IRL* & R. Libeer *FRA*
1960	G. Török *HUN*	S. Sivko *URS*	K. Tanabe *JPN* & A. Elgvindi *UAR*
1964	F. Atzori *ITA*	A. Olech *POL*	S. Sorokin *URS* & R. Carmody *USA*
1968	R. Delgado *MEX*	A. Olech *POL*	S. de Oliveira *BRA* & L. Rwabwogo *UGA*
1972	G. Kostadinov *BUL*	L. Rwabwogo *UGA*	I. Błażyński *POL* & D. Rodríguez *CUB*
1976	L. Randolph *USA*	R. Duvalon *CUB*	D. Torosyan *URS* L. Błażyński *POL*

Bantamweight

Not held before 1904. In 1904 weight limit 52.1kg (115lb); 1908 52.6kg (116lb); 1920 53.6kg (118lb 2oz); 1924–36 53.5kg (118lb); from 1948 54kg (119lb).

	Gold	Silver	Bronze
1904	O. L. Kirk *USA*	G. Finnegan *USA*	
1908	H. Thomas *GBR*	J. Condon *GBR*	W. Webb *GBR*
1912	*Not held*		
1920	C. Walker *SAF*	C. J. Graham *CAN*	J. McKenzie *GBR*
1924	W. Smith *SAF*	S. Tripoli *USA*	J. Ces *FRA*
1928	V. Tamagnini *ITA*	J. Daley *USA*	H. Isaacs *SAF*
1932	H. Gwynne *CAN*	H. Ziglarski *GER*	J. Villanueva *PHI*
1936	U. Sergo *ITA*	J. Wilson *USA*	F. Ortiz *MEX*
1948	T. Csik *HUN*	G. Zuddas *ITA*	J. Venegas *PUR*
1952	P. Hämäläinen *FIN*	J. McNally *IRL*	G. Garbuzov *URS* & J. H. Kang *KOR*
1956	W. Behrendt *GER*	S. C. Song *KOR*	F. Gilroy *IRL* & C. Barrientos *CHI*
1960	O. Grigoriev *URS*	P. Zamparini *ITA*	O. Taylor *AUS* & B. Bendig *POL*
1964	T. Sakurai *JPN*	S. C. Chung *KOR*	B. J. Fabila *MEX* & W. Rodríguez *URU*
1968	V. Sokolov *URS*	E. Mukwanga *UGA*	E. Morioka *JPN* & K. C. Chang *KOR*
1972	O. Martínez *CUB*	A. Zamora *MEX*	G. Turpin *GBR* & R. Carreras *USA*
1976	Y. J. Gu *PRK*	C. Mooney *USA*	P. Cowdell *GBR* & V. Rybakov *URS*

Featherweight

Not held before 1904. In 1904 weight limit 56.7kg (125lb); 1908–36 57.15kg (126lb); 1948 58kg (127lb 14oz); from 1952 57kg (125lb $10\frac{1}{2}$oz).

	Gold	Silver	Bronze
1904	O. L. Kirk *USA*	F. Haller *USA*	
1908	R. Gunn *GBR*	C. W. Morris *GBR*	H. Roddin *GBR*
1912	*Not held*		
1920	P. Fritsch *FRA*	J. Gachet *FRA*	E. Garzena *ITA*
1924	J. Fields *USA*	J. Salas *USA*	P. Quartucci *ARG*
1928	L. van Klaveren *HOL*	V. Peralta *ARG*	H. Devine *USA*
1932	C. Robledo *ARG*	J. Schleinkofer *GER*	C. Carlsson *SWE*

	Gold	Silver	Bronze
1936	O. Casanovas *ARG*	C. Catterall *SAF*	J. Miner *GER*
1948	E. Formenti *ITA*	D. Shepherd *SAF*	A. Antkiewicz *POL*
1952	J. Zachara *TCH*	S. Caprari *ITA*	L. Leisching *SAF* & J. Ventaja *FRA*
1956	V. Safronov *URS*	T. Nicholls *GBR*	H. Niedźwiedzki *POL* & P. Hämäläinen *FIN*
1960	F. Musso *ITA*	J. Adamski *POL*	W. Meyers *SAF* & J. Limmonen *FIN*
1964	S. Stepashkin *URS*	A. Villaneuva *PHI*	C. Brown *USA* & H. Schulz *GER*
1968	A. Roldan *MEX*	A. Robinson *USA*	P. Waruinge *KEN* & I. Mikhailov *BUL*
1972	B. Kusnetsov *URS*	P. Waruinge *KEN*	C. Rojas *COL* & A. Botos *HUN*
1976	A. Herrera *CUB*	R. Nowakowski GDR	J. Paredes *MEX* & L. Kosedowski *POL*

Lightweight

Not held before 1904. In 1904 weight limit 61.2kg (135lb); 1908 63.5kg (140lb); 1920–36 61.24kg (135lb); 1948 62kg (136lb 11oz); from 1952 60kg (132lb 4½oz).

	Gold	Silver	Bronze
1904	H. Spanger *USA*	J. Eagan *USA*	R. Van Horn *USA*
1908	F. Grace *GBR*	F. Spiller *GBR*	H. H. Johnson *GBR*
1912	*Not held*		
1920	S. Mosberg *USA*	G. Johanssen *DEN*	C. Newton *CAN*
1924	H. Nielsen *DEN*	A. Copello *ARG*	F. Boylstein *USA*
1928	C. Orlandi *ITA*	S. Halaiko *USA*	G. Berggren *SWE*
1932	L. Stevens *SAF*	T. Ahlqvist *SWE*	N. Bor *USA*
1936	I. Harangi *HUN*	N. Stepulov *EST*	E. Ågren *SWE*
1948	G. Dreyer *SAF*	J. Vissers *BEL*	S. Wad *DEN*
1952	A. Bolognesi *ITA*	A. Antkiewicz *POL*	G. Fiat *ROM* & E. Pakkanen *FIN*
1956	R. McTaggart *GBR*	H. Kurschat *GER*	A. Byrne *IRL* & A. Lagetko *URS*
1960	K. Paździor *POL*	S. Lopopolo *ITA*	R. McTaggart *GBR* & A. Laudonio *ARG*
1964	J. Grudzień *POL*	V. Baranikov *URS*	R. Harris *USA* & J. McCourt *IRL*
1968	R. Harris *USA*	J. Grudzień *POL*	C. Cutov *ROM* & Z. Vujin *YUG*
1972	J. Szczepanski *POL*	L. Orban *HUN*	S. Mbugua *KEN* & A. Pérez *COL*
1976	H. Davis *USA*	S. Cutov *ROM*	A. Rusevski *YUG* & V. Solomin *URS*

Light Welterweight

Not held before 1952. Weight limit 63.5kg (140lb).

	Gold	Silver	Bronze
1952	C. Adkins *USA*	V. Mednov *URS*	E. Mallenius *FIN* & B. Visintin *ITA*
1956	V. Yengibaryan *URS*	F. Nenci *ITA*	H. Loubscher *SAF* & C. Dumitrescu *ROM*
1960	B. Nemeček *TCH*	C. Quartey *GHA*	Q. Daniels *USA* & M. Kasprzyk *POL*
1964	J. Kulej *POL*	Y. Frolov *URS*	E. Blay *GHA* & H. Galhia *TUN*
1968	J. Kulej *POL*	E. Regueiferos *CUB*	A. Nilsson *FIN* & J. Wallington *USA*
1972	R. Seales *USA*	A. Anghelov *BUL*	Z. Vujin *YUG* & I. Daborg *NIG*
1976	R. Leonard *USA*	A. Aldama *CUB*	V. Kolev *BUL* & K. Szczerba *POL*

Welterweight

Not held before 1904. In 1904 weight limit 65.27kg (144lb); 1920–36 66.68kg (147lb); from 1968 67kg (147lb 11⅓oz). In 1924 this weight category was called 'Light Middleweight'.

	Gold	Silver	Bronze
1904	A. Young *USA*	H. Spanger *USA*	J. Lydon *USA*
1908–1912	*Not held*		
1920	J. Schneider *CAN*	A. Ireland *GBR*	F. Colberg *USA*
1924	J. Delarge *BEL*	H. Mendez *ARG*	D. Lewis *CAN*
1928	E. Morgan *NZL*	R. Landini *ARG*	R. Smillie *CAN*
1932	E. Flynn *USA*	E. Campe *GER*	B. Ahlberg *FIN*
1936	S. Suvio *FIN*	M. Murach *GER*	G. Petersen *DEN*
1948	J. Torma *TCH*	H. Herring *USA*	A. d'Ottavio *ITA*
1952	Z. Chychla *POL*	S. Shcherbakov *URS*	V. Jørgensen *DEN* & G. Heidemann *GER*
1956	N. Linca *ROM*	F. Tiedt *IRL*	K. Hogarth *AUS* & N. Gargano *GBR*
1960	G. Benvenuti *ITA*	Y. Radonyak *URS*	L. Drogosz *POL* & James Lloyd *GBR*
1964	M. Kasprzyk *POL*	R. Tamulis *URS*	P. Purhonen *FIN* & S. Bertini *ITA*
1968	M. Wolke *GDR*	J. Bessala *CMR*	V. Masalimov *URS* & M. Guilloti González *ARG*
1972	E. Correa *CUB*	J. Kajdi *HUN*	D. Murunga *KEN* & J. Valdez *USA*
1976	J. Bachfield *GDR*	P. J. Gamarro *VEN*	R. Skricek *GER* & V. Zilberman *ROM*

Light Middleweight

Not held before 1952. Weight limit 71kg (156lb 8½oz).

	Gold	Silver	Bronze
1952	L. Papp *HUN*	T. van Schalkwyk *SAF*	B. Tishin *URS* & E. Herrera *ARG*
1956	L. Papp *HUN*	J. Torres *USA*	J. McCormack *GBR* & Z. Pietrzykowski *POL*
1960	W. McClure *USA*	C. Bossi *ITA*	B. Lagutin *URS* & W. Fisher *GBR*
1964	B. Lagutin *URS*	J. Gonzales *FRA*	N. Maiyegun *NGR* & J. Grzesiak *POL*
1968	B. Lagutin *URS*	R. Garbey *CUB*	J. Baldwin *USA* & G. Meier *GER*
1972	D. Kottysch *GER*	W. Rudkowski *POL*	A. Minter *GBR* & P. Tiepold *GDR*
1976	J. Rybicki *POL*	T. Kacar *YUG*	R. Garbey *CUB* & V. Savchenko *URS*

Middleweight

Not held before 1904. In 1904–8 weight limit 71.67kg (158lb); 1920–36 72.57kg (160lb); 1948 73kg (169lb 15oz); from 1952 75kg (165lb 5¾oz).

	Gold	Silver	Bronze
1904	C. Mayer *USA*	B. Spradley *USA*	
1908	J. Douglas *GBR*	R. Baker *AUS*	W. Philo *GBR*
1912	*Not held*		
1920	H. Mallin *GBR*	G. A. Prud'homme *CAN*	M. H. Herscovitch *CAN*
1924	H. Mallin *GBR*	J. Elliott *GBR*	J. Beecken *BEL*
1928	P. Toscani *ITA*	J. Heřmánek *TCH*	L. Steyaert *BEL*
1932	C. Barth *USA*	A. Azar *ARG*	E. Pierce *SAF*
1936	J. Despeaux *FRA*	H. Tiller *NOR*	R. Villareal *ARG*
1948	L. Papp *HUN*	J. Wright *GBR*	I. Fontana *ITA*
1952	F. Patterson *USA*	V. Tita *ROM*	B. Nikolov *BUL* & K. Sjölin *SWE*
1956	G. Shatkov *URS*	R. Tapia *CHI*	G. Chapron *FRA* & V. Zalazar *ARG*
1960	E. Crook *USA*	T. Walasek *POL*	I. Monea *ROM* & Y. Feofanov *URS*
1964	V. Popenchenko *URS*	E. Schulz *GER*	F. Valla *ITA* & T. Walasek *POL*
1968	C. Finnegan *GBR*	A. Kiselyov *URS*	A. Zaragoza *MEX* & A. Jones *USA*
1972	V. Lemechev *URS*	R. Virtanen *FIN*	P. Amartey *GHA* & M. Johnson *USA*
1976	M. Spinks *USA*	R. Riskiev *URS*	A. Nastac *ROM* & L. Martinez *CUB*

Light Heavyweight

Not held before 1920. Weight limit 1920–36 79.38kg (175lb); 1948 80kg (176lb 6oz); from 1952 81kg (178lb 9oz).

	Gold	Silver	Bronze
1920	E. Eagan *USA*	S. Sørsdal *NOR*	H. Franks *GBR*
1924	H. Mitchell *GBR*	T. Petersen *DEN*	S. Sørsdal *NOR*
1928	V. Avendaño *ARG*	E. Pistulla *GER*	K. L. Miljon *HOL*
1932	D. Carstens *SAF*	G. Rossi *ITA*	P. Jørgensen *DEN*
1936	R. Michelot *FRA*	R. Vogt *GER*	F. Risiglione *ARG*
1948	G. Hunter *SAF*	D. Scott *GBR*	M. Cia *ARG*
1952	N. Lee *USA*	A. Pacenza *ARG*	A. Perov *URS* & H. Siljander *FIN*
1956	J. F. Boyd *USA*	G. Negrea *ROM*	C. Lucas *CHI* & R. Murauskas *URS*
1960	C. Clay *USA*	Z. Pietrzykowski *POL*	A. Madigan *AUS* & G. Saraudi *ITA*
1964	C. Pinto *ITA*	A. Kiselyov *URS*	A. Nicolov *BUL* & Z. Pietrzykowski *POL*
1968	D. Poznyak *URS*	I. Monea *ROM*	G. Stankov *BUL* & S. Dragan *POL*
1972	M. Parlov *YUG*	G. Carrillo *CUB*	I. Ikhouria *NGR* & J. Gortat *POL*
1976	L. Spinks *USA*	S. Ssoria *CUB*	C. Dafinioiu *ROM* & J. Gortat *POL*

Heavyweight

Not held before 1904. In 1904–8 weight limit over 71.67kg (158lb); 1920–36 79.38kg (175lb); 1948 80kg (176lb 6oz); from 1952 81kg (178lb 9oz).

	Gold	Silver	Bronze
1904	S. Berger *USA*	C. Mayer *USA*	
1908	A. L. Oldham *GBR*	S. C. H. Evans *GBR*	F. Parks *GBR*
1912	*Not held*		
1920	R. Rawson *GBR*	S. Petersen *DEN*	X. Eluère *FRA*
1924	O. von Porat *NOR*	S. Petersen *DEN*	A. Porzio *ARG*
1928	A. R. Jurado *ARG*	N. Ramm *SWE*	M. J. Michaelsen *DEN*
1932	S. Lovell *ARG*	L. Rovati *ITA*	F. Feary *USA*
1936	H. Runge *GER*	G. Lovell *ARG*	E. Nilsen *NOR*
1948	R. Iglesias *ARG*	G. Nilsson *SWE*	J. Arthur *SAF*
1952	H. E. Sanders *USA*	*Not awarded*	A. Nieman *SAF* & I. Koski *FIN*
1956	T. P. Rademacher *USA*	L. Mukhin *URS*	D. Bekker *SAF* & G. Bozzano *ITA*
1960	F. de Piccoli *ITA*	D. Bekker *SAF*	J. Nemec *TCH* & G. Siegmund *GER*
1964	J. Frazier *USA*	H. Huber *GER*	G. Ros *ITA* & V. Yemelyanov *URS*
1968	G. Foreman *USA*	I. Chepulis *URS*	G. Bambini *ITA* & J. Rocha *MEX*
1972	T. Stevenson *CUB*	I. Alexe *ROM*	P. Hussing *GER* & H. Thomsen *SWE*
1976	T. Stevenson *CUB*	M. Simon *ROM*	J. Tate *USA* & C. Hill *BER*

Canoeing (Men)

Canadian Singles

Course 1,000m (1,094yd). Not held before 1936.

	Gold	Silver	Bronze
1936	F. Amyot *CAN* 5min 32.1sec	B. Karlik *TCH* 5min 36.9sec	E. Koschik *GER* 5min 39.0sec
1948	J. Holeček *TCH* 5min 42.0sec	D. Bennett *CAN* 5min 53.3sec	R. Boutigny *FRA* 5min 55.9sec
1952	J. Holeček *TCH* 4min 56.3sec	J. Parti *HUN* 5min 03.6sec	O. Ojanperä *FIN* 5min 08.5sec
1956	L. Rotman *ROM* 5min 05.3sec	I. Hernek *HUN* 5min 06.2sec	G. Bukharin *URS* 5min 12.7sec
1960	J. Parti *HUN* 4min 33.93sec	A. Silayev *URS* 4min 34.41sec	L. Rotman *ROM* 4min 35.87sec
1964	J. Eschert *GER* 4min 35.14sec	A. Igorov *ROM* 4min 37.89sec	Y. Penyaev *URS* 4min 38.31sec
1968	T. Tatai *HUN* 4min 36.14sec	D. Lewe *GER* 4min 38.31sec	V. Galkov *URS* 4min 40.42sec
1972	I. Patzaichin *ROM* 4min 08.94sec	T. Wichmann *HUN* 4min 12.42sec	D. Lewe *GER* 4min 13.63sec
1976	M. Ljubek *YUG* 4min 09.51sec	V. Urchenko *URS* 4min 12.57sec	T. Wichmann *HUN* 4min 14.11sec

Canadian Pairs

Course 1,000m (1,094yd). Not held before 1936.

	Gold	Silver	Bronze
1936	TCH 4min 50.1sec	AUT 4min 53.8sec	CAN 4min 56.7sec
1948	TCH 5min 07.1sec	USA 5min 08.2sec	FRA 5min 15.2sec
1952	DEN 4min 38.3sec	TCH 4min 42.9sec	GER 4min 48.3sec
1956	ROM 4min 47.4sec	URS 4min 48.6sec	HUN 4min 54.3sec
1960	URS 4min 17.94sec	ITA 4min 20.77sec	HUN 4min 20.89sec
1964	URS 4min 04.64sec	FRA 4min 06.52sec	DEN 4min 07.48sec
1968	ROM 4min 07.18sec	HUN 4min 08.77sec	URS 4min 11.30sec
1972	URS 3min 52.60sec	ROM 3min 52.63sec	BUL 3min 58.10sec
1976	URS 3min 52.76sec	ROM 3min 54.28sec	HUN 3min 55.66sec

Kayak Singles

Course 1,000m (1,094yd). Not held before 1936.

	Gold	Silver	Bronze
1936	G. Hradetzky *AUT* 4min 22.9sec	H. Cämmerer *GER* 4min 25.6sec	J. Kraaier *HOL* 4min 35.1sec
1948	G. Fredriksson *SWE* 4min 33.2sec	J. F. Kobberup Andersen *DEN* 4min 39.9sec	H. Eberhardt *FRA* 4min 41.4sec
1952	G. Fredriksson *SWE* 4min 07.9sec	T. Strömberg *FIN* 4min 09.7sec	L. Gantois *FRA* 4min 20.1sec
1956	G. Fredriksson *SWE* 4min 12.8sec	I. Pisarev *URS* 4min 15.3sec	L. Kiss *HUN* 4min 16.2sec
1960	E. Hansen *DEN* 3min 53.0sec	I. Szöllösi *HUN* 3min 54.02sec	G. Fredriksson *SWE* 3min 55.89sec
1964	R. Peterson *SWE* 3min 57.13sec	M. Hesz *HUN* 3min 57.28sec	A. Vernescu *ROM* 4min 00.77sec
1968	M. Hesz *HUN* 4min 02.63sec	A. Shaparenko *URS* 4min 03.58sec	E. Hansen *DEN* 4min 04.39sec
1972	A. Shaparenko *URS* 3min 48.06sec	R. Peterson *SWE* 3min 48.35sec	G. Csapo *HUN* 3min 49.38sec
1976	R. Helm *GDR* 3min 48.20sec	G. Csapo *HUN* 3min 48.84sec	V. Diba *ROM* 3min 49.65sec

Kayak Pairs

Course 1,000m (1,094yd). Not held before 1936.

	Gold	Silver	Bronze
1936	AUT 4min 03.8sec	GER 4min 08.9sec	HOL 4min 12.2sec
1948	SWE 4min 07.3sec	DEN 4min 07.5sec	FIN 4min 08.7sec
1952	FIN 3min 51.1sec	SWE 3min 51.1sec	AUT 3min 51.4sec
1956	GER 3min 49.6sec	URS 3min 51.4sec	AUT 3min 55.8sec
1960	SWE 3min 34.73sec	HUN 3min 34.91sec	POL 3min 37.34sec
1964	SWE 3min 38.54sec	HOL 3min 39.30sec	GER 3min 40.69sec
1968	URS 3min 37.54sec	HUN 3min 38.44sec	AUT 3min 40.71sec
1972	URS 3min 31.23sec	HUN 3min 32.00sec	POL 3min 33.83sec
1976	URS 3min 29.01sec	GDR 3min 29.33sec	HUN 3min 30.36sec

Kayak Fours

Course 1,000m (1,094yd). Not held before 1964.

	Gold	Silver	Bronze
1964	URS 3min 14.67sec	GER 3min 15.39sec	ROM 3min 15.51sec
1968	NOR 3min 14.38sec	ROM 3min 14.81sec	HUN 3min 15.10sec
1972	URS 3min 14.02sec	ROM 3min 15.07sec	NOR 3min 15.27sec
1976	URS 3min 08.69sec	ESP 3min 08.95sec	GDR 3min 10.76sec

Slalom – Canadian Singles

Not held before 1972.

	Gold	Silver	Bronze
1972	R. Eiben *GDR* 315.84 pts	R. Kauder *GER* 327.89 pts	J. McEwan *USA* 335.95 pts
1976	*Not held.*		

Slalom - Canadian Pairs

Not held before 1972.

	Gold	Silver	Bronze
1972	GDR 310.68 pts	GER 311.90 pts	FRA 315.10 pts
1976	*Not held.*		

Slalom - Kayak Singles

Not held before 1972.

	Gold	Silver	Bronze
1972	S. Horn *GDR* 268.56 pts	N. Sattler *AUT* 270.76 pts	H. Gimpel *GDR* 277.95 pts
1976	*Not held.*		

Canoeing (Women)

Kayak Singles

Course 500m (547yd). Not held before 1948.

	Gold	Silver	Bronze
1948	K. Hoff *DEN* 2min 31.9sec	A. van der Anker-Doedans *HOL* 2min 32.8sec	F. Schwingl *AUT* 2min 32.9sec
1952	S. Saimo *FIN* 2min 18.4sec	G. Liebhart *AUT* 2min 18.8sec	N. Savina *URS* 2min 21.6sec
1956	E. Dementieva *URS* 2min 18.9sec	T. Zenz *GER* 2min 19.6sec	T. Søby *DEN* 2min 22.3sec
1960	A. Seredina *URS* 2min 08.08sec	T. Zenz *GER* 2min 08.22sec	D. Pilecka (Walkowiakówna) *POL* 2min 10.46sec
1964	L. Khvedosyuk *URS* 2min 12.87sec	H. Lauer *ROM* 2min 15.35sec	M. Jones *USA* 2min 15.68sec
1968	L. Pinaeva *URS* 2min 11.09sec	R. Breuer *GER* 2min 12.71sec	V. Dumitru *ROM* 2min 13.22sec
1972	Y. Ryabchinskaya *URS* 2min 03.17sec	M. Jaapies *HOL* 2min 04.03sec	A. Pfeffer *HUN* 2min 05.50sec
1976	C. Zirzow *GDR* 2min 01.05sec	T. Korshunova *URS* 2min 03.07sec	K. Rajnai *HUN* 2min 05.01sec

Kayak Pairs

Course 500m (547yd). Not held before 1960.

	Gold	Silver	Bronze
1960	URS 1min 54.76sec	GER 1min 56.66sec	HUN 1min 58.22sec
1964	GER 1min 56.95sec	USA 1min 59.16sec	ROM 2min 00.25sec
1968	GER 1min 56.44sec	HUN 1min 58.60sec	URS 1min 58.61sec
1972	URS 1min 53.50sec	GDR 1min 54.30sec	ROM 1min 55.01sec
1976	URS 1min 51.15sec	HUN 1min 51.69sec	GDR 1min 51.81sec

Slalom - Kayak Singles

Not held before 1972.

	Gold	Silver	Bronze
1972	A. Bahmann *GDR* 364.50 pts	G. Grothaus *GER* 398.15 pts	M. Wunderlich *GER* 400.50 pts
1976	*Not held.*		

Cycling

1,000 Metres Sprint

In 1896–1900 the distance was 2,000m. From 1924 only times over the last 200m have been recorded.

	Gold	Silver	Bronze
1896	P. Masson *FRA* 4min 56.0sec	S. Nikolopoulos *GRE* 5min 00.2sec	L. Flameng *FRA* nda
1900	G. Taillandier *FRA* 2min 52.0sec	F. Sanz *FRA* nda	Lake *USA* nda
1904	*Not held.*		
1908	*Final declared void because time limit was exceeded.*		
1912	*Not held*		
1920	M. Peeters *HOL* 1min 38.3sec	H. T. Johnson *GBR* nda	H. Ryan *GBR* nda
1924	L. Michard *FRA* 12.8sec	J. Meijer *HOL*	J. Cugnot *FRA*
1928	R. Beaufrand *FRA* 13.2sec	A. Mazairac *HOL*	W. Falck-Hansen *DEN*
1932	J. van Egmond *HOL* 12.6sec	L. Chaillot *FRA*	B. Pellizzari *ITA*
1936	T. Merkens *GER* 11.8sec	A. van Vliet *HOL*	L. Chaillot *FRA*
1948	M. Ghella *ITA* 12.0sec	R. Harris *GBR*	A. Schandorff *DEN*
1952	E. Sacchi *ITA* 12.0sec	L. Cox *AUS*	W. Potzernheim *GER*
1956	M. Rousseau *FRA* 11.4sec	G. Pesenti *ITA*	R. Ploog *AUS*
1960	S. Gaiardoni *ITA* 11.1sec	L. Sterckx *BEL*	V. Gasparella *ITA*
1964	G. Pettenella *ITA* 13.69sec	S. Bianchetto *ITA*	D. Morelon *FRA*
1968	D. Morelon *FRA* 10.68sec	G. Turrini *ITA*	P. Trentin *FRA*
1972	D. Morelon *FRA* 11.69sec	J. M. Nicholson *AUS*	O. Pkhakadze *URS*
1976	A. Tkak *TCH*	D. Morelon *FRA*	H. J. Geschke *GDR*

1,000 Metres Time Trial

Not held before 1928.

	Gold	Silver	Bronze
1928	W. Falck-Hansen *DEN* 1min 14.4sec	G. D. H. Bosch van Drakestein *HOL* 1min 15.2sec	E. Gray *AUS* 1min 15.6sec
1932	E. Gray *AUS* 1min 13.0sec	J. van Egmond *HOL* 1min 13.3sec	G. Rampelberg *FRA* 1min 13.4sec
1936	A. van Vliet *HOL* 1min 12.0sec	P. Georget *FRA* 1min 12.8sec	R. Karsch *GER* 1min 13.2sec
1948	J. Dupont *FRA* 1min 13.5sec	P. Nihant *BEL* 1min 14.5sec	T. Godwin *GBR* 1min 15.0sec
1952	R. Mockridge *AUS* 1min 11.1sec	M. Morettini *ITA* 1min 12.7sec	R. Robinson *SAF* 1min 13.0sec
1956	L. Faggin *ITA* 1min 09.8sec	L. Fouček *TCH* 1min 11.4sec	A. Swift *SAF* 1min 11.6sec
1960	S. Gaiardoni *ITA* 1min 07.27sec	D. Gieseler *GER* 1min 08.75sec	R. Vargashkin *URS* 1min 08.86sec
1964	P. Sercu *BEL* 1min 09.59sec	G. Pettenella *ITA* 1min 10.09sec	P. Trentin *FRA* 1min 10.42sec
1968	P. Trentin *FRA* 1min 03.91sec	N. C. Fredborg *DEN* 1min 04.61sec	J. Kierzkowski *POL* 1min 04.63sec
1972	N. C. Fredborg *DEN* 1min 06.44sec	D. Clark *AUS* 1min 06.87sec	J. Schütze *GDR* 1min 07.02sec
1976	K. J. Grunke *GDR* 1min 05.927sec	M. Vaarten *BEL* 1min 07.516sec	N. C. Fredborg *DEN* 1min 07.617sec

4,000 Metres Pursuit (Individual)

Not held before 1964.

	Gold	Silver	Bronze
1964	J. Daler *TCH* 5min 04.75sec	G. Ursi *ITA* 5min 05.96sec	P. Isaksson *DEN* 5min 01.90sec
1968	D. Rebillard *FRA* 4min 41.71sec	M. F. Jensen *DEN* 4min 42.43sec	X. Kurmann *SUI* 4min 39.42sec
1972	K. Knudsen *NOR* 4min 45.74sec	X. Kurmann *SUI* 4min 51.96sec	H. Lutz *GER* 4min 50.80sec
1976	G. Braun *GER* 4min 47.61sec	H. Ponsteen *HOL* 4min 49.72sec	T. Huschke *GDR* 4min 52.71sec

4,000 Metres Pursuit (Team)

Not held before 1920.

	Gold	Silver	Bronze
1920	ITA 5min 20.0sec	GBR nda	SAF nda
1924	ITA 5min 15.0sec	POL nda	BEL nda
1928	ITA 5min 01.8sec	HOL 5min 06.2sec	GBR 5min 02.4sec
1932	ITA 4min 53.0sec	FRA 4min 55.7sec	GBR 4min 56.0sec
1936	FRA 4min 45.0sec	ITA 4min 51.0sec	GBR 4min 53.6sec
1948	FRA 4min 57.8sec	ITA 5min 36.7sec	GBR 5min 55.8sec
1952	ITA 4min 46.1sec	SAF 4min 53.6sec	GBR 4min 51.5sec
1956	ITA 4min 37.4sec	FRA 4min 39.4sec	GBR 4min 42.2sec
1960	ITA 4min 30.90sec	GER 4min 35.78sec	URS 4min 34.05sec
1964	GER 4min 35.67sec	ITA 4min 35.74sec	HOL 4min 38.99sec
1968	DEN 4min 22.44sec	GER 4min 18.92sec	ITA 4min 18.35sec
1972	GER 4min 22.14sec	GDR 4min 25.25sec	GBR 4min 23.78sec
1976	GER 4min 21.06sec	URS 4min 27.15sec	GBR 4min 22.41sec

2,000 Metres Tandem

Not held before 1908. From 1928 only times over the last 200m have been recorded.

	Gold	Silver	Bronze
1908	FRA 3min 07.6sec	GBR nda	GBR nda
1912	*Not held.*		
1920	GBR 2min 49.4sec	SAF nda	HOL nda
1924	FRA 2min 40.0sec	DEN nda	HOL nda
1928	HOL 11.8sec	GBR	GER
1932	FRA 12.0sec	GBR	DEN
1936	GER 11.8sec	HOL	FRA
1948	ITA 11.3sec	GBR	FRA
1952	AUS 11.0sec	SAF	ITA
1956	AUS 10.8sec	TCH	ITA
1960	ITA 10.7sec	GER	URS
1964	ITA 10.75sec	URS	GER
1968	FRA 9.83sec	HOL	BEL
1972	URS 10.52sec	GDR	POL
1976	*Not held.*		

Road Race (Individual)

In 1896 the distance was 87km (54 miles); in 1912 320km (199 miles); in 1920 175km (109 miles); in 1924 188km (117 miles); in 1928 169km (105 miles); in 1932 and 1936 100km (62 miles); in 1948 199.6km (124 miles); in 1952 190.4km (118 miles); in 1956 187.7km (117 miles); in 1960 175.4km (109 miles); in 1964 194.8km (121 miles); in 1968 196.2km (122 miles); in 1972 182.4km (113 miles).

	Gold	Silver	Bronze
1896	A. Konstantinidis *GRE* 3hr 22min 31.0sec	A. Goedrich *GER* 3hr 42min 18.0sec	F. Battel *GBR* nda
1900–1908	*Not held.*		
1912	R. Lewis *SAF* 10hr 42min 39.0sec	F. Grubb *GBR* 10hr 51min 24.2sec	C. Schutte *USA* 10hr 52min 38.8sec
1920	H. Stenqvist *SWE* 4hr 40min 01.8sec	H. J. Kaltenbrun *SAF* 4hr 41min 26.6sec	F. Canteloupe *FRA* 4hr 42min 54.4sec
1924	A. Blanchonnet *FRA* 6hr 20min 48.0sec	H. Hoevenaers *BEL* 6hr 30min 27.0sec	R. Hamel *FRA* 6hr 30min 51.6sec
1928	H. Hansen *DEN* 4hr 47min 18.0sec	F. W. Southall *GBR* 4hr 55min 06.0sec	G. Carlsson *SWE* 5hr 00min 17.0sec
1932	A. Pavesi *ITA* 2hr 28min 05.6sec	G. Segato *ITA* 2hr 29min 21.4sec	B. Britz *SWE* 2hr 29min 45.2sec
1936	R. Charpentier *FRA* 2hr 33min 05.0sec	G. Lapébie *FRA* 2hr 33min 05.2sec	E. Nievergelt *SUI* 2hr 33min 05.8sec
1948	J. Beyaert *FRA* 5hr 18min 12.6sec	G. P. Voorting *HOL* 5hr 18min 16.2sec	L. Wouters *BEL* 5hr 18min 16.2sec
1952	A. Noyelle *BEL* 5hr 06min 03.4sec	R. Grondelaers *BEL* 5hr 06min 51.2sec	E. Ziegler *GER* 5hr 07min 47.5sec
1956	E. Baldini *ITA* 5hr 21min 17.0sec	A. Geyre *FRA* 5hr 23min 16.0sec	A. Jackson *GBR* 5hr 23min 16.0sec
1960	V. Kapitonov *URS* 4hr 20min 37.0sec	L. Trapè *ITA* 4hr 20min 37.0sec	W. van den Berghen *BEL* 4hr 20min 57.0sec
1964	M. Zanin *ITA* 4hr 39min 51.63sec	K. Å. Rodian *DEN* 4hr 39min 51.65sec	W. Godefroot *BEL* 4hr 39min 51.74sec
1968	P. Vianelli *ITA* 4hr 41min 25.24sec	L. Mortensen *DEN* 4hr 42min 49.71sec	G. Pettersson *SWE* 4hr 43min 15.24sec
1972	H. Kuiper *HOL* 4hr 14min 37.0sec	K. C. Sefton *AUS* 4hr 15min 04.0sec	*Not awarded*
1976	B. Johansson *SWE* 4hr 46min 52.0sec	G. Martinelli *ITA* 4hr 47min 23.0sec	M. Noeicki *POL* 4hr 47min 23.0sec

Road Race (Team)

Although team medals were awarded from 1912, a separate team event was not held until 1960. From 1960 it has been a 100-km (62-miles) time trial.

	Gold	Silver	Bronze
1912	SWE 44hr 35min 33.6sec	GBR 44hr 44min 39.2sec	USA 44hr 47min 55.5sec
1920	FRA 19hr 16min 43.2sec	SWE 19hr 23min 10.0sec	BEL 19hr 28min 44.4sec
1924	FRA 19hr 30min 14.0sec	BEL 19hr 46min 55.4sec	SWE 19hr 59min 41.6sec
1928	DEN 15hr 09min 14.0sec	GBR 15hr 14min 49.0sec	SWE 15hr 27min 49.0sec
1932	ITA 7hr 27min 15.2sec	DEN 7hr 38min 50.2sec	SWE 7hr 39min 12.6sec
1936	FRA 7hr 39min 16.2sec	SUI 7hr 39min 20.4sec	BEL 7hr 39min 21.0sec
1948	BEL 15hr 58min 17.4sec	GBR 16hr 03min 31.6sec	FRA 16hr 08min 19.4sec
1952	BEL 15hr 20min 46.6sec	ITA 15hr 33min 27.3sec	FRA 15hr 38min 58.1sec
1956	FRA 22pts (16hr 10min 36sec)	GBR 23 pts (16hr 10min 46sec)	GER 27 pts (16hr 11min 10sec)
1960	ITA 2hr 14min 33.53sec	GER 2hr 16min 56.31sec	URS 2hr 18min 41.67sec
1964	HOL 2hr 26min 31.19sec	ITA 2hr 26min 55.39sec	SWE 2hr 27min 11.52sec
1968	HOL 2hr 07min 49.06sec	SWE 2hr 09min 26.60sec	ITA 2hr 10min 18.74sec
1972	URS 2hr 11min 17.8sec	POL 2hr 11min 47.5sec	*Not awarded*
1976	URS 2hr 08min 53.0sec	POL 2hr 09min 13.0sec	DEN 2hr 12min 20.0sec

Equestrian Sports

Show Jumping (Individual)

Not held before 1900.

	Gold	Silver	Bronze
1900	A. Haegeman (Benton II) *BEL* 2min 16.0sec	G. van der Poele (Windsor Squire) *BEL* 2min 17.6sec	de Champsavin (Terpsichore) *FRA* 2min 26.0sec
1904–1908	*Not held.*		

	Gold	Silver	Bronze
1912	J. Cariou (Mignon) *FRA* 186 pts	R. W. von Kröcher (Dohna) *GER* 186 pts	E. de Blommaert (Clonmore) *BEL* 185 pts
1920	T. Lequio (Trebecco) *ITA* 2 flts	A. Valerio (Cento) *ITA* 3 flts	G. Lewenhaupt (Mon Coeur) *SWE* 4 flts
1924	A. Gemuseus (Lucette) *SUI* 6 flts	T. Lequio (Trebecco) *ITA* 8.75 flts	A. Królikiewicz (Picador) *POL* 10 flts
1928	F. Ventura (Eliot) *TCH* 0 flts	P. Bertran de Balanda (Papillon) *FRA* 2 flts	C. Kuhn (Pepita) *SUI* 4 flts
1932	T. Nishi (Uranus) *JPN* 8 flts	H. Chamberlin (Show Girl) *USA* 12 flts	C. von Rosen (Empire) *SWE* 16 flts
1936	K. Hasse (Tora) *GER* 4 flts	H. Rang (Delfis) *ROM* 4 flts	J. von Platthy (Sellö) *HUN* 8 flts
1948	H. Mariles-Cortés (Arete) *MEX* 6.25 flts	R. Uriza (Hatvey) *MEX* 8 flts	J. F. d'Orgeix (Sucre de Pomme) *FRA* 8 flts
1952	P. J. d'Oriola (Ali Baba) *FRA* 8 flts	O. Cristi (Bambi) *CHI* 8 flts	F. Thiedemann (Meteor) *GER* 8 flts
1956	H. G. Winkler (Halla) *GER* 4 flts	R. d'Inzeo (Merano) *ITA* 8 flts	P. d'Inzeo (Uruguay) *ITA* 11 flts
1960	R. d'Inzeo (Posillipo) *ITA* 12 flts	P. d'Inzeo (The Rock) *ITA* 16 flts	D. Broome (Sunsalve) *GBR* 23 flts
1964	P. J. d'Oriola (Lutteur B) *FRA* 9 flts	H. Schridde (Dozent) *GER* 13.75 flts	P. Robeson (Firecrest) *GBR* 16 flts
1968	W. Steinkraus (Snowbound) *USA* 4 flts	M. Coakes (Stroller) *GBR* 8 flts	D. Broome (Mister Softee) *GBR* 12 flts
1972	G. Mancinelli (Ambassador) *ITA* 8 flts	A. Moore (Psalm) *GBR* 8 flts	N. Shapiro (Sloopy) *USA* 8 flts
1976	A. Schockemoehle (Warwick Rex) *GER* 0 flts	M. Vaillancourt (Branch County) *CAN* 12 flts	F. Mathy (Gai Luron) *BEL* 12 flts

Show Jumping (Team) (Nations' Cup)

Not held before 1912.

	Gold	Silver	Bronze
1912	SWE 545 pts	FRA 538 pts	GER 530 pts
1920	SWE 14 flts	BEL 16.25 flts	ITA 18.75 flts
1924	SWE 42.5 flts	SUI 50 flts	POR 53 flts
1928	ESP 4 flts	POL 8 flts	SWE 10 flts
1932	*Not awarded (no nation completed the course with three riders)*		
1936	GER 44 flts	HOL 51.5 flts	POR 56 flts
1948	MEX 34.25 flts	ESP 56.5 flts	GBR 67 flts
1952	GBR 40.75 flts	CHI 45.75 flts	USA 52.25 flts
1956	GER 40 flts	ITA 66 flts	GBR 69 flts
1960	GER 46.5 flts	USA 66 flts	ITA 80.5 flts
1964	GER 68.50 flts	FRA 77.75 flts	ITA 88.50 flts
1968	CAN 102.75 flts	FRA 110.50 flts	GER 117.25 flts
1972	GER 32.00 flts	USA 32.25 flts	ITA 48.00 flts
1976	FRA 40 flts	GER 44 flts	BEL 63 flts

Dressage (Individual)

Not held before 1912.

	Gold	Silver	Bronze
1912	C. Bonde (Emperor) *SWE* 15 flts	G. A. Boltenstern (Neptun) *SWE* 21 flts	H. von Blixen-Finecke (Maggie) *SWE* 32 flts
1920	J. Lundblad (Uno) *SWE* 27.937 pts	B. Sandström (Sabel) *SWE* 26.312 pts	H. von Rosen (Running Sister) *SWE* 25.125 pts
1924	E. Linder (Piccolomini) *SWE* 276.4 pts	B. Sandström (Sabel) *SWE* 275.8 pts	F. X. Lesage (Plumard) *FRA* 265.8 pts
1928	C. F. Frhr von Langen (Draufgänger) *GER* 237.42 pts	P. Marion (Linon) *FRA* 231.00 pts	R. Olson (Günstling) *SWE* 229.78 pts
1932	F. X. Lesage (Taine) *FRA* 343.75 pts	P. Marion (Linon) *FRA* 305.42 pts	H. Tuttle (Olympic) *USA* 300.50 pts
1936	H. Pollay (Kronos) *GER* 1,760.0 pts	F. Gerhard (Absinth) *GER* 1,745.5 pts	A. Podhajsky (Nero) *AUT* 1,721.5 pts
1948	H. Moser (Hummer) *SUI* 492.5 pts	A. Jousseaume (Harpagon) *FRA* 480.0 pts	G. A. Boltenstern (Trumf) *SWE* 447.5 pts
1952	H. St Cyr (Master Rufus) *SWE* 561.0 pts	L. Hartel (Jubilee) *DEN* 541.5 pts	A. Jousseaume (Harpagon) *FRA* 541.0 pts
1956	H. St Cyr (Juli) *SWE* 860 pts	L. Hartel (Jubilee) *DEN* 850 pts	L. Linsenhoff (Adular) *GER* 832 pts
1960	S. Filatov (Absent) *URS* 2,144 pts	G. Fischer (Wald) *SUI* 2,087 pts	J. Neckermann (Asbach) *GER* 2,082 pts
1964	H. Chammartin (Woermann) *SUI* 1,504 pts	H. Boldt (Remus) *GER* 1,503 pts	S. Filatov (Absent) *URS* 1,486 pts
1968	I. Kizimov (Ikhor) *URS* 1,572 pts	J. Neckermann (Mariano) *GER* 1,546 pts	R. Klimke (Dux) *GER* 1,537 pts
1972	L. Linsenhoff (Piaff) *GER* 1,229 pts	E. Petushkova (Pepel) *URS* 1,185 pts	J. Neckermann (Venetia) *GER* 1,177 pts
1976	E. Stueckelberger (Granat) *SUI* 1,486 pts	H. Boldt (Woycek) *GER* 1,435 pts	R. Klimke (Mehmed) *GER* 1,395 pts

Dressage (Team)

Not held before 1928.

	Gold	Silver	Bronze
1928	*GER* 669.72 pts	SWE 650.86 pts	HOL 642.96 pts
1932	FRA 2,818.75 pts	SWE 2,678.00 pts	USA 2,576.75 pts
1936	GER 5,074 pts	FRA 4,856 pts	SWE 4,660.5 pts
1948	FRA 1,269 pts	USA 1,256 pts	POR 1,182 pts
1952	SWE 1,597.5 pts	SUI 1,579.0 pts	GER 1,501.0 pts
1956	SWE 2,475 pts	GER 2,346 pts	SUI 2,346 pts
1960	*Not held*		
1964	GER 2,558 pts	SUI 2,526 pts	URS 2,311 pts
1968	GER 2,699 pts	URS 2,657 pts	SUI 2,547 pts
1972	URS 5,095 pts	GER 5,083 pts	SWE 4,849 pts
1976	GER 5,155 pts	SUI 4,684 pts	USA 4,647 pts

Three-Day Event (Individual)

Not held before 1912.

	Gold	Silver	Bronze
1912	A. Nordlander (Lady Artist) *SWE* 46.59 pts	H. von Rochow (Idealist) *GER* 46.42 pts	J. Cariou (Cocotte) *FRA* 46.32 pts
1920	H. Mörner (Germania) *SWE* 1,775 pts	Å. Lundström (Yrsa) *SWE* 1,738.75 pts	E. Caffaratti (Traditore) *ITA* 1.733.75 pts

	Gold	Silver	Bronze
1924	A. D. C. van der Voort van Zijp (Silver Piece) *HOL* 1,976 pts	F. Kirkebjerg (Meteor) *DEN* 1,873.5 pts	S. Doak (Pathfinder) *USA* 1,845.5 pts
1928	C. F. Pahud de Mortanges (Marcroix) *HOL* 1,969.82 pts	G. P. de Kruyff (Va-t-en) *HOL* 1,967.26 pts	B. Neumann (Ilja) *GER* 1,944.42 pts
1932	C. F. Pahud de Mortanges (Marcroix) *HOL* 1,813.83 pts	E. F. Thomson (Jenny Camp) *USA* 1,811 pts	C. von Rosen (Sunnyside Maid) *SWE* 1,809.42 pts
1936	L. Stubbendorf (Nurmi) *GER* 37.70 flts	E. F. Thomson (Jenny Camp) *USA* 99.90 flts	H. M. Lunding (Jason) *DEN* 102.20 flts
1948	B. Chevalier (Aiglonne) *FRA* +4 pts	F. Henry (Swing Low) *USA* 21 flts	R. Selfelt (Claque) *SWE* 25 flts
1952	H. von Blixen-Finecke (Jubal) *SWE* 28.33 flts	G. Lefrant (Verdun) *FRA* 54.50 flts	W. Büsing (Hubertus) *GER* 55.50 flts
1956	P. Kastenman (Iluster) *SWE* 66.53 flts	A. Lütke-Westhues (Trux von Kamax) *GER* 84.87 flts	F. Weldon (Kilbarry) *GBR* 85.48 flts
1960	L. Morgan (Salad Days) *AUS* +7.15 pts	N. Lavis (Mirrabooka) *AUS* 16.50 flts	A. Bühler (Gay Spark) *SUI* 51.21 flts
1964	M. Checcoli (Surbean) *ITA* 64.40 pts	C. Moratorio (Chalan) *ARG* 56.40 pts	F. Ligges (Donkosak) *GER* 49.20 pts
1968	J. J. Guyon (Pitou) *FRA* 38.86 flts	D. Allhusen (Lochinvar) *GBR* 41.61 flts	M. Page (Foster) *USA* 52.31 flts
1972	R. Meade (Laurieston) *GBR* 57.73 pts	A. Argenton (Woodland) *ITA* 43.33 pts	J. Jonsson (Sarajevo) *SWE* 39.67 pts
1976	E. Coffin (Bally-Cor) *USA* 114.99 flts	J. Plumb (Better & Better) *USA* 125.85 flts	K. Schultz (Madrigal) *GER* 129.45 flts

Three-Day Event (Team)

Not held before 1912.

	Gold	Silver	Bronze
1912	SWE 139.06 pts	GER 138.48 pts	USA 137.33 pts
1920	SWE 5,057.5 pts	ITA 4,735 pts	BEL 4,560 pts
1924	HOL 5,297.5 pts	SWE 4,743.5 pts	ITA 4,512.5 pts
1928	HOL 5,865.68 pts	NOR 5,395.68 pts	POL 5,067.92 pts
1932	USA 5,038.083 pts	HOL 4,689.083 pts	
1936	GER 676.65 flts	POL 991.70 flts	GBR 9,195.50 flts
1948	USA 161.50 flts	SWE 165.00 flts	MEX 305.25 flts
1952	SWE 221.94 flts	GER 235.49 flts	USA 587.16 flts
1956	GBR 355.48 flts	GER 475.91 flts	CAN 572.72 flts
1960	AUS 128.18 flts	SUI 386.02 flts	FRA 515.71 flts
1964	ITA 85.80 pts	USA 65.86 pts	GER 56.73 pts
1968	GBR 175.93 flts	USA 245.87 flts	AUS 331.26 flts
1972	GBR 95.53 pts	USA 10.81 pts	GER −18.00 flts
1976	USA 441.00 flts	GER 584.60 flts	AUS 599.64 flts

Fencing (Men)

Foil (Individual)

	Gold	Silver	Bronze
1896	E. Gravelotte *FRA* 4 wins	H. Callot *FRA* 3 wins	P. Mavromichalis Pierrakos *GRE* 2 wins
1900	E. Coste *FRA* 6 wins	H. Masson *FRA* 5 wins	J. Boulenger *FRA* 4 wins
1904	R. Fonst *CUB* nda	A. Van Zo Post *CUB* nda	C. Tatham *CUB* nda
1908	*Not held*		
1912	N. Nadi *ITA* 7 wins	P. Speciale *ITA* 5 wins	R. Verderber *AUT* 4 wins
1920	N. Nadi *ITA* 10 wins	P. Cattiau *FRA* 9 wins	R. Ducret *FRA* 9 wins
1924	R. Ducret *FRA* 6 wins	P. Cattiau *FRA* 5 wins	M. van Damme *BEL* 4 wins
1928	L. Gaudin *FRA* 9 wins	E. Casmir *GER* 9 wins	G. Gaudini *ITA* 9 wins
1932	G. Marzi *ITA* 9 wins	J. Levis *USA* 6 wins	G. Gaudini *ITA* 5 wins
1936	G. Gaudini *ITA* 7 wins	E. Gardère *FRA* 6 wins	G. Bocchino *ITA* 4 wins
1948	J. Buhan *FRA* 7 wins	C. d'Oriola *FRA* 5 wins	L. Maszlay *HUN* 4 wins
1952	C. d'Oriola *FRA* 8 wins	E. Mangiarotti *ITA* 6 wins	M. di Rosa *ITA* 5 wins
1956	C. d'Oriola *FRA* 6 wins	G. Bergamini *ITA* 5 wins	A. Spallino *ITA* 5 wins
1960	V. Zhdanovich *URS* 7 wins	Y. Sisikin *URS* 4 wins	A. Axelrod *USA* 3 wins
1964	E. Franke *POL* 3 wins	J. C. Magnan *FRA* 2 wins	D. Revenu *FRA* 1 win
1968	I. Drimba *ROM* 4 wins	J. Kamuti *HUN* 3 wins	D. Revenu *FRA* 3 wins
1972	W. Woyda *POL* 5 wins	J. Kamuti *HUN* 4 wins	C. Noël *FRA* 2 wins
1976	F. Dal Zotto *ITA* 4 wins	A. Romankov *URS* 4 wins	B. Talvard *FRA* 3 wins

Foil (Team)

Not held before 1920, except in 1904 when there was a competition won by Cuba from an international team.

	Gold	Silver	Bronze
1920	ITA	FRA	USA
1924	FRA	BEL	HUN
1928	ITA	FRA	ARG
1932	FRA	ITA	USA
1936	ITA	FRA	GER
1948	FRA	ITA	BEL
1952	FRA	ITA	HUN
1956	ITA	FRA	HUN
1960	URS	ITA	GER
1964	URS	POL	FRA
1968	FRA	URS	POL
1972	POL	URS	FRA
1976	GER	ITA	FRA

Epée (Individual)

Not held before 1900.

	Gold	Silver	Bronze
1900	R. Fonst *CUB* nda	L. Perrée *FRA* nda	L. Sée *FRA* nda
1904	R. Fonst *CUB* nda	C. Tatham *CUB* nda	A. Van Zo Post *CUB* nda
1908	G. Alibert *FRA* 5 wins	A. Lippmann *FRA* 4 wins	E. Olivier *FRA* 4 wins
1912	P. Anspach *BEL* 6 wins	I. Osiier *DEN* 5 wins	P. Le Hardy de Beaulieu *BEL* 4 wins
1920	A. Massard *FRA* 9 wins	A. Lippmann *FRA* 7 wins	G. Buchard *FRA* 6 wins
1924	C. Delporte *BEL* 8 wins	R. Ducret *FRA* 7 wins	N. Hellsten *SWE* 7 wins
1928	L. Gaudin *FRA* 8 wins	G. Buchard *FRA* 7 wins	G. Calnan *USA* 6 wins
1932	G. Cornaggia-Medici *ITA* 8 wins	G. Buchard *FRA* 8 wins	C. Agostini *ITA* 7 wins
1936	F. Riccardi *ITA* 5 wins	S. Ragno *ITA* 6 wins	G. Cornaggia-Medici *ITA* 6 wins

	Gold	Silver	Bronze
1948	L. Cantone *ITA* 7 wins	O. Zappelli *SUI* 5 wins	E. Mangiarotti *ITA* 5 wins
1952	E. Mangiarotti *ITA* 7 wins	D. Mangiarotti *ITA* 6 wins	O. Zappelli *SUI* 6 wins
1956	C. Pavesi *ITA* 5 wins	G. Delfino *ITA* 5 wins	E. Mangiarotti *ITA* 5 wins
1960	G. Delfino *ITA* 5 wins	A. Jay *GBR* 5 wins	B. Khabarov *URS* 4 wins
1964	G. Kriss *URS* 2 wins	W. Hoskyns *GBR* 2 wins	G. Kostava *URS* 1 win
1968	G. Kulcsár *HUN* 4 wins	G. Kriss *URS* 4 wins	G. Saccaro *ITA* 4 wins
1972	C. Fenyvesi *HUN* 4 wins	J. La Degaillerie *FRA* 3 wins	G. Kulcsár *HUN* 3 wins
1976	A. Pusch *GER* 3 wins	J. Hehn *GER* 3 wins	E. Kulcsár *HUN* 3 wins

Epée (Team)

Not held before 1908.

	Gold	Silver	Bronze
1908	FRA	GBR	BEL
1912	BEL	GBR	HOL
1920	ITA	BEL	FRA
1924	FRA	BEL	ITA
1928	ITA	FRA	POR
1932	FRA	ITA	USA
1936	ITA	SWE	FRA
1948	FRA	ITA	SWE
1952	ITA	SWE	SUI
1956	ITA	HUN	FRA
1960	ITA	GBR	URS
1964	HUN	ITA	FRA
1968	HUN	URS	POL
1972	HUN	SUI	URS
1976	SWE	GER	SUI

Sabre (Individual)

	Gold	Silver	Bronze
1896	I. Georgiadis *GRE* 4 wins	T. Karakalos *GRE* 3 wins	H. Nielsen *DEN* 2 wins
1900	G. de la Falaise *FRA* nda	L. Thiébaut *FRA* nda	S. Flesch *AUT* nda
1904	M. De Diaz *CUB* nda	W. Grebe *USA* nda	A. Van Zo Post *CUB* nda
1908	J. Fuchs *HUN* 6 wins	B. Zulavsky *HUN* 6 wins	V. Goppold de Lobsdorf *BOH* 4 wins
1912	J. Fuchs *HUN* 6 wins	B. Békéssy *HUN* 5 wins	E. Mészáros *HUN* 5 wins
1920	N. Nadi *ITA* 11 wins	A. Nadi *ITA* 9 wins	A. E. W. de Jong *HOL* 7 wins
1924	S. Posta *HUN* 5 wins	R. Ducret *FRA* 5 wins	J. Garai *HUN* 5 wins
1928	Ö. Tersztyánszky *HUN* 9 wins	A. Petschauer *HUN* 9 wins	B. Bini *ITA* 8 wins
1932	G. Piller *HUN* 8 wins	G. Gaudini *ITA* 7 wins	E. Kabos *HUN* 5 wins
1936	E. Kabos *HUN* 7 wins	G. Marzi *ITA* 6 wins	A. Gerevich *HUN* 6 wins
1948	A. Gerevich *HUN* 7 wins	V. Pinton *ITA* 5 wins	P. Kovács *HUN* 5 wins
1952	P. Kovács *HUN* 8 wins	A. Gerevich *HUN* 7 wins	T. Berczelly *HUN* 5 wins
1956	R. Kárpáti *HUN* 6 wins	J. Pawlowski *POL* 5 wins	L. Kuznetsov *URS* 4 wins
1960	R. Kárpáti *HUN* 5 wins	Z. Horváth *HUN* 4 wins	W. Calarese *ITA* 4 wins
1964	T. Pézsa *HUN* 2 wins	C. Arabo *FRA* 2 wins	U. Mavlikhanov *URS* 1 win
1968	J. Pawlowski *POL* 4 wins	M. Rakita *URS* 4 wins	T. Pésza *HUN* 3 wins
1972	V. Sidiak *URS* 4 wins	P. Maroth *HUN* 3 wins	V. Nazlymov *URS* 3 wins
1976	V. Krovopousky *URS* 5 wins	V. Nazlymov *URS* 4 wins	V. Sidiak *URS* 3 wins

Sabre (Team)

Not held before 1908.

	Gold	Silver	Bronze
1908	HUN	ITA	BOH
1912	HUN	AUT	HOL
1920	ITA	FRA	HOL
1924	ITA	HUN	HOL
1928	HUN	ITA	POL
1932	HUN	ITA	POL
1936	HUN	ITA	GER
1948	HUN	ITA	USA
1952	HUN	ITA	FRA
1956	HUN	POL	URS
1960	HUN	POL	ITA
1964	URS	ITA	POL
1968	URS	ITA	HUN
1972	ITA	URS	HUN
1976	URS	ITA	ROM

Fencing (Women)

Foil (Individual)

Not held before 1924.

	Gold	Silver	Bronze
1924	E. Osiier *DEN* 5 wins	G. M. Davis *GBR* 4 wins	G. Heckscher *DEN* 3 wins
1928	H. Mayer *GER* 7 wins	M. Freeman *GBR* 6 wins	O. Oelkers *GER* 4 wins
1932	E. (Preis) Müller *AUT* 8 wins	J. H. Guiness *GBR* 8 wins	E. Bogen *HUN* 7 wins
1936	I. Elek *HUN* 6 wins	H. Mayer *GER* 5 wins	E. (Preis) Müller *AUT* 5 wins
1948	I. Elek *HUN* 6 wins	K. Lachmann *DEN* 5 wins	E. (Preis) Müller *AUT* 5 wins
1952	I. Camber *ITA* 5 wins	I. Elek *HUN* 5 wins	K. Lachmann *DEN* 4 wins
1956	G. Sheen *GBR* 6 wins	O. Orban *ROM* 6 wins	R. Garilhe *FRA* 5 wins
1960	H. Schmid *GER* 6 wins	V. Rastvorova *URS* 5 wins	M. Vicol *ROM* 4 wins
1964	I. (Ujlaki) Rejtö *HUN* 2 wins	H. Mees *GER* 2 wins	A. Ragno *ITA* 2 wins
1968	Y. Novikova *URS* 4 wins	P. Roldan *MEX* 3 wins	I. Rejtö *HUN* 3 wins
1972	A. (Ragno) Lonzi *ITA* 4 wins	I. Bobis *HUN* 3 wins	G. Gorokhova *URS* 3 wins
1976	I. Schwarczenberger *HUN* 4 wins	M. C. Collino *ITA* 4 wins	E. Belova *URS* 3 wins

Foil (Team)

Not held before 1960.

	Gold	Silver	Bronze
1960	URS	HUN	ITA
1964	HUN	URS	GER
1968	URS	HUN	ROM
1972	URS	HUN	ROM
1976	URS	FRA	HUN

Gymnastics (Men)

Combined Exercises (Individual)

Not held before 1900.

Year	Gold	Silver	Bronze
1900	G. Sandras *FRA* 302 pts	N. Bas *FRA* 295 pts	L. Démanet *FRA* 295 pts
1904	J. Lenhart *AUT* 69.80 pts	W. Weber *GER* 69.10 pts	A. Spinnler *SUI* 67.99 pts
1908	A. Braglia *ITA* 317 pts	S. W. Tysal *GBR* 312 pts	L. Ségura *FRA* 297 pts
1912	A. Braglia *ITA* 135 pts	L. Ségura *FRA* 132.5 pts	A. Tunesi *ITA* 131.5 pts
1920	G. Zampori *ITA* 88.35 pts	M. Torrès *FRA* 87.62 pts	J. Gounot *FRA* 87.45 pts
1924	L. Štukelj *YUG* 110.340 pts	R. Pražák *TCH* 110.323 pts	B. Supčik *TCH* 106.930 pts
1928	G. Miez *SUI* 247.500 pts	H. Hänggi *SUI* 246.625 pts	L. Štukelj *YUG* 244.875 pts
1932	R. Neri *ITA* 140.625 pts	I. Pelle *HUN* 134.925 pts	H. Savolainen *FIN* 134.575 pts
1936	A. Schwarzmann *GER* 133.100 pts	E. Mack *SUI* 112.334 pts	K. Frey *GER* 111.532 pts
1948	V. Huhtanen *FIN* 229.7 pts	W. Lehmann *SUI* 229.0 pts	P. Aaltonen *FIN* 228.8 pts
1952	V. Chukarin *URS* 115.70 pts	G. Shaginyan *URS* 114.95 pts	J. Stalder *SUI* 114.75 pts
1956	V. Chukarin *URS* 114.25 pts	T. Ono *JPN* 114.20 pts	Y. Titov *URS* 113.80 pts
1960	B. Shakhlin *URS* 115.95 pts	T. Ono *JPN* 115.90 pts	Y. Titov *URS* 115.60 pts
1964	Y. Endo *JPN* 115.95 pts	S. Tsurumi *JPN*, B. Shakhlin *URS* & V. Lisitski *URS* 115.40 pts	
1968	S. Kato *JPN* 115.90 pts	M. Voronin *URS* 115.85 pts	A. Nakayama *JPN* 115.65 pts
1972	S. Kato *JPN* 114.650 pts	E. Kenmotsu *JPN* 114.575 pts	A. Nakayama *JPN* 114.325 pts
1976	N. Andrianov *URS* 116.650 pts	S. Kato *JPN* 115.650 pts	M. Tsukahara *JPN* 115.575 pts

Combined Exercises (Team)

Not held before 1904.

Year	Gold	Silver	Bronze
1904	USA 374.43 pts	USA 356.37 pts	USA 349.69 pts
1908	SWE 438 pts	NOR 425 pts	FIN 405 pts
1912	ITA 265.75 pts	HUN 227.25 pts	GBR 184.50 pts
1920	ITA 359.855 pts	BEL 346.785 pts	FRA 340.100 pts
1924	ITA 839.058 pts	FRA 820.528 pts	SUI 816.661 pts
1928	SUI 1,718.625 pts	TCH 1,712.250 pts	YUG 1,648.750 pts
1932	ITA 541.850 pts	USA 522.275 pts	FIN 509.995 pts
1936	GER 657.430 pts	SUI 654.802 pts	FIN 638.468 pts
1948	FIN 1,358.30 pts	SUI 1,356.70 pts	HUN 1,330.85 pts
1952	URS 574.40 pts	SUI 567.50 pts	FIN 564.20 pts
1956	URS 568.25 pts	JPN 566.40 pts	FIN 555.95 pts
1960	JPN 575.20 pts	URS 572.70 pts	ITA 559.05 pts
1964	JPN 577.95 pts	URS 575.45 pts	GER 565.10 pts
1968	JPN 575.90 pts	URS 571.10 pts	GDR 557.15 pts
1972	JPN 571.25 pts	URS 564.05 pts	GDR 559.70 pts
1976	JPN 576.85 pts	URS 576.45 pts	GDR 564.65 pts

Floor Exercises

Not held before 1932.

Year	Gold	Silver	Bronze
1932	I. Pelle *HUN* 9.60 pts	G. Miez *SUI* 9.47 pts	M. Lertora *ITA* 9.23 pts
1936	G. Miez *SUI* 18.666 pts	J. Walter *SUI* 18.500 pts	K. Frey *GER*, E. Mack *SUI* 18.466 pts
1948	F. Pataki *HUN* 38.70 pts	J. Mogyorósi-Klencs *HUN* 38.40 pts	Z. Ružička *TCH* 38.10 pts
1952	W. Thoresson *SWE* 19.25 pts	T. Uesako *JPN* & J. Jokiel *POL* 19.15 pts	
1956	V. Muratov *URS* 19.20 pts	N. Aihara *JPN*, W. Thoresson *SWE* & V. Chukarin *URS* 19.10 pts	
1960	N. Aihara *JPN* 19.45 pts	Y. Titov *URS* 19.325 pts	F. Menichelli *ITA* 19.275 pts
1964	F. Menichelli *ITA* 19.45 pts	V. Lisitski *URS* 19.35 pts	Y. Endo *JPN* 19.35 pts
1968	S. Kato *JPN* 19.475 pts	A. Nakayama *JPN* 19.400 pts	T. Kato *JPN* 19.275 pts
1972	N. Andrianov *URS* 19.175 pts	A. Nakayama *JPN* 19.125 pts	S. Kasamatsu *JPN* 19.025 pts
1976	N. Andrianov *URS* 19.450 pts	V. Marchenko *URS* 19.425 pts	P. Kormann *USA* 19.300 pts

Horizontal Bar

Year	Gold	Silver	Bronze
1896	H. Weingärtner *GER*	A. Flatow *GER*	
1900	*Not held*		
1904	A. Heida *USA* & E. Hennig *USA* 40 pts		G. Eyser *USA* 39 pts
1908–1920	*Not held*		
1924	L. Štukelj *YUG* 19.73 pts	J. Gutweniger *SUI* 19.236 pts	A. Higelin *FRA* 19.163 pts
1928	G. Miez *SUI* 19.17 pts	R. Neri *ITA* 19.00 pts	E. Mack *SUI* 18.92 pts
1932	D. Bixler *USA* 18.33 pts	H. Savolainen *FIN* 18.07 pts	E. Teräsvirta *FIN* 18.07 pts
1936	A. Saarvala *FIN* 19.367 pts	K. Frey *GER* 19.267 pts	A. Schwarzmann *GER* 19.233 pts
1948	J. Stalder *SUI* 39.7 pts	W. Lehmann *SUI* 39.4 pts	V. Huhtanen *FIN* 39.2 pts
1952	J. Günthard *SUI* 19.55 pts	J. Stalder *SUI* & A. Schwarzmann *GER* 19.50 pts	
1956	T. Ono *JPN* 19.60 pts	Y. Titov *URS* 19.40 pts	M. Takemoto *JPN* 19.30 pts
1960	T. Ono *JPN* 19.60 pts	M. Takemoto *JPN* 19.52 pts	B. Shakhlin *URS* 19.475 pts
1964	B. Shakhlin *URS* 19.625 pts	Y. Titov *URS* 19.55 pts	M. Cerar *YUG* 19.50 pts
1968	M. Voronin *URS* & A. Nakayama *JPN* 19.550 pts		E. Kenmotsu *JPN* 19.375 pts
1972	M. Tsukahara *JPN* 19.725 pts	S. Kato *JPN* 19.525 pts	S. Kasamatsu *JPN* 19.450 pts
1976	M. Tsukahara *JPN* 19.675 pts	E. Kenmotsu *JPN* 19.500 pts	E. Gienger *GER* 19.475 pts

Parallel Bars

Year	Gold	Silver	Bronze
1896	A. Flatow *GER*	J. A. Zutter *SUI*	H. Weingärtner *GER*
1900	*Not held*		
1904	G. Eyser *USA* 44 pts	A. Heida *USA* 43 pts	J. Duha *USA* 40 pts
1908–1920	*Not held*		
1924	A. Güttinger *SUI* 21.63 pts	R. Pražák *TCH* 21.61 pts	G. Zampori *ITA* 21.45 pts
1928	L. Vácha *TCH* 18.83 pts	J. Primožič *YUG* 18.50 pts	H. Hänggi *SUI* 18.08 pts
1932	R. Neri *ITA* 18.97 pts	I. Pelle *HUN* 18.60 pts	H. Savolainen *FIN* 18.27 pts
1936	K. Frey *GER* 19.067 pts	M. Reusch *SUI* 19.034 pts	A. Schwarzmann *GER* 18.967 pts

	Gold	Silver	Bronze
1948	M. Reusch *SUI* 39.50 pts	V. Huhtanen *FIN* 39.30 pts	C. Kipfer *SUI* & J. Stalder *SUI* 39.10 pts
1952	H. Eugster *SUI* 19.65 pts	V. Chukarin *URS* 19.60 pts	J. Stalder *SUI* 19.50 pts
1956	V. Chukarin *URS* 19.20 pts	M. Kubota *JPN* 19.15 pts	T. Ono *JPN* & M. Takemoto *JPN* 19.10 pts
1960	B. Shakhlin *URS* 19.40 pts	G. Carminucci *ITA* 19.375 pts	T. Ono *JPN* 19.35 pts
1964	Y. Endo *JPN* 19.675 pts	S. Tsurumi *JPN* 19.45 pts	F. Menichelli *ITA* 19.35 pts
1968	A. Nakayama *JPN* 19.475 pts	M. Voronin *URS* 19.425 pts	V. Klimenko *URS* 19.225 pts
1972	S. Kato *JPN* 19.475 pts	S. Kasamatsu *JPN* 19.375 pts	E. Kenmotsu *JPN* 19.250 pts
1976	S. Kato *JPN* 19.675 pts	N. Andrianov *URS* 19.500 pts	M. Tsukahara *JPN* 19.475 pts

Pommelled Horse

In 1948 Zanetti (4th) and Figone (5th) received the silver and bronze medals respectively because it was not then the rule to pass over subsequent places when there was a tie for first place.

	Gold	Silver	Bronze
1896	J. A. Zutter *SUI*	H. Weingärtner *GER*	
1900	*Not held*		
1904	A. Heida *USA* 42 pts	G. Eyser *USA* 33 pts	W. Merz *USA* 29 pts
1908–1920	*Not held*		
1924	J. Wilhelm *SUI* 21.23 pts	J. Gutweniger *SUI* 21.13 pts	A. Rebetez *SUI* 20.73 pts
1928	H. Hänggi *SUI* 19.75 pts	G. Miez *SUI* 19.25 pts	H. Savolainen *FIN* 18.83 pts
1932	I. Pelle *HUN* 19.07 pts	O. Bonoli *ITA* 18.87 pts	F. Haubold *USA* 18.57 pts
1936	K. Frey *GER* 19.333 pts	E. Mack *SUI* 19.167 pts	A. Bachmann *SUI* 19.067 pts
1948	P. Aaltonen *FIN*, V. Huhtanen *FIN* & H. Savolainen *FIN* 38.7 pts	L. Zanetti *ITA* 38.30 pts	G. Figone *ITA* 38.20 pts
1952	V. Chukarin *URS* 19.50 pts	Y. Korolkov *URS* & G. Shaginyan *URS* 19.40 pts	
1956	B. Shakhlin *URS* 19.25 pts	T. Ono *JPN* 19.20 pts	V. Chukarin *URS* 19.10 pts
1960	E. Ekman *FIN* & B. Shakhlin *URS* 19.375 pts		S. Tsurumi *JPN* 19.150 pts
1964	M. Cerar *YUG* 19.525 pts	S. Tsurumi *JPN* 19.325 pts	Y. Tsapenko *URS* 19.20 pts
1968	M. Cerar *YUG* 19.325 pts	O. E. Laiho *FIN* 19.225 pts	M. Voronin *URS* 19.200 pts
1972	V. Klimenko *URS* 19.125 pts	S. Kato *JPN* 19.000 pts	E. Kenmotsu *JPN* 18.950 pts
1976	Z. Magyar *HUN* 19.700 pts	E. Kenmotsu *JPN* 19.575 pts	N. Andrianov *URS* 19.525 pts

Long Horse Vault

	Gold	Silver	Bronze
1896	C. Schuhmann *GER*	J. A. Zutter *SUI*	
1900	*Not held*		
1904	A. Heida *USA* & G. Eyser *USA* 36 pts		W. Merz *USA* 31 pts
1908–1920	*Not held*		
1924	F. Kriz *USA* 9.98 pts	J. Koutny *TCH* 9.97 pts	B. Mořkovsky *TCH* 9.93 pts
1928	E. Mack *SUI* 9.58 pts	E. Löffler *TCH* 9.50 pts	S. Derganc *YUG* 9.46 pts
1932	S. Guglielmetti *ITA* 18.03 pts	A. Jochim *GER* 17.77 pts	E. Carmichael *USA* 17.53 pts
1936	A. Schwarzmann *GER* 19.20 pts	E. Mack *SUI* 18.967 pts	M. Volz *GER* 18.467 pts
1948	P. Aaltonen *FIN* 39.1 pts	O. Rove *FIN* 39.0 pts	J. Mogyorósi-Klencs *HUN*, F. Pataki *HUN* & L. Sotornik *TCH* 38.5 pts
1952	V. Chukarin *URS* 19.20 pts	M. Takemoto *JPN* 19.15 pts	T. Uesako *JPN* & T. Ono *JPN* 19.10 pts
1956	H. Bantz *GER* & V. Muratov *URS* 18.85 pts		Y. Titov *URS* 18.75 pts
1960	T. Ono *JPN* & B. Shakhlin *URS* 19.35 pts		V. Portnoi *URS* 19.225 pts
1964	H. Yamashita *JPN* 19.660 pts	V. Lisitski *URS* 19.325 pts	H. Rantakari *FIN* 19.300 pts
1968	M. Voronin *URS* 19.000 pts	Y. Endo *JPN* 18.950 pts	S. Diomidov *URS* 18.925 pts
1972	K. Köste *GDR* 18.850 pts	V. Klimenko *URS* 18.825 pts	N. Andrianov *URS* 18.800 pts
1976	N. Andrianov *URS* 19.450 pts	M. Tsukahara *JPN* 19.375 pts	H. Kajiyama *JPN* 19.275 pts

Rings

	Gold	Silver	Bronze
1896	I. Mitropoulos *GRE*	H. Weingärtner *GER*	P. Persakis *GRE*
1900	*Not held*		
1904	H. Glass *USA* 45 pts	W. Merz *USA* 35 pts	E. Voight *USA* 32 pts
1908–1912	*Not held*		
1924	F. Martino *ITA* 21.553 pts	R. Pražák *TCH* 21.483 pts	L. Vácha *TCH* 21.430 pts
1928	L. Štukelj *YUG* 19.25 pts	L. Vácha *TCH* 19.17 pts	E. Löffler *TCH* 18.83 pts
1932	G. Gulack *USA* 18.97 pts	W. Denton *USA* 18.60 pts	G. Lattuada *ITA* 18.50 pts
1936	A. Hudec *TCH* 19.433 pts	L. Štukelj *YUG* 18.670 pts	M. Volz *GER* 18.670 pts
1948	K. Frei *SUI* 39.6 pts	M. Reusch *SUI* 39.1 pts	Z. Ružička *TCH* 38.5 pts
1952	G. Shaginyan *URS* 19.75 pts	V. Chukarin *URS* 19.55 pts	D. Leonkin *URS* & H. Eugster *SUI* 19.40 pts
1956	A. Azarian *URS* 19.35 pts	V. Muratov *URS* 19.15 pts	M. Takemoto *JPN* & M. Kubota *JPN* 19.10 pts
1960	A. Azarian *URS* 19.725 pts	B. Shakhlin *URS* 19.500 pts	V. Kapsazov *BUL* & T. Ono *JPN* 19.425 pts
1964	T. Hayata *JPN* 19.475 pts	F. Menichelli *ITA* 19.425 pts	B. Shakhlin *URS* 19.400 pts
1968	A. Nakayama *JPN* 19.450 pts	M. Voronin *URS* 19.325 pts	S. Kato *JPN* 19.225 pts
1972	A. Nakayama *JPN* 19.350 pts	M. Voronin *URS* 19.275 pts	M. Tsukahara *JPN* 19.225 pts
1976	N. Andrianov *URS* 19.650 pts	A. Ditiatin *URS* 19.550 pts	D. Greco *ROM* 19.500 pts

Gymnastics (Women)

Combined Exercises (Individual)

Not held before 1952.

	Gold	Silver	Bronze
1952	M. Gorokhovskaya *URS* 76.78 pts	N. Bocharova *URS* 75.94 pts	M. Korondi *HUN* 75.82 pts
1956	L. Latynina *URS* 74.933 pts	Á. Keleti *HUN* 74.633 pts	S. Muratova *URS* 74.466 pts
1960	L. Latynina *URS* 77.031 pts	S. Muratova *URS* 76.696 pts	P. Astakhova *URS* 76.164 pts
1964	V. Čáslavská *TCH* 77.564 pts	L. Latynina *URS* 76.998 pts	P. Astakhova *URS* 76.965 pts

	Gold	Silver	Bronze
1968	V. Čáslavská *TCH* 78.25 pts	Z. Voronina *URS* 76.85 pts	N. Kuchinskaya *URS* 76.75 pts
1972	L. Turischeva *URS* 77.025 pts	K. Janz *GDR* 76.875 pts	T. Lazakovich *URS* 76.850 pts
1976	N. Comaneci *ROM* 79.275 pts	N. Kim *URS* 78.675 pts	L. Turischeva *URS* 78.625 pts

Combined Exercises Team

Not held before 1928.

	Gold	Silver	Bronze
1928	HOL 316.75 pts	ITA 289.00 pts	GBR 258.25 pts
1932	*Not held*		
1936	GER 506.50 pts	TCH 503.60 pts	HUN 499.00 pts
1948	TCH 445.45 pts	HUN 440.55 pts	USA 422.63 pts
1952	URS 527.03 pts	HUN 520.96 pts	TCH 503.32 pts
1956	URS 444.80 pts	HUN 443.50 pts	ROM 438.20 pts
1960	URS 382.320 pts	TCH 373.323 pts	ROM 372.053 pts
1964	URS 380.890 pts	TCH 379.989 pts	JPN 377.889 pts
1968	URS 382.85 pts	TCH 382.20 pts	GDR 379.10 pts
1972	URS 380.50 pts	GDR 376.55 pts	HUN 368.25 pts
1976	URS 380.35 pts	ROM 387.15 pts	GDR 385.10 pts

Beam

Not held before 1952.

	Gold	Silver	Bronze
1952	N. Bocharova *URS* 19.22 pts	M. Gorokhovskaya *URS* 19.13 pts	M. Korondi *HUN* 19.02 pts
1956	Á. Keleti *HUN* 18.800 pts	E. Bosáková *TCH* & T. Manina *URS* 18.633 pts	
1960	E. Bosáková *TCH* 19.283 pts	L. Latynina *URS* 19.233 pts	S. Muratova *URS* 19.232 pts
1964	V. Čáslavská *TCH* 19.449 pts	T. Manina *URS* 19.399 pts	L. Latynina *URS* 19.382 pts
1968	N. Kuchinskaya *URS* 19.650 pts	V. Čáslavská *TCH* 19.575 pts	L. Petrik *URS* 19.250 pts
1972	O. Korbut *URS* 19.400 pts	T. Lazakovich *URS* 19.375 pts	K. Janz *GDR* 18.975 pts
1976	N. Comaneci *ROM* 19.950 pts	O. Korbut *URS* 19.725 pts	T. Ungureanu *ROM* 19.700 pts

Asymmetrical Bars

Not held before 1952.

	Gold	Silver	Bronze
1952	M. Korondi *HUN* 19.40 pts	M. Gorokhovskaya *URS* 19.26 pts	Á. Keleti *HUN* 19.16 pts
1956	Á. Keleti *HUN* 18.966 pts	L. Latynina *URS* 18.833 pts	S. Muratova *URS* 18.800 pts
1960	P. Astakhova *URS* 19.616 pts	L. Latynina *URS* 19.416 pts	T. Lyukhina *URS* 19.399 pts
1964	P. Astakhova *URS* 19.332 pts	K. Makray *HUN* 19.216 pts	L. Latynina *URS* 19.199 pts
1968	V. Čáslavská *TCH* 19.650 pts	K. Janz *GDR* 19.500 pts	Z. Voronina *URS* 19.425 pts
1972	K. Janz *GDR* 19.675 pts	O. Korbut *URS* & E. Zuchold *GDR* 19.450 pts	
1976	N. Comaneci *ROM* 20.000 pts	T. Ungureanu *ROM* 19.800 pts	M. Egervari *HUN* 19.775 pts

Horse Vault

Not held before 1952.

	Gold	Silver	Bronze
1952	Y. Kalinchuk *URS* 19.20 pts	M. Gorokhovskaya *URS* 19.19 pts	G. Minaicheva *URS* 19.16 pts
1956	L. Latynina *URS* 18.833 pts	T. Manina *URS* 18.800 pts	A. S. Colling *SWE* & O. Tass *HUN* 18.733 pts
1960	M. Nikolaeva *URS* 19.316 pts	S. Muratova *URS* 19.049 pts	L. Latynina *URS* 19.016 pts
1964	V. Čáslavská *TCH* 19.483 pts	L. Latynina *URS* 19.283 pts	B. Radochia *GER* 19.283 pts
1968	V. Čáslavská *TCH* 19.775 pts	E. Zuchold *GDR* 19.625 pts	Z. Voronina *URS* 19.500 pts
1972	K. Janz *GDR* 19.525 pts	E. Zuchold *GDR* 19.275 pts	L. Turischeva *URS* 19.250 pts
1976	N. Kim *URS* 19.800 pts	L. Turischeva *URS* 19.650 pts	C. Dombeck *GDR* 19.650 pts

Floor Exercises

Not held before 1952.

	Gold	Silver	Bronze
1952	Á. Keleti *HUN* 19.36 pts	M. Gorokhovskaya *URS* 19.20 pts	M. Korondi *HUN* 19.00 pts
1956	L. Latynina *URS* & Á. Keleti *HUN* 18.733 pts		E. Leuştean *ROM* 18.700 pts
1960	L. Latynina *URS* 19.583 pts	P. Astakhova *URS* 19.532 pts	T. Lyukhina *URS* 19.449 pts
1964	L. Latynina *URS* 19.599 pts	P. Astakhova *URS* 19.500 pts	A. Jánosi *HUN* 19.300 pts
1968	V. Čáslavská *TCH* & L. Petrik *URS* 19.675 pts		N. Kuchinskaya*URS* 19.650 pts
1972	O. Korbut *URS* 19.575 pts	L. Turischeva *URS* 19.550 pts	T. Lazakovich *URS* 19.450 pts
1976	N. Kim *URS* 19.850 pts	L. Turischeva *URS* 19.825 pts	N. Comaneci *ROM* 19.750 pts

Handball (Men)

Not held before 1972.

	Gold	Silver	Bronze
1972	YUG	TCH	ROM
1976	URS	ROM	POL

Handball (Women)

Not held before 1976.

	Gold	Silver	Bronze
1976	URS	GDR	HUN

Hockey

Not held before 1908.

	Gold	Silver	Bronze
1908	ENG	IRL	SCO & WAL
1912	*Not held*		
1920	ENG	DEN	BEL
1924	*Not held*		
1928	IND	HOL	GER
1932	IND	JPN	USA
1936	IND	GER	HOL
1948	IND	GBR	HOL
1952	IND	HOL	GBR
1956	IND	PAK	GER
1960	PAK	IND	ESP
1964	IND	PAK	AUS
1968	PAK	AUS	IND
1972	GER	PAK	IND
1976	NZL	AUS	PAK

Judo

Lightweight

Weight limit 1964 68kg (149lb 14½oz); from 1972 63kg (138lb 14¼oz). Not held before 1964.

	Gold	Silver	Bronze
1964	T. Nakatani *JPN*	E. Hänni *SUI*	O. Stepanov *URS* & A. Bogolubov *URS*
1968	*Not held*		
1972	T. Kawaguchi *JPN*	*Not awarded*	Y. I. Kim *PRK* & I. Mounier *FRA*
1976	H. Rodriguez *CUB*	E. Chang *KOR*	F. Mariani *ITA* & J. Tuncsik *HUN*

	Gold	Silver	Bronze

Welterweight

Weight limit 70 kg (154lb 5oz). Not held before 1972.

	Gold	Silver	Bronze
1972	T. Nomura *JPN*	A. Zajkowski *POL*	D. Hoetger *GDR* & A. Novikov *URS*
1976	V. Nevzorov *URS*	K. Kuramoto *JPN*	P. Vial *FRA*

Middleweight

Weight limit 80kg (176lb 6oz). Not held before 1964.

	Gold	Silver	Bronze
1964	I. Okano *JPN*	W. Hofmann *GER*	J. Bregman *USA* & E. T. Kim *KOR*
1968	*Not held*		
1972	S. Sekine *JPN*	S. L. Oh *PRK*	B. Jacks *GBR* & J. P. Cochet *FRA*
1976	I. Sonoda *JPN*	V. Dvoinikov *URS*	S. Obadov *YUG* & Y. C. Park *KOR*

Light Heavyweight

Weight limit 93kg (205lb 0½oz). Not held before 1972.

	Gold	Silver	Bronze
1972	S. Khokhoshvili *URS*	D. C. Starbrook *GBR*	P. Barth *GER* & C. Ishii *BRA*
1976	K. Ninomiya *JPN*	R. Harshiladze *URS*	D. Starbrook *GBR* & J. Roethlisberger *SUI*

Heavyweight

Weight limit 1964 over 80kg (176lb 6oz); from 1972 over 93kg (205lb 0½oz). Not held before 1964.

	Gold	Silver	Bronze
1964	I. Inokuma *JPN*	A. H. Rogers *CAN*	A. Kiknadze *URS* & P. Chikviladze *URS*
1968	*Not held*		
1972	W. Ruska *HOL*	K. Glahn *GER*	G. Onashvili *URS* & M. Nishimura *JPN*
1976	S. Novikov *URS*	G. Neureuther *GER*	S. Endo *JPN* & A. Coage *USA*

Open

No weight limit. Not held before 1964.

	Gold	Silver	Bronze
1964	A. Geesink *HOL*	A. Kaminaga *JPN*	K. Glahn *GER* & T. Boronovskis *AUS*
1968	*Not held*		
1972	W. Ruska *HOL*	V. Kusnetsov *URS*	A. Parisi *GBR* & J. C. Brondani *FRA*
1976	H. Uemura *JPN*	K. Remfry *GBR*	S. Chochishvili *URS* & J. Cho *KOR*

Modern Pentathlon

The five events are horse-riding, fencing, pistol-shooting, swimming and cross-country running. From 1912 to 1952 a point for each place achieved in the separate events was awarded, i.e. 1 for the winner, 2 for the second, etc. In 1956 a scoring system evaluating performance rather than position in each event was introduced.

Modern Penthathlon (Individual)

Not held before 1912.

	Gold	Silver	Bronze
1912	G. Lilliehöök *SWE* 27 pts	G. Åsbrink *SWE* 28 pts	G. de Laval *SWE* 30 pts
1920	G. Dyrssen *SWE* 18 pts	E. de Laval *SWE* 23 pts	G. Runö *SWE* 27 pts
1924	B. Lindman *SWE* 18 pts	G. Dyrssen *SWE* 39.5 pts	B. Uggla *SWE* 45 pts
1928	S. Thofelt *SWE* 47 pts	B. Lindman *SWE* 50 pts	H. Kahl *GER* 52 pts
1932	J. Oxenstierna *SWE* 32 pts	B. Lindman *SWE* 35.5 pts	R. Mayo *USA* 38.5 pts
1936	G. Handrick *GER* 31.5 pts	C. Leonard *USA* 39.5 pts	S. Abba *ITA* 45.5 pts
1948	W. Grut *SWE* 16 pts	G. Moore *USA* 47 pts	G. Gärdin *SWE* 49 pts
1952	L. Hall *SWE* 32 pts	G. Benedek *HUN* 39 pts	I. Szondi *HUN* 41 pts
1956	L. Hall *SWE* 4,833 pts	O. Mannonen *FIN* 4,774.5 pts	V. Korhonen *FIN* 4,750 pts
1960	F. Németh *HUN* 5,024 pts	I. Nagy *HUN* 4,988 pts	R. Beck *USA* 4,981 pts
1964	F. Török *HUN* 5,116 pts	I. Novikov *URS* 5,067 pts	A. Mokeyev *URS* 5,039 pts
1968	B. Ferm *SWE* 4,964 pts	A. Balczó *HUN* 4,953 pts	P. Lednev *URS* 4,795 pts
1972	A. Balczó *HUN* 5,412 pts	B. Onishenko *URS* 5,335 pts	P. Lednev *URS* 5,328 pts
1976	J. Pyciak-Peciak *POL* 5,520 pts	P. Lednev *URS* 5,485 pts	J. Bartu *TCH* 5,466 pts

Modern Pentathlon (Team)

Not held before 1952.

	Gold	Silver	Bronze
1952	HUN 166 pts	SWE 182 pts	FIN 213 pts
1956	URS 13,690.5 pts	USA 13,482.0 pts	FIN 13,185.5 pts
1960	HUN 14,863 pts	URS 14,309 pts	USA 14,192 pts
1964	URS 14,961 pts	USA 14,189 pts	HUN 14,173 pts
1968	HUN 14,325 pts	URS 14,248 pts	FRA 13,289 pts
1972	URS 15,968 pts	HUN 15,348 pts	FIN 14,812 pts
1976	GBR 15,559 pts	TCH 15,451 pts	HUN 15,395 pts

Rowing

The course for all events has been 2,000m (1 mile 427 yd) since 1952. In 1904 it was 3,219m (2 miles); in 1908 2,414m (1½ miles); in 1948 1,880m (1 mile 296 yd). In 1928 third and fourth places were decided in a special race.

Single Sculls

Not held before 1900.

	Gold	Silver	Bronze
1900	H. Barrelet *FRA* 7min 35.6sec	A. Gaudin *FRA* 7min 41.6sec	St George Ashe *GBR* 8min 15.6sec
1904	F. Greer *USA* 10min 08.5sec	J. Juvenal *USA* 2 lengths	C. Titus *USA* 1 length
1908	H. Blackstaffe *GBR* 9min 26.0sec	A. McCulloch *GBR* 1 length	B. von Gaza *GER* & K. Levitzky *HUN* nda
1912	W. D. Kinnear *GBR* 7min 47.6sec	P. Veirman *BEL* 7min 56.0sec	E. B. Butler *CAN* & M. Kusik *URS* nda
1920	J. B. Kelly *USA* 7min 35.0sec	J. Beresford *GBR* 7min 36.0sec	C. H. d'Arcy *NZL* 7min 48.0sec
1924	J. Beresford *GBR* 7min 49.2sec	W. E. G. Gilmore *USA* 7min 54.0sec	J. Schneider *SUI* 8min 01.0sec
1928	H. Pearce *AUS* 7min 11.0sec	K. Myers *USA* 7min 20.8 sec	T. D. Collet *GBR* 7min 19.8 sec
1932	H. Pearce *AUS* 7min 44.4sec	W. Miller *USA* 7min 45.2sec	G. Douglas *URU* 8min 13.6sec
1936	G. Schäfer *GER* 8min 21.5sec	J. Hasenöhrl *AUT* 8min 25.8sec	D. Barrow *USA* 8min 28.0sec
1948	M. Wood *AUS* 7min 24.4sec	E. Risso *URU* 7min 38.2sec	R. Catasta *ITA* 7min 51.4sec
1952	Y. Tyukalov *URS* 8min 12.8sec	M. Wood *AUS* 8min 14.5sec	T. Kocerka *POL* 8min 19.4sec
1956	V. Ivanov *URS* 8min 02.5sec	S. Mackenzie *AUS* 8min 07.7sec	J. Kelly *USA* 8min 11.8sec

	Gold	Silver	Bronze
1960	V. Ivanov *URS* 7min 13.96sec	A. Hill *GER* 7min 20.21 sec	T. Kocerka *POL* 7min 21.26sec
1964	V. Ivanov *URS* 8min 22.51 sec	A. Hill *GER* 8min 26.24sec	G. Kottman *SUI* 8min 29.68sec
1968	H. J. Wienese *HOL* 7min 47.80sec	J. Meissner *GER* 7min 52.00sec	A. Demiddi *ARG* 7min 57.19sec
1972	Y. Malyshev *URS* 7min 10.12sec	A. Demiddi *ARG* 7min 11.53sec	W. Güldenpfennig *GDR* 7min 14.45sec
1976	P. Karppinen *FIN* 7min 29.03sec	P. M. Kolbe *GER* 7min 31.67sec	J. Dreifke *GDR* 7min 38.03sec

Double Sculls

Not held before 1904.

	Gold	Silver	Bronze
1904	USA 10min 03.2sec	USA nda	USA nda
1908–1912	*Not held*		
1920	USA 7min 09.0sec	ITA 7min 19.0sec	FRA 7min 21.0sec
1924	USA 6min 34.0sec	FRA 6min 38.0sec	SUI 3 lengths
1928	USA 6min 41.4sec	CAN 6min 51.0sec	AUT
1932	USA 7min 17.4sec	GER 7min 22.8sec	CAN 7min 27.6sec
1936	GBR 7min 20.8sec	GER 7min 26.2sec	POL 7min 36.2sec
1948	GBR 6min 51.3sec	DEN 6min 55.3sec	URU 7min 12.4sec
1952	ARG 7min 32.2sec	URS 7min 38.2sec	URU 7min 43.7sec
1956	URS 7min 24.0sec	USA 7min 32.2sec	AUS 7min 37.4sec
1960	TCH 6min 47.50sec	URS 6min 50.49sec	SUI 6min 50.59sec
1964	URS 7min 10.66sec	USA 7min 13.16sec	TCH 7min 14.23sec
1968	URS 6min 51.82sec	HOL 6min 52.80sec	USA 6min 54.21sec
1972	URS 7min 01.77sec	NOR 7min 02.58sec	GDR 7min 05.55sec
1976	NOR 7min 13.20sec	GBR 7min 5.26sec	GDR 7min 17.45sec

Coxless Pairs

Not held before 1900.

	Gold	Silver	Bronze
1900	BEL 7min 49.6sec	BEL 7min 52.4sec	FRA 8min 0.6sec
1904	USA 10min 57.0sec	USA nda	USA nda
1908	GBR 9min 41.0sec	GBR 2½ lengths	CAN nda
1912–1920	*Not held*		
1924	HOL 8min 19.4sec	FRA 8min 21.6sec	
1928	GER 7min 06.4sec	GBR 7min 08.8sec	USA 7min 20.4sec
1932	GBR 8min 00.0sec	NZL 8min 02.4sec	POL 8min 08.2sec
1936	GER 8min 16.1sec	DEN 8min 19.2sec	ARG 8min 23.0sec
1948	GBR 7min 21.1sec	SUI 7min 23.9sec	ITA 7min 31.5sec
1952	USA 8min 20.7sec	BEL 8min 23.5sec	SUI 8min 32.7sec
1956	USA 7min 55.4sec	URS 8min 03.9sec	AUT 8min 11.8sec
1960	URS 7min 02.00sec	AUT 7min 03.69sec	FIN 7min 03.80sec
1964	CAN 7min 32.94sec	HOL 7min 33.40sec	GER 7min 38.63sec
1968	GDR 7min 26.56sec	USA 7min 26.71sec	DEN 7min 31.84sec
1972	GDR 6min 53.16sec	SUI 6min 57.06sec	HOL 6min 58.70sec
1976	GDR 7min 23.31sec	USA 7min 26.73sec	GER 7min 30.03sec

Coxed Pairs

Not held before 1900.

	Gold	Silver	Bronze
1900	HOL 7min 34.2sec	FRA 7min 34.4sec	FRA 7min 57.2sec
1904–1912	*Not held*		
1920	ITA 7min 56.0sec	FRA 7min 57.0sec	SUI nda
1924	SUI 8min 39.0sec	ITA 8min 39.1sec	USA nda
1928	SUI 7min 42.6sec	FRA 7min 48.4sec	BEL 7min 59.4sec
1932	USA 8min 25.8sec	POL 8min 31.2sec	FRA 8min 41.2sec
1936	GER 8min 36.9sec	ITA 8min 49.7sec	FRA 8min 54.0sec
1948	DEN 8min 05.0sec	ITA 8min 12.2sec	HUN 8min 25.2sec
1952	FRA 8min 28.6sec	GER 8min 32.1sec	DEN 8min 34.9sec
1956	USA 8min 26.1sec	GER 8min 29.2sec	URS 8min 31.0sec
1960	GER 7min 29.14sec	URS 7min 30.17sec	USA 7min 34.58sec
1964	USA 8min 21.23sec	FRA 8min 23.15sec	HOL 8min 23.42sec
1968	ITA 8min 04.81sec	HOL 8min 06.80sec	DEN 8min 08.07sec
1972	GDR 7min 17.25sec	TCH 7min 19.57sec	ROM 7min 21.36sec
1976	GDR 7min 58.99sec	URS 8min 01.82sec	TCH 8min 03.28sec

Coxless Fours

Not held before 1904.

	Gold	Silver	Bronze
1904	USA 9min 53.8sec	USA nda	
1908	GBR 8min 34.0sec	GBR 1½ lengths	
1912–1920	*Not held*		
1924	GBR 7min 08.6sec	CAN 1¼ lengths	SUI nda
1928	GBR 6min 36.0sec	USA 6min 37.0sec	ITA 6min 31.6sec
1932	GBR 6min 58.2sec	GER 7min 03.0sec	ITA 7min 04.0sec
1936	GER 7min 01.8sec	GBR 7min 06.5sec	SUI 7min 10.6sec
1948	ITA 6min 39.0sec	DEN 6min 43.5sec	USA 6min 47.7sec
1952	YUG 7min 16.0sec	FRA 7min 18.9sec	FIN 7min 23.3sec
1956	CAN 7min 08.8sec	USA 7min 18.4sec	FRA 7min 20.9sec
1960	USA 6min 26.26sec	ITA 6min 28.78sec	URS 6min 29.62sec
1964	DEN 6min 59.30sec	GBR 7min 00.47sec	USA 7min 01.37sec
1968	GDR 6min 39.18sec	HUN 6min 41.64sec	ITA 6min 44.01sec
1972	GDR 6min 24.27sec	NZL 6min 25.64sec	GER 6min 28.41sec
1976	BUL 6min 41.36sec	USA 6min 43.06sec	ROM 6min 43.96sec

Coxed Fours

Not held before 1900. In 1900 there was a dispute and two finals were held, (1) for the crews with the fastest times in the heats and (2) for the winners of the three heats.

	Gold	Silver	Bronze
1900	(1) FRA 7min 11.0sec	FRA 7min 18.0sec	GER 7min 18.2sec
	(2) GER 5min 59.0sec	HOL 6min 33.0sec	GER 6min 35.0sec
1904–1908	*Not held*		
1912	GER 6min 59.4sec	GBR 2 lengths	DEN nda
1920	SUI 6min 54.0sec	USA 6min 58.0sec	NOR 7min 02.0sec
1924	SUI 7min 18.4sec	FRA 7min 21.6sec	USA nda
1928	ITA 6min 47.8sec	SUI 7min 03.4sec	POL 7min 12.8sec
1932	GER 7min 19.0sec	ITA 7min 19.2sec	POL 7min 26.8sec
1936	GER 7min 16.2sec	SUI 7min 24.3sec	FRA 7min 33.3sec
1948	USA 6min 50.3sec	SUI 6min 53.3sec	DEN 6min 58.6sec
1952	TCH 7min 33.4sec	SUI 7min 36.5sec	USA 7min 37.0sec
1956	ITA 7min 19.4sec	SWE 7min 22.4sec	FIN 7min 30.9sec
1960	GER 6min 39.12sec	FRA 6min 41.62sec	ITA 6min 43.12sec
1964	GER 7min 00.44sec	ITA 7min 02.84sec	HOL 7min 06.46sec
1968	NZL 6min 45.62sec	GDR 6min 48.20sec	SUI 6min 49.04sec
1972	GER 6min 31.85sec	GDR 6min 33.30sec	TCH 6min 35.64sec
1976	URS 6min 40.22sec	GDR 6min 42.70sec	GER 6min 46.96sec

Eights

Not held before 1900.

	Gold	Silver	Bronze
1900	USA 6min 09.8sec	BEL 6min 13.8sec	HOL 6min 23.0sec
1904	USA 7min 50.0sec	CAN nda	
1908	GBR 7min 52.0sec	BEL 2 lengths	CAN nda
1912	GBR 6min 15.02sec	GBR 1 length	GER nda
1920	USA 6min 02.6sec	GBR 6min 05.0sec	NOR 6min 36.0sec
1924	USA 6min 33.4sec	CAN 6min 49.0sec	ITA nda
1928	USA 6min 03.2sec	GBR 6min 05.6sec	CAN 6min 03.8sec
1932	USA 6min 37.6sec	ITA 6min 37.8sec	CAN 6min 40.4sec
1936	USA 6min 25.4sec	ITA 6min 26.0sec	GER 6min 26.4sec
1948	USA 5min 46.7sec	GBR 6min 06.9sec	NOR 6min 10.3sec
1952	USA 6min 25.9sec	URS 6min 31.2sec	AUS 6min 33.1sec
1956	USA 6min 35.2sec	CAN 6min 37.1sec	AUS 6min 39.2sec
1960	GER 5min 57.18sec	CAN 6min 01.52sec	TCH 6min 04.84sec

	Gold	Silver	Bronze
1964	USA 6min 18.23sec	GER 6min 23.29sec	TCH 6min 25.11sec
1968	GER 6min 07.00sec	AUS 6min 07.98sec	URS 6min 09.11sec
1972	NZL 6min 08.94sec	USA 6min 11.61sec	GDR 6min 11.67sec
1976	GDR 5min 58.29sec	GBR 6min 00.82sec	NZL 6min 03.51sec

Shooting

Free Pistol

Range 50m (55yd).

	Gold	Silver	Bronze
1896	S. Paine *USA* 442 pts	V. Jensen *DEN* 285 pts	H. Nielsen *DEN* nda
1900	K. Röderer *SUI* 503 pts	A. Paroche *FRA* 466 pts	K. Staeheli *SUI* 453 pts
1904–1908	*Not held*		
1912	A. Lane *USA* 499 pts	P. Dolfen *USA* 474 pts	C. E. Stewart *GBR* 470 pts
1920	C. Frederick *USA* 496 pts	A. da Costa *BRA* 489 pts	A. Lane *USA* 481 pts
1924–1932	*Not held*		
1936	T. Ullman *SWE* 559 pts	E. Krempel *GER* 544 pts	C. des Jammonières *FRA* 540 pts
1948	E. Vasquez Cam *PER* 545 pts	R. Schnyder *SUI* 539 pts	T. Ullman *SWE* 539 pts
1952	H. Benner *USA* 553 pts	A. Léon Gozalo *ESP* 550 pts	A. Balogh *HUN* 549 pts
1956	P. Linnosvuo *FIN* 556 pts	M. Umarov *URS* 556 pts	O. Pinion *USA* 551 pts
1960	A. Gushchin *URS* 560 pts	M. Umarov *URS* 552 pts	Y. Yoshikawa *JPN* 552 pts
1964	V. Markkanen *FIN* 560 pts	F. Green *USA* 557 pts	Y. Yoshikawa *JPN* 554 pts
1968	G. Kosykh *URS* 562 pts	H. Mertel *GER* 562 pts	H. Vollmar *GDR* 560 pts
1972	R. Skanåker *SWE* 567 pts	D. Iuga *ROM* 562 pts	R. Dollinger *AUT* 560 pts
1976	U. Potteck *GDR* 573 pts	H. Vollmar *GDR* 567 pts	R. Dollinger *AUT* 562 pts

Moving Target (Running Boar)

Not held in its present form before 1972. Range 50m (55yd).

	Gold	Silver	Bronze
1972	L. Zhelezniak *URS* 569 pts	H. Bellingrodt *COL* 565 pts	K. Kynoch *GBR* 562 pts
1976	A. Gazov *URS* 579 pts	A. Kedyarov *URS* 576 pts	J. Greszkiewicz *POL* 571 pts

Rapid-Fire Pistol

Range 25m (27yd 1ft).

	Gold	Silver	Bronze
1896	I. Frangudis *GRE* 344 pts	G. Orphanidis *GRE* 249 pts	H. Nielsen *DEN* nda
1900	M. Larrouy *FRA* 58 pts	L. Moreaux *FRA* 57 pts	E. Balme *FRA* 57 pts
1904	*Not held*		
1908	P. van Asbroeck *BEL* 490 pts	R. Storms *BEL* 487 pts	J. E. Gorman *USA* 485 pts
1912	A. Lane *USA* 287 pts	P. Palén *SWE* 286 pts	J. H. von Holst *SWE* 283 pts
1920	G. Paraense *BRA* 274 pts	R. Bracken *USA* 272 pts	F. Zulauf *SUI* 269 pts
1924	H. N. Bailey *USA* 18 pts	V. Carlberg *SWE* 18 pts	L. Hannelius *FIN* 18 pts
1928	*Not held*		
1932	R. Morigi *ITA* 36 pts	H. Hax *GER* 36 pts	D. Matteucci *ITA* 36 pts
1936	C. van Oyen *GER* 36 pts	H. Hax *GER* 35 pts	T. Ullman *SWE* 34 pts
1948	K. Takács *HUN* 580 pts	C. E. Diaz Sáenz Valiente *ARG* 571 pts	S. Lundqvist *SWE* 569 pts
1952	K. Takács *HUN* 579 pts	S. Kun *HUN* 578 pts	G. Lichiardopol *ROM* 578 pts
1956	S. Petrescu *ROM* 587 pts	Y. Cherkassov *URS* 585 pts	G. Lichiardopol *ROM* 581 pts
1960	W. McMillan *USA* 587 pts	P. Linnosvuo *FIN* 587 pts	A. Zabelin *URS* 587 pts
1964	P. Linnosvuo *FIN* 592 pts	I. Tripşa *ROM* 591 pts	L. Nacovsky *TCH* 590 pts
1968	J. Zapedski *POL* 593 pts	M. Roşca *ROM* 591 pts	R. Suleimanov *URS* 591 pts
1972	J. Zapedski *POL* 595 pts	L. Falta *TCH* 594 pts	V. Torshin *URS* 593 pts
1976	N. Klaar *GDR* 597 pts	J. Wiefel *GDR* 596 pts	R. Ferraris *ITA* 595 pts

Free Rifle

Range 300m (330yd) except in 1924 when it was 400–800m (440–880yd).

	Gold	Silver	Bronze
1896	G. Orphanidis *GRE* 1,583 pts	I. Frangudis *GRE* 1,312 pts	V. Jensen *DEN* 1,305 pts
1900–1904	*Not held*		
1908	A. Helgerud *NOR* 909 pts	H. Simon *USA* 887 pts	O. Sæther *NOR* 883 pts
1912	P. Colas *FRA* 987 pts	L. J. Madsen *DEN* 981 pts	N. H. D. Larsen *DEN* 962 pts
1920	M. Fisher *USA* 997 pts	N. H. D. Larsen *DEN* 985 pts	O. Østensen *NOR* 980 pts
1924	M. Fisher *USA* 95 pts	C. T. Osburn *USA* 95 pts	N. H. D. Larsen *DEN* 93 pts
1928–1936	*Not held*		
1948	E. Grünig *SUI* 1,120 pts	P. Janhonen *FIN* 1,114 pts	W. Røgeberg *NOR* 1,112 pts
1952	A. Bogdanov *URS* 1,123 pts	R. Bürchler *SUI* 1,120 pts	L. Vainshtain *URS* 1,109 pts
1956	V. Borisov *URS* 1,138 pts	A. Erdman *URS* 1,137 pts	Y. Ylönen *FIN* 1,128 pts
1960	H. Hammerer *AUT* 1,129 pts	H. Spillmann *SUI* 1,127 pts	V. Borisov *URS* 1,127 pts
1964	G. Anderson *USA* 1,153 pts	S. Kveliashvili *URS* 1,144 pts	M. Gunnarsson *USA* 1,136 pts
1968	G. Anderson *USA* 1,157 pts	V. Kornev *URS* 1,151 pts	K. Müller *SUI* 1,148 pts
1972	L. Wigger *USA* 1,155 pts	B. Melnik *URS* 1,155 pts	L. Pap *HUN* 1,149 pts
1976	*Not held*		

Smallbore Rifle (Prone)

Not held before 1908. Range 50m (55yd) except in 1908 when range was 45.7 and 91.4m (50 and 100yd), 40 shots. In 1908–12 competitors could fire from any position; in 1920 standing; from 1924 prone.

	Gold	Silver	Bronze
1908	A. A. Carnell *GBR* 387 pts	H. R. Humby *GBR* 386 pts	G. Barnes *GBR* 385 pts
1912	F. Hird *USA* 194 pts	W. Milne *GBR* 193 pts	H. Burt *GBR* 192 pts
1920	L. A. Nuesslein *USA* 391 pts	A. Rothrock *USA* 386 pts	D. Fenton *USA* 385 pts
1924	P. C. de Lisle *FRA* 398 pts	M. Dinwiddie *USA* 396 pts	J. Hartmann *SUI* 394 pts
1928	*Not held*		
1932	B. Rönnmark *SWE* 294 pts	G. Huet *MEX* 294 pts	Z. Hradetzky-Sóos *HUN* 293 pts
1936	W. Røgeberg *NOR* 300 pts	R. Berzsenyi *HUN* 296 pts	W. Karaś *POL* 296 pts
1948	A. Cook *USA* 599 pts	W. Tomsen *USA* 599 pts	J. Jonsson *SWE* 597 pts
1952	I. Sarbu *ROM* 400 pts	B. Andreev *URS* 400 pts	A. Jackson *USA* 399 pts

	Gold	Silver	Bronze
1956	G. R. Quellette *CAN* 600 pts	V. Borisov *URS* 599 pts	G. S. Boa *CAN* 598 pts
1960	P. Kohnke *GER* 590 pts	J. Hill *USA* 589 pts	E. Forcella Pelliccioni *VEN* 587 pts
1964	L. Hammerl *HUN* 597 pts	L. Wigger *USA* 597 pts	T. Pool *USA* 596 pts
1968	J. Kurka *TCH* 598 pts	L. Hammerl *HUN* 598 pts	I. Ballinger *NZL* 597 pts
1972	H. J. Li *PRK* 599 pts	V. Auer *USA* 598 pts	N. Rotaru *ROM* 598 pts
1976	K. Smieszek *GER* 599 pts	U. Lind *GER* 597 pts	G. Lushchikov *URS* 595 pts

Smallbore Rifle (Three Positions)

Not held before 1952. Range 50m (55yd), standing, kneeling, prone.

	Gold	Silver	Bronze
1952	E. Kongshaug *NOR* 1,164 pts	V. Ylönen *FIN* 1,164 pts	B. Andreev *URS* 1,163 pts
1956	A. Bogdanov *URS* 1,172 pts	O. Hořínek *TCH* 1,172 pts	N. J. Sundberg *SWE* 1,167 pts
1960	V. Shamburkin *URS* 1,149 pts	M. Niasov *URS* 1,145 pts	K. Zähringer *GER* 1,139 pts
1964	L. Wigger *USA* 1,164 pts	V. Khristov *BUL* 1,152 pts	L. Hammerl *HUN* 1,151 pts
1968	B. Klingner *GER* 1,157 pts	J. Writer *USA* 1,156 pts	V. Parkhimovich *URS* 1,154 pts
1972	J. Writer *USA* 1,166 pts	L. Bassham *USA* 1,157 pts	W. Lippoldt *GDR* 1,153 pts
1976	L. Bassham *USA* 1,162 pts	M. Murdoch *USA* 1,162 pts	W. Seibold *GER* 1,160 pts

Trap Shooting

Not held before 1900. 200 pigeons, except in 1908 when there were 80.

	Gold	Silver	Bronze
1900	R. de Barbarin *FRA* 17 pts	R. Guyot *FRA* 17 pts	J. de Clary *FRA* 17 pts
1904	*Not held*		
1908	W. H. Ewing *CAN* 72 pts	G. Beattie *CAN* 60 pts	A. Maunder *GBR* & A. Metaxas *GRE* 57 pts
1912	J. Graham *USA* 96 pts	A. Göldel *GER* 94 pts	H. Blau *URS* 91 pts
1920	M. Arie *USA* 95 pts	F. Troeh *USA* 93 pts	F. Wright *USA* 87 pts
1924	G. Halasy *HUN* 98 pts	K. Huber *FIN* 98 pts	F. Hughes *USA* 97 pts
1928–1948	*Not held*		
1952	G. P. Généreux *CAN* 192 pts	K. Holmqvist *SWE* 191 pts	H. Liljedahl *SWE* 190 pts
1956	G. Rossini *ITA* 195 pts	A. Smelczyński *POL* 190 pts	A. Ciceri *ITA* 188 pts
1960	I. Dumitrescu *ROM* 192 pts	G. Rossini *ITA* 191 pts	S. Kalinin *URS* 190 pts
1964	E. Mattarelli *ITA* 198 pts	P. Senichev *URS* 194 pts	W. Morris *USA* 194 pts
1968	J. R. Braithwaite *GBR* 198 pts	T. Garrigus *USA* 196 pts	K. Czekalla *GDR* 196 pts
1972	A. Scalzone *ITA* 199 pts	M. Carrega *FRA* 198 pts	S. Basagni *ITA* 195 pts
1976	D. Haldeman *USA* 190 pts	A. Silva Marques *POR* 189 pts	U. Baldi *ITA* 189 pts

Skeet

Not held before 1968.

	Gold	Silver	Bronze
1968	Y. Petrov *URS* 198 pts	R. Garagnani *ITA* 198 pts	K. Wirnhier *GER* 198 pts
1972	K. Wirnhier *GER* 195 pts	Y. Petrov *URS* 195 pts	M. Buchheim *GDR* 195 pts
1976	J. Panacek *TCH* 198 pts	E. Swinkels *HOL* 198 pts	W. Gawlikowski *POL* 196 pts

Swimming and Diving (Men)

100 Metres Freestyle

In 1904 the distance was 91.44m (100 yd).

	Gold	Silver	Bronze
1896	A. Hajós (Guttmann) *HUN* 1min 22.2sec	E. Choraphas *GRE* 1min 23.0sec	O. Herschmann *AUT* nda
1900	*Not held*		
1904	Z. von Halmay *HUN* 1min 02.8sec	C. Daniels *USA* nda	J. S. Leary *USA* nda
1908	C. Daniels *USA* 1min 05.6sec	Z. von Halmay *HUN* 1min 06.2sec	H. Julin *SWE* 1min 08.8sec
1912	D. P. Kahanamoku *USA* 1min 03.4sec	C. Healy *AUS* 1min 04.6sec	K. Huszagh *USA* 1min 05.6sec
1920	D. P. Kahanamoku *USA* 1min 01.4sec	P. K. Kealoha *USA* 1min 02.2sec	W. Harris *USA* 1min 03.0sec
1924	J. Weissmuller *USA* 59.0sec	D. P. Kahanamoku *USA* 1min 01.4sec	S. Kahanamoku *USA* 1min 01.8sec
1928	J. Weissmuller *USA* 58.6sec	I. Bárány *HUN* 59.8sec	K. Takaishi *JPN* 1min 00.0sec
1932	Y. Miyazaki *JPN* 58.2 sec	T. Kawaishi *JPN* 58.6sec	A. Schwartz *USA* 58.8sec
1936	F. Csik *HUN* 57.6sec	M. Yusa *JPN* 57.9sec	S. Arai *JPN* 58.0sec
1948	W. Ris *USA* 57.3sec	A. Ford *USA* 57.8sec	G. Kádas *HUN* 58.1sec
1952	C. Scholes *USA* 57.4sec	H. Suzuki *JPN* 57.4sec	G. Larsson *SWE* 58.2sec
1956	J. Henricks *AUS* 55.4sec	J. Devitt *AUS* 55.8sec	G. Chapman *AUS* 56.7sec
1960	J. Devitt *AUS* 55.2sec	L. Larson *USA* 55.2sec	M. Dos Santos *BRA* 55.4sec
1964	D. Schollander *USA* 53.4sec	R. McGregor *GBR* 53.5sec	H. J. Klein *GER* 54.0sec
1968	M. Wenden *AUS* 52.2sec	K. Walsh *USA* 52.8sec	M. Spitz *USA* 53.0sec
1972	M. Spitz *USA* 51.22sec	J. Heidenreich *USA* 51.65sec	V. Bure *URS* 51.77sec
1976	J. Montgomery *USA* 49.99sec	J. Babashoff *USA* 50.81sec	P. Nocke *GER* 51.31sec

200 Metres Freestyle

Not held before 1900. In 1904 the distance was 201.17m (220yd).

	Gold	Silver	Bronze
1900	F. Lane *AUS* 2min 25.2sec	Z. von Halmay *HUN* 2min 31.0sec	K. Ruberl *AUT* 2min 32.0sec
1904	C. Daniels *USA* 2min 44.2sec	F. Gailey *USA* 2min 46.0sec	E. Rausch *GER* 2min 56.0sec
1908–1964	*Not held*		
1968	M. Wenden *AUS* 1min 55.2sec	D. Schollander *USA* 1min 55.8sec	J. Nelson *USA* 1min 58.1sec
1972	M. Spitz *USA* 1min 52.78sec	S. Genter *USA* 1min 53.73sec	W. Lampe *GER* 1min 53.99sec
1976	B. Furniss *USA* 1min 50.29sec	J. Naber *USA* 1min 50.50sec	J. Montgomery *USA* 1min 50.58sec

400 Metres Freestyle

Not held before 1904. In 1904 the distance was 402.3m (440yd).

	Gold	Silver	Bronze
1904	C. Daniels *USA* 6min 16.2sec	F. Gailey *USA* 6min 22.0sec	O. Wahle *AUT* 6min 39.0sec
1908	H. Taylor *GBR* 5min 36.8sec	F. Beaurepaire *AUS* 5min 44.2sec	O. Scheff *AUT* 5min 46.0sec
1912	G. Hodgson *CAN* 5min 24.4sec	J. Hatfield *GBR* 5min 25.8sec	H. Hardwick *AUS* 5min 31.2sec

	Gold	Silver	Bronze
1920	N. Ross *USA* 5min 26.8sec	L. Langer *USA* 5min 29.0sec	G. Vernot *CAN* 5min 29.6sec
1924	J. Weissmuller *USA* 5min 04.2sec	A. Borg *SWE* 5min 05.6sec	A. Charlton *AUS* 5min 06.6sec
1928	A. Zorilla *ARG* 5min 01.6sec	A. Charlton *AUS* 5min 03.6sec	A. Borg *SWE* 5min 04.6sec
1932	C. Crabbe *USA* 4min 48.4sec	J. Taris *FRA* 4min 48.5sec	T. Oyokota *JPN* 4min 52.3sec
1936	J. Medica *USA* 4min 44.5sec	S. Uto *JPN* 4min 45.6sec	S. Makino *JPN* 4min 48.1sec
1948	W. Smith *USA* 4min 41.0sec	J. McLane *USA* 4min 43.4sec	J. Marshall *AUS* 4min 47.4sec
1952	J. Boiteux *FRA* 4min 30.7sec	F. Konno *USA* 4min 31.3sec	P. O. Östrand *SWE* 4min 35.2sec
1956	M. Rose *AUS* 4min 27.3sec	T. Yamanaka *JPN* 4min 30.4sec	G. Breen *USA* 4min 32.5sec
1960	M. Rose *AUS* 4min 18.3sec	T. Yamanaka *JPN* 4min 21.4sec	J. Konrads *AUS* 4min 21.8sec
1964	D. Schollander *USA* 4min 12.2sec	F. Wiegand *GER* 4min 14.9sec	A. Wood *AUS* 4min 15.1sec
1968	M. Burton *USA* 4min 09.0sec	R. Hutton *CAN* 4min 11.7sec	A. Mosconi *FRA* 4min 13.3sec
1972	B. Cooper *AUS* 4min 00.27sec	S. Genter *USA* 4min 01.94sec	T. McBreen *USA* 4min 02.64sec
1976	B. Goodell *USA* 3min 51.93sec	T. Shaw *USA* 3min 52.54sec	V. Raskatov *URS* 3min 55.76sec

1,500 Metres Freestyle

In 1896 the distance was 1,200m (1,310yd 1ft 5½in); in 1900 1,000m (1,093yd 1ft 10in); in 1904 1,609.34m (1 mile).

	Gold	Silver	Bronze
1896	A. Hajós *HUN* 18min 22.2sec	I. Andreou *GRE* 21min 03.4sec	E. Choraphas *GRE* nda
1900	J. Jarvis *GBR* 13min 40.2sec	O. Wahle *AUT* 14min 53.6sec	Z. von Halmay *HUN* 15min 16.4sec
1904	E. Rausch *GER* 27min 18.2sec	G. Kiss *HUN* 28min 28.2sec	F. Gailey *USA* 28min 54.0sec
1908	H. Taylor *GBR* 22min 48.4sec	T. S. Battersby *GBR* 22min 51.2sec	F. Beaurepaire *AUS* 22min 56.2sec
1912	G. Hodgson *CAN* 22min 00.0sec	J. Hatfield *GBR* 22min 39.0sec	H. Hardwick *AUS* 23min 15.4sec
1920	N. Ross *USA* 22min 23.2sec	G. Vernot *CAN* 22min 36.4sec	F. Beaurepaire *AUS* 23min 04.0sec
1924	A. Charlton *AUS* 20min 06.6sec	A. Borg *SWE* 20min 41.4sec	F. Beaurepaire *AUS* 20min 48.4sec
1928	A. Borg *SWE* 19min 51.8sec	A. Charlton *AUS* 20min 02.6sec	C. Crabbe *USA* 20min 28.8sec
1932	K. Kitamura *JPN* 19min 12.4sec	S. Makino *JPN* 19min 14.1sec	J. Cristy *USA* 19min 39.5sec
1936	N. Terada *JPN* 19min 13.7sec	J. Medica *USA* 19min 34.0sec	S. Uto *JPN* 19min 34.5sec
1948	J. McLane *USA* 19min 18.5sec	J. Marshall *AUS* 19min 31.3sec	G. Mitró *HUN* 19min 43.2sec
1952	F. Konno *USA* 18min 30.3sec	S. Hashizume *JPN* 18min 41.4sec	T. Okamoto *BRA* 18min 51.3sec
1956	M. Rose *AUS* 17min 58.9sec	T. Yamanaka *JPN* 18min 00.3sec	G. Breen *USA* 18min 08.2sec
1960	J. Konrads *AUS* 17min 19.6sec	M. Rose *AUS* 17min 21.7sec	G. Breen *USA* 17min 30.6sec
1964	R. Windle *AUS* 17min 01.7sec	J. Nelson *USA* 17min 03.0sec	A. Wood *AUS* 17min 07.7sec
1968	M. Burton *USA* 16min 38.9sec	J. Kinsella *USA* 16min 57.3sec	G. Brough *AUS* 17min 04.7sec
1972	M. Burton *USA* 15min 52.58sec	G. Windeatt *AUS* 15min 58.48sec	D. Northway *USA* 16min 09.25sec
1976	B. Goodell *USA* 15min 02.40sec	B. Hackett *USA* 15min 03.91sec	S. Holland *AUS* 15min 04.66sec

100 Metres Backstroke

Not held before 1904. In 1904 the distance was 91.44m (100yd).

	Gold	Silver	Bronze
1904	W. Brack *GER* 1min 16.8sec	G. Hoffmann *GER* nda	G. Zacharias *GER* nda
1908	A. Bieberstein *GER* 1min 24.6sec	L. Dam *DEN* 1min 26.6sec	H. Haresnape *GBR* 1min 27.0sec
1912	H. Hebner *USA* 1min 21.2sec	O. Fahr *GER* 1min 22.4sec	P. Kellner *GER* 1min 24.0sec
1920	W. P. Kealoha *USA* 1min 15.2sec	R. Kegeris *USA* 1min 16.2sec	G. Blitz *BEL* 1min 19.0sec
1924	W. P. Kealoha *USA* 1min 13.2sec	P. Wyatt *USA* 1min 15.4sec	K. Bartha *HUN* 1min 17.8sec
1928	G. Kojac *USA* 1min 08.2sec	W. Laufer *USA* 1min 10.0sec	P. Wyatt *USA* 1min 12.0sec
1932	M. Kiyokawa *JPN* 1min 08.6sec	T. Irie *JPN* 1min 09.8sec	K. Kawatsu *JPN* 1min 10.0sec
1936	A. Kiefer *USA* 1min 05.9sec	A. Van de Weghe *USA* 1min 07.7sec	M. Kiyokawa *JPN* 1min 08.4sec
1948	A. Stack *USA* 1min 06.4sec	R. Cowell *USA* 1min 06.5sec	G. Vallerey *FRA* 1min 07.8sec
1952	Y. Oyakawa *USA* 1min 05.4sec	G. Bozon *FRA* 1min 06.2sec	J. Taylor *USA* 1min 06.4sec
1956	D. Theile *AUS* 1min 02.2sec	J. Monckton *AUS* 1min 03.2sec	F. McKinney *USA* 1min 04.5sec
1960	D. Theile *AUS* 1min 01.9sec	F. McKinney *USA* 1min 02.1sec	R. Bennett *USA* 1min 02.3sec
1964	*Not held*		
1968	R. Matthes *GDR* 58.7sec	C. Hickcox *USA* 1min 00.2sec	R. Mills *USA* 1min 00.5sec
1972	R. Matthes *GDR* 56.58sec	M. Stamm *USA* 57.70sec	J. Murphy *USA* 58.35sec
1976	J. Naber *USA* 55.49sec	P. Rocca *USA* 56.34sec	R. Matthes *GDR* 57.22sec

200 Metres Backstroke

Not held before 1900.

	Gold	Silver	Bronze
1900	E. Hoppenberg *GER* 2min 47.0sec	K. Ruberl *AUT* 2min 56.0sec	J. Drost *HOL* 3min 01.0sec
1904–1960	*Not held*		
1964	J. Graef *USA* 2min 10.3sec	G. Dilley *USA* 2min 10.5sec	R. Bennett *USA* 2min 13.1sec
1968	R. Matthes *GDR* 2min 09.6sec	M. Ivey *USA* 2min 10.6sec	J. Horsley *USA* 2min 10.9sec
1972	R. Matthes *GDR* 2min 02.82sec	M. Stamm *USA* 2min 04.09sec	M. Ivey *USA* 2min 04.33sec
1976	J. Naber *USA* 1min 59.19sec	P. Rocca *USA* 2min 00.55sec	D. Harrigan *USA* 2min 01.35sec

100 Metres Breaststroke

Not held before 1968

	Gold	Silver	Bronze
1968	D. McKenzie *USA* 1min 07.7sec	V. Kosinski *URS* 1min 08.0sec	N. Pankin *URS* 1min 08.0sec
1972	N. Taguchi *JPN* 1min 04.94sec	T. Bruce *USA* 1min 05.43sec	J. Hencken *USA* 1min 05.61sec
1976	J. Hencken *USA* 1min 03.11sec	D. Wilkie *GBR* 1min 03.43sec	A. Ivozaytis *URS* 1min 04.23sec

200 Metres Breaststroke

Not held before 1908.

	Gold	Silver	Bronze
1908	F. Holman *GBR* 3min 09.2sec	W. Robinson *GBR* 3min 12.8sec	P. Hansson *SWE* 3min 14.6sec
1912	W. Bathe *GER* 3min 01.8sec	W. Lützow *GER* 3min 05.0sec	K. Malisch *GER* 3min 08.0sec
1920	H. Malmroth *SWE* 3min 04.4sec	T. Henning *SWE* 3min 09.2sec	A. Aaltonen *FIN* 3min 12.2sec
1924	R. Skelton *USA* 2min 56.6sec	J. de Combe *BEL* 2min 59.2sec	W. Kirschbaum *USA* 3min 01.0sec
1928	Y. Tsuruta *JPN* 2min 48.8sec	E. Rademacher *GER* 2min 50.6sec	Y. Yldefonso *PHI* 2min 56.4sec
1932	Y. Tsuruta *JPN* 2min 45.4sec	R. Koike *JPN* 2min 46.6sec	T. Yldefonso *PHI* 2min 47.1sec

	Gold	Silver	Bronze
1936	T. Hamuro *JPN* 2min 41.5sec	E. Sietas *GER* 2min 42.9sec	R. Koike *JPN* 2min 44.2sec
1948	J. Verdeur *USA* 2min 39.3sec	K. Carter *USA* 2min 40.2sec	R. Sohl *USA* 2min 43.9sec
1952	J. Davies *AUS* 2min 34.4sec	B. Stassforth *USA* 2min 34.7sec	H. Klein *GER* 2min 35.9sec
1956	M. Furukawa *JPN* 2min 34.7sec	M. Yoshimura *JPN* 2min 36.7sec	K. Yunichev *URS* 2min 36.8sec
1960	W. Mulliken *USA* 2min 37.4sec	Y. Osaki *JPN* 2min 38.0sec	W. Mensonides *HOL* 2min 39.7sec
1964	I. O'Brien *AUS* 2min 27.8sec	G. Prokopenko *URS* 2min 28.2sec	C. Jastremski *USA* 2min 29.6sec
1968	F. Muñoz *MEX* 2min 28.7sec	V. Kosinski *URS* 2min 29.2sec	B. Job *USA* 2min 29.9sec
1972	J. Hencken *USA* 2min 21.55sec	D. Wilkie *GBR* 2min 23.67sec	N. Taguchi *JPN* 2min 23.88sec
1976	D. Wilkie *GBR* 2min 15.11sec	C. Keating *USA* 2min 17.26sec	R. Colella *USA* 2min 19.20sec

100 Metres Butterfly

Not held before 1968.

	Gold	Silver	Bronze
1968	D. Russell *USA* 55.9sec	M. Spitz *USA* 56.4sec	R. Wales *USA* 57.2sec
1972	M. Spitz *USA* 54.27sec	B. Robertson *CAN* 55.56sec	J. Heidenreich *USA* 55.74sec
1976	M. Vogel *USA* 54.35sec	J. Bottom *USA* 54.50sec	G. Hall *USA* 54.65sec

200 Metres Butterfly

Not held before 1956.

	Gold	Silver	Bronze
1956	W. Yorzyk *USA* 2min 19.3sec	T. Ishimoto *JPN* 2min 23.8sec	G. Tumpek *HUN* 2min 23.9sec
1960	M. Troy *USA* 2min 12.8sec	N. Hayes *AUS* 2min 14.6sec	D. Gillanders *USA* 2min 15.3sec
1964	K. Berry *AUS* 2min 06.6sec	C. Robie *USA* 2min 07.5sec	F. Schmidt *USA* 2min 09.3sec
1968	C. Robie *USA* 2min 08.7sec	M. Woodroffe *GBR* 2min 09.0sec	J. Ferris *USA* 2min 09.3sec
1972	M. Spitz *USA* 2min 00.70sec	G. Hall *USA* 2min 02.86sec	R. Backhaus *USA* 2min 03.23sec
1976	M. Bruner *USA* 1min 59.23sec	S. Gregg *USA* 1min 59.54sec	B. Forrester *USA* 1min 59.96sec

200 Metres Individual Medley

Not held before 1968. Order of strokes: butterfly, backstroke, breaststroke, freestyle.

	Gold	Silver	Bronze
1968	C. Hickcox *USA* 2min 12.0sec	G. Buckingham *USA* 2min 13.0sec	J. Ferris *USA* 2min 13.3sec
1972	G. Larsson *SWE* 2min 07.17sec	T. McKee *USA* 2min 08.37sec	S. Furniss *USA* 2min 08.45sec
1976	*Not held.*		

400 Metres Individual Medley

Not held before 1964. Order of strokes: butterfly, backstroke, breaststroke, freestyle.

	Gold	Silver	Bronze
1964	R. Roth *USA* 4min 45.4sec	R. Saari *USA* 4min 47.1sec	G. Hetz *GER* 4min 51.0sec
1968	C. Hickcox *USA* 4min 48.4sec	G. Hall *USA* 4min 48.7sec	M. Holthaus *GER* 4min 51.4sec
1972	G. Larsson *SWE* 4min 31.98sec	T. McKee *USA* 4min 31.98sec	A. Hargitay *HUN* 4min 32.70sec
1976	R. Strachan *USA* 4min 23.68sec	T. McKee *USA* 4min 24.62sec	A. Smirnov *URS* 4min 26.90sec

4 x 100 Metres Freestyle Relay

Not held before 1964.

	Gold	Silver	Bronze
1964	USA 3min 33.2sec	GER 3min 37.2sec	AUS 3min 39.1sec
1968	USA 3min 31.7sec	URS 3min 34.2sec	AUS 3min 34.7sec
1972	USA 3min 26.42sec	URS 3min 29.72sec	GDR 3min 32.42sec
1976	*Not held.*		

4 x 200 Metres Freestyle Relay

Not held before 1908.

	Gold	Silver	Bronze
1908	GBR 10min 55.6sec	HUN 10min 59.0sec	USA 11min 02.8sec
1912	AUS 10min 11.6sec	USA 10min 20.2sec	GBR 10min 28.2sec
1920	USA 10min 04.4sec	AUS 10min 25.4sec	GBR 10min 37.2sec
1924	USA 9min 53.4sec	AUS 10min 02.0sec	SWE 10min 06.8sec
1928	USA 9min 36.2sec	JPN 9min 41.4sec	CAN 9min 47.8sec
1932	JPN 8min 58.4 sec	USA 9min 10.5sec	HUN 9min 31.4sec
1936	JPN 8min 51.5sec	USA 9min 03.0sec	HUN 9min 12.3sec
1948	USA 8min 46.0sec	HUN 8min 48.4sec	FRA 9min 08.0sec
1952	USA 8min 31.1sec	JPN 8min 33.5sec	FRA 8min 45.9sec
1956	AUS 8min 23.6sec	USA 8min 31.5sec	URS 8min 34.7sec
1960	USA 8min 10.2sec	JPN 8min 13.2sec	AUS 8min 13.8sec
1964	USA 7min 52.1sec	GER 7min 59.3sec	JPN 8min 03.8sec
1968	USA 7min 52.3sec	AUS 7min 53.7sec	URS 8min 01.6sec
1972	USA 7min 35.78sec	GER 7min 41.69sec	URS 7min 45.76sec
1976	USA 7min 23.22sec	URS 7min 27.97sec	GBR 7min 32.11sec

4 x 100 Metres Medley Relay

Not held before 1960. Order of strokes: backstroke, breaststroke, butterfly, freestyle.

	Gold	Silver	Bronze
1960	USA 4min 05.4sec	AUS 4min 12.0sec	JPN 4min 12.2sec
1964	USA 3min 58.4sec	GER 4min 01.6sec	AUS 4min 02.3sec
1968	USA 3min 54.9sec	GDR 3min 57.5sec	URS 4min 00.7sec
1972	USA 3min 48.16sec	GDR 3min 52.1sec	CAN 3min 52.26sec
1976	USA 3min 42.22sec	CAN 3min 45.94sec	GER 3min 47.29sec

Highboard Diving

Not held before 1904. In 1904 and 1908 this was a combined highboard and springboard event. In 1928 Desjardins gained a superior aggregate of placings to Simaika although the latter gained more points.

	Gold	Silver	Bronze
1904	G. Sheldon *USA* 12.66 pts	G. Hoffmann *GER* 11.66 pts	F. Kehoe *USA* & A. Braunschweiger *GER* 11.33 pts
1908	H. Johansson *SWE* 83.75 pts	K. Malmström *SWE* 78.73 pts	A. Spångberg *SWE* 74.00 pts
1912	E. Adlerz *SWE* 73.94 pts	A. Zürner *GER* 72.60 pts	G. Blomgren *SWE* 69.56 pts
1920	C. Pinkston *USA* 100.67 pts	E. Adlerz *SWE* 99.08 pts	H. Prieste *USA* 93.73 pts
1924	A. White *USA* 97.46 pts	D. Fall *USA* 97.30 pts	C. Pinkston *USA* 94.60 pts
1928	P. Desjardins *USA* 98.74 pts	F. Simaika *EGY* 99.58 pts	M. Galitzen *USA* 92.34 pts
1932	H. Smith *USA* 124.80 pts	M. Galitzen *USA* 124.28 pts	F. Kurtz *USA* 121.98 pts
1936	M. Wayne *USA* 113.58 pts	E. Root *USA* 110.60 pts	H. Stork *GER* 110.31 pts
1948	S. Lee *USA* 130.05 pts	B. Harlan *USA* 122.30 pts	J. Capilla Pérez *MEX* 113.52 pts
1952	S. Lee *USA* 156.28 pts	J. Capilla Pérez *MEX* 145.21 pts	G. Haase *GER* 141.31 pts
1956	J. Capilla Pérez *MEX* 152.44 pts	G. Tobian *USA* 152.41 pts	R. Connor *USA* 149.79 pts
1960	R. Webster *USA* 165.56 pts	G. Tobian *USA* 165.25 pts	B. Phelps *GBR* 157.13 pts
1964	R. Webster *USA* 148.58 pts	K. Dibiasi *ITA* 147.54 pts	T. Gompf *USA* 146.57 pts
1968	K. Dibiasi *ITA* 164.18 pts	A. Gaxiola *MEX* 154.49 pts	E. Young *USA* 153.93 pts
1972	K. Dibiasi *ITA* 504.12 pts	R. Rydze *USA* 480.75 pts	F. Cagnotto *ITA* 475.83 pts

	Gold	Silver	Bronze
1976	K. Dibiasi *ITA* 600.51 pts	G. Louganis *USA* 576.99 pts	V. Aleynik *URS* 548.61 pts

Springboard Diving

Not held before 1908.

	Gold	Silver	Bronze
1908	Albert Zürner *GER* 85.5 pts	K. Behrens *GER* 85.3 pts	G. Gaidzik *USA* 80.8 pts
1912	P. Günther *GER* 79.23 pts	H. Luber *GER* 76.78 pts	K. Behrens *GER* 73.73 pts
1920	L. Kuehn *USA* 675.40 pts	C. Pinkston *USA* 655.30 pts	L. Balbach *USA* 649.50 pts
1924	A. White *USA* 696.40 pts	P. Desjardins *USA* 693.20 pts	C. Pinkston *USA* 653.00 pts
1928	P. Desjardins *USA* 185.04 pts	M. Galitzen *USA* 174.06 pts	F. Simaika *EGY* 172.46 pts
1932	M. Galitzen *USA* 161.38 pts	H. Smith *USA* 158.54 pts	R. Degener *USA* 151.82 pts
1936	R. Degener *USA* 163.57 pts	M. Wayne *USA* 159.56 pts	A. Greene *USA* 146.29 pts
1948	B. Harlan *USA* 163.64 pts	M. Anderson *USA* 157.29 pts	S. Lee *USA* 145.52 pts
1952	D. Browning *USA* 205.29 pts	M. Anderson *USA* 199.84 pts	R. Clotworthy *USA* 184.92 pts
1956	R. Clotworthy *USA* 159.56 pts	D. Harper *USA* 156.23 pts	J. Capilla Pérez *MEX* 150.69 pts
1960	G. Tobian *USA* 170.00 pts	S. Hall *USA* 167.08 pts	J. Botella *MEX* 162.30 pts
1964	K. Sitzberger *USA* 159.90 pts	F. Gorman *USA* 157.63 pts	L. Andreasen *USA* 143.77 pts
1968	B. Wrightson *USA* 170.15 pts	K. Dibiasi *ITA* 159.74 pts	J. Henry *USA* 158.09 pts
1972	V. Vasin *URS* 594.09 pts	F. Cagnotto *ITA* 591.63 pts	C. Lincoln *USA* 577.29 pts
1976	P. Boggs *USA* 619.05 pts	F. Cagnotto *ITA* 570.48 pts	A. Kosenkov *URS* 567.24 pts

Water Polo

Not held before 1900.

	Gold	Silver	Bronze
1900	GBR	BEL	FRA
1904	USA	USA	USA
1908	GBR	BEL	SWE
1912	GBR	SWE	BEL
1920	GBR	BEL	SWE
1924	FRA	BEL	USA
1928	GER	HUN	FRA
1932	HUN	GER	USA
1936	HUN	GER	BEL
1948	ITA	HUN	HOL
1952	HUN	YUG	ITA
1956	HUN	YUG	URS
1960	ITA	URS	HUN
1964	HUN	YUG	URS
1968	YUG	URS	HUN
1972	URS	HUN	USA
1976	HUN	ITA	HOL

Swimming and Diving (Women)

100 Metres Freestyle

Not held before 1912.

	Gold	Silver	Bronze
1912	F. Durack *AUS* 1min 22.2sec	W. Wylie *AUS* 1min 25.4sec	J. Fletcher *GBR* 1min 27.0sec
1920	E. Bleibtrey *USA* 1min 13.6sec	I. Guest *USA* 1min 17.0sec	F. Schroth *USA* 1min 17.2sec
1924	E. Lackie *USA* 1min 12.4sec	M. Wehselau *USA* 1min 12.8sec	G. Ederle *USA* 1min 14.2sec
1928	A. Osipowich *USA* 1min 11.0sec	E. Garatti *USA* 1min 11.4sec	J. Cooper *GBR* 1min 13.6sec
1932	H. Madison *USA* 1min 06.8sec	W. den Ouden *HOL* 1min 07.8sec	E. (Garatti) Saville *USA* 1min 08.2sec
1936	H. Mastenbroek *HOL* 1min 05.9sec	J. Campbell *ARG* 1min 06.4sec	G. Arendt *GER* 1min 06.6sec
1948	G. Andersen *DEN* 1min 06.3sec	A. Curtis *USA* 1min 06.5sec	M. L. Vaessen *HOL* 1min 07.6sec
1952	K. Szoke *HUN* 1min 06.8sec	J. Termeulen *HOL* 1min 07.0sec	J. Temes *HUN* 1min 07.1sec
1956	D. Fraser *AUS* 1min 02.0sec	L. Crapp *AUS* 1min 02.3sec	F. Leech *AUS* 1min 05.1sec
1960	D. Fraser *AUS* 1min 01.2sec	C. Von Saltza *USA* 1min 02.8sec	N. Steward *GBR* 1min 03.1sec
1964	D. Fraser *AUS* 59.5sec	S. Stouder *USA* 59.9sec	K. Ellis *USA* 1min 00.8sec
1968	J. Henne *USA* 1min 00.0sec	S. Pedersen *USA* 1min 00.3sec	L. Gustavson *USA* 1min 00.3sec
1972	S. Neilson *USA* 58.59sec	S. Babashoff *USA* 59.02sec	S. Gould *AUS* 59.06sec
1976	K. Ender *GDR* 55.65sec	P. Priemer *GDR* 56.49sec	E. Brigitha *HOL* 56.65sec

200 Metres Freestyle

Not held before 1968.

	Gold	Silver	Bronze
1968	D. Meyer *USA* 2min 10.5sec	J. Henne *USA* 2min 11.0sec	J. Barkman *USA* 2min 11.2sec
1972	S. Gould *AUS* 2min 03.56sec	S. Babashoff *USA* 2min 04.33sec	K. Rothhammer *USA* 2min 04.92sec
1976	K. Ender *GDR* 1min 59.26sec	S. Babashoff *USA* 2min 01.22sec	E. Brigitha *HOL* 2min 01.40sec

400 Metres Freestyle

Not held before 1920. In 1920 the distance was 300m (328yd 4in).

	Gold	Silver	Bronze
1920	E. Bleibtrey *USA* 4min 34.0sec	M. Woodbridge *USA* 4min 42.8sec	F. Schroth *USA* 4min 52.0sec
1924	M. Norelius *USA* 6min 02.2sec	H. Wainwright *USA* 6min 03.8sec	G. Ederle *USA* 6min 04.8sec
1928	M. Norelius *USA* 5min 42.8sec	M. J. Braun *HOL* 5min 57.8sec	J. McKim *USA* 6min 00.2sec
1932	H. Madison *USA* 5min 28.5sec	L. (Kight) Wingard *USA* 5min 28.6sec	J. Makaal *SAF* 5min 47.3sec
1936	H. Mastenbroek *HOL* 5min 26.4sec	R. Hveger *DEN* 5min 27.5sec	L. (Kight) Wingard *USA* 5min 29.0sec
1948	A. Curtis *USA* 5min 17.8sec	K. M. Harup *DEN* 5min 21.2sec	C. Gibson *GBR* 5min 22.5sec
1952	V. Gyenge *HUN* 5min 12.1sec	É. Novák *HUN* 5min 13.7sec	E. Kawamoto *USA* 5min 14.6sec
1956	L. Crapp *AUS* 4min 54.6sec	D. Fraser *AUS* 5min 02.5sec	S. Ruuska *USA* 5min 07.1sec
1960	C. Von Saltza *USA* 4min 50.6sec	J. Cederqvist *SWE* 4min 53.9sec	C. Lagerberg *HOL* 4min 56.9sec
1964	V. Duenkel *USA* 4min 43.3sec	M. Ramenofsky *USA* 4min 44.6sec	T. L. Stickles *USA* 4min 47.2sec
1968	O. Meyer *USA* 4min 31.8sec	L. Gustavson *USA* 4min 35.5sec	K. Moras *AUS* 4min 37.0sec
1972	S. Gould *AUS* 4min 19.04sec	N. Calligaris *ITA* 4min 22.44sec	G. Wegner *GDR* 4min 23.11sec
1976	P. Thumer *GDR* 4min 09.89sec	S. Babashoff *USA* 4min 10.46sec	S. Smith *CAN* 4min 14.60sec

800 Metres Freestyle

Not held before 1968.

	Gold	Silver	Bronze
1968	D. Meyer *USA* 9min 24.0sec	P. Kruse *USA* 9min 35.7sec	M. T. Ramirez *MEX* 9min 38.5sec
1972	K. Rothhammer *USA* 8min 53.68sec	S. Gould *AUS* 8min 56.39sec	N. Calligaris *ITA* 8min 57.46sec
1976	P. Thumer *GDR* 8min 37.14sec	S. Babashoff *USA* 8min 37.59sec	W. Weinberg *USA* 8min 42.60sec

100 Metres Backstroke

Not held before 1924.

	Gold	Silver	Bronze
1924	S. Bauer *USA* 1min 23.2sec	P. Harding *GBR* 1min 27.4sec	A. Riggin *USA* 1min 28.2sec
1928	M. J. Braun *HOL* 1min 22.0sec	E. E. King *GBR* 1min 22.2sec	J. Cooper *GBR* 1min 22.8sec
1932	E. Holm *USA* 1min 19.4sec	P. Mealing *AUS* 1min 21.3sec	V. Davies *GBR* 1min 22.5sec
1936	D. Senff *HOL* 1min 18.9sec	H. Mastenbroek *HOL* 1min 19.2sec	A. Bridges *USA* 1min 19.4sec
1948	K. M. Harup *DEN* 1min 14.4sec	S. Zimmerman *USA* 1min 16.0sec	J. J. Davies *AUS* 1min 16.7sec
1952	J. Harrison *SAF* 1min 14.3sec	G. Wielema *HOL* 1min 14.5sec	J. Stewart *NZL* 1min 15.8sec
1956	J. Grinham *GBR* 1min 12.9sec	C. Cone *USA* 1min 12.9sec	M. Edwards *GBR* 1min 13.1sec
1960	L. Burke *USA* 1min 09.3sec	N. Steward *GBR* 1min 10.8sec	S. Tanaka *JPN* 1min 11.4sec
1964	C. Ferguson *USA* 1min 07.7sec	C. Caron *FRA* 1min 07.9sec	V. Duenkel *USA* 1min 08.0sec
1968	K. Hall *USA* 1min 06.2sec	E. Tanner *CAN* 1min 06.7sec	J. Swagerty *USA* 1min 08.1sec
1972	M. Belote *USA* 1min 05.78sec	A. Gyarmati *HUN* 1min 06.26sec	S. Atwood *USA* 1min 06.34sec
1976	U. Richter *GDR* 1min 01.83sec	B. Treiber *GDR* 1min 03.41sec	N. Garapick *CAN* 1min 03.71sec

200 Metres Backstroke

Not held before 1968.

	Gold	Silver	Bronze
1968	L. Watson *USA* 2min 24.8sec	E. Tanner *CAN* 2min 27.4sec	K. Hall *USA* 2min 28.9sec
1972	M. Belote *USA* 2min 19.19sec	S. Atwood *USA* 2min 20.38sec	D. M. Gurr *CAN* 2min 23.22sec
1976	U. Richter *GDR* 2min 13.43sec	B. Treiber *GDR* 2min 14.97sec	N. Garapick *CAN* 2min 15.60sec

100 Metres Breaststroke

Not held before 1968.

	Gold	Silver	Bronze
1968	D. Bjedov *YUG* 1min 15.8sec	G. Prosumenshchikova *URS* 1min 15.9sec	S. Wichman *USA* 1min 16.1sec
1972	C. Carr *USA* 1min 13.58sec	G. Stepanova *URS* 1min 14.99sec	B. Whitfield *AUS* 1min 15.73sec
1976	H. Anka *GDR* 1min 11.16sec	L. Rusanov *URS* 1min 13.04sec	M. Koshevaia *URS* 1min 13.30sec

200 Metres Breaststroke

Not held before 1924.

	Gold	Silver	Bronze
1924	L. Morton *GBR* 3min 33.2sec	A. Geraghty *USA* 3min 34.0sec	G. Carson *GBR* 3min 35.4sec
1928	H. Schrader *GER* 3min 12.6sec	M. Baron *HOL* 3min 15.2sec	L. (Hildesheim) Mühe *GER* 3min 17.6sec
1932	C. Dennis *AUS* 3min 06.3sec	H. Maehata *JPN* 3min 06.4sec	E. Jacobsen *DEN* 3min 07.1sec
1936	H. Maehata *JPN* 3min 03.6sec	M. Genenger *GER* 3min 04.2sec	I. Sørensen *DEN* 3min 07.8sec
1948	P. van Vliet *HOL* 2min 57.2sec	B. Lyons *AUS* 2min 57.7sec	É. Novák *HUN* 3min 00.2sec
1952	É. Székely *HUN* 2min 51.7sec	É. Novák *HUN* 2min 54.4sec	H. Gordon *GBR* 2min 57.6sec
1956	U. Happe *GER* 2min 53.1sec	É. Székely *HUN* 2min 54.8sec	E. M. Ten Elsen *GER* 2min 55.1sec
1960	A. Lonsbrough *GBR* 2min 49.5sec	W. Urselmann *GER* 2min 50.0sec	B. Göbel *GER* 2min 53.6sec
1964	G. Prosumenshchikova *URS* 2min 46.4sec	C. Kolb *USA* 2min 47.6sec	S. Babanina *URS* 2min 48.6sec
1968	S. Wichman *USA* 2min 44.4sec	D. Bjedov *YUG* 2min 46.4sec	G. Prosumenshchikova *URS* 2min 47.0sec
1972	B. Whitfield *AUS* 2min 41.71sec	D. Schoenfield *USA* 2min 42.05sec	G. Stepanova *URS* 2min 42.36sec
1976	M. Koshevaia *URS* 2min 33.35sec	M. Iurchenia *URS* 2min 36.08sec	L. Rusanov *URS* 2min 36.22sec

100 Metres Butterfly

Not held before 1956.

	Gold	Silver	Bronze
1956	S. Mann *USA* 1min 11.0sec	N. Ramey *USA* 1min 11.9sec	M. J. Sears *USA* 1min 14.4sec
1960	C. Schuler *USA* 1min 09.5sec	M. Heemskerk *HOL* 1min 10.4sec	J. Andrew *AUS* 1min 12.2sec
1964	S. Stouder *USA* 1min 04.7sec	A. Kok *HOL* 1min 05.6sec	K. Ellis *USA* 1min 06.0sec
1968	L. McClements *AUS* 1min 05.5sec	E. Daniel *USA* 1min 05.8sec	S. Shields *USA* 1min 06.2sec
1972	M. Aoki *JPN* 1min 03.34sec	R. Beier *GDR* 1min 03.61sec	A. Gyarmati *HUN* 1min 03.73sec
1976	K. Ender *GDR* 1min 00.13sec	A. Pollack *GDR* 1min 00.98sec	W. Boglioli *GDR* 1min 01.17sec

200 Metres Butterfly

Not held before 1968.

	Gold	Silver	Bronze
1968	A. Kok *HOL* 2min 24.7sec	H. Lindner *GDR* 2min 24.8sec	E. Daniel *USA* 2min 25.9sec
1972	K. Moe *USA* 2min 15.57sec	L. Colella *USA* 2min 16.34sec	E. Daniel *USA* 2min 16.74sec
1976	A. Pollack *GDR* 2min 11.41sec	U. Tauber *GDR* 2min 12.50sec	R. Gabriel *GDR* 2min 12.86sec

200 Metres Individual Medley

Not held before 1968. Order of strokes: butterfly, backstroke, breaststroke, freestyle.

	Gold	Silver	Bronze
1968	C. Kolb *USA* 2min 24.7sec	S. Pedersen *USA* 2min 28.8sec	J. Henne *USA* 2min 31.4sec
1972	S. Gould *AUS* 2min 23.07sec	K. Ender *GDR* 2min 23.59sec	L. Vidali *USA* 2min 24.06sec
1976	*Not held.*		

400 Metres Individual Medley

Not held before 1964. Order of strokes: butterfly, backstroke, breaststroke, freestyle.

	Gold	Silver	Bronze
1964	D. De Varona *USA* 5min 18.7sec	S. Finneran *USA* 5min 24.1sec	M. Randall *USA* 5min 24.2sec
1968	C. Kolb *USA* 5min 08.5sec	L. Vidali *USA* 5min 22.2sec	S. Steinbach *GDR* 5min 25.3sec
1972	G. Neall *AUS* 5min 02.97sec	L. Cliff *CAN* 5min 03.57sec	N. Calligaris *ITA* 5min 03.99sec
1976	U. Tauber *GDR* 4min 42.77sec	C. Gibson *CAN* 4min 48.10sec	B. Smith *CAN* 4min 50.48sec

4 x 100 Metres Freestyle Relay

Not held before 1912.

	Gold	Silver	Bronze
1912	GBR 5min 52.8sec	GER 6min 04.6sec	AUT 6min 17.0sec
1920	USA 5min 11.6sec	GBR 5min 40.8sec	SWE 5min 43.6sec
1924	USA 4min 58.8sec	GBR 5min 17.0sec	SWE 5min 35.8sec
1928	USA 4min 47.6sec	GBR 5min 02.8sec	SAF 5min 13.4sec
1932	USA 4min 38.0sec	HOL 4min 47.5sec	GBR 4min 52.4sec
1936	HOL 4min 36.0sec	GER 4min 36.8sec	USA 4min 40.2sec
1948	USA 4min 29.2sec	DEN 4min 29.6sec	HOL 4min 31.6sec
1952	HUN 4min 24.4sec	HOL 4min 29.0sec	USA 4min 30.1sec
1956	AUS 4min 17.1sec	USA 4min 19.2sec	SAF 4min 25.7sec
1960	USA 4min 08.9sec	AUS 4min 11.3sec	GER 4min 19.7sec
1964	USA 4min 03.8sec	AUS 4min 06.9sec	HOL 4min 12.0sec

	Gold	Silver	Bronze
1968	USA 4min 02.5sec	GDR 4min 05.7sec	CAN 4min 07.2sec
1972	USA 3min 55.19sec	GDR 3min 55.55sec	GER 3min 57.93sec
1976	USA 3min 44.82sec	GDR 3min 45.50sec	CAN 3min 48.81sec

4 x 100 Metres Medley Relay

Not held before 1960. Order of strokes: backstroke, breaststroke, butterfly, freestyle.

	Gold	Silver	Bronze
1960	USA 4min 41.1sec	AUS 4min 45.9sec	GER 4min 47.6sec
1964	USA 4min 33.9sec	HOL 4min 37.0sec	URS 4min 39.2sec
1968	USA 4min 28.3sec	AUS 4min 30.0sec	GER 4min 36.4sec
1972	USA 4min 20.75sec	GDR 4min 24.91sec	GER 4min 26.46sec
1976	GDR 4min 07.95sec	USA 4min 14.55sec	CAN 4min 15.22sec

Highboard Diving

Not held before 1912. In 1924 Smith gained a superior aggregate of placings to Becker although the latter gained more points.

	Gold	Silver	Bronze
1912	G. Johansson *SWE* 39.90 pts	L. Regnell *SWE* 36.00 pts	I. White *GBR* 34.00 pts
1920	S. (Clausen) Fryland *DEN* 34.60 pts	E. Armstrong *GBR* 33.30 pts	E. Ollivier *SWE* 33.30 pts
1924	C. Smith *USA* 33.20 pts	E. Becker *USA* 33.40 pts	H. Töpel *SWE* 32.80 pts
1928	E. (Becker) Pinkston *USA* 31.60 pts	G. Coleman *USA* 30.60 pts	L. Sjöqvist *SWE* 29.20 pts
1932	D. (Poynton) Hill *USA* 40.26 pts	G. Coleman *USA* 35.56 pts	M. Roper *USA* 35.22 pts
1936	D. (Poynton) Hill *USA* 33.93 pts	V. Dunn *USA* 33.63 pts	K. Köhler *GER* 33.43 pts
1948	V. Draves *USA* 68.87 pts	P. Elsener *USA* 66.28 pts	B. Christoffersen *DEN* 66.04 pts
1952	P. McCormick *USA* 79.37 pts	P. J. Myers *USA* 71.63 pts	J. Irwin *USA* 70.49 pts
1956	P. McCormick *USA* 84.85 pts	J. Irwin *USA* 81.64 pts	P. J. Myers *USA* 81.58 pts
1960	I. (Krämer) Engel *GER* 91.28 pts	P. J. (Myers) Pope *USA* 88.94 pts	N. Krutova *URS* 86.99 pts
1964	L. Bush *USA* 99.80 pts	I. (Krämer) Engel *GER* 98.45 pts	G. Alekseeva *URS* 97.60 pts
1968	M. Duchková *TCH* 109.59 pts	N. Lobanova *URS* 105.14 pts	A. Peterson *USA* 101.11 pts
1972	U. Knape *SWE* 390.00 pts	M. Duchková *TCH* 370.92 pts	M. Janicke *GDR* 360.54 pts
1976	E. Vaytsekhovskaya *URS* 406.59 pts	U. Knape *SWE* 402.60 pts	D. Wilson *USA* 401.07 pts

Springboard Diving

Not held before 1920

	Gold	Silver	Bronze
1920	A. Riggin *USA* 539.90 pts	H. Wainwright *USA* 534.80 pts	T. Payne *USA* 534.10 pts
1924	E. Becker *USA* 474.50 pts	A. Riggin *USA* 460.40 pts	C. Fletcher *USA* 436.40 pts
1928	H. Meany *USA* 78.62 pts	D. Poynton *USA* 75.62 pts	G. Coleman *USA* 73.38 pts
1932	G. Coleman *USA* 87.52 pts	K. Rawls *USA* 82.56 pts	J. Fauntz *USA* 82.12 pts
1936	M. Gestring *USA* 89.27 pts	K. Rawls *USA* 88.35 pts	D. (Poynton) Hill *USA* 82.36 pts
1948	V. Draves *USA* 108.74 pts	Z. A. (Olsen) Jensen *USA* 108.23 pts	P. Elsener *USA* 101.30 pts
1952	P. McCormick *USA* 147.30 pts	M. Moreau *FRA* 139.34 pts	Z. A. (Olsen) Jensen *USA* 127.57 pts
1956	P. McCormick *USA* 142.36 pts	J. Stunyo *USA* 125.89 pts	I. MacDonald *CAN* 121.40 pts
1960	I. (Krämer) Engel *GER* 155.81 pts	P. J. (Myers) Pope *USA* 141.24 pts	E. Ferris *GBR* 139.09 pts
1964	I. (Krämer) Engel *GER* 145.00 pts	J. Collier *USA* 138.36 pts	P. Willard *USA* 138.18 pts
1968	S. Gossick *USA* 150.77 pts	T. Pogosheva *URS* 145.30 pts	K. O'Sullivan *USA* 145.23 pts
1972	M. King *USA* 450.03 pts	U. Knape *SWE* 434.19 pts	M. Janicke *GDR* 430.92 pts
1976	J. Chandler *USA* 506.19 pts	C. Kohler *GDR* 469.41 pts	C. McIngvale *USA* 466.83 pts

Volleyball (Men)

Not held before 1964

	Gold	Silver	Bronze
1964	URS	TCH	JPN
1968	URS	JPN	TCH
1972	JPN	GDR	URS
1976	POL	URS	CUB

Volleyball (Women)

Not held before 1964.

	Gold	Silver	Bronze
1964	JPN	URS	POL
1968	URS	JPN	POL
1972	URS	JPN	PRK
1976	JPN	URS	KOR

Weightlifting

The official results are recorded in kilograms. In order to give approximate equivalents in pounds, we have followed the International Weightlifting Federation's system of converting from kilos to pounds to the nearest quarter pound below (because Imperial scales for weighing competitors and barbells weigh to the nearest quarter pound). Since in each case we have converted the total (of two lifts, or, in the early days, three lifts), the total as given in pounds is not quite the same as it would be if we had converted each lift separately into pounds, and therefore is only approximate.

Flyweight

Not held before 1972. Weight limit 52kg (114½lb).

	Gold	Silver	Bronze
1972	Z. Smalcerz *POL* 337.5kg (744lb)	L. Szücs *HUN* 330.00kg (727½lb)	S. Holczreiter *HUN* 327.5kg (722lb)
1976	A. Voronin *URS* 242.5kg (534¼lb)	G. Koszegi *HUN* 237.5kg (523¼lb)	M. Nassiri *IRN* 235.0kg (517¾lb)

Bantamweight

Not held before 1948. Weight limit 56kg (123¼lb).

	Gold	Silver	Bronze
1948	J. De Pietro *USA* 307.5kg (677¾lb)	J. Creus *GBR* 297.5kg (655¾lb)	R. Tom *USA* 295.0kg (650¼lb)
1952	I. Udodov *URS* 315.0kg (694¼lb)	M. Namdjou *IRN* 307.5kg (677¾lb)	A. Mirzai *IRN* 300.0kg (661¼lb)
1956	C. Vinci *USA* 342.5kg (755lb)	V. Stogov *URS* 337.5kg (744lb)	M. Namdjou *IRN* 332.5kg (733lb)
1960	C. Vinci *USA* 345.0kg (760½lb)	Yoshinobu Miyake *JPN* 337.5kg (744lb)	E. Elmkhah *IRN* 330.0kg (727½lb)
1964	A. Vakhonin *URS* 357.5kg (788lb)	I. Földi *HUN* 355.0kg (782½lb)	S. Ichinoseki *JPN* 347.5kg (766lb)
1968	M. Nassiri *IRN* 367.5kg (810lb)	I. Földi *HUN* 367.5kg (810lb)	H. Trebicki *POL* 357.5kg (788lb)
1972	I. Földi *HUN* 377.5kg (832lb)	M. Nassiri *IRN* 370.0kg (815½lb)	G. Chetin *URS* 367.5kg (810lb)
1976	N. Nurikyan *BUL* 262.0kg (578½lb)	G. Cziura *POL* 252.0kg (554½lb)	K. Ando *JPN* 250.0kg (551lb)

Featherweight

Not held before 1920. Weight limit 60kg (132¼lb).

	Gold	Silver	Bronze
1920	F. de Haes *BEL* 220.0kg (485lb)	A. Schmidt *EST* 212.5kg (486¼lb)	E. Ritter *SUI* 210.0kg (462¾lb)
1924	P. Gabetti *ITA* 402.5kg (887¼lb)	A. Stadler *AUT* 385.0kg (848¾lb)	A. Reinmann *SUI* 382.5kg (843¼lb)

	Gold	Silver	Bronze
1928	F. Andrysek *AUT* 287.5kg (633¾lb)	P. Gabetti *ITA* 282.5kg (622¾lb)	H. Wölpert *GER* 282.5kg (622¾lb)
1932	R. Suvigny *FRA* 287.5kg (633¾lb)	H. Wölpert *GER* 282.5kg (622¾lb)	A. Terlazzo *USA* 280.0kg (617¼lb)
1936	A. Terlazzo *USA* 312.5kg (688¾lb)	S. Soliman *EGY* 305.0kg (672¼lb)	I. Shams *EGY* 300.0kg (661¼lb)
1948	M. Fayad *EGY* 332.5kg (733lb)	R. Wilkes *TRI* 317.5kg (699¾lb)	J. Salmassi *IRN* 312.5kg (688¾lb)
1952	R. Chimishkian *URS* 337.5kg (744lb)	N. Saksonov *URS* 332.5kg (733lb)	R. Wilkes *TRI* 322.5kg (710¾lb)
1956	I. Berger *USA* 352.5kg (777lb)	Y. Minaev *URS* 342.5kg (755lb)	M. Zieliński *POL* 335.0kg (738½lb)
1960	Y. Minaev *URS* 372.5kg (821lb)	I. Berger *USA* 362.5kg (799lb)	S. Mannironi *ITA* 352.5kg (777lb)
1964	Yoshinobu Miyake *JPN* 397.5kg (876¼lb)	I. Berger *USA* 382.5kg (843¼lb)	M. Nowak *POL* 377.5kg (832lb)
1968	Yoshinobu Miyake *JPN* 392.5kg (865¼lb)	D. Zhanidze *URS* 387.5kg (854¼lb)	Yoshuyike Miyake *JPN* 385.0kg (848¾lb)
1972	N. Nurikyan *BUL* 402.5kg (887¼lb)	D. Zhanidze *URS* 400.0kg (881¾lb)	J. Benedek *HUN* 390.0kg (859¾lb)
1976	N. Kolesnikov *URS* 285.0kg (628lb)	G. Todorov *BUL* 280.0kg (617lb)	K. Hirai *JPN* 275.0kg (606lb)

Lightweight

Not held before 1920. Weight limit 67.5kg (148¾lb).

	Gold	Silver	Bronze
1920	A. Neuland *EST* 257.5kg (567½lb)	L. Williquet *BEL* 240.0kg (529lb)	F. Rooms *BEL* 230.0kg (507lb)
1924	E. Décottignies *FRA* 440.0kg (970lb)	A. Zwerina *AUT* 427.5kg (942¼lb)	B. Durdis *TCH* 425.0kg (936¾lb)
1928	K. Helbig *GER* & H. Haas *AUT* 322.5kg (710¾lb)		F. Arnout *FRA* 302.5kg (666¾lb)
1932	R. Duverger *FRA* 325.0kg (716½lb)	H. Haas *AUT* 307.5kg (677¾lb)	G. Pierini *ITA* 302.5kg (666¾lb)
1936	A. M. Mesbah *EGY* & R. Fein *AUT* 342.5kg (755lb)		K. Jansen *GER* 327.5kg (722lb)
1948	I. H. Shams *EGY* 360.0kg (793½lb)	A. Hamouda *EGY* 360.0kg (793½lb)	J. Halliday *GBR* 340.0kg (749½lb)
1952	T. Kono *USA* 362.5kg (799lb)	Y. Lopatin *URS* 350.0kg (771½lb)	V. Barberis *AUT* 350.0kg (771½lb)
1956	I. Rybak *URS* 380.0kg (837¾lb)	R. Khabutdinov *URS* 372.5kg (821lb)	C. H. Kim *KOR* 370.0kg (815½lb)
1960	V. Bushuev *URS* 397.5kg (876¼lb)	H. L. Tan *SIN* 380.0kg (837¾lb)	A. W. Aziz *IRQ* 380.0kg (837¾lb)
1964	W. Baszanowski *POL* 432.5kg (953½lb)	V. Kaplunov *URS* 432.5kg (953½lb)	M. Zieliński *POL* 420.0kg (925¾lb)
1968	W. Baszanowski *POL* 437.5kg (963½lb)	P. Jalayer *IRN* 422.5kg (931¼lb)	M. Zieliński *POL* 420.0kg (925¾lb)
1972	M. Kirzhinov *URS* 460.0kg (1,014lb)	M. Kuchev *BUL* 450.0kg (992lb)	Z. Kaczmarek *POL* 437.5kg (964½lb)
1976	P. Korol *URS* 305.0kg (672¼lb)	D. Senet *FRA* 300.0kg (661¼lb)	K. Czarnecki *POL* 295.0kg (650¼lb)

Middleweight

Not held before 1920. Weight limit 75kg (165¼lb).

	Gold	Silver	Bronze
1920	H. Gance *FRA* 245.0kg (540lb)	P. Bianchi *ITA* 237.5kg (523½lb)	A. Pettersson *SWE* 237.5kg (523½lb)
1924	C. Galimberti *ITA* 492.5kg (1,085¾lb)	A. Neuland *EST* 455.0kg (1,003lb)	J. Kikas *EST* 450.0kg (992lb)
1928	R. François *FRA* 335.0kg (738½lb)	C. Galimberti *ITA* 332.5kg (733lb)	A. Scheffer *HOL* 327.5kg (722lb)
1932	R. Ismayr *GER* 345.0kg (760½lb)	C. Galimberti *ITA* 340.0kg (749½lb)	K. Hipfinger *AUT* 337.5kg (744lb)
1936	K. S. el Touni *EGY* 387.5kg (854¼lb)	R. Ismayr *GER* 352.5kg (777lb)	A. Wagner *GER* 352.5kg (777lb)
1948	F. Spellman *USA* 390.0kg (859¾lb)	P. George *USA* 382.5kg (843¼lb)	S. J. Kim *KOR* 380.0kg (837¾lb)
1952	P. George *USA* 400.0kg (881¾lb)	G. Gratton *CAN* 390.0kg (859¾lb)	S. J. Kim *KOR* 382.5kg (843¼lb)
1956	F. Bogdanovski *URS* 420.0kg (925¾lb)	P. George *USA* 412.5kg (909¼lb)	E. Pignatti *ITA* 382.5kg (843¼lb)
1960	A. Kurinov *URS* 437.5kg (964½lb)	T. Kono *USA* 427.5kg (942¼lb)	G. Veres *HUN* 405.0kg (892¾lb)
1964	H. Zdražila *TCH* 445.0kg (981lb)	V. Kurentsov *URS* 440.0kg (970lb)	M. Ohuchi *JPN* 437.5kg (964½lb)
1968	V. Kurentsov *URS* 475.0kg (1,047lb)	M. Ohuchi *JPN* 455.0kg (1,003lb)	K. Bakos *HUN* 440.0kg (970lb)
1972	Y. Bikov *BUL* 485.0kg (1,069lb)	M. Trabulsi *LIB* 472.5kg (1,041¼lb)	A. Silvino *ITA* 470.0kg (1,036lb)
1976	Y. Mitkov *BUL* 335.0kg (738½lb)	V. Militosyan *URS* 330.0kg (729lb)	P. Wenzel *GDR* 327.5kg (721lb)

Light Heavyweight

Not held before 1920. Weight limit 82.5kg (181¾lb).

	Gold	Silver	Bronze
1920	E. Cadine *FRA* 290.0kg (131½lb)	F. Hünenberger *SUI* 275.0kg (124½lb)	E. Pettersson *SWE* 272.5kg (124½lb)
1924	C. Rigoulot *FRA* 502.5kg (1,107¾lb)	F. Hünenberger *SUI* 490.0kg (1,080¼lb)	L. Friedrich *AUT* 490.0kg (1,080¼lb)
1928	S. Nosseir *EGY* 355.0kg (782½lb)	L. Hostin *FRA* 352.5kg (777lb)	J. Verheijen *HOL* 337.5kg (744lb)
1932	L. Hostin *FRA* 365.0kg (804½lb)	S. Olsen *DEN* 360.0kg (793½lb)	H. Duey *USA* 330.0kg (727½lb)
1936	L. Hostin *FRA* 372.5kg (821lb)	E. Deutsch *GER* 365.0kg (804½lb)	I. Wasif *EGY* 360.0kg (793½lb)
1948	S. Stanczyk *USA* 417.5kg (920¼lb)	H. Sakata *USA* 380.0kg (837¾lb)	G. Magnusson *SWE* 375.0kg (826¾lb)
1952	T. Lomakhin *URS* 417.5kg (920½lb)	S. Stanozyk *USA* 415.0kg (914¾lb)	A. Vorobev *URS* 407.5kg (898¼lb)
1956	T. Kono *USA* 447.5kg (986½lb)	V. Stepanov *URS* 427.5kg (942¼lb)	J. George *USA* 417.5kg (920¼lb)
1960	I. Paliński *POL* 442.5kg (975½lb)	S. George *USA* 430.0kg (947¾lb)	J. Bochenek *POL* 420.0kg (925¾lb)
1964	R. Plyukfelder *URS* 475.0kg (1,047lb)	G. Tóth *HUN* 467.5kg (1,030½lb)	G. Veres *HUN* 467.5kg (1,030½lb)
1968	B. Selitski *URS* 485.0kg (1,069lb)	V. Belyaev *URS* 485.0kg (1,069lb)	N. Ozimek *POL* 472.5kg (1,041¼lb)
1972	L. Jensen *NOR* 507.5kg (1,118¾lb)	N. Ozimek *POL* 497.5kg (1,096¾lb)	G. Horváth *HUN* 495.0kg (1,091¼lb)
1976	V. Shary *URS* 365.0kg (804¼lb)	T. Stoichev *BUL* 360.0kg (793¼lb)	P. Baczako *HUN* 345.0kg (760½lb)

Middle Heavyweight

Not held before 1952. Weight limit 90kg (198¼lb).

	Gold	Silver	Bronze
1952	N. Schemansky *USA* 445.0kg (981lb)	G. Novak *URS* 410.0kg (902¾lb)	L. Kilgour *TRI* 402.5kg (887¼lb)
1956	A. Vorobev *URS* 462.5kg (1,019½lb)	D. Sheppard *USA* 442.5kg (975½lb)	J. Debuf *FRA* 425.0kg (936¾lb)
1960	A. Vorobev *URS* 472.5kg (1,041¼lb)	T. Lomakhin *URS* 457.5kg (1,008½lb)	L. Martin *GBR* 445.0kg (981lb)
1964	V. Golovanov *URS* 487.5kg (1,074¾lb)	L. Martin *GBR* 475.0kg (1,047lb)	I. Paliński *POL* 467.5kg (1,030½lb)
1968	K. Kangasniemi *FIN* 517.5kg (1,140¾lb)	Y. Talts *URS* 507.5kg (1,118¾lb)	M. Golab *POL* 495.0kg (1,091¼lb)
1972	A. Nikolov *BUL* 525.0kg (1,157¼lb)	A. Shopov *BUL* 517.5kg (1,140¾lb)	H. Bettembourg *SWE* 512.5kg (1,129¾lb)
1976	D. Rigert *URS* 382.5kg (843lb)	L. James *USA* 362.5kg (798¾lb)	A. Shopov *BUL* 360.0kg (793¼lb)

Heavyweight

For results before 1972 see Super Heavyweight. Weight limit 110kg (242½lb).

	Gold	Silver	Bronze
1972	Y. Talts *URS* 580.0kg (1,278½lb)	A. Kraichev *BUL* 562.5kg (1,240lb)	S. Grützner *GDR* 555.0kg (1,223½lb)
1976	Y. Zaitsev *URS* 385.0kg (848½lb)	K. Semerdjiev *BUL* 385.0kg (848½lb)	T. Rutkowski *POL* 377.5kg (832lb)

Super Heavyweight

This class was described as Heavyweight until 1972. In 1896 and 1904 two separate competitions were held. (1) one-hand lift and (2) two-hand lift. Weight limits 1896–1904 open; 1920–48 over 82.5kg (181¾lb); 1952–68 over 90kg (198¼lb); from 1972 over 110kg (242½lb).

Gold	Silver	Bronze
1896 (1) L. Elliott *GBR* 71.0kg (156½lb)	V. Jensen *DEN* 57.2kg (126lb)	A. Nikolopoulos *GRE* 57.2kg (126lb)
(2) V. Jensen *DEN* 111.5kg (245¾lb)	L. Elliott *GBR* 111.5kg (245¾lb)	S. Versis *GRE* 100.0kg (220½lb)
1900 *Not held*		
1904 (1) O. P. Osthoff *USA* 48 pts	F. Winters *USA* 45 pts	F. Kungler *USA* 10 pts
(2) P. Kakousis *GRE* 111.58kg (245lb)	O. P. Osthoff *USA* 84.36kg (185lb)	F. Kungler *USA* 79.83kg (175lb)
1908–1912 *Not held*		
1920 F. Bottino *ITA* 270.0kg (595¼lb)	J. Alzin *LUX* 255.0kg (562lb)	L. Bernot *FRA* 250.0kg (551lb)
1924 G. Tonani *ITA* 517.5kg (1,140¾lb)	F. Aigner *AUT* 515.0kg (1,135¼lb)	H. Tammer *EST* 497.5kg (1,096¾lb)
1928 J. Strassberger *GER* 372.5kg (821lb)	A. Luhaäär *EST* 360.0kg (793½lb)	J. Skobla *TCH* 357.5kg (788lb)
1932 J. Skobla *TCH* 380.0kg (837¾lb)	V. Pšenička *TCH* 377.5kg (832lb)	J. Strassberger *GER* 377.5kg (832lb)
1936 J. Manger *GER* 410.0kg (902¾lb)	V. Pšenička *TCH* 402.5kg (887¼lb)	A. Luhaäär *EST* 400.0kg (881¾lb)
1948 J. Davis *USA* 452.5kg (997½lb)	N. Schemansky *USA* 425.0kg (936¾lb)	A. Charité *HOL* 412.5kg (909¼lb)
1952 J. Davis *USA* 460.0kg (1,014lb)	J. Bradford *USA* 437.5kg (964½lb)	H. Selvetti *ARG* 432.5kg (953½lb)
1956 P. Anderson *USA* 500.0kg (1,102¼lb)	H. Selvetti *ARG* 500.0kg (1,102¼lb)	A. Pigaiani *ITA* 452.5kg (997½lb)
1960 Y. Vlasov *URS* 537.5kg (1,184¾lb)	J. Bradford *USA* 512.5kg (1,129¾lb)	N. Schemansky *USA* 500.0kg (1,102¼lb)
1964 L. Zhabotinski *URS* 572.5kg (1,262lb)	Y. Vlasov *URS* 570.0kg (1,256½lb)	N. Schemansky *USA* 537.5kg (1,184¾lb)
1968 L. Zhabotinski *URS* 572.5kg (1,262lb)	S. Reding *BEL* 555.0kg (1,223½lb)	J. Dube *USA* 555.0kg (1,223½lb)
1972 V. Alekseev *URS* 640.0kg (1,410¾lb)	R. Mang *GER* 612.0kg (1,344¾lb)	G. Bonk *GDR* 572.5kg (1,262lb)
1976 V. Alekseev *URS* 440.0kg (969¾lb)	G. Bonk *GDR* 405.0kg (892½lb)	H. Losch *GDR* 387.5kg (854lb)

Wrestling Freestyle

Not held before 1904. Weight limit 1904 47.6kg (105lb); from 1972 48kg (105lb 13oz). In 1909 this weight category was called Light flyweight.

Gold	Silver	Bronze
1904 R. Curry *USA*	J. Heim *USA*	G. Thiefenthaler *USA*
1908–1968 *Not held*		
1972 R. Dmitriev *URS*	O. Nikolov *BUL*	E. Javadpour *IRN*
1976 K. Issaev *BUL*	R. Dmitriev *URS*	A. Kudo *JPN*

Flyweight

Not held before 1904. Weight limit 1904 52.16kg (115lb); from 1948 52kg (114lb 10oz). In 1904 this weight category was called 'Bantamweight'.

Gold	Silver	Bronze
1904 G. Mehnert *USA*	G. Bauers *USA*	M. Nelson *USA*
1908–1936 *Not held*		
1948 L. Viitala *FIN*	H. Balamir *TUR*	T. Johansson *SWE*
1952 H. Gemici *TUR*	Y. Kitano *JPN*	M. Mollaghassemi *IRN*
1956 M. Tsalkalamanidze *URS*	M. Khojastehpour *IRN*	H. Akbaş *TUR*
1960 A. Bilek *TUR*	M. Matsubara *JPN*	M. Saifpour Saidabadi *IRN*
1964 Y. Yoshida *JPN*	C. S. Chang *KOR*	S. Aliaakbar Haydari *IRN*
1968 S. Nakata *JPN*	R. Sanders *USA*	S. Sukhbaatar *MGL*
1972 K. Kato *JPN*	A. Alakhverdiev *URS*	H. K. Gwong *PRK*
1976 Y. Takada *JPN*	A. Ivanov *URS*	H. S. Jeon *KOR*

Bantamweight

Not held before 1904. Weight limit 1904 56.80kg (125lb); 1908 54kg (119lb); 1924–36 56kg (123lb 7½oz); from 1948 57kg (125lb 10½oz). In 1904 this weight category was called 'Featherweight'.

Gold	Silver	Bronze
1904 I. Niflot *USA*	A. Wester *USA*	Z. Strebler *USA*
1908 G. Mehnert *USA*	W. J. Press *GBR*	B. A. Côté *CAN*
1912–1920 *Not held*		
1924 K. Pihlajamäki *FIN*	K. E. Mäkinen *FIN*	B. Hines *USA*
1928 K. E. Mäkinen *FIN*	E. Spapen *BEL*	J. Trifunov *CAN*
1932 R. Pearce *USA*	Ö Zombori *HUN*	A. Jaskari *FIN*
1936 Ö Zombori *HUN*	R. Flood *USA*	J. Herbert *GER*
1948 N. Akkar *TUN*	G. Leeman *USA*	C. Kouyos *FRA*
1952 S. Ishii *JPN*	R. Mamedbekov *URS*	K. S. Jadav *IND*
1956 M. Dagistanli *TUR*	M. Yaghoubi *IRN*	M. Shakhov *URS*
1960 T. McCann *USA*	N. Zalev *BUL*	T. Trojanowski *POL*
1964 Y. Uetake *JPN*	H. Akbas *TUR*	A. Ibragimov *URS*
1968 Y. Uetake *JPN*	D. Behm *USA*	A. Gorgori *IRN*
1972 H. Yanagida *JPN*	R. Sanders *USA*	L. Klinga *HUN*
1976 V. Umin *URS*	H. D. Bruchert *GDR*	M. Arai *JPN*

Featherweight

Not held before 1904. Weight limit 1904 61.24kg (135lb); 1908 60.30kg (133lb); 1920 60kg (132lb 4½oz); 1924–36 61kg (134lb 7½oz); 1948–60 62kg (136lb 11oz); 1964–68 63kg (138lb 12oz); from 1972 62kg (136lb 11oz). In 1904 this weight category was called 'Lightweight'.

Gold	Silver	Bronze
1904 B. Bradshaw *USA*	T. McLear *USA*	B. C. Clapper *USA*
1908 G. Dole *USA*	J. Slim *GBR*	W. McKie *GBR*
1912 *Not held*		
1920 C. Ackerley *USA*	S. Gerson *USA*	P. W. Bernard *GBR*
1924 R. Reed *USA*	C. Newton *USA*	K. Naito *JPN*
1928 A. Morrison *USA*	K. Pihlajamäki *FIN*	H. Minder *SUI*
1932 K. Pihlajamäki *FIN*	E. Nemir *USA*	E. Karlsson *SWE*
1936 K. Pihlajamäki *FIN*	F. Millard *USA*	G. Jönsson *SWE*
1948 G. Bilge *TUR*	I. Sjölin *SWE*	A. Müller *SUI*
1952 B. Şit *TUR*	N. Guivehtchi *IRN*	J. Henson *USA*
1956 S. Sasahara *JPN*	J. Mewis *BEL*	E. Penttilä *FIN*
1960 M. Dagistani *TUR*	S. Ivanov *BUL*	V. Rubashvili *URS*
1964 O. Watanabe *JPN*	S. Ivanov *BUL*	N. Khokhashvili *URS*
1968 M. Kaneko *JPN*	E. Todorov *BUL*	S. Seyed-Abassy *IRN*
1972 Z. Abdulbekov *URS*	V. Akdag *TUR*	I. Krastev *BUL*
1976 J. M. Yang *KOR*	Z. Oidov *MGL*	G. Davis *USA*

Lightweight

Not held before 1904. Weight limit 1904 65.77kg (145lb); 1908 66.60kg (146lb 13¼oz); 1920 67.50kg (148lb 13 oz); 1924–36 66kg (145lb 8oz); 1948–60 67kg (147lb 11¼oz); 1964–68 70kg (154lb 5oz); from 1972 68kg (149lb 14½oz). In 1904 this weight category was called 'Light Middleweight'.

Gold	Silver	Bronze
1904 O. Roehm *USA*	S. R. Tesing *USA*	A. Zirkel *USA*
1908 G. de Relwyskow *GBR*	W. Wood *GBR*	A. Gingell *GBR*

	Gold	Silver	Bronze
1912	*Not held*		
1920	K. Anttila *FIN*	G. Svensson *SWE*	P. Wright *GBR*
1924	R. Vis *USA*	V. Vikström *FIN*	A. Haavisto *FIN*
1928	O. Käpp *EST*	C. Pacôme *FRA*	E. Leino *FIN*
1932	C. Pacôme *FRA*	K. Kárpáti *HUN*	G. Klarén *SWE*
1936	K. Kárpáti *HUN*	W. Ehrl *FIN*	H. Pihlajamäki *FIN*
1948	C. Atiki *TUR*	G. Frändfors *SWE*	H. Baumann *SUI*
1952	O. Anderberg *SWE*	J. T. Evans *USA*	D. Tovfighe *IRN*
1956	E. Habibi *IRN*	S. Kasahara *JPN*	A. Bestaev *URS*
1960	S. Wilson *USA*	V. Sinyavski *URS*	E. Dimov (Valchev) *BUL*
1964	E. Valchev *BUL*	K. J. Rost *GER*	I. Horiuchi *JPN*
1968	A. Movahed Ardabili *IRN*	E. Valchev *JPN*	S. Danzandarjaa *MGL*
1972	D. Gable *USA*	K. Wada *JPN*	R. Ashuraliev *URS*
1976	D. Pinigin *URS*	L. Keaser *USA*	Y. Sugawara *JPN*

Welterweight

Not held before 1904. Weight limit 1904 71.67kg (158lb); 1924–36 72kg (158lb $11\frac{1}{2}$oz); 1948–60 73kg (160lb 15oz); 1964–68 78kg (171lb $15\frac{1}{4}$oz); from 1972 74kg (163lb $2\frac{1}{4}$oz). In 1904 this weight category was called 'Middleweight'; in 1924 it was called 'Light Middleweight'.

	Gold	Silver	Bronze
1904	C. Erikson *USA*	W. Beckmann *USA*	J. Winholtz *USA*
1908–1920	*Not held*		
1924	H. Gehri *SUI*	E. Leino *FIN*	O. Müller *SUI*
1928	A. J. Haavisto *FIN*	L. O. Appleton *USA*	M. E. Letchford *CAN*
1932	J. Van Bebber *USA*	D. MacDonald *CAN*	E. Leino *FIN*
1936	F. Lewis *USA*	T. Andersson *SWE*	J. Schleimer *CAN*
1948	Y. Dogu *TUR*	R. Garrard *AUS*	L. Merrill *USA*
1952	W. Smith *USA*	P. Berlin *SWE*	A. Modjtabavi *IRN*
1956	M. Ikeda *JPN*	I. Zengin *TUR*	V. Balavadze *URS*
1960	D. Blubaugh *USA*	I. Ogan *TUR*	M. Bashir *PAK*
1964	I. Ogan *TUR*	G. Sagaradze *URS*	M. A. Sanatkaran *IRN*
1968	M. Atalay *TUR*	D. Robin *FRA*	D. Purev *MGL*
1972	W. Wells *USA*	J. Karlsson *SWE*	A. Seger *GER*
1976	J. Date *JPN*	M. Barzegar *IRN*	S. Dziedzic *USA*

Middleweight

Not held before 1908. Weight limit 1908 73kg (161lb); 1920 75kg (165lb $5\frac{1}{2}$oz); 1924–60 79kg (174lb $2\frac{3}{4}$oz); 1964–68 87kg (191lb $12\frac{3}{4}$oz); from 1972 82kg (180lb $12\frac{1}{2}$oz).

	Gold	Silver	Bronze
1908	S. Bacon *GBR*	G. de Relwyskow *GBR*	F. Beck *GBR*
1912	*Not held*		
1920	E. Leino *FIN*	V. Penttala *FIN*	C. Johnson *USA*
1924	F. Hagmann *SUI*	P. Ollivier *BEL*	V. F. Pekkala *FIN*
1928	E. Kyburz *SUI*	D. P. Stockton *CAN*	S. Rabin *GBR*
1932	I. Johansson *SWE*	K. Luukko *FIN*	J. Tunyogi *HUN*
1936	E. Poilvé *FRA*	R. Voliva *USA*	A. Kireççi *TUR*
1948	G. Brand *USA*	A. Candemir *TUR*	E. Lindén *SWE*
1952	D. Tsimakuridze *URS*	G. R. Takhti *IRN*	G. Gurics *HUN*
1956	N. Stanchev *BUL*	D. Hodge *USA*	G. Skhirtladze *URS*
1960	H. Güngör *TUR*	G. Skhirtladze *URS*	H. Y. Antonsson *SWE*
1964	P. Gardshev *BUL*	H. Güngör *TUR*	D. Brand *USA*
1968	B. Gurevich *URS*	M. Jigjid *MGL*	P. Gardshev *BUL*
1972	L. Tediashvili *URS*	J. Peterson *USA*	V. Jorga *ROM*
1976	J. Peterson *USA*	V. Novojilov *URS*	A. Seger *GER*

Light Heavyweight

Not held before 1920. Weight limit 1920 82.5kg (181lb 8oz); 1924–60 87kg (191lb $12\frac{3}{4}$oz); 1964–68 97kg (213lb $13\frac{1}{2}$oz); from 1972 90kg (198lb $6\frac{3}{4}$oz).

	Gold	Silver	Bronze
1920	A. Larsson *SWE*	C. Courant *SUI*	W. Maurer *USA*
1924	J. Spellman *USA*	R. Svensson *SWE*	C. Courant *SUI*
1928	T. Sjöstedt *SWE*	A. Bögli *SUI*	H. Lefebvre *FRA*
1932	P. Mehringer *USA*	T. Sjöstedt *SWE*	E. Scarf *AUS*
1936	K. Fridell *SWE*	A. Neo *EST*	E. Siebert *GER*
1948	H. Wittenberg *USA*	F. Stöckli *SUI*	B. Fahlkvist *SWE*
1952	V. Palm *SWE*	H. Wittenberg *USA*	A. Atan *TUR*
1956	G. R. Takhti *IRN*	B. Kulaev *URS*	P. S. Blair *USA*
1960	A. Atli *TUR*	G. R. Takhti *IRN*	A. Albul *URS*
1964	A. Medved *URS*	A. Ayik *TUR*	S. Mustafov *BUL*
1968	A. Ayik *TUR*	S. Lomidze *URS*	J. Csatári *HUN*
1972	B. Peterson *USA*	G. Strakhov *URS*	K. Bajko *HUN*
1976	L. Tediashvili *URS*	B. Peterson *USA*	S. Morcov *ROM*

Heavyweight

Not held before 1904. Weight limit 1904 over 71.67kg (158lb); 1908 over 73kg (161lb); 1920 over 82.5kg (181lb 14oz); 1924–60 over 87kg (191lb $12\frac{3}{4}$oz); 1964–68 over 97kg (213lb $13\frac{1}{2}$oz); from 1972 under 100kg (200lb $7\frac{1}{4}$oz).

	Gold	Silver	Bronze
1904	B. Hansen *USA*	F. Kungler *USA*	F. Warmbold *USA*
1908	G. C. O'Kelly *GBR/IRL*	J. Gundersen *NOR*	E. Barrett *GBR/IRL*
1912	*Not held*		
1920	R. Roth *SUI*	N. Pendleton *USA*	E. Nilsson *SWE* & F. Meyer *USA*
1924	H. Steele *USA*	H. Wernli *SUI*	A. McDonald *GBR*
1928	J. Richthoff *SWE*	A. Sihvola *FIN*	E. Dame *FRA*
1932	J. Richthoff *SWE*	J. Riley *FIN*	N. Hirschl *AUT*
1936	K. Palusalu *EST*	J. Klapuch *TCH*	H. Nyström *FIN*
1948	G. Bóbis *HUN*	B. Antonsson *SWE*	J. Armstrong *AUS*
1952	A. Mekokishvili *URS*	B. Antonsson *SWE*	K. Richmond *GBR*
1956	H. Kaplan *TUR*	H. Mekhmedov *BUL*	T. Kangasniemi *FIN*
1960	W. Dietrich *GER*	H. Kaplan *TUR*	S. Tsarasov *URS*
1964	A. Ivanitski *URS*	L. Djiber *BUL*	H. Kaplan *TUR*
1968	A. Medved *URS*	O. Duralyev *BUL*	W. Dietrich *GER*
1972	I. Yarygin *URS*	K. Baianmunkh *MGL*	J. Csatári *HUN*
1976	I. Yarygin *URS*	R. Hellickson *USA*	D. Kostov *BUL*

Super Heavyweight

Not held before 1972. Weight limit over 100kg (220lb $7\frac{1}{4}$oz).

	Gold	Silver	Bronze
1972	A. Medved *URS*	O. Duralyev *BUL*	C. Taylor *USA*
1976	S. Andiev *URS*	J. Balla *HUN*	L. Simon *ROM*

Wrestling Greco-Roman Style

Light Flyweight

Not held before 1972. Weight limit under 48kg (105lb 13oz).

	Gold	Silver	Bronze
1972	G. Berceanu *ROM*	R. Aliabadi *IRN*	S. Anghelov *BUL*
1976	A. Shumakov *URS*	G. Berceanu *ROM*	S. Anghelov *BUL*

Flyweight

Not held before 1948. Weight limit under 52kg (114lb $10\frac{1}{4}$oz).

	Gold	Silver	Bronze
1948	P. Lombardi *ITA*	K. Olcay *TUR*	R. Kangasmäki *FIN*
1952	B. Gurevich *URS*	I. Fabra *ITA*	L. Honkala *FIN*
1956	N. Solovyev *URS*	I. Fabra *ITA*	D. A. Egribas *TUR*
1960	D. Pirvulescu *ROM*	O. Sayed *EGY*	M. Paziraye *IRN*
1964	T. Hanahara *JPN*	A. Kerezov *BUL*	D. Pirvulescu *ROM*
1968	P. Kirov *BUL*	V. Bakulin *URS*	M. Zeman *TCH*
1972	P. Kirov *BUL*	K. Hirayama *JPN*	G. Bognanni *ITA*
1976	V. Kostanjinov *URS*	N. Ginga *ROM*	K. Hirayama *JPN*

Bantamweight

Not held before 1924. Weight limit 1924–28 under 58kg (128lb); 1932–36 under 56kg (123lb 7½oz); from 1948 under 57kg (125lb 10½oz).

	Gold	Silver	Bronze
1924	E. Pütsep *EST*	A. Ahlfors *FIN*	V. Ikonen *FIN*
1928	K. Leucht *GER*	J. Maudr *TCH*	G. Gozzi *ITA*
1932	J. Brendel *GER*	M. Nizzola *ITA*	L. François *FRA*
1936	M. Lörincz *HUN*	E. Svensson *SWE*	J. Brendel *GER*
1948	K. Pettersén *SWE*	A. M. Hassan *EGY*	H. Kaya *TUR*
1952	I. Hódes *HUN*	Z. Khihab *LIB*	A. Terian *URS*
1956	K. Vyrupaev *URS*	E. Vesterby *SWE*	F. Horvat *ROM*
1960	O. Karavaev *URS*	I. Cernea *ROM*	P. Dinko *BUL*
1964	M. Ichiguchi *JPN*	V. Trostyanski *URS*	I. Cernea *ROM*
1968	J. Varga *HUN*	I. Baciu *ROM*	I. Kochergin *URS*
1972	R. Kazakov *URS*	H. J. Veil *GER*	R. Bjoerlin *FIN*
1976	P. Ukkola *FIN*	I. Frgic *YUG*	F. Mustafin *URS*

Featherweight

Not held before 1912. Weight limit 1912–20 60kg (132lb 4½oz); 1924–28 62kg (136lb 11oz); 1932–36 61kg (134lb 7¾oz); 1948–60 62kg (136lb 11oz); 1964–68 63kg (138lb 14½oz); from 1972 62kg (136lb 11oz).

	Gold	Silver	Bronze
1912	K. Koskelo *FIN*	G. Gerstacker *GER*	O. Lasanen *FIN*
1920	O. Friman *FIN*	H. Kähkönen *FIN*	F. Svensson *SWE*
1924	K. Anttila *FIN*	A. Toivola *FIN*	E. Malmberg *SWE*
1928	V. Väli *EST*	E. Malmberg *SWE*	G. Quaglia *ITA*
1932	G. Gozzi *ITA*	W. Ehrl *GER*	L. Koskela *FIN*
1936	Y. Erkan *TUR*	A. Reini *FIN*	E. Karlsson *SWE*
1948	M. Oktav *TUR*	O. Anderberg *SWE*	F. Tóth *HUN*
1952	Y. Punkin *URS*	I. Polyák *HUN*	A. Rashed *EGY*
1956	R. Mäkinen *FIN*	I. Polyák *HUN*	R. Zhneladze *URS*
1960	M. Sille *TUR*	I. Polyák *HUN*	K. Vyrupaev *URS*
1964	I. Polyák *HUN*	R. Rurura *URS*	B. Martinović *YUG*
1968	R. Rurura *URS*	H. Fujimoto *JPN*	S. Popescu *ROM*
1972	G. Markov *BUL*	H. H. Wehling *GDR*	K. Lipień *POL*
1976	K. Lipień *POL*	N. Davidyan *URS*	L. Reczi *HUN*

Lightweight

Not held before 1908. Weight limit 1908 66.6kg (147lb); 1912–28 67.5kg (148lb 13oz); 1932–36 66kg (145lb 8oz); 1948–60 67kg (147lb 11¼oz); 1964–68 70kg (154lb 5oz); from 1972 68kg (149lb 14½oz).

	Gold	Silver	Bronze
1908	E. Porro *ITA*	N. Orlov *RUS*	A. (Lindén) Linko *FIN*
1912	E. Väre *FIN*	G. Malmström *SWE*	E. Matiasson *SWE*
1920	E. Väre *FIN*	T. Tamminen *FIN*	F. Andersen *NOR*
1924	O. Friman *FIN*	L. Keresztes *HUN*	K. Westerlund *FIN*
1928	L. Keresztes *HUN*	E. Sperling *GER*	E. Westerlund *FIN*
1932	E. Malmberg *SWE*	A. Kurland *DEN*	E. Sperling *GER*
1936	L. Koskela *FIN*	J. Herda *TCH*	V. Väli *EST*
1948	G. Freij *SWE*	A. Eriksen *NOR*	K. Ferencz *HUN*
1952	S. Safin *URS*	G. Freij *SWE*	M. Athanasov *TCH*
1956	K. Lehtonen *FIN*	R. Dogan *TUR*	G. Tóth *HUN*
1960	A. Koridze *URS*	B. Martinović *YUG*	G. Freij *SWE*
1964	K. Ayvaz *TUR*	V. Bularca *ROM*	D. Gvantseladze *URS*
1968	M. Munemura *JPN*	S. Horvath *YUG*	P. Galaktopoulos *GRE*
1972	S. Khisamutdinov *URS*	S. Apostolov *BUL*	G. M. Ranzi *ITA*
1976	S. Nalbandyan *URS*	S. Rusu *ROM*	H. H. Wehling *GDR*

Welterweight

Not held before 1932. Weight limit 1932–36 72kg (158lb 11¾oz); 1948–60 73kg (160lb 15oz); 1964–68 78kg (171lb 15½oz); from 1972 74kg (163lb 2¼oz).

	Gold	Silver	Bronze
1932	I. Johansson *SWE*	V. Kajander *FIN*	E. Gallegati *ITA*
1936	R. Svedberg *SWE*	F. Schäfer *GER*	E. Virtanen *FIN*
1948	G. Andersson *SWE*	M. Szilvási *HUN*	H. Hansen *DEN*
1952	M. Szilvási *HUN*	G. Andersson *SWE*	K. Taha *LIB*
1956	M. Bayrak *TUR*	V. Maneev *URS*	P. Berlin *SWE*
1960	M. Bayrak *TUR*	G. Maritschnigg *GER*	R. Schiermeyer *FRA*
1964	A. Koleslov *URS*	C. Todorov *BUL*	B. Nyström *SWE*
1968	R. Vesper *GDR*	D. Robin *FRA*	K. Bajkó *HUN*
1972	V. Macha *TCH*	P. Galaktopoulos *GRE*	J. Karlsson *SWE*
1976	A. Bykov *URS*	V. Macha *TCH*	K. H. Helbing *GER*

Middleweight

Not held before 1908. Weight limit 1908 73kg (161lb); 1912–28 75kg (165lb 5¾oz); 1932–60 79kg (174lb 2¾oz); 1964–68 87kg (191lb 12¾oz); from 1972 82kg (180lb 12½oz). In 1912 this weight category was called 'Middleweight A'; in 1928 'Welterweight'.

	Gold	Silver	Bronze
1908	F. Mårtensson *SWE*	M. Andersson *SWE*	A. Andersen *DEN*
1912	C. Johansson *SWE*	M. Klein *RUS*	A. Asikainen *FIN*
1920	C. Westergren *SWE*	A. Lindfors *FIN*	M. Perttilä *FIN*
1924	E. Westerlund *FIN*	A. Lindfors *FIN*	R. Steinberg *EST*
1928	V. Kokkinen *FIN*	L. Papp *HUN*	A. Kuznets *EST*
1932	V. Kokkinen *FIN*	J. Földeák *GER*	A. Cadier *SWE*
1936	I. Johansson *SWE*	L. Schweikert *GER*	J. Palotás *HUN*
1948	A. Grönberg *SWE*	M. Tayfur *TUR*	E. Gallegati *ITA*
1952	A. Grönberg *SWE*	K. Rauhala *FIN*	N. Belov *URS*
1956	G. Kartozia *URS*	D. Dobrev *BUL*	R. Jansson *SWE*
1960	D. Dobrev *BUL*	L. Metz *GDR*	I. Taranu *ROM*
1964	B. Simić *YUG*	J. Kormanik *TCH*	L. Metz *GER*
1968	L. Metz *GDR*	V. Olenik *URS*	B. Simić *YUG*
1972	C. Hegedus *HUN*	A. Nazarenko *URS*	M. Nenadić *YUG*
1976	M. Petkovic *YUG*	V. Cheboksarov *URS*	I. Kolev *BUL*

Light Heavyweight

Not held before 1908. Weight limit 1908 93kg (205lb); 1912–28 82.5kg (181lb 14oz); 1932–60 87kg (191lb 12¾oz); 1964–68 97kg (213lb 13¾oz); from 1972 90kg (198lb 6¾oz). In 1912 this weight category was called 'Middleweight B'; in 1928 'Middleweight'.

	Gold	Silver	Bronze
1908	V. Weckman *FIN*	Y. Saarela *FIN*	C. Jensen *DEN*
1912	*Not awarded*	A. Ahlgren *SWE* & I. Böhling *FIN*	B. Varga *HUN*
1920	C. Johansson *SWE*	E. Rosenqvist *FIN*	J. Eriksen *DEN*
1924	C. Westergren *SWE*	J. R. Svensson *SWE*	O. Pellinen *FIN*
1928	I. Mustafa *EGY*	A. Riger *GER*	O. Pellinen *FIN*
1932	R. Svensson *SWE*	O. Pellinen *FIN*	M. Gruppioni *ITA*
1936	A. Cadier *SWE*	E. Bietags *LIT*	A. Neo *EST*
1948	K. E. Nilsson *SWE*	K. Gröndahl *FIN*	I. Orabi *EGY*
1952	K. Gröndahl *FIN*	S. Shikhladze *URS*	K. E. Nilsson *SWE*
1956	V. Nikolaev *URS*	P. Sirakov *BUL*	K. E. Nilsson *SWE*
1960	T. Kiş *TUR*	K. Bimbalov *BUL*	G. Kartozia *URS*
1964	B. Radev (Aleksandrov) *BUL*	P. Svensson *SWE*	H. Kiehl *GER*
1968	B. Radev *BUL*	N. Yakovenko *URS*	N. Martinescu *ROM*
1972	V. Rezantsev *URS*	J. Corak *YUG*	C. Kwieciński *POL*
1976	V. Retzansev *URS*	S. Ivanov *BUL*	C. Kwieciński *POL*

Heavyweight

Weight limit 1896 none; 1908 over 93kg (205lb); 1912–28 over 82.5kg (181lb 14oz); 1932–60 over 87kg (191lb 12¾oz); 1964–68 over 97kg (213lb 13¾oz); from 1972 under 100kg (220lb 7¼oz).

	Gold	Silver	Bronze
1896	C. Schuhmann *GER*	G. Tsitas *GRE*	S. Christopoulos *GRE*

	Gold	Silver	Bronze
1900–1904	*Not held*		
1908	R. Weisz *HUN*	A. Petrov *RUS*	S. M. Jensen *DEN*
1912	Y. Saarela *FIN*	J. Olin *FIN*	S. M. Jensen *DEN*
1920	A. Lindfors *FIN*	P. Hansen *DEN*	M. Nieminen *FIN*
1924	H. Deglane *FRA*	E. Rosenqvist *FIN*	R. Badó *HUN*
1928	J. R. Svensson *SWE*	H. E. Nyström *FIN*	G. Gehring *GER*
1932	C. Westergren *SWE*	J. Urban *TCH*	N. Hirschl *AUT*
1936	K. Palusalu *EST*	J. Nyman *SWE*	K. Hornfischer *GER*
1948	A. Kireççi *TUR*	T. Nilsson *SWE*	G. Fantoni *ITA*
1952	Y. Kotkas *URS*	J. Ružička *TCH*	T. Kovanen *FIN*
1956	A. Parfenov *URS*	W. Dietrich *GER*	A. Bulgarelli *ITA*
1960	I. Bogdan *URS*	W. Dietrich *GER*	B. Kubat *TCH*
1964	I. Kozma *HUN*	A. Roshchin *URS*	W. Dietrich *GER*
1968	I. Kozma *HUN*	A. Roshchin *URS*	P. Kment *TCH*
1972	N. Martinescu *ROM*	N. Iakovenko *URS*	F. Kiss *HUN*
1976	N. Bolboshin *URS*	K. Goranov *BUL*	A. Skrzylewski *POL*

Super Heavyweight

Not held before 1972. Weight over 100kg (220lb 7¼oz).

	Gold	Silver	Bronze
1972	A. Roshchin *URS*	A. Tomov *BUL*	V. Dolipschi *ROM*
1976	A. Kolchinski *URS*	A. Tomov *BUL*	R. Codreanu *ROM*

Yachting

5.5 Metres

Not held before 1952.

	Gold	Silver	Bronze
1952	USA 5,751 pts	NOR 5,325 pts	SWE 4,554 pts
1956	SWE 5,527 pts	GBR 4,050 pts	AUS 4,022 pts
1960	USA 6,900 pts	DEN 5,679 pts	SUI 5,122 pts
1964	AUS 5,981 pts	SWE 5,254 pts	USA 5,106 pts
1968	SWE 8.0 pts	SUI 32.0 pts	GBR 39.8 pts
1972	*Not held*		
1976	*Not held*		

Tempest

Not held before 1972.

	Gold	Silver	Bronze
1972	URS 28.1 pts	GBR 34.4 pts	USA 47.7 pts
1976	SWE 14.00 pts	URS 30.40 pts	USA 32.70 pts

Soling

Not held before 1972.

	Gold	Silver	Bronze
1972	USA 8.7 pts	SWE 31.7 pts	CAN 47.1 pts
1976	DEN 46.70 pts	USA 47.70 pts	GDR 47.40 pts

Flying Dutchman

Not held before 1960.

	Gold	Silver	Bronze
1960	NOR 6,774 pts	DEN 5,991 pts	GER 5,882 pts
1964	NZL 6,255 pts	GBR 5,556 pts	USA 5,158 pts
1968	GBR 3.0 pts	GER 43.7 pts	BRA 48.4 pts
1972	GBR 22.7 pts	FRA 40.7 pts	GER 51.1 pts
1976	GER 34.70 pts	GBR 51.70 pts	BRA 52.10 pts

Dragon

Not held before 1948.

	Gold	Silver	Bronze
1948	NOR 4,746 pts	SWE 4,621 pts	DEN 4,223 pts
1952	NOR 6,130 pts	SWE 5,556 pts	GER 5,352 pts
1956	SWE 5,723 pts	DEN 5,723 pts	GBR 4,547 pts
1960	GRE 6,733 pts	ARG 5,715 pts	ITA 5,704 pts
1964	DEN 5,854 pts	GER 5,826 pts	USA 5,523 pts
1968	USA 6.0 pts	DEN 26.4 pts	GDR 32.7 pts
1972	AUS 13.7 pts	GDR 41.7 pts	USA 47.7 pts
1976	*Not held*		

Star

Not held before 1932.

	Gold	Silver	Bronze
1932	USA 46 pts	GBR 35 pts	SWE 28 pts
1936	GER 80 pts	SWE 64 pts	HOL 63 pts
1948	USA 5,828 pts	CUB 4,949 pts	HOL 4,731 pts
1952	ITA 7,635 pts	USA 7,216 pts	POR 4,903 pts
1956	USA 5,876 pts	ITA 5,649 pts	BAH 5,223 pts
1960	URS 7,619 pts	POR 6,665 pts	USA 6,269 pts
1964	BAH 5,664 pts	USA 5,585 pts	SWE 5,527 pts
1968	USA 14.4 pts	NOR 43.7 pts	ITA 44.7 pts
1972	AUS 28.1 pts	SWE 44.0 pts	GER 44.4 pts
1976	*Not held*		

Tornado

Not held before 1976.

	Gold	Silver	Bronze
1976	GBR 18 pts	USA 36 pts	GER 37.70 pts

Finn

Not held before 1924. This single-handed class was not for Finn boats until 1952; before then it was for various types.

	Gold	Silver	Bronze
1924	L. Huybrechts *BEL* 2 pts	H. Robert *NOR* 7 pts	H. Dittmar *FIN* 8 pts
1928	S. Thorell *SWE* nda	H. Robert *NOR* nda	B. Broman *FIN* nda
1932	J. Lebrun *FRA* 87 pts	A. L. J. Maas *HOL* 85 pts	S. A. Cansino *ESP* 76 pts
1936	D. M. J. Kagchelland *HOL* 163 pts	W. Krogmann *GER* 150 pts	P. M. Scott *GBR* 131 pts
1948	P. Elvstrøm *DEN* 5,543 pts	R. Evans *USA* 5,408 pts	J. H. de Jong *HOL* 5,204 pts
1952	P. Elvstrøm *DEN* 8,209 pts	C. Currey *GBR* 5,449 pts	R. Sarby *SWE* 5,051 pts
1956	P. Elvstrøm *DEN* 7,509 pts	A. Nelis *BEL* 6,254 pts	J. Marvin *USA* 5,953 pts
1960	P. Elvstrøm *DEN* 8,171 pts	A. Chuchelov *URS* 6,520 pts	A. Nelis *BEL* 5,934 pts
1964	W. Kuhweide *GER* 7,638 pts	P. Barrett *USA* 6,373 pts	H. Wind *DEN* 6,190 pts
1968	V. Mankin *URS* 11.7 pts	H. Raudaschl *AUT* 53.4 pts	F. Albarelli *ITA* 55.1 pts
1972	S. Maury *FRA* 58.0 pts	I. Hatzipavlis *GRE* 71.0 pts	V. Potapov *URS* 74.7 pts
1976	J. Shumann *GDR* 35.40 pts	A. Balashov *URS* 39.70 pts	J. Bertrand *AUS* 46.40 pts

470

Not held before 1976.

	Gold	Silver	Bronze
1976	GER 42.40 pts	ESP 49.70 pts	AUS 57 pts

The Winter Games

Before the first Winter Games at Chamonix, winter sports were held at the Olympic Games in London (1908) and Antwerp (1920). At each there were official competitions in figure skating (for men, women and pairs). At Antwerp there was also a competition in ice hockey.

Biathlon

20-km ($12\frac{1}{2}$-mile) cross-country race with four shooting exercises. Not held before 1960.

	Gold	Silver	Bronze
1960	K. Lestander *SWE* 1hr 33min 21.6sec	A. Tyrväinen *FIN* 1hr 33min 57.7sec	A. Privalov *URS* 1hr 34min 54.2sec
1964	V. Melanin *URS* 1hr 20min 26.8sec	A. Privalov *URS* 1hr 23min 32.5sec	O. Jordet *NOR* 1hr 24min 38.8sec
1968	M. Solberg *NOR* 1hr 13min 45.9sec	A. Tikhonov *URS* 1hr 14min 40.4sec	V. Gundartsev *URS* 1hr 18min 27.4sec
1972	M. Solberg *NOR* 1hr 15min 55.50sec	H. Knauthe *GDR* 1hr 16min 07.60sec	L. Arwidson *SWE* 1hr16min 27.03sec
1976	N. Kruglov *URS* 1hr 14min 12.26sec	H. Ikola *FIN* 1hr 15min 54.10sec	A. Elizarov *URS* 1hr16min 05.57sec

Biathlon Relay

4 x 7.5km ($4\frac{1}{2}$ miles) with two shooting exercises. Not held before 1968.

	Gold	Silver	Bronze
1968	URS 2hr 13min 02.4sec	NOR 2hr 14min 50.2sec	SWE 2hr 17min 26.3sec
1972	URS 1hr 51min 44.92sec	FIN 1hr 54min 37.25sec	GDR 1hr54min 57.67sec
1976	URS 1hr 57min 55.64sec	FIN 2hr 01min 45.58sec	GDR 2hr04min 08.61sec

Bobsleighing

Two-Man Bob

Not held before 1932.

	Gold	Silver	Bronze
1932	USA I 8min 14.74sec	SUI II 8min 16.28sec	USA II 8min 29.15sec
1936	USA I 5min 29.29sec	SUI II 5min 30.64sec	USA II 5min 33.96sec
1948	SUI II 5min 29.20sec	SUI I 5min 30.40sec	USA II 5min 35.30sec
1952	GER I 5min 24.54sec	USA I 5min 26.89sec	SUI I 5min 27.71sec
1956	ITA I 5min 30.14sec	ITA II 5min 31.45sec	SUI I 5min 37.46sec
1960	*Not held*		
1964	GBR I 4min 21.90sec	ITA II 4min 22.02sec	ITA I 4min 22.63sec
1968	ITA I 4min 41.54sec	GER I 4min 41.54sec	ROM I 4min 44.46sec
1972	GER II 4min 57.07sec	GER I 4min 58.84sec	SUI I 4min 59.33sec
1976	GDR II 3min 44.42sec	GER I 3min 44.99sec	SUI I 3min 45.70sec

Four-Man Bob

Not held before 1924.

	Gold	Silver	Bronze
1924	SUI II 5min 45.54sec	GBR II 5min 48.83sec	BEL I 6min 02.29sec
1928	USA II 3min 20.50sec	USA I 3min 21.00sec	GER II 3min 21.90sec
1932	USA I 7min 53.68sec	USA II 7min 55.70sec	GER I 8min 00.04sec
1936	SUI II 5min 19.85sec	SUI I 5min 22.73sec	GBR I 5min 23.41sec
1948	USA II 5min 20.10sec	BEL I 5min 21.30sec	USA I 5min 21.50sec
1952	GER I 5min 07.84sec	USA I 5min 10.48sec	SUI I 5min 11.70sec
1956	SUI I 5min 10.44sec	ITA II 5min 12.10sec	USA I 5min 12.39sec
1960	*Not held*		
1964	CAN I 4min 14.46sec	AUT I 4min 15.48sec	ITA II 4min 15.60sec
1968	ITA I 2min 17.39sec	AUT I 2min 17.48sec	SUI I 2min 18.04sec
1972	SUI I 4min 43.07sec	ITA I 4min 43.83sec	GER I 4min 43.92sec
1976	GDR I 3min 40.43sec	SUI II 3min 40.89sec	GER I 3min 41.37sec

Ice Hockey

	Gold	Silver	Bronze
1920	CAN	USA	TCH
1924	CAN	USA	GBR
1928	CAN	SWE	SUI
1932	CAN	USA	GER
1936	GBR	CAN	USA
1948	CAN	TCH	SUI
1952	CAN	USA	SWE
1956	URS	USA	CAN
1960	USA	CAN	URS
1964	URS	SWE	TCH
1968	URS	TCH	CAN
1972	URS	USA	TCH
1976	URS	TCH	GER

Luge

Single-Seater (Men)

Not held before 1964.

	Gold	Silver	Bronze
1964	T. Köhler *GER* 3min 26.77sec	K. Bonsack *GER* 3min 27.04sec	H. Plenk *GER* 3min 30.15sec
1968	M. Schmid *AUT* 2min 52.48sec	T. Köhler *GDR* 2min 52.66sec	K. Bonsack *GDR* 2min 53.33sec
1972	W. Scheidel *GDR* 3min 27.58sec	H. Ehrig *GDR* 3min 28.39sec	W. Fiedler *GDR* 3min 28.73sec
1976	D. Guenther *GDR* 3min 27.688sec	J. Fendt *GER* 3min 28.196sec	H. Rinn *GDR* 3min 28.574sec

Two-seater (Men)

Not held before 1964.

	Gold	Silver	Bronze
1964	AUT 1min 41.62sec	AUT 1min 41.91sec	ITA 1min 42.87sec
1968	GDR 1min 35.85sec	AUT 1min 36.34sec	GER 1min 37.29sec
1972	ITA & GDR 1min 28.35sec		GDR 1min 29.16sec
1976	GDR 1min 25.604sec	GER 1min 25.889sec	AUT 1min 25.919sec

Single-seater (Women)

Not held before 1964.

	Gold	Silver	Bronze
1964	O. Enderlein *GER* 3min 24.67sec	I. Geisler *GER* 3min 27.42sec	H. Thurner *AUT* 3min 29.06sec
1968	E. Lechner *ITA* 2min 28.66sec	C. Schmuck *GER* 2min 29.37sec	A. Dünhaupt *GER* 2min 29.56sec
1972	A. M. Müller *GDR* 2min 59.18sec	U. Rührold *GDR* 2min 59.49sec	M. Schumann *GDR* 2min 59.54sec
1976	M. Schumann *GDR* 2min 50.621sec	U. Ruehroid *GDR* 2min 50.846sec	E. Demleitner *GER* 2min 51.056sec

Figure Skating (Men)

	Gold	Silver	Bronze
1908	U. Salchow *SWE* 1,886.5 pts	R. Johansson *SWE* 1,826.0 pts	P. Thorén *SWE* 1,787.0 pts
1920	G. Grafström *SWE* 2,838.50 pts	A. Krogh *NOR* 2,634.00 pts	M. Stixrud *NOR* 2,561.00 pts
1924	G. Grafström *SWE* 2,575.25 pts	W. Böckl *AUT* 2,518.75 pts	G. Gautschi *SUI* 2,223.50 pts
1928	G. Grafström *SWE* 2,698.25 pts	W. Böckl *AUT* 2,682.50 pts	R. van Zeebroeck *BEL* 2,578.75 pts
1932	K. Schäfer *AUT* 2,602.0 pts	G. Grafström *SWE* 2,514.5 pts	M. Wilson *CAN* 2,448.3 pts
1936	K. Schäfer *AUT* 2,959.0 pts	E. Baier *GER* 2,805.3 pts	F. Kaspar *AUT* 2,801.0 pts
1948	R. Button *USA* 1,720.6 pts	H. Gerschwiler *SUI* 1,630.1 pts	E. Rada *AUT* 1,603.2 pts
1952	R. Button *USA* 1,730.3 pts	H. Seibt *AUT* 1,621.3 pts	J. Grogan *USA* 1,627.4 pts
1956	H. A. Jenkins *USA* 1,497.75 pts	R. Robertson *USA* 1,492.15 pts	D. Jenkins *USA* 1,465.41 pts
1960	D. Jenkins *USA* 1,440.2 pts	K. Divin *TCH* 1,414.3 pts	D. Jackson *CAN* 1,401.0 pts
1964	M. Schnelldörfer *GER* 1,916.9 pts	A. Calmat *FRA* 1,876.5 pts	S. Allen *USA* 1,873.6 pts
1968	W. Schwartz *AUT* 1,904.1 pts	T. Wood *USA* 1,891.6 pts	P. Pera *FRA* 1,864.5 pts
1972	O. Nepela *TCH* 2,739.1 pts	S. Chetverukhin *URS* 2,672.4 pts	P. Pera *FRA* 2,653.1 pts
1976	J. Curry *GBR* 192.74 pts	V. Kovalev *URS* 187.64 pts	T. Cranston *CAN* 187.38 pts

Figure Skating (Women)

	Gold	Silver	Bronze
1908	M. Syers (-Cave) *GBR* 1,262.5 pts	E. Rendschmidt *GER* 1,055.0 pts	D. Greenhough Smith *GBR* 960.5 pts
1920	M. Julin-Mauroy *SWE* 913.50 pts	S. Norén *SWE* 887.75 pts	T. Weld *USA* 898.00 pts
1924	H. Plank-Szabo *AUT* 2,094.25 pts	B. S. Loughran *USA* 1,959.0 pts	E. Muckelt *GBR* 1,750.50 pts
1928	S. Henie *NOR* 2,452.25 pts	F. Burger *AUT* 2,248.50 pts	B. Loughran *USA* 2,254.50 pts
1932	S. Henie *NOR* 2,302.5 pts	F. Burger *AUT* 2,167.1 pts	M. Vinson *USA* 2,158.5 pts
1936	S. Henie *NOR* 2,971.4 pts	C. Colledge *GBR* 2,926.8 pts	V. A. Hultén *SWE* 2,763.2 pts
1948	B. A. Scott *CAN* 1,467.7 pts	E. Pawlik *AUT* 1,418.3 pts	J. Altwegg *GBR* 1,405.5 pts
1952	J. Altwegg *GBR* 1,455.8 pts	T. Albright *USA* 1,432.2 pts	J. du Bief *FRA* 1,422.0 pts
1956	T. Albright *USA* 1,866.39 pts	C. Heiss *USA* 1,848.24 pts	I. Wendl *AUT* 1,753.91 pts
1960	C. Heiss *USA* 1,490.1 pts	S. Dijkstra *HOL* 1,424.8 pts	B. Roles *USA* 1,414.9 pts
1964	S. Dijkstra *HOL* 2,018.5 pts	R. Heitzer *AUT* 1,945.5 pts	P. Burka *CAN* 1,940.0 pts
1968	P. Fleming *USA* 1,970.5 pts	G. Seyfert *GDR* 1,882.3 pts	H. Masková *TCH* 1,828.8 pts
1972	B. Schuba *AUT* 2,751.5 pts	K. Magnussen *CAN* 2,673.2 pts	J. Lynn *USA* 2,663.1 pts
1976	D. Hamill *USA* 193.80 pts	D. De Leeuw *HOL* 190.24 pts	C. Errath *GDR* 188.16 pts

Figure Skating (Pairs)

	Gold	Silver	Bronze
1908	A. Hübler & H. Burger *GER* 56.0 pts	P. W. Johnson & J. H. Johnson *GBR* 51.5 pts	M. Syers (-Cave) & E. Syers *GBR* 48.0 pts
1920	L. Jakobsson (-Eilers) & W. Jakobsson *FIN* 80.75 pts	A. Bryn (-Schøyen) & Y. Bryn *NOR* 72.75 pts	P. W. Johnson & B. Williams *GBR* 66.25 pts
1924	H. Engelmann & A. Berger *AUT* 74.50 pts	L. Jakobsson (-Eilers) & W. Jakobsson *FIN* 71.75 pts	A. Joly & P. Brunet *FRA* 69.25 pts
1928	A. Joly & P. Brunet *FRA* 100.50 pts	L. Scholz & O. Kaiser *AUT* 99.25 pts	M. Brunner & L. Wrede *AUT* 93.25 pts
1932	A. Brunet & P. Brunet *FRA* 76.7 pts	B. Loughran & S. Badger *USA* 77.5 pts	E. Rotter & L. Szollás *HUN* 76.4 pts
1936	M. Herber & E. Baier *GER* 103.3 pts	I. Pausin & E. Pausin *AUT* 102.7 pts	E. Rotter & L. Szollás *HUN* 97.6 pts
1948	M. Lannoy & P. Baugniet *BEL* 123.5 pts	A. Kékessy & E. Király *HUN* 122.2 pts	S. Morrow & W. Diestelmeyer *CAN* 121.0 pts
1952	R. Falk & P. Falk *GER* 102.6 pts	K. E. Kennedy & M. Kennedy *USA* 100.6 pts	M. Nagy & L. Nagy *HUN* 97.4 pts
1956	E. Schwartz & K. Oppelt *AUT* 101.8 pts	F. Dafoe & N. Bowden *CAN* 101.9 pts	M. Nagy & L. Nagy *HUN* 99.3 pts
1960	B. Wagner & R. Paul *CAN* 80.4 pts	M. Kilius & H. J. Bäumler *GER* 76.8 pts	N. Ludington & R. Ludington *USA* 76.2 pts
1964	L. Belousova & O. Protopopov *URS* 104.4 pts	M. Kilius & H. J. Bäumler *GER* 103.6 pts	D. Wilkes & G. Revell *CAN* 98.5 pts
1968	L. Belousova & O. Protopopov *URS* 315.2 pts	T. Yukchesternava & A. Gorelik *URS* 312.3 pts	M. Glockshuber & W. Danne *GER* 304.4 pts
1972	I. Rodnina & A. Ulanov *URS* 420.4 pts	L. Smirnova & A. Suraikin *URS* 419.4 pts	M. Gross & U. Kagelmann *GDR* 411.8 pts
1976	I. Rodnina & A. Zaitsev *URS* 140.54 pts	R. Kermer & R. Oestereich *GDR* 136.35 pts	M. Gross & U. Kagelmann *GDR* 134.57 pts

Speed Skating (Men)

500 Metres

Not held before 1924.

	Gold	Silver	Bronze
1924	C. Jewtraw *USA* 44.0sec	O. Olsen *NOR* 44.2sec	R. M. Larsen *NOR* & C. Thunberg *FIN* 44.8sec
1928	C. Thunberg *FIN* & B. Evensen *NOR* 43.4sec		J. O. Farrell *USA*, R. M. Larsen *NOR* & J. Friman *FIN* 43.6sec
1932	J. A. Shea *USA* 43.4sec	B. Evensen *NOR* nda	A. Hurd *CAN* nda
1936	I. Ballangrud *NOR* 43.4sec	G. Krog *NOR* 43.5sec	L. Freisinger *USA* 44.0sec
1948	F. Helgesen *NOR* 43.1sec	K. Bartholomew *USA*, T. Byberg *NOR* & R. Fitzgerald *USA* 43.2sec	
1952	K. Henry *USA* 43.2sec	D. McDermott *USA* 43.9sec	A. Johansen *NOR* & G. Audley *CAN* 44.0sec
1956	Y. Grishin *URS* 40.2sec	R. Grach *URS* 40.8sec	A. Gjestvang *NOR* 41.0sec
1960	Y. Grishin *URS* 40.2sec	W. Disney *USA* 40.3sec	R. Grach *URS* 40.4sec
1964	R. McDermott *USA* 40.1sec	Y. Grishin *URS*, V. Orlov *URS* & A. Gjestvang *NOR* 40.6sec	
1968	E. Keller *GER* 40.3sec	M. Thomassen *NOR* & R. McDermott *USA* 40.5sec	
1972	E. Keller *GER* 39.44sec	H. Börjes *SWE* 39.69sec	V. Muratov *URS* 39.80sec
1976	E. Kulikov *URS* 39.17sec	V. Muratov *URS* 39.25sec	D. Immerfall *USA* 39.54sec

1,500 Metres

Not held before 1924.

	Gold	Silver	Bronze
1924	C. Thunberg *FIN* 2min 20.8sec	R. M. Larsen *NOR* 2min 22.0sec	S. O. Moen *NOR* 2min 25.6sec
1928	C. Thunberg *FIN* 2min 21.1sec	B. Evensen *NOR* 2min 21.9sec	I. Ballangrud *NOR* 2min 22.6sec
1932	J. A. Shea *USA* 2min 57.5sec	A. Hurd *CAN* nda	W. F. Logan *CAN* nda
1936	C. Mathiesen *NOR* 2min 19.2sec	I. Ballangrud *NOR* 2min 20.2sec	B. Wasenius *FIN* 2min 20.9sec
1948	S. Farstad *NOR* 2min 17.6sec	Å. Seyffarth *SWE* 2min 18.1sec	O. Lundberg *NOR* 2min 18.9sec
1952	H. Andersen *NOR* 2min 20.4sec	W. van der Voort *HOL* 2min 20.6sec	R. Aas *NOR* 2min 21.6sec
1956	Y. Grishin *URS* & Y. Mikhailov *URS* 2min 08.6sec		T. Salonen *FIN* 2min 09.4sec
1960	R. Aas *NOR* & Y. Grishin *URS* 2min 10.4sec		B. Stenin *URS* 2min 11.5sec
1964	A. Anston *URS* 2min 10.3sec	C. Verkerk *HOL* 2min 10.6sec	V. Haugen *NOR* 2min 11.2sec
1968	C. Verkerk *HOL* 2min 03.4sec	A. Schenk *HOL* & I. Eriksen *NOR* 2min 05.0sec	
1972	A. Schenk *HOL* 2min 02.96sec	R. Grønvold *NOR* 2min 04.26sec	G. Claesson *SWE* 2min 05.89sec
1976	J. Storholt *NOR* 1min 59.38sec	T. Kondokov *URS* 1min 59.97sec	H. Van Helden *HOL* 2min 00.87sec

5,000 Metres

Not held before 1924.

	Gold	Silver	Bronze
1924	C. Thunberg *FIN* 8min 39.0sec	J. Skutnabb *FIN* 8min 48.4sec	R. M. Larsen *NOR* 8min 50.2sec
1928	I. Ballangrud *NOR* 8min 50.5sec	J. Skutnabb *FIN* 8min 59.1sec	B. Evensen *NOR* 9min 01.1sec
1932	I. Jaffee *USA* 9min 40.8sec	E. S. Murphy *USA* nda	W. F. Logan *CAN* nda
1936	I. Ballangrud *NOR* 8min 19.6sec	B. Vasenius *FIN* 8min 23.3sec	A. Ojala *FIN* 8min 30.1sec
1948	R. Liaklev *NOR* 8min 29.4sec	O. Lundberg *NOR* 8min 32.7sec	G. Hedlund *SWE* 8min 34.8sec
1952	H. Andersen *NOR* 8min 10.6sec	C. Broekman *HOL* 8min 21.6sec	S. Haugli *NOR* 8min 22.4sec
1956	B. Shilkov *URS* 7min 48.7sec	S. Ericsson *SWE* 7min 56.7sec	O. Goncharenko *URS* 7min 57.5sec
1960	V. Kosychkin *URS* 7min 51.3sec	K. Johannesen *NOR* 8min 00.8sec	J. Pesman *HOL* 8min 05.1sec
1964	K. Johannesen *NOR* 7min 38.4sec	P. I. Moe *NOR* 7min 38.6sec	F. A. Maier *NOR* 7min 42.00sec
1968	F. A. Maier *NOR* 7min 22.4sec	C. Verkerk *HOL* 7min 23.2sec	P. Nottet *HOL* 7min 25.5sec
1972	A. Schenk *HOL* 7min 23.61sec	R. Grønvold *NOR* 7min 28.13sec	S. Stensen *NOR* 7min 33.39sec
1976	S. Stensen *NOR* 7min 24.48sec	P. Kleine *HOL* 7min 26.47sec	H. Van Helden *HOL* 7min 26.54sec

10,000 Metres

Not held before 1924.

	Gold	Silver	Bronze
1924	J. Skutnabb *FIN* 18min 04.8sec	C. Thunberg *FIN* 18min 07.8sec	R. M. Larsen *NOR* 18min 12.2sec
1928	*Event officially annulled because of the condition of the ice.*		
1932	I. Jaffee *USA* 19min 13.6sec	I. Ballangrud *NOR* nda	F. Stack *CAN* nda
1936	I. Ballangrud *NOR* 17min 24.3sec	B. Vasenius *FIN* 17min 28.2sec	M. Stiepl *AUT* 17min 30.0sec
1948	Å. Seyffarth *SWE* 17min 26.3sec	L. Parkkinen *FIN* 17min 36.0sec	P. Lammio *FIN* 17min 42.7sec
1952	H. Andersen *NOR* 16min 45.8sec	C. Broekman *HOL* 17min 10.6sec	C. E. Asplund *SWE* 17min 16.6sec
1956	S. Ericsson *SWE* 16min 35.9sec	K. Johannesen *NOR* 16min 36.9sec	O. Goncharenko *URS* 16min 42.3sec
1960	K. Johannesen *NOR* 15min 46.6sec	V. Kosychkin *URS* 15min 49.2sec	K. Bäckman *SWE* 16min 14.2sec
1964	J. Nilsson *SWE* 15min 50.1sec	F. A. Maier *NOR* 16min 06.0sec	K. Johannesen *NOR* 16min 06.3sec
1968	J. Höglin *SWE* 15min 23.6sec	F. A. Maier *NOR* 15min 23.9sec	Ö. Sandler *SWE* 15min 31.8sec
1972	A. Schenk *HOL* 15min 01.35sec	C. Verkerk *HOL* 15min 04.70sec	S. Stensen *NOR* 15min 07.08sec
1976	P. Kleine *HOL* 14min 50.59sec	S. Stensen *NOR* 14min 53.30sec	H. Van Helden *HOL* 15min 02.02sec

Speed Skating (Women)

500 Metres

Not held before 1960 although there were three demonstration events for women speed skaters in 1932.

	Gold	Silver	Bronze
1960	H. Haase *GER* 45.9sec	N. Donchenko *URS* 46.0sec	J. Ashworth *USA* 46.1sec
1964	L. Skoblikova *URS* 45.0sec	I. Yegorova *URS* 45.4sec	T. Sidorova *URS* 45.5sec
1968	L. Titova *URS* 46.1sec	M. Meyers *USA*, D. Holum *USA* & J. Fish *USA* 46.3sec	
1972	A. Henning *USA* 43.33sec	V. Krasnova *URS* 44.01sec	L. Titova *URS* 44.45sec
1976	S. Young *USA* 42.76sec	C. Priestner *CAN* 43.12sec	T. Averina *URS* 43.17sec

1,000 Metres

Not held before 1960.

	Gold	Silver	Bronze
1960	K. Guseva *URS* 1min 34.1sec	H. Haase *GER* 1min 34.3sec	T. Rylova *URS* 1min 34.8sec
1964	L. Skoblikova *URS* 1min 33.2sec	I. Yegorova *URS* 1min 34.3sec	K. Mustonen *FIN* 1min 34.8sec
1968	C. Geijssen *HOL* 1min 32.6sec	L. Titova *URS* 1min 32.9sec	D. Holum *USA* 1min 33.4sec
1972	M. Pflug *GER* 1min 31.40sec	A. Keulen-Deelstra *HOL* 1min 31.61sec	A. Henning *USA* 1min 31.62sec
1976	T. Averina *URS* 1min 28.43sec	L. Poulos *USA* 1min 28.57sec	S. Young *USA* 1min 29.14sec

1,500 Metres

Not held before 1960.

	Gold	Silver	Bronze
1960	L. Skoblikova *URS* 2min 25.2sec	E. Seroczynska *POL* 2min 25.7sec	H. Pilejczyk *POL* 2min 27.1sec
1964	L. Skoblikova *URS* 2min 22.6sec	K. Mustonen *FIN* 2min 25.5sec	B. Kolokoltseva *URS* 2min 27.1sec
1968	K. Mustonen *FIN* 2min 22.4sec	C. Geijssen *HOL* 2min 22.7sec	C. Kaiser *HOL* 2min 24.5sec
1972	D. Holum *USA* 2min 20.85sec	C. Baas-Kaiser *HOL* 2min 21.05sec	A. Keulen-Deelstra *HOL* 2min 22.05sec
1976	G. Stepanskaya *URS* 2min 16.58sec	S. Young *USA* 2min 17.06sec	T. Averina *URS* 2min 17.96sec

3,000 Metres

Not held before 1960.

	Gold	Silver	Bronze
1960	L. Skoblikova *URS* 5min 14.3sec	V. Stenina *URS* 5min 16.9sec	E. Huttunen *FIN* 5min 21.0sec
1964	L. Skoblikova *URS* 5min 14.9sec	V. Stenina *URS* & P. H. Han *PRK* 5min 18.5sec	
1968	J. Schut *HOL* 4min 56.2sec	K. Mustonen *FIN* 5min 01.0sec	C. Kaiser *HOL* 5min 01.3sec
1972	C. Baas-Kaiser *HOL* 4min 52.14sec	D. Holum *USA* 4min 58.67sec	A. Keulen-Deelstra *HOL* 4min 59.91sec

	Gold	Silver	Bronze
1976	T. Averina *URS* 4min 45.19sec	A. Mitscherlich *GDR* 4min 45.23sec	L. Korsmo *NOR* 4min 45.24sec

Alpine Skiing (Men)

Downhill

Not held as a separate competition before 1948.

	Gold	Silver	Bronze
1948	H. Oreiller *FRA* 2min 55.0sec	F. Gabl *AUT* 2min 59.1sec	K. Molitor & R. Olinger *SUI* 3min 00.3sec
1952	Z. Colò *ITA* 2min 30.8sec	O. Schneider *AUT* 2min 32.0sec	C. Pravda *AUT* 2min 32.4sec
1956	A. Sailer *AUT* 2min 52.2sec	R. Fellay *SUI* 2min 55.7sec	A. Molterer *AUT* 2min 56.2sec
1960	J. Vuarnet *FRA* 2min 06.0sec	H. P. Lanig *GER* 2min 06.5sec	G. Perillat *FRA* 2min 06.9sec
1964	E. Zimmermann *AUT* 2min 18.16sec	L. Lacroix *FRA* 2min 18.90sec	W. Bartels *GER* 2min 19.48sec
1968	J. C. Killy *FRA* 1min 59.85sec	G. Perillat *FRA* 1min 59.93sec	J. D. Dätwyler *SUI* 2min 00.32sec
1972	B. Russi *SUI* 1min 51.43sec	R. Collombin *SUI* 1min 52.07sec	H. Messner *AUT* 1min 52.40sec
1976	F. Klammer *AUT* 1min 45.73sec	B. Russi *SUI* 1min 46.06sec	H. Plank *ITA* 1min 46.59sec

Giant Slalom

Not held before 1952.

	Gold	Silver	Bronze
1952	S. Eriksen *NOR* 2min 25.0sec	C. Pravda *AUT* 2min 26.9sec	T. Spiss *AUT* 2min 28.8sec
1956	A. Sailer *AUT* 3min 00.1sec	A. Molterer *AUT* 3min 06.3sec	W. Schuster *AUT* 3min 07.2sec
1960	R. Staub *SUI* 1min 48.3sec	J. Stiegler *AUT* 1min 48.7sec	E. Hinterseer *AUT* 1min 49.1sec
1964	F. Bonlieu *FRA* 1min 46.71sec	K. Schranz *AUT* 1min 47.09sec	J. Stiegler *AUT* 1min 48.05sec
1968	J. C. Killy *FRA* 3min 29.28sec	W. Favre *SUI* 3min 31.50sec	H. Messner *AUT* 3min 31.83sec
1972	G. Thoeni *ITA* 3min 09.62sec	E. Bruggmann *SUI* 3min 10.75sec	W. Mattle *SUI* 3min 10.99sec
1976	H. Hemmi *SUI* 3min 26.97sec	E. Good *SUI* 3min 27.17sec	I. Stenmark *SWE* 3min 27.41sec

Slalom

Not held before 1948.

	Gold	Silver	Bronze
1948	E. Reinalter *SUI* 2min 10.3sec	J. Couttet *FRA* 2min 10.8sec	H. Oreiller *FRA* 2min 12.8sec
1952	O. Schneider *AUT* 2min 00.00sec	S. Eriksen *NOR* 2min 01.2sec	G. Berge *NOR* 2min 01.7sec
1956	A. Sailer *AUT* 3min 14.7sec	C. Igaya *JPN* 3min 18.7sec	S. Sollander *SWE* 3min 20.2sec
1960	E. Hinterseer *AUT* 2min 08.9sec	M. Leitner *AUT* 2min 10.3sec	C. Bozon *FRA* 2min 10.4sec
1964	J. Stiegler *AUT* 2min 11.13sec	W. W. Kidd *USA* 2min 11.27sec	J. F. Heuga *USA* 2min 11.52sec
1968	J. C. Killy *FRA* 1min 39.73sec	H. Huber *AUT* 1min 39.82sec	A. Matt *AUT* 1min 40.09sec
1972	F. F. Ochoa *ESP* 1min 49.27sec	G. Thoeni *ITA* 1min 50.28sec	R. Thoeni *ITA* 1min 50.30sec
1976	P. Gros *ITA* 2min 13.29sec	G. Thoeni *ITA* 2min 03.73sec	W. Frommelt *LIE* 2min 04.28sec

Alpine Skiing (Women)

Downhill

Not held before 1948.

	Gold	Silver	Bronze
1948	H. Schlunegger *SUI* 2min 28.3sec	T. Beiser *AUT* 2min 29.1sec	R. Hammerer *AUT* 2min 30.2sec
1952	T. Jochum-Beiser *AUT* 1min 47.1sec	A. Buchner *GER* 1min 48.0sec	G. Minuzzo *ITA* 1min 49.0sec
1956	M. Berthod *SUI* 1min 40.7sec	F. Dänzer *SUI* 1min 45.4sec	L. Wheeler *CAN* 1min 45.9sec
1960	H. Beibl *GER* 1min 37.6sec	P. Pitou *USA* 1min 38.6sec	G. Hecher *AUT* 1min 38.9sec
1964	C. Haas *AUT* 1min 55.39sec	E. Zimmermann *AUT* 1min 56.42sec	G. Hecher *AUT* 1min 56.66sec
1968	O. Pall *AUT* 1min 40.87sec	I. Mir *FRA* 1min 41.33sec	C. Haas *AUT* 1min 41.41sec
1972	M. T. Nadig *SUI* 1min 36.68sec	A. M. Pröll *AUT* 1min 37.00sec	S. Corrock *USA* 1min 37.68sec
1976	R. Mittermaier *GER* 1min 46.16sec	B. Totschnig *AUT* 1min 46.68sec	C. Nelson *USA* 1min 47.50sec

Giant Slalom

Not held before 1952.

	Gold	Silver	Bronze
1952	A. (Mead) Lawrence *USA* 2min 06.8sec	D. Rom *AUT* 2min 09.0sec	A. Buchner *GER* 2min 10.0sec
1956	O. Reichert *GER* 1min 56.5sec	J. Frandl *AUT* 1min 57.8sec	D. Hochleitner *AUT* 1min 58.2sec
1960	Y. Rügg *SUI* 1min 39.9sec	P. Pitou *USA* 1min 40.0sec	G. (Minuzzo) Chenal *ITA* 1min 40.2sec
1964	M. Goitschel *FRA* 1min 52.24sec	C. Goitschel *FRA* & J. Saubert *USA* 1min 53.11sec	
1968	N. Greene *CAN* 1min 51.97sec	A. Famose *FRA* 1min 54.61sec	F. Bochatay *SUI* 1min 54.74sec
1972	M. T. Nadig *SUI* 1min 29.90sec	A. M. Pröll *AUT* 1min 30.75sec	W. Drexel *AUT* 1min 32.35sec
1976	K. Kreiner *CAN* 1min 29.13sec	R. Mittermaier *GER* 1min 29.25sec	D. Debernard *FRA* 1min 29.95sec

Slalom

Not held before 1948.

	Gold	Silver	Bronze
1948	G. Fraser *USA* 1min 57.2sec	A. Meyer *SUI* 1min 57.7sec	E. Mahringer *AUT* 1min 58.0sec
1952	A. (Mead) Lawrence *USA* 2min 10.6sec	O. Reichert *GER* 2min 11.4sec	A. Buchner *GER* 2min 13.3sec
1956	R. Colliard *SUI* 1min 52.3sec	R. Schöpf *AUT* 1min 55.4sec	Y. Sidorova *URS* 1min 56.7sec
1960	A. Heggtveit *CAN* 1min 49.6sec	B. Snite *USA* 1min 52.9sec	B. Henneberger *GER* 1min 56.6sec
1964	C. Goitschel *FRA* 1min 29.86sec	M. Goitschel *FRA* 1min 30.77sec	J. Saubert *USA* 1min 31.36sec
1968	M. Goitschel *FRA* 1min 25.86sec	N. Greene *CAN* 1min 26.15sec	A. Famose *FRA* 1min 27.89sec
1972	B. Cochran *USA* 1min 31.24sec	D. Debernard *FRA* 1 min 31.26sec	F. Steurer *FRA* 1min 32.69sec
1976	R. Mittermaier *GER* 1min 30.54sec	G. Giordani *ITA* 1min 30.87sec	H. Wenzel *LIE* 1min 32.20sec

Nordic Skiing (Men)

15 Kilometres Cross-Country

Not held before 1924. From 1924 to 1952 it was decided over 18km (11.18 miles).

	Gold	Silver	Bronze
1924	T. Haug *NOR* 1hr 14min 31.0sec	J. Grøttumsbraaten *NOR* 1hr 15min 51.0sec	T. Niku *FIN* 1hr 26min 26.0sec
1928	J. Grøttumsbraaten *NOR* 1hr 37min 01.0sec	O. Hegge *NOR* 1hr 39min 01.0sec	R. Ødegaard *NOR* 1hr 40min 11.0sec
1932	S. Utterström *SWE* 1hr 23min 07.0sec	A. T. Wikström *SWE* 1hr 25min 07.0sec	V. Saarinen *FIN* 1hr 25min 24.0sec
1936	E. A. Larsson *SWE* 1hr 14min 38.0sec	O. Hagen *NOR* 1hr 15min 33.0sec	P. Niemi *FIN* 1hr 16min 59.0sec

	Gold	Silver	Bronze
1948	M. Lundström *SWE* 1hr 13min 50.0sec	N. Östensson *SWE* 1hr 14min 22.0sec	G. Eriksson *SWE* 1hr 16min 06.0sec
1952	H. Brenden *NOR* 1hr 1min 34.0sec	T. Mäkelä *FIN* 1hr 2min 09.0sec	P. Lonkila *FIN* 1hr 2min 20.0sec
1956	H. Brenden *NOR* 49min 39.0sec	S. Jernberg *SWE* 50min 14.0sec	P. Kolchin *URS* 50min 17.0sec
1960	H. Brusveen *NOR* 51min 55.5sec	S. Jernberg *SWE* 51min 58 6sec	V. Hakulinen *FIN* 52min 03.0sec
1964	E. Mäntyranta *FIN* 50min 54.1sec	H. Grønningen *NOR* 51min 34.8sec	S. Jernberg *SWE* 51min 42.2sec
1968	H. Grønningen *NOR* 47min 54.2sec	E. Mäntyranta *FIN* 47min 56.1sec	G. Larsson *SWE* 48min 33.7sec
1972	S. Å. Lundbäck *SWE* 45min 28.24sec	F. Simashov *URS* 46min 00 84sec	I. Førmø *NOR* 46min 02.68sec
1976	N. Bajukov *URS* 43min 58.47sec	E. Beliaev *URS* 44min 01 10sec	A. Koivisto *FIN* 44min 19.25sec

30 Kilometres Cross-Country

Not held before 1956.

Year	Gold	Silver	Bronze
1956	V. Hakulinen *FIN* 1hr 44min 06.0sec	S. Jernberg *SWE* 1hr 44min 30.0sec	P. Kolchin *URS* 1hr 45min 45.0sec
1960	S. Jernberg *SWE* 1hr 51min 03.9sec	R. Rämgård *SWE* 1hr 51min 16.9sec	N. Anikin *URS* 1hr 52min 28.2sec
1964	E. Mäntyranta *FIN* 1hr 30min 50.7sec	H. Grønningen *NOR* 1hr 32min 02.3sec	I. Voronchikhin *URS* 1hr 32min 15.8sec
1968	F. Nones *ITA* 1hr 35min 39.2sec	O. Martinsen *NOR* 1hr 36min 28.9sec	E. Mäntyranta *FIN* 1hr 36min 55.3sec
1972	V. Vedenin *URS* 1hr 36min 31.15sec	P. Tyldum *NOR* 1hr 37min 25.30sec	J. Harviken *NOR* 1hr 37min 32.44sec
1976	S. Saveliev *URS* 1hr 30min 29.38sec	W. Koch *USA* 1hr 30min 57.84sec	I. Geranin *URS* 1hr 31min 09.29sec

50 Kilometres Cross-Country

Not held before 1924.

Year	Gold	Silver	Bronze
1924	T. Haug *NOR* 3hr 44min 32.0sec	T. Strømstad *NOR* 3hr 46min 23.0sec	J. Grøttumsbraaten *NOR* 3hr 47min 46.0sec
1928	P. E. Hedlund *SWE* 4hr 52min 03.0sec	G. Jonsson *SWE* 5hr 05min 30.0sec	V. Andersson *SWE* 5hr 05min 46.0sec
1932	V. Saarinen *FIN* 4hr 28min 00.0sec	V. Liikkanen *FIN* 4hr 28min 20.0sec	A. Rustadstuen *NOR* 4hr 31min 53.0sec
1936	E. Wiklund *SWE* 3hr 30min 11.0sec	A. Wikström *SWE* 3hr 33min 20.0sec	N. J. Englund *SWE* 3hr 34min 10.0sec
1948	N. Karlsson *SWE* 3hr 47min 48.0sec	H. Eriksson *SWE* 3hr 52min 20.0sec	B. Vanninen *FIN* 3hr 57min 28.0sec
1952	V. Hakulinen *FIN* 3hr 33min 33.0sec	E. Kolehmainen *FIN* 3hr 38min 11.0sec	M. Estenstad *NOR* 3hr 38min 28.0sec
1956	S. Jernberg *SWE* 2hr 50min 27.0sec	V. Hakulinen *FIN* 2hr 51min 45.0sec	F. Terentyev *URS* 2hr 53min 32.0sec
1960	K. Hämäläinen *FIN* 2hr 59min 06.3sec	V. Hakulinen *FIN* 2hr 59min 26.7sec	R. Rämgård *SWE* 3hr 02min 46.7sec
1964	S. Jernberg *SWE* 2hr 43min 52.6sec	A. Rönnlund *SWE* 2hr 44min 58.2sec	A. Tiainen *FIN* 2hr 45min 30.4sec
1968	O. Ellefsæter *NOR* 2hr 28min 45.8sec	V. Vedenin *URS* 2hr 29min 02.5sec	J. Haas *SUI* 2hr 29min 14.8sec
1972	P. Tyldum *NOR* 2hr 43min 14.75sec	M. Myrmo *NOR* 2hr 43min 29.45sec	V. Vedenin *URS* 2hr 44min 00.19sec
1976	I. Formo *FIN* 2hr 37min 30.05sec	G. D. Klaus *GDR* 2hr 38min 13.21sec	B. Sodergren *SWE* 2hr 39min 39.21sec

4 x 10 Kilometres Relay

Not held before 1936.

Year	Gold	Silver	Bronze
1936	FIN 2hr 41min 33.0sec	NOR 2hr 41min 39.0sec	SWE 2hr 43min 03.0sec
1948	SWE 2hr 32min 08.0sec	FIN 2hr 41min 06.0sec	NOR 2hr 44min 33.0sec
1952	FIN 2hr 20min 16.0sec	NOR 2hr 23min 13.0sec	SWE 2hr 24min 13.0sec
1956	URS 2hr 15min 30.0sec	FIN 2hr 16min 31.0sec	SWE 2hr 17min 42.0sec
1960	FIN 2hr 18min 45.6sec	NOR 2hr 18min 46.4sec	URS 2hr 21min 21.6sec
1964	SWE 2hr 18min 34.6sec	FIN 2hr 18min 42.4sec	URS 2hr 18min 46.9sec
1968	NOR 2hr 08min 33.5sec	SWE 2hr 10min 13.2sec	FIN 2hr 10min 56.7sec
1972	URS 2hr 04min 47.94sec	NOR 2hr 04min 57.06sec	SUI 2hr 07min 00.06sec
1976	FIN 2hr 07min 59.72sec	NOR 2hr 09min 58.36sec	URS 2hr 10min 51.46sec

Ski Jumping

70 Metres Jump

Not held before 1924. 1924–60 held on one hill.

Year	Gold	Silver	Bronze
1924	J. T. Thams *NOR* 18.960 pts	N. Bonna *NOR* 18.689 pts	T. Haug *NOR* 18.000 pts
1928	A. Andersen *NOR* 19.208 pts	S. Ruud *NOR* 18.542 pts	R. Burkert *TCH* 17.937 pts
1932	B. Ruud *NOR* 228.1 pts	H. Beck *NOR* 227.0 pts	K. Wahlberg *NOR* 219.5 pts
1936	B. Ruud *NOR* 232.0 pts	S. Eriksson *SWE* 230.5 pts	R. Andersen *NOR* 228.9 pts
1948	P. Hugsted *NOR* 228.1 pts	B. Ruud *NOR* 226.6 pts	T. Schjelderup *NOR* 225.1 pts
1952	A. Bergmann *NOR* 226.0 pts	T. Falkanger *NOR* 221.5 pts	K. Holmström *SWE* 219.5 pts
1956	A. Hyvärinen *FIN* 227.0 pts	A. Kallakorpi *FIN* 225.0 pts	H. Glass *GER* 224.5 pts
1960	H. Recknagel *GER* 227.2 pts	N. Halonen *FIN* 222.6 pts	O. Leodolter *AUT* 219.4 pts
1964	V. Kankkonen *FIN* 229.9 pts	T. Engan *NOR* 226.3 pts	T. Brandtzäg *NOR* 222.9 pts
1968	J. Raska *TCH* 216.5 pts	B. Bachler *AUT* 214.2 pts	B. Preiml *AUT* 212.6 pts
1972	Y. Kasaya *JPN* 244.2 pts	A. Konno *JPN* 234.8 pts	S. Aochi *JPN* 229.5 pts
1976	H. G. Aschenbach *GDR* 252.0 pts	J. Danneberg *GDR* 246.2 pts	K. Schnabl *AUT* 242.0 pts

90 Metres Jump

In 1964 the hill was 80m (87yd 1ft).

Year	Gold	Silver	Bronze
1964	T. Engan *NOR* 230.7 pts	V. Kankkonen *FIN* 228.9 pts	T. Brandtzäg *NOR* 227.2 pts
1968	V. Beloussov *URS* 231.3 pts	J. Raska *TCH* 229.4 pts	L. Grini *NOR* 214.3 pts
1972	W. Fortuna *POL* 219.9 pts	W. Steiner *SUI* 219.8 pts	R. Schmidt *GDR* 219.3 pts
1976	K. Schnabl *AUT* 234.8 pts	A. Innauer *AUT* 232.9 pts	H. Glass *GDR* 221.7 pts

Nordic Combined

15-km (9.3 miles) cross-country and jumping. Not held before 1924. After 1928 the scoring system was altered.

Year	Gold	Silver	Bronze
1924	T. Haug *NOR* 18,906 pts	T. Strømstad *NOR* 18,219 pts	J. Grøttumsbraaten *NOR* 17,854 pts
1928	J. Grøttumsbraaten *NOR* 17,833 pts	H. Vinjarengen *NOR* 15,303 pts	J. Snersrud *NOR* 15,021 pts
1932	J. Grøttumsbraaten *NOR* 446.00 pts	O. Stenen *NOR* 436.05 pts	H. Vinjarengen *NOR* 434.60 pts
1936	O. Hagen *NOR* 430.30 pts	O. Hoffsbakken *NOR* 419.80 pts	S. Brodahl *NOR* 408.10 pts
1948	H. Hasu *FIN* 448.80 pts	M. Huhtala *FIN* 433.65 pts	S. Israelsson *SWE* 433.40 pts
1952	S. Slåttvik *NOR* 451.621 pts	H. Hasu *FIN* 447.500 pts	S. Stenersen *NOR* 436.335 pts

	Gold	Silver	Bronze
1956	S. Stenersen *NOR* 455.000 pts	B. Eriksson *SWE* 437.400 pts	F. Gron-Gasienica *POL* 436.800 pts
1960	G. Thoma *GER* 457.952 pts	T. Knutsen *NOR* 453.000 pts	N. Gusakov *URS* 452.000 pts
1964	T. Knutsen *NOR* 469.28 pts	N. Kiselev *URS* 453.04 pts	G. Thoma *GER* 452.88 pts
1968	F. Keller *GER* 449.04 pts	A. Kälin *SUI* 447.94 pts	A. Kunz *GDR* 444.10 pts
1972	U. Wehling *GDR* 413.340 pts	R. Miettinen *FIN* 405.505 pts	K. H. Luck *GDR* 398.800 pts
1976	U. Wehling *GDR* 423.39 pts	U. Hettich *GER* 418.90 pts	K. Winkler *GDR* 417.47 pts

Nordic Skiing (Women)

5 Kilometres Cross-Country

Not held before 1964.

1964	K. Boyarskikh *URS* 17min 50.5sec	M. Lehtonen *FIN* 17min 52.9sec	A. Kolchina *URS* 18min 08.4sec
1968	T. Gustafsson *SWE* 16min 45.2sec	G. Kulakova *URS* 16min 48.4sec	A. Kolchina *URS* 16min 51.6sec
1972	G. Kulakova *URS* 17min 00.50sec	M. Kajosmaa *FIN* 17min 05.50sec	H. Sikolová *TCH* 17min 07.32sec
1976	H. Takalo *FIN* 15min 48.69sec	R. Smetanina *URS* 15min 49.73sec	G. Kulakova *URS* 16min 07.36sec

10 Kilometres Cross-Country

Not held before 1952.

1952	L. Wideman *FIN* 41min 40.0sec	M. Hietamies *FIN* 42min 39.0sec	S. Rantanen *FIN* 42min 50.0sec
1956	L. Kosyreva *URS* 38min 11.0sec	R. Yeroshina *URS* 38min 16.0sec	S. Edström *SWE* 38min 23.0sec
1960	M. Gusakova *URS* 39min 46.6sec	L. (Kosyreva) Baranova *URS* 40min 04.2sec	R. Yeroshina *URS* 40min 06.0sec
1964	K. Boyarskikh *URS* 40min 24.3sec	E. Mekshilo *URS* 40min 26.6sec	M. Gusakova *URS* 40min 46.6sec
1968	T. Gustafsson *SWE* 36min 46.5sec	B. Mørdre *NOR* 37min 54.6sec	I. Aufles *NOR* 37min 59.9sec
1972	G. Kulakova *URS* 34 min 17.82sec	A. Olunina *URS* 34min 54.11sec	M. Kajosmaa *FIN* 34min 56.45sec
1976	R. Smetanina *URS* 30min 13.41sec	H. Takalo *FIN* 30min 14.28sec	G. Kulakova *URS* 30min 38.61sec

4 x 50 Kilometres Relay

Not held before 1956.

1956	FIN 1hr 9min 01.0sec	URS 1hr 9min 28.0sec	SWE 1hr 9min 48.0sec
1960	SWE 1hr 4min 21.4sec	URS 1hr 5min 02.6sec	FIN 1hr 6min 27.5sec
1964	URS 59min 20.2sec	SWE 1hr 1min 27.0sec	FIN 1hr 2min 45.1sec
1968	NOR 57min 30.0sec	SWE 57min 51.0sec	URS 58min 13.6sec
1972	URS 48min 46.15sec	FIN 49min 19.37sec	NOR 49min 51.49sec
1976	URS 1hr 7min 49.75sec	FIN 1hr 8min 36.57sec	GDR 1hr 9min 57.95sec

ACKNOWLEDGMENTS AND NOTES ON ILLUSTRATIONS

The publishers are indebted to the International Olympic Committee for permission to quote from their publications. We should also like to acknowledge the help of M. Geoffroy de Navacelle in supplying us with photographs of his uncle, Coubertin, and in giving us permission to reproduce many of his writings, some previously unpublished.

The editors of this book would like to express their grateful thanks to all the contributors and many others who provided or suggested sources of information and illustrations; in particular the officials and staff of the International Olympic Committee, of many International Sports Federations, National Olympic Committees and National Sports Associations; and many individuals. We should also like to express our gratitude to previous Olympic historians, in particular Dr Ference Mező, author of *The Modern Olympic Games* (English edition 1956; originally published in 1930) and Erich Kamper, author of *Encyclopedia of the Olympic Winter Games* (1964), *Encyclopedia of the Olympic Games* (1972) and *Who's Who at the Olympics* (1975) whose books have been invaluable references.

The producers are also indebted to all those who are indicated by the following list of illustrations, especially the staffs of the agencies and libraries and individual owners of photographs. Every effort has been made to trace the primary sources of illustrations; in one or two cases where it has not been possible, the producers wish to apologize if the acknowledgment proves to be inadequate; in no case is such inadequacy intentional and if any owner of copyright who has remained untraced will communicate with the producers a reasonable fee will be paid and the required acknowledgment made in future editions of the book.

6 John Morris, courtesy International Olympic Committee
10 Rex Features Ltd
15 British Olympic Association; John R Freeman Ltd
16 Keystone
17 Library of Congress
19 David Cotton
21 a. Jean-Paul Maeder, courtesy International Olympic Committee b. British Olympic Association; John R Freeman Ltd
22 Geoffroy de Navacelle
23 British Olympic Association; John R Freeman Ltd
24 Mansell Collection
25 Jean-Paul Maeder, courtesy International Olympic Committee
26 Jean-Paul Maeder, courtesy International Olympic Committee
27 Jean-Paul Maeder, courtesy International Olympic Committee
28 Jean-Paul Maeder, courtesy International Olympic Committee
29 a. and b. British Olympic Association; John R Freeman Ltd
31 a. Associated Press. b. Colorsport
32 British Olympic Association; John R Freeman Ltd
33 Jean-Paul Maeder, courtesy International Olympic Committee
34 a. and b. Jean-Paul Maeder, courtesy International Olympic Committee
35 Keystone
38 National Postal Museum
39 National Postal Museum
41 All Sport
42 International Olympic Committee
43 Presse-Sports
44 Otto Szymiczek
46 London Electrotype Agency
48 Presse-Sports
50 Missouri Historical Society
51 a. and b. Missouri Historical Society
53 Missouri Historical Society
54 Missouri Historical Society
55 British Olympic Association; John R Freeman Ltd
56 All-Sport
57 British Olympic Association; John R Freeman Ltd
58 Radio Times Hulton Picture Library
59 All-Sport
60 British Olympic Association; John R Freeman Ltd
61 Popperfoto
62 British Olympic Association; John R Freeman Ltd
63 British Olympic Association; John R Freeman Ltd
64 British Olympic Association; John R Freeman Ltd
65 R. Wilsher, courtesy E. R. L. Powell
66 R. Wilsher, courtesy E. R. L. Powell
67 British Olympic Association; John R Freeman Ltd
68 British Olympic Association; John R Freeman Ltd
69 a. British Olympic Association; John R Freeman Ltd. b. British Athletics Publicity and Information Unit
70 a. and b. British Olympic Association; John R Freeman Ltd
71 British Olympic Association; John R Freeman Ltd
72 British Olympic Association; John R Freeman Ltd
74 British Olympic Association; John R Freeman Ltd
75 R. Wilsher, courtesy E. R. L. Powell
76 a. Reproduction Jean-Paul Maeder, courtesy International Olympic Committee. b. R. Wilsher, courtesy E. R. L. Powell
77 British Olympic Association; John R Freeman Ltd
78 British Olympic Association; John R Freeman Ltd
79 British Olympic Association; John R Freeman Ltd
80 British Olympic Association; John R Freeman Ltd
81 Reproduction Jean-Paul Maeder, courtesy International Olympic Committee
82 R. Wilsher, courtesy E. R. L. Powell
83 a., b. and c. British Olympic Association; John R Freeman Ltd
84 H. Roger Viollet

85 R. Wilsher, courtesy E. R. L. Powell
86 British Olympic Association; John R Freeman Ltd
88 a. British Olympic Association; John R Freeman Ltd. b. ANP/PA Photos
89 Reproduction Jean-Paul Maeder, courtesy International Olympic Committee
90 Reproduction Jean-Paul Maeder, courtesy International Olympic Committee
91 British Olympic Association; John R Freeman Ltd
92 British Olympic Association; John R Freeman Ltd
93 ANP/PA Photos
95 British Olympic Association; John R Freeman Ltd
96 Associated Press
97 U S National Olympic Committee; John R Freeman Ltd courtesy British Olympic Association
98 U S National Olympic Committee; John R Freeman Ltd, courtesy British Olympic Association
99 U S National Olympic Committee; John R Freeman Ltd, courtesy British Olympic Association
100 a. and b. U S National Olympic Committee; John R Freeman Ltd, courtesy British Olympic Association
101 Associated Press
102 a. British Olympic Association; John R Freeman Ltd. b. U S National Olympic Committee; John R Freeman Ltd, courtesy British Olympic Association
103 Associated Press
104 U S National Olympic Committee; John R Freeman Ltd, courtesy British Olympic Association
105 British Olympic Association; John R Freeman Ltd
106 Presse-Sports
107 All-Sport
108 Reproduction Jean-Paul Maeder, courtesy International Olympic Committee
109 British Olympic Association; John R Freeman Ltd
110 Library of Congress
111 a. Leni Riefenstahl-Produktion. b. British Olympic Association; John R Freeman Ltd
112 British Olympic Association; John R Freeman Ltd, courtesy German Olympic Committee
113 a. Library of Congress. b. British Olympic Association; John R Freeman Ltd
114 British Olympic Association; John R Freeman Ltd
115 a. All-Sport. b. British Olympic Association; John R Freeman Ltd
117 Sport & General
118 Radio Times Hulton Picture Library
120 Racecourse Technical Services Ltd
123 Keystone
124 Popperfoto
127 PA Photos
129 PA Photos
130 PA Photos
132 PA Photos
133 PA Photos
134 PA Photos
139 Associated Press
140 Melbourne Herald-Sun
143 Keystone
144 Italian National Olympic Committee
145 Associated Press
146 Keystone
148 Keystone
151 Italian National Olympic Committee
152 Presse-Sports
153 Popperfoto
154 Japanese National Olympic Committee
155 Associated Press
156 Associated Press
157 Japanese National Olympic Committee
158 Popperfoto
161 E. D. Lacey
162 Mark Shearman
163 Popperfoto
164 Derek Cattini/All-Sport
165 Mark Shearman
166 Presse-Sports
167 Popperfoto
168 Popperfoto
170 E. D. Lacey
171 Colorsport
173 Colorsport
174 Keystone
177 Colorsport
178 Keystone
179 Associated Press
180 Colorsport
181 Popperfoto
182 Presse-Sports
183 Mark Shearman
184 Mark Shearman
185 Colorsport
186 Mark Shearman
187 All-Sport
188 a., b., c. and d. Colorsport
192 Associated Press
198 All-Sport
202 Mansell Collection
205 Popperfoto
209 Presse-Seeger
210 Frischauf-Bild
212 Colorsport
213 Tony Duffy/All-Sport
214 Colorsport
215 Colorsport
216 Colorsport
218 Colorsport
220 Colorsport
222 Colorsport
223 a. Kishimoto. b. Colorsport
224 a. E. D. Lacey. b. Popperfoto
225 Tony Duffy/All-Sport
227 a. Keystone. b. Japanese National Olympic Committee
228 Associated Press
229 a. Melbourne Herald-Sun. b. Associated Press
230 Associated Press
231 Keystone
232 a. Tony Duffy/All-Sport. b. Radio Times Hulton Picture Library. c. George Konig/All-Sport
233 British Olympic Association; John R Freeman Ltd
234 Kishimoto
235 Tony Duffy/All-Sport
236 Presse-Sports
237 a. Presse-Sports. b. All-Sport
238 a. British Olympic Association; John R Freeman Ltd. b. Melbourne Herald-Sun
239 a. Mark Shearman. b. Colorsport. c. British Olympic Association; John R Freeman Ltd
240 Mark Shearman
241 British Olympic Association; John R Freeman Ltd
242 a. Colorsport. b. R. Wilsher, courtesy E. R. L. Powell
243 Melbourne Herald-Sun
244 Keystone
245 Missouri Historical Society
246 Sport & General
247 a. Leslie Lane. b. Colorsport
248 Colorsport
249 a. Mark Shearman. b. R. Wilsher, courtesy E. R. L. Powell. c. Reproduction Jean-Paul Maeder, courtesy International Olympic Committee
250 Presse-Sports
251 a. All-Sport. b. Associated Press
253 a. Leni Riefenstahl Produktion. b. E. D. Lacey. c. Sport & General
254 a. Novosti. b. British Olympic Association; John R Freeman Ltd courtesy German Olympic Committee
255 a. All-Sport. b. Votava
256 a. Mark Shearman. b. George Konig/All-Sport
257 a. Presse-Sports. b. Kishimoto
258 a. Horst Muller. b. All-Sport
259 Mark Shearman
260 a. R. Wilsher, courtesy E. R. L. Powell. b. Reproduction Jean-Paul Maeder, courtesy

International Olympic Committee
261 a. Mark Shearman. b. Associated Press. c. Keystone
262 Presse-Sports
263 Tony Duffy/All-Sport
264 a. Colorsport. b. Presse-Sports. c. Presse-Sports
266 PA Photos
267 Popperfoto

INDEX

Page numbers in *italics* refer to illustrations.